T0185401

# Lecture Notes in Computer Science 9299

Commenced Publication in 1973
Founding and Former Series Editors:
Gerhard Goos, Juris Hartmanis, and Jan van Leeuwen

Julio Abascal · Simone Barbosa
Mirko Fetter · Tom Gross
Philippe Palanque · Marco Winckler (Eds.)

# Human-Computer Interaction – INTERACT 2015

15th IFIP TC 13 International Conference
Bamberg, Germany, September 14–18, 2015
Proceedings, Part IV

 Springer

*Editors*

Julio Abascal
Universidad del País Vasco/Euskal Herriko
   Unibertsitatea
Donostia-San Sebastián
Spain

Simone Barbosa
PUC-Rio
Rio de Janeiro
Brazil

Mirko Fetter
University of Bamberg
Bamberg
Germany

Tom Gross
University of Bamberg
Bamberg
Germany

Philippe Palanque
University Paul Sabatier
Toulouse
France

Marco Winckler
University Paul Sabatier
Toulouse
France

ISSN 0302-9743          ISSN 1611-3349 (electronic)
Lecture Notes in Computer Science
ISBN 978-3-319-22722-1          ISBN 978-3-319-22723-8 (eBook)
DOI 10.1007/978-3-319-22723-8

Library of Congress Control Number: 2015945606

LNCS Sublibrary: SL3 – Information Systems and Applications, incl. Internet/Web, and HCI

Springer Cham Heidelberg New York Dordrecht London

Springer International Publishing AG Switzerland is part of Springer Science+Business Media
(www.springer.com)

in the discipline of HCI and its current applications. Experienced HCI researchers and professionals, as well as newcomers to the HCI field, interested in the design or evaluation of interactive software, development of new technologies for interaction, and research on general theories of HCI met in Bamberg.

We thank all the authors who chose INTERACT 2015 as the venue to publish their research. This was again an outstanding year for the conference in terms of submissions in all the technical categories.

We received 651 submissions. Of these, the following were accepted: 93 full research papers; 74 short research papers; eight demos; 30 interactive posters; four organizational overviews; three panels; six tutorials; 11 workshops; and 13 doctoral consortium papers.

The acceptance rate for the full papers was 29.6 % and 26.8 % for short papers.

In order to select the highest-quality contributions, an elaborate review system was organized including shepherding of 38 full research papers that went through a second and sometimes a third round of review. That process was primarily handled by the 32 meta-reviewers who willingly assisted and ensured the selection of high-quality full research papers to be presented at INTERACT 2015.

The final decision on acceptance or rejection of papers was taken in a plenary Program Committee meeting held in Tampere (Finland) in February 2015, aimed to discuss a consistent set of criteria to deal with inevitable differences among the large number of reviewers who were recruited and supported by the meta-reviewers. The technical program chairs and the track chairs, the general chairs, and the members of IFIP Technical Committee 13 participated in the meeting.

Special thanks must go to the track chairs and all the reviewers, who put in an enormous amount of work to ensure that quality criteria were maintained throughout the selection process. We also want to acknowledge the excellent work of the co-chairs of the different sections of the conference and the meta-reviewers of the full research paper track.

We also thank the members of the Organizing Committee, especially Mirko Fetter, local organization chair, who provided us with all the necessary resources to facilitate our work. Finally, we wish to express a special thank you to the proceedings publication chair, Marco Winckler, who did extraordinary work to put this volume together.

September 2015
Tom Gross
Julio Abascal
Simone Barbosa
Philippe Palanque

# Foreword

The 15th IFIP TC.13 International Conference on Human–Computer Interaction, INTERACT 2015, was held during September 14–18, 2015, in Bamberg, Germany, organized by the University of Bamberg. The city of Bamberg is proud of its more than 1,000-year-old center. It has more than 2,400 historically listed buildings and became a UNESCO World Cultural Heritage Site in 1993. With 70,000 inhabitants, Bamberg is a small town in the heart of Europe.

The theme of the 2015 edition was "Connection, tradition, innovation." In its relatively short history, the human–computer interaction (HCI) area has experienced impressive development. Theories, methodologies, procedures, guidelines, and tools have been progressively proposed, discussed, tested, and frequently adopted by academia and industry. The protagonists of this development created in a short period of time a scientific and technological tradition able to produce high-quality interaction systems. However, the evolution of the computers and networks pose new challenges to all stakeholders. Innovation, based on tradition, is the only way to face these challenges, even if innovation often requires breaking the tradition. In order to make this process possible, INTERACT 2015 provides diverse and abundant connection opportunities. A multidisciplinary approach is characteristic of the HCI field. INTERACT 2015 aimed to connect all the matters able to contribute to the quality of the future interactions among people and computers.

The series of INTERACT international conferences (started in 1984) is supported by Technical Committee 13 on Human–Computer Interaction of the International Federation for Information Processing (IFIP). This committee aims at developing the science and technology of the interaction between humans and computing devices.

IFIP was created in 1960 under the auspices of UNESCO with the aim of balancing worldwide the development of computer technology and Science. Technical Committee 13 is fully conscious of the social importance of information and communication technologies for our world, today and in the future. Therefore, INTERACT 2015 made efforts to attract and host people from all over the world, and to pay attention to the constraints imposed on HCI by differences in culture, language, technological availability, physical, as well as sensory and cognitive differences, among other dimensions of interest.

INTERACT 2015 gathered a stimulating collection of research papers and reports of development and practice that acknowledge the diverse disciplines, abilities, cultures, and societies, and that address all the aspects of HCI, including technical, human, social, and esthetic.

Like its predecessors, INTERACT 2015 aimed to be an exciting forum for communication with people of similar interests, to foster collaboration and learning. Being by nature a multidisciplinary field, HCI requires interaction and discussion among diverse people with different interests and backgrounds. INTERACT 2015 was directed both to the academic and industrial world, always highlighting the latest developments

# IFIP TC13

Established in 1989, the International Federation for Information Processing Technical Committee on Human–Computer Interaction (IFIP TC13) is an international committee of 37 national societies and nine working groups, representing specialists in human factors, ergonomics, cognitive science, computer science, design, and related disciplines. INTERACT is its flagship conference, staged biennially in different countries in the world. From 2017 the conference series will become an annual conference.

IFIP TC13 aims to develop the science and technology of human–computer interaction (HCI) by: encouraging empirical research, promoting the use of knowledge and methods from the human sciences in design and evaluation of computer systems; promoting better understanding of the relation between formal design methods and system usability and acceptability; developing guidelines, models, and methods by which designers may provide better human-oriented computer systems; and, cooperating with other groups, inside and outside IFIP, to promote user orientation and humanization in system design. Thus, TC13 seeks to improve interactions between people and computers, encourage the growth of HCI research and disseminate these benefits worldwide.

The main orientation is toward users, especially non-computer professional users, and how to improve human–computer relations. Areas of study include: the problems people have with computers; the impact on people in individual and organizational contexts; the determinants of utility, usability, and acceptability; the appropriate allocation of tasks between computers and users; modeling the user to aid better system design; and harmonizing the computer to user characteristics and needs.

While the scope is thus set wide, with a tendency toward general principles rather than particular systems, it is recognized that progress will only be achieved through both general studies to advance theoretical understanding and specific studies on practical issues (e.g., interface design standards, software system consistency, documentation, appropriateness of alternative communication media, human factors guidelines for dialogue design, the problems of integrating multimedia systems to match system needs and organizational practices, etc.).

In 1999, TC13 initiated a special IFIP Award, the Brian Shackel Award, for the most outstanding contribution in the form of a refereed paper submitted to and delivered at each INTERACT. The award draws attention to the need for a comprehensive human-centered approach in the design and use of information technology in which the human and social implications have been taken into account. 2007 IFIP TC 13 also launched an accessibility award to recognize an outstanding contribution with international impact in the field of accessibility for disabled users in HCI. In 2013, IFIP TC 13 launched the Interaction Design for International Development (IDID) Award, which recognizes the most outstanding contribution to the application of interactive systems for social and economic development of people in developing countries. Since the process to decide the award takes place after papers are submitted for publication, the awards are not identified in the proceedings.

IFIP TC 13 also recognizes pioneers in the area of HCI. An IFIP TC 13 pioneer is one who, through active participation in IFIP Technical Committees or related IFIP groups, has made outstanding contributions to the educational, theoretical, technical, commercial, or professional aspects of analysis, design, construction, evaluation, and use of interactive systems. IFIP TC 13 pioneers are appointed annually and awards are handed over at the INTERACT conference.

IFIP TC13 stimulates working events and activities through its working groups (WGs). WGs consist of HCI experts from many countries, who seek to expand knowledge and find solutions to HCI issues and concerns within their domains, as outlined here.

WG13.1 (Education in HCI and HCI Curricula) aims to improve HCI education at all levels of higher education, coordinate and unite efforts to develop HCI curricula and promote HCI teaching.

WG13.2 (Methodology for User-Centered System Design) aims to foster research, dissemination of information and good practice in the methodical application of HCI to software engineering.

WG13.3 (HCI and Disability) aims to make HCI designers aware of the needs of people with disabilities and encourage development of information systems and tools permitting adaptation of interfaces to specific users.

WG13.4 (also WG2.7; User Interface Engineering) investigates the nature, concepts, and construction of user interfaces for software systems, using a framework for reasoning about interactive systems and an engineering model for developing user interfaces.

WG 13.5 (Resilience, Reliability, Safety, and Human Error in System Development) seeks a framework for studying human factors relating to systems failure, develops leading-edge techniques in hazard analysis and safety engineering of computer-based systems, and guides international accreditation activities for safety-critical systems.

WG13.6 (Human–Work Interaction Design) aims at establishing relationships between extensive empirical work-domain studies and HCI design. It will promote the use of knowledge, concepts, methods, and techniques that enable user studies to procure a better apprehension of the complex interplay between individual, social, and organizational contexts and thereby a better understanding of how and why people work in the ways that they do.

WG13.7 (Human–Computer Interaction and Visualization) aims to establish a study and research program that will combine both scientific work and practical applications in the fields of HCI and visualization. It will integrate several additional aspects of further research areas, such as scientific visualization, data mining, information design, computer graphics, cognition sciences, perception theory, or psychology, into this approach.

WG13.8 (Interaction Design and International Development) are currently working to reformulate their aims and scope.

WG13.9 (Interaction Design and Children) aims to support practitioners, regulators, and researchers to develop the study of interaction design and children across international contexts.

New Working Groups are formed as areas of significance to HCI arise. Further information is available on the IFIP TC13 website: http://ifip-tc13.org/

# IFIP TC13 Members

## Officers

**Chair**
Jan Gulliksen, Sweden

**Vice-chair**
Philippe Palanque, France

**Vice-Chair for WG and SIG**
Simone D.J. Barbosa, Brazil

**Treasurer**
Anirudha Joshi, India

**Secretary**
Marco Winckler, France

**Webmaster**
Helen Petrie, UK

## Country Representatives

**Australia**
Henry B.L. Duh
Australian Computer Society

**Austria**
Geraldine Fitzpatrick
Austrian Computer Society

**Belgium**
Monique Noirhomme-Fraiture
Fédération des Associations
   Informatiques de Belgique

**Brazil**
Raquel Oliveira Prates
Brazilian Computer Society (SBC)

**Bulgaria**
Kamelia Stefanova
Bulgarian Academy of Sciences

**Canada**
Heather O'Brien
Canadian Information Processing Society

**Chile**
Jaime Sánchez
Chilean Society of Computer Science

**Croatia**
Andrina Granic
Croatian Information Technology
   Association (CITA)

**Cyprus**
Panayiotis Zaphiris
Cyprus Computer Society

**Czech Republic**
Zdeněk Míkovec
Czech Society for Cybernetics &
   Informatics

**Denmark**
Torkil Clemmensen
Danish Federation for Information
   Processing

**Finland**
Kari-Jouko Räihä
Finnish Information Processing
   Association

**France**
Philippe Palanque
Société des Electriciens et des
   Electroniciens (SEE)

**Germany**
Tom Gross
Gesellschaft fur Informatik

**Hungary**
Cecilia Sik Lanyi
John V. Neumann Computer
   Society

**Iceland**
Marta Kristin Larusdottir
The Icelandic Society for Information
  Processing (ISIP)

**India**
Anirudha Joshi
Computer Society of India

**Ireland**
Liam J. Bannon
Irish Computer Society

**Italy**
Fabio Paternò
Italian Computer Society

**Japan**
Yoshifumi Kitamura
Information Processing Society of Japan

**Korea**
Gerry Kim
KIISE

**Malaysia**
Chui Yin Wong
Malaysian National Computer
  Confederation

**The Netherlands**
Vanessa Evers
Nederlands Genootschap voor
  Informatica

**New Zealand**
Mark Apperley
New Zealand Computer Society

**Nigeria**
Chris C. Nwannenna
Nigeria Computer Society

**Norway**
Dag Svanes
Norwegian Computer Society

**Poland**
Marcin Sikorski
Poland Academy of Sciences

**Portugal**
Pedro Campos
Associação Portuguesa para o Desen-
  volvimento da Sociedade da Infor-
  mação (APDSI)

**Slovakia**
Vanda Benešová
The Slovak Society for Computer
  Science

**South Africa**
Janet L. Wesson
The Computer Society of South Africa

**Spain**
Julio Abascal
Asociación de Técnicos de Informática
  (ATI)

**Sweden**
Jan Gulliksen
Swedish Computer Society

**Switzerland**
Solange Ghernaouti
Swiss Federation for Information
Processing

**Tunisia**
Mona Laroussi
Ecole Supérieure des Communications
  De Tunis (SUP'COM)

**UK**
Andy Dearden
British Computer Society (BCS)

**USA**
Gerrit van der Veer
Association for Computing Machinery
  (ACM)

# Expert Members

Nikos Avouris (Greece)
Simone D.J. Barbosa (Brazil)
Peter Forbrig (Germany)
Joaquim Jorge (Portugal)
Paula Kotzé (South Africa)
Masaaki Kurosu (Japan)

Gitte Lindgaard (Australia)
Zhengjie Liu (China)
Fernando Loizides (Cyprus)
Dan Orwa (Kenya)
Frank Vetere (Australia)

# Working Group Chairs

**WG13.1 (Education in HCI and HCI Curricula)**
Konrad Baumann, Austria

**WG13.2 (Methodologies for User-Centered System Design)**
Marco Winckler, France

**WG13.3 (HCI and Disability)**
Helen Petrie, UK

**WG13.4 (also 2.7) (User Interface Engineering)**
Jürgen Ziegler, Germany

**WG13.5 (Resilience, Reliability, Safety and Human Error in System Development)**
Chris Johnson, UK

**WG13.6 (Human–Work Interaction Design)**
Pedro Campos, Portugal

**WG13.7 (HCI and Visualization)**
Achim Ebert, Germany

**WG 13.8 (Interaction Design and International Development)**
José Adbelnour Nocera, UK

**WG 13.9 (Interaction Design and Children)**
Janet Read, UK

# Conference Organizing Committee

**General Conference Co-chairs**
Tom Gross, Germany
Julio Abascal, Spain

**Tutorials Co-chairs**
Christoph Beckmann, Germany
Regina Bernhaupt, France

**Full Papers Chairs**
Simone D.J. Barbosa, Brazil
Philippe Palanque, France

**Workshops Co-chairs**
Christoph Beckmann, Germany
Víctor López-Jaquero, Spain

**Short Papers Co-chairs**
Fabio Paternò, Italy
Kari-Jouko Räihä, Finland

**Doctoral Consortium Co-chairs**
Geraldine Fitzpatrick, Austria
Panayiotis Zaphiris, Cyprus

**Posters and Demos Co-chairs**
Stephen Brewster, UK
David McGookin, UK

**Proceedings Chair**
Marco Winckler, France

**Madness Co-chairs**
Artur Lugmayr, Finland
Björn Stockleben, Germany
Tim Merritt, Denmark

**Organization Overviews Co-chairs**
Melanie Fitzgerald, USA
Kori Inkpen, USA

**Panels Co-chairs**
Anirudha N. Joshi, India
Gitte Lindgaard, Australia

**Local Organization Co-chairs**
Mirko Fetter, Germany
Claudia Tischler, Germany

**Open Space Co-chairs**
Christoph Beckmann, Germany
Achim Ebert, Germany

**Student Volunteers Co-chairs**
Robert Beaton, USA
Sascha Herr, Germany

## Program Committee

**Meta-reviewers**

Birgit Bomsdorf, Germany
Gaëlle Calvary, France
José Campos, Portugal
Pedro Campos, Portugal
Luca Chittaro, Italy

Torkil Clemmensen, Denmark
Paul Curzon, UK
Achim Ebert, Germany
Peter Forbrig, Germany
Michael Harrison, UK

Anirudha Joshi, India
Denis Lalanne, Switzerland
Effie Law, UK
Célia Martinie, France
Laurence Nigay, France
Monique Noirhomme, Belgium
Fabio Paternò, Italy
Helen Petrie, UK
Antonio Piccinno, Italy
Aaron Quigley, UK
Kari-Jouko Räihä, Finland
Virpi Roto, Finland

Luciana Salgado Cardoso de Castro,
   Brazil
Paula Alexandra Silva, Ireland
Frank Steinicke, Germany
Simone Stumpf, UK
Allistair Sutcliffe, UK
Jean Vanderdonckt, Belgium
Gerhard Weber, Germany
Astrid Weiss, Austria
Marco Winckler, France
Panayiotis Zaphiris, Cyprus

# Reviewers

José Abdelnour-Nocera, UK
Al Mahmud Abdullah, Australia
Silvia Abrahão, Spain
Funmi Adebesin, South Africa
Ana Paula Afonso, Portugal
David Ahlström, Austria
Pierre Akiki, Lebanon
Deepak Akkil, Finland
Hannu Alen, Finland
Jan Alexandersson, Germany
José Carlos Bacelar Almeida, Portugal
Florian Alt, Germany
Julian Alvarez, France
Junia Coutinho Anacleto, Brazil
Leonardo Angelini, Switzerland
Craig Anslow, New Zealand
Mark Apperley, New Zealand
Nathalie Aquino, Paraguay
Liliana Ardissono, Italy
Carmelo Ardito, Italy
Oscar Javier Ariza Núñez, Germany
Myriam Arrue, Spain
Ilhan Aslan, Austria
Simon Attfield, UK
Nikolaos Avouris, Greece
Chris Baber, UK
Myroslav Bachynskyi, Germany
Jonathan Back, UK
Gilles Bailly, France
Liam Bannon, Ireland

Emilia Barakova, The Netherlands
Javier Barcenila, France
Louise Barkhuus, USA
Barbara Rita Barricelli, Italy
Valentina Bartalesi, Italy
Mohammed Basheri, Saudi Arabia
Christoph Beckmann, Germany
Yacine Bellik, France
Vanda Benešová, Slovak Republic
Kawtar Benghazi, Spain
David Benyon, UK
François Bérard, France
Regina Bernhaupt, Austria
Karsten Berns, Germany
Nadia Berthouze, UK
Raymond Bertram, Finland
Mark Billinghurst, New Zealand
Dorrit Billman, USA
Silvia Amelia Bim, Brazil
Fernando Birra, Portugal
Renaud Blanch, France
Ann Blandford, UK
Mads Boedker, Denmark
Davide Bolchini, USA
Birgit Bomsdorf, Germany
Rodrigo Bonacin, Brazil
Paolo Gaspare Bottoni, Italy
Fatma Bouali, France
Chris Bowers, UK
Giorgio Brajnik, Italy

Anke Brock, France
Barry Brown, Sweden
Judith Brown, Canada
Gerd Bruder, Germany
Duncan Brumby, UK
Nick Bryan-Kinns, UK
Stéphanie Buisine, France
Sabin-Corneliu Buraga, Romania
Paris Buttfield-Addison, Australia
Maria Claudia Buzzi, Italy
Marina Buzzi, Italy
Cristina Cachero, Spain
Sybille Caffiau, France
Paul Cairns, UK
Roberto Caldara, Switzerland
Gaëlle Calvary, France
Licia Calvi, The Netherlands
José Campos, Portugal
Pedro Campos, Portugal
Katia Canepa Vega, Brazil
Maria-Dolores Cano, Spain
Maria Beatriz Carmo, Portugal
Francesco Carrino, Switzerland
Stefano Carrino, Switzerland
Luis Carriço, Portugal
Marcus Carter, Australia
Daniel Cernea, Germany
Teresa Chambel, Portugal
Stéphane Chatty, France
Monchu Chen, Portugal
Yu Chen, Switzerland
Kelvin Cheng, Singapore
Yoram Chisik, Portugal
Luca Chittaro, Italy
Elizabeth Churchill, USA
Torkil Clemmensen, Denmark
Gilbert Cockton, UK
Karin Coninx, Belgium
Tayana Conte, Brazil
Stéphane Conversy, France
Jeremy Cooperstock, Canada
Nuno Correia, Portugal
Joëlle Coutaz, France
Céline Coutrix, France
Nadine Couture, France
Chris Creed, UK

Martin Cronel, France
James Crowley, France
Jácome Cunha, Portugal
Paul Curzon, UK
Marie d'Udekem, Belgium
Florian Daiber, Germany
Girish Dalvi, India
José Danado, UK
Antonella De Angeli, Italy
Alexander De Luca, Switzerland
Maria De Marsico, Italy
Giorgio De Michelis, Italy
Leonardo Cunha de Miranda, Brazil
Boris De Ruyter, The Netherlands
Clarisse de Souza, Brazil
Alexandre Demeure, France
Giuseppe Desolda, Italy
Ines Di Loreto, France
Paulo Dias, Portugal
Shalaka Dighe, India
Christian Dindler, Denmark
Anke Dittmar, Germany
Pierre Dragicevic, France
Carlos Duarte, Portugal
Cathy Dudek, Canada
Henry Been-Lirn Duh, Australia
Bruno Dumas, Belgium
Sophie Dupuy-Chessa, France
Achim Ebert, Germany
Florian Echtler, Germany
Rob Edlin-White, UK
Jan Engelen, Belgium
Thomas Erickson, USA
Elina Eriksson, Sweden
Dominik Ertl, UK
Parisa Eslambolchilar, UK
Marc Fabri, UK
Carla Faria Leitão, Brazil
Ava Fatah gen Schieck, UK
Xavier Ferre, Spain
Eija Ferreira, Finland
Mirko Fetter, Germany
Sebastian Feuerstack, Germany
Vagner Figueredo de Santana, Brazil
Daniela Fogli, Italy
Joan Fons, Spain

Manuel Fonseca, Portugal
Peter Forbrig, Germany
Marcus Foth, Australia
Andre Freire, Brazil
Carla D.S. Freitas, Brazil
Jonas Fritsch, Denmark
Luca Frosini, Italy
Dominic Furniss, UK
Nestor Garay-Vitoria, Spain
Jérémie Garcia, France
Roberto García, Spain
Jose Luis Garrido, Spain
Franca Garzotto, Italy
Isabela Gasparini, Brazil
Miguel Gea, Spain
Patrick Gebhard, Germany
Cristina Gena, Italy
Giuseppe Ghiani, Italy
Patrick Girard, France
Kentaro Go, Japan
Daniel Gonçalves, Portugal
Rúben Gouveia, Portugal
Nicholas Graham, Canada
Andrina Granic, Croatia
Toni Granollers, Spain
Saul Greenberg, Canada
John Grundy, Australia
Nuno Guimaraes, Portugal
Jan Gulliksen, Sweden
Rebecca Gulotta, USA
Mieke Haesen, Belgium
Hans Hagen, Germany
Jonna Häkkilä, Finland
Jukka Häkkinen, Finland
Jaakko Hakulinen, Finland
Lynne Hall, UK
Arnaud Hamon, France
Chris Harrison, USA
Daniel Harrison, UK
Michael Harrison, UK
Ruediger Heimgaertner, Germany
Tomi Heimonen, Finland
Matthias Heintz, UK
Ingi Helgason, UK
Susan Catherine Herring, USA
Wilko Heuten, Germany

Martin Hitz, Austria
Thuong Hoang, Australia
Rüdiger Hoffmann, Germany
Jennifer Horkoff, UK
Heiko Hornung, Brazil
Ko-Hsun Huang, Taiwan,
   Republic of China
Alina Huldtgren, The Netherlands
Ebba Thora Hvannberg, Iceland
Aulikki Hyrskykari, Finland
Ioanna Iacovides, UK
Netta Iivari, Finland
Mirja Ilves, Finland
Yavuz İnal, Turkey
Poika Isokoski, Finland
Minna Isomursu, Finland
Howell Istance, Finland
Ido A. Iurgel, Germany
Mikkel R. Jakobsen, Denmark
Francis Jambon, France
Jacek Jankowski, Poland
Maddy Janse, The Netherlands
Nuno Jardim Nunes, Portugal
Caroline Jay, UK
Kasper Løvborg Jensen, Denmark
Mikael Johnson, Finland
Matt Jones, UK
Joaquim Jorge, Portugal
Rui Jose, Portugal
Anirudha Joshi, India
Christophe Jouffrais, France
Anne Joutsenvirta, Finland
Marko Jurmu, Finland
Eija Kaasinen, Finland
Jari Kangas, Finland
Anne Marie Kanstrup, Denmark
Victor Kaptelinin, Sweden
Evangelos Karapanos, Portugal
Kristiina Karvonen, Finland
Dinesh Katre, India
Manolya Kavakli, Australia
Patrick Gage Kelley, USA
Ryan Kelly, UK
Rabia Khan, UK
Hideki Koike, Japan
Christophe Kolski, France

Harri Siirtola, Finland
Paula A. Silva, Ireland
Bruno S. Silva, Brazil
Carlos CL Silva, Portugal
João Carlos Silva, Portugal
Jose Luis Silva, Portugal
Paula Alexandra Silva, Ireland
Milene Silveira, Brazil
Carla Simone, Italy
Shamus Smith, Australia
Andreas Sonderegger, Switzerland
Keyur Sorathia, India
Fabio Sorrentino, Italy
Hamit Soyel, UK
Oleg Spakov, Finland
Lucio Davide Spano, Italy
Mark Vincent Springett, UK
Jan Stage, Denmark
Christian Stary, Austria
Katarzyna Stawarz, UK
Frank Steinicke, Germany
Gerald Stollnberger, Austria
Markus Stolze, Switzerland
Simone Stumpf, UK
Noi Sukaviriya, USA
Allistar Sutcliffe, UK
David Mark Swallow, UK
Tapio Takala, Finland
Chee-wee Tan, Denmark
Franck Tarpin-Bernard, France
Carlos Teixeira, Portugal
Luis Teixeira, Portugal
Daniel Tetteroo, The Netherlands
Jakob Tholander, Sweden
Nigel Thomas, UK
Liisa Tiittula, Finland
Nava Tintarev, UK
Martin Tomitsch, Australia
Ilaria Torre, Italy
Marilyn Tremaine, USA
Daniela Trevisan, Brazil
Sanjay Tripathi, India
Janice Tsai, USA
Manfred Tscheligi, Austria
Huawei Tu, UK
Outi Tuisku, Finland
Phil Turner, UK

Susan Ellen Turner, UK
Markku Turunen, Finland
Blase Ur, USA
Heli Väätäjä, Finland
Stefano Valtolina, Italy
Judy van Biljon, South Africa
Jos P. van Leeuwen, The Netherlands
Paul van Schaik, UK
Jeroen Vanattenhoven, Belgium
Jean Vanderdonckt, Belgium
Jari Varsaluoma, Finland
Radu-Daniel Vatavu, Romania
Angel Velazquez-Iturbide, Spain
Hanna Venesvirta, Finland
Jayant Venkatanathan, India
Gilles Venturini, France
Arnold Vermeeren, The Netherlands
Karel Vermeulen, UK
Frédéric Vernier, France
Markel Vigo, UK
Nadine Vigouroux, France
Chris Vincent, UK
Giuliana Vitiello, Italy
Arnd Vitzthum, Germany
Dhaval Vyas, Australia
Mike Wald, UK
Jim Wallace, Canada
Tanja Carita Walsh, Finland
Robert Walter, Germany
Leon Watts, UK
Gerhard Weber, Germany
Rina Wehbe, Canada
Astrid Weiss, Austria
Janet Louise Wesson, South Africa
Graham Wilson, UK
Stephanie Wilson, UK
Marco Winckler, France
Theophilus Winschiers, Namibia
Chui Yin Wong, Malaysia
Wolfgang Wörndl, Germany
Volker Wulf, Germany
Yeliz Yesilada, Turkey
Salu Ylirisku, Finland
Nur Haryani Zakaria, Malaysia
Massimo Zancanaro, Italy
Panayiotis Zaphiris, Cyprus
Jürgen Ziegler, Germany

## Sponsors and Supporters

### Sponsors

 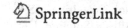

### Supporters

# Contents – Part IV

**Touch and Haptic**

**User and Task Modelling**

## Visualization

## Visualization 3D

## Visualization in Virtual Spaces

## Wearable Computing

## Demonstrations

**Interactive Posters**

**Organizational Overview**

## Panels

## Tutorials

# Workshops

# Child or Adult? Inferring Smartphone Users' Age Group from Touch Measurements Alone

Radu-Daniel Vatavu[1]([✉]), Lisa Anthony[2], and Quincy Brown[3]

[1] University Stefan cel Mare of Suceava, Suceava, Romania
vatavu@eed.usv.ro
[2] Department of CISE, University of Florida, Gainesville, FL, USA
lanthony@cise.ufl.edu
[3] Bowie State University, Bowie, MD, USA
qbrown@bowiestate.edu

**Abstract.** We present a technique that classifies users' age group, *i.e.*, *child* or *adult*, from touch coordinates captured on touch-screen devices. Our technique delivered 86.5 % accuracy (user-independent) on a dataset of 119 participants (89 children ages 3 to 6) when classifying each touch event one at a time and up to 99 % accuracy when using a window of 7+ consecutive touches. Our results establish that it is possible to reliably classify a smartphone user *on the fly* as a *child* or an *adult* with high accuracy using only basic data about their touches, and will inform new, automatically adaptive interfaces for touch-screen devices.

**Keywords:** Touch input · Children · Adults · Age group · Tap time · Offset distance · Touch accuracy · Classifier · Bayes' rule · Touch-screen · Smartphone · Experiment

## 1 Introduction

As of 2013, 43 % of adult Americans over age 16 own a tablet or e-reader and 56 % of adult Americans own a smartphone [7, 8], and touch-screen input has rapidly become the primary way many users interact with these mobile computing devices. This trend is especially true for children of pre-school and elementary school age (ages 3 to 10) [5]. Previous work has determined that touch and stroke gesture interaction behaviors differ between adults and children in ways that significantly impact gesture recognition and processing of users' touch input [2, 3, 6], *e.g.*, children's touches are more likely to be just outside the boundaries of their intended target [3] and their gestures are less likely to be recognized correctly than adults' gestures [2, 3].

If touch-screen interfaces were able to determine on the fly whether the user is a child or an adult, applications could switch ad hoc to processing or recognition algorithms tailored for one age group or the other. Such *adaptive touch interaction* mechanisms would assist users in their touch input, making them more accurate and more successful during touch-screen interaction. Unfortunately, research on age-detection classification is sparse, and what work exists so far focuses on gesture input [6], which provides a far richer source of classification features than simple taps; see for instance Blagojevic et al. [4] for an examination of 114 such features. On the other hand, touch

© IFIP International Federation for Information Processing 2015
J. Abascal et al. (Eds.): INTERACT 2015, Part IV, LNCS 9299, pp. 1–9, 2015.
DOI: 10.1007/978-3-319-22723-8_1

input on its own is more challenging to interpret, because of the rudimentary features provided by current touch-screen hardware, typically limited to touch coordinates and timestamps and, in the best-case scenario, to rough approximations of touch pressure and area size.

We present in this work a technique for classifying users' age group, *i.e.*, *child* or *adult*, from touch input alone. In this work, a *child* is a person having 6 years at most; at this age, children's touch input behaviors are the most different from those of adults knowing that children's input performance and touch accuracy improve with age [3]. Our technique, using a Bayes' rule classifier, delivered 86.5 % user-independent accuracy on a dataset of 119 participants (89 children ages 3 to 6) when classifying each touch event one at a time and 99 % accuracy with a window of 7+ consecutive touch events. These results establish that it is possible to classify a user as a *child* or *adult* with high accuracy using only minimal data provided by all existing touch-screen hardware. Our contributions will inform the next generation of *adaptive user interfaces for touch-screen devices* that will be able to respond appropriately and *on the fly* to their users, without pre-configuration or the need of specialized sensors.

## 2   Touch Input Analysis to Inform Classifier Design

We analyze in this section adults' and small children's touch input patterns using two measures that can be readily computed for any touch-screen device, *i.e.*, (1) the time between the moment when the user's finger touches the screen and the moment when the finger lifts off (TAP-TIME) and (2) the distance between the actual touch point where the user's finger was placed and the center of the touch target (OFFSET-DISTANCE); see Fig. 1 for an illustration of these measures. We generate frequency distributions of adults' and children's tap times and offset distances (see Fig. 2, next page) using the touch dataset of Vatavu et al. [9]. This dataset contains 587 samples from 119 participants (89 children with ages between 3 and 6 years old and 30 young adults).[1]

**Fig. 1.** TAP-TIME ($\tau$) and OFFSET-DISTANCE ($d$) touch measures.

---

[1] The dataset of Vatavu et al. [9] is available to download at http://www.eed.usv.ro/∼vatavu/ Note that, though there are more samples in the dataset from children than adults, all classification tests that we report in this paper were done with balanced data samples.

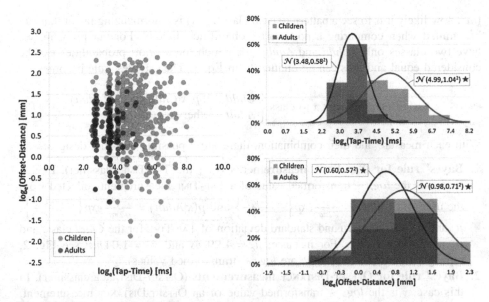

**Fig. 2.** Distribution of the *Child* and *Adult* classes in the TAP-TIME × OFFSET-DISTANCE space (left) and frequency histograms of each feature (right) with normal distributions superimposed. NOTE: we use $log_e$ – transformed TAP-TIME and OFFSET-DISTANCE; a star symbol (★) indicates that the Kolmogorov-Smirnov test found no significant difference ($p > .01$) between our $log_e$-transformed data and a normal distribution $N(\mu, \sigma^2)$ with same mean and standard deviation.

Figure 2 plots the *Child* and *Adult* classes in the TAP-TIME × OFFSET-DISTANCE space and the frequency distributions of the two measures. We found that all 4 distributions deviated significantly from normality, so we applied a $log_e$ transform on our data. Follow-up Kolmogorov-Smirnov tests confirmed the normality of 3 out of the 4 $log_e$ transformed distributions (*i.e.*, TAP-TIME for *Child*, OFFSET-DISTANCE for *Adult*, and OFFSET-DISTANCE for *Child*, which are marked with a star symbol ★ in Fig. 2). The only distribution that still deviated significantly from normality was TAP-TIME for the *Adult* class ($D_{(149)} = 0.171, p < .01$). However, the effect size of the Kolmogorov-Smirnov test was considerably smaller than Cohen's suggested limit for small effect sizes ($r = .014 < .100$), while both skewness and kurtosis were close to zero ($s = -0.62$, CI$_{95\%}$= $[-0.81, -0.42]$ and $k = -0.76$, CI$_{95\%}$= $[-1.16, -0.36]$). These results support modeling $log_e$(TAP-TIME) and $log_e$(OFFSET-DISTANCE) data with normal distributions, which in turn leverage the option of designing a Bayes' rule classifier to discriminate between *Child* and *Adult* classes.

Bayes' rule assigns a candidate measurement $x$ to class $j$ for which the a posteriori probability $p(class_j|x)$ is maximized [11] (p. 7):

$$p(class_j|x) = \frac{p(x|class_j) \cdot p(class_j)}{p(x)} \qquad (1)$$

knowing the class-conditional density functions $p(x|class_j)$ (*i.e.*, the probability of a randomly chosen pattern $x$ to lie with class $j$) and the a priori probabilities $p(class_j)$

(*i.e.*, how likely it is to see a pattern of each class); $p(x)$ is a normalizing factor that can be omitted when comparing a posteriori probabilities directly. For our problem, we have two classes only (*Child* and *Adult*), for which the a priori probabilities can be considered equal and thus can be omitted from Eq. 1. Then, Bayes' rule becomes:

$$\text{Assign measurement } x \text{ to class} \begin{cases} Child & \text{if } p(x|Child) > p(x|Adult) \\ Adult & \text{otherwise} \end{cases} \quad (2)$$

With each measure and their combination, there are 3 possible classifier designs:

1. **Bayes' rule for Tap-Time measurements** (*i.e.*, the Tap-Time classifier). In this case, $x$ is the $log_e$ − transformed value of a Tap-Time measurement collected from the user, $p(x|Child) = \frac{1}{\sqrt{2\pi}\sigma_c} exp\left\{-\frac{(x-\mu_c)^2}{2\sigma_c^2}\right\}$ and $p(x|Adult) = \frac{1}{\sqrt{2\pi}\sigma_a} exp\left\{-\frac{(x-\mu_a)^2}{2\sigma_a^2}\right\}$; $\mu_c$ and $\sigma_c$ are the mean and standard deviation of Tap-Time for the *Child* class, and $\mu_a$ and $\sigma_a$ for *Adults*. For instance, $\mu_c = 4.99\,ms$ and $\sigma_c = 1.04\,ms$; see Fig. 2, top-right (remember that these are $log_e$ − transformed values).

2. **Bayes' rule for Offset-Distance measurements** (Offset-Distance classifier). In this case, $x$ is the $log_e$ − transformed value of an Offset-Distance measurement, $p(x|Child) = \frac{1}{\sqrt{2\pi}\sigma_c} exp\left\{-\frac{(x-\mu_c)^2}{2\sigma_c^2}\right\}$ and $p(x|Adult) = \frac{1}{\sqrt{2\pi}\sigma_a} exp\left\{-\frac{(x-\mu_a)^2}{2\sigma_a^2}\right\}$; $\mu_c$ and $\sigma_c$ are the mean and standard deviation of Offset-Distance for the *Child* class, and $\mu_a$ and $\sigma_a$ for *Adults*. For instance, $\mu_a = 0.60\,ms$ and $\sigma_a = 0.57\,ms$; see Fig. 2, bottom-right (remember that these are $log_e$ − transformed values).

3. **Combined Time & Offset-Distance rule** (*i.e.*, the Time-Offset classifier). In this case, $x$ is a vector consisting of one Tap-Time and one Offset-Distance measurement, $p(x|Child) = \frac{1}{2\pi\sqrt{|\Sigma_c|}} exp\left\{-\frac{1}{2}(x - \mu_c)^T \Sigma_c^{-1}(x - \mu_c)\right\}$, $p(x|Adult) = \frac{1}{2\pi\sqrt{|\Sigma_a|}} exp\left\{-\frac{1}{2}(x - \mu_a)^T \Sigma_a^{-1}(x - \mu_a)\right\}$; $\mu_c$ is a vector containing the mean values of Tap-Time and Offset-Distance for the *Child* class and $\mu_a$ the mean vector for *Adults*; $\Sigma_c$ and $\Sigma_a$ represent the covariance matrices for the two classes. For instance, $\mu_c = [4.99, 0.98]$ and $\Sigma_c = \begin{bmatrix} 1.08 & -0.11 \\ -0.11 & 0.50 \end{bmatrix}$, where 1.08 is the variance (*i.e.*, square standard deviation) of Tap-Time, 0.50 the variance of Offset-Distance, and −0.11 the covariance between Tap-Time and Offset-Distance for the *Child* class (Fig. 2, right).

## 3   Experiment #1: Classifying Age Group with One Touch Point Only

We conducted a first experiment to evaluate the accuracy of the Bayes' rule classifiers to predict age group using measurements from *one touch point only*. We employed the touch dataset of Vatavu et al. [9], which contains 587 touch samples collected from 119 participants (89 children with ages between 3 and 6 years old and 30 young adults). The experiment was a within-subject design with two independent factors:

1. CLASSIFIER, nominal with 3 levels: TAP-TIME, OFFSET-DISTANCE, TIME-OFFSET.
2. The number of training participants P from which we estimated the mean and standard deviation values for TAP-TIME and OFFSET-DISTANCE employed by the class-conditional density functions $p(x|Child)$ and $p(x|Adult)$. We varied P between 2 and 30 participants for each class. (P = 10 participants means that data from 5 children and 5 adults was used for training.) For each participant, a maximum of 5 samples are available in the dataset [9], making the size of the training set for estimating $p(x|Child)$ and $p(x|Adult)$ between 10 and 150.

We compute one dependent variable, the recognition ACCURACY of our classifiers, according to the following user-independent procedure from [10]: (1) for each P, we randomly select P children and P adults for training; (2) we randomly select 1 child and 1 adult for testing from the remaining participants, and we classify one randomly-selected touch point for each; (3) we repeat step 2 for 100 times for each training set, and we repeat step 1 for 100 times (i.e., 100 different training sets). Overall, we report classification results from 15 (number of training participants P) × 100 (repetitions of each P) × 200 (classifications for each training set) = 300,000 classification trials. All tests are user-independent, so different data is used for the training and testing sets.

Friedman's test showed a significant effect of CLASSIFIER on recognition ACCURACY $(\chi^2_{(2,N=1500)} = 2304.714, p < .001)$, and post hoc Wilcoxon signed-rank tests showed significant differences for all classifier pairs ($p < .001$) with medium to large effect sizes ($r$ between .27 and .61); see Fig. 3. The highest accuracy was delivered by the TIME-OFFSET classifier, which had an average performance of 83.9 % and reached 86.5 % with training data from 15 adults and 15 children. The TAP-TIME classifier came second with an average performance of 82.8 % and maximum accuracy of 84.9 %. The OFFSET-DISTANCE classifier exhibited the lowest performance with only 63.8 % accuracy for the maximum number of P = 30 training participants. Friedman's tests showed significant effects of P over all classifiers ($p < .001$), with ACCURACY increasing considerably for both TIME-OFFSET and TAP-TIME from P = 2 to 8 participants (71 % to 83 %), after which it continued to increase slowly up to 86.5 %.

## 4 Experiment #2: Classifying Age Group with a Touch Window

The results from the previous section show good potential for two Bayes' rule classifiers to discriminate between *Child* and *Adult* classes, with accuracy up to 86.5 %. In this section, we show how this accuracy rate can be much improved by employing a majority vote for which the classification decision is taken after analyzing several touch measurements in a row. A *touch window* represents a sequence of W consecutive touches. We classify each touch with one of our Bayes' rules and then count the number of *Child* and *Adult* votes. The majority count wins the classification and selecting an odd number for W guarantees no ties for our 2-class problem.

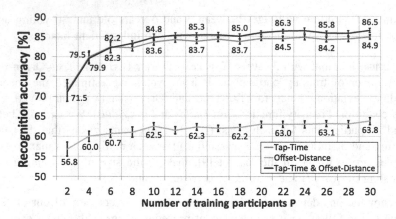

**Fig. 3.** Recognition accuracy of Bayes' rule classifiers. NOTES: P = 10 participants means that touch data from 5 children and 5 adults was used for training. Five touch measurements were used for each training participant. Error bars show 95 % CIs.

We conducted a second experiment to evaluate the accuracy of the Bayes' rule classifiers to predict users' age group using measurements from *touch windows*. The experiment was a within-subject design with three independent factors:

CLASSIFIER, nominal with 3 levels: TAP-TIME, OFFSET-DISTANCE, TIME-OFFSET. The number of training participants $2 \leq P \leq 30$ from which we estimated the mean and standard deviation values for TAP-TIME and OFFSET-DISTANCE employed by the class-conditional density functions $p(x|Child)$ and $p(x|Adult)$. The size of the touch window W with 1, 3, 5, 7, 9, 11, 13, and 15 touches.

We compute one dependent variable, the recognition ACCURACY of our classifiers, according to the following user-independent procedure [10]: (1) for each P value, we randomly select P children and P adults for training; (2) for each W, we randomly select W children touch samples and W adult touch samples from the remaining participants, and classify the two W-touch windows as *Child* or *Adult*; (3) we repeat step 2 for 100 times for each training set, and we repeat step 1 for 100 times (*i.e.*, 100 different training sets). Overall, we report results from 15 (number of training partic-ipants P) × 8 (sizes W of the touch window) × 100 (repetitions of each P) × 200 (classifications for each training set) = 2,400,000 classification trials. Because the dataset has a maximum of 5 touch samples per participant, we simulate larger windows by sampling across participants for this experiment. Since the training set shares no users in common with the testing set (user-independent), this approach is equivalent to off-the-shelf use cases.

Friedman's test detected a significant effect of CLASSIFIER on ACCURACY $(\chi^2_{(2,N=12000)} = 18362.182, p < .001)$ and post hoc Wilcoxon signed-rank tests revealed significant differences between all classifier pairs (at $p < .001$) with medium to large effect sizes ($r$ between .24 and .60). The OFFSET-DISTANCE classifier exhibited again the poorest performance (70.9 % average accuracy), much lower than the other two classifiers (93.5 % and 94.2 %, respectively), so we disregard it from subsequent analysis. We found a significant effect of touch window size W on ACCURACY

$(\chi^2_{(7,N=1500)} = 5975.910, p < .001$ for the TAP-TIME classification rule and $\chi^2_{(7,N=1500)} = 6280.743, p < .001$ for the TIME-OFFSET rule), with the average ACCURACY improving for both TAP-TIME and TIME-OFFSET from 83.1 % and 83.9 % for W = 1 up to 97.2 % and 97.5 % for W = 15; see Fig. 4. For each touch window, performance improved with more training participants, *e.g.*, the TIME-OFFSET classifier delivered 97.1 % accuracy with W = 11 and P = 4 participants (2 children + 2 adults), which increased to 99.4 % when training data from P = 30 participants (15 children + 15 adults) was used. Overall, the TIME-OFFSET classification rule delivered significantly better performance than TAP-TIME ($Z = -38.073, p < .001$), with a medium effect size ($r = .25$), while the actual average difference in accuracy was only 1.1 %.

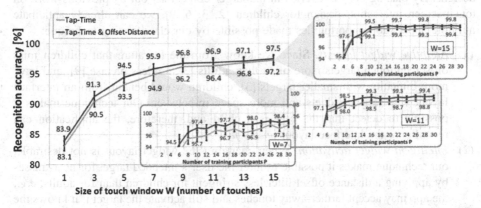

**Fig. 4.** Recognition accuracy of Bayes' rule classifiers on *touch windows*. The effect of number of participants P on accuracy shows an increasing trend overall; we highlight the effect of P for some of the touch windows (W = 7, 11, and 15). For W = 1, see Fig. 3. Error bars show 95 % CIs.

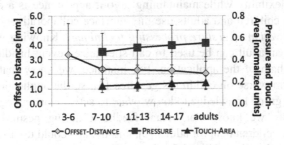

**Fig. 5.** Potential touch features for multi-class age group classification that show a descending trend in OFFSET-DISTANCE and ascending trends in PRESSURE and TOUCH-AREA. Error bars show ± 1 SD.

## 5 Discussion, Conclusions, and Future Work

We showed that distance offset and tap time are enough to classify whether the user is a small *child* or an *adult* with reasonable accuracy (86.5 %) using only one touch point and very high accuracy (>99 %) with a window of 7+ touches. Although there are some limitations to our study, as we focused only on children ages 3 to 6 years, accuracy results are promising given the rudimentary data we worked with, *i.e.*, touch coordinates and timestamps alone. These results recommend our technique for discrimination of age groups at much finer granularity. However, we must leave such detailed investigations for future work, as they will most likely need examination of additional features to reach similar levels of accuracy. For example, Fig. 5 shows two such measures, PRESSURE and TOUCH-AREA for 5 age groups and 185 participants [3, 9]. Because such measurements may not be available for all touch-screen hardware, fine age group discrimination may be restricted to some devices only. While we point the community to these opportunities, the exploration of such tradeoffs is future work.

Meanwhile, our technique can already be incorporated by practitioners into their designs. By placing our discoveries in the larger context set out by previous work on touch-screen interaction design for children [2, 3, 6, 9], we can already anticipate multiple application opportunities made possible by our classification technique:

(1) *Adaptive widget layouts.* Since we know from the literature that children miss on-screen touch targets more often than adults [3], are less precise [9], and have more difficulty with smaller targets [3], children would benefit from an interface layout with larger widgets and more space in-between. Our technique makes it possible to detect that the user is a child and, therefore, the application can reconfigure the interface layout *on the fly*.

(2) *Intelligent widget activation.* When changing the widget layout is not desirable, our technique makes it possible to infer the user's intended target for near-misses by applying a distance offset filter less stringent for children than for adults, *e.g.*, the app may accept farther-away touches and still activate the target if it knows the user is a child. The layout and size of the widgets stay the same, but the application will apply different age-group-dependent processing. This mechanism will provide more flexibility for the application developer by allowing them to use the same interface for multiple target age groups. The increase in touch target acquisition flexibility while maintaining layout appearance is a desirable design option when children and adults use the interface collaboratively.

(3) *Adaptive activation of gesture processing techniques.* Knowing whether the user is a child or an adult can be used to call specialized event handlers in the touch processing chain of the application. For instance, we know that gesture recognizers perform worse on children's gestures [3], so the application could benefit from the age group knowledge to know *when* to activate one recognizer or another [4, 10]. Also, we know that visual feedback during gesture input is more important for children than for adults [2], and the app could use the age group data to increase or dim down visual feedback as necessary, which will provide more cues for children and more screen space for adults to display other app widgets and data.

(4) *Adaptive filtering of content and access to applications.* Knowing whether the user is a child or an adult can be used to automatically filter Internet content and to disable access to applications according to parental monitoring settings [1]. However, in contrast to existing approaches, our technique can inform the app

*right away* (from the first touch or just a few touches) that the ownership of the device has changed and can enforce or disable parental settings automatically.

All these application opportunities can be easily incorporated into existing interfaces, increasing adaptiveness to users. We hope that this first examination of age group classification with basic, readily collectable touch data will empower the community with a new tool to make touch interfaces even more adaptable for users, and will inspire researchers to gain richer understanding of touch input for different age groups.

**Acknowledgment.** This work was supported by the project MappingBooks, no. PN-II-PT-PCCA-2013-4-1878, 4/01.07.2014, funded by UEFISCDI, Romania.

# References

1. Álvarez, M., Torres, A., Rodríguez, E., Padilla, S., Rodrigo, M.J.: Attitudes and parenting dimensions in parents' regulation of Internet use by primary and secondary school children. Comput. Educ. **67**, 69–78 (2013)
2. Anthony, L., Brown, Q., Nias, J., Tate, B.: Examining the need for visual feedback during gesture interaction on mobile touchscreen devices for kids. In: Proceeding of IDC 2013. ACM, New York, USA, pp. 157–164 (2013)
3. Anthony, L., Brown, Q., Tate, B., Nias, J., Brewer, R., Irwin, G.: Designing smarter touch-based interfaces for educational contexts. Pers. Ubiquit. Comput. **18**(6), 1471–1483 (2014)
4. Blagojevic, R., Chang, S.H.H., Plimmer, B.: The power of automatic feature selection: rubine on steroids. In: Proceeding of SBIM 2010, pp. 79–86 (2010)
5. Kang, C.: Survey: For young children, mobile devices such as tablets, smart phones now a mainstay. The Washington Post (2013)
6. Kim, H., Taele, P., Valentine, S., McTigue, E., Hammond, T.: KimCHI: a sketch-based developmental skill classifier to enhance pen-driven educational interfaces for children. In: Proceeding of SBIM 2013. ACM, New York, NY, USA, pp. 33–42 (2013)
7. Rainie, L., Smith, A.: Tablet and e-reader ownership update. Pew Research Center (2013)
8. Smith, A.: Smartphone ownership 2013. Pew Research Center (2013)
9. Vatavu, R.D., Cramariuc, G., Schipor, D.M.: Touch interaction for children aged 3 to 6 years: Experimental findings and relationship to motor skills. Int. J. Hum Comput Stud. **74**, 54–76 (2015)
10. Vatavu, R.D., Anthony, L., Wobbrock, J.O. Gestures as point clouds: A $P recognizer for user interface prototypes. In: Proceeding of ICMI 2012. ACM, NY, USA, pp. 273–280 (2012)
11. Webb, A.: Statistical Pattern Recognition, 2nd edn. John Wiley & Sons, UK (2003)

# Designing of 2D Illusory Tactile Feedback
# for Hand-Held Tablets

Youngsun Kim, Jaedong Lee, and Gerard J. Kim[(✉)]

Digital Experience Laboratory, Korea University, Seoul, Korea
{zyoko85,jdlee,gjkim}@korea.ac.kr

**Abstract.** In this paper, we investigate whether the "out of body" tactile illusion can be extended or applied to a relatively large hand-held device such as a tablet for which the hands/fingers would not be in direct contact with the vibration motors. We derived guidelines for applying tactile illusion techniques in 2D space with regards to operational conditions such as the size of the device, holding position, minimally required vibration amplitudes, and the effects of matching visual feedback. For this purpose, a series of exploratory pilot experiments were first conducted in 1D space. Based on the results, a 2D illusory tactile rendering method was devised and tested for its effectiveness. We have found that for a tablet sized device (e.g. *iPad mini* and *iPad*), the illusory perception was possible with a rectilinear grid resolution of $5 \times 7$ (with a grid size of 2.5 cm) with matching visual feedback.

**Keywords:** Funneling · Illusory feedback · Vibro-tactile feedback · User experience · Mobile/Hand-held interaction

## 1 Introduction

Smart hand-held devices nowadays come in many different sizes: from smart phones (10–15 cm in diagonal length) to larger tablet devices and hand-held computers (18–25 cm). There have been increasing interests in improving the user experience on hand-held devices by providing richer and more dynamic feedback through vibro-tactile actuators [6, 11, 12]. To avoid resorting to vibro-tactile arrays which would require a sizable and continuous contact area with the hand or body parts, researchers have proposed to apply tactile illusion techniques so that similar effects can be realized with only a few number of vibration motors [6, 11]. In addition, Miyazaki has demonstrated that tactile illusory feedback could be elicited at the "out of the body" space [8]. Kim has applied the "out of the body" tactile illusory feedback for a small-sized smartphone (9.4 cm in diagonal length), and demonstrated the illusory feedback was indeed applicable and extendable for interaction in 2D screen space using only four vibrators [6].

In this paper, we investigate whether the "out of body" tactile illusion can be extended or applied also to larger hand-held devices such as tablet devices. The extension is not expected to be straightforward for few reasons. First the original "out of body" tactile illusion was only validated when the body parts (e.g. fingertips) were stimulated directly and set apart by 7–8 cm span [6], similar to when the phenomenon was originally

© IFIP International Federation for Information Processing 2015
J. Abascal et al. (Eds.): INTERACT 2015, Part IV, LNCS 9299, pp. 10–17, 2015.
DOI: 10.1007/978-3-319-22723-8_2

discovered [8]. With tablet devices, the operating conditions are quite different (see Fig. 1(c) and (d)). For one, the vibratory stimulations are indirect, and the hands/fingers may not be in equidistance from the actuators. No relevant study has been reported for when the size of the hand-held object goes larger than the "8 cm" span, not to mention for the 2D extension.

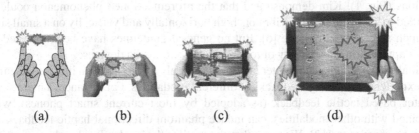

(a)       (b)       (c)       (d)

**Fig. 1.** The concept of "out of body" tactile experience from a hand-held object. (a) When vibratory stimulations are given to the fingertips properly, phantom tactile sensations can be felt as if occurring from the middle of the hand-held object [7]. The 1D tactile illusion is extended to 2D for (b) a small smart phone where fingers are in direct contact with the vibration motors [6], (c) a small tablet (e.g. *iPad mini*), and (d) a larger tablet (e.g. *iPad*).

Thus, to find out how to apply the "out of body" tactile illusion to tablet devices, we ran a series of pilot exploratory experiments to first observe the effects of the tactile illusion e.g. with regards to various operational conditions such as the size of the device, holding position, minimal vibration amplitudes and effects of accompanying visual feedback for a fair perception of the illusion. The findings and observations would form the basis for designing a proper 2D tactile illusory rendering method for the tablet device. We shortly describe these experiments, report the newly derived guidelines, propose for a 2D tactile illusory rendering method for a tablet, and empirically validate its effectiveness.

## 2  Related Work

Funneling is one of the major perceptual illusion techniques specifically for vibro-tactile feedback (along with saltation which we do not consider in this work for now). It refers to stimulating the skin at two different locations simultaneously with different amplitudes and eliciting phantom sensations in between the two (i.e. 1D phenomenon) [1, 3]. The intended location of the phantom sensation (ITL) can be changed by modulating the stimulation intensity.

Several researchers have applied this phenomenon to human interfaces, experimenting with different ways of modulating the vibration amplitudes for detailed controlling of the target phantom sensation locations [1, 2, 5, 9, 10]. For example, the SemFeel was a vibro-tactile feedback system for a mobile touch screen device [11] using five vibrators attached to the backside of the device (4 corners and 1 center). It was capable of producing 10 different perceptible vibration patterns for expressing richer semantic information compared to the usual single vibrator scheme.

Recently, researchers have discovered such phantom sensations can be extended to the "out of body" [8] (see Fig. 1(a)), thus making it possible to generate phantom tactile sensations as if coming from an external object. This result is appealing in its application possibility to mobile devices. That is, there now is a potential method to make a user feel (phantom) sensations indirectly emanating from the hand-held device (e.g. middle of the display), but supplying actual vibrations only to the "natural" holding finger/hand locations (Fig. 1). Kim demonstrated that the aforementioned phenomenon could be extended to 2D by employing vibrators both horizontally and vertically on a small sized (3.5 inch screen) smart phone [6]. But no general guidelines have been reported for further applications to a variety of today's hand-held media devices.

Finally, many human computer interfaces also rely on cross modal illusions to enrich user experience by fusing feedbacks of different modalities. For instance, a mere single vibrator based tactile feedback (as adopted by most current smart phones), when combined with other modalities, can induce phantom directional haptic feedback and rich user experience [12]. We posit that the tactile illusion feedback, when combined with other usual modalities such as the visual and aural, can similarly improve the inter-action experience even further.

Thus, to summarize, the distinguishing point of our work is that we seek to newly extend funneling to an enlarged 2D space, and identify important design guidelines. This would open doors for a more flexible design of vibro-tactile feedback techniques for a wide variety of hand-held devices.

# 3 Pilot Experiments: "Out of Body" Funneling Effects Along Longer 1D Separation Span

Due to lack of space, we only provide a very short description of how the exploratory pilot experiments were run. Funneling stimulations were given through vibrators attached to an *iPad mini* and *iPad*, along three horizontal (along the top/middle/bottom row) or vertical directions (along the left/middle/right column) using two vibrators attached at the respective ends (i.e. six vibrators used for each case). Sixteen participants were asked to report the existence of any illusory tactile perception and indicate where they came from, if any (along the respective row or column). Various rendering param-eters were changed and results observed.

## 3.1 Perception Resolution and Extent

Our data showed the smallest perceptible linear interval size to be comparable to that of the smart phone case (~1.6 cm) [6], "regardless of the size of the device (or distance between the vibration motors)," but only so in the middle part (40–60 % of the bands). The perception resolution was notably lower (or discernable grid size "stretched", e.g. to as long as 7 cm depending on where the device was held) near the horizontal or vertical ends (see Fig. 2). This was more evident in the vertical direction, because the hands were holding the device along the horizontal direction.

It seems the increased size of the devices and the fact that the hands/fingers are not in direct contact with the vibration motors somehow affect the "out of body" illusory perception near the holding positions. Based on this finding, we conjectured that for 2D situation, the perception resolution pattern and extent would look like what are depicted in Fig. 2 (dotted lines).

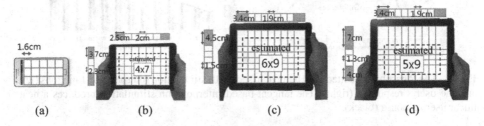

**Fig. 2.** Perceptible grid sizes in horizontal and vertical directions (a) smart phone: ~1.6 cm [6] (b) *iPad mini*: 2–3.7 cm, (c) *iPad* (held in the middle): 1.5–4.5 cm, (d) *iPad* (held in the lower part): 1.3–7 cm. The grids and the dotted area on the *iPad mini* and *iPad* show the "projected" effective perception area in 2D. Shaded regions represent the "stretched" grids.

## 3.2  Tactile Rendering Function and Interpolated Stimulation Strength

In the pilot experiment described in Sect. 3.1, we initially tested the three most popular and arguably reliable (in terms of eliciting the phantom sensation from the intended location) stimulation rendering methods for funneling, namely, interpolating the two vibration amplitudes using linear, logarithmic, and tangent functions [1]. Among the three, the tangent based interpolation showed the widest perception band (e.g. 6 intervals vertically and 9 horizontally on an *iPad* as shown in Fig. 2). However, in the later main experiment, this finding did not carry over to the 2D case. The responses were inaccurate and irregular. This was due to the fact that when tangent-based interpolation was applied in 2D, the interpolated amplitudes at the middle region became relatively too low (compare the two interpolating functions in Fig. 3). Thus, the logarithmic interpolation was chosen to render the tactile vibration amplitude with slightly less effective perception resolution ($5 \times 7$) but with higher accuracy and response regularity.

## 3.3  Hand Location

Finally, the finger/hand grabbing positions were varied between the middle and lower part on the sides of the tablets. When the users held the lower part of the tablets, the middle effective perception region also shifted in the lower direction and toward the user (see Fig. 2). In the main experiment, we asked the participants to hold the middle part of the device.

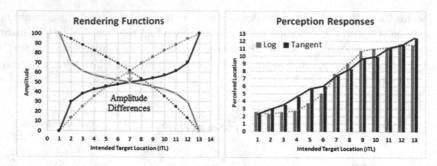

**Fig. 3.** The logarithmic (dotted) and tangent based (full) stimulation interpolation functions (left) and the user's responses (right). The tangent-based interpolation stimulation produces a near-linear user response (black).

# 4   Main Experiment: Extending "Out of Body" Funneling to Tablets

## 4.1   Experimental Design and Set up

In the main experiment, we used four single vibrators attached in the four rear corners of the *iPad* (see Fig. 1). We used the same rendering algorithm as in Kim's study for the smart phone [6] but with the few parameters adjusted according to our pilot experiment findings described in the previous section. The main purpose of the experiment was (1) to assess the illusory tactile perception behavior and effectiveness of the newly adjusted rendering algorithm with the larger tablet device and (2) how combining the illusory tactile feedback with the visual would further improve the accuracy and user experience. Two cases of 2D illusory tactile renderings were compared: without any visual feedback (NV), and with visual feedback (VF).

For NV, users were given 2D illusory tactile stimulations on an *iPad* held in the middle part (e.g. as shown in Fig. 1(d)) at the resolution of 5 × 7 (conservatively chosen based on the results of the pilot experiment). Participants were asked to pinpoint (using a stylus pen) where they felt the tactile feedback to be coming from.

For VF, when the stimulation was given, 5 visual icons (matching feedback), only one of them corresponding to the true intended target location (ITL), were shown and the user had to choose the correct one.

Vibrators were controlled by a voltage input using a PWM signal with an amplitude between 0 to 5 V, which in turn produced vibrations with frequency between 0 and 250 Hz and associated amplitudes between 0 to 2G (measured in acceleration, or 0 to 18 μm in position) respectively.

## 4.2   Detailed Procedure

Seven paid participants (4 men and 3 women) participated in the experiment with the mean age of 24.7. After collecting one's basic background information, the participant was briefed about the purpose of the experiment and instructions for the experimental task.

A short training was given for the participant to get familiarized to the experimental process. The participants wore ear muffs to prevent any bias from the sounds of the vibration. For both NV and VF conditions, the funneling stimulation was given by activating 4 vibrators simultaneously with logarithmically interpolated amplitudes according to the intended target location of phantom sensation (Fig. 4).

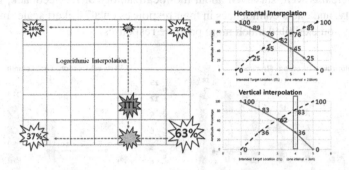

**Fig. 4.** Funneling stimulations for the 5 × 7 grid on an *iPad*. Amplitudes of four vibrators in the corners are logarithmically interpolated to produce an illusory sensation in the 2D screen space.

# 5  Results

## 5.1  NV Experiment

ANOVA was applied for analyzing the perception resolution illustrated in the horizontal and vertical directions separately for simplicity. Figure 5 shows the cases for the first row and column where 5 and 3 distinct intervals were perceived respectively. Other rows and columns showed similar statistics. This lead us to project that the 2D perception resolution to be about only 3 × 5, lower than the expected (Fig. 2). The graphs in Fig. 5 show a similar pattern of lowered resolution at the periphery of the screen, i.e. elongated/enlarged grid size (e.g. ITLs at 1, 2 and 6, 7 in Fig. 5(a) and 1, 2 and 4, 5 in 5(b)). Also note that the user response was not linear as desired, an artifact of resorting back to using the logarithmic interpolation and a possible interaction among the stimulations in 2D. Thus, we believe that better and linear responses can be obtained by employing vibration motors with larger amplitude capabilities and a "mixed" interpolation technique (e.g. logarithmic + tangent-based). Although the main purpose of NV experiment was observing user behavior for 2D response in 2D tactile feedback, correct responses for each ITL grid were recorded (Fig. 6).

## 5.2  VF Experiment

As for the case of VF, Fig. 6 shows the percentages of correct response for each ITL grid with an average of 78.6 % (right part of Fig. 6). Note that with the user having to select from five possible responses, the pure chance performance was only 20 %.

Thus the average of near 80 % is considered a psychophysically meaningful response [4, 7]. While the performance is relatively lower in the middle upper and middle lower region (denoted darker), we claim that with the accompanying matching visual feedback, the non-regular and distorted perception pattern was much rectified and resolution improved as well (compare the left and right parts of Fig. 6). In both NV and VF treatments, participants were surveyed about the localizability of the feedback, its clarity, task difficulty, and one's confidences in their responses on a 7-Likert scale. In all cases, the VF condition exhibited much more positive responses.

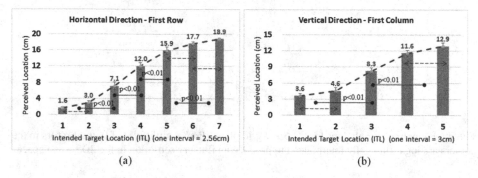

**Fig. 5.** Average percentage of correct responses in the horizontal (left) and vertical directions (right). The graphs show the same pattern of lowered resolution at the periphery of the screen (horizontal ITLs at 1, 2 and 6, 7 and vertical ITLs at 1, 2 and 4, 5).

| 47.8 | 17.4 | 26.1 | 13.1 | 0 | 13.1 | 73.9 | 73.9 | 65.2 | 56.5 | 60.8 | 52.1 | 82.6 | 86.9 |
|------|------|------|------|------|------|------|------|------|------|------|------|------|------|
| 26.1 | 52.2 | 39.1 | 21.7 | 8.7 | 17.4 | 52.2 | 78.2 | 91.3 | 65.2 | 69.5 | 78.2 | 73.9 | 78.2 |
| 4.3 | 27.3 | 43.5 | 65.2 | 21.7 | 26.1 | 21.7 | 86.9 | 86.3 | 78.2 | 86.9 | 91.3 | 73.9 | 91.3 |
| 43.5 | 39.1 | 30.4 | 13.1 | 21.7 | 34.8 | 43.5 | 95.6 | 91.3 | 56.5 | 69.5 | 73.9 | 95.6 | 91.3 |
| 65.2 | 4.3 | 8.7 | 0 | 17.4 | 8.7 | 43.4 | 91.3 | 73.9 | 73.9 | 52.1 | 73.9 | 69.5 | 73.9 |

**Fig. 6.** Overall performance of the NV (left) and VF (right) experiments. The percentages of the correct response are indicated in the grid.

# 6   Conclusion and Future Work

In this paper, we carried out pilot experiments to explore how to extend 2D illusory tactile rendering to tablet devices. Tablet devices exceed in length for which "out of body" tactile illusion is known to work, and the stimulations become more indirect and their interactions in 2D more complex. Based on the experimental findings, we have devised a 2D illusory tactile rendering algorithm and have found that for an *iPad* sized device, approximately 5 × 7 regular resolution (grid size = ~2.5 cm) of illusory perception was achievable, when a matching visual feedback was provided.

For future work, we will apply our findings to real world examples such as interactive videos and mobile games, and assess whether the UX can be improved by the proposed vibro-tactile rendering method. At the same time, we plan to investigate additional ways to improve the 2D sensation localization accuracy by adjusting various rendering parameters, combining with the aural modality and employing other vibro-tactile illusion techniques such as the saltation and apparent motion.

**Acknowledgements.** This research was supported by Basic Science Research Program through the National Research Foundation of Korea (NRF) funded by the Ministry of Science, ICT & Future Planning (No. 2011-0030079) and funded by the Forensic Research Program of the National Forensic Service (NFS), Ministry of Government Administration and Home Affairs, Korea (NFS-2015-DIGITAL-04).

# References

1. Alles, D.S.: Information transmission by phantom sensations. IEEE Trans. Man-Mach. Syst. **11**(1), 85–91 (1970)
2. Barghout, A., Kammerl, J., Cha, J., Steinbach, E., El Saddik, A.: Spatial resolution of vibrotactile perception on the human forearm when exploiting funneling illusion. In: Proceeding of IEEE International Workshop on HAVE, pp. 19–23 (2009)
3. Bekesy, G.V.: Funneling in the nervous system and its role in loudness and sensation intensity on the skin. J. Acoust. Soc. Am. **30**(5), 399–412 (1958)
4. Geshelder, G.: Psychophysics: The Fundamentals. Lawrence Erlbaum Associates, Mahwah (1997)
5. Israr, A., Poupyrev, I.: Control space of apparent haptic motion. In: IEEE World Haptics Conference (2011)
6. Kim, Y., Lee, J., Kim, G. J.: Extending "out of the body" saltation to 2D mobile tactile interaction. In: Proceedings of APCHI, pp. 67–74 (2012)
7. Kingdom, F., Prins, N.: Psychophysics: A Practical Introduction. Elsevier-Academic Press, London (2010)
8. Miyazaki, M., Hirashima, M., Nozaki, D.: The "cutaneous rabbit" hopping out of the body. J. Neurosci. **30**(5), 1856–1860 (2010)
9. Mizukami, Y., Sawada, H.: Tactile information transmission by apparent movement phenomenon using shape-memory alloy device. Intl. J. Disabil. Hum. Dev. **5**(3), 277–284 (2006)
10. Seo, J., Choi, S.: Initial study for creating linearly moving vibrotactile sensation on mobile device. In: Proceedings of IEEE Haptics Symposium, pp. 67–70 (2010)
11. Yatani, K., Truong, K.: SemFeel: a user interface with semantic tactile feedback for mobile touch-screen devices. In: Proceedings of UIST, pp. 111–120 (2009)
12. Nokia, Bouncing ball on Nokia N900 (2013). http://bit.ly/x2-bouncingball

# Need for Touch in Human Space Exploration: Towards the Design of a Morphing Haptic Glove – ExoSkin

Sue Ann Seah[1](✉), Marianna Obrist[2], Anne Roudaut[1],
and Sriram Subramanian[1]

[1] Department of Computer Science, University of Bristol, Bristol, UK
{s.a.seah,anne.roudaut,
sriram.subramanian}@bristol.ac.uk
[2] School of Engineering and Informatics, University of Sussex, Brighton, UK
m.obrist@sussex.ac.uk

**Abstract.** The spacesuit, particularly the spacesuit glove, creates a barrier between astronauts and their environment. Motivated by the vision of facilitating full-body immersion for effortless space exploration, it is necessary to understand the sensory needs of astronauts during *extra-vehicular activities* (EVAs). In this paper, we present the outcomes from a two-week field study performed at the Mars Desert Research Station, a facility where crews carry out Mars-simulated missions. We used a combination of methods (a haptic logbook, technology probes, and interviews) to investigate user needs for haptic feedback in EVAs in order to inform the design of a haptic glove. Our results contradict the common belief that a haptic technology should always convey as much information as possible, but should rather offer a controllable transfer. Based on these findings, we identified two main design requirements to enhance haptic feedback through the glove: (i) transfer of the shape and pressure features of haptic information and (ii) control of the amount of haptic information. We present the implementation of these design requirements in the form of the concept and first prototype of ExoSkin. ExoSkin is a morphing haptic feedback layer that augments spacesuit gloves by controlling the transfer of haptic information from the outside world onto the astronauts' skin.

**Keywords:** Space · Touch · Haptic feedback · Haptic glove · User experience · Extra-vehicular activities · Haptic jamming · Field study · Technology probes

## 1 Introduction

The idea of space travel and exploring other planets in the solar system has long fascinated and inspired humans. Even before Apollo 11 landed the first humans on the Moon in 1969, researchers had already been planning and developing mission profiles to Mars [27]. NASA and ESA have both expressed plans for permanently manned lunar bases in the future [13, 15]. A base in the Moon can serve as a testbed for new technologies and the exploration of interactive techniques that enable eventual extra-terrestrial settlement and develop future space missions [28]. This ever-increasing

© IFIP International Federation for Information Processing 2015
J. Abascal et al. (Eds.): INTERACT 2015, Part IV, LNCS 9299, pp. 18–36, 2015.
DOI: 10.1007/978-3-319-22723-8_3

interest in long-term missions and space settlements necessitates tackling astronauts' needs for full-body immersion and interaction with the environment.

However, the spacesuit creates an unnatural barrier resulting in the inability to feel, smell, or touch when exploring their surroundings. Since the human hand plays a major role when performing extra-vehicular activities (EVAs), the lack of haptic feedback has implications on any interaction with tools and the environment as astronauts often have to rely on visual cues. This is not always sufficient as the field of view is limited through the spacesuit and the helmet itself, which ironically makes astronauts dependent on their limited sense of touch to find objects and tools [34]. Both points suggest that astronauts cannot rely on intuitiveness when interacting with their environment, making EVAs a difficult and tedious experience. These limitations on the human senses, especially on touch, might result in a reduced ability of astronauts' to focus on their main tasks (e.g., geological sampling, scientific instrument setup and testing). With these issues in mind, technologies in human-computer interaction (HCI) should be exploited in the design context of space exploration, which will be common in the near future [18].

In this paper we focus on haptic experiences astronauts have when performing EVAs by looking at: (i) the details of the task and what they want to achieve; (ii) how they approach a task; (iii) what role their hands play in completing the task; and (iv) the types of haptic feedback that are relevant to the task. We carried out a two-week field study at the Mars Desert Research Station (MDRS), an analogue simulation environment, on a six-member crew. The MDRS reproduces an environment close to what an actual space mission is (zero gravity aside) and thus ensures a high level of ecological validity for our user study.

Over the two weeks, each crew member kept a logbook recording all their experiences whenever they performed an EVA. Inspired by work on technology probes [14], we introduced three low-level mechanical glove prototypes in the second week of the study to gain insight on the usefulness of haptic feedback in EVAs and for the completion of specific tasks assigned to the different crew members. The study concluded with an interview with each crew member capturing a more holistic understanding of the experiences from the last two weeks and highlighting the experienced difficulties and limitations when performing EVAs wearing gloves. We analysed the data and extracted individual user requirements (linked to different crew member roles or tasks), with a focus on the specific needs for haptic feedback design.

Based on the findings from the field study, we identified two key design criteria of a spacesuit glove with haptic feedback: (i) transfer of the shape and pressure features of haptic information; and (ii) control of the amount of haptic information. We present the implementation of these design requirements in the form of concept and first prototype of ExoSkin (Fig. 1). ExoSkin combines both a passive mechanical and an active electrical layer in its design. The mechanical layer of the glove transfers the shape of touched objects onto the user's skin while the electrical layer controls the amount of this transfer by tuning the stiffness of the layer. This concept represents a step towards a more intuitive and natural interaction of astronauts with the environment.

Here, we not only aim to make a design contribution, but also enhance our understanding of this specific context of use, user group, and its opportunities for further experimentations in HCI and interaction design.

**Fig. 1.** ExoSkin (right) is a morphing haptic feedback layer that augments spacesuit gloves by controlling the transfer of tactile information from the outside world onto the skin. To design ExoSkin, we carried out a two-week field study at the Mars Desert Research Station (left).

## 2  Related Work

Extra-vehicular activities (EVAs) require the astronaut to wear a spacesuit in order to perform operations away from Earth and outside spacecrafts. Due to the need to balance the protective function of a spacesuit in such harsh environments and the ergonomics of wearing one, the design of the spacesuit has gained lots of attention from space agencies, aerospace engineers, and also from HCI researchers. In this section we review previous work in two relevant areas: first, the current and future spacesuit and EVA glove designs, and second, haptic glove technology in HCI.

### 2.1  Spacesuit and EVA Glove Designs

Currently, spacesuits used by the United States, Russia and China are gas-filled full pressure suits. Gas-filled pressure suits have been used since the 1960s; for both lunar surface exploration and spacewalks at the International Space Station (ISS) [33]. However, there are many limitations with this type of suit such as their weight (more than 110 kgs) and limited mobility and dexterity due to the need to work against the pressure of the suit [35]. The number of EVA hours for the exploration of the Moon and Mars is projected to be more than all previous decades of EVAs combined [11]. Therefore, these suits are not suitable for long hours of human planetary surface exploration where EVAs can include difficult geological traverses [35, 37].

Thus, the 'space activity suit' has been proposed as a lightweight solution that provides enhanced mobility when performing EVAs [26]. These suits are essentially skin-tight elastic bodysuits that provide mechanical counter-pressures (MCPs) to uniformly compress the skin and therefore circumvent the need for a pressure suit [35]. One of the main research efforts into realizing this type of suit is the MIT Bio-Suit system [24]. The Bio-Suit aims to allow astronauts to work, with little resistance of the spacesuits, on Mars as they would do on Earth and thus avoiding the need for task simulation or non-standard equipment [26].

Current EVA gloves are pressurized like the spacesuits, meaning the astronauts' hand will also have to work against pressure when performing a task. The effect of

EVA gloves, due to its thickness and pressure, on hand-performance such as reduced grip strength, pinch strength and tactile sensations have been documented and observed [3, 34]. However, as hand and arm fatigue has been considered the main issue, most EVA technologies focus on reducing this by implementing power-assisted exoskeletons on the gloves [7, 36]. Similar to the MCP suits, there is also research into MCP gloves. Although these gloves provide the increased dexterity needed for the hand and fingers, sensory feedback is still reduced as the thickness of the Bio-Suit is aimed at 5 mm [12]. Although some studies have implemented tactile sensations for EVA gloves [1, 36], few have conducted user studies such as [1] which found that vibration feedback in the gloves to augment 'button-clicks' on a virtual keyboard increases text-entry rates and reduces errors. In this paper, we aim to investigate in detail how haptic feedback can improve the experience when performing a variety of EVA tasks drawing on haptic technologies designed and developed within HCI.

## 2.2 Haptic Glove Technology in HCI

Glove-based systems have been designed and developed since the 1970s to accurately track and measure hand configurations, movements and gestures [6]. These gloves, embedded with multiple sensors and trackers, have been mainly used for applications involving object selection and manipulation in virtual environments. Some of these glove-based systems also have actuators mounted to provide haptic feedback to the user's hands [5, 22, 32].

There are a variety of actuation technologies that can be used to generate haptic feedback; for example using motors, peltier elements, pin arrays and shape memory alloys [2]. Nevertheless, due to their complexity, not all technologies have been exploited in glove designs. Vibration actuators are most common as they are small and lightweight [5, 22]. The Teletact and Teletact II gloves [32] use air pressurized bladders to create force feedback in the palm. However, as far as we know, none of these glove-based systems have been applied to real-world scenarios involving the use of an actual glove with the exception of [4], which uses vibration feedback to augment obstacle distance information to firefighters.

Generally, there are three types of tactile displays [10]. The first type is pin arrays or sometimes called shape displays. These transfer vertical shape information and spatial patterns via the up-and-down movement of pins [9, 17]. Although effective at transferring most tactile information, it has been shown that lateral forces can also afford shape perception through active touch [29]. The second type uses vibration actuators and has been implemented not only in glove-based systems but many other prototype devices [2]. Although vibrations generate a 'buzzing' sensation, they can be used to produce different textures [21] and even 3D shapes [22]. The third method of producing tactile sensations is by creating lateral skin deformation using a simple comb-like system [10, 20]. This method has been shown to display Braille dots [20] and shapes and textures [19].

In this paper, we explore each of these types of tactile displays via three low-level mechanical glove prototypes, which we deployed as technology probes in the second week of our field study at MDRS.

# 3  Field Study

The study was conducted during a two-week field mission at the Mars Desert Research Station[1] (MDRS). The MDRS, based in the southern Utah desert, is one of several purpose-built analogue habitats that are located where environmental conditions, geological and biological features are similar to those on Mars. These habitats serve as field laboratories for researchers to run experiments that simulate the physical and psychological aspects of a Mars mission.

The MDRS is designed based on NASA's Design Reference Mission 3 and consists of a $10 \text{ m}^2$ two-story cylindrical habitat, a greenhouse and a small observatory. Researchers have to apply to participate and crews usually consist of six people who conduct their own independent Mars-related research. For one of the rotations, one of the authors was successfully recruited as part of a six-person crew (C6 – see Table 1). The crew was made up of four females and two males (aged between 25 and 53 years, mean 33), each with a specific role and main EVAs. C6 (author) facilitated the field study onsite and was not included in the data collection and analysis. There was a seventh person, a documentary film-maker, who was also not included in the data collection. Apart from C1 who took part two years ago, none of the other crew members had previously participated in a field rotation at the MDRS.

During the two weeks, crew members conducted all their EVAs in analogue spacesuits, which consist of the suit, a helmet, a backpack containing the life support system (fans with portable batteries), gloves and boots (see Fig. 2). Although the setup aims to be as realistic as possible, real spacesuits cannot be provided as they are too expensive and customized for size. Thus to mimic an envisioned field mission, the analogue suits used are coveralls, the gloves used are 4 mm thick ski gloves, the boots are hiking boots and the weight combination of the helmet and backpack is around 10 kg. For transport during their EVAs, crew members either walked or used all-terrain vehicles (ATVs). Each EVA generally lasts around 3 h and an average of two EVAs are carried out every other day.

Our field study offers a high level of ecological validity, which is crucial when designing interfaces for unfamiliar environments, such as space exploration. The users are

**Table 1.** Crew members' roles and main extra-vehicular activities at MDRS.

| Crew members | Roles and main extra-vehicular activities |
|---|---|
| C1 | *Crew commander.* Radiation dosage mitigation and radio signal measurements |
| C2 | *Crew medical officer.* Tele-surgery and tele-anaesthesia protocols for space |
| C3 | *Crew engineer.* Rover terrain testing |
| C4 | *Crew geochemist.* Hydrogen extraction from soil |
| C5 | *Crew astrobiologist.* Geological and biological sampling for extremophiles |
| C6 | *Crew engineer.* Exploration of haptic needs during EVAs |

---

[1] http://mdrs.marssociety.org/.

**Fig. 2.** Mars Desert Research Station in the southern Utah desert (left), and a crew member wearing the analogue spacesuit (right).

in a particular context and set of mind incorporating a plethora of factors (e.g., pressure to complete a task successfully, heavy equipment, time-delaying repercussions due to visual constraints of a spacesuit) that are very difficult to reproduce in laboratory settings. With our field study, we were able to reproduce an environment very close to what an actual space mission is (zero gravity aside), thus allowing our results to have higher external validity. Below we present the details on the conducted field study and methods used.

### 3.1  Study Design and Methods

The field study was divided into three parts: (i) a haptic logbook kept over two weeks, (ii) technology probes introduced in the second week, and (iii) individual interviews at the end of the two weeks. We describe each part in the following sections.

#### (i) Haptic Logbook: Need for Haptic Feedback in EVAs

The main aim of the logbook was to gather information on the types of EVAs that were carried out and the crew members' needs and requirements for haptic feedback when performing EVAs. Upon their return to the habitat, each crew member was asked to record and reflect about the difficulties they experienced when executing tasks during the EVA. They were also asked to describe as well as to rate their performance of the specific EVA on the day. As each crew member had their own research project and EVAs to carry out, they had their own specific tasks and equipment. A selection of these tools is shown in Fig. 3.

The logbook contained questions related to the following four aspects:

(1)  the details and characteristics of the conducted EVA (short narrative on the experience and title);
(2)  the context in which the EVA experience took place (presence of other crew members, physical environment, equipment used);
(3)  the experienced workload during the EVA (based on the NASA TLX[2]);

---

[2] NASA TLX: http://humansystems.arc.nasa.gov/groups/tlx/.

**Fig. 3.** Tools used by crew members during EVAs; ranging from geological hammers, spatulas, clinometer and thermometer, to pens, GPS and camera.

(4) the relevance of haptic feedback to the specific EVA (focused on the interaction wearing the glove, desirable haptic feedback).

In the second week, the logbook was enhanced with an additional question on:

(5) how, if any, of the technology probes (described in the next section) could have assisted them in the particular EVA.

### (ii) Technology Probes: Three Glove Prototypes

At the beginning of the second week, we introduced three glove prototypes as technology probes [14]. Technology probes is a simple and flexible approach with three interdisciplinary goals: *"the social science goal of understanding the needs and desires of users in a real-world setting, the engineering goal of field-testing the technology, and the design goal of inspiring users and researchers to think about new technologies"* [14]. This approach was particularly suitable for our field study as it enabled us to deepen our understanding of the need for haptic feedback in specific situations and for performing different tasks. The crew members were enabled to think beyond current limitations and express ideas about new solutions in the logbook and later on in the concluding interview.

For the design of the technology probes, we selected the following three types of haptic feedback mechanisms (as shown in Fig. 4):

(a) *Shape transfer mechanism (ST)*: This consisted of a rigid base holding an array of metal pins that can slide up and down. When the user makes contact with an object, the pins in contact with the object are displaced, thus transferring the shape with a resolution that depends on the density of the pins.

(b) *Vibration transfer mechanism (VT)*: This consisted of a rigid base holding an array of metal pins that has minimal horizontal and vertical movements (a few micrometres). When the user actively explores an object, the pins vibrate as a result of that action.

(c) *Lateral deformation transfer mechanism (LT)*: This consisted of a flexible silicone base onto which a matrix of comb-like plastic pins was embedded. When the user touches an object, the flexible base bends and causes the pins to move away or towards each other creating lateral stretching of the skin.

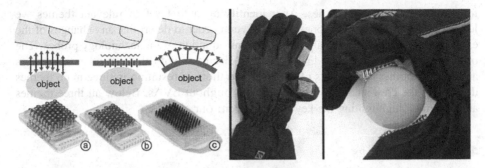

**Fig. 4.** (Left) The three different transfer mechanisms in the technology probes integrated into individual prototype gloves; (a) shape, (b) vibration and (c) lateral deformation. (Middle) Example of the glove prototypes: vibration transfer mechanism implemented on the index and thumb. (Right) The pins of the shape transfer mechanism deforming with the contour of a ball.

We chose these three mechanisms based on typical methods of providing tactile sensations (as discussed in the *Related Work* section) and the ability to implement them without use of complicated sensors and/or actuators, so as to have no expectation of the users, environment or objects. Thus they fit the purpose of a technology probe; being simple, flexible and adaptable technologies [14].

The gloves were introduced by C6 to each crew member individually in a 15-min session. Initial reactions were captured when the crew members were asked to use each prototype with some of the tools shown in Fig. 3. Each crew member was then asked to explore the gloves throughout the second week in relation to their EVAs and logbook entries, but not to discuss the details with the others to avoid a bias on the usefulness of three glove mechanisms. The gloves were placed on a common desk in the main habitat for the crew members to freely access whenever they wanted to.

**(iii) Individual Interviews: Overall Experience**

At the end of the two weeks, we conducted an interview with each crew member individually to capture their overall experiences over the two-week field mission, their EVA experiences, and their reflections on the challenges, surprises, and frustrations related to their sense of touch and the technology probes. The interviews were conducted by another researcher (co-author) on the last day at the MDRS. The interviews, which lasted about 45 min, took place in the greenhouse and were also based on the crew members' logbook entries (previously shared with the interviewer). All interviews were audio-video recorded for transcription and analysis purposes.

## 3.2   Data Analysis

The analysis process followed an open coding approach [30]. The two researchers involved in the role as crew member (C6) and interviewer conducted the first step of the qualitative coding process. To begin with, we looked at relevant themes across all collected data by carefully and repeatedly reading through the transcripts from the interviews and logbook entries. After identifying a first set of relevant themes we looked at the data from a temporal perspective in order to determine any changes of the experiences over time, especially due to the introduction of the technology probes. The outcomes from this initial coding effort was discussed with the two other co-authors and lead to further refinements of the identified themes, resulting in three main themes describing the crew members' experiences throughout EVAs. Below all three themes are described highlighting the key findings from our study.

## 4 Study Findings

From our analysis of the logbook and interview data, we identified three main themes that support the classification of crew members' experiences in EVAs:

(a) *Rethinking the hand/s*: Crew members became aware of the limitations and unexpected challenges of wearing both the spacesuit and gloves for EVAs, especially when performing precision work. This led crew members to re-think the 'familiar use' of their hands and focus on other and more specific parts of their hands (e.g., fingernails, palm) to complete the EVAs.

(b) *Changing practices*: The lack of haptic feedback resulted in crew members having to modify their work practices during EVAs. To complete their work, crew members exploited and enforced new strategies over time, as they could not perform tasks the same way as they would normally do with their bare hands. Specifically, they would explore new ways of using their hands (e.g., grasping with their fingertips, holding with their palm, engaging their wrist) and make use of other senses (e.g., vision) to help inform their actions.

(c) *Varying needs for touch*: Crew members have a specific understanding on how to complete their tasks; what is necessary for a successful EVA, and what they are willing to invest (e.g., taking safety and health risks into account). Despite a clear commitment to the vision of preparing humanity for life on Mars and the acceptance of challenges when wearing a spacesuit, crew members clearly expressed instances when haptic feedback was more or less desired in the interaction. When offered the three glove prototypes, crew members were able to reflect on the glove designs and their specific qualities in relation to their individual tasks and EVAs.

The first two themes represent the relevant understanding established about the specific use context, encountered limitations when wearing gloves, and crew members' experiences and exploited strategies over time. Based on this contextualisation of the design space for a haptic glove, the third and last theme represents the most relevant insights gained to inform the design process, as it narrows the interaction features down to the specific elements and needs for touch in different EVAs. Before we highlight our design solution to enhance haptic feedback, we describe three typical EVA scenarios exemplified through findings from the study and crew member quotes.

## 4.1 Findings Exemplified Through EVA Scenarios

In the following we elaborate on each of these themes through three specific scenarios representing typical EVAs from the two-week field study and crew members' feedback: (i) soil sampling for hydrogen extraction, (ii) geological sampling of rocks and soil surface and (iii) ATV terrain scouting (illustrated in Fig. 5).

**Fig. 5.** A few examples of EVAs performed during the field study: (a) soil sampling for hydrogen extraction; (b) examining rocks during geological sampling and (c) ATV terrain scouting.

**Soil Sampling for Hydrogen Extraction**

In this EVA, the crew member had to extract soil samples between 5 cm and 10 cm below the surface. The samples will later be brought back to the habitat for water content analysis. The tools used were a hammer to loosen up the soil, a spade to collect it, a bag to contain the soil and an infrared thermometer to measure the temperature of it. The crew member had to kneel down to perform the tasks.

As the whole crew, apart from C1, were wearing an analogue spacesuit for the first time, their excitement was coupled with the realisation of how the spacesuit impacts on their tasks within the EVA. The feeling of enjoying the challenge but also acknowledging its difficulty was captured by C4 as follows: *"I was like, 'Wow, I'm going to be like an astronaut!' But, after wearing it [spacesuit], it was really a heavy task...The first time was kind of exciting, but slowly, as I started walking and when I had to sit and dig it was very difficult for me to keep my legs in the right position".*

On establishing a new understanding of the hands, C4 comments in the interview: *"So, you will work according to that [limitations]. It's just that for 27 years, I am working with these fingers, I'm comfortable with that. It's like that. So, I just took some time in the beginning. It was difficult to understand how my hands are behaving with those gloves".*

C4 expressed frustration on the difficulty of moving with the heavy spacesuit: *"Wearing the backpack and the helmet, it was very uncomfortable, very uncomfortable... your backpack is heavy and you have to walk with it"* and the tools slipping out of the hand when digging for soil due to incorrect grip and not being able to feel the buttons on the thermometer; *"Oh my God, I never thought it would be so difficult"* but at the same time states that *"I was trying to cope with it, because I knew that it was a challenging task. I can't expect that things are going to be rosy".*

In the logbook, C4 mentions that although the task with the gloves became easier after the first EVA, grasping of tools was still difficult. C4 states; *"It was quite difficult to grasp the tools like the spade and the hammer for digging. With one hand, I felt as if I was not able to apply the right pressure to the tools [for] hitting or digging the soil. I could apply the right pressure to the radio button and it was much easier. It was so probably because of my understanding of the gloves from the first EVA".*

In the logbook, C4 also comments that haptic feedback would be helpful to *"... which can make easy to sense where the fingers not just the palm [are on the tool] as fingers help hold the tool and have the right grip on it".* When presented with the technology probes, C4 preferred a combination of the shape transfer (ST) and the lateral deformation transfer (LT) mechanism. In the interview, C4 states that *"This one [ST] I felt was very good for such devices ... If you have this one button to press, this would also work, because this is quite hard as a surface and you know what you're hitting. You know the difference of the protrusion of the button and the flatness of the other part... they are better for this precision type of work".*

Overall, this example on soil sampling highlights the initial reactions of crew members on the new situation and the realisation of the limitations of their hands in use. While the statements exemplify that the difficulties of wearing gloves were expected, it still took them time to realise and adjust to the unfamiliar behaviour of their hands and the lack of sensations and accuracy when performing simple tasks.

## Geological Sampling of Rocks and Soil Surface

In this EVA, the crew members had to collect geological samples from various locations. This EVA involved examining the outcrop and its density (whether hard and solid or soft and easy to break up), look at patterns in the rock (e.g., layer or signs of deformation) and inspect its grain size. The tools used were a geological hammer to break the rocks, a shovel for digging the soil, a camera to take photos of the samples, bags to contain the samples, a compass-clinometer to perform some measurements and a pen and notebook to record observations. If a sample is small, a spatula is used.

C5 recalled some thoughts before going on the first EVA: *"Oh, no, doing biological sampling and writing, how am I going to do it? But I find that when you have to, you have to. You find a way to do things".*

Upon realising the limitations on the EVA tasks, C5 noted in the logbook: *"My main problem was the decreased agility caused by the gloves. It made all the tasks much more difficult, time consuming and messy. It was trickier because I couldn't feel the edges of the aluminium foil around the spatula and cannot apply pressure to properly peel it off. However, writing with the gloves was a challenge and the writing in my notebook is very messy as the glove was thick and I could not hold the pen properly. For geological samples it would be good to touch the samples and feel the grain size (whether it's gritty or not). This is currently inhibited by the gloves."*

As in the previous scenario, the hands were sometimes not used in the normal way. C1 describes employing different methods for writing; *"I'd have to grip it as tight as I could, just to make sure the pen was secure, even though I couldn't quite tell where my fingers were in contact with the pen, just such that there was a solid surface".*

C1 also pointed out that haptic feedback was not always necessary for all tasks: *"For this EVA in particular, such sensation would have made writing easier, brushing items clean easier, peeling tinfoil off wrapping, open/closing the briefcase, and opening/closing zip-lock bags. Due to the loads required, I think very little would have been gained when using the digging shovel. In fact, less sensation helped in terms of mitigating against fatigue".*

C5 reflected on a combination of the ST and LT technology probes in relation to the task: *"Well, because [ST] takes the shape of what you're trying to press and touch. I think I found it easier to identify the buttons and things. But then, on the other hand, this glove [LT], the advantage was that because this is flexible, unlike [ST] It's thinner, I felt like I had, I guess, a bit more control of what I'm touching, I was able to feel the size of the button, not just the button coming at me."*

Overall, this example on geological sampling advances on the observations from soil sampling by giving more insights into the need for more fine-granular haptic feedback when touching a rock or handling small tools. However, at the same time, it brings to the fore the desire for an adaptable glove; so that it allows for less haptic feedback when digging on hard surfaces to avoid hand fatigue. It demonstrates the importance of finding a balance between increased haptic sensations for one task versus limiting the transfer of haptic sensations onto the human hand in another task, when performing the same type of EVA.

**ATV Terrain Scouting**

In this EVA, the crew members used the ATV to scout terrain for either rover testing or collecting geological samples. The other tool mainly used here was a walkie-talkie for communications between crew members and with the habitat.

From the logbook, C1 mentions safety implications of the lack of haptic feedback when driving the ATVs as it was difficult to feel the controls of buttons and throttle properly. C1 also mentions that he would make mistakes when carrying out certain tasks especially when using the walkie-talkie. C1 comments: *"I sometimes did not make the correct contact with the walkie-talkie communication button and would accidently release it half-way through a 10-count."*

From the logbook, C1 states; *"The gloves impeded my ability somewhat regarding the controls of the ATV, the buttons and the throttle - a necessary evil as without them, my fingers would have gotten very cold very quickly and my senses would have been in a far worse state...Where my thumb was, exactly in relation to the throttle level, was sometimes difficult to tell if I didn't look down. This could be considered dangerous when moving. My thumb could be half a centimetre below or above the throttle making the force I needed to input for a given amount of throttle variable. With the vibrations through the ATV (engine and interaction with trail surface) coupled to this lack of sensation, could lead to accidents."*

The glove, in most of the cases, does not allow enough haptic feedback, and thus limits one's ability to feel or receive any confirmation on an action. Most of the crew members start employing other senses, especially vision, to get their work done. C1 summarises as follows: *"The gloves are like oven mittens; you can't quite... It's like you've lost your senses in your hands. More than feel, you're using your eyes to see exactly what your hands are doing".*

In terms of haptic feedback based on the technology probes, C1 refers to the combination of ST and LT mechanisms as ideal as it will allow for more tactility and also increases precision when performing a task through ensuring grip on a tool (so that there is no need to exaggerate the pressure too much).

Overall, this example on terrain scouting further highlights that the need for more tactile sensations varies throughout an EVA (pressing buttons versus ensuring grip when steering the ATV). Moreover it also clearly points to the cross-sensory compensation for the lack of haptic information (i.e., through visual cues).

## 4.2    Crew Preferences Based on the Technology Probes

Overall, all crew members preferred the ST glove because it projects the shape, curvature and texture onto the hand which is useful for interacting with tools and objects. Three crew members (C1, C4 and C5) however saw this glove ideally combined with the LT glove, because its flexibility allows it to amplify pressure feedback. The VT glove was not preferred by anyone specifically because of the drawbacks of limited flexibility and shape and pressure feedback (Table 2).

**Table 2.**  Summary of crew experiences of glove design based on logbook and interview

| Shape transfer (ST) | Vibration transfer (VT) | Lateral transfer (LT) |
|---|---|---|
| The pins conform to the object's shape allowing one to be precise when pressing different buttons or when feeling and holding tools. This provides a high shape resolution allowing easy identification of general shapes and subtle differences in objects. | Different textures can be felt, but it is difficult to feel edges, sharpness or curvatures of objects. | Some shapes and textures can be felt, but edges of objects are not so clear. Compared to ST, this has a poorer shape resolution. However, it can transmit pressure sensations when pressing buttons or gripping tools. |

## 4.3    Summary and Implications for the Glove Design

Overall, crew members felt that the spacesuit and gloves created an additional burden to their work and made it more stressful and frustrating, especially considering the limited time they can spend on each EVA. Haptic feedback would have easily allowed them to perform some of their tasks more efficiently. More importantly, in terms of designing for haptic feedback, we found that there is not only a need for touch, but a need for varied levels of touch in different scenarios.

Based on the field study, which provided us with a clear understanding of the environment astronauts are operating and the limitations they face during EVAs, we started a design process that took not only the findings from the technology probes (the initial prototypes) into account but in particular the lessons from the varied needs of haptic feedback in the diverse sets of tasks and EVAs carried out by the crew.

In the following section, we present our conceptual and prototypical design of ExoSkin, which is based on two main design requirements:

(1) *Transfer of the shape and pressure features of haptic information*: The glove needs to be designed in a way that haptic information is transferred from the outside world onto the hand supporting differences in the shape contours (e.g., edges, curves, surface irregularities) to help astronauts easily identify objects. Pressure information is also important to enable astronauts to better judge the amount of pressure and grip to apply onto objects or tools.

(2) *Control of the amount of haptic information*: The variety of EVA tasks needs to be considered in the glove design such that it can equally support more sensations when needed for fine motor skills involved in geological sampling and less haptic feedback when driving an ATV through an uneven terrain.

## 5  Exoskin

In this section, we propose the concept of ExoSkin; a spacesuit haptic feedback layer that is able to selectively transmit haptic information from outside of the suit to the inside, i.e. onto the human skin. Based on the two main design criteria summarised in the previous section, we implemented ExoSkin in two layers: first, a passive mechanically actuated layer consisting of free-moving pins on a flexible material; and second, an active electrically-controlled jamming layer for programmable stiffness (Fig. 6).

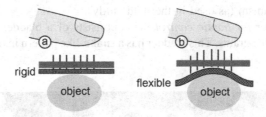

**Fig. 6.** ExoSkin layers. (a) When the jamming layer is rigid, haptic feedback is minimally transferred; and (b) when the jamming layer is flexible, the amount of haptic feedback that is transferred depends on the amount of air in the jamming layer.

### 5.1  Implementation

In the field study, we found that the shape transfer mechanism to be the preferred method for haptic feedback. We also found that a combination of the shape and lateral deformation transfer mechanisms was preferred by a few of the crew members. With both these points in mind, instead of implementing the shape transfer mechanism on a rigid base, we now implement it on a flexible silicon layer. A similar device [16] has shown that a pin array on a flexible base can even increase the sensitivity to surface asperities as it produces both normal and tangential forces to the skin.

As we observed for some tasks, the crew members did not want the gloves to transfer all of the haptic feedback. Thus, we added a second layer that is able to control the amount of haptic information that is being transferred. Although this layer can be implemented with actuated pins, we decided to create this second layer of ExoSkin using the principles of jamming due to its advantages as described below.

Jamming interfaces have been used to create a variety of objects and layers with electronically programmable stiffness [8, 25]. [25] demonstrated that thin layers of jamming can be used to create a shoe with different stiffness distributed all across its frame. Thus, the shoe can be configured for different scenarios such as walking, hiking or running. We draw inspiration from this and apply it to ExoSkin.

From initial prototyping tests, we found that jamming has the following advantages. Firstly, it allows us to control the rigidity of the layer in a continuous way, thus we can control the amount of haptic information that gets transferred. Secondly, due to its ability to deform and maintain rigidity, we are also able to use it for take shape and also grip objects (Fig. 7). The jamming layer can potentially act as an exoskeleton by retaining its shape when it is stiff. This is useful, especially for astronauts, as it can also be exploited as an exoskeleton for holding onto objects or surfaces. If the jamming layer was implemented in the whole hand, the glove can stiffen up and maintain form around tools thus avoiding occurrences of losing grip on tools.

We implemented ExoSkin in the form of fingertips of a glove as shown in Fig. 8. The ExoSkin prototype consists of two layers as described below:

(1) *Mechanical layer for haptic transfer:* This consists of a flexible layer made from 4 mm polyester fabric embedded with a matrix of free-moving plastic pins. This corresponds to implementing a combination of the shape and lateral deformation transfer mechanism (as used in the field study).

(2) *Electronic layer for haptic control:* This consists of a bladder made of silicone containing coffee grains. This bladder has a snake-like pattern in order for the coffee

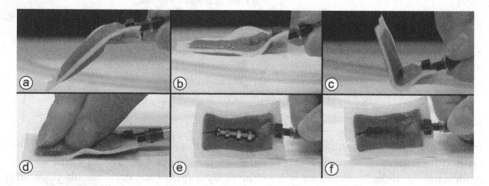

**Fig. 7.** Jamming layer implementation. (a) Layer is flexible; (b) it is rigid when air is removed; (c) a rigid layer can take shape; (d) when holding onto objects; (e) the layer can maintain grip on them and (f) it can hold the shape of the objects.

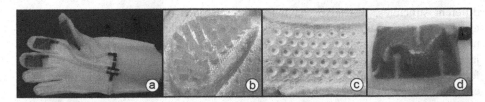

**Fig. 8.** First prototype of ExoSkin. (a) Glove prototype; (b) pin array on the inside which contacts the skin; (c) pin array on the outside and (d) jamming layer with chambers to ensure the grains stay homogeneously distributed.

grains to remain homogenously distributed. Due to the gravity, having a bladder without any patterns or chambers would cause the grains to collect on the sides depending on the orientation of the glove. Each bladder is then connected to a peristaltic pump that controls the amount of air in the bladder and thus its flexibility.

The design of ExoSkin offers three advantages: (a) transfer of shapes and pressure information; (b) continuous control of this transfer and (c) the ability to maintain grip on objects. Although implemented at the fingertips at the moment, ExoSkin can be extended to the whole hand and even to other parts of the body (e.g. arms or feet).

## 6   Conclusion and Future Work

Our research focused on the need for haptic feedback during extra-vehicular activities. The combination of the field study at the Mars Desert Research Station and the use of initial ExoSkin prototypes as technology probes within the study initiated a promising design process towards a morphing haptic feedback glove.

We have identified that not only is there a need to enhance haptic feedback when wearing gloves, there is also a need to reduce haptic feedback for certain tasks to improve an EVA experience. Moreover, depending on a crew member's role and task, more specialised glove design need to be considered. Apart from the three scenarios discussed in this paper, other crew member roles need to be taken into account. For example, a crew scientist could require sterile gloves and a crew medic could require intelligent gloves for capturing biometrics from a patient. These specialised EVA scenarios open up future design directions for HCI and haptic technology.

Further investigations are needed to create higher-fidelity prototypes and evaluate their usefulness for specific tasks. Although we can build on previous works on perception studies of pin arrays [e.g. 23, 31], future studies will also need to investigate perception thresholds with varying stiffness and thickness of the jamming layer.

Moreover, in order to achieve a functional device, we believe our work can be supported with new technologies from areas such as material engineering. Active materials, such as shape memory polymers, and textile architectures, which these materials are built into, are already being investigated to create morphing structures that can actively compress to provide the pressures needed for the Bio-Suit system [12]. For the jamming layers, [25] demonstrated that thin layers can be weaved together to form different structures. Instead of having pins embedded through a fabric, 3D textile technologies drawn upon to create pin-like structures, so that the mechanical layer does not have holes. Although we implemented ExoSkin using a pin array combined with a jamming layer, many other technologies could be used (e.g., pin array combined with ferrofluid or just an array of actuated pins). ExoSkin could be applied in other work environments, which involve both the need to wear gloves and precision work. For example, tactile sensation is highly important for extreme work conditions like fire-fighting where there is impaired vision due to smoke and low light levels [4].

In conclusion, the insights gained from our field study did not only inform and steer the design of a new haptic glove, but also enabled us to establish a richer understanding of a use and interaction context – human space exploration – not yet mainstream within HCI and interaction design research. This is only the first of many studies to come considering the global ambition to prepare humanity for life on Mars.

**Acknowledgements.** The authors thank all members of MarsCrew134 for participating in the field study and for some of the photos and videos. This work was supported by the EC within the 7th framework programme through the FET Open scheme for the GHOST project (Grant Agreement 309191) and within the Horizon2020 programme through the ERC (Starting Grant Agreement 638605).

# References

1. Adams, R.J. et al.: Glove-enabled computer operations (GECO): design and testing of an EVA glove adapted for human-computer interface. In: 42nd AIAA ICES, pp. 1–23 (2013)
2. Benali-Khoudja, M., Hafez, M., Alexandre, J.M., Kheddar, A.: Tactile interfaces: a state-of-the-art survey. In: 35th International Symposium on Robotics, pp. 721–726 (2004)
3. Bishu, R.R., Klute, G.: The effects of extra vehicular activity (EVA) gloves on human performance. Int. J. Ind. Ergonomics **16**(3), 165–174 (1995)
4. Carton, A., Dunne, L.E.: Tactile distance feedback for firefighters: design and preliminary evaluation of a sensory augmentation glove. In: Proceedings of the 4th Augmented Human International Conference, pp. 58–64 (2013)
5. CyberTouch. http://www.cyberglovesystems.com/
6. Dipietro, L., Sabatini, A.M., Dario, P.: A survey of glove-based systems and their applications. IEEE Trans. Syst. Man. Cybern. C Appl. Rev. **38**(4), 461–482 (2008)
7. Favetto, A., Chen, F.C., Ambrosio, E.P., Manfredi, D., Calafiore, G.C.: Towards a hand exoskeleton for a smart EVA glove. In: IEEE ROBIO, pp. 1293–1298 (2010)
8. Follmer, S., Leithinger, D., Olwal, A., Cheng, N., Ishii, H.: Jamming user interfaces: programmable particle stiffness and sensing for malleable and shape-changing devices. In: 25th UIST, pp. 519–528 (2010)
9. Garcia-Hernandez, N., Tsagarakis, N.G., Caldwell, D.G.: Feeling through tactile displays: a study on the effect of the array density and size on the discrimination of tactile patterns. IEEE Trans. Haptics **4**(2), 100–110 (2011)
10. Hayward, V., Cruz-Hernandez, M.: Tactile display device using distributed lateral skin stretch. In: Proceedings Haptics Interfaces for Virtual Environment and Teleoperator Systems Symposium, pp. 1309–1314 (2000)

11. Hoffman, S.J.: Advanced EVA Capabilities: a study for NASA's revolutionary aerospace systems concept Programs. NASA/TP—2004-212068 (2004)
12. Holschuh, B., Obropta, E., Buechley, L., Newman, D.: Materials and textile architecture analyses for mechanical counter-pressure space suits using active materials. In: AIAA SPACE Conference and Exposition (2012)
13. Hovland, S.: ESA human lunar architecture activities. In: International Lunar Conference (2005)
14. Hutchinson, H., et al.: Technology probes: inspiring design for and with families. In: CHI, pp. 17–24 (2003)
15. Kennedy, K.J., Toups, L.D., Rudisill, M.: Constellation architecture team–lunar scenario 12.0 habitation overview. In: Earth and Space, pp. 989–1011 (2010)
16. Kikuuwe, R., Sano, A., Mochiyama, H., Takesue, N., Fujimoto, H.: Enhancing haptic detection of surface undulation. ACM Trans. Appl. Percept. 2(1), 46–67 (2005)
17. Killebrew, J.H., Bensmaia, S.J., Dammann, J.F., Denchev, P., Hsiao, S.S., Craig, J.C., Johnson, K.O.: A dense array stimulator to generate arbitrary spatio-temporal tactile stimuli. J. Neurosci. Methods 161(1), 62–74 (2007)
18. Kostakos, V.: The challenges and opportunities of designing pervasive systems for deep-space colonies. Pers. Ubiquit. Comput. 15(5), 479–486 (2011)
19. Lévesque, V., Hayward, V.: Tactile graphics rendering using three laterotactile drawing primitives. In: Haptics Symposium (HAPTICS), pp. 429–436 (2008)
20. Lévesque, V., Pasquero, J., Hayward, V., Legault, M.: Display of virtual braille dots by lateral skin deformation: feasibility study. ACM Trans. Appl. Perct. 2(2), 132–149 (2005)
21. Martínez, J., Garcíia, A.S., Martínez, D., Molina, J.P., González, P.: Texture recognition: evaluating force, vibrotactile and real feedback. In: Campos, P., Graham, N., Jorge, J., Nunes, N., Palanque, P., Winckler, M. (eds.) INTERACT 2011, Part IV. LNCS, vol. 6949, pp. 612–615. Springer, Heidelberg (2011)
22. Martínez, J., García, A., Oliver, M., Molina Masso, J., González, P.: Identifying 3D geometric shapes with a vibrotactile glove. In: IEEE CGA, p. 99 (2014)
23. Nakatani, M., Kawakami, N., Tachi, S.: How human can discriminate between convex and concave shape from the tactile stimulus. In: Annual Conference Cognitive Science (2007)
24. Newman, D.J., Canina, M., Trotti, G.L.: Revolutionary design for astronaut exploration - beyond the bio-suit system. Proc. STAIF 880(1), 975–986 (2007)
25. Ou, J., Yao, L., Tauber, D., Steimle, J., Niiyama, R., Ishii, H.: jamSheets: thin interfaces with tunable stiffness enabled by layer jamming. In: Proceedings of the TEI, pp. 65–72 (2014)
26. Pitts, B., Brensinger, C., Saleh, J., Carr, C., Schmidt, P., Newman, D.: Astronaut bio-suit for exploration class missions. NIAC Phase I Final report, MIT, Cambridge (2001)
27. Portree, D.S. Humans to Mars: Fifty Years of Mission Planning, 1950–2000. NASA/SP-2001-4521 (2001)
28. Purves, L.R.: Use of a lunar outpost for developing space settlement technologies. In: Proceedings of the AIAA Space (2008)
29. Robles-De-La-Torre, G., Hayward, V.: Force can overcome object geometry in the perception of shape through active touch. Nature 412(6845), 445–448 (2001)
30. Saldana, J.: The Coding Manual for Qualitative Researchers. SAGE Publications, Thousand Oaks (2012)
31. Shimojo, M., Shinohara, M., Fukui, Y.: Human shape recognition performance for 3d tactile display. IEEE Trans. Syst. Man Cybern. Part A Syst. Hum. 29(6), 637–644 (1999)
32. Stone, R.J.: Haptic feedback: a brief history from telepresence to virtual reality. In: Brewster, S., Murray-Smith, R. (eds.) Haptic HCI. LNCS, vol. 2058, pp. 1–16. Springer, Heidelberg (2001)

33. Thomas, K.S., McMann, H.J.: US Spacesuits. Springer, Heidelberg (2011)
34. Thompson, S., Mesloh, M., England, S., Benson, E., Rajulu, S.: The effects of extravehicular activity (EVA) glove pressure on tactility. In: Proceedings of the Human Factors and Ergonomics Society, vol. 55, issue 1, pp. 1385–1388 (2001)
35. Webb, P., Cole, C., Hargens, A.: The elastic space suit: its time has come. In: Proceedings of the ICES (2011)
36. Yamada, Y., et al.: Proposal of a SkilMate hand and its component technologies for extravehicular activity gloves. Adv. Robot. **18**(3), 269–284 (2004)
37. Young, D., Newman, D.: Augmenting exploration: aerospace, earth and self. In: Bonfiglio, A., De Rossi, D. (eds.) Wearable Monitoring Systems, pp. 221–249. Springer, Heidelberg (2011)

# Tactile Communication in Extreme Contexts: Exploring the Design Space Through Kiteboarding

André Schmidt[1], Mads Kleemann[1], Timothy Merritt[2(✉)], and Ted Selker[3]

[1] Aarhus University, Åbogade 34, 8200 Aarhus N, Denmark
andre@andsch.com, madskleemann@me.com
[2] Aarhus School of Architecture, Nørreport 20, 8000 Aarhus C, Denmark
timothy.merritt@aarch.dk
[3] CITRIS, University of California, Berkeley, USA
ted.selker@gmail.com

**Abstract.** This paper uses kiteboarding as an experimental platform to find ways in which technologies could support communication needs in mentally and physically demanding contexts. A kite control bar with embedded sensors and actuators communicates instructions through voice or tactile cues to explore facilitating communication for control guidance. Tactile cues were shown to be productive in changing behavior. Voice, however, communicated planning models and directional guidance better than tactile cues. Still, voice may negatively impact experience. The experiments highlight the need for better ways for communication tools to support mental models.

**Keywords:** Tactile communication · Research through design · Extreme sports · Kiteboarding

## 1 Introduction

This study explores communication modalities to provide feedback using kiteboarding as a platform to examine the design space and better understand the experience. Kiteboarding (also referred to as kitesurfing) is a water-sport, inspired by wakeboarding, windsurfing, and paragliding. The kite pulls a person standing on a special purpose surfboard or a kiteboard across the surface of the water. It requires expert control of a 6–17 square meter kite producing considerable pulling power and speed similar to a ski boat. The kite is connected to the rider typically by four lines 20 m in length, which are controlled through a hand-held control bar and a harness worn around the waist. The activity is commonly described as one of the most complex coordinated activities people engage in. Common to all kiteboarding skills is that kite and board control and timing of maneuvers is crucial to success. Giving and receiving feedback on technique is challenging as the rider is separated from others on a windy day during the activity. Hand-over-hand training is inappropriate and post session reviews do not provide real-time feedback.

© IFIP International Federation for Information Processing 2015
J. Abascal et al. (Eds.): INTERACT 2015, Part IV, LNCS 9299, pp. 37–54, 2015.
DOI: 10.1007/978-3-319-22723-8_4

**Fig. 1.** Kiteboarding – a rider is sailing on the water surface using a kite as the power source.

Discrete signals can be effectively communicated with voice and tactile means, for example the instructor can yell, "Let go of the bar!" and a student will drop the control bar. In a similar way, a sharp tactile pulse might be used to carry the same meaning. This would seem to be a natural feedback, aligned with and transmitted through the control bar. In the context of scuba diving, instructors often carry a metal rod to tap against an air tank propagating a sharp noise through the water, an effective blunt communication for alerting student divers to attend to the instructor. We are only beginning to understand the impact to human performance and experience when multimodal communication technologies support performance and skill acquisition [19]. There is similar interest in exploring directional control and communicating continuous values, as well as directional guidance in real-time tasks of navigation using a mix of tactile and visual cues [4, 5, 30].

It is an interesting direction for research to explore how communication channels impact cognitive resources and experiential effects of activities. Existing research often involves building of prototypes with isolated tests of individual modalities. In this paper we explore the language of multimodal interactions to support performance and experience in the extreme sport of kiteboarding by focusing on the modes of voice and tactile feedback.

We present an augmented kiteboarding control bar prototype that provides tactile communication between the rider and the instructor. It will be used in studies that examine the performance of steering a kite with the help of three different types of feedback including vibrotactile feedback alone, vibrotactile feedback combined with voice feedback, and voice feedback alone.

The rest of this paper is organised as follows. First we describe the sport of kiteboarding to provide a better understanding of the disciplines, demands on the rider, experiential goals and identify opportunities for technology to support the experience. We identify communication as an area to explore further and describe the development of a prototype control bar that facilitates communication. We then describe two user evaluations that explore the usefulness and experiences of voice and vibrotactile feedback separately and combined. We then relate the results of the evaluations to the existing research to provide insights for designers focused on the context of extreme sports.

## 2   Kiteboarding

In this section kiteboarding will be described; this emerged from expert and instructor interviews, observations and the authors' combined experience of more than 20 years in the sport. Kites are usually between 6 m$^2$ and 17 m$^2$ depending on the wind speed and rider weight. It is controlled through lines between 10–30 m long (see Fig. 1). Steering left is done by pulling the left side of the control bar, same for right. Some novices think turning the bar like a steering wheel will cause the kite to turn – this is not the case, tension on the steering line must be applied. Power is controlled by either pushing the whole bar away, which depowers the kite, or by pulling the bar towards the body, which powers up the kite. Board control including edging and balance are also crucial skills for kitesurfing.

### 2.1   Communication

While kite instructors might demonstrate their skills next to a student, interviews with 5 kiteboarding instructors revealed the preferred method of communication between students and instructors is through voice. However, during training and riding, the athletes are quickly separated. In these situations, hand signals are used to communicate commands and requests. Radio communication helmets are used by some kite-schools, however, they are expensive and delicate, and students often become overwhelmed with the water noise and poor sound. Instructors reported to us that students stop responding to voice commands during high levels of excitement. Perhaps the overloaded audio channel leads to confusion, change blindness, or that instructions blend in with environmental noise.

### 2.2   Progression

There are different ways a rider typically progresses in training depending on their skill level. Kitesurfing is very difficult to learn without taking a beginner's course [16], while an intermediate rider or expert typically learns through watching others, viewing instructional videos, and through much practice. For feedback, riders often return to shore for critique from others. Kite control is a crucial component for the progression of riders at all levels. Training could involve moving the kite to a position in the sky requested by the instructor, holding it steady at one position, or moving it through various positions in a sequence. The kite position is typically explained according to the positions of a clock face as shown in Fig. 2. The entire face is referred to as the wind window as shown in Fig. 3. Holding at 12 o'clock is directly overhead, while a kite positioned at 9 or 3 is nearly touching the ground.

### 2.3   Technology for Kiteboarding

Already within the sport of kiteboarding there are various technologies used including a personal video documentation camera (e.g. GoPro) to capture video, GPS or a

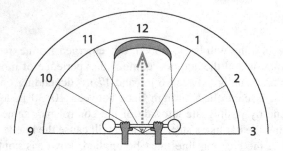

**Fig. 2.** A clock face is used to describe the kite position in the wind window.

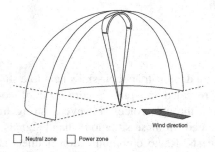

**Fig. 3.** The wind window that shows where the kite can fly.

smartphone to map a route. Other products promise to track and replay kite board movements in virtual replay [33]. This enables riders to evaluate height, length and speed of jumps etc. We recognized the challenges and needs for communicating guidance and suggestions for skill improvement, yet we find few examples of technology to support this. Furthermore, there has not been sufficient attention given to the physical equipment including control bar, board, harness, which provide opportunities for contact to the body and capacity for holding embedded technology.

# 3  Related Work

Work that has examined technologies supporting physical activities include research focused on technologies in sports and physical activities, technologies supporting navigation, and research exploring the limits of human perception in various modalities. Of particular interest is the research that involves embedding communication technologies into activities to better understand the context and to explore the performance and responses to the technology-based interventions.

## 3.1  Technologies in Sports and Physical Activity

Research has gone into exploring interactive technologies and how it can support physical activities by improving performance, experience and motivating physical activity. Much research has focused on exertion interfaces which examine technologies to foster exercise interactions [25], enhancing social play through familiar activities, using elements from computer games to motivate physical activity and new forms of expression and performance. Various examples of research explore how technology can improve the performance and technique of athletes [2, 8, 34], the experience of performing the exertion activities [26, 28], and designing for such interactions [12, 29]. Research has distinguished between interactive sport-training games and integrated systems [19]. These games refer to systems that train activities that could translate back into the sport activity. These systems include technologies that embed directly into the activity and seek to improve performance and training. Training systems have been studied using tactile instructions to give athletes cues on navigation, timing and posture in different sports [8, 35].

## 3.2  Technologies for Navigation

We examine research involving audio, tactile, and/or haptic means of delivering feedback, as these modalities might free the rider's visual sense that is generally focused on their equipment, spotting and avoiding obstacles. Navigational cues are delivered using simple, symbolic, ambient and spatial representations of directions. Various examples of research using audio technologies for navigation include simple directional voice commands for visually impaired [22], and spatial sounds presenting general directions [15, 41]. Research projects have focused on aiding navigation and orientation through the use of tactile feedback as described in [6] including tactile feedback delivered to various parts of the body through wearable and mobile devices. Research explored smartphones [27], tactile belts [14, 38] and shoes [21] to give simple directional cues, as well as symbolic cues for communicating direction [39] and ambient guidance [9, 37]. In terms of haptic research, simple directional signals have been explored for guiding pedestrians [24] and navigation through symbolic haptic means in the form of shape and weight shifting technologies [13]. More direct forms of guidance are also relevant including examples of actually pulling the user's body [1, 20] or providing guidance through shape-changing mobile devices that simulate a physical guide or handrail [17].

## 3.3  Human Factors in Multimodal Interfaces

The capacity and limits of human perception and attention in a high cognitive workload environment have been explored through research focused on human modalities, attention and processing resources, as well as insights about mapping the modality to the appropriate information. Multiple Resource Theory proposes that humans can process information from multiple sensory channels simultaneously, and that in some situations it can be more effective to divide attention between visual and auditory channels rather than loading a single sensory channel [40]. Changes in modalities can be easily overlooked due to lack of attention [32]. Change blindness can occur in vision, in the audition (change deafness), or even within the tactile modality [10]. There are also attempts at providing overall guidance in selection of communication modality and task [7].

## 4   Research Problem

While there is much work focused on technologies to support various activities, there has been less focus on communication in the demanding context of extreme sports. With kiteboarding as a platform for exploration of high demands on the user, we examine the use of voice and tactile communication technology to support the needs of kiteboarders. How does choice of modality (voice or tactile) impact the effectiveness of control guidance? Are there any interactions or complimentary effects of using voice and tactile feedback together? Aside from objective measurements of performance, are there subjective measures that reveal any preferences and experiential differences?

## 5   Design and Implementation

When a student is learning how to sail a boat, an instructor is sitting beside the student and is able to assert direct control and manipulate the same controls as the student. This is known as hand-over-hand training through a shared object. However in the context of kiteboarding this is not possible due to the separation of instructor and student/rider. This is problematic for both the beginner but also for the intermediate or expert rider who wants direct feedback on his technique. The overall vision with our design has been to capture the benefits of hand-over-hand instructions. We present the current prototype that aims to capture this vision followed by details about the issues we explored during the design process.

### 5.1   Current Implementation

By adopting haptic feedback technologies in a "shared object" model as illustrated in the inTouch system [3], the design vision is a control bar that connects two people through vibrotactile feedback. In Fig. 4A, both the instructor and the student are

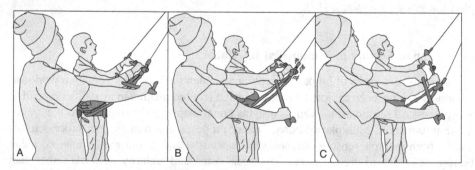

**Fig. 4.**  Design vision: (A) Instructor and student have the control bars in the same orientation thus no vibrotactile signals are sent. (B) When the instructor moves the control bar to a new position, the student control bar vibrates on the side of the bar indicating direction to move. (C) The student matches the instructed position and the vibrotactile signals cease.

holding a control bar, however the instructor bar is not attached to a kite. When the instructor moves the bar to a new position the student bar will vibrate in the corresponding side of the bar, indicating the direction to move, and thereby which side to pull as shown in Fig. 4B. This mapping is similar to the metaphor of "tapping on one's shoulder" [31]. When the student bar is at the same position as the instructor bar, the directional vibrotactile signal will stop and a short tactile confirmation cue could be given. For testing purposes, only the student bar is part of the current implementation. It consists of the tactile kite control bar and a Java-based test control system on a PC for facilitating evaluations and logging of performance data. The tactile bar prototype is shown in Fig. 5, and consists of (A) a waist harness for holding an Arduino Leonardo microcontroller inside a box (B), a kite control bar equipped with two large mass Eccentric Rotating Mass (ERM) vibrotactile actuators from a Playstation controller at each end of the bar (C and E), (D) a Sparkfun MMA7361 3-axis accelerometer and a 6 mm ERM vibrotactile actuator in the middle of the bar. The bar is attached to the harness using a leash (G) ensuring that the kite cannot fly away accidentally. A signal wire along the leash (F) is attached making communication between the bar and micro controller possible. Based on accelerometer readings, the prototype is able to provide tactile feedback in the right and left hand side, or both, simultaneously. A smoothing algorithm provides stable accelerometer readings. Further, a small center-mounted vibrator can distribute stimuli all over the bar. The prototype can be used as a research platform to study teaching different kinds of feedback for a variety of kiting skills (like "Let go of the bar!") and even multi-kite coordination (like kiting in formation).

### 5.2   Design Exploration

The current prototype is a result of several iterations, where different technologies for feedback were considered. During the process the design has been evaluated by 5 instructors, 2 kiteboarding equipment designers from the CrazyFly kiteboarding

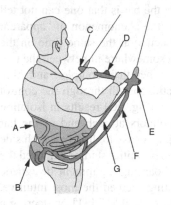

**Fig. 5.** (Left) Elements of prototype: (A) harness, (B) microcontroller enclosure, (C) left vibrotactile actuator, (D) accelerometer and center vibrotactile actuator, (E) right vibrotactile actuator, (G) safety leash, (F) signal wire. (Right) Control bar prototype in use during study session.

company and various kiteboarders including the authors of this paper. The process has been centered around four factors: placement, number of actuators, intensity as identified in [11] and mapping of the system logic to the actuation events. Regarding intensity, two different types of vibrotactile actuators have been considered, the ERM type and the Linear Resonant Actuator (LRA) type. The ERM feedback is often bigger and more intense than the smaller, more precise and faster LRA feedback. Figure 6 illustrates different options regarding the placement and number of vibrotactile actuators.

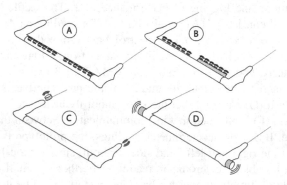

**Fig. 6.** Different stimuli explored in number and placement. (A) LRA actuators inside the bar. (B) LRA actuators outside the bar, both isolated with fabric and direct mount. (C) Vibrotactile actuators on the lines, both with ERM and LRA type. (D) ERM actuators on bar ends

Adding small LRA vibrators inside the control bar (Fig. 6A) will cause the stimuli to resonate all over the bar, because of tight contact to the material. This challenge is also faced when mounting LRA's outside the bar (Fig. 6B). Isolating the actuators from the bar is possible with an insulating material such as foam (Fig. 6B), but when applying pressure, contact will again be present. This is problematic if trying to create an animated stimulus for example from the middle of the bar to the ends of the bar. The overall result of adding more actuators inside or outside the bar is that one can not tell the difference in where the stimulus is active. It reflects the phenomenon of "apparent location", which is when two separated vibrations are active at the same time on the skin, they can be perceived as one single vibration from somewhere in between the two [11]. That suggests an approach of choosing simple rather than complex and high positional fidelity when it comes to communicating tactile stimuli through the control bar. Mounting vibrotactile actuators directly on the lines (Fig. 6C) results in isolation from the bar. Mounting powerful large-mass ERM actuators at each end of the bar turned out to be very effective (Fig. 6D). With this setup it is easy to discern which side is vibrating, therefore this setup is part of the current design. Initial studies explored the options of mapping. Evaluations with instructors, kiteboarding equipment designers, and others showed that pulling in the side that is vibrating seemed the most intuitive. This is also similar to the metaphor of "tapping on one's shoulder" [31] or steering a motorcycle to the same side as the active tactile stimuli [30]. Some use the opposite analogy when steering a car, but here the driver must steer *away* from the cue felt [36].

In the case of driving, that approach seems optimal, because the driver would steer *away* from the road barrier.

# 6 Evaluation

The evaluation of the system is aimed at performance in kite control. In order to examine this, two study sessions were conducted. To avoid the learning effect, each session was conducted with a new set of 10 participants. In each session participants performed a kite control task involving three conditions providing different modes of guidance including tactile feedback only (tactile only), voice feedback only (voice only), and voice commands with tactile feedback (tactile + voice). The order presented to the subjects was balanced and randomized. In each of these the participant should steer the kite to 7 different positions. The sessions took place at the beach in order to provide a context that is as close to the real world scenario as possible. From the results of session I, opportunities for improvements were identified and implemented in session II and evaluated with a different set of participants.

## 6.1  Participants and Task

As mentioned, 10 participants took part in each session including 3 females and 17 males between the ages of 19 and 41 with an average age of 25.9 years. This included 3 novices and 17 proficient kiteboarders. Participants were briefed on the kite control task and were asked to fill out a consent form and a questionnaire before and after the study session. The participants completed a kite control task in each of the three conditions. The task is based on a typical kite control exercise. Participants must orient the control bar to the 12 o'clock position in order to begin the session. The participant is then guided through a series of 7 target positions mapped to positions on the clock face. Upon reaching each target position, one is required to hold the position for 5 s, after which they are guided to the next position in the task sequence. This sequence was provided to the participants, always beginning and ending with the 12 o'clock position. Half of the participants proceeded through the positions of 2, 10, 1, 12, 11, 2, and the other half proceeded in reverse order. This was balanced and randomized.

## 6.2  Study Session Protocol and Measures

The participants were asked to answer a demographic questionnaire. Participants were then asked to hold and orient the control bar to explore the tactile sensations in order to understand the mapping between the position of the bar and the vibrotactile sensations. When the participant was satisfied with their control abilities and were able to maintain an indicated position, the specific tasks for the study were introduced. After completing the tasks in all conditions, a second questionnaire about the experience was given. The participant performance and response to the tasks was measured through logged system events and self-reported feedback. Performance data was logged by the test control system running on a PC connected to the control bar microcontroller. The log includes events for when the target range is achieved, number of times the position deviates from the target range (drift), and when the position has been held steady within the target range for 5 s. During the study sessions the wind speed was tracked using an anemometer to ensure similar conditions across participants. Both before and after the session, participants were asked to answer forced selection questions and provide additional open ended feedback.

**Q1-2: Preferences.** In order to explore which condition the participant preferred the most and least, they were asked to indicate by circling the words, "tactile only", "voice + tactile", or "voice only". Participants were permitted to provide supporting details about their choice if they desired.

**Q3: Reflection on Performance.** In order to explore the self-reported belief about their performance, participants were asked to indicate in which of the three conditions they believed their performance was best. Again, they could choose tactile only, voice + tactile, or voice only and provide additional supporting details if desired.

**Q4: Improvements and Suggestions.** In order to better understand the impressions of the system, the participants were asked to provide suggestions for improvements.

## 6.3   Session I: Controlling a Kite

Both sessions were conducted at the beach with a 3 $m^2$ trainer kite on land with average windspeed of 8 m/sec. The settings of the system in session I are illustrated in Fig. 7. Here the clock face is shown, with 12 o'clock as an example target position. There are 4 layers on the figure including the clock positions, the vibration events, logged events, and angle in degrees. In the tactile only and tactile + voice conditions the tactile feedback was provided as indicated "vibration events". If the kite is steered away from the example target of 12 o'clock to 2 o'clock, full vibration will be active in the left side (L), and when passing 1 o'clock it transforms to weak vibration. When within 18° of the target, vibration stops. When giving voice commands in the tactile + voice and voice only conditions the logging remains the same. The facilitator calls out the position, e.g. "move the kite to 2 o'clock", then uses the voice commands equivalent to the vibration signals (strong/weak) to give guidance – "more left/right", "a little more left/right" and "hold it". The system alerts the facilitator when, and which command to verbalize.

## 6.4   Results of Session I

While all of the experienced kiteboarders completed the study session successfully, 3 novice participants were not able to complete the kite control task and their partial results have been withheld. Insights gathered from their behavior revealed a mismatch in the mental model for how to control a kite which we discuss in more detail later in the paper. While participants were able to quickly complete the control task in all conditions, the tactile only condition resulted in longer average times to achieve a target as shown in Fig. 9 and moved outside the target range more as shown in Fig. 10. The results are summarized in Table 1 and explained in more detail in the coming sections.

**Self-reported Feedback from Session I.** Q1-2 explored the participant preferences for the three conditions. Three participants preferred tactile only, while two preferred it the least. Two participants preferred voice + tactile and three indicated this as least preferred. Results from Q3 revealed that four participants believed they did best in the voice only condition. Two participants believed they did best in voice + tactile.

A review of the open-ended feedback suggests various motivations for their answers. Those who least preferred voice + tactile said that they only relied on one modality in the condition, as participant 3, 4 and 5 stated:

P3:   "Too much information."
P4:   "Not using the vibrations because I concentrate on the voice instructions."
P5:   "It was a bit confusing to both be listening and feeling simultaneously."

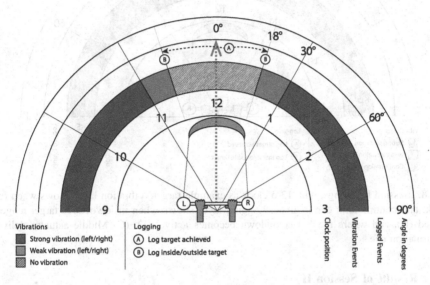

**Fig. 7.** Session I system settings, with 12 o'clock as example target. Vibration layer shows when full, weak and no vibration is present. Logging layer shows when inside/outside target range is logged (B), and where the 5 s countdown becomes active (A).

## 6.5   Session II: Vibrotactile Refinements

From the results of session I, we recognized that participants responded differently to voice and tactile feedback not only in the amount of time to complete the tasks, but their steering behavior varied noticeably. When tactile cues alone were provided, participants hovered near the target range or oscillated between the boundaries of the range, yet when tactile was combined with voice and when guided by voice alone, participants did not engage in these wandering behaviors. We discuss this in more detail in the discussion section. Feedback suggested that additional guidance was needed. Therefore, we developed a tighter range of guidance signals as shown in

Fig. 8B and a vibrotactile confirmation cue to alert when the target position was reached, yet we maintained the previous target range. This was intended to guide the participant closer to the center of the target. The confirmation cue was delivered by the middle vibrotactile actuator as indicated in Figs. 5D and 8C. The enhancements to the new settings were evaluated with new participants at the beach, following the same study protocol as in study session I.

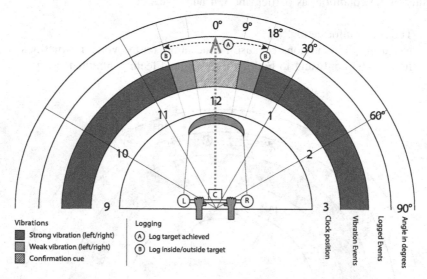

**Fig. 8.** Session II settings, with 12 o'clock as example target. Vibration layer shows when full, weak, and confirmation cue is given. Logging layer shows when inside/outside target range is logged (B), and where the 5 s countdown becomes active (A). (C) Middle actuator delivers confirmation cue.

## 6.6    Results of Session II

Analysis of variance (ANOVA) within subjects did not reveal differences to be significant. However independent samples t-test between session I and session II, suggest that the improvements made to the prototype resulted in improvements to the performance and these differences were not due to chance. Comparing sessions I and II, there were improvements across all conditions in session II. This includes the time to reach a target position in the tactile only condition for session I (M = 17.86 s, SD = 5.68 s) and session II (M = 12.57 s, SD = 2.57 s), t(15) = 2.618, p = 0.019. For the tactile + voice condition there is significant difference between session I (M = 12.33 s, SD = 1.57 s) and the improved settings in session II (M = 10.36 s, SD = 1.07 s), t(15) = 3.084, p = 0.008. Differences with "voice only" cues were not found to be significant p = 0.555. With "tactile only" cues, kiters had statistically fewer average drifts from target (M = 1.1, SD = 0.69) with refined tactile cues compared to original thresholds (M = 2.67, SD = 1.63), t(15) = 2.755, p = 0.015. With "tactile + voice" cues, kiters had statistically fewer average drifts from target (M = 0.56, SD = 0.31) with refined tactile cues compared to original thresholds (M = 0.94, SD = 0.28), t(15) = 2.572, p = 0.021. Differences with "voice only" cues were not found to be significant p = 0.974.

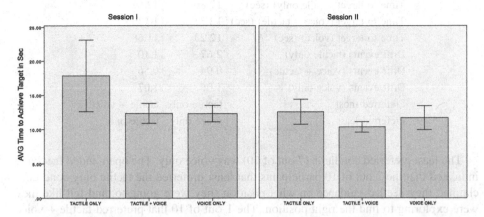

**Fig. 9.** Average time in seconds to reach each target session I (left), II (right).

These results suggest that voice can be more effective than haptic feedback for planning tasks when it provides a model (such as "move the kite to 2 o'clock") for the user to test their actions against, and that the refinements to feedback with confirmation of target acquisition can lead to better performance.

**Self-reported Feedback from Session II.** In session II the majority (7 out of 10) preferred the condition with tactile and voice combined, and none preferred voice feedback alone. Those who prefer tactile + voice, mention they like that voice gives a precise idea of where the target is, while the tactile feedback supports with precise information for final adjustments. The remaining 3 out of 10 preferred the tactile only condition claiming to notice a sense of control, quick response time and precise feedback.

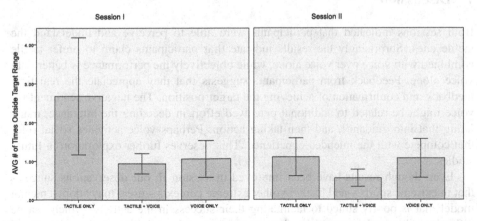

**Fig. 10.** Average number of times participant moved the bar position outside of each target range in session I (left), II (right).

Table 1. Summary of results from session I and II.

|  | Session I | Session II |
|---|---|---|
| Time to target (tactile only) (sec) | 17.86 | 12.57 |
| Time to target (voice + tactile) (sec) | 12.33 | 10.36 |
| Time to target (voice) (sec) | 12.23 | 11.68 |
| Drift events (tactile only) | 2.67 | 1.10 |
| Drift events (voice + tactile) | 0.94 | 0.56 |
| Drift events (voice only) | 1.06 | 1.07 |
| Preferred most | tactile only | tactile + voice |
| Preferred least | voice only | tactile only |

The least preferred condition (7 out of 10) was voice only. The open-ended feedback indicated that the 2 out of 10 participants that least preferred the tactile only condition, claimed they needed guidance on what position they were going to, and felt like they were exploring to find the right position. The 1 out of 10 that preferred tactile + voice least, indicated that they did not like the redundancy in the feedback and 7 out of 10 expressed claims that the voice feedback was too slow and imprecise. Every participant reported they did the best in the condition they preferred the most. The majority (7 out of 10) preferred tactile + voice, and none preferred the session with voice only. In contrast to the self-reported feedback in session II, the logged data shows that there were no statistically significant differences between the average time it took the participant to achieve the desired target in the tactile + voice condition compared to the tactile only condition. Surprisingly, in session I, the open-ended feedback indicated that participants did not like the additional feedback in the tactile + voice condition, however, it was the most preferred condition in session II. Various participants noted the confirmation signal from the center of the bar helped them understand when they achieved the target.

## 7  Discussion

Both sessions indicated that participants were able to perceive and understand the tactile cues. Surprisingly the results indicate that participants claim to prefer tactile combined with voice over voice alone, while objectively the performance is better with voice alone. Feedback from participants suggests that they appreciate the real time feedback and confirmation of achieving the target position. The negative sentiment for voice might be related to additional perceived effort in decoding the utterance, translating that into guidance, and then taking action. Perhaps voice activates social rules that compete with the intended experience. This deserves further exploration in future studies.

Even though results have been improved in session II, our observations suggests that in extreme sports – and likely in other extreme contexts – users may adopt a mental model that is poorly suited to facilitating their success in the activity, which can be difficult to change. We provide further explanation of these findings in this section and discuss the limitations of our work.

## 7.1    Improvements to Tactile Communication

Voice feedback resulted in better performance, compared to tactile cues alone, as participants quickly adopt the semantic map and move to the target position, and upon reaching it, they were told to stop. This is challenging for tactile feedback, as it is not well suited in communicating the angle in clock positions. Instead, simple guidance (left/right) has been provided, which is not always enough as some participants were stopping right at the acceptable boundary, or oscillating between the 2 edges of the target range. The reason for this was identified as (1) a missing confirmation, and (2) guidance that stops too soon. By adding a tactile confirmation cue and by moving the weak vibration inside the acceptable target range, guiding the participants away from the edge (Fig. 8), improved the results. Even tough tactile feedback can communicate basic guidance, mental models of novices for how a kite is controlled can be mismatched, making guidance difficult.

## 7.2    Mental Models

In session I, 2 people were not able to complete the tasks. The main obstacle was typical for beginners – they failed to adopt an effective mental model for how the kite responds to the control bar movements, leading to inability to maintain a stable position. In order to control the position of the kite, the rider shortens the line connected to one side of the kite in the desired direction of travel. Experienced kiters adopt a habit of holding the control bar parallel to the leading edge of the kite, so that pulling on one side of the bar maps to the direction the kite will move. Skilled riders on the water usually follow the same practice adjusting the orientation of the bar while riding. It is possible to control the kite without holding the bar like this, however, it becomes much more difficult to control and predict movements.

## 7.3    Limitations

Our work provides some initial steps towards developing technologies to support participants in kiteboarding, however, there are possible limitations to this work which are worthwhile to discuss. In terms of the prototype design and evaluation, there may be concerns about the nature of the evaluation task and its relation to the real world experience of kiteboarding. While the choice of logged data for the evaluations has been useful in highlighting the differences in response to voice and tactile feedback – we would like to expand to more measures including tension of the lines, position of the body, orientation of the board, and bar to identify bad habits.

## 8    Conclusion and Future Work

Designers have explored technologies to support physical activities, however, there is less research focused on technologies supporting communication in physically and mentally demanding contexts such as extreme sports. We explore kiteboarding as an experimental platform to find ways in which technologies can support communication needs. Kiteboarding is a complex dynamic activity with intense demands of control and diminished opportunities for communication. We developed a kite control bar with embedded sensors and actuators to communicate instructions through voice or tactile cues to explore how technology can facilitate communication for control guidance. Evaluations suggest that familiar voice communication is effective, yet may negatively impact the experience. We show that tactile cues can also be effective at changing behavior. However, tactile feedback was not as flexible as voice for presenting a mental model.

Our work demonstrates the value of voice commands providing quick, high level semantic models. We found that tactile cues can provide effective feedback that might be preferred in contexts that place extreme demands on the user. Evaluations reveal how small changes in tactile feedback can yield significant improvements. This work is a celebration of the capacities of human performance and signals opportunities for computer controlled feedback across modalities. There is a need for continued exploration of cyber-physical systems to examine signals for appropriateness and capacity to support interactions. This paper calls for building an understanding of how to explore scenarios and contexts using multimodal feedback systems. We encourage the continued investigation into exploring languages of various modalities and interactions among them. This seems to be an area ripe for exploration in the challenge of designing for extreme sports or other contexts in which people are pushed to their limits.

Aside from the existing goals of kiteboarders, it would be interesting to explore other forms of play that can be supported through the use of digital augmentations along the lines of work involving augmentations to expand the experience of a game platform [18] and new forms of social expression through an exertion interfaces approach [28], perhaps exploring opportunities for social interaction among participants and even spectators [23].

# References

1. Amemiya, T., Ando, H., Maeda, T.: Lead-me interface for a pulling sensation from handheld devices. ACM Trans. Appl. Percept. 5(3), 1–17 (2008)
2. Baca, A., Kornfeind, P.: Rapid feedback systems for elite sports training. IEEE Pervasive Comput. 5(4), 70–76 (2006)
3. Brave, S.: inTouch. In: SIGGRAPH 1998. ACM, New York, NY, USA (1998)
4. Cao, Y., van der Sluis, F., Theune, M., op den Akker, R., Nijholt, A.: Evaluating informative auditory and tactile cues for in-vehicle information systems. In: Proceedings of Automotive UI 2010 (2010)
5. Ege, E.S., Cetin, F., Basdogan, C.: Vibrotactile feedback in steering wheel reduces navigation errors during GPS-guided car driving. In: Haptics 2011 (2011)
6. van Erp, J.B.F., Van Veen, H.A.H.C., Jansen, C., Dobbins, T.: Waypoint navigation with a vibrotactile waist belt. ACM Trans. Appl. Percept. 2(2), 106–117 (2005)
7. van Erp, J.B., Kooi, F.L., Bronkhorst, A.W., van Leeuwen, D.L., van Esch, M.P., van Wijngaarden, S.J.: Multimodal interfaces: a framework based on modality appropriateness. In: Proceedings of the HFES 2006, vol. 50, pp. 1542–1546. SAGE Publications (2006)

8. van Erp, J.B., lan Saturday, Jansen, C.: Application of tactile displays in sports: where to, how and when to move. In: EuroHaptics, pp. 90–95 (2006)
9. Frey, M.: CabBoots: shoes with integrated guidance system. In: Proceedings of the TEI 2007, pp. 245–246. ACM, New York, NY, USA (2007)
10. Gallace, A., Tan, H.Z., Spence, C.: The failure to detect tactile change: a tactile analogue of visual change blindness. Psychon. Bull. Rev. 13, 300–303 (2006)
11. Gallace, A., Tan, H.Z., Spence, C.: Numerosity judgments for tactile stimuli distributed over the body surface. Perception 35, 247–266 (2006)
12. Graether, E., Mueller, F.: Joggobot: a flying robot as jogging companion. In: Proceedings of the CHI 2012. pp. 1063–1066. ACM, New York, NY, USA (2012)
13. Hemmert, F., Hamann, S., Löwe, M., Wohlauf, A., Zeipelt, J., Joost, G.: Take me by the hand: haptic compasses in mobile devices through shape change and weight shift. In: Proceedings of the NordiCHI 2010. pp. 671–674. ACM, New York, NY, USA (2010)
14. Heuten, W., Henze, N., Boll, S., Pielot, M.: Tactile wayfinder: a non-visual support system for wayfinding. In: Proceedings of the NordiCHI 2008, pp. 172–181. ACM, NY, USA (2008)
15. Holland, S., Morse, D.R., Gedenryd, H.: Audiogps: spatial audio navigation with a minimal attention interface. Pers. Ub.Comp. 6(4), 253–259 (2002)
16. Internation Kiteboarding Organization (2014). http://www.ikointl.com/
17. Imamura, Y., Arakawa, H., Kamuro, S., Minamizawa, K., Tachi, S.: HAPMAP: haptic walking navigation system with support by the sense of handrail. In: SIGGRAPH 2011. ACM, NY, USA (2011)
18. Ishii, H., Wisneski, C., Orbanes, J., Chun, B., Paradiso, J.: PingPongPlus: design of an athletic-tangible interface for computer-supported cooperative play. In: Proceedings CHI 1999. pp. 394–401. ACM, NY, USA (1999)
19. Jensen, M.M., Rasmussen, M.K., Grønbaek, K.: Design sensitivities for interactive sport-training games. In: Proceedings of the DIS 2014, pp. 685–694. ACM, New York, NY, USA (2014)
20. Kojima, Y., Hashimoto, Y., Fukushima, S., Kajimoto, H.: Pull-navi: a novel tactile navigation interface by pulling the ears. In: ACM SIGGRAPH 2009, p. 19. ACM (2009)
21. Lechal website (2014). http://lechal.com
22. Loomis, J.M., Golledge, R.G., Klatzky, R.L.: Navigation system for the blind: auditory display modes and guidance. Presence: Teleoperators Virtual Environ. 7(2), 193–203 (1998)
23. Ludvigsen, M., Veerasawmy, R.: Designing technology for active spectator experiences at sporting events. In: Proceedings of the OZCHI 2010, pp. 96–103. ACM, NY, USA (2010)
24. Maeda, T., Ando, H., Amemiya, T., Nagaya, N., Sugimoto, M., Inami, M.: Shaking the world: galvanic vestibular stimulation as a novel sensation interface. In: ACM SIGGRAPH 2005 Emerging technologies, p. 17. ACM (2005)
25. Mueller, F., Agamanolis, S., Picard, R.: Exertion interfaces: sports over a distance for social bonding and fun. In: Proceedings of the CHI 2003. pp. 561–568. ACM, NY, USA (2003)
26. Mueller, F., Edge, D., Vetere, F., Gibbs, M.R., Agamanolis, S., Bongers, B., Sheridan, J.G.: Designing sports: a framework for exertion games. In: Proceedings of the CHI 2011, pp. 2651–2660. ACM, New York, NY, USA (2011)
27. Pielot, M., Poppinga, B., Heuten, W., Boll, S.: Pocketnavigator: studying tactile navigation systems in-situ. In: Proceedings of the CHI 2012, pp. 3131–3140. ACM (2012)
28. Pijnappel, S., Mueller, F.: 4 design themes for skateboarding. In: Proceedings of the CHI 2013, pp. 1271–1274. ACM, NY, USA (2013)
29. Pijnappel, S., Mueller, F.: Designing interactive technology for skateboarding. In: Proceedings TEI 2014, pp. 141–148. ACM, New York, NY, USA (2013)

30. Prasad, M., Taele, P., Goldberg, D., Hammond, T.A.: Haptimoto: turn-by-turn haptic route guidance interface for motorcyclists. In: Proceedings of the CHI 2014, pp. 3597–3606. ACM (2014)

31. Prasad, M., Taele, P., Olubeko, A., Hammond, T.A.: Haptigo: a navigational "tap on the shoulder". In: HAPTICS 2014, p. 1. IEEE (2014)

32. Rensink, R.A., O'Regan, J.K., Clark, J.J.: To see or not to see: The need for attention to perceive changes in scenes. Psychol. Sci. **8**(5), 368–373 (1997)

33. ShadowBox board tracking (2014). http://bit.ly/shadowbx

34. Solomon, C., Banerjee, A., Horn, M.S.: Ultimate trainer: instructional feedback for ultimate frisbee players. In: Proceedings of the TEI 2014 (2014)

35. Spelmezan, D.: An investigation into the use of tactile instructions in snowboarding. In: Proceedings of the MobileHCI 2012 (2012)

36. Sucu, B., Folmer, E.: Haptic interface for non-visual steering. In: Proceedings of the IUI 2013, pp. 427–434. ACM, New York, NY, USA (2013)

37. Takeuchi, Y.: Gilded gait: reshaping the urban experience with augmented footsteps. In: Proceedings of the UIST 2010, pp. 185–188. ACM, NY, USA (2010)

38. Tsukada, K., Yasumura, M.: ActiveBelt: belt-type wearable tactile display for directional navigation. In: Mynatt, E.D., Siio, I. (eds.) UbiComp 2004. LNCS, vol. 3205, pp. 384–399. Springer, Heidelberg (2004)

39. Velazquez, R., Bazan, O., Magana, M.: A shoe-integrated tactile display for directional navigation. In: Proceedings of the IROS 2009, pp. 1235–1240. IEEE Press, Piscataway, NJ, USA (2009)

40. Wickens, C.D.: Multiple resources and performance prediction. Theor. Issues Ergonomics Sci. **3**, 159–177 (2002)

41. Zwinderman, M., Zavialova, T., Tetteroo, D., Lehouck, P.: Oh music, where art thou? In: Proceedings of the MobileHCI 2011, pp. 533–538. ACM (2011)

# Glass+Skin: An Empirical Evaluation of the Added Value of Finger Identification to Basic Single-Touch Interaction on Touch Screens

Quentin Roy[1,2(✉)], Yves Guiard[1], Gilles Bailly[1], Éric Lecolinet[1], and Olivier Rioul[1]

[1] Telecom ParisTech, CNRS LTCI UMR 5141, Paris, France
quentin@quentinroy.fr,
{yves.guiard,gilles.bailly,eric.lecolinet,olivier.rioul}
@telecom-paristech.fr
[2] GE Healthcare, Buc, France

**Abstract.** The usability of small devices such as smartphones or interactive watches is often hampered by the limited size of command vocabularies. This paper is an attempt at better understanding how finger identification may help users invoke commands on touch screens, even without recourse to multi-touch input. We describe how finger identification can increase the size of input vocabularies under the constraint of limited real estate, and we discuss some visual cues to communicate this novel modality to novice users. We report a controlled experiment that evaluated, over a large range of input-vocabulary sizes, the efficiency of single-touch command selections with vs. without finger identification. We analyzed the data not only in terms of traditional time and error metrics, but also in terms of a throughput measure based on Shannon's theory, which we show offers a synthetic and parsimonious account of users' performance. The results show that the larger the input vocabulary needed by the designer, the more promising the identification of individual fingers.

**Keywords:** Input modality · Multitouch · Finger identification · Evaluation methodology · Throughput · Information theory

## 1 Introduction

The number of buttons on small touchscreens (e.g. watches, wearable devices, smartphones) is strongly limited by the Fat Finger Problem [7, 30, 36]. Increasing the number of commands requires users to navigate through menus, lists or tabs, thus slowing down the interaction. This problem also arises on larger touch screens, such as tablets, where applications need to save as much space as possible for the display of objects of interest, rather than controls. For instance, users of photo-editing, 3D drawing, or medical imagery applications want to see large high-resolution images, but at the same time they want to see large command menus. Possible responses to this challenge are a drastic reduction in the number of available commands and functionalities (e.g., Photoshop

© IFIP International Federation for Information Processing 2015
J. Abascal et al. (Eds.): INTERACT 2015, Part IV, LNCS 9299, pp. 55–71, 2015.
DOI: 10.1007/978-3-319-22723-8_5

offers 648 menu commands on a PC, and only 35 on a tablet [37]), and intensive recourse to hierarchical menus, at the cost of efficiency. For frequently used commands, the lack of hotkeys on touch-based devices badly aggravates this problem.

Many different approaches have been proposed in the literature to provide input methods that save screen real estate. Most of them rely on gestures [20, 24, 25, 29, 41, 42] such as Marking menus [20, 42], rolling gestures [32], multi-finger chords [23, 37], finger-counting [3, 4] etc. Another approach exploits additional sensors such as motion sensors or accelerometers [17] or pressure sensors [31]. In this paper we focus on finger identification and investigate to which extent it can augment the expressivity of touch input and allow larger command vocabularies while saving screen space.

Recognition of finger identity provides several advantages for command selection. Finger identification allows increasing the input vocabulary while being compatible with already existing interaction styles: For instance, the same button may serve to invoke different commands depending on which finger is pressing it. This strategy will increase the total number of commands for a *given interface*. But it will also reduce the number of necessary buttons for a given set of commands while maintaining a direct access to these commands (i.e. without the need to open menus, scrolling lists, etc.). Buttons can then be designed with larger sizes, thus easing interaction on small touchscreens. It is worth noticing that on such devices interaction is usually more constrained by (touch) input than by (visual) output. Because of the high pixel resolution of modern screens, icons — and often even text — can remain recognizable at sizes that preclude their selection using a finger tip. Finger identification can be exploited for displaying several icons (one for each available command) on *finger-dependent buttons* and thus make all commands discoverable, as we will see in Sect. 3.

Finger identification can also serve to provide shortcuts for invoking frequent or favorite commands instead of opening context menus. For instance, "copy", "paste", "select" and other heavily used commands could be invoked in this way on smartphones.

Finger identification may facilitate the transition to complex chording gestures: Novice users will sequentially press two different buttons with two different fingers (e.g. index and middle fingers). More experienced users will execute these operations faster and faster until they perform these two actions simultaneously and perform a chording gesture.

To explore this promising modality a number of finger-identification prototypes have been described in the HCI literature, which in the near future are likely to become practical and robust.

Below we will call GLASS the usual input channel that considers only the $xy$ coordinates of the contact on the screen, and GLASS+SKIN the augmentation of this channel with the skin (categorical, or non-metrical) coordinates, which requires finger identification.

In this paper, we try to better understand how interaction techniques relying on finger identification may help users invoke commands on touch screens. To progress towards this goal, we conducted a user study comparing the performance of finger-dependent buttons with traditional, finger-agnostic buttons, for various sizes of the command vocabulary. One of our concerns was to figure out when finger-identification starts outperforming traditional button-based interfaces.

The results showed that if the standard channel is perfect for very few commands, it is soon outperformed by the GLASS+SKIN option, in a given amount of real estate, as the number of commands increases. The main finding is that with GLASS+SKIN the error rate increases at a considerably reduced pace with vocabulary size, which makes it possible to handle much larger sets of commands. We found that the maximum obtainable bandwidth (or, more precisely, the maximal level of possible throughput, in Shannon's [33] sense) is higher and that users can handle larger vocabularies with finger-sensitive than finger-agnostic touch detections.

## 2 Related Work

### 2.1 Augmenting the Expressivity of Touch Input

In the face of the small size of the screen and the fat finger problem [19, 30, 36], several modalities have been proposed to augment the expressivity of touch input. The most widespread of all seems to be multi-touch input [22], especially with the most successful zoom-and-rotate gesture that the iPhone popularized. One particular exploitation of the multi-touch was Finger-Count [3, 4], which determines command selection based on just the *number* of finger contacts from both hands.

Other modalities have also been proposed such as touch in motion [17] or pressure +touch input [7, 15, 28, 31], whose input bandwidth unfortunately is low because selection time is long (from ~1.5 s to more than 2 s with no feedback) and whose users distinguish hardly more than 5–7 values [28].

Our motivation is to understand what happens if screen and skin coordinates of touch input are distinguished. In this spirit, Roudaut et al. recognize the signature of fingers' micro-rolls on the surface [32]. Wang et al. used the orientation of the finger to control parameters [39]. Holz and Baudish detect fingerprint to improve touch accuracy [19]. And more recently, TapSense uses acoustic signatures to distinguish the taps from four different part of users' fingers: tip, nail, knuckle and pad [14].

In this class of interaction, proper finger identification — with screen and skin coordinates jointly taken into account — seems highly promising [1, 6, 9, 11, 12, 18, 23, 26, 37, 40]. Many studies have concentrated on triggering finger-dependent commands or action [1, 6, 23, 26, 37]. For instance, Adoiraccourcix maps different modifiers to the fingers of the non-dominant hand and different commands to fingers of the dominant hand [12]. Finger identification can also be coupled with physical buttons as in recent Apple Smartphones [35, 40]. The advantage of this method is that the identification can be performed even if the button is not pressed, adding a supplementary state to the interaction [8]. Finger-dependent variants of chords and Marking Menus have also been investigated [23].

Some researchers have examined the discoverability of finger-dependent commands. For example, Sugiura and Koseki [35] identify the finger as soon as a user touches a (physical) button. They use this property to show a feedback on the corresponding command name prior to the actual button press. This, however, is not compatible with most touch systems, which more often than not lack a passive state [8]. In Au et al. [1] a menu is displayed showing the commands under each fingers, but users must depress their whole hand on the surface to invoke it. In Sect. 3.3 we will consider various techniques of informing users about the availability of finger-dependent commands.

## 2.2  Finger Identification Technologies

Under certain circumstances, fingers can be identified using the default hardware of hand-held computers. Specific chord gestures are typically used for this purpose. Assuming a relaxed hand posture, the user must touch the surface with a certain combination of fingers or perform a specific temporal sequence [1, 37]. Some other multi-touch techniques such as MTM [2] or Arpege [10] do not directly identify fingers but infer them based on the likely positions of individual fingers relative to some location of reference.

Computer-vision can be used to identify fingers without requiring chording gestures. The camera can either be located behind the interactive surface such as with FTIR multi-touch tables (e.g. [23]) or placed above with a downward orientation (e.g. [5]). The idea is to compare fingertip locations (obtained through computer-vision) with touch event locations (provided by the interactive surface). Basic solutions identify fingers by considering their relative positions. But this approach fails if some fingers are flexed (e.g. [9]). Markers can be attached to the fingers to solve this problem (e.g. color [40] or fiduciary tag [26]). But, this cumbersome solution, which demands that the users be instrumented, is workable only in research laboratories. Some commercial systems are able to track the mid-air motion of individual fingers (e.g. Microsoft Kinect and Leap Motion). This approach makes it possible to identify which fingers come in contact with a surface [21].

Hardware-based approaches have also been proposed. Sugiura and Koseki [35] used a fingerprint scanner to identify fingers. They were able to trigger finger-dependent commands but not to track finger positions. Holtz and Baudish extended this work to touchpads [19] and more recently to the touch-screen of interactive tables [18]. Another approach consists of analyzing EMG signals on the forearm to determine which finger is applying pressure to the surface [6]. In yet another approach, Goguet et al. attached *GameTraks*[1] to user's fingers [11, 12]. Of course, digital gloves can also serve to track user fingers [34]. A drawback of these approaches is that they require user instrumenting and/or a calibration phase.

## 3  GLASS+SKIN: A Class of Promising Interaction Techniques

Several widgets such as toolbars or menus exclusively rely on the spatial arrangement of buttons on the screen. During interaction with these widgets the system only exploits the *screen* coordinates of finger contacts to interpret the decisions of users. In this section, we show how finger identification can offer interesting properties to improve command selection on touch screens. In this section, we give some insights in how application designers may leverage GLASS+SKIN, a class of interaction techniques that augment traditional interaction with finger identification.

---

[1] *GameTrak* is a game controller designed for the Sony PlayStation 2. It is equipped with two retractable strings usually attached to the player's wrists. It is able to track the 3D position of the attached limbs on top of the device.

## 3.1 Multi-function Buttons

**Increasing the Input Vocabulary.** With GLASS+SKIN input, a button can invoke more than one command. From the moment individual fingers are identified, more commands can be handled for the same amount of screen real estate. For instance, the main screen of the iPhone can provide a direct access to 20–24 applications (a 4x5 or 4x6 array of buttons, depending on the model). Whether useful or not, with five fingers discriminated, these numbers could be multiplied by 5.

**Reducing the Number of Buttons.** More interestingly, perhaps, on a given screen with a given set of commands, GLASS+SKIN input can just as well reduce the number of buttons. Direct access to these commands is maintained, without the need to open a hierarchical menu or scroll a list. Moreover, if more space is available, buttons can be designed with larger sizes, facilitating the interaction with small touchscreens.

**Compatibility.** One concern is to make GLASS+SKIN interaction compatible with users' habits. To this end the default button behavior might be assigned to the index finger that most users prefer for touch-screen interaction. Only experienced users would be concerned with the set of additional commands (four extra possibilities per button).

**Input vs. Output.** If a button can invoke different commands, it should communicate the different options it offers. It is worth noticing that interaction is usually more constrained by (touch) input than by (visual) output on such devices. Because of the high pixel resolution of modern screens, icons - and even text to a certain extent - can remain recognizable at sizes for which they could hardly be selected using a finger. Displaying several icons (one for each available command) on multi-function buttons it is thus possible to make all commands discoverable. After all, buttons on hardware keyboard already contain several symbols that can be accessed from different modifiers (i.e. Ctrl, Shift, Alt).

**Cancel.** Users pressing a button with the wrong finger can cancel the current selection by moving their finger away from the target or just waiting for a delay. The mapping then appears and users can release the finger without triggering a command.

## 3.2 Menus

GLASS+SKIN can reduce the needs for menus from small to medium applications. However, when the number of commands is very large, it is difficult to avoid menus, which are useful for organizing commands. This section considers how GLASS+SKIN fares with menus.

Menu shortcuts, such as keyboard shortcuts, are generally not present on mobile devices. We propose to use finger identification as a substitute for menu shortcuts on touchscreens. This makes it possible both to interact in the usual way (by opening menus and clicking on their items) and to activate frequent or favorite commands quickly (by pressing the appropriate finger on the touchscreen). Finger identification can thus serve to (partly) compensate for the lack of keyboard shortcuts on mobile devices (see Fig. 1c).

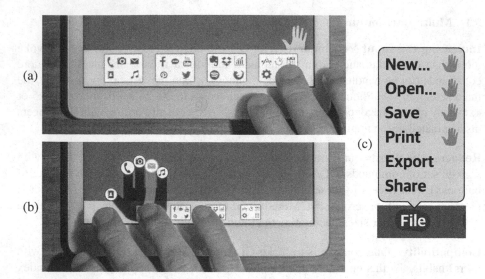

**Fig. 1.** GLASS+SKIN menu instances.

**Context Menus.** GLASS+SKIN can provide an expert mode to context menus. Novice users continue to press and wait for a delay to open the menu. However, more experienced users can invoke commands without waiting for the delay. The five most frequent or favorite commands of the menu are assigned to the five fingers. This can be especially useful for selecting repeatedly used commands such as "copy", "paste" or "select". Alternatively, one can choose to sacrifice one shortcut to remove the menu delay: e.g., the thumb could open the menu instantly.

**Menu Bar, Tool Bar and Folders.** Some persistent buttons give access to pull-down menus. In this case, the index finger is still used to navigate in the hierarchy of commands as usual. However, the other fingers provide a direct access (shortcuts) to favorite (or frequent) menu items deeper in the hierarchy. Suppose the index finger is still used to open a folder on smartphone. The four remaining fingers are shortcuts to select pre-defined items within this folder. This class of interaction strongly differs from approaches relying on finger chords [4, 10, 37] which specify not one but several contact points (one per finger) making it difficult to predict their behavior on small widgets (smaller than the required surface to contain all contact points).

### 3.3 Communicating GLASS+SKIN

**Discovering.** Some users can be unaware of this novel input modality. Some visual cues can help them to discover this modality without using video tutorial or documentation. We consider two of them in this project illustrated in Fig. 1a, b. The first one is static and displays a ghost hand on top of the toolbar to indicate that different fingers can be used. The second one is dynamic and shows a short animation showing several surface contacts with different fingers. Further studies are necessary to evaluate the ability of users to understand the meaning of these icons.

**Mapping.** When a button have several commands, it is important to communicate which finger activates which command. Figure 1 illustrates 3 visual cues to understand the mapping. The first one uses the location of the icon inside the button to convey the target finger. The second one builds on the previous and appears only on demand. Users should press and wait for 100 ms to see the mapping. This approach reduces the total amount of information on the screen for expert users but can be less intuitive for novice users. The last example uses fingers as a menu shortcut. Symbols representing the target finger are shown on the right of the command name similarly to keyboard shortcuts on linear menus.

**Toward Chording Gestures.** Finger identification may facilitate the transition to complex chording gestures: Novice users will sequentially press two different buttons with two different fingers (e.g. index and middle fingers). More experienced users will execute these operations faster and faster until they perform these two actions simultaneously and perform a chording gesture.

### 3.4   Limitations

GLASS+SKIN also has some limitations. For instance, the different interaction techniques are not compatible with each other, e.g. a GLASS+SKIN button cannot launch five applications and open a menu. Designers should make compromises according to the users' needs and the coherence between applications/systems.

In some situations, it can be difficult to use a specific finger on the touch screen. Though the current smartphone trend is to large screens precluding a single hand use, some users still often use their smartphone this way. In this case, not only is the novel input resource unavailable to users, but errors may also arise if the application does not consider the thumb as the default finger. One solution would consist of constraining GLASS+SKIN to a subset of applications (e.g. games). Another would require sensing and recognizing grab [13] to avoid accidental activations. GLASS+SKIN is probably more useful for tablets or watches where "thumb interaction" is less common.

## 4   A Controlled Experiment

The experiment was designed in light of Shannon's theory [33]. A communication channel permits a source of information (the user) to transmit information to a destination (the system), the user's hand serving as the emitter and the touch screen as the receiver of the coded message. The code shared by the source and the destination is some mapping of a set of touch events to a set of commands. The larger the sets, the more entropy in our vocabulary of commands. For simplicity, below we will assume equally probable commands: in this case the input entropy (or the vocabulary entropy $H_V$) is just the $\log_2$ of the number of possible commands.

Although we will not ignore traditional time and error metrics, our analysis will focus on the *throughput* (*TP*), the rate of successful message transmission over a communication channel. We simply define the *TP* (in bits/s) as the ratio of Shannon's mutual information transmitted per command to the time taken on average to enter the command. Our main concern is the particular vocabulary size that maximizes the throughput — i.e., the optimal level of vocabulary entropy ($H_{opt}$, in bits) — in the two conditions of interest. In the GLASS condition, our baseline, the command vocabulary leveraged only the entropy offered at the surface of the glass (the $\log_2$ of the number $N$ of graphical buttons), as usual; in the GLASS+SKIN condition we also leveraged the entropy available on the skin side. The vocabulary size is then $NN'$, where $N'$ denotes the number of identifiable bodily regions that may touch the screen (in practice the experiment involved the five finger tips of the right hand). The entropies of these two independent variables add up — i.e., $\log_2(NN') = \log_2(N) + \log_2(N')$ — allowing the creation of larger command vocabularies. Our problem was to experimentally evaluate the actual usability of such enlarged vocabularies.

We were able to formulate several straightforward predictions.

(1) As the vocabulary entropy is raised, the amount of transmitted information $I_t$ must level off at some point, just as has long been known to be the case in absolute-judgment tasks [27].
(2) On the other hand, mean selection time $\mu_T$ must increase about linearly with $H_V$, due to Hick's law and Fitts' law.
(3) It follows from (1) and (2) that the dependency of $TP = I_t/\mu_T$ upon $H_V$ must be bell shaped — for any given input technique there must exist an optimal level of entropy.

Thus we will focus on the maximum of *TP* ($TP_{max}$) reached at the optimal level of entropy, and on the particular level of entropy, which we will designate as optimal ($H_{opt}$), at which that maximum takes place. One faces two independent pieces of empirical information: The higher the $TP_{max}$, the better the information transmission; the higher the $H_{opt}$, the larger the range of usable vocabulary sizes.

We conjectured that when contacting a touch screen users have control not only over the selection of one screen region, but also over the selection of one region of their own body surface. Put differently, the glass surface and the skin surface should be usable as more or less independent input channels. Therefore both $TP_{max}$ and $H_{opt}$ should be raised with GLASS+SKIN, relative to the GLASS baseline.

### 4.1 Participants and Apparatus

14 right-handers (5 females) ranging in age from 21 to 33 years, recruited from within the university community in our institution, volunteered.

The apparatus consisted of an iPad tablet (9.7 in./24.6 cm in diagonal) reproducing the screen of an iPhone (see Fig. 2). A start button, on which participants had to rest their forefinger, middle finger, and ring finger, was displayed below the smartphone, so as to standardize the position and the posture of the hand at trial start. The target area was displayed as a horizontal layout extending over the complete width of the phone screen (2.3 in./59 mm), simulating the common toolbars/docks of smartphones. Buttons height was a constant 0.90 mm (as on an iPhone). We considered manipulating the size of the target area and the layout of buttons as factor, however we decided to focus on this configuration to keep the experiment short enough. Pilot studies, in which we also tested 2D grid layouts, showed that simple 1D layouts produced essentially the same results. The software was implemented with Javascript.

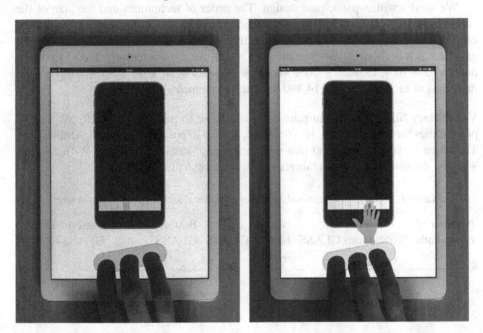

**Fig. 2.** The display at the time of appearance of the stimulus in the GLASS (left) and the GLASS +SKIN (right) conditions.

## 4.2    Method

**Task and Stimulus.** In response to a visual stimulus, participants were to select a command as fast and accurately as possible by touching a target button highlighted in gray. In the GLASS+SKIN condition, a ghost hand was also shown (Fig. 2 right), the target finger, highlighted in blue, coinciding with the target button.

**Procedure.** The participants started the trial by placing their three longer fingers on an oblique start button located at the bottom of the screen. The system responded by presenting the stimulus (depending on the condition either just a button highlight or a button highlight plus the ghost hand). The stimulus remained as long as the start button was occupied.

If correctly hit the target button turned green. A mistakenly-hit button was highlighted in red. If for any reason no touch was recorded, the participant was supposed to return to the start button to reset the trial. The finger identity of touch events was not recorded. Video recordings in a pilot experiment using our ghost-hand stimuli having revealed a remarkably low error rate for finger selection (2.3 % on average, $\sigma = 2.0$ %), it seemed reasonably safe to trust participants. Video recordings of a sample of 3 participants during the present experiment showed similar results (1.5 % on average, $\sigma = 0.52$ %).

We used a within-participant design. The order of techniques and the size of the command vocabulary were counter-balanced between participants with Latin squares, each command randomly appearing three times per block. The total duration of the experiment was about 30 min/participant. Overall the experiment involved 14 participants x (5 + 10 + 15 + 20 + 30 + 40 + 5 + 10 + 20 + 30 + 40 + 50 + 70) trials x 3 iterations of each trial type = 14,490 selection movements.

**Vocabulary Size.** Relying on pilot data, we chose to use 5, 10, 15, 20, 30, and 40 possibilities for GLASS and 5, 10, 20, 30, 40, 50 and 70 possibilities for GLASS+SKIN. The more possibilities in a 60 mm-wide array, the smaller the target. With GLASS +SKIN, the number of *screen* targets was divided by 5 (Table 1).

**Table 1.** Number of commands, number of buttons, and horizontal button size

| Number of commands | Number of buttons GLASS | Number of buttons GLASS +SKIN | Button width GLASS | Button width GLASS+SKIN |
|---|---|---|---|---|
| 5 | 5 | 1 | 12 mm/0.46 in. | 58 mm/2.3 in. |
| 10 | 10 | 2 | 5.8 mm/ 0.23 in. | 29 mm/1.2 in. |
| 15 | 15 | | 3.9 mm/ 0.15 in. | |
| 20 | 20 | 4 | 2.9 mm/ 0.11 in. | 15 mm/0.58 in. |
| 30 | 30 | 6 | 1.9 mm/ 0.077 in. | 9.7 mm/ 0.38 in. |
| 40 | 40 | 8 | 1.4 mm/ 0.058 in. | 7.3 mm/ 0.29 in. |
| 50 | | 10 | | 5.8 mm/ 0.23 in. |
| 70 | | 14 | | 4.2 mm/ 0.16 in. |

## 4.3    Results

**Classic Time/Error Analysis.** The relevant dependent variables are the reaction time (*RT*, the time elapsed between stimulus onset time and the release of the start button), movement time (*MT*, the time elapsed between release of the start button and the first detection of a screen contact), and the error rate.

Significance was estimated using ANOVA. Non-common values of *number of commands* are ignored in the time and error analysis so that the comparisons between GLASS and GLASS+SKIN are relevant.

Reaction Time (*RT*) was faster with GLASS than GLASS+SKIN (Fig. 3), a result observed in all our 14 participants ($p < .001$). The mean difference, computed over the common range of abscissas, was 132 ms. The number of commands slightly affected *RT* for GLASS, but not GLASS+SKIN.

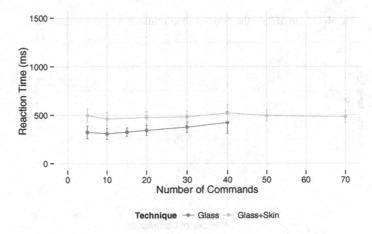

**Fig. 3.** Mean *RT* vs. the number of commands for each condition.

Overall, mean movement time (*MT*) was shorter with GLASS+SKIN than GLASS (Fig. 4). The mean difference amounted to 43 ms. The effect of vocabulary size, more pronounced on *MT* than *RT*, was approximately linear, with a steeper slope for GLASS ($F_{1,13} = 26, p = .0001$).

On average, over the common range of abscissas, total task completion time ($TT = RT + MT$) was slightly (89 ms) higher with GLASS+SKIN (Fig. 5). Much more importantly, *TT* increased at a much slower pace as vocabulary size was raised ($F_{1,13} = 16.5, p = .001$). With more than 30 commands, GLASS+SKIN was faster.

We conclude from this classic analysis of our data that taking into account the skin (categorical) coordinates of the touch event *together with* the glass (metrical) coordinates of the event enhances both the speed and accuracy of input selection, for large vocabularies. The error rate increasing at a considerably reduced pace with vocabulary size, GLASS+SKIN makes it possible to handle much larger sets of commands (Fig. 6). This error rate does not include potential mistakenly-used finger. However, video

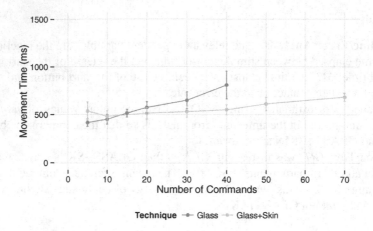

**Fig. 4.** Mean *MT* vs. the number of commands for each condition.

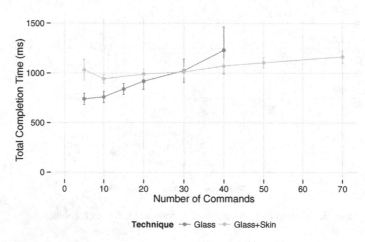

**Fig. 5.** *Total Time* vs. the number of commands for each condition.

recordings from a sample of 3 participants showed that it is particularly rare (1.5 % of the trials on average, $\sigma = 0.52$ %).

**Information-Theoretic Analysis.** One reason why we felt the throughput (*TP*) analysis was worth a try is because this quantity combines the speed and the accuracy information into a single, theoretically well-justified quantity. Let us ask how the amount of successfully transmitted information $I_t$ (bits), and then the *TP* (bits/s) vary with the entropy of the vocabulary (simplified to $\log_2 N$ and $\log_2 NN'$).

In both conditions, $I_t$ tended to level off as $H_V$ was gradually raised, confirming the limited capacity (in bits per selection) of the tested transmission channels. Had we investigated larger vocabularies, the leveling off would have been more spectacular, but exploring very high levels of entropy is not just time consuming — also recall that in general humans hate to make errors. Below we will report evidence that in fact our range of *x* values, chosen in light of our pilot results, was adequate.

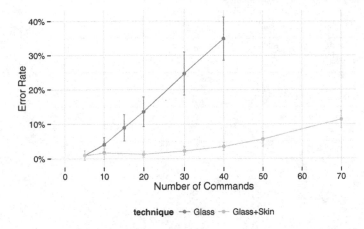

**Fig. 6.** *Error rate* vs. the number of commands for each condition.

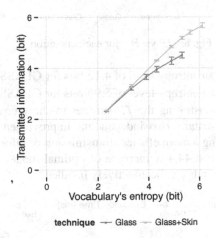

**Fig. 7.** $I_t$ vs. $H_V$, for each condition

The two curves of Fig. 7 tend to asymptote to different capacity limits. With GLASS +SKIN not only was the average amount of transmitted information higher than it was with GLASS (this difference was observed in all 14 participants), the capacity limit suggested to the eye by the curvature of the plot was invariably higher (14/14).

We may now turn to the *TP*, which in both conditions reached a maximum, as predicted (Fig. 8). Fitting second-order polynomials to the data, we obtained:

$y = -0.389x^2 + 3.2043x - 2.1714$ ($r^2 = .985$) for GLASS and $y = -0.1941x^2 + 2.3115x - 2.0004$ ($r^2 = .997$) for GLASS+SKIN.

From these equations, shown graphically in Fig. 8, one can estimate the *xy* coordinates of the maxima (both maxima take place within the tested range of entropies, and so no extrapolation is required):

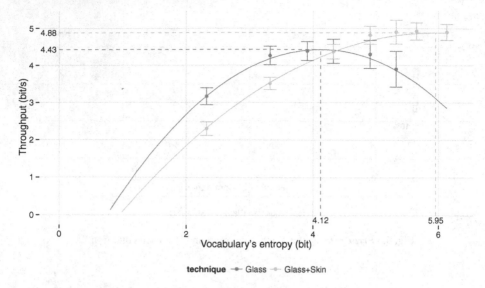

**Fig. 8.** *TP* vs. $H_V$, for each condition.

$TP_{\max} = 4.43$ bits/s at an entropy level of 4.12 bits for GLASS and

$TP_{\max} = 4.88$ bits/s at an entropy level of 5.95 bits for GLASS+SKIN.

Thus a single figure illustrating the *TP* suffices to show unambiguously that the GLASS+SKIN resource entails two independent improvements. One is a 10.1 % increase of the *TP*, meaning a more efficient transmission of information from the user to the system. The other is a 44.4 % increase of optimal input entropy, meaning that much larger sets of commands can be effectively handled.

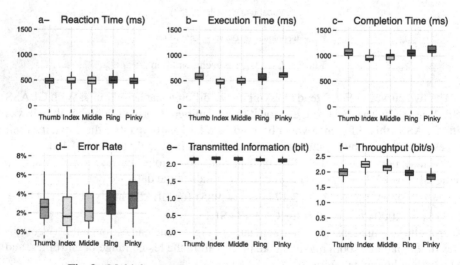

**Fig. 9.** Multiple quantitative characterization of finger performance

**Differential Finger Performance.** Obviously our fingers are not all equally suitable to serve in the GLASS+SKIN approach, for reasons unlikely to have much to do with entropy. Figure 9 suggests, unsurprisingly, that our best performer is the forefinger and the worse is the pinky, as summarized most compactly by the *TP* data of Fig. 9f. Any attempt to leverage the GLASS+SKIN principle in some interaction technique should probably consider focusing on the three central fingers of the human hand. Bearing in mind the current proliferation of small devices, however, the possibility to multiply the vocabulary by just 3 (thus adding up to $\log_2 3 = 1.58$ bits to $H_V$) seems of non-negligible interest.

## 5 Conclusion and Perspectives

In view of the specialized literature there is no doubt that finger identification has a potential to considerably enhance input expressivity on touch screens in the near future, even (but not exclusively) in the simplest case of single-touch input that was considered in the present research. The data of the above-reported experiment suggest that touch-screen input may certainly benefit from the substantial functional parallelism of the skin and glass channels, as we called them. We discovered that surprisingly little effort is demanded of users to adapt their hand posture, during hand motion to the target object, so as to touch this one target with this one finger. Importantly, our pilot experiments revealed that the latter choice, unlike the former, is essentially errorless.

One reason why the skin channel is of interest in the face of the real-estate scarcity challenge is that exploiting this additional channel makes it possible to increase the width of hierarchical command systems and hence to reduce their depth. For example with just three fingers rather than one, and the GLASS+SKIN principle, one may escape the problematic design imagined by Apple in which 20 control buttons are displayed on a watch (Apple Watch Sport).

In the theoretical introduction to our experiment we offered a schematic view of the input problem. In particular, we left aside the complex *code* issue (movement-to-command mapping) and we deliberately ignored the fact that in the real world some commands are far more frequent than others, meaning the real levels of entropy are less than we assumed. These obviously are subtle and important issues that will deserve sustained attention in future research if the GLASS+SKIN principle is ever to be optimally leveraged. One important question in this direction is, What part of the information should be transmitted through which channel? One obvious constraint is that while screen regions (buttons) can be, and are invariably marked with text or symbols reminding users of which button does what, it is more difficult to imagine tricks that will remind which fingers does what without consuming screen space.

## References

1. Au, O.K.-C., Tai, C.-L.: Multitouch finger registration and its applications. In: OZCHI 2010, pp. 41–48. ACM, New York, NY, USA (2010)
2. Bailly, G., Demeure, A., Lecolinet, E., Nigay, L.: MultiTouch menu (MTM). In: IHM 2008, pp. 165–168. ACM, New York, NY, USA (2008)

3. Bailly, G., Lecolinet, E., Guiard, Y.: Finger-count and radial-stroke shortcuts: 2 techniques for augmenting linear menus on multi-touch surfaces. In: CHI 2010, pp. 591–594. ACM, New York, NY, USA (2010)

4. Bailly, G., Müller, J., Lecolinet, E.: Design and evaluation of finger-count interaction: combining multitouch gestures and menus. IJHCS **70**, 673–689 (2012)

5. Benko, H., Ishak, E.W., Feiner, S.: Cross-dimensional gestural interaction techniques for hybrid immersive environments. In: VR 2005, pp. 209–216 (2005)

6. Benko, H., Saponas, T.S., Morris, D., Tan, D.: Enhancing input on and above the interactive surface with muscle sensing. In: ITC, pp. 93–100. ACM, New York, NY, USA (2009)

7. Benko, H., Wilson, A.D., Baudisch, P.: Precise selection techniques for multi-touch screens. In: CHI 2006, pp. 1263–1272. ACM, New York, NY, USA (2006)

8. Buxton, W.: A three-state model of graphical input. In: Interact 1990, pp. 449–456. North-Holland Publishing Co. (1990)

9. Ewerling, P., Kulik, A., Froehlich, B.: Finger and hand detection for multi-touch interfaces based on maximally stable extremal regions. In: ITS 2012, pp. 173–182. ACM Press, New York, NY, USA (2012)

10. Ghomi, E., Huot, S., Bau, O., Beaudouin-Lafon, M., Mackay, W.E.: Arpège: learning multitouch chord gestures vocabularies. In: ITS 2013, pp. 209–218. ACM, New York, NY, USA (2013)

11. Goguey, A., Casiez, G., Pietrzak, T., Vogel, D., Roussel, N.: Adoiraccourcix: multi-touch command selection using finger identification. In: IHM 2014, pp. 28–37. ACM, New York, NY, USA (2014)

12. Goguey, A., Casiez, G., Vogel, D., Chevalier, F., Pietrzak, T., Roussel, N.: A Three-step interaction pattern for improving discoverability in finger identification techniques. In: UIST 2014 Adjunct, pp. 33–34. ACM, New York, NY, USA (2014)

13. Harrison, B.L., Fishkin, K.P., Gujar, A., Mochon, C., Want, R.: Squeeze me, hold me, tilt me! An exploration of manipulative user interfaces. In: CHI 1998, pp. 17–24. ACM Press, New York, NY, USA (1998)

14. Harrison, C., Schwarz, J., Hudson, S.E.: TapSense: enhancing finger interaction on touch surfaces. In: UIST 2011, pp. 627–636. ACM, New York, NY, USA (2011)

15. Herot, C.F., Weinzapfel, G.: One-point touch input of vector information for computer displays. In: SIGGRAPH 1978, pp. 210–216. ACM, New York, NY, USA (1978)

16. Hinckley, K., Baudisch, P., Ramos, G., Guimbretière, F.: Design and analysis of delimiters for selection-action pen gesture phrases in Scriboli. In: CHI 2005, pp. 451–460. ACM, New York, NY, USA (2005)

17. Hinckley, K., Song, H.: Sensor synaesthesia: touch in motion, and motion in touch. In: CHI 2011, pp. 801–810. ACM, New York, NY, USA (2011)

18. Holz, C., Baudisch, P.: Fiberio: a touchscreen that senses fingerprints. In: UIST 2013, pp. 41–50. ACM Press, New York, NY, USA (2013)

19. Holz, C., Baudisch, P.: The generalized perceived input point model and how to double touch accuracy by extracting fingerprints. In: CHI 2010, pp. 581–590. ACM, New York, NY, USA (2010)

20. Kurtenbach, G.P.: The Design and Evaluation of Marking Menus. University of Toronto, Toronto (1993)

21. Kung, P., Küser, D., Schroeder, C., DeRose, T., Greenberg, D., Kin, K.: An augmented multi-touch system using hand and finger identification. In: CHI EA 2012, pp. 1431–1432. ACM, New York, NY, USA (2012)

22. Lee, S.K., Buxton, W., Smith, K.C.: A multi-touch three dimensional touch-sensitive tablet. In: Proceedings of the SIGCHI Conference on Human Factors in Computing Systems, pp. 21–25. ACM, New York, NY, USA (1985)
23. Lepinski, J., Grossman, T., Fitzmaurice, G.: The design and evaluation of multitouch marking menus. In: CHI 2010, pp. 2233–2242. ACM, New York, NY, USA (2010)
24. Li, Y.: Gesture search: a tool for fast mobile data access. In: UIST 2010, p. 87. ACM Press, New York, NY, USA (2010)
25. Malacria, S., Lecolinet, E., Guiard, Y.: Clutch-free panning and integrated pan-zoom control on touch-sensitive surfaces: the cyclostar approach. In: CHI 2010, pp. 2615–2624. ACM, New York, NY, USA (2010)
26. Marquardt, N., Kiemer, J., Greenberg, S.: What caused that touch?: expressive interaction with a surface through fiduciary-tagged gloves. In: ITS 2010, pp. 139–142. ACM, New York, NY, USA (2010)
27. Miller, G.A.: The magical number seven, plus or minus two: some limits on our capacity for processing information. Psychol. Rev. **63**, 81–97 (1956)
28. Mizobuchi, S., Terasaki, S., Keski-Jaskari, T., Nousiainen, J., Ryynanen, M., Silfverberg, M.: Making an impression: force-controlled pen input for handheld devices. In: CHI 2005 Extended Abstracts, pp. 1661–1664. ACM, New York, NY, USA (2005)
29. Pook, S., Lecolinet, E., Vaysseix, G., Barillot, E.: Control menus: execution and control in a single interactor. In: CHI 2000, pp. 263–264. ACM, New York, NY, USA (2000)
30. Potter, R.L., Weldon, L.J., Shneiderman, B.: Improving the accuracy of touch screens: an experimental evaluation of three strategies. In: CHI 1988, pp. 27–32. ACM, New York, NY, USA (1988)
31. Ramos, G., Boulos, M., Balakrishnan, R.: Pressure widgets. In: CHI 2004, pp. 487–494. ACM, New York, NY, USA (2004)
32. Roudaut, A., Lecolinet, E., Guiard, Y.: MicroRolls: expanding touch-screen input vocabulary by distinguishing rolls vs. slides of the thumb. In: CHI 2009, pp. 927–936. ACM, New York, NY, USA (2009)
33. Shannon, C.E.: A mathematical theory of communication. Bell Syst. Tech. J. **27**(379–423), 623–656 (1948)
34. Sturman, D.J., Zeltzer, D.: A survey of glove-based input. IEEE Comput. Graph. Appl. **14**, 30–39 (1994)
35. Sugiura, A., Koseki, Y.: A user interface using fingerprint recognition: holding commands and data objects on fingers. In: UIST 1998, pp. 71–79. ACM, New York, NY, USA (1998)
36. Vogel, D., Baudisch, P.: Shift: a technique for operating pen-based interfaces using touch. In: CHI 2007, pp. 657–666. ACM, New York, NY, USA (2007)
37. Wagner, J., Lecolinet, E., Selker, T.: Multi-finger chords for hand-held tablets: recognizable and memorable. In: CHI 2014, pp. 2883–2892. ACM, New York, NY, USA (2014)
38. Wang, F., Cao, X., Ren, X., Irani, P.: Detecting and leveraging finger orientation for interaction with direct-touch surfaces. In: UIST 2009, p. 23. ACM Press, New York, NY, USA (2009)
39. Wang, F., Ren, X.: Empirical evaluation for finger input properties in multi-touch interaction. In: CHI 2009, pp. 1063–1072. ACM Press, New York, NY, USA (2009)
40. Wang, J., Canny, J.: FingerSense: augmenting expressiveness to physical pushing button by fingertip identification. In: CHI 2004 Extended Abstracts, pp. 1267–1270. ACM, New York, NY, USA (2004)
41. Wobbrock, J.O., Morris, M.R., Wilson, A.D.: User-defined gestures for surface computing. In: CHI 2009, p. 1083. ACM Press, New York, NY, USA (2009)
42. Zhao, S., Balakrishnan, R.: Simple vs. compound mark hierarchical marking menus. In: UIST 2004, pp. 33–42. ACM, New York, NY, USA (2004)

# Physical Playlist: Bringing Back the Mix-Tape

Daniel Burnett[1(✉)], Adrian Gradinar[1], Joel Porter[1], Mike Stead[1],
Paul Coulton[1], and Ian Forrester[2]

[1] ImaginationLancaster, Lancaster University,
LICA Building, Lancaster LA1 4YW, UK
{d.burnett,a.gradinar,j.porter,m.stead,
p.coulton}@lancaster.ac.uk
[2] Dock House, MediaCity, Salford, UK
ian.forresterl@bbc.co.uk

**Abstract.** To those of a certain age the concept of the mix-tape holds fond memories, and generally not of the musical content they contained, but rather the emotional and physical connection they represented with either its creator or recipient. They provided an embodiment of the time and effort it its creation and thus presented the same qualities of other handmade gifts. The advent of digital content, and particularly the mp3, for storage and streaming meant that audio content could be shared more quickly and easily than ever before. However, the creation of a digital playlist does not embody the same qualities present in a mix-tape and thus has not gained the same cultural significance. This research re-imagines the mix-tape for digital content as physical customizable jewellery that can once again embody values not generally attributed to digital content. Through a discussion of the design process and the results of preliminary evaluation, the potential benefits on the user experience of sharing digital content through physical objects have been highlighted.

**Keywords:** Tangible · Embodied · NFC · Customizable · Jewellery

## 1 Introduction

The shared mix-tape had an emotional and physical connection for people that digitally shared content often lacks. This connection comes from the fact that objects or artefacts often symbolize something more than their intrinsic value, and this is often preserved over the years. Our personal associations with objects often gain subjective meaning based on the memories that we have about them, although such memories are generally hidden and intangible [2]. Where once time was spent decorating the cover of the mix-tape[1] and carefully cultivating the tracks and possibly taking upwards of an hour to make, it now takes mere seconds with digital services such as Spotify, where on average nine playlists are created each second[2]. Between the mix-tape and Spotify was the writeable CD but they came too late, or too close, to the emergence of the mp3 to

---

[1] A mix-tape is the name given to any compilation of songs recorded onto any audio format although it is primarily associated with the compact audiocassette.
[2] https://press.spotify.com/uk/information/.

© IFIP International Federation for Information Processing 2015
J. Abascal et al. (Eds.): INTERACT 2015, Part IV, LNCS 9299, pp. 72–78, 2015.
DOI: 10.1007/978-3-319-22723-8_6

become a shareable treasured object akin to the mix-tape. The project presented in this research and developed in conjunction with BBC R&D at Media City UK resulted in the creation of a system, The Physical Playlist, that can be used to explore users experience of a physical shareable personalized object that has digital content embedded within it. Thus the project differs from those that have used objects as a means of storing memories, such as Memory Boxes [4] or Stevens et al.'s Living Memory Box [9], as the object itself primarily represents the embodiment of the time and effort the creator took to personalize the gift thus making it more meaningful than a purely digital playlist.

## 2 Design Process

This research is part of a larger AHRC[3] project The Creative Exchange[4] whose aim is to bring together academics and businesses to improve the way they work together through a series of workshops exploring different themes around the concept of The Digital Public Space [7]. The theme of the workshop from which this project emerged was "Making the Digital Physical" and the Physical Playlist was one of the ideas generated by the group who went on to develop the project. The core idea was to recreate the concept of the mix-tape using digital content associated with physical objects. The physical objects could take almost any form imaginable although the original idea was for customizable jewellery and its format chosen for the initial prototype presented in this paper.

As the design was to be created collaboratively it was felt a 'research through design' [3] approach would be adopted, as it would allow all parties to reflect upon the design in an agile and emergent manner. One of the earliest considerations was how to embed digital content within an object that could be used easily by a user. The obvious solution to this was Near Field Communications (NFC) tags as they are relatively cheap, come in a variety of form factors, and now can be easily programmed via a mobile phone [1].

After deciding upon NFC tags as the bearer of the playlist, a method of personalizing the tags and then reading them back to play the associated media would have to be created. The tags chosen needed to be relatively small and robust, in the end a 14 mm laundry tag was settled upon. Given its resilient nature and small footprint it was ideal for the application as the jewellery it is attached to may be worn out and about in diverse environments.

While different ideas for embedding the tag emerged a design was settled on that would allow easy programming of the tag and individual customization when incor-

---

[3] Arts and Humanities Research Council.
[4] http://www.thecreativeexchange.org/.

porated within a piece of jewellery, which in this case was a bracelet. This resulted in the definition of a widget to hold the required tag and after a number of design iterations, shown in Fig. 1, a widget was produced that fulfilled this purpose.

**Fig. 1.** Prototypes of widget from left (initial) to right (final).

With the NFC tags suitably housed the next step was to create a means to turn this individual item into a playlist. A simple bracelet was chosen as shown in Fig. 2 below, as each widget could then be customized to produce something akin to a charm bracelet.

**Fig. 2.** Original prototype bracelet with an NFC tag embedded in a widget

With the playlist form factor created a method for embedding content and then reading and playing the tracks was required.

## 2.1   Embedding Content Within Tags

An elegant solution was required for the process of storing the track data within the tag, as the chosen tags were only capable of storing 48 bytes. A simplified protocol was created where the first part of the data would be the type of track i.e. *s* for Spotify, *y* for YouTube and *i* for iPlayer, followed by a comma and finished with the URI (Unique Resource Identifier) for that track. The whole string was then enclosed within chevrons to give an indication of the start and end of the tag. For example:

```
<s, 6JEKOCvvjDjjMUBFoXShNZ>
```

The most viable option was to create a mobile app for the Android platform due to its open nature and the prevalence of NFC technology already contained within a large number of the phones running the operating system.

With the player capable of playing a multitude of different media types from different services, in this project the media to be embedded came from YouTube[5], Spotify[6], and BBC iPlayer[7] and the developed app had to accommodate all of these in one simple interface. The most effective way to do this was to provide a single text entry space with the option to then search any of the three services; the interface is shown in Fig. 3.

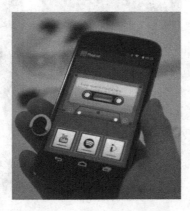

**Fig. 3.** The Android Application, Buttons can be seen for the three services.

Of course the utility of the App is not limited only to the initial writing of the data to the tag, it can also be used to re-write the tag so playlists can be edited on the fly to personalize them even further.

Once a playlist has been created the next step would be to play it back, for this a working device that can read the NFC tags and create a playlist and ultimately play the tracks was required.

## 2.2 Playing the Tracks

For the design team maintaining the order of the playlist was crucial and so it was decided that any player developed would have to respect the creators' order of the playlist. Working from a position of slow technology [5, 6] the process of building the playlist and the act of placing the tags into the bracelet then fixing them in place,

---

[5] http://www.youtube.com/.

[6] https://www.spotify.com/.

[7] http://www.bbc.co.uk/iplayer/.

creates a time for self reflection and allows the creator to contemplate how best to actually curate the playlist.

From this standpoint a player design was formed that read the bracelet from top to bottom through the use of a rotating rod that moves a platform which can be seen in the left most image in Fig. 4 below. This image also shows the subsequent refined design showcased at MozFest 2014[8] in the middle and the 3D model that has become the finalised design.

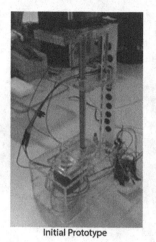  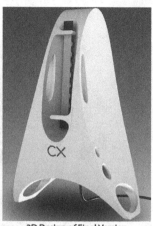

Initial Prototype              Second Prototype              3D Design of Final Version

**Fig. 4.** Initial prototype to Proposed Final Player (Left to Right)

As for the actual playback of the playlist itself, the player, is in fact an Arduino[9] connected to a RaspberryPi[10] and transmits the data read from the tag via serial connection where it is then decoded and added to the playlist stored on the RaspberryPi. The playlist begins to play when the first tag is scanned and the arm continues to move down the playlist scanning until it encounters the next unread tag, this is then added to the playlist and the player ceases its movement until the previous track is completed. This is slow technology as was originally coined but also represents its more recent consideration as a way of slowing down the consumption of media [8]. The playback screen on the monitor is shown in Fig. 5.

---

[8] http://2014.mozillafestival.org.

[9] http://www.arduino.cc/.

[10] http://www.raspberrypi.org.

**Fig. 5.** Playback screen of the Physical Playlist.

## 3  Initial Prototype Evaluation

The customizable physical shareable and a bespoke media content player were taken to MozFest 2014 for preliminary evaluation where participants were invited to create and play their own bracelets. At the end of the exercise 24 of the participants completed a simple visual tool to indicate how they currently share data and how likely they are to share that data in the future with different peer groups. The tool was designed to encourage comment and debate and enabled the researchers not only to ascertain that the users were able to create and play the produced objects easily it also drew information from the users which suggested that in the future they would be more likely to share a larger amount of personal information with friends and family if it were embedded in a physical object compared to current social network platforms.

In terms of the acceptance of slow technology perhaps surprisingly the younger participants enjoyed that they couldn't skip a track and had to listen in order whereas the older participants wanted to rush through and get to the next part faster. These initial insights allowed us to move forward in the design process towards the forthcoming iterations discussed in the following section.

## 4  Future Work

The forthcoming stage of the project the 3D modelled version of the reader, shown in Fig. 4, will be created along with some custom made and designed bracelets to give the whole project a cleaner aesthetic and allow users to see the potential of the objects created. Further, plans are also underway to run a series of more in depth workshops with a range of potential user demographics through which a detailed analysis can be produced of how physical embodiment of digital content may affect users relationship with that content.

# 5  Conclusions

Whilst the original mix tapes offered elements of personalization, the flexibility of the potential objects that can be combined to form a physical playlist is considerably greater as they can take almost any form. Further, as the playlist is digitally enabled they can also be made to use other information, for instance they could be made so that they could only be played on a specific day, such as a birthday, or at a specific time, or when the weather is warm and sunny, thus allowing the creator to produce a very unique personalized experience.

Overall it is believed that the advent of 3D printing coupled with readily available means of embedding digital content in physical objects has enormous potential in creating new ways of sharing and this project offers a glimpse of the potential of this.

**Acknowledgments.** The research presented in this paper has been made possible through the support of a number of organizations most notably the Arts and Humanities Research Council (AHRC) project The Creative Exchange at Lancaster University and BBC Research and Development at Media City UK.

# References

1. Coulton, P., Omer, R., William, B.: Experiencing 'touch' in mobile mixed reality games. In: The Fourth International Game Design and Technology Workshop and Conference, GDTW 2006, pp. 68–75. Liverpool John Moores University, Liverpool (2006)
2. Csikszentmihalyi, M., Halton, E.: The Meaning of Things Domestic Symbols and the Self. Cambridge University Press, Cambridge (1981)
3. Frayling, C.: Research in art and design. Royal College of Art Research Papers **1**(1), 1–9 (1993)
4. Frohlich, D., Murphy, R.: The memory box. Pers. Ubiquit. Comput. **4**(4), 238–240 (2000)
5. Hallnas, L., Redstrom, J.: Slow technology – designing for reflection. Pers. Ubiquit. Comput. **5**(3), 201–212 (2001)
6. Hallnas, L., Jaksetic, P., Ljungstrand, P., Redstrom, J., Skog, T.: Expressions: towards a design practice of slow technology. In: Proceedings of IFIP INTERACT 2001: Human-Computer Interaction 2001, Tokyo, pp. 447–454 (2001)
7. Hemment, D., Thompson, B., de Vicente, J., Cooper, R. (eds.): Digital Public Spaces. FutureEverything (2013)
8. Odom, W., Banks, R., Durant, A., Kirk, D., Pierce, J.: Slow technology: critical reflection and future directions. In: Proceedings of the Designing Interactive Systems Conference, DIS 2012, pp. 816–817. ACM, New York (2012)
9. Stevens, M.M., Abowd, G.D., Truong, K.N., Vollmer, F.: Getting into the Living Memory Box: family archives & holistic design. Pers. Ubiquit. Comput. **7**, 210–216 (2003)

# Tangible Voting: A Technique for Interacting with Group Choices on a Tangible Tabletop

Valérie Maquil[✉], Eric Tobias, and Thibaud Latour

IT for Innovative Services, Luxembourg Institute of Science and Technology
(LIST), 5, Avenue des Hauts-Fourneaux, Esch-sur-Alzette, Luxembourg
{valerie.maquil, eric.tobias, thibaud.latour}@list.lu

**Abstract.** The tangible tabletop has been exploited in many different application domains as one of the most popular setups of Tangible User Interfaces. Proposed interaction techniques are based on, for instance, direct manipulation, dual hand input, or physical actuation. This paper reports on the design and implementation of a new interaction technique to support multiple users in their specifying and manipulating individual choices on a tangible tabletop. The proposed tangible widget consists of both a physical enclosing with several separated zones, and a number of tokens that can be distributed in these zones to specify the individual choices of the group. We present the rationale used in design, the technical implementation, and report on the use of the interaction technique during workshops with children.

**Keywords:** Tangible User Interfaces · Tabletop interaction · Widgets · Interaction technique · Collaboration

## 1 Introduction

One of the most popular setups of Tangible User Interfaces (TUI) is the tangible tabletop. This setup allows groups of people to simultaneously touch and manipulate a shared space and thus supports collaboration in different kinds of tasks [1]. To date, a variety of application scenarios have been implemented, such as landscape modelling [2], urban planning [3], musical performance [4], or logistics training [5].

Various interaction techniques have been proposed up to now for such application scenarios. While the first approaches had exploited the paradigm of direct manipulation (e.g. [6]), more recent works propose technical solutions for creating generic, reusable interaction objects, which are inspired by well-known GUI widgets (e.g., [7, 8]). Patten et al. propose a technique that allows dual hand input, requiring the concurrent use of two pucks [9]. Finally, we can find physical handles that are able to alter their position or shape (e.g., [10, 11]), with the aim to provide haptic feedback.

In this paper, we report on the design and implementation of a new interaction technique to support multiple users in their specifying and manipulating individual choices on a tangible tabletop. While previous work has focussed on improving individual interactions on a tangible tabletop, this paper presents a solution which facilitates group interactions. The aim of our work is to explore the designs of the tangibles to facilitate the potential interactions in a collaborative setting.

© IFIP International Federation for Information Processing 2015
J. Abascal et al. (Eds.): INTERACT 2015, Part IV, LNCS 9299, pp. 79–86, 2015.
DOI: 10.1007/978-3-319-22723-8_7

## 2 Methodology

The interaction technique has been developed in a participatory design approach as part of a research and development project dealing with the use of TUIs to support children in exploring and understanding the effects of their daily life decisions onto the emissions of $CO_2$ and the increase in global average temperature.

The TUI was designed in a multidisciplinary design group across several competencies, covering Software Engineering, Interaction Design, Graphic Design, and Pedagogy. In this group we iteratively designed and the widgets, the visual feedback, the selected parameters of daily life decisions, the underlying equations describing the effects onto the environment, and the scenario of use as part of one-day workshops on Climate Change. Intermediate designs were first visualized as sketches, and then implemented as low-fidelity prototypes that were improved in each iteration. Each of these was then discussed and refined collaboratively in the design team. Two of the preliminary versions were further tested with several groups of children (Fig. 1).

**Fig. 1.** The Tangible Voting technique has been developed in four iterations

In total, we created four different prototypes. The first was set up as semi-functional prototype, to test the technical feasibility of the interaction technique. For the second prototype, we used magnets and a poster on a magnetic board, in order to validate the Tangible Voting technique in a scenario of discussing Climate Change with children. The third prototype was fully functional and operated on the TUI. For the fourth and final version, we improved the design of the different components based on observations collected during the evaluation of the previous version (Table 1).

**Table 1.** Prototypes generated during the participatory design process

| Version | Evaluation |
|---|---|
| Semi-functional prototype | Inside design team |
| Non-functional poster and magnets | With 2 groups of children |
| Fully-functional prototype | With 2 groups of children |
| Improved, fully-functional prototype | With 27 groups of children |

## 3  The Tangible Voting Interaction Technique

Global Warming is a complex phenomenon influenced by a high number of parameters. Human activities are considered to be a significant cause of this change. Concentrations of greenhouse gases are increasing, with carbon dioxide ($CO_2$) being the largest contributor. Based on these scientific facts, we agreed that the learning goals of the TUI are to understand:

- Which human activities have the most negative impact on the climate.
- The children's individual lifestyle having a negative impact on the climate.
- The individual person having little impact; changing the climate is a group effort.

In order to allow individual children to reflect upon their own lifestyle and explore the impact of the group, we were looking for an interaction technique that takes into account individual choices of the group members. We realized that this could not be done in the traditional way with tangibles imitating knobs or sliders.

Inspired by Runaround[1], the popular gameshow, we created an interaction technique that allows groups of users to individually provide input to questions with a set of predefined answers, while still being able to differentiate between multiple users' inputs. Subsequently, and due to the physical nature of the interface and the persistent nature of the interface components, users are able to consult previously given answers - either individual answers or group consensus - at any time, and adapt their individual inputs freely and concurrently.

The physical design consists of an enclosing with multiple, non-overlapping zones, one for each possible answer. Each of the group members can add a provided token into one of the zones in order to indicate their selected input. The system then counts the number of tokens in each zone and calculates the distribution.

In the following, we describe the major components related to the design of the Tangible Voting technique in the context of the Climate Change scenario. We will describe the design decisions regarding object shape and visual feedback in particular.

### 3.1  Object Shape

The original layout from the game show which inspired the Tangible Voting technique had three separate zones aligned on one axis. As the typical widget design we are

---

[1] http://en.wikipedia.org/wiki/Runaround_(game_show).

working with features a marker, we chose to align the different input zones in a circular manner with the marker hidden in their centre (see Fig. 2 left). This makes the widget resemble a pie chart. We used a diameter of 15 cm and three zones. The enclosing is physical, with its bottom supported by a thin transparent plastic film to allow users to lift, drop, and reposition the widget without impacting votes that have already been cast. We embedded the widget label indicating the question on a flat, vertical board (third prototype) first, then on a cylinder placed in the centre of the widget (fourth prototype). The rationale was that such a 3D label may facilitate reading the text from a lower perspective and be memorized more easily compared to a flat, horizontal label.

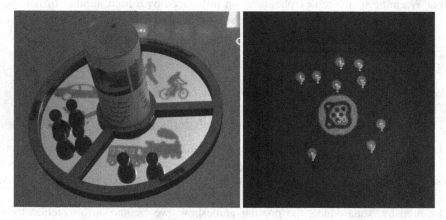

**Fig. 2.** The final design of the Tangible Voting widget (left); detection via reacTIVision (right).

Users cast their votes using small tokens (Ø 1,5 cm). While for the first version we chose small cylinders as tokens, we decided to use pawns for the third prototype. Their simple shape was expected to facilitate correct orientation during placement as well as grasping and positioning them. For the fourth prototype we decided to use different colours for each child, to allow them to better retrace their individual answer and identify with their choice.

## 3.2  Visual Feedback

We decided to provide feedback for the question asked, the three answers, and the current impact of the already provided answers by making use of the hybrid nature of the TUI, i.e. capitalizing on the possibilities of the digital and the physical nature of the widget. The question was indicated on a 3D cylinder in the centre of the widget. The answers, which exclusively related to quantities, were displayed as digital icons projected in the centre of each zone. A short text describing each answer was engraved on the physical border next to each zone. Feedback of the current status was, on one hand, provided by the pawns. We expected users to be able to quickly approximate their number, which was confirmed by the test sessions. To visualize the result of the distribution, we added a bar as visual cue on top of the widget which showed the impact of already cast votes.

## 4 Implementation

The implementation of the Tangible Voting technique was done for the Climate Change application developed in Java using TULIP [12] a software framework for implementing widgets on TUI and developed in-house. The framework allows to define the physical qualities of the widget, such as handles, identifiers, and dimensions, and to link it with digital components such as different types of visualizations. The framework hides much of the complexity related to the connection to the Computer Vision Framework, reacTIVision in this instance, and handles the receipt of protocol messages such as TUIO [13]. It will drive the changes of the interface as well.

To implement required widgets, we first defined a set of questions and answers as well as the underlying model we wanted to influence with the inputs. For each widget, we created three zones, one per answer. We defined the shape of the zones and added images and text to visualize the answers. With the look and feel defined, the input zones as well as any feedback was then tied to the underlying model using the Observer pattern.

To detect the position of the tokens, we added a round white dot underneath each token. This could be recognised as cursor in the reacTIVision framework (see Fig. 2 right). In each frame, we counted the number of tokens per zone, and compared it with their number in the previous frame in order to recognise token placements and removals. To detect the position and orientation of the physical enclosing(s), we added a small fiducial marker recognized by reacTIVision.

## 5 Evaluation

First insights regarding the functionality and the usability of the implemented interaction technique were collected as part of a case study with 27 groups of 3–9 children aged 8–10 years. Each session around the tabletop was animated by a pedagogue and a researcher and lasted about 30 min. Two video cameras were installed to capture speech and bodily interactions after consent was given. At the end of the session, a group interview was conducted, asking children questions about what they learned and how they liked it. While detailed analysis of the collected data will be published in a forthcoming publication, this paper provides a preliminary evaluation of the functionality of the Tangible Voting technique, based on collected direct observations.

The course of action adopted in the sessions consisted of three phases. In a first phase, children were asked to answer questions defined by eight widgets lying next to the interactive surface. The questions turned around the children's daily life, for instance, the kind of food they were eating, or the way they travel to school. For each of these questions, three different answers were provided by the widgets, with each having a different impact on the climate model: either low, medium, high, or none at all.

The children were each provided with a cup of coloured tokens. The questions were then asked by a moderator, one by one. The moderator read the question on the widget which they placed onto the tabletop. Each child then answered the question by placing one of their tokens in the respective zone, then sliding the widget to their neighbour. While continuing to answer the questions, the children saw the levels of $CO_2$ and temperature rise. The input approach was quickly adopted by each child, and answering questions using the pawns and the physical zones was done naturally and without further explanation regarding the input method itself, allowing the participants to focus on the questions and the impact.

In the second phase, children were asked to individually reflect on whether they would be willing to change their own lifestyle in order to try and alleviate their negative impact on the climate. Children then changed, if they were so inclined, the position of their tokens in some of the widgets. As in the first phase, this was a straightforward interaction, which did not require any further explanation. To reach the different widgets, the children either moved around the table, or asked someone else to slide the widget closer to them.

In the third phase children were asked to explore in detail multiple "what-if" scenarios provided by the moderator on four of the widgets, in order to understand the impact of each of the parameters. The children freely moved the pawns and observed the effects. After their exploration, the moderator provided a concrete goal, expressed as a target $CO_2$ value for the children to reach. To answer this question, children needed to reposition the pawns until the value was reached. We observed that, during this highly collaborative phase, children were rather possessive of their pawns and preferred to make adjustments to their previous choices on their own. After being encouraged by the moderators, they then started to work simultaneously in subgroups, each group focussing on one widget. Only when the value had been sufficiently approached, children started to coordinate their actions and focused on one widget at a time, methodologically manipulating individual pawns in order to obtain the exact value.

In this last phase, two usability problems were observed. As the manipulation of the widgets is based on removing and adding pawns, changing the position of a pawn required the application to interpret two actions. Therefore, when changing a position, the calculated outcome subsequently showed two different values. One value indicated the result when the pawn was removed, then a second indicated the result when the pawn was placed at a new position. This was slightly confusing for the children and they began asking questions as to why the $CO_2$ emissions were constantly changing.

A second issue dealt with the coordination of manual activity and visual feedback. Changing the position of pawn inside a widget could not be done blindly and required the children to look at their hands. Therefore, they were not able to look at the projected level of $CO_2$ to understand whether it was increasing or decreasing. This resulted in confusion regarding to whether the manipulation had changed anything. Some of the groups then distributed roles regarding who would take care of the manipulation of the pawns and who would observe the results.

In order to address these problems, we suggest enhancing the provided feedback. For instance, to enhance retracing the modifications of the output, we will explore the possibility to display the previous value in the visualisation of the output. To avoid confusion due to frequent changes in output, we suggest providing more feedback related to the validity of configurations. For instance, the output could adopt a different transparency if a pawn is momentarily lifted and turning opaque again once the pawn is set on the board again.

## 6 Conclusion and Future Work

In this paper, we have presented a new technique for groups to interact on tangible tabletops. Tangible Voting uses a physical enclosing with several separated zones, as well as multiple small tokens that can be distributed in these zones to specify the individual choices of the group.

A limitation of the current implementation is that the system does not differentiate between the pawns of each user. Tracking individual pawns could allow for new possibilities regarding logging of interactions and related feedback, a topic to be investigated in future work.

The instantiation of the technique in the context of a pedagogical workshop about climate change targeting children 8–10 years has shown that the Tangible Voting technique supported the planned group activities towards the three expected learning goals well. During phase one and two, the children reflected upon their individual lives and indicated their own answers. On the other hand, in the third phase the users were able to collaboratively modify the distribution of the whole group, thus creating a collaborative learning situation where the impact could be analysed and understood.

While the activities of answering questions and modifying their own answers were straightforward for all children, the conduction of small experiments in order to understand the relation between the parameters required a higher mental effort. To better support the users in these types of tasks, we suggest enriching the provided feedback.

The case study conducted with the Tangible Voting interaction technique has provided us with a large amount of video data of a scenario consisting of both individual and collaborative activities. We believe that this interaction technique is particularly interesting for the analysis of social interactions as it allows a high variety of usage patterns. In future work, we will analyse the collected video data, with the aim of enhancing the understanding of how users interact with tangible resources in a collaborative setting.

**Acknowledgments.** We would like to thank all those who contributed to the design of the Tangible Voting interaction technique, in particular Dany Blum, Luc Ewen, Roland Gilbertz, Monique Mathieu, and Ralph Theisen from the CAPEL service of the city of Luxembourg. We further thank all the school children and their teachers who tested the technique and provided us with valuable insights.

# References

1. Fleck, R., Rogers, Y., Yuill, N., Marshall, P., Carr, A., Rick, J., Bonnett, V.: Actions speak loudly with words: unpacking collaboration around the table. Paper Presented at the ACM International Conference on Interactive Tabletops and Surfaces, Banff, Canada (2009)
2. Piper, B., Ratti, C., Ishii, H.: Illuminating clay: a 3-D tangible interface for landscape analysis. In: Proceedings of the SIGCHI Conference on Human Factors in Computing Systems, pp. 355–362 (2002)
3. Maquil, V., Psik, T., Wagner, I., Wagner, M.: Expressive interactions - supporting collaboration in urban design. In: Proceedings of the International ACM Conference on Supporting Group Work - GROUP 2007, pp. 69–78. ACM, New York (2007)
4. Kaltenbrunner, M., Jorda, S., Geiger, G., Alonso, M.: The reacTable*: a collaborative musical instrument. In: 15th IEEE International Workshops on Enabling Technologies: Infrastructure for Collaborative Enterprises, pp. 406–411. IEEE Computer Society (2006)
5. Jermann, P., Zufferey, G., Schneider, B., Lucci, A., Lépine, S., Dillenbourg, P.: Physical space and division of labor around a tabletop tangible simulation. In: Proceedings of the 9th International Conference on Computer Supported Collaborative Learning, vol. 1, pp. 345–349. International Society of the Learning Sciences (2009)
6. Underkoffler, J., Ishii, H.: Urp: a luminous-tangible workbench for urban planning and design. In: Proceedings of the SIGCHI Conference on Human Factors in Computing Systems (1999)
7. Weiss, M., Wagner, J., Jansen, Y., Jennings, R., Khoshabeh, R., Hollan, J., Borchers, J.: SLAP widgets: bridging the gap between virtual and physical controls on tabletops. In: Proceedings of the SIGCHI Conference on Human Factors in Computing Systems (CHI 2009), pp. 481–490. ACM, New York (2009)
8. Simon, T., Thomas, B., Smith, R., Smith, M.: Adding input controls and sensors to RFID tags to support dynamic tangible user interfaces. In: Proceedings of Tangible, Embedded and Embodied Interaction (TEI 2014), pp. 165–172. ACM, New York (2014)
9. Patten, J., Recht, B., Ishii, H.: Audiopad: a tag-based interface for musical performance. In: Brazil, E. (ed.) Proceedings of 2002 Conference on New Interfaces for Musical Expression (NIME 2002), pp. 1–6. National University of Singapore, Singapore (2002)
10. Pedersen, E., Hornbæk, K.: Tangible bots: interaction with active tangibles in tabletop interfaces. In: Proceedings of the SIGCHI Conference on Human Factors in Computing Systems (2011)
11. Vonach, E., Gerstweiler, G., Kaufmann, H.: ACTO: a modular actuated tangible user interface object. In: Proceedings of Interactive Tabletops and Surfaces (ITS 2014), pp. 259–268. ACM, New York (2014)
12. Tobias, E., Maquil, V., Latour, T.: TULIP: a widget-based software framework for tangible tabletop interfaces. In: Proceedings of the 2015 ACM SIGCHI Symposium on EICS (2015)
13. Kaltenbrunner, M., Bovermann, T., Bencina, R., Costanza, E.: TUIO - a protocol for table-top tangible user interfaces. In: Proceedings of the 6th International Workshop on Gesture in Human-Computer Interaction and Simulation (GW 2005), Vannes, France (2005)

# Dico: A Conceptual Model to Support the Design and Evaluation of Advanced Search Features for Exploratory Search

Emanuel Felipe Duarte[1]([⊠]), Edson Oliveira Jr.[1], Filipe Roseiro Côgo[2],
and Roberto Pereira[3]

[1] DIN, UEM, Maringá, PR, Brazil
contato@emanuelfelipe.net, edson@din.uem.br
[2] DACOM, UTFPR, Campo Mourão, PR, Brazil
filiper@utfpr.edu.br
[3] IC, UNICAMP, Campinas, SP, Brazil
rpereira@ic.unicamp.br

**Abstract.** The design of models and tools to support Exploratory Search acquires more importance as the amount of information on the Web grows. The use of advanced search features is a viable approach for query exploration during Exploratory Search. However, the usage of advanced search features remains relatively low since Web search engines became popular, partially because of design decisions that ignore the complex and flexible nature of search activities. In this paper, we introduce Dico: a conceptual model for advanced search features for Exploratory Search, presenting and evaluating a set of guidelines created to support designers and evaluators to design better advanced search features, promoting its usage. Results from an evaluation activity with prospective designers indicated participants were able to make sense of Dico's guidelines, suggesting the guidelines as a promising artifact to support the evaluation of search engines.

**Keywords:** Design and evaluation guidelines · Information Seeking · Exploratory Search · Advanced search · Search user interfaces

## 1 Introduction

According to White and Roth [28], exploration is part of human nature and we aim to expand our knowledge through exploration. Continuous advances in information technology and the advent of the Web have revolutionized the way people interact with information, and the amount of information available to be explored has become abundant. However, the abundance of information became a significant problem in recent years as information consumes the attention of its recipients [21]. Therefore, White and Roth [28] express the need for systems capable of safeguarding users' attention through information filtering.

White *et al.* [25] discussed how search technologies available in 2005 already provided adequate support for users with well-defined information needs. However,

© IFIP International Federation for Information Processing 2015
J. Abascal et al. (Eds.): INTERACT 2015, Part IV, LNCS 9299, pp. 87–104, 2015.
DOI: 10.1007/978-3-319-22723-8_8

the authors highlighted how these technologies lacked support for situations where users do not have the knowledge or the contextual awareness to formulate queries or navigate on complex information spaces. According to White *et al.* [24], current search technologies still provide insufficient support for this kind of activity, denominated **Exploratory Search**: an activity in which users perform a search with open and abstract goals and need to build knowledge about a particular subject. There is a growing need for models and tools to support Exploratory Search.

In this paper we introduce Dico (Latin for "say", "speak", "mean"): a conceptual model for advanced search features for Exploratory Search, presenting and evaluating a set of guidelines created to support designers and evaluators of Exploratory Search tools. These guidelines are intended to support the design and evaluation of advanced search features to provide new possibilities of exploration for people engaged in Exploratory Search activities, such as modifying, refining, restricting, or expanding a search query.

This paper is structured as follows: in Sect. 2 we briefly present and discuss the literature review; in Sect. 3 we present Dico, the methodology for creating the guidelines and the guidelines themselves; in Sect. 4 we present an evaluation of Dico's guidelines and discuss the main results; finally, in Sect. 5 we present the main conclusions and directions for future research.

## 2   Literature Review

According to White and Roth [28], most Web search engines operate by means of a classic query-response paradigm: users formulate a query and the search engine returns a collection of documents for the given query. However, this paradigm represents a narrow understanding about the Information Seeking process and the way people interact with information. Dico is grounded on Information Seeking models because a better understanding of the Information Seeking process can benefit the creation of models and tools for supporting Information Seeking activities, such as the Exploratory Search.

### 2.1   Information Seeking

As a research area, Information Seeking focus on Information Science and benefits from the advances of Computer Science, including Human-Computer Interaction (HCI). According to Marchionini [15], Information Seeking investigates the search for information centered on users and their activities. Attfield and Blandford [5] state that many Information Seeking models have been proposed with focus on temporal and behavioral aspects. However, several studies argue the users' iterative process is transversal to both temporal and behavioral aspects, and need to be considered [4,14,15].

Marchionini [15], for instance, describes the Information Seeking process in eight stages where iterations can occur, *e.g.* when the examination of the query results guides users to formulate a new query. According to Kuhlthau [14], cognitive processes and users' feelings throughout the activity also play an important role. Furthermore, the users' activity of finding meaning from information to extend their state of knowledge about a particular subject is considered in the author's Information Search Process. Negative feelings, such as uncertainty and anxiety, are common when there is little knowledge on the subject.

Bates' Berrypicking model [4] focus on the identification of new search opportunities, proposing a process in which users starts with only an open subject and shape their own path according to their evolving interests by navigating through different sources. The Berrypicking model emphasizes that: both information need and queries are constantly evolving; information is collected gradually and continuously; users perform a variety of search strategies according to the search topic and the proficiency with the involved technologies; and users navigate through various information sources to gradually and continuously build knowledge.

In a biological analogy, Pirolli [19] describes the Information Seeking process in terms of foraging. The author's Information Foraging theory explains how people explore information sources and decide whether to continue exploring the same region or identify a new and more "fruitful" area. This decision is motivated by a perceived information quality indicator named "information scent". In a vast information environment such as the Web, the perceived "information scent" of search results may define, or at least influence, the next steps of users.

To Dervin [8], people interact with an information system to build a "picture" or "model" of a domain. This process, called Sensemaking, can be described as "the deliberate effort to understand events" [13]. According to Zhang *et al.* [30], Sensemaking occurs when people face problems in unfamiliar situations where their current knowledge proves insufficient. Sensemaking plays an important role in search, specially when users' current knowledge on the topic is limited. Targeting for a holistic and high-level abstraction model about how people interact with information, Blandford and Attfield [5] created the Information Journey Framework. The Information Journey Framework suggests the design of tools to interact with information, such as Exploratory Search tools, should consider users' cognition process (*i.e.* the creation of mental models) and the iterative nature of the Information Seeking process, which may accommodate various techniques and interaction styles in addition to a variety of feelings from users.

## 2.2 Exploratory Search

White *et al.* [26] argue that Exploratory Search is an elusive concept, suggesting that every search is somewhat exploratory. Marchionini [16] develops a conceptual discussion and proposes a categorization with three types of search activities: "lookup", "learn" and "investigate", whereas Exploratory Search is concentrated on the last two. They are explained as follows:

- **lookup:** users already know the format of the information and how to find it, therefore well-defined queries are formulated generating accurate results.

  Example: a search for weather conditions;
- **learn:** involves multiple iterations and a greater cognitive effort to handle and interpret the results. Possible goals are the acquisition of knowledge and

skills, and the understanding of concepts. Example: a researcher seeking to learn what is quantum physics; and

– **investigate:** it also involves multiple iterations that may occur during long periods of time. This activity has higher-level goals, such as analysis, synthesis and evaluation. Example: a consumer interested in purchasing a television set investigating which model is the most appropriate for his needs.

According to White and Roth [28], Exploratory Search tools should "support querying and rapid query refinement" and "offer facets and metadata-based result filtering", among other features. In practical terms, these tools should support users to (re)formulate their queries, allowing them to constantly explore and filter the obtained results. In the literature, there are related works reporting results from investigations on Exploratory Search tools, such as Flamenco [9] and Relation Browser [7]. Although these tools feature important contributions, both Flamenco and Relation Browser are not suitable for the Web as a whole, they are limited to specific closed sets of documents because they need very carefully structured metadata.

In the sense of frameworks and design recommendations, there are related works such as Wilsons's [29] design recommendations and Campos and Silva's [6] framework. Aiming to propose a framework for search user interface features, Wilson [29] proposes four categories: (1) input; (2) control; (3) informational; and (4) personalisable, and twenty design recommendations distributed between these categories. The recommendations are succinct and direct in order to be easily applied. However, there is little room for discussion on human factors, and there is no clear connection with the domain of Exploratory Search. Campos and Silva [6], in turn, consider Exploratory Search directly and propose a framework with six dimensions that can be addressed in Exploratory Search tools: (1) documents quality; (2) information presentation; (3) time; (4) cognition and knowledge acquisition; (5) personalization; and (6) collaboration. Initially only time was directly explored with a history tool. Therefore, there is still need for subsequent studies to address other dimensions and their interrelations.

The aforementioned studies feature important contributions, however none of them considered the advanced search features' potential of exploration in the context of Exploratory Search activities. Morville and Callender [17] describe advanced search as a "clumsy" and rarely used complement, like Google Advanced Search[1]. To Russel-Rose and Tate [20], advanced search is a set of features that goes beyond what is provided by the conventional search user interface. Wilson [29] points out most advanced search features can be expressed as filters or operators in a query, as long as users memorize the proper syntax. However, Hearst [10] argues many users do not even understand how these operators work. Boolean algebra operators such as AND and OR can cause confusion.

Studies show only a small fraction of submitted queries makes use of advanced search features [2,11,12]. For instance, White and Morris [27] report that only 1.1 % of analysed queries contained advanced search features, and only 8.7 % of

---

[1] http://www.google.com/advanced_search.

users used at least one advanced search feature at some point. Summarizing the views of Hearst [10], Morville and Callender [17], Wilson [29] and Russell-Rose and Tate [20], we enumerate four major advanced search problems:

1. **it displaces users from their context:** memorization of filters and operators syntax is problematic for most users, therefore they need to access a separated "advanced search" page to make use of these features;
2. **features are difficult to find:** the link to access the separated "advanced search" page is usually concealed inside drop down menus or positioned in low visibility areas of the page;
3. **features are presented in intimidating form:** once users access the separated "advanced search" page, they usually find a long form full of fields with little or no help on how to fill them properly; and
4. **the applied logic of the features can be misunderstood:** it is common for people to have difficulties to understand the employed logic of some filters and operators, like the ones involving Boolean algebra.

As enumerated, advanced search features usage is relatively low due to several factors, some of them related to how these features are designed. However, because the use of advanced search features empowers users to explore new search possibilities, such as modifying, refining, restricting or expanding a search query, they are a plausible and viable approach to support Exploratory Search. Therefore, there is a need for studies that help to understand how to design better solutions that favour the use of advanced search features. Dico is intended to contribute in this direction and is presented in the next section.

## 3   Dico

Dico is a conceptual model for advanced search features to support Exploratory Search. Dico is composed by three principles derived from the four major problems pointed out in Sect. 2.2: (1) **context**, (2) **presence** and (3) **simplicity**, and has guidelines to promote the usage of advanced search features by addressing one or more of these principles. The conceptual model can be applied to any query-response paradigm search engine, such as *Google*[2], *Bing*[3], *Google Scholar*[4] and *Springer Link*[5]. Figure 1 illustrates Dico's composition and its application, which promotes the creation of Exploratory Search tools that favour the use of advanced search features. The main difference between Dico's guidelines and other examples of design recommendations, such as Nielsen's [18] heuristics or Wilson's [29] search user interface design recommendations, is the focus on promotion of advanced search features usage during Exploratory Search activities, an objective that may not be achieved without specific design recommendations such as Dico's guidelines.

---

[2] http://www.google.com/.
[3] http://bing.com/.
[4] http://scholar.google.com/.
[5] http://link.springer.com/.

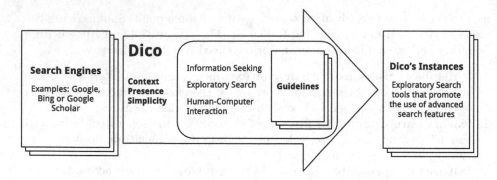

**Fig. 1.** Illustration of Dico's composition and its application.

## 3.1 Methodology for Creating Dico's Guidelines

Dico has three key principles that cover the major advanced search features problems identified in the literature: (1) **context**: provide features when and where they can be useful to users; (2) **presence**: make features easily found or perceivable by users; and (3) **simplicity**: present features without intimidating users and in formats they can understand what the feature is, what it does, and how to use it. Grounded on these principles, we carried out four steps to identify and propose guidelines for Dico. The methodology is illustrated in Fig. 2 and detailed in sequence:

- **step 1**: analyse how the studies discussed in the literature review are related to one or more of Dico's principles. If a study contributes to at least one principle it was a candidate to compose a new guideline or complement an already outlined one. Finally, compile a set of guidelines in which each one must be theoretically justified by at least one study. The guidelines' structure is inspired by Design Patterns [1], containing:
  - **name:** presents an identification number and the guideline name. The number is for reference only and does not indicate importance or priority;

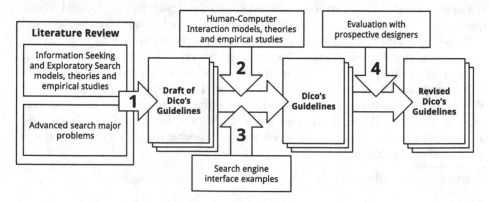

**Fig. 2.** Illustration of the methodological steps to create Dico's guidelines.

- **description:** presents a more detailed explanation of the guideline;
- **theoretical foundation:** describes the theoretical foundation used to support the guideline, which may be related studies on Information Seeking, Exploratory Search and HCI;
- **category:** relates the guideline to at least one of three Dico's principles, which are context, presence and simplicity; and
- **example:** presents and discusses an example of the guideline implementation (*i.e.*, how it can be understood and put into practice).

- **step 2:** analyse the composed guidelines and complement the theoretical foundation with HCI studies. The considered studies are Nielsen's [18] heuristics, the communicability concept from Semiotic Engineering [22], and Weinschenk's [23] study on human aspects relevant to design decisions. These studies cover a wide range of factors, such as design questions and human factors (*e.g.*, memory and cognition);
- **step 3:** create an illustrated example of how to apply the guideline within a search user interface. Examples consist of an analysis of certain features of search user interfaces from search engines or academic tools. It is discussed how the example satisfies the guideline, or why it does not and what could be done to solve the problem; and
- **step 4:** evaluate the guidelines description and illustrated example with prospective designers. The guidelines were revisited based on the results from their usage and evaluation with a group of prospective designers. The evaluation details and results are presented in Sect. 4.

As a result of this process, we created a set of eight guidelines for Dico, which means we were able to approach Dico's principles with eight different perspectives inspired by our literature review. Due to space restrictions, we present only a summary of the guidelines. The summary contains the number, name and description for each guideline, and can be seen in Table 1. For demonstration purposes, guideline #1 is presented in detail in Sect. 3.2. A document describing Dico and containing all the guidelines in their complete structure is available at http://din.uem.br/gsii/dico/.

## 3.2  Guideline #1: Users Should Be Able to Reformulate Their Query at Any Time in an Easy Way

- **Description:** the search user interface should always allow users to reformulate their query easily according to their evolving state of knowledge on the subject. The query reformulation can be in the format of modification, refinement, restriction, or expansion, and to do so the search field and the current query must always be available to users.
- **Theoretical Foundation:** as evidenced by Bates [4], Marchionini [15] and Blandford and Attfield [5], users go through an iterative process during a search. Among other aspects, this process is characterized by query reformulation according to the new acquired knowledge. Therefore, it is critical the interface does not prevent or make it difficult for users to reformulate queries,

**Table 1.** Summary of Dico's guidelines.

| # | Name and description |
|---|---|
| 1 | **Users should be able to reformulate their query at any time in an easy way:** the search user interface should always allow users to reformulate their query easily according to their evolving state of knowledge on the subject. The query reformulation can be in the format of modification, refinement, restriction, or expansion, and to do so the search field and the current query must always be available to users |
| 2 | **Advanced search features must be present in the main search page:** advanced search features should not be limited to the fields of a separate and specific page, such features should be included in the main search page which users are already used to operate. More specifically, advanced search features should be included in the search results page, because it is there where they will possibly be more useful |
| 3 | **Users should be able to start their search in a conventional search user interface:** to take advantage of advanced search features offered by the search engine, users should not be required to access an unfamiliar and possibly intimidating page. They should be able to start their search in a conventional search user interface they are already used to operate (*e.g.*, the default home page of the selected search engine) |
| 4 | **Advanced search features should complement information when applicable:** when filters and operators relate to the presented information, interaction elements for advanced search features should be inserted in the search user interface next to the information or even contained in it. Such elements are intended to allow users to directly use the information of their interest to formulate and submit new queries without being moved from their context |
| 5 | **The interface should assist users to understand concepts and relationships present in the results:** users should be assisted in forming a mental model of the researched topic, because this is an important step in the construction of knowledge in an Exploratory Search activity. The interface can provide a visual representation of the information space in which the main concepts and how they relate to the retrieved documents can be highlighted. Such relationships, for example, may be interactive so that users make further queries with related advanced search features |
| 6 | **Advanced search features must be presented in a manner that does not intimidate users:** the search user interface should not have the format of a page with several fields to be filled or complex controls, it is necessary to provide search features that are as simples as possible according to the context. The advanced search features should be presented with simple controls, and the presentation of these features must be diluted along the search activity, with different features presented at different times as they become useful for a given context |
| 7 | **Users should be able to identify and manage advanced search features easily in the current query:** the query must be processed so the features can be identified and presented in a format that highlights them individually. Presenting features individually also facilitates its management, like removing or editing a specific feature present in the query. When presented individually, the features may also receive an individual explanation in a language that makes sense to users, assisting them to associate syntax and functionality |
| 8 | **The search user interface should communicate technical information of advanced search features in a manner that makes sense to users:** users must be able to understand the logical operation of advanced search features. For this, the visual and verbal communication used to display the features and related technical information must have a simple language that makes sense to users |

because this is a recurring step during Exploratory Search activities. From the HCI perspective, this guideline can be related to Nielsen's third heuristic "user control and freedom", described by the author as "Users often choose system functions by mistake and will need a clearly marked 'emergency exit' to leave the unwanted state without having to go through an extended dialogue.

**Fig. 3.** Guideline #1 example: lack of current query on the search field in the search results page of *Submarino*. Accessed 01 August 2014.

Support undo and redo." Finally, considering the advanced search perspective, freedom and easiness to submit new queries can be incentives for users to explore the provided advanced search features.
- **Category:** context, presence and simplicity.
- **Example:** the search results page of the Brazilian e-commerce *Submarino*[6], illustrated in Fig. 3 for the query "**seo**", makes use of features such as breadcrumbs, faceted navigation and visual highlight of the found terms. However, there are problems considering the scope of this guideline. Although the search field remains present on the Web page, it appears without the current query filled in, making it difficult to reformulate in case users wish to modify only a part of the query. The interface would be in compliance with the guideline if the search field remained filled after submitting a query.

## 4   Evaluation

To evaluate Dico's guidelines, we conducted a study to investigate whether prospective designers would make sense of the guidelines' descriptions and their illustrated examples, and whether they would find the guidelines useful to support their practical activities. First, participants carried out an inspection of two Web search engines using Dico's guidelines. This task was designed to introduce the guidelines to the participants, enabling them to subsequently evaluate the applied guidelines based on their experience with them. Both qualitative and quantitative data were collected and analysed, therefore we considered this a mixed evaluation. We used the Goal Question Metric (GQM) template [3] to

---

[6] http://www.submarino.com.br/.

summarize the nature of the study and the main aspects involved: **we evaluated** Dico's guidelines; **for the purpose of** assessing whether they make sense to designers who may apply them; **with respect to** description clarity and illustrated examples usefulness; **from the viewpoint of** designers using Dico's guidelines to inspect search engines; and **in the context of** Computer Science undergraduate students attending to a HCI course.

## 4.1 Study Planning

The study planning consisted of the activities described as follows.

**Participant Selection:** 15 Computer Science undergraduate students attending to a HCI course in the third semester were invited to participate. Participants were all males, with ages ranging from 18 to 31 years old. They were chosen for knowing basic principles of evaluation by inspection and heuristic evaluation, for being used to conduct Exploratory Search activities on the Web, and for being the target audience of Dico's guidelines: prospective designers who will probably work in the design and evaluation of computer systems. The study was applied as an HCI theoretical and practical activity, however it was up to the students to decide whether they want to anonymously supply their data to this study. A total of 14 students consented, and one of them had incoherent answers with the asked questions and was removed, resulting in a sample $N = 13$. As the study involved human beings, the applicable ethical aspects were adequately addressed. Participation was voluntary, unpaid, with the possibility to leave the study at any time without justification, and all participants registered their consent.

**Planning the Inspection of Search Engines with Dico:** two search engines were selected to be inspected: *Google* (general purpose) and *Google Scholar* (scholarly literature), and participants were randomly assigned to inspect one of them. Individually, participants inspected whether the search engine was in compliance with each of Dico's guidelines. Participants did not receive any kind of prior training or information about Dico's guidelines beyond what is already presented in the guidelines. For data collection, we selected mandatory multiple-choice questions with three options: (1) "Yes"; (2) "No"; or (3) "N/A", followed by a required text field to justify the answer. This activity was considered sufficient to provide an initial experience with the application of Dico, qualifying the participants to later evaluate its guidelines directly.

**Planning the Evaluation of Dico's Guidelines:** participants evaluated the guidelines individually. For each guideline they evaluated the clarity of its description and the usefulness of its example. For data collection, we selected the format of an assertion for which participants select their degree of agreement using a five-point Likert scale. The first assertion is "The Guideline #$X$ is clear and can be easily understood", where $X$ is the guideline number. The possible answers were: (1) "Strongly agree"; (2) "Partially agree"; (3) "Indifferent"; (4)

"Partially disagree"; and (5) "Strongly disagree". Participants have the option (not mandatory due to time constraints and possible fatigue effects) to justify their answer. The second statement is "The given example assists to understand the Guideline #X". Again, participants must select an answer between the same degree of agreement options and optionally justify their answer.

**Instrumentation:** we created three *ad hoc* instruments for this study: (1) a document containing an overview of Dico's guidelines with their names and descriptions; (2) an online form for the inspection of search engines with Dico; and (3) an online form for the evaluation of Dico's guidelines. The first instrument contains a summary of all guidelines in the same page for a holistic view, because they can be viewed only one at a time in the online forms. The second instrument introduces and supports the search engine inspection with Dico, where each guideline along with the respective fields are presented in detail in separated pages. Finally, the third instrument introduces and presents Dico's guidelines evaluation, repeating the format in which each guideline along with the respective fields are presented in detail in separated pages.

## 4.2   Operation

Participation was in person during a HCI class inside a computer lab, and all participants had access to a computer and Internet. The first instrument was handed to each participant, and also contained an anonymous identification code and the search engine to be inspected. The other two instruments were given as URLs to be accessed. The participants were instructed to access them in order, starting with the form for the inspection of the search engines (second instrument), and then, after finishing filling it, accessing the form for the evaluation of Dico's guidelines (third instrument). Participants were instructed the purpose of the study was to obtain their opinion as prospective designers, and therefore there were no "correct" or "wrong" answers. The tasks were performed individually, without exchange of information between participants, and submitted in digital format.

## 4.3   Results Analysis and Interpretation

For the search engine inspection with Dico, Fig. 4 shows the summary of responses for both *Google* and *Google Scholar* inspections. (In Fig. 4, "#X" stands for compliance with guideline #X according to participants' responses.) It can be noted that even though both search engines are from the same company, there is a clear difference in responses between them. This difference is positive for this study because both groups of participants had different experiences with the application of Dico's guidelines, enriching the results. As participants inspected the search engines with Dico, this experience properly qualified them to evaluate Dico's guidelines directly.

For Dico's guideline evaluation, Fig. 5 illustrate all responses (in the first activity participants 1, 3, 5, 7, 9, 11 and 13 inspected *Google*, and participants

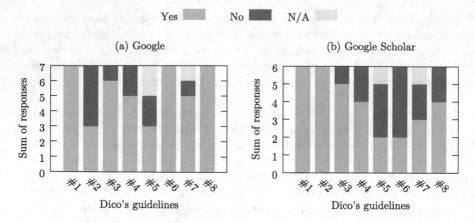

**Fig. 4.** Summary of search engines inspection with Dico responses.

2, 4, 6, 8, 10 and 12 inspected *Google Scholar*), and Fig. 6 a summary of the responses. (In Figs. 5 and 6, "#XD" stands for the statement "The Guideline #X is clear and can be easily understood" and "#XE" for "The given example assists to understand the Guideline #X".) Summarizing, there were 155 (74.52 %) responses for "Strongly agree", 30 (14.42 %) for "Partially agree" (summarizing 88.94 % of agreeing responses), 12 (5.77 %) for "Indifferent", 8 (3.85 %) for "Partially disagree" and 3 (1.44 %) for "Strongly disagree" (summarizing 5.29 % of disagreeing responses). It can be noted participants 7 and 8 had together 16 of the 30 "Partially agree" responses. Aside from that, responses were relatively equally distributed among participants. The 11 disagreeing responses, for instance, were distributed among 7 participants, therefore we did not detect dramatic differences regarding individual participants. These results indicate participants approved Dico's guidelines descriptions and illustrated examples. Additionally, because participants were all prospective designers, it was expected them to experience some difficulty when using the guidelines for the first time. Only 5.29 % of responses indicated difficulty, what is another indication the guidelines were well received and understood. However, a more detailed analysis regarding individual guidelines and differences between the responses of participants who inspected *Google* and *Google Scholar* can provide more specific results and highlight opportunities for improvement.

For guidelines #2 and #8, all the participants strongly or partially agreed their descriptions are clear and can be easily understood and the illustrated example assists to understand the guideline. One participant, for instance, justified his "Strongly agree" choice for guideline #8 as "*Very easily understood.*" for description clarity and "*Clear and easily understood example.*" for illustrated example usefulness — all translations of participants answers were made by the authors. Therefore, guidelines #2 and #8 were considered useful and well elaborated by all the participants. It can be noted that among participants who inspected *Google* there were 3 "Partially agree" responses, while for those who inspected *Google Scholar* there were 6, indicating these two guidelines were bet-

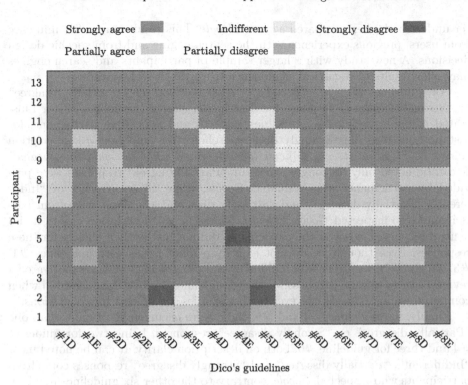

**Fig. 5.** Dico's guidelines evaluation responses.

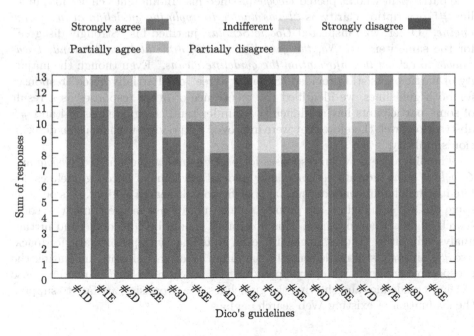

**Fig. 6.** Summary of Dico's guidelines evaluation responses.

ter understood when compared against *Google*. This result may suffer influence from users' previous experience with the search engine and from specific design decisions. A new study with a larger sample of participants and search engines may offer results of statistical significance to verify these hypothesis.

For guidelines #1, #3, #6 and #7, each received one "Partially disagree" or "Strongly disagree" response for description clarity (guideline #3) or illustrated example usefulness (guidelines #1, #6 and #7). One participant, for instance, justified his "Strongly disagree" choice for guideline #3 description clarity as "*I found it very difficult to understand what the guideline means.*" It can be noted only "Strongly agree" or "Partially agree" responses were provided by participants who evaluated *Google*, while all occurrences of "Indifferent", "Partially disagree" and "Strongly disagree" responses were from participants who inspected *Google Scholar*. Guideline #7 description clarity had 3 neutral responses, however the participants did not justify their choices for these responses. Even though we did not identify evident issues with guidelines #1, #3, #6 and #7, the presence of indifferent and disagreeing responses motivated a review of them. Again, it is possible these guidelines are better understood when compared against *Google*, however further studies are needed for conclusions.

Finally, for guidelines #4 and #5, there were occurrences of more than one "Partially disagree" or "Strongly disagree" responses, being two for guideline #4 and three for guideline #5, both on description clarity. It can be noted most "Indifferent", "Partially disagree" and "Strongly disagree" responses come from participants who inspected *Google*, contrary to the other six guidelines in which all these type of responses came from participants who inspected *Google Scholar*. One participant who inspected *Google* justified his "Indifferent" choice for guideline #5 description clarity as "*I was unable to apply the guideline in the search engine.*" Other, who inspected *Google Scholar*, justified his "Strongly disagree" for the same item as "*No, the guideline is very difficult to understand, I was unable to extract the information the guideline means.*" Even though the majority of participants still provided "Strongly agree" or "Partially agree" responses for both guidelines, we identified the recurrence of other responses as a result of some participants having difficulty to understand the guidelines #4 and #5 abstraction level, therefore they were improved by a review with focus on description simplicity.

The difference between responses for participants who evaluated *Google* and *Google Scholar* indicate designers may understand some of Dico's guidelines differently in different contexts, such as specific domain search engines. It is possible some of Dico's guidelines are prone to make more sense in the context of some search engines than in others. This possibility should be considered and further analysed in future studies. In general, even guidelines with problematic feedback, like #4 and #5, still made sense to the majority of participants, indicating the prospective designers who participated in this study succeeded in making sense of Dico's guidelines and showing the guidelines as a promising artifact to support the evaluation of existing Web search engines.

## 4.4   Validity Evaluation

Following, we present the potential threats to the study's validity we anticipated, and the efforts taken to minimize them.

**Conclusion Validity:** the study sample size ($N = 13$) does not provide results with statistical significance, and participants applied Dico to only two different search engines. However, our objective was to obtain feedback from prospective designers because they are Dico's target audience. Even though a larger sample of participants and search engines is needed for results with statistical significance, the study sample size was considered enough to obtain initial evidence Dico's guidelines descriptions and illustrated examples made sense to the participants. Therefore, sample size was not considered a threat.

**Construct Validity:** we were very careful for participants to properly understand what should be done in the activity. Instructions for every step were explained clearly and succinctly before the study, the tasks performed by participants were coherent with their qualification and educational level and they were allowed to ask for help at any time if they had questions about how to proceed. To ensure the same treatment for all the participants, questions about how to proceed in the study were answered to the whole class. No participant showed significant difficulty in understanding and carrying out the activity. Therefore, the threat of participants not understanding what should be done was considered under control, not affecting the results.

**Internal Validity:** we anticipated the following two threats:

1. **fatigue effects:** participants took between 1 h and 1 h 30 min to complete the study, and it required a considerable cognitive workload from them. However, the participants are used to perform similar activities during the 1 h 40 min duration HCI classes in which the study took place, and they could have abandoned the study at any time if they became uncomfortable with it. Therefore, the threat of participants becoming fatigued was considered under control, not affecting the results; and
2. **influence among participants:** because we requested participants to carry out the activity individually, and no significant interaction between them was observed, the threat of participants influencing each others' responses was considered under control, not affecting the results.

**External Validity:** the selection of prospective designers as participants does not guarantee experienced designers would show similar responses. However, we intentionally selected prospective designers to evaluate Dico because they are its target audience. Because low experienced prospective designers were able to make sense of Dico's guidelines descriptions and illustrated examples, it is reasonable to expect experienced designers to also be able to make sense of them, possibly even better than prospective designers. Therefore, we did not consider the selection of prospective designers a threat.

## 5   Conclusions

Current search engines still lack support for Exploratory Search. Therefore, there is a need for models and tools to support users in Exploratory Search activities. Even though the use of advanced search features is a plausible approach for Exploratory Search tools because it empowers users with new exploration possibilities, currently the usage of such features is relatively low.

To promote the use of advanced search features we introduced Dico. Dico is composed of three principles and eight guidelines to address the current major problems of advanced search. Inspired by Design Patterns, each guideline has: identification number and name; description; theoretical foundation on Information Seeking, Exploratory Search and HCI; category according to the three principles; and illustrated example demonstrating how it can be applied.

We evaluated Dico's guidelines and provided evidence prospective designers were able to make sense of them when inspecting existing Web search engines. Even though most responses evidenced no problems, the few who did also provided useful insights to further improve some of Dico's guidelines. For further studies regarding Dico, we consider:

- evaluate Dico's guidelines with a larger sample and more search engines to obtain results of statistical significance and possibly new insights on how different contexts affect the ability to make sense of Dico's guidelines;
- analyse designers using Dico's guidelines to identify problems in search engines and propose design solutions to analyse how differently people may apply the guidelines and, by evaluating the solutions, whether Dico's guidelines are serving their purpose in assisting the design better tools; and
- instantiate Dico as an Exploratory Search tool based on a search engine and evaluate it both qualitatively and quantitatively to analyse aspects such as how participants feel about using the tool, and measure the usage of advanced search features to compare with data from the literature.

**Acknowledgements.** This study was partially funded by Coordenação de Aperfeiçoamento de Pessoal de Nível Superior (CAPES). We would like to dedicate this work to Professor Sérgio R.P. da Silva who is dearly missed.

## References

1. Alexander, C.: The Timeless Way of Building. Center for Environmental Structure Berkeley, Calif: Center for Environmental Structure series, vol. 8. Oxford University Press, New York (1979)
2. Aula, A., Khan, R.M., Guan, Z.: How does search behavior change as search becomes more difficult? In: Proceedings of the SIGCHI Conference on Human Factors in Computing Systems, CHI 2010, pp. 35–44. ACM, New York (2010)
3. Basili, V., Caldiera, G., Rombach, H.D.: The goal question metric approach. In: Marciniak, J.J. (ed.) Encyclopedia of Software Engineering, pp. 528–532. Wiley, New York (1994)

4. Bates, M.J.: The design of browsing and berrypicking techniques for the online search interface. Online Inf. Rev. **13**(5), 407–424 (1989)
5. Blandford, A., Attfield, S.: Interacting with information. Synth. Lect. Hum. Centered Inf. **3**(1), 1–99 (2010)
6. Campos, T.P., Silva, S.R.P.: Um framework e uma ferramenta para apoiar a pesquisa exploratória na web. In: Proceedings of the 12th Brazilian Symposium on Human Factors in Computing Systems, IHC 2013, pp. 198–207. Brazilian Computer Society, Porto Alegre (2013)
7. Capra, R.G., Marchionini, G.: The relation browser tool for faceted exploratory search. In: Proceedings of the 8th ACM/IEEE-CS Joint Conference on Digital Libraries, JCDL 2008, pp. 420–420. ACM, New York (2008)
8. Dervin, B.: An Overview of Sense-making Research: Concepts, Methods, and Results to Date. Sense-making packet, The Author (1983)
9. Hearst, M.A.: Next generation web search: setting our sites. IEEE Data Eng. Bull. **23**(3), 38–48 (2000)
10. Hearst, M.A.: Search User Interfaces. Cambridge University Press, Cambridge (2009)
11. Jansen, B.J., Spink, A.: How are we searching the world wide web? A comparison of nine search engine transaction logs. Inf. Process. Manage. **42**(1), 248–263 (2006)
12. Jansen, B.J., Spink, A., Koshman, S.: Web searcher interaction with the dogpile.com metasearch engine. J. Am. Soc. Inf. Sci. Technol. **58**(5), 744–755 (2007)
13. Klein, G., Phillips, J.K., Rall, E.L., Peluso, D.A.: A data-frame theory of sense-making. In: Expertise Out of Context: Proceedings of the Sixth International Conference on Naturalistic Decision Making, p. 113. Psychology Press (2007)
14. Kuhlthau, C.C.: Inside the search process: information seeking from the user's perspective. J. Am. Soc. Inf. Sci. **42**(5), 361–371 (1991)
15. Marchionini, G.: Information Seeking in Electronic Environments. Cambridge Series on Human-Computer Interaction. Cambridge University Press, Cambridge (1997)
16. Marchionini, G.: Exploratory search: from finding to understanding. Commun. ACM **49**(4), 41–46 (2006)
17. Morville, P., Callender, J.: Search Patterns. O'Reilly Media, Sebastopol (2010)
18. Nielsen, J.: Usability Engineering (Interactive Technologies). Morgan Kaufmann, New York (1993)
19. Pirolli, P.: Information Foraging Theory: Adaptive Interaction with Information. Human Technology Interaction Series. Oxford University Press, Oxford (2009)
20. Russell-Rose, T., Tate, T.: Designing the Search Experience: The Information Architecture of Discovery. Morgan Kaufmann, Amsterdam (2013)
21. Simon, H.A.: Designing organizations in an information-rich world. In: Greenberger, M. (ed.) Computers, communications, and the public interest, pp. 37–53. Johns Hopkins University Press, Baltimore (1971)
22. Souza, C.S.D.: Semiotic engineering: bringing designers and users together at interaction time. Interact. Comput. **17**(3), 317–341 (2005)
23. Weinschenk, S.: 100 Things Every Designer Needs to Know About People, 1st edn. New Riders Publishing, Thousand Oaks (2011)
24. White, R.W., Capra, R., Golovchinsky, G., Kules, B., Smith, C., Tunkelang, D.: Introduction to special issue on human-computer information retrieval. Inf. Process. Manage. **49**(5), 1053–1057 (2013)

25. White, R.W., Kules, B., Bederson, B.: Exploratory search interfaces: categorization, clustering and beyond: report on the XSI 2005 workshop at the human-computer interaction laboratory, university of Maryland. SIGIR Forum **39**(2), 52–56 (2005)
26. White, R.W., Kules, B., Drucker, S.M., Schraefel, M.: Introduction. Commun. ACM **49**(4), 36–39 (2006)
27. White, R.W., Morris, D.: Investigating the querying and browsing behavior of advanced search engine users. In: Proceedings of the 30th Annual International ACM SIGIR Conference on Research and Development in Information Retrieval, SIGIR 2007, pp. 255–262. ACM, New York (2007)
28. White, R.W., Roth, R.A.: Exploratory search: beyond the query-response paradigm. Synth. Lect. Inf. Concepts Retrieval Serv. **1**(1), 1–98 (2009)
29. Wilson, M.L.: Search user interface design. Synth. Lect. Inf. Concepts Retrieval Serv. **3**(3), 1–143 (2011)
30. Zhang, X., Qu, Y., Giles, C.L., Song, P.: Citesense: supporting sensemaking of research literature. In: Proceedings of the SIGCHI Conference on Human Factors in Computing Systems, CHI 2008, pp. 677–680. ACM, New York (2008)

# Revealing Differences in Designers' and Users' Perspectives

## A Tool-Supported Process for Visual Attention Prediction for Designing HMIs for Maritime Monitoring Tasks

Sebastian Feuerstack(✉) and Bertram Wortelen

OFFIS – Institute for Information Technology,
Escherweg 2, 26121 Oldenburg, Germany
{Feuerstack, Wortelen}@offis.de

**Abstract.** Monitoring complex systems includes scanning, aggregating and processing data from various sources. The design of graphical interfaces for monitoring tasks involves a fine-grained exploration of the importance and expected frequency of events that an operator needs to be informed about.

The Human Efficiency Evaluator is a tool for the prediction of human behavior. We extended it to predict the distribution of operator's attention while monitoring interfaces. The prediction is based on the SEEV model. We show that our tool can be used by experts with different backgrounds to generate predictions following a structured, semi-automated process.

In a qualitative study with subject matter experts, we analyzed different HMI designs for a navigation task in the maritime domain. We evaluated their modeling time, tested different prediction result visualizations, and investigated in the model differences between the subjects. Different to what we originally expected, the study revealed that the models created by the subjects substantially differ depending on their perspectives. Heat maps visualizing the predicted attention allocation were appreciated by the subjects and enabled them to argue about their perspective.

**Keywords:** Visual attention · HMI analysis · Monitoring task

## 1 Introduction

Controlling safety-critical systems often includes several monitoring tasks to observe the current system state and to predict future system states that might affect the controlling activities. A ship bridge is an example for such a safety-critical system. Modern bridge systems offer a broad range of automation of routine tasks and most of the navigation decisions (passage planning for instance) can be performed prior to the voyage. Therefore most of the time on a ship bridge is spent on the navigation monitoring task. This includes observing the ships status, its navigation path and watching out for future events that require adjusting the planned route of the vessel's by changing its speed and heading to prevent dangerous situations.

© IFIP International Federation for Information Processing 2015
J. Abascal et al. (Eds.): INTERACT 2015, Part IV, LNCS 9299, pp. 105–122, 2015.
DOI: 10.1007/978-3-319-22723-8_9

Studies show that in between 75 % – 80 % of accidents in ship navigation happen because the human operator had not access to information that could have prevented the accident [1]. A study that investigated the lack of situation awareness of mariners revealed the importance of situation awareness for the decision making process in the maritime domain. From the 177 maritime accident reports analyzed, 71 % percent of the human errors were situation awareness related. 58.5 % of those could be classified as caused by failures in correctly perceiving information [2]. These types of failures are caused by data not being available, data not being easy to discriminate, misperceptions or failures in monitoring or observing data [2].

Electronic integrated bridge concepts are driving future navigation system planning [3]. Such systems aggregate data from various ship sensors and support the vessel navigation task with a map-centric view augmented with current and future navigation paths of the own vessel and real-time information of other vessels in the current area of the ship [3]. Monitoring such complex systems demands intermittently for the human operator's attention to observe and interpret several information sources [4].

This contribution presents a tool, the Human Efficiency Evaluator (HEE), which supports subject matter experts (SMEs), such as HMI designers and domain experts, with no background in cognitive modeling to generate and benefit from attention predictions. With the HEE predictions can be performed by a cognitive human operator simulation in a very early design phase where only HMI design images or sketches of future interfaces are available. The HEE uses the Adaptive Information Expectancy model (AIE model) [5], which is based on the SEEV model [6] and is a dynamic simulation model of attention distribution.

The following section discusses related work. Thereafter we detail the theoretical background of our approach, the process and the underlying models in Sect. 3. Section 4 describes how the process is implemented in the HEE. Section 5 illustrates a use case in the maritime domain that we used to evaluate our approach. This qualitative study with SMEs in Sect. 6 reports about the evaluation of the HEE, which was focused on analyzing the modeling differences between different potential users of the HEE: domain experts, HMI designers, cognitive modelers, and situation awareness experts. Different to what we originally expected, we found much more differences in modeling than similarities between the different SMEs. We close by discussing and summarizing the study results and elaborate a list of hypothesizes derived from observations made during the study. Finally, Sect. 8 concludes and states future work.

## 2   Related Work

The Adaptive Information Expectancy (AIE) model is a predictive simulation model of attention distribution [7, 8]. It is an integral part of the CASCaS (Cognitive Architecture for Safety Critical Task Simulation) architecture [9]. It simulates the attention distribution of a human operator based on two sets of input parameters: *Expectancy* and *Task Value*. They describe how often new information can be expected from an information source (IS) and how valuable the information is for accomplishing the tasks of the human operator. These factors are relevant for showing optimal monitoring behavior and have been shown to be the main drivers for skilled operators like pilots and drivers [10]. An expectancy coefficient $u_g$ and a value coefficient $v_g$ is assigned to each goal $g$ of a cognitive model executed in CASCaS.

A cognitive architecture like CASCaS can be understood as a generic interpreter that executes formalized procedures of a human operator in a psychological plausible way. An overview of cognitive computational models like ACT-R, MIDAS and others is provided in [11, 12]. Computational cognitive models have got the potential to automate parts of human factor analyses during system design. In order to leverage this potential the models have to be embedded in a design tool which can be readily applied by design experts.

Monitoring involves detecting and reacting to events and is composed of a set of monitoring goals. To execute such a goal the human operator looks to the IS that can signal the event. Upon event detection the operator utilizes the perceived information to react to this event. If no event is detected, the operator's attention shifts to another monitoring goal probabilistically based on the expectancy and value coefficients. The probability of switching to goal $g$ among a set $G$ of monitoring goals is defined as (cf. [7]):

$$P(g) = \frac{u_g}{\sum_{g_i \in G} u_{g_i}} \cdot \frac{v_g}{\sum_{g_i \in G} v_{g_i}}$$

Several tools already support cognitive model creation. CogTool [13] supports the generation of ACT-R [14] models implementing deterministic sequences of actions. These models are based on GOMS and KLM and therefore CogTool targets on evaluating Windows-, Icons, Menus, and Pointer (WIMP) user interfaces but also considers speech-commands and basic gestures. For monitoring simulations the HEE generates a probabilistic sequence of actions. Based on CASCaS and the AIE model prediction of average values (percentage dwell times, gaze frequencies) and prediction of distributions (reaction times, duration of diversion) are possible.

MIDAS is a system developed by NASA [15], which uses cognitive models to analyze tasks and interfaces in the aerospace domain. It simulates visual attention distribution similar to CASCaS, but uses the SEEV model of Wickens et al. [6] instead of the AIE model. Both models are strongly related, but differ in some aspects [7].

## 3 Approach

Cognitive models require input from an expert to predict the attention. In our case these inputs are the identification and location of ISs on a graphical display. Because we use the AIE model (see Sect. 2) for prediction of attention distribution, for each Information Source (IS) an expectancy coefficient and a value coefficient need to be defined by an expert. Figure 1 illustrates this. We explain the theory of how to derive the expectancy and value coefficients from the experts' inputs and formalize it for both in the two upcoming subsections. Based on these information and the identification of one IS that most probably make the expert aware of a specific unexpected event (Subsect. 3.4) the cognitive operator model (Subsect. 3.5) and the HMI model are generated. After the theoretical foundation, Sect. 4 explains how forms and visualizations support the

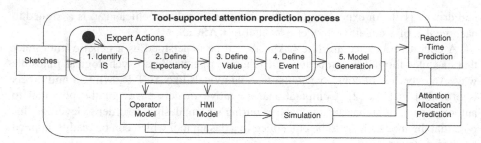

**Fig. 1.** Main activities of the process to generate the models that are then feed into a simulation to predict reaction times and the attention allocation of the operator.

coefficient derivation, which is then feed into the Human Efficiency Evaluator for running the simulation and generating the predictions.

### 3.1 Identification of Information Sources

Information sources (IS) are regions of a display or on a design sketch that communicate a single piece of information to the operator. The process requires that an expert collects all information that can be extracted from a graphical display. Each information is marked as an IS by specifying as exactly as possible its graphical position, its size and by unambiguously naming the IS so that it can be referred to by its name.

### 3.2 Definition of Expectancy Coefficients

Earlier AIE model applications extracted the expectancy coefficients during the simulation of the cognitive model in interaction with realistic environment simulations [5, 8]. Since this approach is focused on evaluating design sketches, we derive them manually using the lowest ordinal heuristic for this purpose as proposed by Wickens et al. [16]. For this heuristic the expert needs to order all IS based on the amount of new information expected. The rank of an IS in this order determines its expectancy coefficient. The heuristic does not require a total order on the IS. It is sufficient to specify a partial order between the IS across all designs. Partial orders are typically visualized by Hasse diagrams. Following, we formally describe the notation that the expert can use to define the partial order. Let $D$ be the set of all considered designs, $S$ be the set of all defined IS, and $S_D : D \to \mathcal{P}(S)$ the function that gives for each design the IS that are defined on it. The same IS can be defined on several designs. The tuple $(s|d)$ specifies the IS $s$ defined on design $d$. By defining relations between different IS such a partial order is established. Relations are formally defined by statements, such as $(s_i|d_j) > (s_k|d_l)$. Which states that IS $s_i$ of design $d_j$ provides relevant events with a higher frequency than IS $s_k$ of design $d_l$. Such statements can relate IS by the operators ">", "<", or "=". Further on, several statements can be condensed into a single one to specify relations time efficiently by comma separating IS and designs and also by using quantors. To support an automatic transformation of the relations with quantors into a partial order (visualized as a Hasse diagram) we specified them formally.

**Comma Separated IS.** Several comma-separated IS and/or designs can be listed on the left hand side and/or right hand side of the relation. Such statements create a set of relationships by using the Cartesian product of the entries on the left hand side and on the right hand side of the statement, e.g.:

$$(s_1, s_2|d) > (s_3, s_4|d) \equiv \{(s_i|d) > (s_k|d)| \, s_i \in \{s_1, s_2\}, s_k \in \{s_3, s_4\}\}$$
$$\equiv \{(s_1|d) > (s_3|d), (s_1|d) > (s_4|d), (s_2|d) > (s_3|d), (s_2|d) > (s_4|d)\}$$

**Quantors.** An Asterix is used as quantor to describe that a relation holds for all IS of a specific design $(*|d)$ or for a specific IS in all designs $(s|*)$. The exact semantic depends on whether a quantor is used on both sides of the relation. Quantor on both sides means Cartesian product of all IS respectively designs. The following specifies that $s_1$ provides information more frequently than $s_2$ regardless of a specific design.

$$(s_1|*) > (s_2|*) \equiv \{(s_1|d_i) > (s_2|d_k)| \, d_i, d_k \in D\}$$

If only one side contains a quantor, it stands for all information sources or designs, except the ones listed on the respective other side. The following specifies that IS $s_1$ on design $d$ provides information more frequently than all other IS on that design.

$$(s_1|d) > (*|d) \equiv \{(s_1|d) > (s|d)| s \in S_D(d) \backslash s_1\}$$

A variable following a quantor can be used to bind two quantors on both sides to the same variable. It prevents that the full Cartesian product is created. The following specifies that for each design $s_1$ provides information more frequently than $s_2$, but this relation cannot be drawn across different designs.

$$(s_1| * Y) > (s_2| * Y) \equiv \{(s_1|d) > (s_2|d)|d \in D\}$$

The expectancy coefficient for $(s|d)$ is determined by the order of $(s|d)$ within the partial order. In the Hasse diagram of the relation this is the greatest length of a path from any minimal element to $(s|d)$ plus 1. More formally: Let $\leq$ be the transitive reduction of the defined partial order and $\Delta_\leq$ be the distance between two elements:

$$\text{expectancy}(s, d) = \max_{d_k \in D, s_i \in S_D(d_k)} (\Delta_\leq((s_i|d_k), (s|d))) + 1$$

## 3.3    Definition of Value Coefficients

Monitoring is typically performed to collect information relevant for tasks a human operator has to perform. The value of an IS depends on the values of the tasks for which it provides information. To obtain the value coefficients for the IS, in a first step the importance of all human operator tasks is rated by the lowest ordinal algorithms as shown above for the expectancy coefficient. Second, the user fills out a relevance matrix $R$ specifying the relevancy $R$ for each IS and each task (cf. [6]). $R(s,t) = 0$ states, that IS $s$ is not relevant for task $t$, $R(s,t) = 0.5$ defines that $s$ supports $t$, but is not mandatory for t, and $R(s,t) = 1$ means, that $s$ is mandatory for $t$. The value of an IS $s$ is determined by (cf. [6]):

$$value(s) = \sum_{t \in T} R(s,t) \cdot value(t)$$

### 3.4  Event Definition

Monitoring is performed in order to maintain suitable situation awareness and to detect events in a timely manner and to react to events if necessary. The reaction time depends on the amount of attention directed to the IS that displays the event. When simulating the allocation of attention, the reaction time to events can also be predicted. An event $e = (s,t)$ is defined by the user by specifying the time $t$ of occurrence and the IS $s$, that most likely will make the operator aware of the occurrence of this specific event. This might vary between designs. Therefor the IS has to be specified for each design.

### 3.5  Generation of Monitoring Operator Model

The operator model specifying the monitoring is automatically created based on the IS markups and the expectancy and the value coefficients. For the overall monitoring, a

```
rule(goal=g_m) {                                                          R1
  ⇒
  Goal(name=monitor_s_1, value=value(s_1), expectancy=expectancy(s_1, d))
  Goal(name=monitor_s_2, value=value(s_2), expectancy= expectancy(s_2, d))
  ...
}
```

```
rule(goal=monitor_s_i) {          R2
  Condition(s_i.event == 'Event')
  ⇒
  <reaction>
}
```

```
rule(goal=monitor_s_i) {          R3
  Condition(s_i.event != 'Event')
  ⇒
  --
}
```

```
rule(goal=monitor_s_i) {          R4
  Condition(s_i.event unknown)
  ⇒
  LookAt(s_i)
}
```

**Fig. 2.** Generic structure of rules for simulation of the operator's monitoring behavior in CASCaS-like pseudo code.

top level goal $g_t$ is created, which has only one associated procedural rule. This rule activates a set of sub-goals – one for monitoring each IS. This structure is reflected by rule R1 in Fig. 2. The sub-goals are annotated with the expectancy and value coefficients as defined above.

Rule R2 is executed, if an event is shown by IS $s_i$. If no event is shown, R3 is executed. However, as the operator usually does not know the current state of information on $s_i$ the conditions of R2 and R3 cannot be evaluated, because this information is unknown. This state triggers rule R4, which commands the perception and motor component of the cognitive architecture to move the gaze to $s_i$. After the information about the event is perceived, the model either triggers R2, in case there is an event, or triggers R3, if there is none.

The resulting model, will constantly switch between the monitoring sub-goals to move visual attention between the IS based on the probability calculated with the expectancy and value coefficients.

## 4 Tool-Supported Attention Prediction with the HEE

The Human Efficiency Evaluator (HEE) is based on CogTool because of two reasons. First, we share the idea of supporting an evaluation of interfaces based by annotating design sketches at a very early stage. Second, the results are also predictions based on a simulation.

But there are several fundamental differences between both. CogTool focuses on performance prediction of WIMP (Windows, Icons, Menus, Pointer) interfaces. Therefore, the annotation of design sketches is based on a fixed palette of the most common WIMP widgets like buttons, menu bars, and radio buttons. The annotation process to construct a user interface model is therefore straight-forward by identifying and marking widgets exactly as they are depicted in the design sketch. However, nautical maps have no fixed widgets (even though there are standards, e.g. color) and new design proposals often intentionally break with some of already existing concepts. As we show later, the

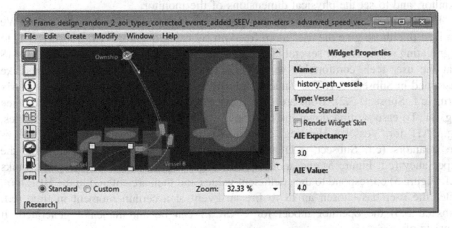

**Fig. 3.** Design Modeling Perspective of the HEE tool.

| Expectancy Relation | | | | C | D | E | F | G |
|---|---|---|---|---|---|---|---|---|
| Information source configuration 1 | | Relation | Information source configuration 2 | IS1 | Design1 | Relation | IS2 | Design2 |
| Information source: *ES &H* | < | Information source: *AH, BH, CH* | | ESH | * | < | AH, BH, CH | * |
| Design: ✳ | | Design: ✳ | | Kol | G, TCPA | > | * | G, TCPA |
| Information source: *KoL* | > | Information source: ✳ | | LF1, U | *X | < | * | *X |
| Design: *G, TCPA* | | Design: *G, TCPA* | | ESP | * | > | ESH | * |

**Fig. 4.** Transcription of the Expectancy relation to an Excel sheet.

identification and markup of IS substantially depends on the background and experience of the tool user and also often on interpretations. With CogTool one annotates what is depicted, with HEE one also marks what one knows. Different to CogTool, that inherently ends up with similar HMI models fed into the simulation, map-centric monitoring HMI models for the same design can substantially differ between users and therefore the resulting predictions as well.

Therefore, we re-implemented the entire backend of CogTool to use our cognitive architecture CASCaS (Cognitive Architecture for Safety Critical Task Simulation) [9, 17, 18] and integrated support for generating operator models. These models support the Adaptive Information Expectancy (AIE) model [5] to predict the distribution of attention and the average reaction time to a certain event. Further on, we exchanged the hard-coded widgets palette of CogTool to annotate the designs with a model-based backend that enables us to define new annotation options (like for the IS in this case) without recompiling the tool.

The HEE currently supports users with the IS identification, automates the operator model generation and the generation of visualizations of the predicted attention distribution and the computed average reaction times (cf. Figure 1).

Figure 3 shows the HMI design modeling perspective of the HEE. The left vertical bar contains a palette of widgets that can be used to annotate a design. For attention allocation prediction, one widget ("i") is used to mark relevant sources of information for each design. The main area of Fig. 3 displays an already annotated design where several IS have been already marked by the user. Further widgets are used from the palette to identify the operator's initial line of sight, the operator's distance to the monitor, and to set the physical dimensions of the monitor.

For specifying the expectancy and value coefficients we use paper forms. We realized that those give the user more freedom by using quantors (c.f. Subsect. 3.1) to aggregating relations over several IS and designs or by introducing abbreviations for IS that the user feels comfortable with. The expectancy is specified by relations like described in Subsect. 3.1. The value is defined by filling in a printed relevance matrix form (c.f. Subsect. 3.2). Both are then transcribed to an interactive excel sheet (see Fig. 4). To ease writing down the relations, we used abbreviations for the IS names, e.g., 'AH' for 'Vessel A Heading'. The sheet is then processed by a script that solves the quantors (c.f. Subsect. 3.1) and generates two Hasse diagrams: one for the expectancy (c.f. Figure 5) and another one for the value coefficient. The graph ranks (c.f. Figure 5) correspond to the coefficient values and then are entered in the HEE tool. After the user has chosen an IS to fire an event at a certain moment in time (c.f. Subsect. 3.3) the operator model for CASCaS can be automatically generated. It consists of:

- An HMI model defining the physical dimensions and spatial locations of the simulated operator and all IS (which we call topology in CASCaS). The HMI model is automatically created based on the rectangular definitions of information sources. The 2-dimensional coordinates are projected onto a 3-dimensonial plane, which is placed at a specific distance in front of the head of the simulated operator.
- An operator model composed of the operator's monitoring goals as a procedural knowledge specified as rules (c.f. Subsect. 3.4).

Both models are fed into CASCaS and executed as a Monte-Carlo simulation. Based on the desired visualization the HEE processes the simulation results and generates a heat map for each design (see Fig. 7). It is also possible to feed the data into interactive excel sheets that currently can generate a diagram with the average attention allocation per IS in percent as a pie chart and display the reaction time to an event while monitoring the interface as a histogram (see Fig. 8).

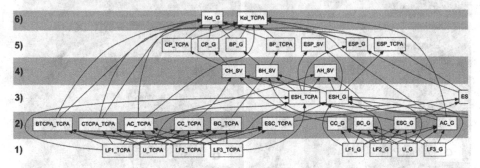

**Fig. 5.** Section of a Hasse diagram depicting the partial ordered graph with ranks on the left side. Node labels contain the abbreviation of an IS and a design name, separated by underscore.

## 5  Use Case

Electronic Chart Display and Information Systems depicting nautical maps enriched by navigation-relevant information are one of the main sources of information of shipmasters and navigation officers and need to be continuously monitored.

Within the Cooperative Shipping and Navigation on Sea project, COSINUS,[1] several new display designs have been proposed. Some of them are depicted in Fig. 6. Figure 6(a) shows a state of the art chart display and Fig. 6(b) the corresponding design sketch, that highlights speed vectors (**SV**) as the current state of the art concept to display vessel behaviors with arrows and a red line illustrating the route of the own ship. All sketches illustrate a prediction. Therefore the speed vectors point to locations of the future vessels' locations in 10 min (with the assumption that they do not change their course and speed).

---

[1] http://www.emaritime.de/projects/cosinus, last checked 04/15/15.

Figure 6(c) depicts the design **G**: the entire routes of all surroundings vessels together with the maximum tolerance for deviations (gates), which have been set beforehand.

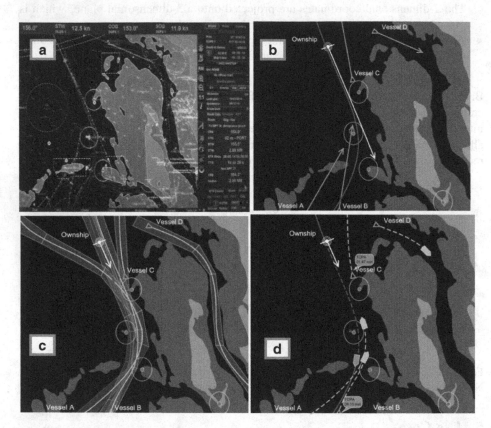

**Fig. 6.** Different variants of showing future vessel positions on a map display: (a) Current version, (b) Abstracted design of the map display: Speed Vectors, (c) Gates, (d) TCPA and position prediction (Color figure online).

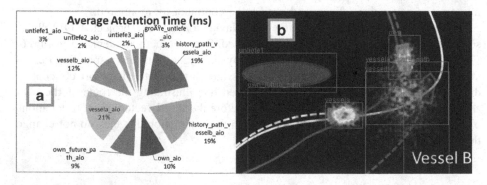

**Fig. 7.** Pie chart of the average attention allocation (a) and a heat map illustrating the monitoring behavior of the simulated operator (b).

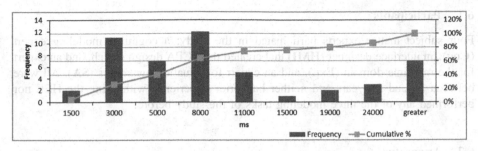

**Fig. 8.** Histogram of the average reaction time. With a probability of 80 % the average reaction time of the operator to a certain event took between 0 and 19 s.

Regions where the temporal and spatial distance to other vessels are very small are marked red. The design **TCPA** of Fig. 6(d) does not present the entire route, but only the future routes of the surrounding vessels. These routes end with displaying the vessels' orientation and position in 10 min. Furthermore the time to closest point of approach (TCPA) is annotated at the vessels position.

## 6   Evaluation

We evaluated the attention prediction process with the HEE by a qualitative study.[2] The main objective was to get first insights into how well the HEE tool can be operated by users, and how helpful the visualizations that HEE creates are for the users. However, this is the first evaluation made for HEE. It therefore has a strong explorative character. Based on its findings, we plan to perform more extensive studies afterwards. The current study had a fixed, scripted procedure and implemented a within-subject design with four subject matter experts. The procedure contained explorative questions and pre-scripted help text (elaborated during a pre-test) that were planned to be read in case a subject is not able to perform a task. We designed the study to test three main hypotheses that were supported by several sub-hypotheses:

$H_1$: "Users without specific prior knowledge are able to use the HEE and end up with results in a reasonable amount of time."
$H_2$: "The variations between the models specified by the participants are small."
$H_3$: "The result visualization of the HEE is clear."

$H_{3a}$: "A pie chart is an easy understandable visualization of the average attention allocation prediction."
$H_{3b}$: "A histogram is an easy to understand visualization of reaction time prediction."
$H_{3c}$: "Heatmaps are an easy understandable visualization of the average attention distribution prediction."

---

[2] A video documentation of the study can be found online at http://multi-access.de/512.

## 6.1 Participants

Four subject matter experts participated in the study: a cognitive modeling expert (**Cog**), an interface designer (**HMI**) that created the TCPA design sketch, and an expert for the maritime domain (**Exp**), and an expert for situation awareness (**SA**). All were between 30 and 55 years and neither had prior experience with using the HEE nor performed any of the three modeling tasks of the study before.

## 6.2 Apparatus

Participants were sat comfortably in front of a computer screen, and the experimenter sat to the side. A current state of the art map display, the three design variants (c.f. Figure 6), and three basic tasks of a ship master (avoid low water sections; avoid dangerous vessel approaches; follow your planned route) were presented as slides to the subjects. The explanation was read from a manuscript.

## 6.3 Software

The HEE was opened with a project were the three designs variants have been al-ready added. The subjects received an explanation of the modeling functions: marking an IS, resizing, moving, deleting, and naming it.

## 6.4 Procedure

The experiment was composed of the four expert activities of the overall prediction process (c.f. Figure 1): (1) IS annotation with the HEE, (2) specifying the expected information update frequency, (3) task ranking by impact and defining the relevancy of each IS for each task and design variant, (4) identifying the IS of a predefined event. Further on, (5) the three resulting visualizations were analyzed. None of the participants was informed about what kind of results the HEE produces.

Between the first four activities that took each participant between 120-180 min in total and the fifth activity that took around 30–60 min there was a break. The break was required by the experimenters to calculate and prepare the visualizations.

## 6.5 Results

Based on the video recordings and notes taken during the study we evaluated the data with respect to each sub-hypothesis.

**H$_1$**: *"Users without specific prior knowledge are able to use the HEE and end up with results in a reasonable amount of time."*

Table 1 shows the overall duration of the entire study for each participant and the total time for performing the three modeling steps. None of the subjects had used the

**Table 1.** Amount of time required to explain and to perform each modelling task in minutes.

| Subject | IS Identification | | Expectancy | | Relevance | | Entire Modelling Time | Entire study |
|---------|---|---|---|---|---|---|---|---|
| Cog | 3 | 23 | 6 | 16 | 1 | 3 | 42 | 94 |
| SA | 6 | 70 | 3 | 55 | 1 | 7 | 132 | 112 |
| HMI | 5 | 52 | 2 | 53 | 1 | 7 | 112 | 105 |
| Exp | 6 | 90 | 3 | 54 | 1 | 16 | 160 | 231 |

tool before. Thus, for each step we gave a scripted introduction and allowed questions before each modeling activity started. The instruction time is listed in the first column of each modeling step. The mean of the modeling time is 2:02 h. The Cog felt most familiar with all modeling steps and intuitively decided to mark the fewest IS (18) of all participants which reduced the work in the proceeding steps substantially. The SA had the most IS marked (47). We all asked the participants to comment on each IS identified, which Exp did in detail. It explains the relative high amount of time for the IS identification step (90 min) of Exp.

$H_2$: *"The variations between the models specified by the participants are small."*

As a first step we compared the IS defined by participants. All participants together defined 130 IS over all designs. During phase 1 participants explained which information they marked with an IS. We created a list of all this information and checked for each participant if it was marked. An excerpt of this list is shown in Table 2. The list contains 68 information elements. Sometimes the classification is not clear, because one participant marked an IS containing several information elements, while another participant marked one IS for each of these information elements. Therefore we distinguished between marking identical information, marking similar information and not marking the information.

**Table 2.** Comparison of IS between participants (excerpt).

| Information | Cog | | SA | | HMI | | Exp | |
|-------------|-----------|---------|-----------|---------|-----------|---------|-----------|---------|
| | Identical | Similar | Identical | Similar | Identical | Similar | Identical | Similar |
| Position beacon center-south | LF1 | | L1 | | LF3 | | L4 | |
| Position beacon south-east | | | L4 | | | | L3 | |
| Ownship Position | ESP | | E | | POwn | | E | |
| Vessel A Position | | | | | | RPLAB | A | |
| Vessel B Position | BP | | V3 | | | RPLAB | B | |

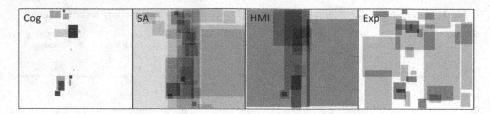

**Fig. 9.** IS marked by the subjects for design G. Darkness of the regions corresponds to the calculated expectancy coefficients.

Only four information elements are marked identical by all participants: 3 out of 4 beacons, the position of ownship and an area with higher danger of collision around the strait in design TCPA. Furthermore 8 information elements are marked by all participants, but not in the same way. These are headings and routes of vessels A, B and C and positions of vessels B and C. In contrast, 26 IS are only marked by one of the participants. Thus the IS models show a high variance.

There are not only differences in the number and kind of information that is marked. Even if the same information is marked by two participants, the marked regions of their IS can be very different. Figure 9 shows for all four subjects the marked IS on design G. It is easy to visually identify differences between the four models. For example it can be seen, that the expert user marked only few small regions in the center of the sketch, while the HMI designer has covered the entire sketch with a focus on the center. As a measure of the similarity between rectangular IS we use the root integrated squared distance (RISD), which is sensitive to differences in size and position of two rectangles. Based on Table 2 the mean RISD between two IS from different participants marking identical information is far smaller ($\overline{M}$ = 66.8 mm), than for two IS marking similar information ($\overline{M}$ = 208.2 mm). For every information in Table 2 that was marked at least by two participants, we calculated the mean RISD between the IS. Not surprisingly it turned out, that the 10 most similarly marked information elements (mean RISD $\leq$ 28.7 mm) are displayed as small icons with clear boundaries: vessel positions, beacon positions, TCPA speech bubbles and labels. However, the 11th-most similar information is an area with high danger of collision in design TCPA. This is surprising, because there is no clear symbol or display on the screen that gives a boundary for this area. All participants marked it solely based on interpretation and aggregation of several other information elements, like predicted vessel positions, routes and strait. It is also one of the very few information elements, which was marked by all four participants. It seems that the TCPA design easily supports the recognition of critical regions, without directly highlighting them.

As a conclusion, we did not find support for the hypothesis, because the number of defined IS greatly varies and also the kind of marked information elements. Furthermore, even the same information was marked differently. However, this difference varies strongly between the information elements.

**H₃:** *"The result visualization of the HEE is clear."*

**H₃ₐ:** *"A pie chart is an easy understandable visualization of the average attention allocation prediction."*

Confronted with the average attention allocation prediction, visualized as a pie chart (Fig. 7a) and without knowing which pie chart reflects which design, all subjects raised the question of how an optimal attention distribution can be identified. Three subjects assumed that most attention should be focused on a few IS only, only HMI argued for a "balanced distribution". Cog assumes "reduced scanning effort" for few big chunks although mentioned that huge chunks might identify IS which require high effort to derive specific information. SA stated that huge chunks combined with only a low amount of IS identify less complex information spaces, but in this case it remains questionable if a small information space still offers all information to perform a task. Different to the others, only Exp analyzed the specific IS that received most attention. Exp considered the own vessel direction and speed as most important IS and preferred to have the attention focused on them. Based on observing the four subject matter experts (SMEs) the pure pie chart did not support H₃ₐ. The biggest problem was the lack of measure to judge about the goodness of overall attention allocation.

**H₃ᵦ:** *"A histogram is a simple to understand visualization of a reaction time prediction."*

Although each participant was given an example on how the cumulative distribution function is read (e.g. "In 80 % of the simulated cases the reaction time was below 10 s"), they focused on the frequency distribution shown as bar diagram, whereas Cog required additional support while initially focusing on the cumulative frequency distribution (line chart). Based on the four subjects we could not found support for H₃ᵦ.

**H₃c:** *"Heatmaps are an easy understandable visualization of the average attention distribution prediction."*

All participants stated that the heat map-based visualization of the attention distribution matches their expectancies. Only for design G HMI missed a hot spot for the crossing gates, Cog missed attention for one vessel and SA could not explain strong focus on the own ship in one design. While looking at the heat map all participants found arguments for their preferred design. The decision for one design based on the heat map visualization was difficult for three participants. SA decided based on the reduction in ergonomic effort (spots are located close to each other) and also looked for equally distributed hotspots of the most relevant IS. HMI based the decision on looking for hotspots covering the most relevant IS. Cog and Exp took their decision instantly based on the design that hot spotted the high traffic area best while Exp also considered the reliability of the IS. We could found support for H₃c since all SMEs understood the visualization, stated that it presents expected hotspots and were able to argue based on the visualization.

# 7   Discussion

In earlier studies we used the HEE to predict task performance and operator workload for HMI designs in the aeronautics domain and the Adaptive Information Expectancy (AIE) model to predict attention distribution in the automotive domain. The analysis of map-centric monitoring tasks is based on different prerequisites. The model creation figured out to be much more based on individual experiences and background unlike for other HMIs: In an automotive HMI or an airplane cockpit instruments communicate clearly defined information and each instrument has a fixed position. Monitoring a nautical map involves interpretation and the amount, size and position of ISs considered as relevant differ greatly between the roles that participate in the design process.

This has an effect on the attention predictions. The SMEs modeled their perspective and understanding of the HMI quite differently and with different inputs the attention predictions results differ as well. Interestingly, this does seem to affect the users' expectancy: None of our participants was really surprised by the results. Especially for the heat maps it could be observed that the predictions offered only few inconsistencies from what was expected and all subjects were able to analyze and argue about the designs ($H_{3c}$) based on their results. Furthermore the overlay of IS on the design sketches were used by participants during arguing to point at exactly the information they were talking about.

We summarize our observations into the following hypotheses:

**Hp:** *"Using the HEE for modeling map-based monitoring tasks makes expert knowledge explicit and can be used as a basis for argumentation of a role specific perspective."*

**Hp$_a$:** "The resulting models differ between different roles."
**Hp$_b$:** "Role-specific IS can be identified and visually communicated."
**Hp$_c$:** "The definition and naming of IS provides a common vocabulary, which supports the discussion between different perspectives."

The average reaction time visualization as a histogram figured out to be complicated to understand ($H_{3b}$). It was hard for the subjects to identify the shortest reaction time. The probability and their respective cumulation were difficult to understand for the subjects. The visualization of the attention allocation as a pie chart did not motivate the subjects to reflect the percentage share of specific IS of the overall attention allocation. Rather the subjects were unsure about a concrete measurement to argue for or against big chunks or for comparing slide sizes ($H_{3a}$).

# 8   Conclusion and Future Work

In this paper we presented a tool-supported, semi-automated process to predict human attention allocation that enables non-experts in cognitive modeling to analyze nautical chart displays. In a qualitative study experts with different backgrounds were able to understand and successfully perform the process and generate HMI-models of three different HMI design variants in a reasonable amount of time.

We initially assumed that the HEE tool helps non-human factor experts to create valid predictions of human attention distribution to map-based HMIs. In contrast this study revealed that different HEE users created very different models, resulting in different predictions. The subjects identified a total amount of 130 information sources, only 4 are equal, 8 more are similar but marked differently. 26 were only identified by one of the participants.

We also tested different types of result visualizations. The visualization of the predicted reaction time distribution by a histogram figured out to be too complicated to understand. Similar, pie-charts depicting the average attention allocation offered only little use for most of the subjects. However, heat maps of attention distributions were understood by all subjects. It turned out that information depicted in the heat maps was in the range of what was expected or learnt by the participants during modeling. We further observed that HEE users easily articulate their respective expert knowledge while referencing their marked IS on the heat map.

It is technically easy to identify differences between models created by different users. We assume that showing these differences with a suitable visualization can help to exchange knowledge between experts with different background and also differences in their mental models can be revealed. Furthermore the explicit definition of IS could help experts of different areas to communicate with a shared vocabulary. These assumptions will be investigated in future studies.

**Acknowledgments.** The HEE is developed in the EU ARTEMIS JU project HoliDes (http://www.holides.eu/) SP-8, GA No.: 332933. Any contents herein reflect only the authors' views. The ARTEMIS JU is not liable for any use that may be made of the information contained herein.

# References

1. International Maritime Organization. Annex 24 – MCA guidance notes for voyage planning. Technical report, IMO RESOLUTION A.893(21) (1999). https://mcanet.mcga.gov.uk/public/c4/solas/solas_v/Annexes/Annex24.htm Accessed 15 April 2015
2. Grech, M.R., Horberry, T., Smith, A.: Human error in maritime operations: analyses of accident reports using the leximancer tool. In: Proceedings of the Human Factors and Ergonomics Society Annual Meeting, vol. 46, pp. 1718–1721. SAGE Publications (2002)
3. Bowditch, N.: The American Practical Navigator: An Epitome of Navigation. Paradise Cay Publications, Arcata (2002)
4. Hollnagel, E., Woods, D.D.: Joint Cognitive Systems: Foundations of Cognitive Systems Engineering. Taylor & Francis, Boca Raton (2005)
5. Wortelen, B., Baumann, M., Lüdtke, A.: Dynamic simulation and prediction of drivers' attention distribution. Transp. Res. Part F: Traffic Psychol. Behav. **21**, 278–294 (2013)
6. Wickens, C.D., Goh, J., Helleberg, J., Horrey, W.J., Talleur, D.A.: Attentional models of multitask pilot performance using advanced display technology. Hum. Factors **45**(3), 360–380 (2003)
7. Wortelen, B.: Das Adaptive-Information-Expectancy-Modell zur Aufmerksamkeitssimulation eines kognitiven Fahrermodells. Ph.D. thesis, Universität Oldenburg, Fakultät II Informatik, Wirtschafts- und Rechtswissenschaften, Department für Informatik (2014)

8. Wortelen, B., Lüdtke, A.: Adaptive simulation of monitoring behavior. In: The Sixth International Conference on Advances in Computer-Human Interaction (2013)

9. Lüdtke, A., Osterloh, J-P., Frische, F.: Multi–criteria evaluation of aircraft cockpit systems by model–based simulation of pilot performance. In: Proceedings of ERTS - Embedded Real Time Software and Systems (2012)

10. Wickens, C.D., McCarley, J.S., Alexander, A.L., Thomas, L.C., Ambinder, M., Zheng, S.: Attention-situation awareness A-SA model of pilot error. In: Foyle, D.C., Hooey, B.L. (eds.) Human Performance Modeling in Aviation, pp. 213–239. CRC Press, New York (2008)

11. Forsythe, C., Bernard, M.L., Goldsmith, T.E. (eds.): Cognitive Systems: Human Cognitive Models in Systems Design. Psychology Press, New York (2006)

12. Wickens, C., Sebok, A., Keller, J., Peters, S., Small, R., Hutchins, S., Algarín, L., Gore, B. F., Hooey, B.L., Foyle, D.C.: Modeling and evaluating pilot performance in nextgen: Review of and recommendations regarding pilot modeling efforts, architectures, and validation studies. Technical report, Human Centered Systems Lab (2013)

13. John, B.E., Prevas, K., Salvucci, D.D., Koedinger, K.: Predictive human performance modeling made easy. In: Proceedings of the SIGCHI Conference on Human Factors in Computing Systems, CHI 2004, pp. 455–462. ACM, New York (2004)

14. Anderson, J.R., Lebiere, C.J. (eds.): The Atomic Components of Thought. Lawrence Erlbaum Associates, Mahwah (1998)

15. Corker, K.M., Smith, B.R.: An architecture and model for cognitive engineering simulation analysis: Application to advanced aviation automation. In: Proceedings of AIAA Computing in Aerospace 9 Conference, San Diego, CA, 21 October 1993

16. Wickens, C.D., Helleberg, J., Goh, J., Xu, X., Horrey, W.J.: Pilot task management: testing an attentional expected value model of visual scanning. Technical report, NASA Ames Research Center Moffett Field, CA (2001)

17. Lüdtke, A., Weber, L., Osterloh, J.-P., Wortelen, B.: Modeling pilot and driver behavior for human error simulation. In: Duffy, V.G. (ed.) ICDHM 2009. LNCS, vol. 5620, pp. 403–412. Springer, Heidelberg (2009)

18. Frische, F., Osterloh, J.-P., Lüdtke, A.: Simulating visual attention allocation of pilots in an advanced cockpit environment. In: Modelling and Simulation (MODSIM) World Conference & Expo, Hampton, Virginia, USA, 13–15 October 2010

# Worth-Centered Design in Practice: Lessons from Experience and Research Agenda

Fatoumata Camara[1]([✉]) and Gaëlle Calvary[2]

[1] Univ. Grenoble Alpes, LIG, 38000 Grenoble, France
fatoumatag.camara@gmail.com
[2] CNRS, LIG, 38000 Grenoble, France
Gaelle.Calvary@imag.fr

**Abstract.** Worth-Centered Design (WCD) provides designers with six principles, five "D"s, a framework, and a set of tools, techniques, and methods for designing interactive systems that deliver worth. Despite its potential, WCD has not received much attention: the related literature is not intensive and the design methodology has not been investigated in many actual design settings. The community lacks of experience with WCD.

This paper first compiles the state-of-the-art on WCD and then relates the worth-centered design of Cocoon, a mobile and context-aware application. It presents further insights about the notion of worth and provides the community with nine lessons from experience for informing future worth-centered designs. Worth maps appear as a treasure also for worth assessment over time, giving rise to the ARROW (Appreciations, Requirements and Rationale Of Worth) framework and research perspectives.

## 1 Introduction

It has long been argued that interactive systems design must consider criteria other than objective and system-oriented ones (e.g., reliability, correctness, effectiveness, efficiency). Over the past decades, we have experienced the introduction of different methodologies seeking to provide designers with means in order to account for more human-oriented criteria, such as human values, user experience (UX) [18], and worth [5], in design projects. Friedman and colleagues have identified several values (e.g., human welfare, privacy, user autonomy, freedom from bias) that should be considered in the design of technology [12–14]. The authors propose Value-Sensitive Design (VSD), a theoretically grounded approach that accounts for human values in a principled and comprehensive manner throughout the design process [13, 14]. Numerous works have been investigating techniques, methods, and frameworks for understanding, designing, and evaluating UX. In another example, Cockton introduces worth [5] and proposes Worth-Centered Design (WCD) for designing worth [5]. The work presented in this paper is related to this last aforementioned methodology WCD.

WCD provides designers with six meta-principles, five "D"s, a framework, and a set of tools, techniques, and methods for designing interactive systems that are worth purchasing, learning, using, and being recommended. If WCD appears, from a theoretical point of view, well suited for the design of today's and tomorrow's interactive

© IFIP International Federation for Information Processing 2015
J. Abascal et al. (Eds.): INTERACT 2015, Part IV, LNCS 9299, pp. 123–139, 2015.
DOI: 10.1007/978-3-319-22723-8_10

systems, the design methodology has not received much attention. Only a few researchers, other than Cockton and colleagues, have investigated WCD in design projects. For example, Otero and José applied WCD to the development of digital artifacts for teachers of a secondary school and for children with cognitive and emotional impairments [16]. Vu utilized the WCD framework in the design of an information system, i.e., a web application dedicated to a golf union employees and golf clubs managers [19].

In our opinion, the main reason to this lack of a strong enthusiasm regarding WCD is that the related literature is not very intensive. Moreover, it is spread up over years and most papers address WCD only partially: there is a lack of a sharp compilation on the topic.

This paper presents a complete operationalization of WCD through the design of Cocoon, a context-aware and mobile application. The design project lasted over 3 years and investigated several design tools and techniques, both general and specific to WCD. The remainder is organized as follows. Next section presents a state-of-the-art on WCD. Section 3 relates the worth-centered design of Cocoon, design phase by phase. Finally, Sect. 4 proposes a discussion and directions for future research.

## 2 Worth-Centered Design in a Nutshell

This section compiles the state-of-the-art on WCD with one subsection per key point.

### 2.1 Concept of Worth

Worth is a motivator. According to Cockton, "*Designing worth means designing things that will motivate people to buy, learn, use or recommend an interactive product, and ideally, most of all these*" [5].

It is important to note that "*worth*" was initially introduced as "*value*" [3]. However, because worth, as a predicative adjective (as in the usage "because you are worth it") better conveys the intended meaning of worth in WCD and, in order to avoid confusion with Value Sensitive Design (VSD) [13, 14] for instance, "worth" has replaced "value".

It is also important to note that worth can be of many forms. According to [3], it can be political, personal, organizational, experiential, and spiritual.

### 2.2 Six Meta-principles

Cockton proposes the following meta-principles for guiding designers [9]: (1) *inclusiveness* for taking all stakeholders into account; (2) *receptiveness* for openness to all ideas; (3) *expressivity* for a good communication; (4) *Credibility* of the design to ensure achievement of worth; (5) *committedness* of the design team for ensuring achievement of worth; and (6) *improvability* for an appropriate assessment of worth and a good understanding of possible problems.

## 2.3    Five "D"s

Cockton proposes four D's for worth achievement assessment: Donation, Delivery, Degrading, and Destruction [5]. According to [5] evaluation leads to Donation when the design offers more than the intended worth. The author highlights Apple products as designs illustrating Donation [3]. Evaluation leads to Delivery, Degrading, and Destruction when the design delivers respectively as much, less, and none of the intended worth.

A fifth D exists within the WCD framework: Denial. In [5], the author points out three causes that can lead to Denial: when causal analysis denies the viability of the worth proposition, the possibility of adequate risk management via appropriate research field, and/or the possibility of any successful design fix with available technology.

## 2.4    The WCD Framework

The WCD framework [4, 5] structures the design process around four phases: (1) study of needs, wants, and unfelt needs, (2) design, (3) evaluation that may lead to (4) iteration. Figure 1 shows the WCD framework.

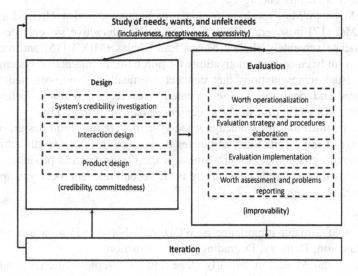

**Fig. 1.**  The WCD framework (resulting from the analysis of related works [4, 5, 9])

## Study of Needs, Wants, and Unfelt Needs

The study of needs, wants, and unfelt needs phase (we will refer to this phase as "study of needs phase" in the remainder of the paper) aims at understanding worth of the system under study. Interviews, cultural probes, competitive analysis, prototyping, envisionment, and performance are examples of techniques that are appropriate for studying worth. In the study of needs phase, involvement of users and other relevant stakeholders is highly recommended. Indeed, according to Cockton, "whenever possible, worth should be expressed using words and images of users, sponsors, and other stakeholders."

During this initial phase of WCD, relevant meta-principles include inclusiveness in order to involve any relevant stakeholder, receptiveness in order to collect all their ideas and, finally, expressivity in order to convey worth in a way that can be understood by the entire design team.

It is important to note that, in order to enhance expressivity, worth enrichment (i.e., association of direct quotes from interviews, photographs, or video material with worth elements) [6] is possible.

## Design

The design phase aims at designing and implementing the system. During this phase, applicable techniques and tools include the ones generally used in interactive systems design, such as mocking-up and prototyping, but also WCD-specific techniques. Specifically, in order to challenge credibility of the design to ensure worth achievement, Worth Delivery Scenarios (WoDS) [5, 7] authoring, worth mapping [6–8, 10, 11], or adapted impact matrices [5] construction has to be carried out.

Briefly, WoDS are stories that clearly demonstrate achievement of worth through design. Stories can be written, storyboarded, performed live, or produced as a video and must have a "happy ending".

Worth Maps (WMs), resulting from worth mapping, revisit Hierarchical Value Maps (HVMs) [17] in several points for supporting interactive systems design [10]. HVMs associate separately elicited Means-End-Chains (MEC) [15] and are used in Marketing to study customers' motivations for purchase. In interactive systems design, WMs are visual representations that connect (vertically) system-oriented attributes (e.g., features and qualities) to user-oriented ones (e.g., emotions, feelings), thus shifting from "*designing as crafting to designing as connecting*" [10].

Finally, the third tool for challenging the system's credibility in design phase, the WCD version of impact matrices, associates design features with worth achievement.

In addition to credibility, committedness of the design team to produce a concrete product that guarantees worth achievement is the second relevant meta-principle for the design phase.

## Evaluation

Evaluation is of a major importance in WCD and should lead to worth assessed in terms of Donation, Delivery, Degrading, and Destruction.

Evaluation should start at an early stage and can employ different methods and techniques. Worth operationalization, i.e., translation of statements about worth into (measurable) criteria, should be part of the evaluation phase activities in WCD. According to [5], the relative role of usability-related attributes has limited relevance when real-world outcomes are achieved. Therefore, field evaluation should be part of the worth evaluation strategy. However, it is worth noting that poor usability may have a negative impact on worth [3]. Therefore, usability testing should also be part of the worth evaluation strategy.

In the evaluation phase, improvability is the key meta-principle for an appropriate assessment of worth and a good understandability of problems.

**Iteration**
In WCD, if required, iteration can be partial or total depending on worth achievement. Indeed, no iteration is necessary in the Donation case, when expectations are exceeded. However, in order to reach perfection, iteration can be considered in the Delivery case. In the Degrading and Destruction cases, iteration is necessary in order to overcome defects that negatively impact the system's worth.

Iteration starting point depends on identified problems. For instance, fixes in design are not enough when problems lie in misconceptions about worth and/or in case of Denial. In such cases, iteration from the initial phase, the study of needs phase, is necessary for a better understanding of worth.

## 3 Worth-Centered Design in Practice

This section reports the operationalization of WCD on a case study, design phase by phase.

### 3.1 Case Study

Prior to engaging to WCD operationalization, we proceeded to opportunity identification through a review of several existing interactive systems. This lead to the vision of Cocoon, a mobile application that automatically provides the user with different types of information in context. Information is of two types: personal vs. impersonal. Personal information is related to the user's contacts (e.g., location, a church where a contact's marriage was celebrated). All non-personal information is considered impersonal (e.g., related to historical buildings and bars; news, music recommendations). Cocoon also provides users with the opportunity to exchange posts, multimedia messages which delivery conditions can be specified according to date and location. Also, Cocoon allows the user to control different parameters: types of received and shared information, numbers of personal and impersonal information notifications on a daily basis, and system activation/deactivation.

It is important to note that our design project did not start with a so well-envisioned system. Rather, outcomes from the opportunity identification phase supported the creation of storyboards illustrating different features for a large design space exploration in terms of target user groups (senior, adult, and young users), platform and interaction paradigms (large display, small display, projector, tactile, speech), and environment (different mobile, sedentary, and social settings). Any criteria suitable to allow users experiencing more than good usability guided the creation of storyboards.

The final version of Cocoon (Fig. 2) was implemented as an Android widget. The Cocoon widget clearly separates personal and impersonal information by two different icons, and gives access to the other features of the system. Information presentation pages look different and offer different possibilities depending on information type (for instance, downloading an item attached to post, accessing to the website of a news provider).

**Fig. 2.** Cocoon on the HTC Desire S: on the left, the Cocoon widget on the Smartphone home screen; in the middle, a post; on the right, a page of information related to news.

## 3.2    Study of Needs, Wants, and Unfelt Needs

Study of needs is the beginning of our experience with WCD. At this stage, two major questions raised: How to start? And, more importantly, how to reach elements other than the ones related to features and User Interface (UI)? We chose to start with interviews because this technique has been proven efficient for information gathering in general but also in a worth-centered design development context [10]. However, in order to surface elements beyond traditional criteria considered in Human-Computer Interaction (HCI), we carried out a state-of-the art on the laddering technique, used for eliciting HVMs elements [17], for inspiration. Therefore, the study of needs focused not only on the "what" (features) and slightly the "how" (UI and interaction) but also on the "why" (motivations). During interviews, the researcher opportunistically came up with "why" questions on the basis of participants' statements. In addition, one closing question was asked to participants: "What is the worth of Cocoon from your point of you?"

We conducted 19 semi-structured interviews. Considering our large design space, a wide range of possible users participated to the study: people ranging from 21 to 63 years old (mean: 30), from different social classes and with different professions. Interviews lasted about one hour and were supported by storyboards illustrating the identified features. During interviews, storyboards were first presented to participants. Then, they were questioned in order to gather their comments and feedback regarding Cocoon. Interviews were recorded and transcribed.

Data analysis was carried out by two researchers (the researcher who conducted interviews and another one) and followed 3 steps: (1) extraction of statements related to both positive and negative sides of the system, (2) translation of the extracted statements into well-defined worth elements and association of relevant verbatims with them (worth enrichment), and (3) classification of worth elements into 'universes' of worth. We relied on existing value lists and outcomes from evaluation of other existing systems (worth spread opportunities inspection [7]) during worth analysis.

### Outcomes About Cocoon

- Cocoon represents a worthwhile system with regard to different aspects

Data analysis revealed that Cocoon's positive sides are related to the following four universes of worth: 'Discovery and Diversity', 'Emotions and Feelings', 'Exchange and Communication', and 'Adaptation and Presentation of information'. Indeed, during interviews, participants mentioned the system's potential to automatically provide them with diverse types of information (according to context), including information related to relatives. Thanks to this core feature, Cocoon was perceived as a system that allows gaining knowledge in different domains and causes emotions such as pleasure, amusement, surprise, etc.

Thanks to posts, Cocoon was also perceived as a system that encourages to share, and contributes to maintaining social ties as well as knowledge sharing.

Interviews also highlighted Cocoon as innovative in terms of information presentation (for instance, using a pico-projector).

- Control is a must

If information push was perceived as a worthwhile feature in Cocoon, participants repeatedly expressed their concerns about privacy with regard to personal information sharing as well as about information overload and redundancy with regard to the push mode. Interviews then highlighted the need for allowing control over different aspects in the system (types and numbers of received and shared information, contextual data information collection).

Based on the outcomes from interviews, the functional core of Cocoon was limited to features that were the most voted in by participants. Consequently, our design space was reduced to: adult and young users in terms of target users groups and small display, tactile interaction, mostly mobile settings respectively in terms of platform, interaction paradigm, and environment.

### Lessons Learned About WCD

- #1. Worth is multidimensional

Our study confirms the multidimensional property of worth. Indeed, users stated opinions in relation to different elements, both system-oriented and human-oriented. System-oriented elements included features (e.g. contextual information push) but also qualities of features (e.g., efficient in use). User-oriented elements included consequences from usage (e.g., discovery of new places and new stories) but also worthwhile outcomes (e.g., maintain of ties). In the specific case of Cocoon, interviews revealed that associations of the aforementioned elements may activate users' personal values such as family, friendship, freedom, and so on. However, we believe that user-oriented worth elements may concern different sensitivities depending on factors such as the application domain, the targeted users group, etc.

- **#2. Worth is twofold: appreciated vs. requested**

During interviews, participants mentioned both the positive and negative sides of Cocoon. By positive, we mean what would motivate them to buy, learn, use, or recommend the system, such as diversity of types of information. We call this positive side: the "*appreciated worth*". By negative we mean what would discourage them from buying, learning, using, or recommending Cocoon, such as information overload. We call elements that compensate this negative side: the "*requested worth*". In the case of Cocoon, user control was part of *requested* worth at the end of the study of needs phase.

- **#3. It is difficult to directly question about worth**

VSD heuristics for interviewing stakeholders suggest asking about values both directly and indirectly [14]. The "why" questions that opportunistically came out during interviews indirectly asked about worth. Our closing question, "what is the worth of Cocoon from your point of view?", was meant to directly ask about worth. Most participants first reacted to the question by asking "what do you mean by worth?". This reaction was not surprising considering that worth can be related to many domains in life, whether financial or not. Then, the interviewer had to reformulate the question using the definition of worth: "What would motivate you to buy, learn, use, and recommend this system". After reformulation, participants managed to start listing points that make Cocoon worthwhile from their point of view. Indeed, most of elements had been already mentioned. Thus, the question represented a good means for summarizing and, sometimes, clarifying statements about the system's worth from participants point of view.

## 3.3   Design

In WCD, the design phase aims to design and implement the interactive product. One of the main goals of the design phase consists in demonstrating the system's credibility, thus ensuring worth achievement. As mentioned in the state-of-the-art, in order to achieve this goal, Worth Delivery Scenarios (WoDS), Worth Maps (WMs), and impact matrices can be applied.

During the development of Cocoon, the first activity of the design phase consisted in challenging the credibility of the adapted version (on the basis of outcomes from interviews) of the system. At this stage, the main question to be addressed was: What tool(s) to apply? We chose to investigate WMs because they also consider connections among worthies and provide a visual representation of the system worth. This choice raised subsequent issues: How to start worth mapping? What tool(s) to use? We achieved an intensive literature review on WMs and related concepts (Hierarchical Value Maps (HVMs) and Means-Ends Chains (MECs)). Outcomes from this work revealed a lack of a method and/or framework supporting worth mapping. Indeed, papers related to worth mapping only show examples of WMs that are different in terms of hierarchy levels and classes of worth elements [6, 7, 9–11, 19]. To fulfill this need, we worked in collaboration with five experts involved in interactive system design (a project manager, a UI and interaction designer, a psychologist, a graphic designer, and a software engineer) and proposed the PEW (Perceived-Expected Worth) framework for supporting worth mapping [2]. This framework suggests that:

- WMs are formed of three main categories of elements: (1) perceived worth, i.e. appreciated worth, (2) expected worth, i.e. requested worth, and (3) Native Software and Hardware Components (NSHC) of the device(s) hosting interaction;
- WMs still follow a vertical representation and clearly separate the three main categories of elements that we propose: appreciated worth on the upper part, requested worth on the lower part, and NSHC in the middle as they may support both appreciated worth and requested worth features.

With this renaming, PEW becomes the ARROW framework (Appreciations, Requirements and Rationale Of Worth).

Outcomes from our literature review on WMs also revealed a lack of appropriate tools for WMs construction. Indeed, for instance, during our review of the WCD-related literature, we discovered LadderUX[1], an online tool supporting quantitative data analysis from laddering. However, even though it represents an interesting tool, LadderUX is not well-suited for WMs construction since it only considers classes of elements specific to MECs (attributes, consequences, and values). Yet, a major difference between HVMs and WMs lies in the refinement and extension of considered classes of elements [10].

In the absence of an appropriate tool, we proceeded to constructing Cocoon's WMs using Microsoft PowerPoint. It is worth noting that WMs construction was also successfully achieved using Microsoft Visio [10]. Figure 3 depicts examples of excerpts of WMs constructed during the development of Cocoon at respectively design and evaluation phases and on the basis of our ARROW framework for worth mapping.

Activities carried out during the development of Cocoon in design phase also include the creation of mock-ups using the Axure software[2]. Since Axure allows mapping desired behavior to UIs, both the system's UI and associated interactions were illustrated through several mock-ups. It is important to note that the first WM of Cocoon, constructed at the end of the study of needs phase, supported the creation of mock-ups particularly regarding the UI design.

After the mock-ups creation completed, usability testing (an evaluation activity) was conducted. Eleven (11) persons, ranging from 16 to 38 years old (mean: 24), participated to usability testing sessions. Sessions lasted about one hour and, during each session, participants had to achieve three scenarios using the interactive mock-ups available via the Web browser of a laptop. During interaction, tasks completion times were measured and sequences of actions recorded.

**Outcomes About Cocoon**

Analyses of usability testing data show first that Cocoon is easy to learn. Indeed, completion times decreased for tasks which were achieved several times during the test: from 0.36 min (the first time) to 0.02 min (the last time) for consulting information and

---

[1] http://ladderux.net/joomla/index.php.

[2] http://www.axure.com/fr.

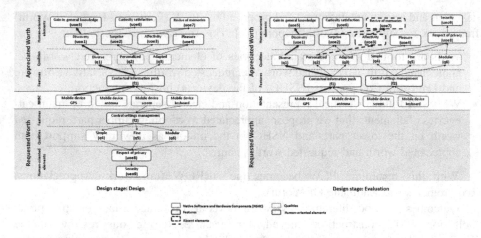

**Fig. 3.** The ARROW framework illustrated on Cocoon. The bold chains of arrows are to be read as follows: the contextual information push feature supported by the mobile device GPS presents the quality of being diverse (because serves the user with different types of information); this diversity enhances discovery of new information (e.g. related to a chateau, a museum) and results in a gain of general knowledge for the user.

from 1.31 min to 0.7 min for sending a post. Second, usability testing showed that Cocoon is globally easy to use. Indeed, in addition to low completion times we computed for repetitive tasks, analyses only revealed misunderstandings regarding particularly one interaction paradigm (sliding buttons) and application-related terms. The system's UI and some associated interactions were updated prior to implementation in order to solve problems highlighted by usability testing sessions.

### Lessons Learned About WCD

During the design phase, we carried out several activities: development of a framework for worth mapping in collaboration with experts involved in interactive systems design, construction of an initial WM for Cocoon, mocking-up, and usability testing. Lessons that we have learned are the following.

- **#4. WMs support design in different ways**

Our main expectation from WMs was to demonstrate the credibility of design. However, our collaboration with expert designers showed that WMs can also help designers as support to UI and interaction design (through (non-functional) qualities of features), support to graphic design (particularly through human-oriented elements), support to software implementation (through (functional) qualities of features). For instance, the requested quality of modularization (see Fig. 3) guided us to organize the UI dedicated to control parameters setting using blocks. According to graphic designer, he would not hesitate to use joyful colors for Cocoon as the study of worth revealed amusement as part of the user experience.

Finally, our collaboration with experts involved in interactive systems design revealed WMs as support to communication as they visually provide an overview of the system as well as information regarding different aspects.

- **#5. Users should be involved in worth mapping**

One of the strength of WMs (compared to WoDS for instance) is the highlight of connections between worth elements. Yet, during interviews conducted in the study of needs phase, we did not put much attention to these connections (our focus was mainly on reaching elements that go beyond usability). As a consequence, during worth mapping sessions, even though most worth elements were clearly expressed (thanks to worth operationalization and worth enrichment), our design team had to rely on interviews transcriptions for clarifying and better understanding links among Cocoon worth elements. We believe that involvement of users in the worth mapping process can help avoid such situations. In our opinion, this can be achieved by paying more attention to possible existing connections among worth elements during study of needs or through special worth mapping sessions with users at design phase.

- **#6. WMs construction is tedious and time consuming**

Experts who participated in the elaboration of our ARROW framework for worth mapping expressed concerns about constructing WMs from scratch without the support of a dedicated tool, manually or with inappropriate tools. Indeed, construction of the Cocoon WM using PowerPoint was tedious and time consuming, thus has proved it possible but still the lack of an appropriate tool could hinder use of WMs by designers.

## 3.4    Evaluation

In WCD, the system evaluation should start at an early stage. As related earlier, in the development of Cocoon, evaluation started at the end of the study of needs phase with worth translation (see Sect. 3.2). The evaluation process continued throughout the system development and usability testing was conducted at design phase (see Sect. 3.3). Here, we focus on the final evaluation of the system implemented on the basis of mock-ups resulting from design phase.

It is important to note that the final version of the Cocoon application was instrumented with a probe collecting actual usage data (received information, sent and received posts, access to control parameters).

Considering the requirements for evaluation in WCD, we elaborated a strategy consisting of a field study for experience with Cocoon in the real word, SUS questionnaires for a subjective assessment of the system's (real) usability, and group interviews for feedback.

We conducted a field study of three weeks with 15 participants ranging from 19 to 31 years old (mean: 25). In order to ensure social interactions, we recruited five groups of three people knowing each other. Most participants were friends. We only had one group of colleagues (working as air-traffic controllers), one group with a couple (partners living in the same house), and one group with two cousins.

About one week after the start of field trials, we sent the SUS questionnaire [1] to participants. After field trials ended, we conducted interviews with the five groups of participants. All group interviews were video-recorded.

Data collected during evaluation was analyzed using different techniques. Participants' discourses were transcribed and analyzed similarly as in the study of needs phase (see Sect. 3.2). The subjective usability score was computed from SUS questionnaires and various statistical treatments were applied to actual usage data.

Outcomes from evaluation data analysis allowed us understanding and highlighting worth of Cocoon. However, a main issue remained unresolved: How to assess worth achievement in terms of the 5Ds as suggested in the WCD literature?

Our review of the WCD literature also revealed the lack of a framework and/or method supporting assessment of worth achievement according to the 5Ds. In order to fulfill this need, we engaged in the development of a method for worth assessment. Giving their potential, we investigated WMs for this purpose. Indeed, WMs based on the ARROW framework are well suited for supporting worth evaluation because the framework proposes that WMs capture the system's global state by considering both perceived positive and missing elements, but clearly separated, and associations between them.

Our approach suggests comparing different WMs, constructed at different stages, in order to trace the evolution of the system. Then, the goal of the design is to transform requested worth to appreciated worth. Taking our framework for worth mapping as the basis for reasoning:

- Worth is donated (the system delivers more than the worth that was intended) when additional appreciated worth elements appear, from a preceding design stage to a current design stage, and when there is no requested worth;
- Worth is delivered (the system delivers as much as the worth that was intended), from a preceding design stage to a current design stage, when the current WM has no requested worth;
- Worth is degraded (the system delivers less than the worth that was intended), from a preceding design stage to a current design stage, when requested worth element(s) remain in the current WM;
- Worth is destroyed from a preceding design stage to a current design stage, when appreciated worth elements in the preceding WM turn to be part of requested worth in the current WM. Note, we define Destruction as of a higher priority than Degrading (i.e., worth is considered as destroyed whenever at least one appreciated worth element turns to be part of requested worth).

Following our approach to worth assessment, we constructed a second WM and compared it to the first one constructed at the end of the study of needs phase. Findings from evaluation of our final system and lessons learned from this phase are summarized below.

**Outcomes About Cocoon**

- Cocoon represents a worthwhile system with regard to different aspects

Actual usage data revealed that participants intensively used Cocoon. Except the universe of worth "Emotions and Feelings", all the other universes of worth identified at that study of needs phase surface from analyses: "Discovery and Diversity", "Exchange and Communication", and "Adaptation and Presentation of Information". Indeed, during interviews, participants declared having learned things about their Cocoon contacts and surroundings. Participants also appreciated the automatic push, adaptation of information according to context, and posts which, according to them (and particularly the group of colleagues), incited them to communicate more.

During interviews, participants also declared that separation of the personal and impersonal information in the UI by two different icons was very helpful since it allows determining the types of received information at notification time.

- System's control is requested but not used

Even though user control appeared as a must during the study of needs, surprisingly, usage data showed that participants accessed to control parameters only a few times. Yet, during interviews, we did not receive complains regarding information overload and redundancy or intrusion in general. In our opinion, this can be explained by the fact that Cocoon relies on a sophisticated information filtering algorithm that also considers time frames between information deliveries and favors diversity of delivered information. This outcome shows that it is, indeed, necessary to provide users with control means but that the system should, by default, take over a part of control.

- Cocoon delivers worth in the real world

Figure 3 compares the WM constructed at design and evaluation phases. We can notice that the second WM has no requested worth. As a consequence, according to our approach to worth assessment, Cocoon delivered (Delivery) the intended worth in the real word. However, a closer analysis shows that this worth delivery is only partial since some appreciated worth elements of the first WM are not present in the second one. In our opinion, absence of deep social ties between participants and the relatively short evaluation period may explain this absence of some elements in the second WM.

## Lessons Learned About WCD

- #7. Not all worth element is measurable

The first evaluation task of WCD – i.e., worth operationalization – suggests translating worth elements into measurable criteria. Unsurprisingly and as our experience confirmed, not all worth element (particularly human-oriented ones) can be (objectively) measured. Our method for worth assessment allows overcoming this issue since its application does not require that worth elements are necessarily measurable.

- #8. WMs comparison favors attention to appreciated worth

Usually, focus is put on negative elements during design. Yet, changes may impact positive elements as well. Since WMs consider both the positive and the negative, changes in appreciated worth elements also attract attention.

- **#9. WMs comparison is complex**

Our approach suggests comparing WMs constructed at different design times. In the absence of an appropriate tool supporting such a task, we proceeded to a paper-based WMs comparison. However, even though WMs of Cocoon were relatively small, this task was difficult to achieve. Therefore, WMs comparison would probably be unmanageable by humans in most actual design settings.

# 4   Discussion and Research Agenda

This paper relates the worth-centered design of Cocoon, a context-aware and mobile application. Our work shows the applicability of WCD in an actual design setting and makes the following contributions:

- In addition to present a compilation of the state-of-the-art in WCD together with a complete operationalization of the WCD framework, the paper provides further insights about worth and introduces the notions of appreciated vs. requested worth.
- The paper highlights strengths and weaknesses of WCD as well as practical issues related to its operationalization through nine lessons from experience.
- The paper makes contributions with respect to the development of tools and techniques supporting worth design and evaluation. It presents the ARROW framework for worth mapping (as chains of arrows) and an approach to worth assessment.

  These contributions open discussion and perspectives.

## 4.1   Discussion

Based on our experience, we summarize WCD as a design philosophy that provides designers with six meta-principles, five "D"s, one framework, and a set of tools, techniques, and methods for designing interactive systems that deliver worth in the real world. The point is not to say whether outcomes from this study could be reached using another approach. The point is to provide further insights about the operationalization of WCD. Clearly the design of Cocoon has proven that WCD is appropriate for accounting for more human-oriented elements but also for system-oriented ones.

WCD meta-principles are well supported by WCD specific tools, techniques, and methods. Indeed, these meta-principles provide a particular mind state which eases communication within the design team, remains designers focused on the design objectives, encourages them to consider human-oriented criteria but also system-oriented criteria that could degrade or destroy worth, and assign importance to positive as well as negative aspects. Our design case witnesses to this last point. On the one hand, because we modeled the positive and the negative sides of Cocoon through WMs, we detected that some elements that had been perceived as worthwhile at the study of needs phase disappeared at the evaluation phase. On the other hand, outcomes from the system's evaluation pointed out some directions for improvement (mainly minor changes of the UI). However, since evaluation did not point out any defect and/or adverse outcome that would hinder the use of the system at its current state (perceived benefits are worth the defects), iteration would rather focus on understanding reasons for disappearance of elements that had been perceived as worthwhile at the study of needs phase.

## 4.2 Future Work

Research agenda is fourfold.

- A better understanding of relationships between WCD and other approaches

This paper presents further insights about worth and WCD. However, during the development of Cocoon questions related to relationships between WCD and other designs approaches, such as VSD, often rose: there is a need for a better understanding of similarities and differences between different methodologies as well as possible relationships between their underlying core notions. For this, in our opinion, reflections and investigations conjointly conducted by practitioners and researchers interested in the different topics would be significantly beneficial to the community.

- Diffusion of WCD

So far, WCD has not received much attention. We believe further understandings about worth and WCD compared to other existing design criteria and methodologies will probably encourage worth-centered developments. However, in our opinion diffusion of WCD also represents a key point to this progress that deserves a special attention through, for instance, a dedicated platform to WCD, workshops and special sessions in conferences on the topic.

- Improvement and development of WCD-specific tools

Many WCD-specific tools and techniques exist. During our experience, we focused on WMs. Even though our work has made contributions in regard to WMs, several challenges still need to be addressed. At the current state, the main issue is the absence of an appropriate tool supporting WMs-based development (particularly WMs construction and comparison). Further developments are also required regarding worth assessment. In the near feature, we plan to improve our approach to assessing worth achievement according to the 5 D's and propose a computerizable version that can be integrated to relevant tools.

- Dynamic WMs for making the adaptation of interactive systems driven by worth

This includes research on how to present WMs to end-users to provide them with control over the adaptation process.

**Acknowledgments.** We warmly thank Orange Labs (Lannion) for its support to this work.

# References

1. Brooke, J.: SUS-A quick and dirty usability scale. In: Jordan, P.W., Weerdmeester, B., Thomas, A., Mclelland, I.L. (eds.) Usability Evaluation in Industry, pp. 189–194. Taylor and Francis, London (1996)
2. Camara, F., Calvary, G., Demumieux, R.: The PEW framework for worth mapping. In: Kotzé, P., Marsden, G., Lindgaard, G., Wesson, J., Winckler, M. (eds.) INTERACT 2013, Part IV. LNCS, vol. 8120, pp. 667–674. Springer, Heidelberg (2013)
3. Cockton, G.: Value-centred HCI. In: Proceedings of the Third Nordic Conference on Human-Computer Interaction, NordiCHI 2004, pp. 149–160. ACM, New York (2004)
4. Cockton, G.: A development framework for value-centred design. In: CHI 2005 Extended Abstracts on Human Factors in Computing Systems, CHI EA 2005, pp. 1292–1295. ACM, New York (2005)
5. Cockton, G.: Designing worth is worth designing. In: Proceedings of the 4th Nordic Conference on Human-Computer Interaction: Changing Roles, NordiCHI 2006, pp. 165–174. ACM, New York (2006)
6. Cockton, G.: Designing worth – connecting preferred means to desired ends. Interactions 15 (4), 54–57 (2008)
7. Cockton, G.: Putting value into evaluation. In: Law, E., et al. (eds.) Maturing Usability. Human Computer Interaction Series, pp. 287–317. Springer, London (2008)
8. Cockton, G.: Sketch worth, catch dreams, be fruity. In: CHI 2008, Extended Abstracts on Human Factors in Computing Systems, CHI EA 2008, pp. 2579–2582. ACM (2008)
9. Cockton, G.: Getting there: six meta-principles and interaction design. In: Proceedings of the 27th International Conference on Human Factors in Computing Systems, CHI 2009, pp. 2223–2232. ACM, New York (2009)
10. Cockton, G., Kirk, D., Sellen, A., Banks, R.: Evolving and augmenting worth mapping for family archives. In: Proceedings of the 23rd British HCI Group Annual Conference on People and Computers: Celebrating People and Technology, BCS-HCI 2009, pp. 329–338. British Computer Society (2009)
11. Cockton, G., Kujala, S., Nurkka, P., Hölttä, T.: Supporting worth mapping with sentence completion. In: Gross, T., Gulliksen, J., Kotzé, P., Oestreicher, L., Palanque, P., Prates, R. O., Winckler, M. (eds.) INTERACT 2009, Part II. LNCS, vol. 5727, pp. 566–581. Springer, Heidelberg (2009)
12. Friedman, B.: Value-sensitive design. Interactions 3(6), 16–23 (1996)
13. Friedman, B., Kahn Jr., P.H.: Human values, ethics, and design. In: The Human-Computer Interaction Handbook, pp 1177–1201. L. Erlbaum Associates Inc., Hillsdale (2003)
14. Friedman, B., Kahn Jr., P.H., Borning, A., Huldtgren, A.: Value sensitive design and information systems. In: Doorn, N., et al. (eds.) Early Engagement and New Technologies: Opening Up the Laboratory, pp. 55–95. Springer, Netherlands (2013)
15. Gutman, J.: A means-end chain model based on consumer categorization processes. J. Mark. 46, 60–72 (1982)
16. Otero, N., José, R.: Considering worth and human values in the design of digital public displays. In: Symonds, J. (ed.) Emerging Pervasive and Ubiquitous Aspects of Information Systems: Cross-Disciplinary Advancements, pp. 248–260 (2011)
17. Reynolds, T.J., Gutman, J.: Laddering theory, method, analysis and interpretation. J. Advertising Res. 28, 11–31 (1988)

18. Roto, V.: User Experience from Product Creation Perspective. Towards a UX Manifesto Workshop (2007)
19. Vu, P.: A worth centered development approach to information management system design. Master thesis, Aalto University, p. 107 (2013)

# Actuated Shear: Enabling Haptic Feedback on Rich Touch Interfaces

Bernhard Maurer[✉], Roland Buchner, Martin Murer,
and Manfred Tscheligi

Center for Human-Computer Interaction, Christian Doppler Laboratory
"Contextual Interfaces", University of Salzburg, Salzburg, Austria
{bernhard.maurer,roland.buchner,martin.murer,
manfred.tscheligi}@sbg.ac.at

**Abstract.** We present an approach of a shear force based touch interface that provides a way of actively changing the possible shear-based input (force tangential to a screens surface) by physically locking the corresponding axis of the device. This approach of *actuated* shear aims at using shear not only as input, but to create a new form of output modality that changes the input affordance of the device itself. It enables a new channel of incorporating physical information and constraints into touch-based interaction (i.e., by changing the input affordance of the device and using shear as a feedback mechanism). With this actuated shear approach, we create a coupling between the digital context created via touch and the actual physical input affordance of the device. Based on the implementation of a prototype, we discuss the design space of actively changing the input affordance of a shear-based touch device, sketch interaction ideas as well as future application scenarios and domains.

**Keywords:** Rich touch · Shear force · Actuated displays · Haptic feedback

## 1 Introduction

Within recent years touch-based interfaces have become more and more pervasive and with the introduction of multi-touch capable touch screens a new level of interaction was possible. However, the resulting interactions were mainly based on using the X and Y coordinates of a user's touch. To further improve the interaction and to create new forms of touch interaction, much research effort has been going on to enrich touch-based interaction by using more data related with the user's touch (e.g., [5, 6]) This research stream was coined by Harrison et al. as "Rich Touch", as these touch interactions go beyond traditional ones. To further study the design space of rich touch Harrison et al. [3] introduced the concept of using shear (the force tangential to a screens surface) as a supplemental 2-dimensional input channel. Thereby, a user exerts a force on the surface of an object (e.g., touchscreen of a mobile phone) into a tangential direction, which in turn moves the object physically. Shear-based interactions on surfaces consist of two forms of force – the tangential force to move the object and friction force that is created by applying pressure on such an object. Previous concepts of incorporating shear force into touch-based interactions, however, only use

© IFIP International Federation for Information Processing 2015
J. Abascal et al. (Eds.): INTERACT 2015, Part IV, LNCS 9299, pp. 140–147, 2015.
DOI: 10.1007/978-3-319-22723-8_11

shear for input purposes. Also, the challenge of how to provide feedback for shear force interactions is still an open issue [3]. The goal of our research was to address this problem of giving feedback in shear-based touch interactions by utilizing *actuated* shear and explore the resulting design space for touch interaction.

Therefore, we built a prototype that extends a touch interface with *actuated* shear for physically limiting the shear-based input, i.e., locking the devices corresponding X and Y-axis. Actuated shear allows us to create a new way of physical output - namely changing the shear-based input affordance of the device itself to regards of the digital context created via the user's touch (i.e., area of touch changes shear input behaviour). This approach provides an opportunity to give feedback during shear force based touch interaction, and to create a coupling between the digital context created via the user's touch and the device's shear input affordance.

Our concept of actuated shear extends prior work (see [3]) as we are able to actively change the possible axis of shear-based input and use this for feedback purposes. In this paper we present our approach of actuated shear for touch-based interaction and our exploratory prototype. We describe several use cases of how the concept of actuated shear can be utilized as a supplemental feedback and output channel. We finish with a discussion on the resulting design space and point out future work in this area.

## 2   Related Work

Rich touch approaches do not only use X and Y coordinates of a user's touch: new interactions are possible by using e.g., different areas of the fingers [6] or thumb gestures [9], therefore enabling an additional layer of input. Harrison et al. [3] investigated how shear force (force applied tangential to the screens surface) could be applied as touch input on a tablet by linking common touch gestures (e.g., double tap) to this new layer of input. Shear force input was further applied to the field of smart watch interaction by creating a device which is capable of being physically tilted, panned, clicked, and twisted for interaction purposes [11]. However, rich touch interactions still lack proper feedback [3]. There is much research effort on how feedback on touch interfaces can be improved, e.g., near-surface feedback [2], or tactile feedback using air [10]. These approaches are mostly concerned to guide the user's touch input. The area of research on actuated displays shows how dynamic, on-demand control of the physical properties of interfaces can improve interaction [7]. Previous work on actuated displays was done by researching shape changing displays [4] or by creating displays that are actuated to dynamically present different physical forms as feedback to the user [1, 8].

Nevertheless, as shear-based touch interfaces still lack proper feedback, we want to address this issue by extending the concept of shear force interaction using *actuated* shear to enable dynamic changes of the physical input affordance presented of a touch device. In that sense, we use shear not only as input but for actively locking the X and Y axis as a new form of output and supplemental feedback modality. We utilize the digital context created via the user's touch to change the devices shear-based input behaviour. This creates a coupling between digital context and the device's shear behavior. With our work, we contribute to the existing research efforts towards con-textually aware rich touch interfaces.

## 3  Prototype Device

To explore the design space of using *actuated* shear, we built a prototype of a touch device that follows the concept of actively constraining the possible shear input axis (see Fig. 1). The prototype was built using a 7″ tablet and a set of Maker Beam[1] as a frame to hold the device. The frame holds buttons on each side of the tablet that are activated when shear force is applied via the user's touch. Each side of the device is actuated via Arduino[2] controlled solenoids that can actively lock the different axis of the shear input. For instance, activating the solenoids on the left and right locks the device's shear input in the corresponding axis. We used solenoids because they are capable of changing their state rapidly. This enables us to quickly adapt the possible shear input based on the users input, resulting in a more seamless interaction. The communication between the tablet and the Arduino hardware was done via Space-brew[3], which is a websocket-based prototyping framework that allowed us to quickly connect the prototypes hardware and software parts.

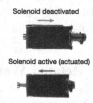

**Fig. 1.** Picture of prototype device. The device captures 2D touch location and 2D shear input. Each solenoid on the side of the tablet can be activated independently to lock a specific axis of the shear input (e.g., based on the touch input of the user).

## 4  Utilizing Actuated Shear

In the following, we describe different aspects of how our approach of actuated shear enables new interaction concepts. These concepts are the result of exploring the design space with our prototype and applying it to different contexts and domains by building a range of application prototypes. The current prototype allows us to explore the following types of interactions: actuated shear as haptic and directional feedback, embodied interaction by coupling digital context with matching actuated shear, and multimodal interaction based on constraining shear input to specific areas of the screen.

### 4.1  Actuated Shear as Haptic and Directional Feedback

Since the lack of feedback on touch screens is still an important issue, we see actuated shear as a further step to improve the feedback on such devices. When designing

---

[1] http://www.makerbeam.eu.

[2] http://www.arduino.cc.

[3] http://docs.spacebrew.cc.

shear-based touch interaction, the question of how to design for visual feedback is also still an open question [3]. We want to address this lack of feedback on shear-based devices via haptic feedback created with actuated shear as it can be used to support the visual feedback presented on screen or to set tangible "boundaries". For instance, when the maximum of a slider is reached, the corresponding shear input axis can be locked as a physical indicator. Further, our approach can be utilized to enable directional feedback. By activating a specific axis of the touch device (e.g., using solenoids as actuators) the device can be moved a short distance within the boundaries of the prototype's frame. Therefore, we can support the visual "snapping" of digital objects e.g., during a drag and drop task with the corresponding directional feedback (slightly pushing the device in the target direction) to create the perception of two items "snapping" to each other (see Fig. 2).

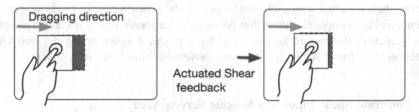

**Fig. 2.** Utilizing actuated shear as directional feedback in a drag and drop task. The user drags a digital object while actuated shear feedback is applied to create a tangible "snapping" effect.

### 4.2   Changing Shear Input Affordance

By constraining the device's shear input capabilities, we create a channel of physical output that can be used to change the device's input affordance. Hence, the digital context (e.g., location of the user's touch) and the device's "shear affordance" can be coupled. For instance, this can be used to create an affordance coupling between physical movement attributes of UI elements (e.g., a slider moving horizontally) and the device's affordance itself (i.e., shear force constrained to X axis). The touch input is used to set the digital context (e.g., the selection of a number value), whereas the shear input changes the value itself. In this example, adjusting a number value corresponds to a slider element, thus, the device locks the corresponding Y axis to make the device moveable only in the X axis. Hence, the properties of a slider, i.e., being able to move left and right, are applied to the shear input affordance of the device (see Fig. 3). In contrast to that, touching on areas related to boolean values (i.e., switching something on or off) conveys the affordance of a toggle, i.e., the ability to move up and down, by locking the corresponding shear input axis of the device.

This mapping between shear input affordance and the digital context created via touch input, can be used to support (semi) blind interaction scenarios in safety critical application domains like the car.

In-car scenarios are often based on peripheral interaction with a touch screen in the middle console, while visually focusing on the main driving task (interaction remains the secondary task). Touch screens become more and more present in nowadays cars,

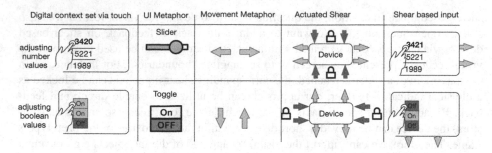

**Fig. 3.** Translation of the physical movement attributes of the UI elements into changes of the device's possible shear input. The touch input, i.e., area of screen, sets the digital context to actuate/lock the corresponding axes.

however, the interaction with such interfaces lack the haptic nature of physical interface elements making peripheral interaction potentially harder. Actuated shear can integrate haptic guidance, that would be conveyed by a physical slider or toggle, into touch interaction (e.g., touch screen incorporates movement affordance of a slider).

### 4.3    Constrain Shear Input to a Specific Screen Area

By actively locking a specific side around the device, we are able to constrain the possible shear force input to specific screen areas (see Fig. 4a and b). Locking a single side of the device, enables "rotational" shear input (i.e., device moves in rotational manner around the locked axis that defines a rotation point). One exemplary use case is to consider actuated in situ manipulation of objects, e.g., selecting an object via touch and rotating it via shear-based input (see Fig. 4a). The digital context (i.e., position of the user's touch and type of object to be manipulated) defines the shear input behaviour and which area of the screen is locked correspondingly. For instance, when the user touches the corner of a digital object (e.g., via long-press), the device locks its axis at the corresponding side by activating its solenoids. That creates a rotation point in the center of this axis enabling a rotate interaction via shear input.

There are more such object manipulation interactions possible like flipping an object horizontally/vertically or turning it for 90 degrees. Such interactions can be utilized for

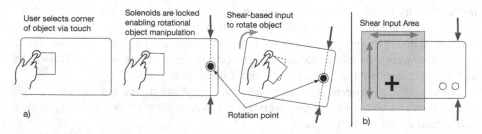

**Fig. 4.** (a) Actuated shear-based in situ manipulation of objects. (b) Game controller overlay on touch screen. Left side with shear-based "joystick" overlay; shear movement on right side is locked.

touch interactions where exact positioning and adjusting is necessary (e.g., touch-based image manipulation). Further, actuated shear could be used for game-based interactions on touch devices. For instance, Fig. 4b illustrates another concept of limiting the possible shear force to a specific screen area. By using a typical overlay of a physical game controller and limiting the shear movement to one side of the device, we create two different parallel interaction modalities on the same touch device.

## 5 Design Space

Based on the exploratory prototype and the above mentioned aspects of how to utilize actuated shear, we describe three levels of information that can be conveyed by actuated shear. We do this by applying a framing introduced by Antolini et al. [1] that also applies to actuated shear as a feedback modality.

**Information Redundancy:** Actuated shear can be used to create feedback redundant to visual on-screen information (i.e., coupling of possible shear movement and digital context). This additional channel of information can be used in (semi) blind/peripheral interaction scenarios or to provide feedback in in situ touch manipulation tasks.

**Information Transposition:** Actuated shear provides a way of giving feedback beyond what is felt via touch. The sensory substitution provided by our approach can be used to provide e.g., directional cues or physically perceivable virtual "boundaries" for touch-based games.

**Information Balance:** Actuated shear can be used to reduce the amount of visual on-screen information needed, based on providing information via this new layer of output. We address the lacking visual feedback of other shear-based approaches with haptic feedback created by actuated shear. Therefore, this haptic feedback channel can be used instead of providing visual feedback in order to save screen real estate.

## 6 Findings and Limitations

First feedback from our explorations showed that the shear "state changes" our approach provides, should be synchronous with the touch input in order to enable seamless interaction between the user's touch input and the feedback conveyed by actuated shear. Otherwise the potential lag in feedback can easily be misinterpreted by the user. Further, an open issue to consider is that by providing feedback via actuation during shear-based touch interaction, the user's touch itself is also influenced. This in turn may lead to potential unintended inputs or loosing the initial focus of touch. The presented prototype acts as a proof of concept and provided a base for our design space explorations of using actuated shear for rich touch interactions. As we focused on the aspect of actively locking specific axis of the possible shear input, the button-based detection of the actual shear force was simplified in our prototype (only stepwise, on/off). Further, the locking of the device's axis movement can thus far only be switched on or off. In future iterations of the hardware we aim at continuously varying the strength of the actuated shear feedback (i.e., pressure applied against the user's shear force vector) to enable more diverse feedback possibilities. For future iterations of the hardware we aim at making the device smaller to be truly handheld in order to explore the resulting design space of utilizing actuated shear on small touch displays (e.g., smart watches).

## 7 Conclusion

With actuated shear we presented a supplemental 2D feedback channel to change the shear-based input affordance of a touch device. By sketching a range of use cases that extend the possible interactions and feedback on a shear-based touch device, we showed how this approach can be applied to different shear-based interactions. The concept of actuation extends and complements the existing concept of using shear force for rich touch interaction. This new modality allows a coupling between the digital context, created by the user's touch and the device's movement affordance, which results in richer touch-based interactions. Existing shear-based rich touch approaches (e.g., [3, 5]) enable a wide range of new input possibilities, whereas our approach extends them by enabling new feedback and interaction mechanisms with the opportunity to lock the device's X and Y shear input axis actively and independently. Combining our approach of actuating the possible shear input with existing approaches of dynamically processing shear force (with more detail compared to our prototype) would result in a substantial extension of what is currently possible on shear-based touch interfaces. We will further conduct a series of user studies to gain insights on the feedback provided by actuated shear and how it affects the user's experience. At the moment only the digital context - created via touch input - is used to influence the shear actuation behaviour. In our future research we aim at incorporating the physical context (e.g., physical surroundings influencing shear input behaviour) to enable couplings between the physical context and potential physically related interactions (e.g., collaborating with other co-located humans). The fact that the affordance changes that actuated shear conveys are not visually perceivable, but have to be sensed via touch, bears potential for interesting touch-based interaction that use "touch" beyond what is currently the case (i.e., not only as input but as a means for sensing) as well as for embodied interaction design to further enrich touch-based input modalities.

**Acknowledgments.** The financial support by the Austrian Federal Ministry of Science, Research and Economy and the National Foundation for Research, Technology and Development is gratefully acknowledged (Christian Doppler Laboratory for Contextual Interfaces).

## References

1. Alexander, J., Lucero, A., Subramanian, S.: Tilt displays: designing display surfaces with multi-axis tilting and actuation. In: MobileHCI 2012, pp. 161–170. ACM, New York (2012)
2. Antolini, M., Bordegoni, M., Cugini, U.: A haptic direction indicator using the gyro effect. In: 2011 IEEE World Haptics Conference (2011)

3. Harrison, C., Hudson, S.: Using shear as a supplemental two-dimensional input channel for rich touchscreen interaction. In: CHI 2012, pp. 3149–3152. ACM, New York (2012)
4. Hemmert, F., Joost, G., Knörig, A., Wettach, R.: Dynamic knobs: shape change as a means of interaction on a mobile phone. In: CHI 2008 EA on Human Factors in Computing Systems, CHI, pp. 2309–2314. ACM, New York (2008)
5. Heo, S., Lee, G.: ForceDrag: using pressure as a touch input modifier. Using pressure as a touch input modifier. In: Proceedings of the 24th Australian Computer-Human Interaction Conference. ACM, New York (2012)
6. Huang, D.Y., Tsai, M.C., Tung, Y.C., Tsai, M.L., Yeh, Y.T., Chan, L., Hung, Y.P., Chen, M.Y.: Touchsense: expanding touchscreen input vocabulary using different areas of users' finger pads. In: CHI 2014, pp. 189–192. ACM, New York (2014)
7. Poupyrev, I., Nashida, T., Okabe, M.: Actuation and tangible user interfaces: the vaucanson duck, robots, and shape displays. In: TEI 2007, pp. 205–212. ACM, New York (2007)
8. Roudaut, A., Karnik, A., Löchtefeld, M., Subramanian, S.: Morphees: toward high "shape resolution" in self-actuated exible mobile devices. In: CHI 2013, pp. 593–602. ACM, New York (2013)
9. Roudaut, A., Lecolinet, E., Guiard, Y.: Microrolls: expanding touch-screen input vocabulary by distinguishing rolls vs. slides of the thumb. In: CHI 2009, pp. 927–936. ACM, New York (2009)
10. Sodhi, R., Poupyrev, I., Glisson, M., Israr, A.: Aireal: interactive tactile experiences in free air. ACM Trans. Graph. 32(4), 134:1–134:10 (2013)
11. Xiao, R., Gierad, L., Harrison, C.: Expanding the input expressivity of smartwatches with mechanical pan, twist, tilt and click. In: CHI 2014, pp. 193–196. ACM, New York (2014)

# Characterizing the Influence of Motion Parameters on Performance When Acquiring Moving Targets

Alexandre Kouyoumdjian[1(✉)], Nicolas Férey[1], Patrick Bourdot[1], and Stéphane Huot[2]

[1] Venise - LIMSI/CNRS, Orsay, France
alexandre.kouyoumdjian@limsi.fr
[2] INRIA, Lille, France

**Abstract.** Current pointing techniques provide no adequate way to select very small objects whose movements are fast and unpredictable, and theoretical tools –such as Fitts' law– do not model unpredictable motion. To inform the design of appropriate selection techniques, we studied how users performed when selecting moving objects in a 2D environment. We propose to characterize selection performance as a function of the predictability of the moving targets, based on three parameters: the speed ($S$) of the target, the frequency ($F$) at which the target changes direction, and the amplitude ($A$) of those direction changes. Our results show that for a given speed, selection is relatively easy when $A$ and $F$ are both low or high, and difficult otherwise.

**Keywords:** Pointing · Picking · Mobile targets · Selection

## 1 Introduction

Interactive systems often rely on animated content and thus require the ability to select moving targets in a rapid and reliable way. For example, scientists working on a molecular dynamics simulation would need to isolate one or several moving particles to study their properties. "Freezing" the animation is a straightforward solution to this problem, but this is not applicable when the movement itself matters (e.g. molecular simulations or games) or when interacting with live data (e.g. air-traffic control).

Several efficient and promising techniques have been proposed to ease the selection of moving targets. For instance, *Hook* [8] relies on an effective target-prediction heuristic, but is not based on any particular theoretical analysis of moving targets. *Comet* or *Target Ghost* [5] rely on assumptions based on Fitts' law [3] in order to improve the effective width of the moving target or to reduce the pointing distance. However, it is not yet clear if this predictive model is appropriate.

While the relevance of Fitts' law to pointing tasks for moving targets has been investigated by psychologists [6, 7], they mostly focused on movements along a straight path or in a regular and relatively predictable way. In interactive systems, however, selectable targets can move in a more erratic and unpredictable fashion (e.g. Brownian motion in molecular simulations, the ball in a video of a ball sport). A better

© IFIP International Federation for Information Processing 2015
J. Abascal et al. (Eds.): INTERACT 2015, Part IV, LNCS 9299, pp. 148–155, 2015.
DOI: 10.1007/978-3-319-22723-8_12

understanding of how the nature of targets' motion affects pointing performance is therefore critical to inform the design of appropriate interaction techniques and to evaluate them as well. Since Fitts' width and amplitude fall short of fully characterizing the task of mobile target acquisition, we propose in this paper to consider also their *speed* and *direction* (frequency of changes and angles) as a way to characterize a broader range of motion, from regular to erratic.

We describe these parameters in the following section, as well as an experiment we conducted in order to assess users' performance when varying these parameters.

## 2    Studying the Acquisition of Erratic Targets

### 2.1    Characterizing Erratic Motion

In order to study performance when acquiring targets with erratic movements, we need a quantifiable, controllable and replicable way to generate such motion. We propose to characterize the nature of motion with three parameters:

- **S:** the speed at which the target moves, in cm/s;
- **F:** the frequency at which the target's direction vector is rotated, in Hz;
- **A:** the maximum angle by which the direction vector of the target can be rotated: after every period $T = 1/F$, the direction vector of the target is rotated by the angle *alpha* which is pseudo-randomly sampled from $[-A; +A]$ (with A in degrees of arc).

These parameters (and their values in the following experiment) only capture a part of all possible types of motion, since simulating all of them would have been too complex and unmanageable, with too many parameters (e.g., acceleration, curvature, etc.). We rather chose a trade-off between simplicity and the potential to simulate types of motion that participants in our experiment would perceive as fundamentally different in nature. In particular, varying *F* and *A* allows the simulation of a wide range of movements, from regular to erratic.

### 2.2    Experiment

We conducted an experiment with 13 right-handed participants, aged 14 to 56. They were asked to click with a mouse on a moving target displayed on a desktop monitor.

**Apparatus.** The input device was a standard mouse without acceleration, moving a standard crosshair pointer on a *Dell UltraSharp U2412 M* 24" display. The task was performed in a square window of 1000 pixels (about 23.87 cm).

**Task and Conditions.** The task consisted in selecting one circular target among 50, with a fixed diameter of 5.4 mm. The 49 "distractors" were displayed in gray, and the target to select in red (see Fig. 3(b)). Both the target and the distractors moved according to the current condition, defined by the *S*, *F* and *A* parameters, and bounced off the edges of the window. To control the pointing amplitude, the motion of the distractors was constrained so that after selecting a target, the distance between the mouse cursor and the next target was constant (of about 7.96 cm). When the participant successfully selected the red target, it briefly turned green while the next target to select turned red at the same time.

Selection involves a trade-off between speed and accuracy [4], and users can adopt different approaches to this trade-off. In order to minimize such variation in selection strategy, participants were instructed to select the target as fast as possible but with at most 5 attempts. The number of remaining attempts for each trial was displayed in the top left corner of the window. After the last try, the word "failure" was displayed and the participant was asked to keep trying to select the target, but without trying to minimize errors. Thus, failures are not absolute, but indicate critical conditions for which selection is very difficult.

We tested all combinations of the following $(S,A,F)$ values, replicated 4 times:

- $S$: 0.73, 1.46 and 2.19 cm/s (3 values);
- $F$: 1, 2, 4, 8, 13, 20 and 30 Hz (6 values);
- $A$: 0, 30, 60, 90, 120 and 180 degrees of arc (7 values).

An additional baseline condition was added with static targets, which was replicated 20 times. When A = 0, targets move in straight lines. In summary, we tested a total of $3 \times 6 \times 7 + 1 = 127$ conditions, and 524 trials ($126 \times 4 + 1 \times 20$) per participant.

**Procedure and Data Collection.** Each session lasted approximately 40 min, including a training phase of over 50 trials, after which participants felt comfortable with the task. Short breaks were allowed after 25 %, 50 % and 75 % of the trials were completed. At the end of the session, participants were administered a short questionnaire about their perception of the different classes of motion and the strategies they had adopted.

We collected *Selection Time* from the moment the target turned red to the successful click, *Erroneous Clicks* (i.e. clicks outside of the target disk), and *Failures* (i.e. last erroneous clicks of the 5 tries).

## 3 Results and Analysis

### 3.1 Selection Performance

All the values presented here are averaged across the subjects. Performance in the easiest conditions was relatively stable across participants: our slowest participant was less than 4 times slower than the fastest one for straight motion. However, there was a considerable amount of variation for the most difficult conditions (by a factor of over 18 from the fastest to the slowest participant). We therefore normalized selection times to avoid bias from the slowest participants: for each participant, the resulting averages of normalized selection times (ANSTs) are the average of selection time per condition, normalized according to the most difficult condition for the given participant. Therefore, if a condition has an ANST of 0.75 for a given participant, it means that this participant needed 75 % as much time on average to select targets in this condition as in the condition he/she found most difficult. Because the condition that was precisely the most difficult may be slightly different for each participant, no condition has an average ANST of 1.0 across all subjects.

The number of errors ranges from 0 to 5. An error rate of 3.5 for a given condition means that on average, participants made 3.5 failed clicks for each trial in that condition. A failure rate of 50 % for a given condition means that on average, 50 % of the trials in that condition were failed, i.e. that participants made at least 5 failed clicks in 50 % of their trials. Note that because of growing concerns in various research fields over the limits of null hypothesis significance testing for reporting and interpreting experimental results [1, 2], our discussions are based on effect sizes (reported as percent differences[1]).

**Speed.** We observed that both selection time and error rate increase when speed increases, as illustrated in Fig. 1(a): average ANST at the highest speed (37 %) is higher than in the lowest one (17 %) with a percent difference of 74 %. We observe that selection time and error rates are roughly affine functions of speed. We only included the plots for $A = 90$, but the results for all other values of $A$ are very similar.

**Angle.** Parameter $A$ exhibits more complicated tendencies, with an interaction with both $S$ and $F$. At low speed, $A$ has a small effect on selection times (for $S = 0.73$ and $F = 4$, when A = 0, ANST = 14 % and when $A = 120$, ANST = 20 %; percent difference of 33 %, the highest observed at this speed) but a bigger effect at high speed (for $S = 2.19$, at the same $A$ and $F$, ANSTs are respectively 21 % and 54 %; percent difference of 90 %). A possible explanation is that at low speed, selection is almost as easy as with static targets, regardless of the nature of the motion. Figure 1(c) illustrates the effect of A at high speed. We observe that as long as frequency is low, higher values of $A$ imply higher selection times. However, as $F$ increases, the effect of $A$ on selection time is changed: after steadily increasing with $A$, selection time reaches a plateau, and then decreases. Furthermore, the value of $A$ associated with this plateau ($A_{peak}$) depends on $F$: as $F$ increases, $A_{peak}$ decreases.

We also observed that the number of errors and failure rates follow the same trends and that at medium speed, these trends are similar but less pronounced.

**Frequency.** A similar pattern can be observed for frequency: F has a smaller effect on selection time when speed is low, but a larger one at high speed. On Fig. 1(d), we observe that for lower values of A, higher frequencies are correlated with higher selection time, but for higher values of A, the trend changes. When A is high, selection time increases with F up to a certain peak ($F_{peak}$) and then decreases. Furthermore, the value of $F_{peak}$ decreases as A increases. Trends for number of errors and failure rates are consistent with those observed for selection time, and as for angle widths, trends at medium speed are similar to those at high speed, although less pronounced.

---

[1] Percent differences between 2 measures ($m_1$, $m_2$) were computed using $p = 100 \times \frac{(m_2 - m_1)}{\frac{1}{2} \times (m_1 + m_2)}$ in order to get symmetric measures of relative differences.

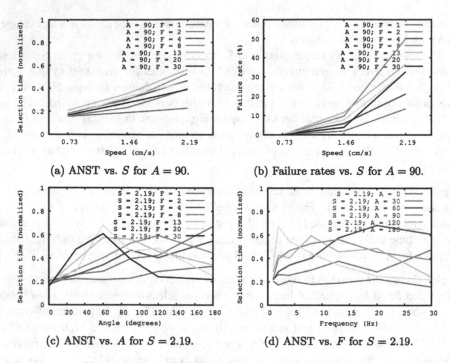

(a) ANST vs. $S$ for $A = 90$.    (b) Failure rates vs. $S$ for $A = 90$.

(c) ANST vs. $A$ for $S = 2.19$.    (d) ANST vs. $F$ for $S = 2.19$.

**Fig. 1.** Selection performance as a function of $S$, $A$ and $F$.

## 3.2  Exploratory Analysis

We also considered our parameter space as a whole in order to identify general trends. The heat maps in Figs. 2(a) and (b) represent the ANSTs for medium and high speeds. In each of those heat maps, $A$ stands on the horizontal axis, and $F$ on the vertical one. Each intersection is thus the average of ANSTs for the corresponding condition. The heat maps in Figs. 2(b), (c) and (d) present the highest speed we tested, since it resulted in the most pronounced effects of $A$ and $F$. In Fig. 2(b), we observe that a region of the heat map approximately centred on the main diagonal (from top-left to bottom-right) exhibits the highest selection times. Figure 2(c) displays the average error rates for each condition, which are correlated with selection times. Finally, failure rates are presented in Fig. 2(d).

These heat maps suggest that selection is especially difficult for combinations of wide angles with low frequencies, narrow angles with high frequencies, or medium angles with moderate frequencies.

**From Angle and Frequency to Predictability.**  The trends highlighted above suggest that the product $A \times F$ (angle width by frequency) might roughly predict selection performance for erratic targets. We plotted this product against selection time in Fig. 3 (a), and it reveals that an index of difficulty (or predictability) for irregular motion could be derived from $A \times F$. Furthermore, when $A \times F$ reaches a certain value $AF_{peak}$, which in our data is around 1,100, selection time is maximal. We suppose that $AF_{peak}$

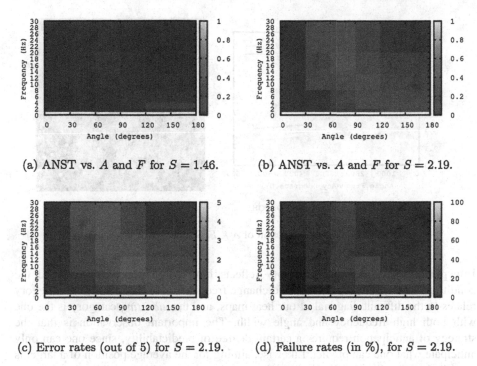

(a) ANST vs. $A$ and $F$ for $S = 1.46$.

(b) ANST vs. $A$ and $F$ for $S = 2.19$.

(c) Error rates (out of 5) for $S = 2.19$.

(d) Failure rates (in %), for $S = 2.19$.

**Fig. 2.** Selection performance as a function of $A$ and $F$, for different values of S.

would vary in different conditions, e.g. target width or pointing distance as described by Fitts' law, but it remains stable for the three different speeds we have tested, and therefore probably independent of this parameter. As mentioned before, we observed error rate to be generally strongly correlated with selection time, and so to also depend on the $A \times F$ product.

**Subjective Impressions.** The answers to our questionnaire were consistent with, and complementary to, our quantitative results. Indeed, 92 % of our participants were able to identify different categories of motion: 77 % of them identified at least three major categories, together with two or three corresponding selection strategies.

**Categories and Strategies.** Participants first described rather steady motion, in roughly straight lines, with few or small deviations. In the second case, they identified "jerky" or "erratic" motion that they characterized by frequent, significant changes in direction. In the third case, they described the motion as "Brownian", or "oscillations" or "vibrations". More interestingly, 92 % of them explained that they would try to anticipate the target's movement and to intercept it, and those who had identified a steady category specifically linked this strategy to it. However, our participants had no "clever" way of catching *jerky* targets, and would simply try to be fast enough and click a lot, thus making many errors. For the *vibrating* category, 69 % of them said they would aim for the "average" position of the target over a short period of time, and either try to intercept it or just click and hope for the best.

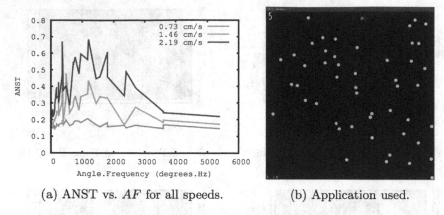

(a) ANST vs. *AF* for all speeds.          (b) Application used.

**Fig. 3.** Selection time as a function of $A \times F$. Screenshot of the application.

**Interpretation.** The *steady* category reflects how our participants perceived the conditions where both angle width and change frequency were low. The *jerky* category relates to the difficult diagonal of our heat maps, and the *vibrating* category is the one with both high frequency and angle width. The important observation is that the strategy of anticipation requires a certain degree of predictability, since one can only anticipate what one can predict. Likewise, aiming for the average position of a target is a prediction. On the other hand, the *jerky* category seems to be very difficult to predict.

We therefore conclude that the *steady* and *vibrating* categories of moving targets are relatively easy to acquire because their movements are quite predictable, whereas *jerky* targets are more difficult because less predictable. Of course, the borders between these categories are hard to determine formally and are likely to depend on the user perception of the movement.

## 4   Conclusion and Perspectives

We have proposed a way to characterize the erratic behavior of moving targets with three parameters: *speed*, *angle width* and *frequency*, and tested pointing performance when varying these parameters. We have shown that the nature of target motion affects pointing performance, which is not captured by Fitts' law's index of difficulty. The latter can only describe the best case, and does not indicate that acquiring fast, highly erratic targets can be extremely difficult.

Although the *(S,A,F)* set of parameters we have proposed models a continuum of target motion, our participants were able to distinguish at least three distinct categories that we have characterized (*steady*, *vibrating* and *jerky*). Our results suggest that for erratic targets, predictability determines pointing performance. And while the *steady* and *vibrating* categories are relatively predictable, the *jerky* one is not.

We have also observed that the $A \times F$ product might be a promising way to assess predictability, although we still need more data to deduce a predictive law for the acquisition of erratic targets. Nevertheless, this preliminary work is a first step toward a more formal study of the acquisition of erratic targets, and introduces a way to better characterize or even control their movement. Ultimately, such a model could be instrumental in the design of new selection techniques.

**Acknowledgements.** We wish to thank the participants for their time and effort.

# References

1. Dragicevic, P., Chevalier, F., Huot, S.: Running an HCI experiment in multiple parallel universes. In: CHI 2014 Extended Abstracts, pp. 607–618. ACM (2014)
2. Cumming, G.: The new statistics: why and how. Psychol. Sci. **25**(1), 7–29 (2014)
3. Fitts, P.M.: The information capacity of the human motor system in controlling the amplitude of movement. J. Exp. Psychol. **47**(6), 381 (1954)
4. Guiard, Y., Olafsdottir, H.B., Perrault, S.T.: Fitts' law as an explicit time/error trade-off. In: Proceedings of CHI 2011, pp. 1619–1628. ACM (2011)
5. Hasan, K., Grossman, T., Irani, P.: Comet and target ghost: techniques for selecting moving targets. In: Proceedings of CHI 2011, pp. 839–848. ACM (2011)
6. Hoffmann, E.R.: Capture of moving targets: a modification of Fitts law. Ergonomics **34**(2), 211–220 (1991)
7. Jagacinski, R.J., Repperger, D.W., Ward, S.L., Moran, M.S.: A test of Fitts' law with moving targets. Hum. Factors: J. Hum. Factors Ergon. Soc. **22**(2), 225–233 (1980)
8. Ortega, M.: Hook: heuristics for selecting 3d moving objects in dense target environments. In: Proceedings of 3DUI 2013, pp. 119–122. IEEE (2013)

# Comparing Fatigue When Using Large Horizontal and Vertical Multi-touch Interaction Displays

Shiroq Al-Megren[1]([⊠]), Ahmed Kharrufa[2], Jonathan Hook[3],
Amey Holden[2], Selina Sutton[2], and Patrick Olivier[2]

[1] School of Computing, University of Leeds, Leeds, UK
scsaml@leeds.ac.uk
[2] Culture Lab, Newcastle University, Newcastle upon Tyne, UK
{ahmed.kharrufa, selina.sutton,
patrick.olivier}@ncl.ac.uk, ameyholden3@gmail.com
[3] Department of Theatre, Film and Television, University of York, York, UK
jonathan.hook@york.ac.uk

**Abstract.** We report on a user study that compared muscle fatigue experienced when using a large multi-touch display in horizontal and vertical configurations over a one-hour period. Muscle fatigue is recognized as the reduction in a muscle's capacity to generate force or power output and was measured objectively and subjectively before and after a puzzle-solving task. While subjective measures showed a significant level of overall arm muscle fatigue after the task for both configurations, objective measures showed a significant level of muscle fatigue on the middle deltoids and the non-dominant extensor digitorum for the vertical configuration only. We discuss the design implications of these findings and suggest relevant future areas of investigation.

**Keywords:** Large displays · Interaction · Tabletops · Fatigue · Ergonomics

## 1 Introduction

Muscle fatigue is the transitory decrease in a muscle's capacity to contract and perform actions, which leads to the development of musculoskeletal imbalance if it persists for longer stretches of time and overruns the body's recovery system [1, 2]. Previous work has reported on subjective perceptions of fatigue [3, 4], which are deemed unreliable for assessing physical demands [5], and objective measures of muscle fatigue [6, 7] on tablet sized vertical touchscreens. Past research has also explored how display angle affects a range of different aspects of users' interaction with large interactive displays (e.g. [8, 9]). However, relatively little attention has been paid to the impact that display angle has on users' physiology over time and consequential musculoskeletal damage. The few studies that have investigated this issue have required subjects to perform a constrained task repeatedly for a relatively short time, rather than exploring the typical varied and longitudinal usage that designers envisage, such as teachers' interaction with interactive boards (e.g., [10] who looked at vertical boards only). Other studies, such as

© IFIP International Federation for Information Processing 2015
J. Abascal et al. (Eds.): INTERACT 2015, Part IV, LNCS 9299, pp. 156–164, 2015.
DOI: 10.1007/978-3-319-22723-8_13

[11, 12], have reported informal and conflicting insights for longitudinal usage of large interactive displays.

We present a study that measured muscle fatigue objectively and subjectively for both horizontal and vertical large interactive displays using an unconstrained task, which required users to perform gestures commonly used in multi-touch interaction. Our results suggest that when designing multi-touch applications that will be used for extended periods, designs that consider fatigue should, in general, favor horizontal over vertical displays, and in both cases should aim at locating interactions at closely accessible locations on the display whenever possible. Our results also suggest that designers should pay close attention to objective measures of fatigue when evaluating the appropriateness of their designs to users' physiology, rather than relying on subjective measures alone.

## 2 Study Design

We performed the study on a Microsoft PixelSense multi-touch tabletop with a 30" rear projected display (21" high, 27" deep, and 42.5" wide). The task was to complete a series of 25-piece puzzles, using the tabletop's Puzzle application, which was adapted to include scaling of pieces. Pieces could be translated, scaled and rotated, or an integrated combination of two or more of these actions, using one or more fingers, uni- or bi-manually. Initially, the pieces of each puzzle were displayed at random orientations, sizes and locations. Two pieces could only connect to form one larger piece if they were a similar size (within 20 %) and orientation (within 30°). Once completed the puzzle was replaced with another. This exercise was repeated for one-hour. The puzzles were displayed in a random order and subjects completed five puzzles on average. This task was chosen because it required participants to complete common types of interactions used when performing different tasks using large interactive displays, along with intermittent periods of no activity.

## 3 Procedure

Surface Electromyography (SEMG) was used to monitor three muscles on each arm before, during and after the task. These muscles are: middle deltoid, bicep brachii, and extensor digitorum muscles (see Fig. 1a). Lozano et al. [7] suggested these muscles are appropriate sites for measuring gestural interaction and fatigue on a multi-touch tablet when using SEMG. The deltoid placement was altered, from anterior to middle, to consider both shoulder abduction and flexion. To locate the placement of the SEMG sensor for each muscle, a specific location on the arm was palpated as the subject performed a movement activating the target muscle. The skin was then shaved, wiped with alcohol and the sensors placed parallel to their prospective muscle at 2 cm apart. We followed Criswell's guidelines [13] to ensure correct placement.

Two measures were then collected: maximal voluntary isometric contractions (MVIC) and ratings using the Borg scale [14] both before and after the task (as described below). The subjects were then asked to sit and familiarize themselves with

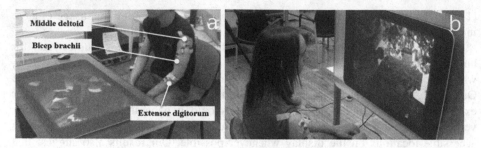

**Fig. 1.** The experimental set up for the horizontal (a) and vertical (b) configurations

the task as the possible interaction techniques were described verbally. They were then asked to wait for the start and the end of the session to be announced. During the session, ten electromyograms (EMG) were recorded for muscle activity analysis. Participants were all males to limit interferences due to anatomical differences [15].

### 3.1    Experiment 1: Horizontal Configuration

Eighteen males, who were familiar with multi-touch technology and were free of musculoskeletal disorders, took part. The mean age was 26.4 (± 4.6). Three were left-handed. The tabletop was raised to a height of 26" using wooden panels to allow comfort and participants sat on a chair 18" in height (Fig. 1a).

### 3.2    Experiment 2: Vertical Configuration

A second participant group of eighteen males took part; all were right-handed, familiar with multi-touch technology and free of musculoskeletal disorder, with an average age of 28.8 (± 4.8). The tabletop was placed on its side on top of a desk and participants were sat on a chair 18" in height (Fig. 1b).

## 4    Objective Measures

Muscle fatigue has objectively been detected non-invasively using sonomyography, near-infrared spectroscopy, mechanomyogram, and SEMG. Recent research has also proposed a novel approach, "Consumed Endurance" [16], which does not necessitate the employment of specialized equipment. A survey carried out by Al-Mulla et al. [17] found SEMG to be the most suited measurement for the detection and quantification of fatigue. Previous applications of SEMG for the assessment of fatigue include interacting with software on a traditional setup [18] and a multi-touch table [6, 7]. Accordingly, SEMG was used to detect and measure physiological changes to skeletal muscles due to contraction. Processed EMG data can provide information about localized fatigue and force.

A MVIC, where the muscle's tension changes while its length remains the same [19], is used to quantify force and localized muscle fatigue. To gain a MVIC the subject is instructed to achieve the greatest possible force of contraction, constantly, for a short period. To do this our subjects were asked to remain seated and maintain a posture for 10 s while holding a 2.5 kg weight. The postures were; (i) Middle deltoid: arm elevated at 90° in the frontal plane; (ii) Bicep brachii: arm held close to the body while elevating the forearm at 90° in the sagittal plane; (iii) Extensor digitorum: the forearm resting on a desk with the wrist resting on the edge of the table. A MVIC is a baseline and so future readings may be greater than 100 %.

**Localized Fatigue.** For fatigue indexing, we adopted the median power frequency (MPF) of the MVIC in the time domain as a reference point [20]. Essentially, a decreasing MPF signal indicates that muscle fatigue is increasing. Previous research corroborates the reliability and consistency of this method of analysis (e.g. [21]) unlike using the amplitude in the time domain, where the literature reports significant contradictions (e.g. [7, 21]).

**Force.** 'Force' quantifies a muscle's electrical activity during contraction and is described as a percentage of a MVIC. To extract force information we integrated a rectified EMG, a long-established technique due to their linear relationship [22].

The SEMG used was ZeroWire, a wireless system with six surface channels, with Biosense's bio-logic disposable press-stud electrodes (Ag-AgCI). This system operates using light autonomous signal processing and power transmission units, each weighing 10gm. Each channel provides a bandwidth of 10-1000 Hz for a signal sampled at 2000 sample/sec. The transmitters wirelessly transfer the signals captured with the electrodes to the main unit, which is directly connected to a computer running the ZeroWire software suite. This minimizes the restriction of a user's movements. Matlab and Microsoft Excel were used to process the EMGs and analyze the results.

## 4.1 Localized Fatigue Analysis

The 10-second MVIC collected before and after the task was divided into 10 segments with a 50 % overlap. This led to 3000 data points for each segment from the original 2000. The last segment was excluded from the analysis because of the overlap. Each segment was then rectified and passed through a low pass fourth-order Butterworth filter with a cut-off frequency of 500 Hz. A fast Fourier transform was then performed to calculate the power spectrum of each segment from which the MPF is obtained. Matlab was used to process the EMG using functions provided by the Signal Processing Toolbox (DSP) and the Biomechanics et al. Toolbox (BEAT) [23].

For normalization (to eliminate variations between the subjects such as age and muscle mass) the data recorded before the task was averaged and used as a reference value for the data collected after the task. These values were averaged to produce singular values representing the MPF of each muscle. A paired t-test was then carried out between the two data sets.

## 4.2   Localized Fatigue Results

**Horizontal.**   While some muscles did show a decrease of MPF indicating some level of fatigue, none of them showed a significant evidence for increased fatigue. The dominant and non-dominant extensor digitorum showed a decrease to 80 % and 63 % respectively, while the dominant and non-dominant bicep brachii showed a decrease to 88 % and 95 % respectively. Moreover, while the dominant middle deltoid also showed evidence of significant increase of MPF indicating decreased fatigue (119 % and $t(17) = 1.74$, $p = 0.01$), no change was noted for the non-dominant middle deltoid.

**Vertical.**   The middle deltoid showed a significant decrease of MPF indicating increased fatigue (63 % and $t(17) = 1.74$, $p = 0.003$ for the dominant, and 71 %, $t(17) = 1.74$, $p = 0.02$ for the non-dominant side). As for the extensor digitorum only the non-dominant side showed a significant decrease of MPF indicating increased fatigue (75 % and $t(17) = 1.74$, $p = 0.01$) with no noted decrease for the dominant hand. The biceps brachii showed non-significant decrease of MPF for the non-dominant hand to 79 % and no-decrease for the dominant hand.

## 4.3   Force Analysis

Ten 1-minute EMGs were collected during the experimental task at 5-minute intervals. Each EMG was passed through a low-pass fourth-order Butterworth filter with a cut-off frequency of 500 Hz. The averaged root mean square was then calculated using BEAT, which was then averaged. Normalization was carried out using the averaged MVICs collected before the start of the task. The normalized values were then averaged to represent the muscle activity as a percentage of the MVIC (see Fig. 2). A one-way repeated measure analysis of variance (ANOVA) was then carried out.

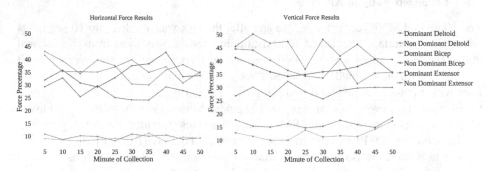

**Fig. 2.**   Force results for 1-minute readings collected every 5 min for both configurations

## 4.4 Force Results

**Horizontal.** A one-way repeated ANOVA for the 10 measures showed that only the dominant extensor digitorum showed significant inconsistency of muscle activity throughout the task (a change of 13 % and $F(17, 9) = 3.09$, $p = 0.002$). No significant evidence was found against the other muscles proving their activity to be consistent. Nevertheless, the non-dominant extensor digitorum showed an increase and decrease of up to 8 % and the bicep brachii showed a change of up to 10 % and 14 % for the dominant and non-dominant sides respectively. The middle deltoids' activity proved relatively stable with activations ranging from 8-11 % for both sides.

**Vertical.** A one-way repeated ANOVA for the 10 measures showed significant inconsistency of muscle activity throughout the task for the dominant extensor digi-torum (a change of 13 % and $F(17, 9) = 2.85$, $p = 0.004$). No significant evidence was found against the other muscles proving their activity to be consistent. Nevertheless, both biceps brachii showed an increase and decrease in activation of up to 13 %, while both middle deltoid muscles showed relatively consistent activation of up to 18 %.

Table 1 marks the muscles that showed significant evidence of increase in level of fatigue after the trial session for both configurations. It also marks significant incon-sistencies in activation of force during task interactions.

**Table 1.** Objective measures summary of significant increase in fatigue and force inconsistency

|  |  | Significant Evidence | | | |
|  |  | Horizontal | | Vertical | |
|  |  | Dom. | Non-Dom. | Dom. | Non-Dom. |
|---|---|---|---|---|---|
| Middle Deltoid | Fatigue | × | × | ✓ | ✓ |
|  | Force | × | × | × | × |
| Bicep Brachii | Fatigue | × | × | × | × |
|  | Force | × | × | × | × |
| Extensor digitorum | Fatigue | × | × | × | ✓ |
|  | Force | ✓ | × | ✓ | × |

# 5 Subjective Measures

When examining fatigue, subjective ratings are commonly used to assess perceived physical exertion and supplement objective measures. We used the Borg CR100 scale [14], which is a fine graded ratio scaling method that estimates the level of exertion and determines the ratio relationship between perceptual responses. The scale contains subjective dynamic ranges with values ranging from 0 to 120 annotated with verbal anchors ranging from "nothing at all" to "absolute maximum". This scale was chosen as the most appropriate after critical assessment and comparison of four other scales. The subjects were asked to rate their perceived muscle exertion after the MVIC had been recorded before and after the experiment.

The average of the scores collected was analyzed for statistical significance using a paired t-test. For the horizontal configuration, the averaged value of the ratings was significantly greater after the task ($t(17) = 1.74$, $p = 0.0003$). Similarly for the vertical configuration, the averaged value was significantly greater after the task ($t(17) = 1.74$, $p = 0.0005$). This indicates an overall increased perceived level of fatigue for both configurations (see Table 2).

**Table 2.** Subjective mean and standard deviation results for the horizontal and vertical configurations

| Configuration | Before | After |
|---|---|---|
| Horizontal | 3.97 (± 7.96) | 15.44 (± 14.93) |
| Vertical | 3.17 (± 5.40) | 12.44 (± 11.92) |

# 6 Discussion and Conclusion

The main aim of the study was to compare the muscle fatigue experienced when using large multi-touch interactive displays in horizontal and vertical configurations, over a one-hour period.

Our findings from the objective measures provide statistically significant evidence for the presence of potentially damaging fatigue for the middle deltoids for the vertical case only and not the horizontal. This can be due to the elevation required of the arms when interacting with the vertical display (i.e. gorilla-arm effect [24]) and the employment of larger force activation percentages. The presence of fatigue was also noted for the non-dominant extensor digitorum despite consistent activation of force. This can be due to the regular use of the non-dominant muscle (either uni- or bi-manually) in the vertical configuration, as can be derived from the significantly inconsistent activation of the dominant extensor digitorum. The inconsistent activation of dominant extensor digitorum suggests that the users were alternating between dominant and non-dominant sides. Unlike the objective measures, the results of the subjective measures showed that the subjects perceived the presence of fatigue in both the vertical and horizontal configurations with statistical significance. This emphasizes the unreliability of a person's perception of fatigue, where objective results found significant levels of muscle fatigue that can be damaging only in the vertical case.

These results have clear implications on interaction design for large interactive displays. Vertical interactive displays, while suitable for intermittent use over short periods of time, are not as suitable for frequent longer use – our study showed presence of fatigue for a one-hour task, but it might occur in shorter durations. Prolonged activities leading to muscle fatigue, which has previously been reported anecdotally, have the potential to lead to musculoskeletal disorders [1, 2]. For tasks that require frequent interactions in the range of one or more hours, designers should choose a horizontal display where possible to minimize damage to the musculoskeletal system, modify the design of interaction techniques to reduce the need for continuous inter-action, or to change the location of distant interactions when possible to more acces-sible locations on the display. Moreover, subjective measures showed a significant level of fatigue for both horizontal and vertical cases, indicating that for either case, designers should locate points of interaction in spaces easily accessible to the user whenever possible. As a simple example, for large displays, the use of contextual commands that are located based on users' interaction location is recommended over the traditional desktop model of showing commands on upper or side toolbars and menus. However, identifying the display space that helps reduce fatigue, whether on horizontal or vertical displays, is the subject of further investigation.

This study has several limitations that point towards future work. We studied fatigue for only male participants to overcome physiological differences. Additional studies with female participants would give insight on sex differences and its effect on measured fatigue when interacting with large interactive displays. Furthermore, our study only considered a small subset of the muscles' activated when interacting with the display and only two angles of interaction. In the future, we plan to assess the fatigability of other muscles (e.g. capitis muscles) at additional angles of interaction.

# References

1. Vøllestad, N.K.: Measurement of human muscle fatigue. J. Neurosci. Methods **74**, 219–227 (1997)
2. Wahlström, J.: Ergonomics, musculoskeletal disorders and computer work. Occ. Med. **55**, 168–176 (2005)
3. Meyer, S., Cohen, O., Nilsen, E.: Device comparisons for goal-directed drawing tasks. In: CHI 1995 Conference Companion, pp. 251–252. ACM, Boston (1994)
4. Sears, A., Shneiderman, B.: High precision touchscreens: design strategies and comparisons with a mouse. Int J Man-Mach Stud **34**, 593–613 (1991)
5. Barriera-Viruet, H., Sobeih, T.M., Daraiseh, N., Salem, S.: Questionnaires vs observational and direct measurements: a systematic review. In: TIES 2006, vol. 7, pp. 261–284 (2006)
6. Young, J.G., Trudeau, M.B., Odell, D., Marinelli, K., Dennerlein, J.T.: Wrist and shoulder posture and muscle activity during touch-screen tablet use. WORK **45**, 59–71 (2013)
7. Lozano, C., Jindrich, D., Kahol, K.: The impact on musculoskeletal system during multitouch tablet interactions. In: ACM CHI 2011, pp. 825–828. ACM, Vancouver (2011)
8. Ichino, J., Isoda, K., Hanai, A., Ueda, T.: Effects of the display angle in museums on user's cognition, behavior, and subjective responses. In: CHI 2013, pp. 2979–2988. ACM, Paris (2013)
9. Muller-Tomfelde, C., Wessels, A., Schremmer, C.: Tilted tabletops: in between horizontal and vertical workspaces. In: TABLETOP 2008, pp. 49–56 (2008)
10. Zerpa, C., Lopez, N., Przysucha, E., Sanzo, P.: The effect of common teaching tools on upper extremity muscle activity. Education **4**, 160–166 (2014)
11. Morris, M.R., Brush, A.J.B., Meyers, B.R.: A field study of knowledge workers'; use of interactive horizontal displays. In: TABLETOP 2008, pp. 105–112 (2008)
12. Wigdor, D., Perm, G., Ryall, K., Esenther, A., Chia, S.: Living with a tabletop: Analysis and observations of long term office use of a multi-touch table. In: TABLETOP'07, pp. 60–67 (2007)
13. Criswell, E.: Cram's Introduction to Surface Electromyography. Jones and Barlett, London (2011)

14. Borg, G., Borg, E.: A new generation for scaling methods: level-anchored ratio scaling. Psychologica **28**, 15–45 (2001)
15. Cioni, R., Giannini, F., Paradiso, C., Battistini, N., Navona, C., Starita, A.: Sex differences in surface EMG interference pattern power spectrum. J. Appl. Physiol. **77**, 2163–2168 (1994)
16. Hincapi-Ramos, J.D., Guo, X., Moghadasian, P., Irani, P.: Consumed endurance: a metric to quantify arm fatigue of mid-air interactions. In: CHI 2014, pp. 1063–1072. ACM, Toronto (2014)
17. Al-Mulla, M.R., Sepulveda, F., Colley, M.: A review of non-invasive techniques to detect and predict localised muscle fatigue. Sensors **11**, 3545–3594 (2011)
18. Peres, S.C., Nguyen, V., Kortum, P.T., Akladios, M., Wood, S.B., Muddimer, A.: Software ergonomics: relating subjective and objective measures. In: CHI 2009 EA, pp. 3949–3954. ACM, Boston (2009)
19. Sherwood, L.: Human physiology: from cells to systems. Cengage Learning, USA (2012)
20. Phinyomark, A., Thongpanja, S., Hu, H., Phukpattaranont, P., Limsakul, C.: The usefulness of mean and median frequencies in electromyography analysis. In: Naik, G.R. (ed.) Computational Intelligence in Electromyography Analysis – A Perspective on Current Applications and Future Challenges, pp. 195–220 (2012)
21. Murata, A., Ishihara, H.: Evaluation of shoulder muscular fatigue induced during mouse operation in a VDT task. IEICE Trans. Inf. Syst. **E88-D**, 223–229 (2005)
22. Lawrence, J.H., De Luca, C.J.: Myoelectric signal versus force relationship in different human muscles. J Appl Physiol Respir Environ Exerc Physiol **54**, 1653–1659 (1983)
23. NISMAT. http://www.nismat.org/software/beat/doc/beat.html
24. Gorilla arm. http://www.computer-dictionary-online.org/index.asp?q=gorilla+arm

# Touch, Movement and Vibration:
# User Perception of Vibrotactile Feedback
# for Touch and Mid-Air Gestures

Christian Schönauer[1], Annette Mossel[1(✉)], Ionuț-Alexandru Zaiți[2],
and Radu-Daniel Vatavu[2]

[1] Vienna University of Technology, Vienna, Austria
{schoenauer,mossel}@ims.tuwien.ac.at
[2] University Stefan Cel Mare of Suceava, Suceava, Romania
ionutzaiti@gmail.com, vatavu@eed.usv.ro

**Abstract.** Designing appropriate feedback for gesture interfaces is an important
aspect of user experience and performance. We conduct the first investigation of
users' perceptions of vibrotactile stimuli during touch and mid-air gesture input
for smart devices. Furthermore, we explore perception of feedback that is
*decoupled* from the smart device and delivered *outside its operating range* by an
accessory wearable, *i.e.*, feedback delivered at arm-level. Results show user
perception of vibrotactile stimuli up to 80 % accurate, which we use to recommend guidelines for practitioners to design new vibrotactile feedback techniques for smart devices.

**Keywords:** Gestures · Vibrotactile feedback · User perception · Mid-air
gestures · Touch · Wearable · Design guidelines · Smartphone · Actuators ·
Interface design

## 1 Introduction

Gesture interfaces are today's standard for interacting with smart mobile devices in the
form of touch and accelerated motion and, recently, mid-air gestures. Related research
has shown that delivering appropriate feedback to users during gesture input can help
with gesture training [7], increase recognition accuracy [8], and improve overall user
experience [5]. However, providing feedback beyond visual and audio cues is still
subject of technical development and investigation of user perception of vibrotactile
stimuli [1, 9, 11]. Nevertheless, prior art has reported many advantages of vibrotactile
stimuli for user feedback, such as more intuitive indication of body part positions than
delivered by visual or audio feedback [11], reduced errors and improved learning rate
for motor training tasks [9], and increased accuracy for mid-air finger gesture articulation [1]. However, no work has compared users' perceptions of vibrotactile stimuli
across the various gesture input modalities enabled by today's smart devices, such as
touch, accelerated hand motion, and mid-air finger and arm gestures. Furthermore, at
the advent of new miniaturized wearables (*e.g.*, smart watches and interactive jewelry)
that enable new interactive contexts, vibrotactile stimuli will likely play an important

© IFIP International Federation for Information Processing 2015
J. Abascal et al. (Eds.): INTERACT 2015, Part IV, LNCS 9299, pp. 165–172, 2015.
DOI: 10.1007/978-3-319-22723-8_14

role for delivering user feedback. These new devices are worn on various body parts and communicate with the user's smartphone, which is emerging as the central unit of a distributed on-body network of devices [2]. Although prior art has investigated vibrotactile feedback delivered *on the smartphone itself* [7], no work has examined users' perceptions of feedback *decoupled from the smartphone* and delivered on the body by an accessory wearable during gesture input with the primary device.

The contributions of this work are: (1) we conduct the first exploration of users' perceptions of vibrotactile feedback for touch, accelerated motion, and mid-air gestures performed on smartphone devices with *decoupled* vibrotactile stimuli delivered *outside the operating range* of the smart device, *i.e.*, feedback delivered at arm-level; (2) we report good levels of user perception of vibrotactile stimuli up to 80 % accuracy with minimal training; (3) we recommend guidelines for practitioners to design vibrotactile patterns for similar multi-device prototypes. We hope that this first exploration into user perception of vibrotactile feedback during gesture input will inspire the community to further investigate cross-device feedback for gesture-controlled multi-device prototypes and to promote new approaches for gesture articulation guidance.

## 2    Experiment

We designed an experiment to understand users' perceptions of vibrotactile feedback at arm level for various interaction contexts involving touch and mid-air gestures.

**Participants.**    Eleven participants volunteered for the experiment (5 females). Participants were young adults with ages between 21 and 25 years old (mean age 22.7 years, SD 1.04 years). No participant had previous experience with vibrotactile feedback.

**Apparatus.**    For the purpose of this study, we developed a wearable vibrotactile device with actuators powered by a control unit attached to the arm near the wrist. The unit was implemented around a Spark Core v1.0 board driving two Precision Microdrives vibration motors (of type 304-108) small in size (4 mm diameter) with short rise and stop times (50 ms and 76 ms, respectively), and a vibration speed of 10,000 rpm, a design that we adopted to optimize mobility and perception at skin-level receptors [3]. The two actuators were encased in an ABS housing to prevent direct contact between their rotational mass and the skin, and a spring was added to decouple the housing from vibrations to maximize the vibrating effect on the surface of the skin. The vibrotactile device weights approximately 6 g/55 g (actuator/control unit) and can be worn effortlessly on the arm at any location (Fig. 1 shows our experimental setup). Feedback delivered by the actuators was generated by a custom software application implementing our experiment design that ran on a smartphone (HTC One S), which communicated with the control unit via a wireless connection.

**Design.**    Our experiment was a within-subject design, with the following factors:

(1) PATTERN, ordinal variable, with 6 values: NO-FEEDBACK (control condition – participants did not receive any vibrotactile feedback, but were still asked afterward what they felt), SHORT-PULSE (a continuous, 250 ms constant-amplitude pulse),

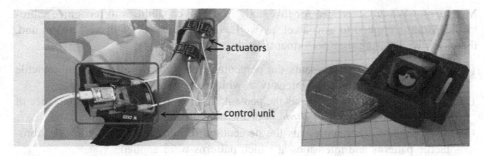

**Fig. 1.** Left: Apparatus employed during our experiment composed of a control unit driving two vibrotactile actuators controlled by a smartphone via a wireless connection. The two actuators were placed around the wrist at a distance of 10 cm. Right: Close-up of one actuator.

    LONG-PULSE (continuous, constant-amplitude pulse of 750 ms), SIMPLE-PATTERN (sequence of two short and long pulses with 250 ms pauses in-between), COMPLEX-PATTERN (sequence of 3 pulses – short, long, and short – with 250 ms pauses in-between), and LINE (amplitude decreases for one actuator as it increases for the other, giving the sensation of a moving point, total duration of 1750 ms).

(2) INTENSITY, ordinal variable, with 3 values: LOW, MEDIUM, and HIGH. The HIGH intensity condition corresponds to typical operating amplitude (0.85 G) and voltage (3 V) for our actuators, which was found close to the upper threshold of the comfortable stimuli range during pre-tests. The LOW intensity condition corresponds to 1/3 of the HIGH intensity (0.2 G at 0.9 V), which was found easily detectable during pre-tests. The MEDIUM intensity level was selected between HIGH and LOW at an amplitude of 0.55 G and 2 V voltage.

(3) HAND-MODE, nominal variable, with 5 conditions: REST (hand is resting on the table or the leg), HOLD (hand holds the smartphone), HOLD-AND-MOVE (hand performs a touch stroke gesture on the smartphone), FINGER-MOTION (fingers move in mid-air), and ARM-MOTION (arm moves in mid-air at low velocity).

(4) To prevent participants from becoming familiar with the gestures they performed in the HOLD-AND-MOVE and ARM-MOTION conditions, we also varied GESTURE type, nominal variable, with 3 conditions: CIRCLE, SWIPE-LEFT, and SWIPE-RIGHT.

**Task.** Participants sat in a comfortable chair, watching instructions delivered on a large display about the hand states and movements to perform according to the HAND-MODE and GESTURE conditions. During this time, a vibrotactile stimuli was delivered to participants' arms according to the PATTERN and INTENSITY experimental conditions. In total, there were 90 trials (= 6 PATTERN × 3 INTENSITY × 5 HAND-MODE) randomized across participants. After each trial, participants were asked to recognize both PATTERN and INTENSITY of the applied vibrotactile stimuli. Before the experiment, participants were familiarized with our vibrotactile prototype, and they were presented with the patterns and intensities for several times until they confirmed good understanding. During the experiment, we had participants wearing headsets and listening to music to prevent them to hear the actuators, which would have affected positively participants' capability to discern patterns and intensities by relying on audio information. The experiment took about 35 min per participant to complete.

**Measures.**  We are interested for this study in users' capabilities to recognize vibro-tactile patterns applied to arm level, as well as the intensities of these patterns and, therefore, we measure user performance at three distinct levels:

(1)  PATTERN-ACCURACY represents the percentage of correctly identified vibrotactile patterns, *regardless* of the intensity at which they were applied.
(2)  INTENSITY-ACCURACY represents the percentage of correctly identified intensities of the vibrotactile stimuli, *regardless* of the actual pattern being applied.
(3)  OVERALL-ACCURACY represents the percentage of correctly identified *both* vibro-tactile patterns and intensities at which patterns were applied.

**Hypotheses.**  We set the following hypotheses to verify in our experiment:

(H1)  The PATTERN type of the applied vibrotactile stimuli will affect participants' OVERALL- and PATTERN-ACCURACY.
(H2)  The INTENSITY level of the applied vibrotactile stimuli will affect participants' OVERALL-ACCURACY and INTENSITY-ACCURACY.
(H3)  The PATTERN type will not affect participants' INTENSITY-ACCURACY, nor will the INTENSITY level affect participants' PATTERN-ACCURACY.
(H4)  The HAND-MODE will affect participants' recognition accuracy of vibrotactile stimuli for all accuracy measures.

## 3  Results

Overall, our participants were successful at recognizing combined vibrotactile patterns and their intensities in only 55.4 % of all trials (OVERALL-ACCURACY). Although the overall performance is modest, PATTERN-ACCURACY and INTENSITY-ACCURACY were significantly higher than the overall performance, as indicated by McNemar tests (79.7 % and 55.4 %, respectively, $\chi^2_{(1,N=990)} = 239.004$, $p < .001$ and 67.8 % and 55.4 %, $\chi^2_{(1,N=990)} = 121.008, p < .001$, respectively). These results show that our participants managed to recognize *either* the vibrotactile pattern *or* its intensity with acceptable rates, but their overall judgment of the multiple characteristics of the vibrotactile stimuli failed significantly more often. To understand more, we performed additional tests for each experimental factor. Figure 2 illustrates participants' recognition accuracy computed for the PATTERN, INTENSITY, and GESTURE conditions.

Cochran's $Q$ tests showed a significant effect of PATTERN on OVERALL-ACCURACY ($\chi^2_{(5,N=165)} = 211.345, p < .001$), PATTERN-ACCURACY ($\chi^2_{(5,N=165)} = 226.065, p < .001$) and INTENSITY-ACCURACY ($\chi^2_{(5,N=165)} = 92.962, p < .001$), see Fig. 2a, d, and g. Participants had no problems detecting the NO-FEEDBACK condition (98.2 %), which confirms an appropriate level for our LOW intensity, and also alleviates concerns regarding a potential vibrotactile after-effect. The SIMPLE and COMPLEX patterns were recognized with 95.2 % and 92.1 % PATTERN-ACCURACY (*n.s.* difference), and were followed by SHORT-PULSE with 86.1 %, see Fig. 2b. Confusion matrix analysis showed that LONG-PULSES were often mistaken for SHORT-PULSES (18.2 % of the time) and as LINES (22.4 %), while LINES were repeatedly perceived as LONG-PULSES (34.5 %), see Fig. 3,

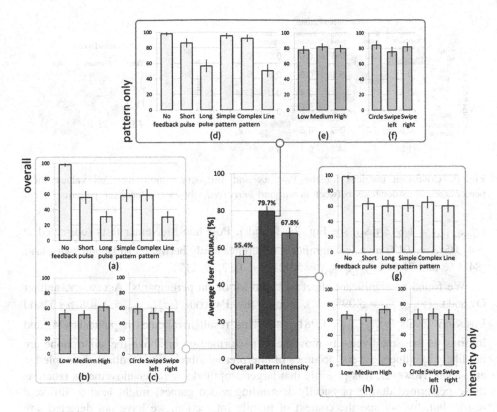

**Fig. 2.** Average user ACCURACY of recognizing vibrotactile feedback measured OVERALL (left), per PATTERN (top), and for each INTENSITY level (right). Error bars show 95 % CIs.

left. When we removed the NO-FEEDBACK condition from the analysis, no significant effect of PATTERN was present any longer on INTENSITY-ACCURACY ($\chi^2_{(4,N=165)}$ = 1.507, n.s.), but the effect was still there for the other two measures. These results validate hypothesis H1 and the first part of H3.

Cochran's $Q$ tests showed a significant effect of INTENSITY on OVERALL-ACCURACY ($\chi^2_{(2,N=330)}$ = 11.385, $p < .005$) and INTENSITY-ACCURACY ($\chi^2_{(2,N=330)}$ = 9.025, $p < .05$), but no effect on PATTERN-ACCURACY ($\chi^2_{(2,N=330)}$ = 2.774, n.s.), see Fig. 2b, e, and h. These results validate hypothesis H2 and the second part of H3. Follow-up post hoc McNemar tests (Bonferroni corrected at the $p = .05/3 = .017$) revealed a significant difference only between the INTENSITY-ACCURACY of MEDIUM and HIGH ($\chi^2_{(1,N=330)}$ = 7.358, $p < .01$, $\phi$=.15), see Fig. 2h. Confusion matrix analysis revealed that LOW intensities were often perceived as MEDIUM (36.7 % of the time), and HIGH as MEDIUM (28.2 %), see Fig. 3, right. At the same time, MEDIUM intensities were perceived more as being HIGH (33.0 %) rather than LOW (14.2 %) by our participants.

We found a significant effect of GESTURE on PATTERN-ACCURACY ($\chi^2_{(2,N=195)}$ = 7.053, $p < .05$), but not on INTENSITY ($\chi^2_{(2,N=195)}$ = 0.019, n.s.) nor on OVERALL-ACCURACY

**Perceived Pattern**

| | | No feedback | Short pulse | Long pulse | Simple pattern | Complex pattern | Line |
|---|---|---|---|---|---|---|---|
| **Actual Pattern** | No feedback | 98.2 | 0.0 | 0.6 | 0.6 | 0.6 | 0.6 |
| | Short pulse | 0.6 | 86.1 | 6.1 | 0.6 | 0.6 | 6.1 |
| | Long pulse | 0.6 | 18.2 | 56.4 | 2.4 | 0.0 | 22.4 |
| | Simple pattern | 1.2 | 1.2 | 0.6 | 95.2 | 0.6 | 1.2 |
| | Complex pattern | 0.0 | 1.2 | 0.6 | 4.8 | 92.1 | 1.2 |
| | Line | 1.2 | 4.2 | 34.5 | 6.1 | 3.6 | 50.3 |

**Perceived Intensity**

| | | Low | Medium | High |
|---|---|---|---|---|
| **Actual Intensity** | Low | 55.8 | 36.7 | 7.6 |
| | Medium | 14.2 | 52.7 | 33.0 |
| | High | 7.9 | 28.2 | 63.9 |

**Fig. 3.** Confusion matrices for the PATTERN and INTENSITY conditions. Cell values show percentages of associations between *actual* and *perceived* vibrotactile feedback patterns.

$(\chi^2_{(2,N=195)} = 1.842, \text{n.s.})$, see Fig. 2c, f, and i. Post hoc McNemar tests (corrected at $p = .05/3 = .017$) revealed significant differences only between CIRCLE and SWIPE-LEFT (84.3 % and 75.5 %, $\chi^2_{(1,N=195)} = 5.921, p < .017, \phi = .17$).

We found no significant effect of HAND-MODE on participants' ACCURACY, neither OVERALL $(\chi^2_{(4,N=198)} = 5.095, \text{n.s.})$, nor at the PATTERN $(\chi^2_{(4,N=198)} = 2.408, \text{n.s.})$ and INTENSITY levels $(\chi^2_{(4,N=198)} = 1.981, \text{n.s.})$. This result invalidates hypothesis H4, and informs us that small-velocity movements performed on or above the smartphone are not likely to influence users' accuracy of interpreting vibrotactile feedback decoupled at arm-level. However, it is possible that larger amplitude or faster movements (such as those performed during physically-demanding video games) might lead to different results but, for our specific context of mobile interaction, we have not detected any such effects. (Consequently, we have not illustrated HAND-MODE results in Fig. 2). There were no significant differences between the performance of women and men, as shown by Mann-Whitney $U$ tests (all $p > .05, \text{n.s.}$).

## 4  Design Guidelines for Vibrotactile Feedback

Our data so far enables us to recommend a number of 4 easy-to-apply guidelines for designing vibrotactile feedback to be delivered by an accessory wearable device at arm level during touch and mid-air gesture input with the primary device:

(1) **Design vibrotactile patterns that vary significantly in their time duration.** In our experiment, we found that PATTERN type affects significantly users' recognition accuracy (hypothesis H1). However, the most elementary and simple patterns were not always the most easily recognized ones. For instance, our participants achieved a modest accuracy for LONG-PULSE rather than for our COMPLEX pattern design. Our data indicates that it is difficult to recognize patterns' duration accurately even when they vary by as much as 500 ms, which is supported by the frequent unidirectional confusion between LONG and SHORT pulses (Fig. 3, left), even when their time duration varied by factor of 3 (*i.e.*, 750 ms *vs.* 250 ms). Furthermore, LONG-PULSE and LINE were often confused by our participants, despite

that LINE took twice as much time as LONG-PULSE (*i.e.*, 1750 ms *vs.* 750 ms). Consequently, we advise practitioners to employ time duration with caution by ensuring enough difference in the duration of vibrotactile stimuli to prevent misrecognition. Our results above suggest rough guidelines of what this difference might be, but we leave this design decision for practitioners, which will ultimately adapt our results to their specific application context.

(2) **Exploit pauses in the design of vibrotactile patterns.** The remarkable accuracy achieved by the COMPLEX pattern suggests that series of discrete pulses are easier to recognize by users when they appear in conjunction with simple, continuous patters, as users can exploit the pauses between pulses to validate and inform their guesses about the applied vibrotactile pattern. Designs with discrete pulses likely determined COMPLEX and LINE to be discriminated accurately, even if they took the same amount of time to complete (1750 ms both).

(3) **Limit the intensity levels of vibrotactile patterns to at most two.** According to van Erp [3], four is the maximum number of levels that should be designed for vibrotactile feedback when using intensity to encode information in the interval ranging between detection and pain. Our experiment shows that three intensity levels were difficult to discriminate (*i.e.*, 67.8 % average accuracy, see Fig. 3, right). Considering that we did not calibrate intensity per participant, nor did we evaluate the perception of intensity alone (*i.e.*, an easier task), this result is not surprising. However, the LOW and HIGH intensities were rarely mistaken one for the other (there was less than 8 % error rate in each direction). Consequently, we recommend the use of two intensity levels for designs of vibrotactile patterns that are easily recognizable with minimal training conditions. Also, we observed a tendency in our participants to overestimate intensity, which might be an indicator that our MEDIUM and HIGH intensities might have been too intense overall. Some participants even complained that HIGH was close to uncomfortable and its intensity should have been reduced, which recommends calibration of intensity levels per participant during training. Our data informs us to recommend normalized vibration amplitudes below 0.85G for devices, which don't have much mass themselves and are attached tightly to the lower arm/wrist.

(4) **Exploit both duration and pattern type for vibrotactile feedback.** Validation of hypothesis H3 shows that feedback can be successfully encoded as both intensity and pattern type, without significantly affecting the users' accuracy of perception of either. For our applied patterns, no temporal enhancement [3] has been observed, which could have affected the perceived intensities for the SIMPLE and COMPLEX patterns. Practitioners are encouraged to explore the design space of PATTERN × INTENSITY for feedback options combining both these characteristics.

# 5   Conclusion

We examined in this work users' perceptions of vibrotactile feedback delivered at arm-level during touch and mid-air gesture input. As more and more miniaturized wearable devices and sensors will become available in conjunction with the smartphone, such investigations are mandatory for the community to build up the required knowledge to design proper feedback during gesture input with these smart devices. It is our hope that this first investigation on decoupled vibrotactile feedback will inspire the community to examine more such scenarios for gesture interaction with smart devices.

**Acknowledgment.** This work was supported by the liFe-StaGE project 740/2014, "Multimodal Feedback for Supporting Gestural Interaction in Smart Environments", co-funded by UEFISCDI & OeAD. The authors would like to thank the graduate student of Vienna University of Technology, Patrick Kühtreiber for his help during the design and implementation of the prototype used in this work.

# References

1. Adams, R.J., Olowin, A.B., Hannaford, B., Sands, O.S.: Tactile data entry for extravehicular activity. In: Proceedings of 2011 IEEE World Haptics, pp. 305–310 (2011)
2. Chen, M., Gonzalez, S., Vasilakos, A., Cao, H., Leung, V.C.M.: Body area networks: a survey. Mobile Netw. Appl. **16**(2), 171–193 (2011)
3. Van Erp, J.B.F.: Guidelines for the use of vibro-tactile displays in human computer interaction. In: Proceedings of Eurohaptics, pp. 18–22 (2002)
4. Geldard, F.A.: Sensory Saltation: Metastability in the Perceptual World. Wiley, New York (1975)
5. Grandhi, S.A, Joue, G., Borchers, J., Mittelberg, I.: How we gesture towards machines: an exploratory study of user perceptions of gestural interaction. In: Proceedings of CHI 2013 Extended Abstracts, pp. 1209–1214. ACM Press (2013)
6. Israr, A., Poupyrev, I.: Tactile brush: drawing on skin with a tactile grid display. In: Proceedings of CHI 2011, pp. 2019–2028. ACM Press (2011)
7. Kamal, A., Li, Y., Lank, E.: Teaching motion gestures via recognizer feedback. In: Proceedings of IUI 2014, pp. 73–82. ACM Press (2014)
8. Kratz, S., Ballagas, R.: Unravelling seams: improving mobile gesture recognition with visual feedback techniques. In: Proceedins of CHI 2009, pp. 937–940. ACM (2009)
9. Lieberman, J., Breazeal, C.: TIKL: development of a wearable vibrotactile feedback suit for improved human motor learning. IEEE Trans. Robotics **23**(5), 919–926 (2007)
10. McDaniel, T., Villanueva, D., Krishna, S., Panchanathan, S.: MOVeMENT: A framework for systematically mapping vibrotactile stimulations to fundamental body movements. In: Proceedings of the 2010 IEEE International Symposium on Haptic Audio-Visual Environments and Games, pp. 1–6 (2010)
11. Spelmezan, D., Jacobs, M., Hilgers, A., Borchers, J.: Tactile motion instructions for physical activities. In: Proceedings of CHI 2009. ACM Press, 2243–2252 (2009)
12. Wulf, G.: Attention and motor skill learning. Human Kinetics (2007)

# Where to Start? Exploring the Efficiency of Translation Movements on Multitouch Devices

Quan Nguyen[1(✉)] and Michael Kipp[2]

[1] DFKI, Saarbrücken, Germany
quan.nguyen@dfki.de
[2] Augsburg University of Applied Sciences, Augsburg, Germany
michael.kipp@hs-augsburg.de

**Abstract.** Predicting the efficiency of interaction techniques can be crucial for designing user interfaces. While models like Fitts' law make general predictions, there is little research on how efficiency varies under different conditions like in which screen region a movement starts and in which direction it is going, and whether the surface is horizontal or vertical. This study investigates these aspects with regard to translation movements on a touch screen, using an extended Fitts' law setup and considering arm kinematics. The results show that on horizontal displays translation is faster and causes less arm fatigue than on vertical ones. Also, on horizontal displays, we identified screen regions and movement directions that allow significantly faster movement compared to others. Finally, movements that employ shorter kinematic chains (e.g. just the wrist) are significantly faster than those that use longer ones (e.g. wrist, elbow, shoulder). We suggest adjustments to Fitts' original formulation. In the future, our findings can inform or partially automate positioning decisions in interaction design.

**Keywords:** Multitouch interaction techniques · Fitts' law · 2D translation

## 1   Introduction

For many devices multitouch has become the standard interaction technique. Predicting the performance of interaction techniques can be important for various reasons, e.g. if an application is highly time/cost critical (industry, logistics, communications) or needs very high precision (medical, military). Even for applications where performance is not the first priority, it is still a criterion to evaluate the user interface [7]: Nielsen and Levy [18] report that in 75 % of the 57 studies they evaluated the user preferred the system with the best performance. Ben-Bassat et al. [2] show that the user would choose the system with the better performance and ignore the design, even if they have to expect monetary loss. Other studies could show that users rate a design worse after usage if the usability was low on effectiveness [22] or efficiency [18].

© IFIP International Federation for Information Processing 2015
J. Abascal et al. (Eds.): INTERACT 2015, Part IV, LNCS 9299, pp. 173–191, 2015.
DOI: 10.1007/978-3-319-22723-8_15

We find multitouch techniques on a broad range of devices, from smartphones and tablets to touch-sensitive tables and display walls. The performance of even basic interaction techniques like the translation and rotation of objects will likely differ depending on the size and orientation (horizontal/vertical) of the device and the position and posture of the user and his or her arm and hand. However, current models like Fitts' law [6] do not take such conditions into account yet. Although Fitts' law has been confirmed for different input devices like mouse, pen input and multitouch [5], there have only been few extensions so far [1,4]. In prior work we have started to look at how the screen region effects the performance of translation and rotation techniques as a first step to explore the conditions under which interaction techniques perform best [17].

In this paper, we focus exclusively on translation movements (dragging). However, in our study we include many different conditions like screen orientation (horizontal vs. vertical), screen regions (20 regions where the movement can start) and movement direction (eight directions). Based on existing work [3,23] we hypothesized that performance will differ with respect to screen orientation and screen region. We also look at the concept of fatigue as a possible cause for performance differences and as an important aspect in the subjective evaluation of multitouch displays [14]. Various studies have shown that the length of the kinematic chains which were used to execute the task play a decisive role in terms of fatigue and performance. Hincapié-Ramos et al. [9] for instance showed that working with extended arms, which constitutes a longer kinematic chain, fatigue increases. Other studies found higher performance for shorter kinematic chains [12].

We hypothesize that there is an increased perceived fatigue for vertical displays [3]. In accordance with [9,12] we hypothesize that users will use longer kinematic chains on vertical displays which decreases performance.

Our main contributions are the following: We present significant empirical findings concerning the performance of translation movements on horizontal vs. vertical displays, considering start points in various screen regions and various movement directions. We show that horizontal displays outperform vertical ones and identified various screen regions, on a horizontal screen, which perform better than others. Finally, we prove correlations between performance and kinematic chains based on a manual video analysis of kinematic chains.

## 2    Related Work

Most of the research for multitouch deals with the problem of selection/tapping in terms of efficiency and precision or both [13,20]. Or they focused on different interaction techniques for manipulating objects (translation, rotation or both) with multiple degrees of freedom in 2D [16] or 3D [11]. There is relatively little research for the translation/dragging task for multitouch in terms of efficiency in different areas of the display [3,23]. Bi et al. [3] divided the multitouch display into different cells to measure the performance of different tasks for the each cell in relationship to the position of the multitouch display. The displays were placed around the keyboard (left, bottom, right and top) and as a vertical screen.

The used task for the study was a one-finger gesture task and two docking tasks with translation, rotation and scaling. In contrast to our experiment they used fewer screen locations (nine) and the direction of the one-finger drag gesture was limited to up, down, left or right. For one-handed tasks cells close to the keyboard performed best. For two-handed tasks the placement on bottom and top had the best performance. The design of Weiss et al. [23] only included up and down movements.

There are two lines of research where vertical and horizontal displays were at the center of attention. In the first line of research, the two orientations are compared in terms of efficiency and performance [8,19]. In the second line of research, solutions for the integration of both screen orientations are explored [23]. Hancock and Booth [8], for instance, compared the direct input with a pen input on a vertical and horizontal display surface. With a selection task on menus they tried to find out which regions are faster and easier to reach for the used hands. Based on their findings they suggested an adaptive interface to detect handedness because handedness influences the performance of the selection. For instance, the left hand is faster for upper-left und lower-right regions while the upper-right and lower-left regions are faster for the right hand. Pedersen and Hornbæk [19] found that tapping was performed 5 % faster on the vertical surface, whereas dragging was performed 5 % faster and with fewer errors on the horizontal surface. In contrast to our experiment they compared tapping and dragging tasks on large multitouch displays where participants were standing. Additionally, the participants where free to choose the left or right hand for interaction. In contrast, the BendDesk [23] was constructed as a combined horizontal and vertical display, connected by a curved region. The authors studied this curved area and, among other things, compared down-up movements that cross through all three areas. One of their findings was that dragging on a planar surface is faster and straighter than dragging across the curve. Given that the distances were constant for all dragging tasks Fitts' law would have expected constant movement durations over all areas.

Since Fitts published his formula which predicts that the time to acquire a target is logarithmically related to the distance over the target size [6], there has been more research on this topic and Fitts' formula has been confirmed for different input devices like mouse, pen input or multitouch [5].

There has also been work claiming that Fitts' law was unsatisfactory and suggesting to extend it for a 2D task [24] or for touch input [4]. Additionally, the authors [17] proposed to consider the direction of the movement. Weiss et al. [23] found indications that the interaction zone has an influence on the task completion time.

## 3    Method

### 3.1    Participants

Participants were recruited via noticeboards on university campus and through academic mailing lists. 16 subjects (7 male, 9 female) took part in the study

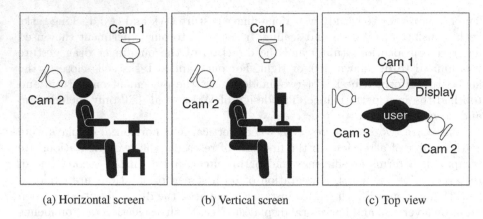

(a) Horizontal screen     (b) Vertical screen     (c) Top view

**Fig. 1.** (a) and (b) show the setup for horizontal and vertical screens, (c) shows the top view (cam 3) in the vertical screen configuration.

and were paid 10 Euros. The age varied between 19 and 33 with an average of 24 years. In terms of handedness 13 subjects were right-handed and three were left-handed but use the right hand for controlling mouse and touch interfaces.

## 3.2 Apparatus

We used a 22-in. multitouch screen (3M model M2256PW) with $1680 \times 1050$ pixels and $<6$ ms touch response time. The application was developed in *Java 8* with *JavaFX* and was run on an iMac.

The screen was used in two orientations, vertical and horizontal. In the vertical setup the display stood on a desk, in the horizontal setup it was placed on a low table so that the surface was at a height of 73 cm = 28.7 in. (Fig. 1a, b). The participants sat on a static chair centered in front of the display. Interactions were tracked by three webcams from the left (side view, cam 3), from above (top view, cam 1) and from behind the participant (shoulder view, cam 2). Figure 1c shows the webcam setup for the vertical display setup.

## 3.3 Tasks

The task required to move a circular cursor (grey circle with a red cross) into a target area marked by a dashed circle (see Fig. 2a). The target area was 1.5 cm in diameter. As soon as the cursor was selected by touching it the cursor changed to monochrome colors (see Fig. 2b). A trial was rated successful if the center of the cross was located inside the target area when lifting the finger off the screen. Success was signaled by a green check mark (Fig. 2c). It was not necessary to achieve a perfect match between cursor and target area. But if the center of the cross remains outside the target area a "sad smiley" appeared to signal failure (see Fig. 2d). In this case, the corresponding trial was repeated at the end of the set. The beginning of a new trial and success or failure of a trial were accompanied by distinct sounds.

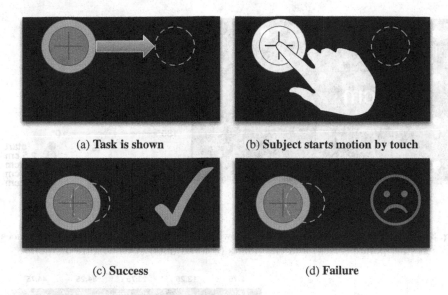

(a) **Task is shown**          (b) **Subject starts motion by touch**

(c) **Success**          (d) **Failure**

**Fig. 2.** Tasks

## 3.4  Material

For a thorough analysis the surface area of the screen needed to be completely covered by movement paths. A movement path was described by a start and an end point, marked by two different circular areas. Start points were evenly distributed through a pattern as broad as possible. The multiplication with end points showed that a high number of start points would have led to an unacceptably high number of trials per orientation. Therefore, the number of start points was set to 20, so that the display was still optimally covered with points in reasonable distances and the study was still feasible in an adequate time frame and with adequate effort (see Fig. 3). Possible end points were computed for each start point with four possible distances (2.5 cm, 5 cm, 10 cm and 20 cm) going in eight possible directions (0°, 45°, 90°, 135°, 180°, 225°, 270° and 315°). The combination of distances and directions resulted in 32 different theoretical end points per start point (see Fig. 3b). Some of the end points were not reachable because of the screen limits, so such points were removed (see Fig. 4a). Figure 4b shows all used configurations for the respective start points. The total number of configurations was thus reduced from 640 to 388. Each configuration occurred once in each set for horizontal and vertical level.

## 3.5  Procedure

The study was conducted in a lab with a supervisor and took about 1:15 h per participant. Each subject was briefed using written instructions while allowing for clarification questions.

Participants completed a pre-test questionnaire for demographic data. To make subjects familiar with the device and its use (strategy and optimal finger

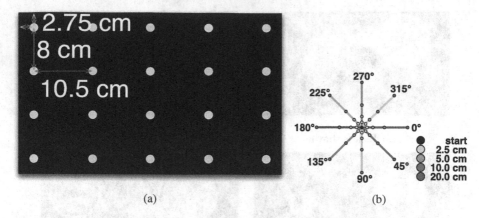

**Fig. 3.** (a) shows all start points, (b) shows all generated directions and distances between start points (black) and end points (colored dots) (Color figure online).

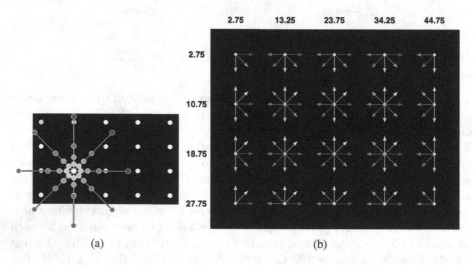

**Fig. 4.** Since some end points are off screen we removed several directions and distances, (a) shows an example where the red points were removed from the configuration set by removing the distance or the angle to this corresponding point, (b) shows all finally used directions for each start point in the experiment (Color figure online).

movements) each session began with a training phase of 30 randomized trials using the same configurations across subjects.

All tasks were conducted first in the horizontal, then in the vertical condition, or vice versa (setup order was balanced across subjects). Each condition took about 30 min to complete with a short break in between. After switching display orientation another training phase was conducted with a different training set. For every orientation condition, the task set consisted of at least 388 trials presented in four blocks separated by three breaks of 20 s. The actual number of trials for each subject depended on the individual error rate. Every failed trial was repeated at the end of the current set. Every subject received different task sets with 388 distinct configurations. The order of configurations was pseudo-random under the condition that neither start point nor movement direction be the same in two immediately subsequent trials.

After completing all tasks, subjects answered a questionnaire with subjective ratings concerning the comparison of both orientation setups.

### 3.6  Design

We devised a within-subject design with two independent variables: (a) display orientation (horizontal, vertical) and (b) configuration (start point, direction). Training phases were not included in the analysis of the trials so that there were 16 subjects × 2 screen orientations × 4 blocks × 97 configurations by block (388 configurations in sum) = 12416 data items were analyzed.

The following data were measured as dependent variables:

1. Distance time (DT): time from start point to end point minus tolerance.
2. Correction time: time from entering the target area to lifting finger off screen
3. Error rate

Correction time and error rate have to be measured for the effective ID ($ID_e$) in the mean-of-means throughput (TP) formula after Soukoreff and MacKenzie [21].

### 3.7  Results

We analyzed our data such that concrete design recommendations could be generated. Therefore, we looked at screen areas. First, we analyzed screen halves (top/bottom half and left/right). Second, we defined three functional areas (see Fig. 5) based on the following observations of current UIs:

1. **Center (yellow):** Translation movements in this area are multidirectional and can be used functionally (e.g. scrollbars, pop up menus etc.) and within different applications (image editing, map navigation etc.).
2. **Edges (blue):** Screen edges are often used for menu bars (e.g. Windows charm bars) or as storage areas. Here, selection requires translation movements vertical to the respective border directed towards the center of the display. Those movements are also relevant for desktop changes or gestures to control browser menus (tab/side forward/backward etc.).
3. **Corners (red):** Corners are treated separately from edges because they seem to be quite important. Often, frequently used functions are placed there (start menu, touch and hold menus, which are optionally used in multitouch and mouse combinations). Translation movements are mainly directed up- or downwards. Gestural interaction in the corners can also require diagonal movements.

We compared the performance of these areas. Performance was measured for horizontal and vertical displays considering start point, movement direction and varying distances. We measured in terms of mean-of-means throughput (TP) after Soukoreff and MacKenzie [21]. The difficulty of each configuration was measured using the Index of Difficulty (ID) with the Shannon formula because it always gives a positive rating for the index of task difficulty [15]. TP combines speed and accuracy into a single dependent measure and is calculated by:

$$TP = \frac{1}{y} \sum_{i=1}^{y} \left( \frac{1}{x} \sum_{j=1}^{x} \frac{ID_{e_{ij}}}{MT_{ij}} \right)$$

where $y$ is the number of subjects, and $x$ represents the movement condition. $MT_{ij}$ is the meantime over all trials for this condition. The units of throughput are bits per second (or bps).

The advantage of TP is the normal distribution of these data (Shapiro-Wilk-Test: $W = 0.9858, p - value = 0.8047$) because normal distribution of the data is often a requirement for statistical tests. In contrast, distance times are log distributed (see Fig. 6).

**Comparing Display Orientation.** A two-tailed paired t-test showed that translation movements on a horizontal surface ($M = 8.67, SD = 2.02$) outperformed the ones on a vertical surface ($M = 7.53, SD = 1.46$); $t(15) = 3.62, p < 0.002, Cohen's\ d = 0.907$ (see Fig. 7) which is also clearly visible in the heat maps in Fig. 8.

**Comparing Screen Halves.** On horizontal screens, the comparison of the left and right half of the display shows that movements which start on the left side ($M = 8.87, SD = 2.13$) of the horizontal display are faster than movements which start on the right side ($M = 8.50, SD = 1.95$); $t(15) = 3.46, p < 0.004, Cohen's\ d = 0.865$. On vertical displays we found the same effect on

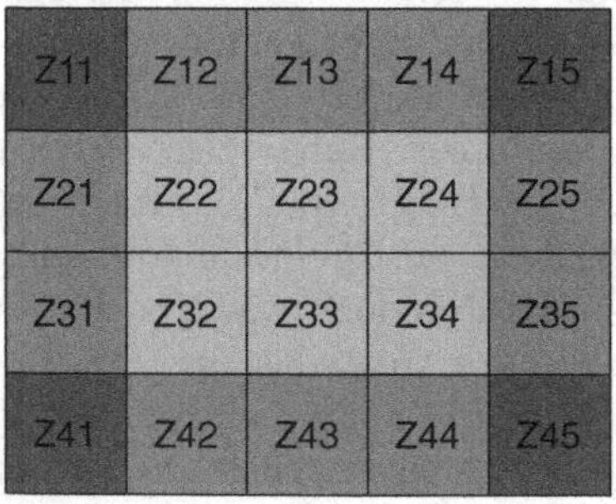

**Fig. 5.** Functional areas: center (yellow), edges (blue) and corners (red) (Color figure online).

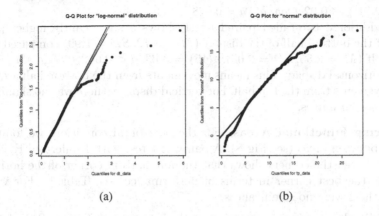

**Fig. 6.** Execution time is log-distributed (a). TP is normal distributed (b).

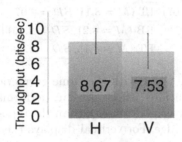

**Fig. 7.** Mean throughput (TP) for horizontal screen (blue) which significantly outperforms the vertical screen (red) (Color figure online).

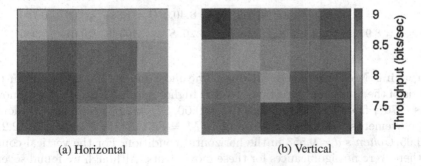

(a) Horizontal                                    (b) Vertical

**Fig. 8.** Performance heat map of the horizontal (a) and vertical (b) screen. Red means high performance, blue low performance (Color figure online).

the left side ($M = 7.61, SD = 1.46$) and the right side ($M = 7.38, SD = 1.48$); $t(15) = 2.71, p < 0.02, Cohen's\ d = 0.678$.

An additional two-tailed paired t-test shows a significantly higher performance of the bottom half of the display ($M = 8.79, SD = 1.99$) compared to the upper half ($M = 8.55, SD = 2.05$), $t(15) = 3.63, p < 0.002, Cohen's\ d = 0.908$ for the horizontal display. This means movements from the bottom half are faster than movements from the top half. For vertical displays there was no significance between screen halves.

**Comparing Functional Areas.** For the horizontal condition, we found differences between areas (see Fig. 8). A pairwise t-test with Bonferroni-Holm correction between the corners shows that the left bottom corner of the horizontal display is the best corner in terms of performance (see Table 1). For vertical displays there were no significances.

**Table 1.** Results of pairwise comparison of the corners: Left-Bottom (LB), Left-Top (LT), Right-Bottom (RB) and Right-Top (RT).

| Corner 1 | Corner 2 | p-Value | Cohen's d |
|---|---|---|---|
| LB ($M = 9.073, SD = 2.07$) | LT ($M = 8.11, SD = 2.07$) | <0.004 | 1.062 |
| LB | RB ($M = 8.21, SD = 2.05$) | <0.01 | 0.925 |
| LB | RT ($M = 8.15, SD = 2.03$) | <0.05 | 0.718 |

An additional pairwise t-test with the same correction for the edges shows significant differences with large effect sizes in performance (see Table 2): the bottom edge allows for better performance than the top and right edge. The left edge outperforms the top edge. For vertical displays there are no significances.

**Table 2.** Results of a pairwise comparison with Bonferroni-Holm correction of the areas on the edges.

| Edge 1 | Edge 2 | p-Value | Cohen's d |
|---|---|---|---|
| Bottom ($M = 8.70, SD = 1.97$) | Top ($M = 8.26, SD = 2.03$) | <0.02 | 0.878 |
| Bottom ($M = 8.70, SD = 1.97$) | Right ($M = 8.40, SD = 1.88$) | <0.03 | 0.780 |
| Left ($M = 8.95, SD = 2.17$) | Top ($M = 8.26, SD = 2.03$) | <0.01 | 0.946 |

**Comparing Movement Directions.** The most interesting finding from the analysis of the movement directions was the higher performance of upward movements ($270°$) from the bottom half ($M = 9.00, SD = 2.06$) compared to downward movements ($90°$) from the top half ($M = 8.61, SD = 2.16, t(15) = 2.21$), $p < 0.05, Cohen's\ d = 0.553$ in the horizontal condition. For the vertical condition there were no significances for these movements. Although we found several statistically significant differences between directions in the horizontal and vertical condition it was difficult to find systematic patterns. Figure 9 illustrates both the best and worst directions. The stars indicates the level of significance: $*p < 0.05; **p < 0.01; ***p < 0.001;$

**Comparing Movement Axes.** We slightly abstracted away from actual directions by collapsing two opposing directions into one *axis* (for the labels see Fig. 10). A pairwise comparison of axes in different areas showed, in some areas, a highly significant difference between the performance of the axes. Figure 11 shows only significant pairs. For instance the V axis showed significant differences to the H axis and the D2 axis in the zones Z21, Z22, Z31, Z32, Z33.

**Kinematic Chains.** For the analysis of the kinematic chains the sessions were recorded by three cameras (see Fig. 1 for the setup and Fig. 12 for an example screenshot of the video). The recorded material was annotated by two independent coders using the ANVIL video annotation tool [10]. For each transla-

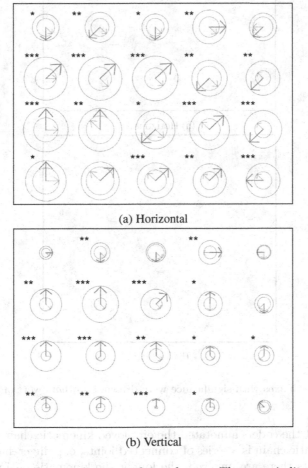

(a) Horizontal

(b) Vertical

**Fig. 9.** The best and worst directions for each area. The stars indicate the level of significance between the corresponding direction vectors ($^*p < 0.05$; $^{**}p < 0.01$; $^{***}$ $p < 0.001$). Note: To make the difference between the vectors visible the view was zoomed in by clipping the start part and enlarging the rest by a factor of 200.

**Fig. 10.** The eight directions (see Fig. 3b) were cumulated to four main axes.

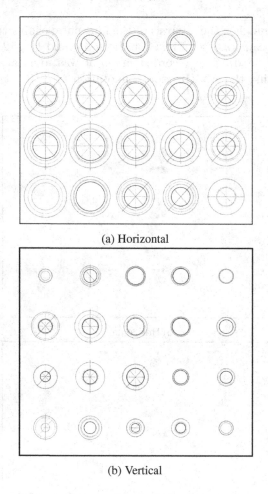

(a) Horizontal

(b) Vertical

**Fig. 11.** All axes with significance were drawn, all others were omitted.

tion movement the coders annotated the employed kinematic chain in the user's arm. A kinematic chain is a series of connected joints, e.g. finger–hand–forearm. The more joints there are involved, the longer the kinematic chain. To categorize a user movement we defined four kinematic chains: **finger**, finger–**hand**, finger–hand–**forearm** and finger–hand–forearm–**upper arm**. Each chain type is denoted by the topmost joint in the chain (printed in bold). For instance, if

**Fig. 12.** Screenshots of the three camera perspectives.

the target was moved by the finger without moving the hand, elbow or shoulder, then we categorized it as "finger". If the elbow was involved, then "forearm" was annotated.

A chi square statistic shows that the orientation of the display influences the usage of the kinematic chain $\chi^2 = (3, n = 12335) = 423.210, p < 0.001$. On horizontal displays, users employed shorter kinematic chains. Table 3 illustrates the usage in percent. We can see that the values for finger, hand and forearm increases up to 200 % in comparison to the vertical display.

T-Tests for the horizontal condition show that shorter chains (finger, hand, forearm) ($M = 9.36, SD = 2.27$) have significantly higher performance than longer chains (upper arm) ($M = 8.47, SD = 1.95$); $t(15) = 6.593, p < 0.000$. The same applies for the vertical orientation: shorter chains ($M = 8.27, SD = 1.66$) compared to upper arm ($M = 7.47, SD = 1.46$), $t(15) = 3.884, p < 0.001$.

**Adjusting Fitts' Law.** We adjusted Fitts' law to include the factors of screen orientation, start point and direction. We performed a multiple (linear) regression with the mentioned factors using the Shannon formulation for index of difficulty (id). For the computation we indexed the real values for start x-point ($startX$), start y-point ($startY$), screen *orientation* and direction (*angle*) to calculate the regression coefficients. We used values from 1 to 5 for the five possible starting x-coordinates, 1 to 4 for the starting y-coordinates and 1 to 8 for the angles in clockwise direction ($1 = 0° \ldots 8 = 315°$). For screen orientation we used 1 for horizontal and 2 for vertical.

**Table 3.** Distribution of kinematic chains in percent.

| | Horizontal | | | | Vertical | | | |
|---|---|---|---|---|---|---|---|---|
| Distance | Finger | Hand | Forearm | Upper arm | Finger | Hand | Forearm | Upper arm |
| 2.5 | 2.02 % | 6.69 % | 24.29 % | 66.99 % | 0.23 % | 1.09 % | 15.09 % | 83.59 % |
| 5 | 0.06 % | 1.14 % | 23.26 % | 75.54 % | 0.00 % | 0.11 % | 10.69 % | 89.20 % |
| 10 | 0.00 % | 0.06 % | 18.33 % | 81.61 % | 0.00 % | 0.00 % | 6.31 % | 93.69 % |
| 20 | 0.00 % | 0.00 % | 8.54 % | 91.46 % | 0.00 % | 0.00 % | 0.33 % | 99.67 % |
| at all | 0.52 % | 1.97 % | 18.61 % | 78.90 % | 0.06 % | 0.30 % | 8.10 % | 91.54 % |

We randomly divided our data into a training set and a test set, each of which contained 50 % of vertical and 50 % of horizontal data points. We used the training set to generate the model and derived the following parameters (**startX**, **orientation** and **angle**) and regression coefficients after the multiple regression (the starting y-coordinate was not significant for this model, $p > 0.1$):

$$MT = 0.0100 + 0.155 * id$$
$$+ 0.008 * startX$$
$$+ 0.053 * orientation$$
$$- 0.006 * angle$$
$$with \quad R^2 = 0.92$$

The first line is the regular Fitts' law formulation (from now on called Fitts' model). We used the training data to compute the coefficients for the regular Fitts' model, too, and derived $y = 0.1605x + 0.089$.

Comparing the actual test data (green) with the predictions of the regular Fitts' model (red) and of our adjusted Fitts' model (blue) over all *ids* (Fig. 13a), both models achieve a similarly high correlation (Fitts' model $R^2 = 0.98$, adjusted model $R^2 = 0.92$). However, if we take the other factors into account like *orientation, starting point* and *direction* we get a better picture of the performance of the two models (see Fig. 13b, c, d). Here, the adjusted model is more precise than the predicted constant time of Fitts' model. It is clearly visible how the adjusted model accounts for our findings: The prediction for surface orientation for instance shows the different performances for horizontal and vertical displays (see Fig. 13b) - horizontal outperforms vertical. In Fig. 13c the prediction shows that the left side is faster than the right side of the display. And as we can see in Fig. 13d the different directions have different performances.

**Questionnaire and Interviews.** The direct comparison between horizontal and vertical display orientation shows an explicit preference for a horizontal multitouch display over all categories among the subjects (find all results in Table 4). Most of the subjects perceive the horizontal orientation as faster, simpler and operable with less effort compared to the vertical orientation. Furthermore, subjects feel safer and even for the correction of errors like re-adjusting due to missing the target area the horizontal display is preferred over the vertical display.

### 3.8 Discussion

Our results first of all show that the performance of a translation movement depends on the orientation of the display, the point where the interaction starts, the direction in which the translation moves and which kinematic chain the user used.

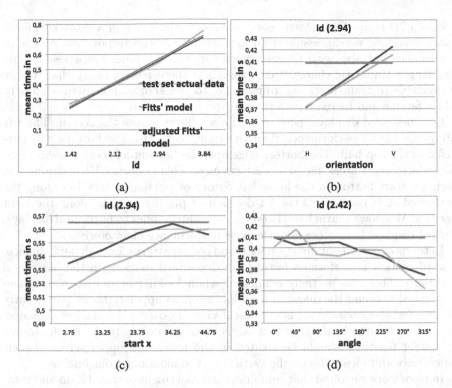

**Fig. 13.** Comparison of two models (Fitts' model, red, and adjusted Fitts' model, blue) against the test data (green): (a) for all *ids* (b) with fixed *id* for both orientations (c) for different x coordinates (d) and different angles (Color figure online).

**Table 4.** Results of questionnaire and interviews.

| Assessment category | Horizontal | Neither nor | Vertical |
|---|---|---|---|
| Faster and safe handling | 62.50 % | 25.00 % | 12.50 % |
| Simpler operation | 75.00 % | 18.75 % | 6.25 % |
| Less effort in operation | 81.25 % | 12.50 % | 6.25 % |
| Easier correctable (precise working) | 50.00 % | 31.25 % | 18.75 % |
| Felt faster | 81.25 % | 12.50 % | 6.25 % |

The horizontal display yielded the best performance and lowest perceived fatigue compared to the vertical one. Additionally, users used shorter kinematic chains. Our results show that kinematic chains influence performance: shorter kinematic chains (involving finger, hand, forearm) yield higher performance than longer ones (involving the upper arm) which is in accordance with earlier findings [12]. However, how do kinematic chains relate to the concept of fatigue? A recent study by Hincapié-Ramos et al. [9] showed that what they call the "bent arm position" is the least tiring of all positions they tested for a selection task on a 2D plane. This clearly corresponds to our notion of a short kinematic chain. Therefore, we can assume that kinematic chains correspond not only with performance but also with fatigue: shorter kinematic chains cause less fatigue than longer kinematic chains. Taken together, these results imply that it may be desirable to train users accordingly, i.e. to use shorter kinematic chains to reduce fatigue and increase performance.

On horizontal displays, performance also differs across the screen. The left half yields higher performance than the right half. Also the bottom half outperforms the top half. The bottom edge and the bottom-left corner seem to be particularly good areas for high performance. This confirms UI decisions like placing a start button in the lower left corner or putting a dock bar along the bottom edge. It contradicts the UI decision of placing a menu along the right edge (e.g. Windows charm bar). However, this only applies to horizontal displays. Vertical displays have more homogeneous performance characteristics.

In terms of movement direction we found some patterns for high performance. Upward motion is performed faster than downward motion (in the horizontal condition). This was partially confirmed when looking at motion axes where the vertical axis and the diagonal from lower-left to upper-right are particularly good performance-wise. This is relevant if virtual objects (UI elements, photos, documents) have to be dragged to a target area. According to our results source and target positions should be located in the lower and upper screen regions respectively and ideally be on the vertical or the mentioned diagonal axis.

In prior work we found that combining the movement of translation and rotation achieves higher performance when directed to the right than when directed to the left [17]. Our current study shows that this does not hold for translation-only movements. It can be concluded that the found direction preference must be due to the rotation part or the combination of rotation and translation which is an interesting refinement of our earlier result.

Regarding Fitts' law, we found contradictory data since there are significant differences in performance depending on the start position and movement direction. However, Fitts' law would have predicted constant movement durations over all areas and direction. This confirms earlier works [17,23]. So we suggest to adapt Fitts' law with additional parameters to factor in the start position, the screen orientation and the direction of the movement. Our adaption of Fitts' law gives a better approximation and prediction of the expected performance although the measured time data were not involved in the modeling of the prediction formula. In our case the adapted version predicted the different performances between the directions, orientations and x-coordinates. We are aware of the fact that our extension is only the simplest approach to adapt Fitts' law, but this should demonstrate the necessary of the extension of Fitts' law to achieve usable predictions.

Finally we would like to point out that the conditions have to be extended to have a higher generalizibility of the outcomes. Possible extensions are outlined in future work (Sect. 5).

# 4    Conclusion

We presented a study to systematically explore the performance of translation movements on a multitouch display. Our results show that the performance varies significantly and with large effect size depending on surface orientation (vertical vs. horizontal), movement start point and movement direction.

We showed that horizontal screens yield the highest performance and are subjectively preferred over vertical ones. We also found specific areas where the performance outperformed other areas of the display in both conditions, vertical and horizontal. Most differences occur on the horizontal display which means that the optimization potential is higher with horizontal displays. And we could show that the direction of the movement influences performance. These findings contradict Fitts' law which predicts constant movement time over all areas and along all directions. Therefore, we suggest to extend Fitts' law using a simple linear combination that factors in display orientation, start point and direction.

In terms of ergonomics we could show that orientation influences how the user executes movements. On horizontal displays user employ shorter kinematic chains compared to movements on a vertical screen. We interpret this as a possible cause for the higher performance and the lower perceived fatigue on horizontal screens.

# 5    Future Work

Future work should investigate more in-depth the correlation between performance, perceived fatigue and the usage of shorter kinematic chains. Our experimental design could be used to examine a wider array of conditions. It would be interesting to include smaller and larger form factors like smartphones and phablets, which are often operated by thumb, or multitouch tables and large touch walls where users may have to stretch or even walk to reach certain areas. Other important aspects to consider are different postures (sitting, standing) and different screen angles (45° and others).

Additionally, we need to check whether and how handedness affects our results. It would also be interesting to look at cultural differences (e.g. different reading and writing directions).

Ultimately, our results should make it possible to generate recommendations e.g. in the form of heat maps for specific devices, and to automatically evaluate user interfaces. Future interfaces may even constantly adapt the UI layout depending on user characteristics based on results such as ours.

**Acknowledgements.** We thank Markus Pospeschill (Saarland University) for his competent advice in the user study and the data analysis. We thank Johanna Nguyen and Dat Ba Nguyen for the help in the execution of the experiments. Parts of this research have been carried out within the framework of the Softwarecampus sponsored by the German Federal Ministry of Education and Research (BMBF), grant "01IS12050".

# References

1. Accot, J., Zhai, S.: Refining fitts' law models for bivariate pointing. In: Proceedings of the SIGCHI Conference on Human Factors in Computing Systems. pp. 193–200. CHI 2003. ACM (2003)
2. Ben-Bassat, T., Meyer, J., Tractinsky, N.: Economic and subjective measures of the perceived value of aesthetics and usability. ACM Trans. Comput.-Hum. Interact. 13(2), 210–234 (2006)
3. Bi, X., Grossman, T., Matejka, J., Fitzmaurice, G.: Magic desk: bringing multi-touch surfaces into desktop work. In: Proceedings of the SIGCHI Conference on Human Factors in Computing Systems, pp. 2511–2520. CHI 2011. ACM (2011)
4. Bi, X., Li, Y., Zhai, S.: Ffitts law: modeling finger touch with fitts' law. In: Proceeding of the SIGCHI Conference on Human Factors in Computing Systems. pp. 1363–1372. CHI 2013. ACM (2013)
5. Cockburn, A., Ahlström, D., Gutwin, C.: Understanding performance in touch selections: tap, drag and radial pointing drag with finger, stylus and mouse. Int. J. Hum. Comput. Stud. 70(3), 218–233 (2012)
6. Fitts, P.M.: The information capacity of the human motor system in controlling the amplitude of movement. J. Exp. Psychol. 47, 381–391 (1954)
7. Frøkjær, E., Hertzum, M., Hornbæk, K.: Measuring usability: are effectiveness, efficiency, and satisfaction really correlated? In: Proceedings of the SIGCHI Conference on Human Factors in Computing Systems, pp. 345–352. CHI 2000. ACM (2000)
8. Hancock, M.S., Booth, K.S.: Improving menu placement strategies for pen input. In: Proceedings of Graphics Interface 2004, pp. 221–230. GI 2004. Canadian Human-Computer Communications Society (2004)
9. Hincapié-Ramos, J.D., Guo, X., Moghadasian, P., Irani, P.: Consumed endurance: a metric to quantify arm fatigue of mid-air interactions. In: Proceedings of the SIGCHI Conference on Human Factors in Computing Systems, pp. 1063–1072. CHI 2014. ACM (2014)
10. Kipp, M.: ANVIL: the video annotation research tool (Chap. 21). In: Durand, J., Gut, U., Kristoffersen, G. (eds.) The Oxford Handbook of Corpus Phonology, pp. 420–436. Oxford University Press, Oxford (2014)
11. Kipp, M., Nguyen, Q.: Multitouch puppetry: creating coordinated 3d motion for an articulated arm. In: ACM International Conference on Interactive Tabletops and Surfaces, pp. 147–156. ITS 2010. ACM (2010)
12. Langolf, G.D., Chaffin, D.B., Foulke, J.A.: An investigation of fitts' law using a wide range of movement amplitudes. J. Motor Behav. 8(2), 113–128 (1976)
13. Lee, S., Zhai, S.: The performance of touch screen soft buttons. In: Proceedings of the SIGCHI Conference on Human Factors in Computing Systems, pp. 309–318. CHI 2009. ACM (2009)
14. Loi, Daria: Ultrabooks™ and Windows 8: a *touchy* UX story. In: Marcus, Aaron (ed.) DUXU 2013, Part IV. LNCS, vol. 8015, pp. 57–66. Springer, Heidelberg (2013)
15. MacKenzie, I.S.: Fitts' law as a research and design tool in human-computer interaction. Hum.-Comput. Interact. 7(1), 91–139 (1992)
16. Moscovich, T., Hughes, J.: Multi-finger cursor techniques. In: Proceedings of Graphics Interface 2006, pp. 1–7. Canadian Information Processing Society (2006)
17. Nguyen, Q., Kipp, M.: Orientation matters: efficiency of translation-rotation multitouch tasks. In: Proceedings of the SIGCHI Conference on Human Factors in Computing Systems, pp. 2013–2016. CHI 2014. ACM (2014)

18. Nielsen, J., Levy, J.: Measuring usability: preference vs. performance. Commun. ACM **37**(4), 66–75 (1994)
19. Pedersen, E.W., Hornbæk, K.: An experimental comparison of touch interaction on vertical and horizontal surfaces. In: Proceedings of the 7th Nordic Conference on Human-Computer Interaction: Making Sense Through Design, pp. 370–379. NordiCHI 2012. ACM (2012)
20. Sasangohar, F., MacKenzie, I.S., Scott, S.D.: Evaluation of Mouse and touch input for a tabletop display using Fitts' reciprocal tapping task. In: Proceedings of the 53rd Annual Meeting of the Human Factors and Ergonomics Society HFES 2009, pp. 839–843. Human Factors and Ergonomics Society (2009)
21. Soukoreff, R.W., MacKenzie, I.S.: Towards a standard for pointing device evaluation, perspectives on 27 years of Fitts' law research in HCI. Int. J. Hum.-Comput. Stud. **61**(6), 751–789 (2004)
22. Tuch, A.N., Roth, S.P., HornbæK, K., Opwis, K., Bargas-Avila, J.A.: Is beautiful really usable? toward understanding the relation between usability, aesthetics, and affect in hci. Comput. Hum. Behav. **28**(5), 1596–1607 (2012)
23. Weiss, M., Voelker, S., Sutter, C., Borchers, J.: Benddesk: dragging across the curve. In: ACM International Conference on Interactive Tabletops and Surfaces, pp. 1–10. ITS 2010. ACM (2010)
24. Zhang, X., Zha, H., Feng, W.: Extending Fitts' law to account for the effects of movement direction on 2d pointing. In: Proceedings of the SIGCHI Conference on Human Factors in Computing Systems, pp. 3185–3194. CHI 2012. ACM, New York, NY, USA (2012)

# Enhanced Task Modelling for Systematic Identification and Explicit Representation of Human Errors

Racim Fahssi, Célia Martinie, and Philippe Palanque[✉]

Institute of Research in Informatics of Toulouse (IRIT), University Toulouse 3,
118, route de Narbonne, 31062 Toulouse Cedex 9, France
{fahssi,martinie,palanque}@irit.fr

**Abstract.** Task models produced from task analysis, are a very important element of UCD approaches as they provide support for describing users goals and users activities, allowing human factors specialists to ensure and assess the effectiveness of interactive applications. As user errors are not part of a user goal they are usually omitted from tasks descriptions. However, in the field of Human Reliability Assessment, task descriptions (including task models) are central artefacts for the analysis of human errors. Several methods (such as HET, CREAM and HERT) require task models in order to systematically analyze all the potential errors and deviations that may occur. However, during this systematic analysis, potential human errors are gathered and recorded separately and not connected to the task models. Such non integration brings issues such as completeness (i.e. ensuring that all the potential human errors have been identified) or combined errors identification (i.e. identifying deviations resulting from a combination of errors). We argue that representing human errors explicitly and systematically within task models contributes to the design and evaluation of error-tolerant interactive system. However, as demonstrated in the paper, existing task modeling notations, even those used in the methods mentioned above, do not have a sufficient expressive power to allow systematic and precise description of potential human errors. Based on the analysis of existing human error classifications, we propose several extensions to existing task modelling techniques to represent explicitly all the types of human error and to support their systematic task-based identification. These extensions are integrated within the tool-supported notation called HAMSTERS and are illustrated on a case study from the avionics domain.

## 1 Introduction

Task analysis and modelling approaches have always focused on the explicit representation of standard behavior of users, leaving user error analysis for later phases in the design processes [2]. This is part of the rationale underlying task analysis which is to provide an exhaustive analysis of user behavior describing goals and activities to reach these goals. Clearly, errors, mistakes and deviations are not part of the users' goals and thus left aside of tasks descriptions. This exhaustive aspect of task analysis is fundamental as it is meant to provide the basics for a global understanding of users

© IFIP International Federation for Information Processing 2015
J. Abascal et al. (Eds.): INTERACT 2015, Part IV, LNCS 9299, pp. 192–212, 2015.
DOI: 10.1007/978-3-319-22723-8_16

behaviors which will serve as a basis for driving evolutions of the interactive system. However, practice (for real-life applications) shows that reaching this comprehensiveness is very hard, especially as it require a vast amount of resources. If cuts have to be made when analyzing standard activities, it is clear that infrequent or abnormal behaviors are often not considered. However, this is precisely where the emphasis should be placed in order to deal efficiently with error tolerance as error prone systems deeply impact efficiency and satisfaction. Beyond these usability-related aspects, in critical systems the cost of an operator error might put people life at stake, and this is the reason why Human Reliability Assessment (HRA) methods (such as HET, CREAM or HERT) provide means for identifying human errors. Such approaches go beyond early work of Norman on typologies of human errors [20] which have then been integrated in the action theory [21]. Indeed, they are usually associated with tasks descriptions in order to relate work and goals with erroneous behaviors of operators. However, they all exploits basic task description techniques making impossible to go beyond qualitative and quantitative temporal descriptions.

In this paper we propose the use of a detailed task description technique called HAMSTERS [18] within a HRA method to support identification of errors related to information, knowledge and devices. Beyond that, we present extensions to HAMSTERS notation in order to describe identified error within the task models. Integrating errors within a task model brings multiple advantages, the most prominent being the seamless representation of activities to reach goals and possible deviations. Such integrated representation can be exploited for building effective and error avoidant interactive systems.

The paper is structured as follows. Section 2 presents the human error domain, human reliability assessment methods and task modeling. This state of the art is used to identify limitations of current HRA methods and to identify requirements for extending task models to encompass information dedicated to user errors. Section 3 presents an extended version of the HAMSTERS notation in which genotypes and phenotypes of errors enrich "standard" task models. This section also proposes a stepwise process based on Human Error Template (HET) [33] HRA method to systematically identify user errors and to represent them in task models. Section 4 shows, on a case study, how this framework can be used and what it brings to the design and verification of error-tolerant safety critical interactive systems. Section 5 highlights benefits and limitations of the approach while Sect. 6 concludes the paper and presents future work.

## 2 Related Work on Human Error and Task Modelling

Human error has received a lot of attention over the years and this section aims at presenting the main concepts related to human errors as well as the existing approaches for analyzing them. This related work section starts with the analysis of taxonomies of human errors followed by processes and methods for **identifying human errors** in socio-technical systems. Last sub-section summarizes work on **representing human errors** with a specific focus on representations based on task description.

## 2.1    Definition and Taxonomies of Human Errors

Several contributions in the human factors domain deal with studying internal human processes that may lead to actions that can be perceived as erroneous from an external view point. In the 1970s, Norman, Rasmussen and Reason have proposed theoretical frameworks to analyze human error. Norman, proposed a predictive model for errors [20], where the concept of "slip" is highlighted and causes of error are rooted in improper activation of patterns of action. Rasmussen proposes a model of human performance which distinguishes three levels: skills, rules and knowledge (SRK model) [28]. This model provides support for reasoning about possible human errors and has been used to classify error types. Reason [30] takes advantages of the contributions of Norman and Rasmussen, and distinguishes three main categories of errors:

1. Skill-based errors are related to the skill level of performance in SRK. These errors can be of one of the 2 following types: (a) Slip, or routine error, which is defined as a mismatch between an intention and an action [20]; (b) Lapse which is defined as a memory failure that prevents from executing an intended action.
2. Rule-based mistakes are related to the rule level of performance in SRK and are defined as the application of an inappropriate rule or procedure.
3. Knowledge-based errors are related to the knowledge level in SRK and are defined as an inappropriate usage of knowledge, or a lack of knowledge or corrupted knowledge preventing from correctly executing a task.

At the same time, Reason proposed a model of human performance called GEMS [30] (Generic Error Modelling System), which is also based on the SRK model and dedicated to the representation of human error mechanisms. GEMS is a conceptual framework that embeds a detailed description of the potential causes for each error types above. These causes are related to various models of human performance. For example, a perceptual confusion error in GEMS is related to the perceptual processor of the Human Processor model [5]. GEMS is very detailed in terms of description and vocabulary (e.g. strong habit intrusion, capture errors, overshooting a stop rule …) and structuring approaches have been proposed as the Human Error Reference Table (HERT) in [22].

Causes of errors and their observation are different concepts that should be separated when analyzing user errors. To do so, Hollnagel [9] proposed a terminology based on 2 main concepts: phenotype and genotype. The phenotype of an error is defined as the erroneous action that can be observed. The genotype of the error is defined as the characteristics of the operator that may contribute to the occurrence of an erroneous action.

These concepts and the classifications above provide support for reasoning about human errors and have been widely used to develop approaches to design and evaluate interactive systems [31]. As pointed out in [23] investigating the association between a phenotype and its potential genotypes is very difficult but is an important step in order to assess the error-proneness of an interactive system. This is why most of the approaches for Human Reliability Assessment focus on this double objective, as presented in next section.

## 2.2   Techniques and Methods for Identifying Human Errors

Many techniques have been proposed for identifying which human errors may occur in a particular context and what could be their consequences in this given context. Several human reliability assessment techniques such as CREAM [10], HEART [39], and THERP [34] are based on task analysis. They provide support to assess the possibility of occurrence of human errors by structuring the analysis around task descriptions. Beyond these commonalities, THERP technique provides support for assessing the probability of occurrence of human errors. Table 1 presents an overview on the existing techniques for identifying potential human errors. For each technique, the following information is highlighted:

- Type of technique: to indicate to which scientific domain this technique is related. Values can be HEI (Human Error Identification), DC (Dependable Computing), SA (Safety Analysis) ...
- Associated task modelling technique: to indicate how the user tasks are described once the task analysis has been performed. Most of them exploit HTA (Hierarchical Task Analysis notation) [1];
- Tool support for task analysis and modelling: to indicate whether or not a particular Computer Aided Software Environment (CASE) tool is available to provide support for the application of the technique;
- Associated error classification: to indicate which human error classification is used to identify possible errors. 'G' and 'S' indicates whether the classification comes from a generic system failures analysis or whether it is specific to human errors;
- Capacity to deal with combination of errors: to indicate whether or not the techniques provides explicit support for identifying possible combinations of errors. Here only 2 values are possible: 'No' and 'NE' (Not Explicitly meaning that the method was not claiming explicitly that combinations of errors are handled).

For all the techniques presented above the process of identifying possible human errors highly relies on the user tasks descriptions. The task descriptions have to be precise, complete and representative of the user activities, in order to be able to identify all the possible errors. Indeed, the task description language as well as the mean to produce the description affect the quality of the analysis. However, most of them exploit Hierarchical Task Analysis (HTA) which only provides support for decomposing user goals into tasks and subtasks and for describing the sequential relationships between these tasks (in a separate textual representation called "plan"). As HTA does not provide support for describing precisely the types of user actions, the temporal ordering types that are different from a sequence of actions (such as concurrent actions, order independent actions...), as well as information and knowledge required to perform an action, errors related to these elements cannot be identified. Furthermore, as most of these techniques do not have tool support it is cumbersome to check coverage of and to store identified errors in a systematic way. For example, as HTA does not provide support for describing knowledge required to perform a task, none of these methods provide explicit support for the identification of all possible knowledge-based mistakes.

**Table 1.** Summary of techniques and methods used for identifying human errors

| Name of the technique | Type of technique | Task modelling | Tool support | Associated error classification (generic/specific) | | Combination of errors |
|---|---|---|---|---|---|---|
| Hazard and operability study (HAZOP) [15] | Safety analysis | HTA | None | Not done, less, more, as well as, other than, repeated, sooner, later, misordered, part of | G | NE |
| Systematic human error reduction and prediction approach (SHERPA) [7] | HEI, HRA | HTA | None | Action errors, checking errors, communication errors, info retrieval errors, selection errors | S | No |
| Potential human error cause analysis (PHECA) [38] | HEI, HRA | HTA | None | HAZOP classification | G | NE |
| Cognitive reliability and error analysis method (CREAM) [10] | HEI, HRA | HTA | None | Timing, duration, sequence, object, force, direction, distance, speed | S | NE |
| Human error assessment and reduction technique (HEART) [39] | HEI, HRA | HTA | None | None (concrete description of the human error) | S | NE |
| Human error identification in systems tool (HEIST) [13] | HEI, HRA | HTA | None | Skill rule knowledge model | S | NE |
| Human error template (HET) [33] | HEI, Human factors | HTA | None | *Fail to execute*: task execution incomplete, task executed in the wrong direction, wrong task executed, task repeated, task executed on the wrong interface element, *Task executed*: too early/too late/too much/too little, misread information, other | S | No |
| System for predictive error analysis and reduction (SPEAR) [35] | HEI, HRA, SA | HTA | None | Action, retrieval, check, selection, transmission | G | No |
| Task analysis for error identification (TAFEI) [2] | HEI, HF | HTA | None | Generic categories | S | NE |

(*Continued*)

**Table 1.** (Continued)

| Name of the technique | Type of technique | Task modelling | Tool support | Associated error classification (generic/specific) | Combination of errors |
|---|---|---|---|---|---|
| Technique for human error assessment (THEA) [27] | HEI, HCI | HTA | None | Goals, plans, performing actions, perception, interpretation and evaluation | S | NE |
| Human error recovery and assessment (HERA) [14] | HEI HRA | HTA | None | Omission, timing, sequence, quality, selection error, information transmission error, rule violation, other | S | No |
| Tech. for human error precision rate (THERP) [34] | HRA | Not specified | None | Omission, commission, selection error, error of sequence, time error, qualitative error | S | No |
| Tech. for the retrospective and predictive analysis of cognitive errors in air traffic control (TRACer) [32] | HEI HRA | HTA | None | Selection and quality Timing and sequence Communication | S | No |
| Task model-based systematic analysis of system failures and human errors [17] | HCI, DC | HAMSTERS | HAMSTERS | HAZOP and reason classifications | G | NE |

## 2.3    Support for Representation of Human Errors in Task Model

As explained above the expressive power of the task modelling notation has a direct impact on how task models produced with these notation are likely to support the identification of errors. Many task modelling notations have been proposed over the years focusing on the representation of standard user behaviors most of the time leaving aside erroneous behaviors.

Table 2 presents a comparison of task modelling notations to assess (depending on their expressive power) their capability in identifying and representing human errors. For each notation, the following information is highlighted:

- Identification of human error: to indicate whether or not the notation provides support to systematically establish a relationship between a task model element and a component of a model of human information processing or model of human performance.
- Explicit representation of human error: to indicate whether or not the notation provides support to systematically represent human error related information in a task model.
- Explicit representation of error recovery: to indicate whether or not the notation provides support to explicitly represent recovery tasks i.e. when an error has occurred, to describe the set of actions to be performed in order to still reach the goal. While this is possible in most task modelling notations (e.g. set of action to perform after entering a wrong PIN when using a cash machine) we identify here the fact that the notation makes explicit (or not) that this set of task is related to a user error.

Even though the content in Table 2 demonstrates the very limited account of error handling in task modeling notation, task models have already been used to take into account possible human errors while interacting with an interactive system. Paterno and Santoro proposed a model-based technique that uses insertion of deviated human actions into task models in order to evaluate the usability of the system and to inform design [25], however, such information is presented in tables outside of the task models. This approach is relevant for human error identification but only in generic terms (as it exploits HAZOP which is a standard hazard analysis method). Palanque and Basnyat proposed a technique based on task patterns (represented in CTT) that supports human routine errors [22] description. Here a specific task model is produced in which recovery actions following errors are explicitly represented, thus ending up with two un-connected task model. Modification in one of the task model has then to be reflected in the other one increasing complexity of task modelling activities. In both contributions, no specific element of the notation are introduced thus leaving the contributions to basic task elements provided in CTT notation (and thus not covering errors related to information, knowledge … as presented above).

In order to overcome the limitations of the current task modelling notations, next section presents extensions to the HAMSTERS notation to specifically represent errors. While the extensions are made explicit on that particular task modelling technique, the underlying concepts are generic making them applicable to others.

**Table 2.** Support for describing errors and errors-related elements

| | Element of representation | CTT [27] | COMM [12] | GOMS [4] | GTA [41] | HAMSTERS [22] | HTA [1] | SAMANTA [42] | TKS [11] |
|---|---|---|---|---|---|---|---|---|---|
| Identification of human error | Representation of refined user tasks | No | No | No | No | Yes | No | No | No |
| | Representation of declarative knowledge | No | No | No | No | Yes | No | Yes | Yes |
| | Representation of manipulated information | No | No | No | No | Yes | No | Yes | No |
| Explicit representation of human error | Representation of cause and observable consequence of errors (Genotype, Phenotype) | No | No | No | No | No | No | No | No |
| | Representation of skill based errors (Slips, Lapse) | No | No | No | No | No | No | No | No |
| | Representation of rule based mistakes | No | No | No | No | No | No | No | No |
| | Representation of knowledge based mistakes | No | No | No | No | No | No | No | No |
| Explicit representation of error recovery | | No | No | No | No | No | No | No | No |

# 3   Extending a Task Modelling Notation to Support the Identification and Representation of Human Errors

This section presents the extensions that have been added to the HAMSTERS notation in order to provide support for systematic identification and representation of human errors in task models. We also present how this extended notation has been integrated within a human error identification technique. This process starts with an extant task model and extends it with explicit genotypes and phenotypes of errors.

## 3.1   HAMSTERS Notation

HAMSTERS (Human – centered Assessment and Modeling to Support Task Engineering for Resilient Systems) is a tool-supported graphical task modeling notation for representing human activities in a hierarchical and structured way. At the higher abstraction level, goals can be decomposed into sub-goals, which can in turn be decomposed into activities. Output of this decomposition is a graphical tree of nodes that can be tasks or temporal operators. Tasks can be of several types (depicted in Table 3) and contain information such as a name, information details, and criticality level. Only the single user high-level task types are presented here but they can be further refined. For instance the cognitive tasks can be refined in Analysis and Decision tasks [19] and collaborative activities can be refined in several task types [16].

**Table 3.** Task types in HAMSTERS

|  | Abstract | Input | Output | I/O | Processing |
|---|---|---|---|---|---|
| **Abstract** | Abstract | Not Applicable | Not Applicable | Not Applicable | Not Applicable |
| **User** | User abstract | Perceptive | Motor | User | Cognitive |
| **Interactive** | Abstract interactive | Input | Output | Input/Output | Not Applicable |
| **System** | Abstract system | Output | Input | Input/Output | System |

Temporal operators (depicted in Table 4 and similar to the ones in CTT) are used to represent temporal relationships between sub-goals and between activities. Tasks can also be tagged by properties to indicate whether or not they are iterative, optional or both. The HAMSTERS notation is supported by a CASE tool for edition and simulation of models. This tool has been introduced in order to provide support for task system integration at the tool level [16]. This tool supported notation also provides support for structuring a large number and complex set of tasks introducing the

**Table 4.** Illustration of the operator type within hamsters

| Operator type | Symbol | Description |
|---|---|---|
| Enable | T1≫T2 | T2 is executed after T1 |
| Concurrent | T1\|\|\|T2 | T1 and T2 are executed at the same time |
| Choice | T1[]T2 | T1 is executed OR T2 is executed |
| Disable | T1[>T2 | Execution of T2 interrupts the execution of T1 |
| Suspend-resume | T1\|>T2 | Execution of T2 interrupts the execution of T1, T1 execution is resumed after T2 |
| Order Independent | T1\|=\| T2 | T1 is executed then T2 OR T2 is executed then T1 |

mechanism of subroutines [19], sub-models and components [8]. Such structuring mechanisms allow describing large and complex activities by means of task models. These structuring mechanisms enables the breakdown of a task model in several ones that can be reused in the same or different task models.

HAMSTERS expressive power goes beyond most other task modeling notations particularly by providing detailed means for describing data that is required and manipulated [16] in order to accomplish tasks. Figure 1 summarizes the notation elements to represent data. Information ("Inf:" followed by a text box) may be required for execution of a system task, but it also may be required by the user to accomplish a task. Physical objects required for performing a task can also be represented ("Phy O") as well as the device (input and/or output) with which the task is performed ("i/o D"). Declarative and situational knowledge can also be made explicit by the "SiK" and "StK" elements.

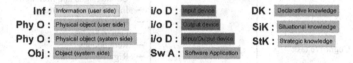

**Fig. 1.**  Representation of objects, information and knowledge with HAMSTERS notation

### 3.2  HAMSTERS Notation Elements and Relationship with Genotypes

All of the above notation elements are required to be able to systematically identify and represent human errors within task models. Indeed, some genotypes (i.e. causes of human errors) can only occur with a specific type of task or with a specific element in a task model described using HAMSTERS. This relationship between classification of genotypes in human error models and task modelling elements is not trivial. For this reason, Table 5 presents the correspondences between HAMSTERS notation elements and error genotypes from the GEMS classification [29]. Such a correspondence is very useful for identifying potential genotypes on an extant task model.

It is important to note that strategic and situational knowledge elements are not present in this table. Indeed, such constructs are similar to the M (Methods) in GOMS and thus correspond to different ways of reaching a goal. As all the methods allow users to reach the goal an error cannot be made at that level and is thus not connected to a genotype.

### 3.3  Extensions to HAMSTERS to Describe User Errors

Several notation elements have been added to HAMSTERS in order to allow explicit representation of both genotypes and phenotypes of errors. Table 6 summarizes these notation elements that can be used to describe an observable consequence of an error (phenotype) and its potential associated causes (genotypes).

In that table the first column lists the types of errors following GEMS classification. The second column makes the connection with the SRK classification as previously

**Table 5.** Correspondence between HAMSTERS elements and genotypes from GEMS [29]

| Element of notation in HAMSTERS | Related genotype from GEMS [32] | |
|---|---|---|
| Perceptive task | Perceptual confusion (Skill Based Error) Interference error (Skill Based Error) | |
| Input task Motor task | Interference error (Skill Based Error) Double capture slip (Skill Based Error) Omissions following interruptions (Skill Based Error) | |
| Cognitive task | Skill based errors | — Double capture slip<br>— Omissions following interruptions<br>— Reduced intentionality<br>— Interference error<br>— Over-attention errors |
| | Rule based mistakes | Misapplication of good rules<br>— First exceptions<br>— Countersigns and non-signs<br>— Informational overload<br>— Rule strength<br>— General rules<br>— Redundancy<br>— Rigidity<br>Application of bad rules<br>— Encoding deficiencies<br>— Action deficiencies |
| | Knowledge based mistakes | — Selectivity<br>— Workspace limitations<br>— Out of sight out of mind<br>— Confirmation bias<br>— Overconfidence<br>— Biased reviewing<br>— Illusory correlation<br>— Halo effects<br>— Problems with causality<br>— Problems with complexity |
| Information **Inf :** Information | Double capture slip, Omissions following interruptions, Interference error, all of the Rule Based Mistakes and Knowledge Based Mistakes | |
| Declarative knowledge **DK :** Declarative | All of the Knowledge Based Mistakes | |

performed in [29]. Third column present the new notation elements in HAMSTERS for describing genotypes of errors as well as how they relate to the classifications on human error. Four new elements are added: Slips, Lapses, Rule-Based Mistakes and Knowledge-Based Mistakes. As for phenotypes only one notation element is proposed. Indeed, the phenotype (i.e. how the errors is made visible) only need to be explicitly represented, the label beneath it providing a textual description while its relationship to the causes is made by connecting genotypes to it. Such connections will be presented in details in the case study section.

**Table 6.** Representation of genotypes and phenotypes in HAMSTERS

| Type of error (GEMS [32]) | Level of Performance from [31] | Representation of genotype in HAMSTERS | Representation of phenotype in HAMSTERS |
|---|---|---|---|
| Slip | Skill-based | Slip | |
| Lapse | | Lapse | |
| Mistake | Rule-based | RBM | |
| | Knowledge-based | KBM | |

## 3.4    Modelling Process

In this section, we show how we have integrated HAMSTERS extended notation with the HET [33] technique. HAMSTERS could be used to replace HTA in any other human error identification method based on task description, but we have chosen HET because it provides a detailed process and because it has been demonstrated in [33] to be more accurate than other techniques such as SHERPA and HAZOP [15].

Figure 2 presents a modified version of the HET process and provides support for identifying genotypes and phenotypes of possible human errors by embedding error descriptions in the task models that have been produced to describe user activities. The extended process starts with a task analysis and description phase (as for the original HET one), but in our case the produced task models are refined to represent perceptive, cognitive and motor user tasks as well as information and knowledge required to perform the tasks. These models take full advantage of the expressive power of HAMSTERS that has been presented in Sect. 3. All the modifications made with respect to the original process have been made explicit by using various shades of grey.

Next step in the process exploits the task type–genotypes correspondence table (Table 5), to provide support for systematic identification of genotypes associated to perceptive, cognitive, motor and interactive input tasks, but also to the related phenotypes. The likelihood and criticality of a genotype are inserted as properties of the instance of represented genotype. This is performed in HAMSTERS tool by specific properties associated to the genotypes icons. Similarly, likelihood and criticality of a phenotype can also be described using properties of the instance of a represented phenotype. Likelihood of a phenotype may be a combination of likelihood of related genotypes. Once all of the possible genotypes and phenotypes have been identified and described in the task model, the human error identification and representation technique is applied to the next task model. Once all of the models have been analyzed, a last step is performed (see bottom left activity in Fig. 2) in order to determine, for each task model that embeds human error descriptions, which phenotypes may be propagated to other task models. Several phenotypes may be associated to an observable task, but not all of them may happen in a particular scenario.

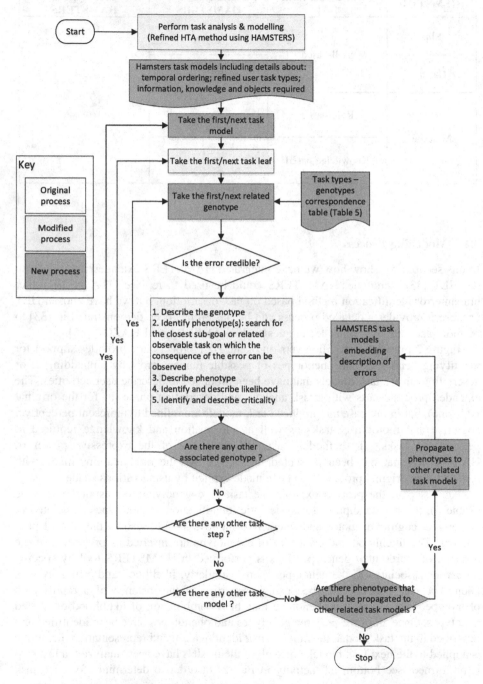

**Fig. 2.** Human error identification and description process extended from HET [33]

# 4  Illustrative Example from an Avionics Case Study

This section presents an excerpt of task models produced by the application of the process presented above for identification and representation to a case study. The case study belongs to the aeronautics domain and more precisely deals with pilot tasks exploiting a weather radar cockpit application. This section aims at illustrating how the HAMSTERS extensions can be applied to human operations on a real-life application. Due to space constraints, the application of all new elements of notation are not shown in this article but most of them are.

## 4.1  Presentation of the Weather Radar Case Study

Weather radar (WXR) is an application currently deployed in many cockpits of commercial aircrafts. It provides support to pilots' activities by increasing their awareness of meteorological phenomena during the flight journey, allowing them to determine if they may have to request a trajectory change, in order to avoid adverse weather conditions such as storms or precipitations. In this case study, we particularly focus on the tasks that have to be performed by a pilot to check the weather conditions on the current flight path.

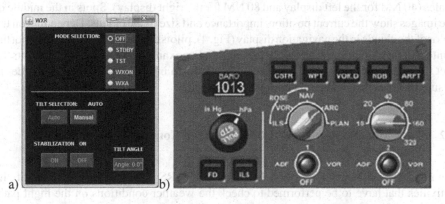

a)                                           b)

**Fig. 3.**  Image of (a) the numeric part of weather radar control panel (b) physical manipulation of the range of the weather radar

Figure 3 presents a screenshot of the weather radar control panels, used to operate the weather radar application. These panels provides two functionalities to the crew. The first one is dedicated to the mode selection of weather radar and provides information about status of the radar, in order to ensure that the weather radar can be set up correctly. The operation of changing from one mode to another can be performed in the upper part of the panel (mode selection section).

The second functionality, available in the lower part of the window, is dedicated to the adjustment of the weather radar orientation (Tilt angle). This can be done in an automatic way or manually (Auto/manual buttons). Additionally, a stabilization function aims to keep the radar beam stable even in case of turbulences. The right-hand part of Fig. 3 (labelled "(b)") presents an image of the controls used to configure radar display, particularly to set up the range scale (right-hand side knob with ranges 20, 40, … nautical miles).

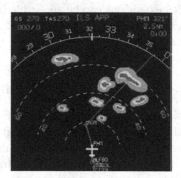

**Fig. 4.** Screenshots of weather radar displays (Color figure online)

Figure 4 shows screenshots of weather radar displays according to two different range scales (40 NM for the left display and 80 NM for the right display). Spots in the middle of the images show the current position, importance and size of the clouds. Depending on the color of the clouds in the navigation display (Fig. 4), pilots can determine whether or not the content of the clouds is dangerous for the aircraft. For example, the red color highlights the fact that the clouds contain heavy precipitations. Such information is needed in order to ensure that the current or targeted flight plan are safe.

### 4.2    Task Model of the Task "Check Weather Conditions on the Flight Path"

Figure 5 presents the description, with HAMSTERS elements of notation, of the activities that have to be performed to check the weather conditions on the flight path.

The tasks presented in this model describe how the pilot builds a mental model of the current weather from information gathered on the navigation display (Fig. 4). For a pilot, checking weather conditions is very important as it provides support for deciding to maintain or change the current trajectory of the aircraft. This task is decomposed into 3 sub tasks:

- "Examine Map": the pilot perceives and examines the radar image of the weather, which is displayed on the navigation display (see Fig. 4). To perform this analysis, the pilot has to know the meaning of the weather representations (described with declarative knowledge notation elements in Fig. 5 such as "Green light clouds mean precipitation").

- "Manage WXR control panel": This sub task is represented by a subroutine, and linked to another task model, which describes the tasks that have to be performed to control the WXR modes.
- "Manage Display Range": This sub task describes the actions that have to be performed by the pilot in order to change the range of the WXR display with using the physical knob "range" (illustrated in Fig. 3b). The pilot has to turn the knob to modify the range, and then to wait for the radar image to be refreshed on the navigation display (Fig. 4).

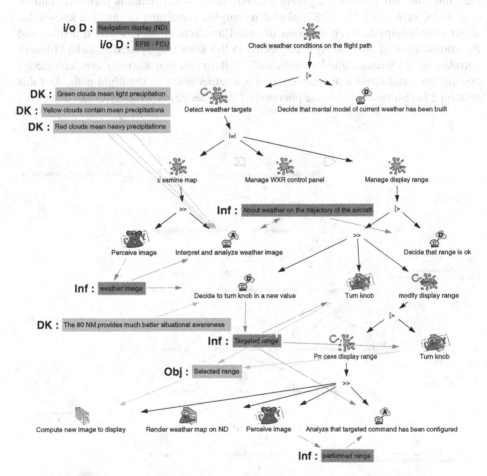

**Fig. 5.** Task model of the "Check weather conditions on the flight path" task (Color figure online)

## 4.3 Task Model with Human Errors

Figure 6 presents a modified version of the "Check weather conditions on the flight path" task model. This new version embeds the descriptions of possible human errors (genotype and phenotypes) which have been identified while applying the human error identification process.

Each human task and interactive input task is connected to one (or several) genotype(s), indicating possible cause(s) of errors. Genotypes are then connected to phenotypes, which are the observable consequences of the errors. For example, the "Perceive image" perception task is connected to the genotype "Perceptual confusion: image badly or not perceived" (zoomed in view in Fig. 7). This genotype is also connected to the phenotype "Weather target wrongly or not detected". In the same way, the "Interpret and analyze" cognitive analysis task, which requires particular knowledge to be performed (the "DK" labeled rectangles containing declarative knowledge about relationships between the color of visual artefacts in the navigation display and the composition of the clouds) is connected to the knowledge based mistake "Illusory correlation: No weather problem detected". This means that a wrong user knowledge association could cause a non-detection of a weather issue on the flight path. And this genotype is also connected to the phenotype "Weather target wrongly or not detected".

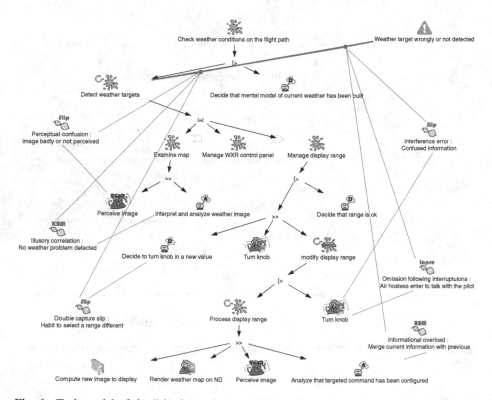

**Fig. 6.** Task model of the "check weather conditions on the flight path" task embedding the description of potential errors

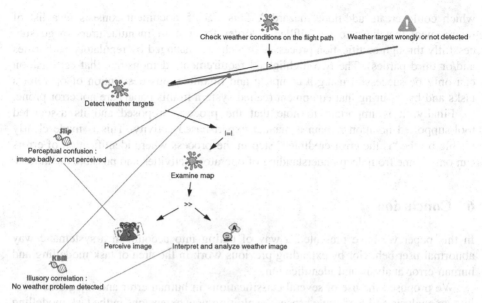

**Fig. 7.** "Examine map" sub-task of the "check weather conditions on the flight path" task embedding the description of potential errors

## 5 Benefits and Limitations of the Approach

The stepwise refinement process of task models presented in Sect. 3.4 and its application to the case study in Sect. 4 have demonstrated the possibility to exploit the extended version of HAMSTERS to support identification and description of operator errors on an existing task model.

While this is critical in order to identify parts in a system that might be error prone or parts in the system that are not tolerant to operators errors it is also true that the task models enriched with error artefacts are gathering a lot of information that might decrease their understandability and modifiability. We currently favor the expressiveness of the notation and of the resulting task models than legibility and understandability. These two aspects are currently being addressed at tool level providing multiple filtering mechanisms for hiding (in a temporary way) information that the analyst is not focusing on. For instance, all the information elements can be hidden, as the genotypes and the phenotypes if the current activity is to focus on sequencing of tasks.

The main objective of the approach is to support redesign activities when error prone designs have been identified. Such redesign would take place through an iterative design process involving co-evolution of tasks and systems as presented in [3] but development costs are clearly increased. This is the reason why such an approach would be also useful for supporting certification activities in critical systems. For instance, as stated in [6] CS25-1302 annex E 1-F-1, "Flight deck controls must be installed to allow accomplishment of these tasks and information necessary to accomplish these tasks must be provided" and in CS 25-1309 "stems and controls, including indications and annunciations must be designed to minimize crew errors, which could create additional hazards". This CS 25 document consists in a list of requirement that have to be fulfilled in order for aircraft manufacturers to go successfully through certification processes (which are managed by regulatory authorities and/or third parties). The two highlighted requirements demonstrate that certification can only be successful using a complete and unambiguous description of operator's tasks and by ensuring that equipment (called system in this paper) are not error prone.

Finally, it is important to note that the process proposed and its associated tool-supported notation remain a manual expert-based activity. This is made clearly visible by the "is the error credible?" step in the process where identification of errors can only come from deep understanding of operators activities and possible deviations.

# 6 Conclusion

In this paper we have presented a way of taking into account in a systematic way abnormal user behavior by extending previous work in the area of task modelling and human error analysis and identification.

We proposed the use of several classifications in human error and integrated them into an analysis and modelling process exploiting new extensions in the task modelling notation HAMSTERS. These extensions make it possible to explicitly represent genotypes and phenotypes of operator errors and to describe their relationships.

These contributions have been applied to a real-life case study in the field of aeronautics demonstrating most of the aspects of the contributions. However, errors related to strategic knowledge and errors related to temporal ordering (e.g. the task model describes a sequence of tasks but the operator performs them in parallel) were not presented even though covered by the approach.

As identified in "Benefits and Limitations" section, this work targets at supporting certification activities for critical systems and more precisely cockpits of large aircrafts. However, thanks to the tool support provided by HAMSTERS (which make human error identification and description less resource consuming) the approach is also applicable to other domains where errors are damaging, in terms of human life, economics, prestige, trust ...

# References

1. Annett, J.: Hierarchical task analysis. In: Hollnagel, E. (ed.) Handbook of Cognitive Task Design, pp. 17–35. Erlbaum, Mahwah (2003)
2. Baber, C., Stanton, N.A.: Task analysis for error identification: a methodology for designing error-tolerant consumer products. Ergonomics 37(11), 1923–1941 (1994)
3. Barboni, E., Ladry, J.-F., Navarre, D., Palanque, P., Winckler, M.: Beyond modelling: an integrated environment supporting co-execution of tasks and systems models. In: ACM SIGCHI conference Engineering Interactive Computing Systems. EICS 2010, pp. 165–174. ACM, DL
4. Card, S.K., Newell, A., Moran, T.P.: The psychology of human-computer interaction. Lawrence Erlbaum Associates, USA (1983)

5. Card, S., Moran, T., Newell, A.: The Model Human Processor: An Engineering Model of Human Performance. Wiley, New York (1986)
6. EASA CS 25: Certification for Large Aeroplanes (2007). http://www.easa.europa.eu/agency-measures/certification-specifications.php#CS-25
7. Embrey, D.E.: SHERPA: a systematic human error reduction and prediction approach. In: International Topical Meeting on Advances in Human Factors in Nuclear Power Systems (1986)
8. Forbrig, P., Martinie, C., Palanque, P., Winckler, M., Fahssi, R.: Rapid task-models development using sub-models, sub-routines and generic components. In: Sauer, S., Bogdan, C., Forbrig, P., Bernhaupt, R., Winckler, M. (eds.) HCSE 2014. LNCS, vol. 8742, pp. 144–163. Springer, Heidelberg (2014)
9. Hollnagel, E.: The phenotype of erroneous actions implications for HCI design. In: Weir, G. R.S., Alty, J.L. (eds.) Human Computer Interaction and the Complex Systems. Academic Press, London (1991)
10. Erik, H.: Cognitive Reliability and Error Analysis Method (CREAM). Elsevier, Oxford (1998)
11. Johnson, H., Johnson, P.: Task knowledge structures: psychological basis and integration into system design. Acta Psychol. 78(1), 3–26 (1991)
12. Jourde, F., Laurillau, Y., Nigay, L.: COMM notation for specifying collaborative and multimodal interactive systems. In: Proceedings of the 2nd ACM SIGCHI Symposium on Engineering Interactive Computing Systems, pp. 125–134. ACM (2010)
13. Kirwan, B.: A Guide to Practical Human Reliability Assessment. CRC Press, London (1994)
14. Kirwan, B.: Human Error Recovery and Assessment (HERA) Guide. Project IMC/GNSR/HF/5011, Industrial Ergonomics Group, School of Manufacturing Engineering, University of Birmingham, March 1996
15. Kletz, T.: HAZOP and HAZAN - Notes on the Identification and Assessment of Hazards. Institute of Chemical Engineers, Rugby (1974)
16. Martinie, C., Barboni, E., Navarre, D., Palanque, P., Fahssi, R., Poupart, E., Cubero-Castan, E.: Multi-models-based engineering of collaborative systems: application to collision avoidance operations for spacecraft. In: Proceedings of EICS 2014, pp. 85–94
17. Martinie, C., Palanque, P., Fahssi, R., Blanquart, J.-P., Fayollas, C., Seguin, C.: Task models based systematic analysis of both system failures and human errors. IEEE Transactions on Human Machine Systems, Special Issue on Systematic Approaches to Human-Machine Interface: Improving Resilience, Robustness, and Stability (to appear)
18. Martinie, C., Palanque, P., Ragosta, M., Fahssi, R.: Extending procedural task models by systematic explicit integration of objects, knowledge and information. In: Proceedings of the 31st European Conference on Cognitive Ergonomics, p. 23. ACM (2013)
19. Martinie, C., Palanque, P., Winckler, M.: Structuring and composition mechanisms to address scalability issues in task models. In: Campos, P., Graham, N., Jorge, J., Nunes, N., Palanque, P., Winckler, M. (eds.) INTERACT 2011, Part III. LNCS, vol. 6948, pp. 589–609. Springer, Heidelberg (2011)
20. Norman, D.A.: Categorization of action slips. Psychol. Rev. 88(1), 1 (1981)
21. Norman, D.A.: The Psychology of Everyday Things. Basic Book, New York (1988)
22. Palanque, P., Basnyat, S.: Task patterns for taking into account in an efficient and systematic way both standard and erroneous user behaviours. In: Proceedings of International Conference on Human Error, Safety and System Development (HESSD), pp. 109–130 (2004)
23. Papatzanis, G., Curzon, P., Blandford, A.: Identifying phenotypes and genotypes: a case study evaluating an in-car navigation system. In: Gulliksen, J., Harning, M.B., Palanque, P., Veer, G.C., Wesson, J. (eds.) EIS 2007. LNCS, vol. 4940, pp. 227–242. Springer, Heidelberg (2008)

24. Paternò, F., Mancini, C., Meniconi, S.: ConcurTaskTrees: a diagrammatic notation for specifying task models. In: Human-Computer Interaction INTERACT 1997, pp. 362–369. Springer US (1997)

25. Paterno, F., Santoro, C.: Preventing user errors by systematic analysis of deviations from the system task model. Int. J. Hum. Comput. Syst. **56**(2), 225–245 (2002)

26. Phipps, D.L., Meakin, G.H., Beatty, P.C.: Extending hierarchical task analysis to identify cognitive demands and information design requirements. Appl. Ergon. **42**(5), 741–748 (2011)

27. Pocock, S., Harrison, M., Wright, P., Johnson, P.: THEA: a technique for human error assessment early in design. In: Human-Computer Interaction: INTERACT, vol. 1, pp. 247–254 (2001)

28. Rasmussen, J.: Skills, rules, knowledge: signals, signs and symbols and other distinctions in human performance models. IEEE Trans. Syst. Man Cybern. **13**, 257–267 (1983)

29. Reason J.: Human Error. Cambridge University Press, New York (1990)

30. Reason, J.T.: Generic error modelling system: a cognitive framework for locating common human error forms. New Technol. Hum. Error **63**, 86 (1987)

31. Rizzo, A., Ferrante, D., Bagnara, S.: Handling human error. In: Hoc, J.M., Cacciabue, P.C. (eds.) Expertise and Technology: Cognition & Human-Computer Cooperation, pp. 195–212. Lawrence Erlbaum Associates, Hillsdale (1995)

32. Shorrock, S.T., Kirwan, B.: Development and application of a human error identification tool for air traffic control. Appl. Ergon. **33**(4), 319–336 (2002)

33. Stanton, N.A., Harris, D., Salmon, P.M., Demagalski, J., Marshall, A., Waldmann, T., Dekker, S., Young, M.S.: Predicting design induced error in the cockpit. J. Aeronaut. Astronaut. Aviat. **42**(1), 001–010 (2010)

34. Swain, A.D., Guttman, H.E.: Handbook of human reliability analysis with emphasis on nuclear power plant applications. Final report. NUREG/CR- 1278. SAND80-0200. RX, AN. US Nuclear Regulatory Commission, August 1983

35. The Center for Chemical Process Safety: Guidelines for Preventing Human Error in Process Safety. American Institute of Chemical Engineers, New York (1994)

36. Van Der Veer, G.C., Lenting, B.F., Bergevoet, B.A.: GTA: groupware task analysis—modeling complexity. Acta Psychol. **91**(3), 297–322 (1996)

37. Villaren, T., Coppin, G., Leal, A.: Modeling task transitions to help designing for better situation awareness. In: ACM SIGCHI EICS Conference, pp. 195–204 (2012)

38. Whailey, S.P.: Minimising the cause of human error. In: Libberton, G.P. (ed.) Proceedings of l0th Advances in Reliability Technology Symposium. Elsevier, London (1988)

39. Williams, J.C.: A data-based method for assessing and reducing human error to improve operational performance. In: Human Factors and Power Plants, pp. 436–450. IEEE (1988)

40. Zapf, D., Reason, J.T.: Introduction: human errors and error handling. Appl. Psychol. Int. Rev. **43**(4), 427–432 (1994)

# EvolutionWorks

## Towards Improved Visualization of Citation Networks

Jason Wilkins[✉], Jaakko Järvi, Ajit Jain, Gaurav Kejriwal,
Andruid Kerne, and Vijay Gumudavelly

Texas A&M University, 3112 TAMU, College Station, TX 77843-3112, USA
jwilkins@tamu.edu

**Abstract.** *EvolutionWorks* supports exploratory browsing of the academic paper citation network with an animated and zoom-able visualization that helps researchers explore the conceptual space that emerges from the relationships between academic papers. Metaphorically speaking, a researcher starts out with the *seed* of an idea that will *grow* into an unwieldy set of potentially useful papers that the researcher must *prune* into a final reading list. Accordingly, EvolutionWorks provides novel affordances to explore the citation network based on this *seed-grow-prune* model. First, *kinetic layering* represents abstract document properties as physical properties in a force-directed layout. Second, a *unified layout* shows the network graph and documents in a single view. Third, the *focus-context-focus hop* is a way to change focus from paper to paper that keeps researchers aware of the immediate context. Finally, if there is a tight cluster of papers, the system automatically creates *cluster summary titles* that are easier to read.

**Keywords:** Citation networks · Graph visualization · Information retrieval

## 1 Introduction

Making sense out of the body of academic literature is a challenge. In this paper, we treat the literature primarily as a *citation network*. The citation network is a large conceptual space embodied in the complex hypertext constructed from all the various connections between academic research papers—such as references, citations, or shared authorship. Although interactive visual presentations of graphs can aid people who need to explore and comprehend complex data [1–3], like the academic literature, only a few experimental search tools currently take advantage of such presentations. More often, open public access catalogs and web-based search tools have user interfaces that unimaginatively present users with pages of text full of hyperlinks. A specific problem is that tools present search results primarily as text, which fails to take advantage of most *retinal variables* [4] (size, color, value, shape, etc.), so the amount of information they can convey about the relationships between research papers is

Support for this work partially provided for by NSF grant CCF-1320092.

© IFIP International Federation for Information Processing 2015
J. Abascal et al. (Eds.): INTERACT 2015, Part IV, LNCS 9299, pp. 213–230, 2015.
DOI: 10.1007/978-3-319-22723-8_17

relatively impoverished. The result is an additional burden placed on the researcher to construct and maintain more of the conceptual space of the academic literature within their own limited working memory. With these issues in mind, we have developed *EvolutionWorks* to help researchers navigate the academic literature effectively by presenting it as an interactive visualization of the citation network that takes advantage of more retinal variables to characterize more strongly the relationships between papers.

The main scenario that guided the design of EvolutionWorks is that of a researcher building a *reading list* for a potentially unfamiliar topic. For our purposes, a reading list is a set of academic research papers, relevant to a particular topic that a researcher saves to consider in more depth after scanning the literature. More broadly, building a reading list is an *information-based ideation task* [5] that requires a researcher to iteratively explore, think about, collect, and develop significant ideas. Further, we define *exploratory browsing* [6] as the creative process that researchers engage in when they seek diverse and novel information as they use the Internet to investigate a conceptual space. In this case, the researcher follows chains of references and citations. We designed the features of EvolutionWorks for the purpose of aiding researchers in exploratory browsing by making it more clear what papers are important and what links to follow-up, with the aim being to paint a clearer picture that grants the researcher greater confidence that their reading list will improve their comprehension of the state of the art.

The contributions of EvolutionWorks that we present here are the *seed-grow-prune design model, kinetic layering,* a *unified presentation, focus-context-focus hopping,* and *cluster title summarization*:

- Our *seed-grow-prune* design model reflects what we discovered from interviewing researchers about how they approach the task of building a reading list. EvolutionWorks supports the metaphorical task of a researcher starting out with the *seed* of an idea that will *grow* into an unwieldy set of potentially useful papers to read that the researcher must *prune* into a final reading list.
- Our *kinetic layering* methodology is the encoding of the abstract properties of documents into the physical properties of the particles that drive a force-directed animation engine that dynamically positions the nodes of a graph visualization. Thus, the physical simulation helps to make complex relationships and properties clear by visual inspection, for example, by causing related papers to group automatically because they attract one another, or by making important papers appear more significant because they are bigger and heavier.
- There are drawbacks to presenting paper content and the citation network in separate views, such as a split screen or by separate paper and network viewing modes. Specifically, a split presentation takes up extra screen real estate (which is scarce on mobile devices), and separate modes create a cognitive disconnect by dividing the researcher's attention between two representations of the same paper. To avoid this, EvolutionWorks combines both papers and the citation network into a single *unified presentation* with papers represented directly as graph nodes.
- The unified presentation alone would have a problematic trade-off between zooming in to view a paper's content and zooming out to keep track of the broader

relationships between papers. We developed a context preserving navigation primitive, the *focus-context-focus* hop, which helps to keep the larger context in mind. When a researcher selects a paper link, the system brings the target paper into focus by smoothly panning from the original view to the subsequent view. In order to give the researcher a sense of the larger context the view also zooms out to reveal more of the citation network before zooming back in to the new focus. The impression given is much like that of physically hopping from paper to paper.

- Another problem with the unified presentation is that zooming out tends to cause paper titles to overlap and become illegible. To solve the problem EvolutionWorks automatically takes tight groups of papers and collapses them into *clusters*, and gives each cluster a single *summary title*, computed based on the metadata of the clustered papers.

To evaluate EvolutionWorks we conducted a small user study. The results were indicative that all in all these contributions work towards creating an improved visualization of citation networks compared to a typical Web browser.

The rest of this paper is organized as follows. Section 2 provides background material that justifies the need for EvolutionWorks and the science that supports its design. Section 3 briefly reviews related work by other researchers in this area. Section 4 explains each contribution of EvolutionWorks in more detail and discusses a few implementation concerns. Section 5 reports the results of a user study that evaluates how well EvolutionWorks steers users towards better papers. Section 6 puts forward possible avenues for further improvement and evaluation of this work and concludes the paper.

## 2 Background

The Google search engine has become so ubiquitous that the term "googling" and research are seen as one and the same [7]. Whether or not this is a good thing, (no consensus has been reached), users have come to expect search tools to be simple [8]. It seems that simplicity and intuition trump the organization and quality of search results; so much so that many would rather search the World Wide Web for academic papers than use online public access catalogs (OPAC) that have been shown to produce higher quality results [9]. Since users find OPACs less intuitive [8, 9]—and the Web is relatively disorganized—there is a need for a more intuitive search tool specifically tailored for the particular structure of the academic literature [10, 11]. This section reviews the research background that we relied on to build such a tool; one that aims to be as friendly as a browser, but leads users to higher quality search results.

The s*eed-grow-prune* methodology is derived from Bates' *berry picking* model for on-line searches [12] and from the *mixed-initiative* ideation engine *combinFormation* [13]. When describing berry picking, Bates made the case that searches evolve as the user gathers more information and zeroes in on what they need—which may actually end up being quite different from what they originally thought they needed. Additionally, the mixed-initiative system combinFormation combines the actions of the system and the user in a single collaborative space. Both the system and the user can modify the collaborative space, with the user providing guidance to improve the system's actions.

*EvolutionWorks* relies on *physically based modeling*, which is a methodology were objects in some model are given physical properties—such as position, velocity, acceleration, and mass—that are acted on by forces. The system simulates the behavior of objects according to the object's given properties, with the goal being that people will recognize the resulting animation as being physically plausible. One case of a physically based simulation is a *force-directed* graph layout, defined as a simulation of the motion of graph nodes as if they were point masses connected through the edges of the graph by springs [14–17]. The system assigns physical properties to the nodes and edges, and the results of the simulation determine node locations. To keep nodes from overlapping, the simulation adds a repulsive force between nodes to push them apart. Interactive force-directed layouts allow the user to tweak the layout while the simulation responds intuitively to the user's intervention.

The *kinetic layering* methodology, build upon force-directed layout, is analogous to the *visual layering* [18] and *kinetic visualization* [19] methodologies. With visual layering, the *retinal variables* [4] of location, size, shape, color, value, texture, and orientation are used to encode information, while with kinetic visualization, animated contours disambiguate 3D surface features. There are several examples of how the perception of motion is an important source of information and is the key to why kinetic layering is useful. First, the *kinetic depth effect* [20] allows the 3D shape of an object to be understood, even if all that is visible is the silhouette of the object, but if and only if the object is moving. More generally, motion allows the brain to segment an image into its separate parts. Second, people are especially sensitive to *biological motion* [21]. People can readily recognize the characteristic motion of plants and animals from relatively sparse information. For instance, a grouping of white dots on a black background might appear completely random if they are static, but it is instantly apparent what they represent if the dots start moving as if attached to a tiger. Certainly, motion that mimics life is compelling. Finally, motion also helps to overcome a certain kind of perceptual glitch caused by the very short-term nature of sensory memory. Under some circumstances, suddenly adding or removing an element from an image might cause an observer to remain oblivious to any change at all. This effect is called *change blindness* [22] and it represents a fundamental limitation in the ability to perceive changes that are not continuous.

## 3 Related Work

There have been many efforts undertaken to meet the need for improved tools for exploring networks and in particular, the academic citation network.

*Vizster* [2] is an interactive visualization tool for exploring the community structure of on-line social networks such as *Facebook*. It draws a springy animated *sociogram* (social graph) driven by force-directed layout, and is in fact one of the main inspirations for *EvolutionWork's* design. Vizster's creators clearly demonstrated the advantage of graph visualization in a party setting where people were surprised to discover *friend of a friend* relationships that were not apparent to them through the ordinary web interface. Although Vizster uses a force-directed layout to create a springy and "fun" visualization, it does not take advantage of physically based modeling to convey any additional information.

There have been several systems built that directly address the problem of exploring the citation network. One such tool is *CiteWiz* [23], which supports multiple visualization techniques. First, the *growing polygon* [24] is used to visualize causality and was found to illustrate partially ordered sets better than Hasse diagrams. Taking advantage of this, CiteWiz uses growing polygons to show the influence of authors on each other as derived from the partial order of the citation network. However, the growing polygon visualization provided by the CiteWiz tool is less intuitive than a Hasse diagram, so it requires some training before users can take full advantage of it. Additionally, its use of color limits accessibility for the colorblind. The second visualization provided by CiteWiz is *Newton's shoulders*, which represents a timeline of when authors started publishing combined with how many citations they have. In the visualization, each stick figure represents an author whose size is determined by that author's total citation count, and later authors are stacked on top of the earlier ones. The final visualization is CiteWiz's *concept map*, which is a force-directed layout that can show the relative importance of either keywords or authors. In the case of keywords, larger nodes represent keywords that are more common and springs connect keywords that appear together. In the case of authors, larger nodes are authors with more citations while springs connect authors that worked on the same paper. Applying force-directed layout to keywords and authors, but not papers, seems like a missed opportunity.

*PaperCube* [25] is a web application that supports several different visualization methods for both papers and authors, but we will only mention the *CircleView* [26] method here. CircleView shows *focus+context* for a single paper by placing the focus paper in the middle and encircling it with the context—the focus paper's citations. CircleView begins to break down when the number of citations is high. The limit appears to be about 15 citations, but papers commonly have many more. The context provided by CircleView is also limited to the immediate relationships between papers. The system does not smoothly animate the transitions between focused papers, which can cause problems due to change blindness.

A *co-citation* occurs when two separate papers both cite another paper. The purpose of *CociteSeer* [27–29] is to visualize the relationships between papers that co-citation implies. Rather than explicit edges between co-citing papers, CociteSeer implies these relationships by placing co-citing papers close to one another.

Physically based modeling has been used to visualize academic *career histories* [30] derived from citation data. Two different visualizations were reported: the first modeled an author's publication patterns as fluid flow through pipes and the second modeled an author's influence as wave propagation through a graph.

A *research front* [31] is a set of documents that cite a base set of fundamental documents that is fixed and time invariant. By visualizing research fronts, it is possible to determine how research splits into different branches over time.

*PaperViz* [32] makes use of the radial filling space and bulls-eye view visualization techniques that attempt to show the relationships between papers while saving screen space.

The *XML3D* [33] web browser demonstrated the potential of novel visualization methods to enhance the user experience. The browser has an interactive hyperbolic 3D graph view of pages and links. The hyperbolic view is a focus+context visualization that keeps global relationships between documents visible to the user. Promisingly, a user study found that the browser increased both user productivity and satisfaction, which corroborates with our results. However, to show the full benefit, the XML3D web browser had to provide the user with two separate views: a hierarchical summary of links, and the hyperbolic view. Neither the link summary nor the hyperbolic view alone showed a clear advantage. EvolutionWorks integrates both views into a single unified presentation.

## 4 EvolutionWorks

This section describes the features of EvolutionWorks in more detail, focusing on the contributions listed in the introduction, and then providing additional details about the implementation.

The EvolutionWorks main window, as shown in Fig. 1, has a search dialog on the left and a *view* of the *workspace* on the right. The workspace is the entire contents of the visualization, while the current view shows only a portion of the workspace at one time. The background of the view is a grid that always displays about ten solid lines and about one-hundred fine lines that become more solid as the view zooms in. The fine lines eventually replace the original ten solid lines (the opposite happens when the view is zoomed out), which gives the impression of a grid with infinite gradation. The purpose of this infinite grid is to enhance the sense of motion as the view pans and

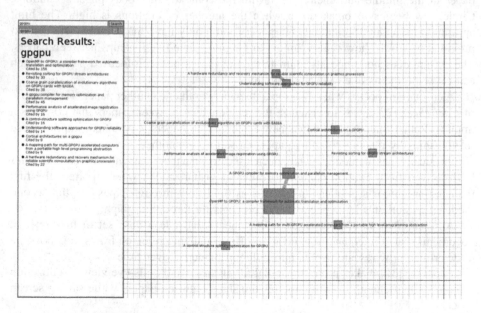

**Fig. 1.** The selected search results seed the workspace.

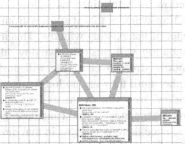

(a) When a paper gets the focus, it fills the view, but leaves a small margin.

(b) After a researcher selects references, they sprout out from the paper like leaves.

**Fig. 2.** Grow

zooms and additionally it provides the user feedback when there are no papers visible in the view.

Clicking on any paper link gives the target paper focus and causes the view of the workspace to smoothly pan and zoom so that the target paper becomes centered in the view and large enough to read as illustrated in Fig. 2a.

### 4.1 Seeding

The system initially presents the user with an empty workspace and a conventional text box for searching. Clicking on a search result opens a window in the workspace that contains the clicked paper's metadata. Entering the direct URL of a paper—say from the ACM Digital Library—is another way to open a window for that paper. The size of the paper's window is proportional to a selected metric, such as the number of citations, or the computed impact. If papers added to the workspace are related, then they are automatically linked by an edge (causing them to be pulled closer together by the force-directed layout), which is illustrated by two separate pairs of papers in Fig. 1.

To determine the placement of a paper in the workspace, the layout engine generates multiple random candidate locations within a bounding rectangle that surrounds all the other windows in the workspace. The layout engine weighs candidates according to the distance to other windows and to the edges of the view, and selects the best candidate. This method keeps windows from overlapping and keeps new windows close to existing ones as the number of windows grows.

### 4.2 Growth

While selecting a paper from the search dialog adds the paper to the workspace, selecting a new paper from a link in an existing paper causes the new paper to "sprout" from the existing paper like a leaf from a branch. As before, new edges connect the new paper to papers already in the workspace. The placement of a new citation or reference window is determined as follows. A new window starts out overlapping with the existing window that it sprouts from with its center point just slightly offset from the center of the existing window. This initial placement determines what direction that the simulation will push the window after it is created. The repulsive force that keeps windows from overlapping will push the existing and new window away from one another until they are no longer overlapping, which gives the appearance that the new window grew out of the exiting one. To determine the initial placement, the layout engine generates several candidate directions and weighs them according to how much free space there is to grow in that direction, and then it chooses the most unused space.

In Fig. 2b, the user has selected three references from the original paper in Fig. 2a, and as a result, three new papers are displayed. Further, the user has followed the chain one step further and selected a reference from one of the new papers, causing a fourth new paper to appear. Notice that the new papers also reference to each other, as indicated by the new edges between them.

## 4.3   Pruning

Pruning a single window from the workspace is simply a matter of clicking the *close* button on that window. The window and all of its associated edges will disappear from the workspace.

Additionally, user can remove an entire branch as long as there is only one edge connecting it to the rest of the graph. Hovering the mouse cursor over an eligible edge reveals a *delete* button on that edge, as shown in Fig. 3a. Clicking the button will prune the entire branch as shown in Fig. 3b. If the edge is not eligible to be pruned, due to not being the sole bridge to a sub-graph, then a circle-backslash will overlay the *delete* button to indicate that pruning is disabled. The user can work around this by pruning windows instead of edges.

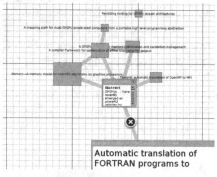

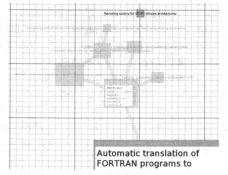

(a) Bringing the mouse close to a graph edge reveals a delete button.

(b) Clicking the delete button prunes the sub-graph if it is a branch; the sub-graph fades away.

**Fig. 3.**   Prune

## 4.4    Kinetic Layering

With visual layering, retinal variables encode information, but with what we call *kinetic layering*, information is encoded in the physical properties of a physically based model. As retinal variables do with visual layering, in EvolutionWorks the motion of the elements in the simulation convey information *metaphorically*. We emphasize the term *metaphorical* here because physically based simulations are typically intended to be taken literally—but this is not the case for kinetic layering. For example, a literal simulation could mean, "this object weighs one thousand *kilograms*," however for kinetic layering the meaning of a physical property is metaphorical, so it might mean, "this object weights one thousand *citations*." As mentioned above, this is the same as with visual layering, which is also metaphorical; for example, in photography or representational art something red is literally red, but in a visualization, red is assigned a metaphorical meaning.

Some variables in a physically based model overlap with retinal variables, for example, location, size, shape, and orientation (particle systems only model location while rigid-body simulations model all of these). Typical physically based simulations use color, value, and texture either for pure aesthetics or metaphorically to convey information, while the physical variables are meant to be taken literally—a literal physical simulation with visual layering. The physical properties are things such as velocity, friction, rotation (angular velocity), and acceleration due to forces. Forces can be between objects and other objects, or forces can come from a force field (e.g. gravity). Kinetic layering uses these purely physical properties metaphorically, which leads to a physically based simulation where *nothing* displayed, neither retinal variables nor motion, is meant to be taken as a literal representation of physical reality.

EvolutionWorks uses kinetic layering by making papers with more citations larger and more massive—they push harder on other papers. Since the simulation is interactive, if a user attempts to pull an important paper around by pulling on a minor paper (like trying to lead a big dog on a leash), the important paper barely moves, which conveys its metaphorical weight. On the other hand, grabbing the important paper and moving it around easily flings about the referring papers because they are so light.

## 4.5    Focus-Context-Focus Hopping

To show as much metadata of a paper as possible, *EvolutionWorks* zooms in fairly close to a paper window that gets focus. This could make it difficult to keep the context of a paper in mind because all the other papers are outside of the view. This is why the view is never panned directly from one paper to another (which would give the impression of passing by a picket fence and looking through it closely), but instead the view is zoomed out first to reveal the context. For example, if the user clicks on a reference in the paper shown in Fig. 2a, the view zooms out to reveal the relationship between the original focus and the next focus. Then, as shown in Fig. 4a, the view pans over to center the selected paper, as shown in Fig. 4b, and then zooms in to focus on the selected paper, as shown in Fig. 4c.

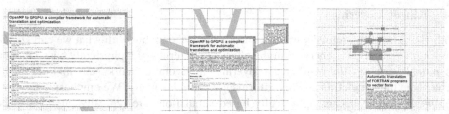

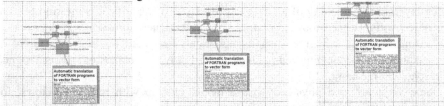

**(a)** To start, a researcher selects a reference from the paper in Fig. 2a, then the view zooms out to reveal the surrounding context

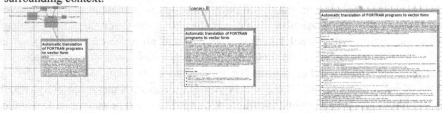

**(b)** Next, the view pans and the referenced paper moves to the center; revealing a new surrounding context.

**(c)** Finally, the view zooms in to focus on the referenced paper.

**Fig. 4.** Focus-context-focus hop

## 4.6 Unified Presentation

Except for the initial search text box, *EvolutionWorks* displays everything in a single unified view. The nodes of the graph are windows containing paper metadata. This presents a couple of challenges, the first being aesthetics, and the second being performance.

Full windows do not look pleasing when scaled down to a small size. Therefore we use a *semantic zoom* [34] that changes windows to a simpler representation depending on their size. Our current implementation only has two levels of semantic zoom—the full window and a simple rectangle with an overlaid title.

When many windows are open, the computational requirements for smooth animation can become overwhelming. Resizing dozens of full windows that contain text that needs to be word-wrapped at sixty frames per second is challenging even for powerful machines. *EvolutionWorks* thus uses a simplified window representation while the view is animating. This way the layout engine only needs to be fully reformat text once the view stops changing. The simplified presentation preserves information, such as the context, during a focus-context-focus hop, but it does not spend time re-computing information that users would most likely not be able to read during animation anyway.

## 4.7    Cluster Title Summarization

Figure 5a shows how difficult it can be to make out individual paper titles once the view is zoomed out far enough, as titles can overlap, and become illegible. EvolutionWorks creates a more concise representation for papers when they become jumbled like this. Small clusters of papers are detected by their proximity in the view. The titles of the papers in the same cluster are then replaced by a selection of common terms that appear in the metadata of cluster members. A set of common stop words like "the" are ignored. The *Porter stemming algorithm* [35] is used to factor out different forms of the same word. The *tf-idf* [36] score of the words appearing in each cluster are counted, and the top six terms are concatenated to make a new title for each cluster, like the ones shown in Fig. 5b.

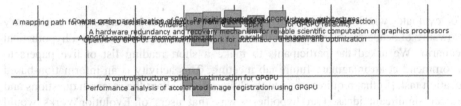

**(a)** Showing full titles of many papers at once in a small space can become an illegible mess.

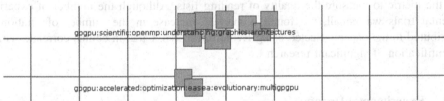

**(b)** Titles are replaced by a list of the most prevalent words, which keeps the view legible.

**Fig. 5.** Cluster title summarization

## 4.8    Implementation

EvolutionWorks relies on several technologies to enable its simulation, animation, and graphics. We use *Gephi* [37, 38] for manipulating graphs and for physically based modeling, and *OpenGL* [39] with the *Themable Widget Library* (TWL) [40] for the user interface. Gephi is a powerful graph visualization application and library for Java—described as "Photoshop for graphs." Specifically, we use Gephi's *ForceAtlas2* layout algorithm for small to medium sized graphs. Additionally, there is a plug-in system for defining new layout algorithms. For visuals, OpenGL and TWL provide the hardware accelerated high performance graphics required for kinetic layering and the unified presentation. Standard Java widget libraries have significant overhead, which is unacceptable for implementing smooth animation. TWL puts a lot of emphasis on efficiency because its purpose is for use in video games. Since TWL is implemented with OpenGL, combining TWL user interface elements with OpenGL graphics primitives is natural.

Another important capability that EvolutionWorks needs is structured access to the Web. For this, EvolutionWorks uses *BigSemantics* [41], an open source system that can provide structured semantic information from the Web even though the Web is only semi-structured. We use the object-oriented *Meta-Metadata* language, provided by BigSemantics, to describe *semantic data types* [42] for scholarly articles. While different digital libraries and repositories—such as Google Scholar [43], ACM Digital Library [44], IEEE Xplore [45], and CiteSeer [46]—use different HTML representations, BigSemantics provides a common base type that allows EvolutionWorks to use scholarly articles from different sources as if they were from the same source.

## 5    User Study

To evaluate whether *EvolutionWorks* improves the experiences of exploratory browsing of academic literature, we devised a user study that simulated a hypothetical scenario. We asked the participants to make a short reading list of five papers to recommend at an imaginary future lab meeting. This activity is an information-based ideation task [5] that requires users to think iteratively about the research questions and collect significant ideas. Our hypothesis was that users of EvolutionWorks would produce reading lists with a higher citation count than those made by users of a regular Web browser. We chose the citation count, as retrieved from the ACM Digital Library, as the metric to measure the quality of reading lists. Although the number of experimental trials was small, we found a marked increase in the number of citations attributed to the papers selected using EvolutionWorks. Citation counts correlate with identification of significant research.

### 5.1    Experimental Design

We created two separate tasks and two separate groups, which resulted in there being four subgroups. The first task was to look up papers relevant to human computer interfaces and *Healthcare*, and the second task was to look up papers relevant to human computer interfaces involving the *Wiimote* controller (by *Nintendo*). The subgroups used either a version of EvolutionWorks that looks similar to a conventional tabbed *Browser*, or the full version that uses EvolutionWorks' *Graph* visualization. The result is four subgroups, *Healthcare-Browser*, *Healthcare-Graph*, *Wiimote-Browser*, and *Wiimote-Graph*. To increase the amount of trials, we asked some users to participate in two subgroups with different tasks. For example, if a user had completed *Healthcare-Browser* then they could also complete *Wiimote-Graph*. To counter any learning effect we randomly determined the order that the users would undertake the *Browser* or *Wiimote* tasks.

### 5.2    Hypothesis

The size and weight given to papers with more citations should draw the user's attention to these papers more than in a list of papers sorted by citation count. The difference should be noticeable in the number of citations attributed to the papers found by users that are in the Graph group. In addition, the mean time taken to complete a reading list by the Graph group should not be significantly different from the mean time of the Browser group.

## 5.3   Results

It turned out that the mean of the time taken by the users in each group was not statistically significant. For the *Wiimote* task, the browser subgroup happened to take less time; the mean time taken of the *Wiimote-Browser* subgroup was 5 min 24 s and that of the *Wiimote-Graph* subgroup was 10 min and 51 s. The opposite was observed of the *Healthcare* task with the *Healthcare-Graph* subgroup seeming to do better by taking a mean time of 7 min and 24 s and the *Healthcare-Browser* group a mean time of 9 min and 14 s. The two-tailed P value for these means was 0.3952, which indicates a 40 % probability that these results were due to variability in the measurements and are not significant. This is similar to the results of tests of the XML3D [33] browser where they found that the use of a non-conventional visualization did not cause a significantly affect the time spent on browsing. Users seem to work until they get bored with a task and want to move on, so any improvement in results is due to more efficient exploration, and not because the user spent more time with EvolutionWorks.

Figures 6 and 7 visualize the results of the user study as a histogram. Each bar represents a paper whose height is based on the citation count scaled by the number of users in each group. In Fig. 8 the same histograms are overlaid on top of one another to

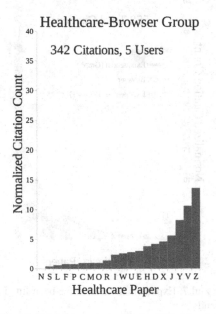
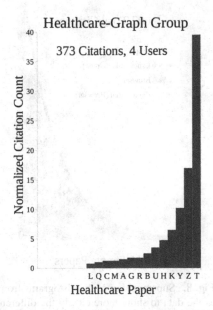

**Fig. 6.** The histograms for the Wiimote task indicate the large advantage we observed that the Graph group had over the Browser group in selecting papers that are more highly cited. The bars in each histogram labeled with the same letter or digit correspond to the same paper.

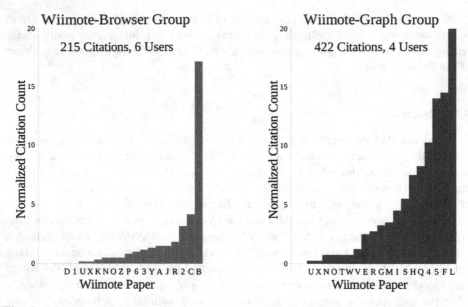

**Fig. 7.** The advantage of the *Graph* group is smaller for the *Healthcare* task than for the *Wiimote* task shown in Fig. 6, but it is still clearly observed. The bars in each histogram labeled with the same letter correspond to the same paper.

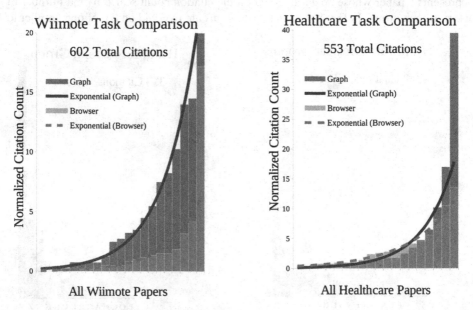

**Fig. 8.** Superposition of the histograms from Figs. 6 and 7. Exponential curves have been fitted to the data to show more clearly the difference in trends.

demonstrate the differences. To help show the difference in the results more clearly, we have fit exponential curves to the histograms. An exponential curve was chosen because it has been shown empirically [47] that the distribution of citation counts in the academic citation network is consistent with a power law governing how quickly the number of citations of a paper grows over time. The general impression is that most of the papers found by the *Graph* group are of higher quality than those found by the *Browser* group, because the area under the curve is greater.

## 6  Conclusion and Future Work

After interviewing researchers about their methods of researchers conducting literature searches, we noticed a pattern that we dubbed *seed-grow-prune*. The *seed* is a research idea that suggests keywords for the researcher to search the web or an online public access catalog. From those initial results, the researcher follows link after link (prioritizing based mostly on paper titles alone), forming a chain, so that eventually the seed ends up *growing* into an unwieldy pile. After looking at the abstracts and contents of papers in more detail, the researcher *prunes* many of the papers away until there is finally a manageable reading list.

The novel features of EvolutionWorks, including: *kinetic layering*, a *unified presentation*, *focus-context-focus hopping*, and *cluster title summarization*, work together to support seed-grow-prune. First, *kinetic layering* allows growth to take place smoothly while conveying abstract document properties in the motion of a physically based simulation. The continuous plant-like motion is compelling, avoids change blindness, and gives a literal meaning to seed-grow-prune. Second, the *unified presentation* displays documents directly in the graph in order to avoid a split in the researcher's attention between the graph and a separate document viewer. Third, *focus-context-focus hopping* keeps the broader context of documents in the mind of the researcher when switching focus between papers. Without hopping, the user might pan from paper to paper in the view without ever seeing much context and lose the benefit of the unified presentation. Finally, *cluster title summarization* keeps the view tidy by simplifying the titles of papers that are too small (in the current view) for the researcher to examine individually, which can happen because the importance metric can cause the size of different papers to vary widely.

To evaluate EvolutionWorks we conducted a user study that gave promising results, but also provides seeds of ideas for future research. The study reported in this paper was small, but we obtained positive indicative results that the quality of papers found by users of EvolutionWorks is higher than that of the papers found with a traditional Web browser. However, for stronger confidence in the benefits of EvolutionWorks, in the future a larger user study is necessary—especially to pinpoint the value of each individual feature. In particular, the benefit of different physical properties used with kinetic layering needs to be further studied. So far, we have purposefully not taken advantage of most retinal variables, which allows us to avoid confusing the benefits of visual layering with the benefits of kinetic layering. We say most, because size is both a retinal variable and a physical property at the same time. Since size is actually the most dominant retinal variable, we need to measure the benefit of kinetic layering where there are no size differences. Another possible experiment could isolate even the effects of paper titles and citation counts by showing that kinetic layering alone is enough to influence users to select papers based on a "quality" metric that assigns papers completely random values.

Another avenue of future work is the application of filtering to kinetic layering. A visualization system normally displays filtered results by making marked variations in visual layering, such as changing the size, color, brightness, etc., of objects. Extending this concept to kinetic layering would give us *kinetic filtering*, where the behavior of a simulation could be modified dynamically by changing the physical properties of objects based on a filter.

Finally, we would like to apply EvolutionWorks to other forms of information-based ideation other than using the academic citation network to build reading lists. *BigSemantics* already includes formats for many other kinds of creative works and social media. Consequently, the system could bring multiple kinds of data into the view at once, such as *Wikipedia* articles, news stories, tweets, social media profiles, etc. — all grown from a user's seed — all connected together in a single workspace.

# References

1. Herman, I., Melançon, G., Marshall, M.S.: Graph visualization and navigation in information visualization: a survey. IEEE Trans. Visual Comput. Graphics **6**, 24–43 (2000)
2. Heer, J., Boyd, D.: Vizster: visualizing online social networks. In: Proceedings of the Proceedings of the 2005 IEEE Symposium on Information Visualization, pp. 532–539. IEEE Computer Society, Washington, DC, USA (2005)
3. Von Landesberger, T., Kuijper, A., Schreck, T., Kohlhammer, J., van Wijk, J.J., Fekete, J.-D., Fellner, D.W.: Visual analysis of large graphs: state-of-the-art and future research challenges. Comput. Graphics Forum **30**, 1719–1749 (2011)
4. Bertin, J.: Semiology of Graphics: Diagrams, Networks, Maps. University of Wisconsin Press, Madison (1983)
5. Kerne, A., Webb, A.M., Smith, S.M., Linder, R., Lupfer, N., Qu, Y., Moeller, J., Damaraju, S.: Using metrics of curation to evaluate information-based ideation. ACM ToCHI **21**, 48 pp. (2014)
6. Jain, A., Lupfer, N., Qu, Y., Linder, R., Kerne, A., Smith, S.M.: Evaluating TweetBubble with ideation metrics of exploratory browsing. In: Proceedings of Creativity and Cognition. ACM (2015)
7. Mostafa, J.: Seeking better web searches. Sci. Am. **292**, 66–73 (2005)
8. Fast, K.V., Campbell, D.G.: "I still like Google": University student perceptions of searching OPACs and the web. Proc. Am. Soc. Inf. Sci. Technol. **41**, 138–146 (2004)
9. Griffiths, J.R., Brophy, P.: Student searching behavior and the web: use of academic resources and Google. Libr. Trends **53**, 539–554 (2005)
10. Bell, S.J.: The Infodiet: how libraries can offer an appetizing alternative to Google. Chronicle Higher Educ. **50**, B15 (2004)
11. Rowlands, I., Nicholas, D., Williams, P., Huntington, P., Fieldhouse, M., Gunter, B., Withey, R., Jamali, H.R., Dobrowolski, T., Tenopir, C.: The Google generation: the information behaviour of the researcher of the future. Aslib Proc. **60**, 290–310 (2008)
12. Bates, M.J.: The design of browsing and Berrypicking techniques for the online search interface. Online Rev. **13**, 407–424 (1989)

13. Koh, E., Dworaczyk, B., Albea, J., Hill, R., Choi, H., Caruso, D., Graeber, R., Mistrot, J.M., Smith, S.M., Webb, A., Kerne, A.: combinFormation: a mixed-initiative system for representing collections as compositions of image and text surrogates. In: Joint Conference on Digital Libraries, vol. 0, pp. 11–20 (2006)

14. Eades, P.: A heuristics for graph drawing. Congressus Numerantium **42**, 146–160 (1984)

15. Fruchterman, T.M., Reingold, E.M.: Graph drawing by force-directed placement. Softw. Pract. Experience **21**, 1129–1164 (1991)

16. Kamada, T., Kawai, S.: An algorithm for drawing general undirected graphs. Inf. Process. Lett. **31**, 7–15 (1989)

17. Frick, A., Ludwig, A., Mehldau, H.: A fast adaptive layout algorithm for undirected graphs (extended abstract and system demonstration). In: Tamassia, R., Tollis, I.G. (eds.) GD 1994. LNCS, vol. 894, pp. 388–403. Springer, Heidelberg (1995)

18. Tufte, E.R.: Envisioning information. Optometry Vision Sci. **68**, 322–324 (1991)

19. Lum, E.B., Stompel, A., Ma, K.-L.: Kinetic visualization: a technique for illustrating 3D shape and structure. In: Visualization, pp. 435–442 (2002)

20. Wallach, H., O'Connell, D.N.: The kinetic depth effect. J. Exp. Psychol. **45**, 205–217 (1953)

21. Johansson, G.: Visual perception of biological motion and a model for its analysis. Percept. Psychophys. **14**, 201–211 (1973)

22. Simons, D.J., Levin, D.T.: Change blindness. Trends Cogn. Sci. **1**, 261–267 (1997)

23. Elmqvist, N., Tsigas, P.: CiteWiz: a tool for the visualization of scientific citation networks. Inf. Visual. **6**, 215–232 (2007)

24. Elmqvist, N., Tsigas, P.: Causality visualization using animated growing polygons. In: IEEE Symposium on Information Visualization, pp. 189–196 (2003)

25. Bergstrom, P., Atkinson, D.C.: Augmenting the exploration of digital libraries with web-based visualizations. In: Fourth International Conference on Digital Information Management, pp. 1–7 (2009)

26. Keim, D.A., Schneidewind, J.O., Sips, M.: CircleView: a new approach for visualizing time-related multidimensional data sets. In: Proceedings of the Working Conference on Advanced Visual Interfaces, pp. 179–182. ACM, Gallipoli, Italy (2004)

27. Small, H.: Co-citation in the scientific literature: a new measure of the relationship between two documents. J. Am. Soc. Inf. Sci. **24**, 265–269 (1973)

28. Chen, T.T., Hsieh, L.C.: On visualization of cocitation networks. In: Proceedings of the 11th International Conference on Information Visualization pp. 470–475. IEEE Computer Society (2007)

29. Chen, T.T., Yen, D.C.: CociteSeer: a system to visualize large cocitation networks. Electron. Libr. **28**, 477–491 (2010)

30. Blythe, J., Patwardhan, M., Oates, T., desJardins, M., Rheingans, P.: Visualization support for fusing relational, spatio-temporal data: building career histories. In: Proceedings of the 9th International Conference on Information Fusion, pp. 1–7 (2006)

31. Morris, S.A., Yen, G., Wu, Z., Asnake, B.: Time line visualization of research fronts. J. Am. Soc. Inform. Sci. Technol. **54**, 413–422 (2003)

32. Chou, J.-K., Yang, C.-K.: PaperVis: literature review made easy. Comput. Graphics Forum **30**, 721–730 (2011)

33. Risden, K., Czerwinski, M.P., Munzner, T., Cook, D.B.: An initial examination of ease of use for 2D and 3D information visualizations of web content. Int. J. Hum. Comput. Stud. **53**, 695–714 (2000)

34. Perlin, K., Fox, D.: Pad: an alternative approach to the computer interface. In: Proceedings of the 20th Annual Conference on Computer Graphics and Interactive Techniques, pp. 57–64. ACM, Anaheim, CA (1993)

35. Van Rijsbergen, C.J., Robertson, S.E., Porter, M.F.: New models in probabilistic information retrieval. Computer Laboratory, University of Cambridge (1980)
36. Jones, K.S.: A statistical interpretation of term specificity and its application in retrieval. In: Peter, W. (ed.) Document Retrieval Systems, pp. 132–142. Taylor Graham Publishing, London (1988)
37. Bastian, M., Heymann, S., Jacomy, M.: Gephi: An open source software for exploring and manipulating networks. In: Third International AAAI Conference on Weblogs and Social Media, pp. 361–362. AAAI Publications (2009)
38. Gephi. http://gephi.github.io. Accessed 12 May 2015
39. OpenGL. http://opengl.org. Accessed 12 May 2015
40. TWL—Themable Widget Library. http://twl.l33tlabs.org/. Accessed 12 May 2015
41. Kerne, A., Qu, Y., Webb, A.M., Damaraju, S., Lupfer, N., Mathur, A.: Meta-metadata: a metadata semantics language for collection representation applications. In: Proceedings of the 19th ACM International Conference on Information and Knowledge Management, pp. 1129–1138. ACM, Toronto, ON, Canada (2010)
42. Qu, Y., Kerne, A., Lupfer, N., Linder, R., Jain, A.: Metadata type system: integrate presentation, data models and extraction to enable exploratory browsing interfaces. In: Proceedings of EICS. ACM (2014)
43. Google Scholar. http://scholar.google.com. Accessed 12 May 2015
44. ACM Digital Library. http://dl.acm.org. Accessed 12 May 2015
45. IEEE Xplore. http://ieeexplore.ieee.org. Accessed 12 May 2015
46. CiteSeer. http://citeseer.ist.psu.edu/index. Accessed 12 May 2015
47. Redner, S.: How popular is your paper? An empirical study of the citation distribution. Eur. Phys. J. B Condens. Matter Complex Syst. **4**, 131–134 (1998)

# Quantifying Object- and Command-Oriented Interaction

Alix Goguey[1(✉)], Julie Wagner[2], and Géry Casiez[3]

[1] Inria, Lille, France
alix.goguey@inria.fr
[2] Human-Computer Interaction Group,
University of Munich (LMU), Munich, Germany
julie.wagner@ifi.lmu.de
[3] University of Lille, Lille, France
gery.casiez@univ-lille1.fr

**Abstract.** In spite of previous work showing the importance of understanding users' strategies when performing tasks, i.e. the order in which users perform actions on objects using commands, HCI researchers evaluating and comparing interaction techniques remain mainly focused on performance (e.g. time, error rate). This can be explained to some extent by the difficulty to characterize such strategies. We propose metrics to quantify if an interaction technique introduces a rather object- or command-oriented task strategy, depending if users favor completing the actions on an object before moving to the next one or in contrast if they are reluctant to switch between commands. On an interactive surface, we compared Fixed Palette and Toolglass with two novel techniques that take advantage of finger identification technology, Fixed Palette using Finger Identification and Finger Palette. We evaluated our metrics with previous results on both existing techniques. With the novel techniques we found that (1) minimizing the required physical movement to switch tools does not necessarily lead to more object-oriented strategies and (2) increased cognitive load to access commands can lead to command-oriented strategies.

**Keywords:** Interaction sequence · Task strategy · Metric · Theory · Finger identification · Finger specific

## 1 Introduction

In HCI research, we sometimes face the problem that two designed interaction techniques might differ in various factors that we cannot control in experiments: individual techniques might require different implementations (*vision-based* hand- vs. *capacitive* touch tracking), different body parts for interaction (e.g. *uni-* vs. *bimanual*) or different modalities (*touch* vs. *mid-air* gestures). For such techniques, comparing performance time becomes either meaningless or does not reveal the exact reasons for the time benefit.

Playing around with the context, Mackay [7] compared floating palette, marking menu and Toolglass [5] when performing two tasks requiring participants to copy or modify Petri-nets. She concluded that the optimal interaction technique in terms of

© IFIP International Federation for Information Processing 2015
J. Abascal et al. (Eds.): INTERACT 2015, Part IV, LNCS 9299, pp. 231–239, 2015.
DOI: 10.1007/978-3-319-22723-8_18

performance varied depending on the task, the user's cognitive context and individual preferences. She further observed that floating palette and marking menu favor *toolby-tool* actions (*e.g.* first creating all *triangles*, then all *circles*) while Toolglass favors frequent switch between tools.

We believe that interaction techniques – the integration of *physical* and *logical* device design [2] – affects how people solve a task; and that exclusive time metrics do not help researchers in understanding *why* one technique performs faster than another. We propose additional metrics to help categorizing interaction techniques by automatically and objectively labeling strategies. We believe that used in an iterative development, they would give insight to designers on whether or not their system leads users to adopt an effective strategy for a given task and helps them choosing one interaction technique or another. We compared two techniques from the literature, Fixed Palette [1] and Toolglass [5], with two novel techniques using finger identification on interactive surfaces, *Fixed Palette with Finger Identification* and *Finger Palette* in a vector drawing task. We found that we can correctly conclude the previously identified results [1, 7] from our metrics: *Fixed Palette* is a highly command-oriented and *Toolglass* a highly object-oriented technique. We found that *Fixed Palette using Finger Identification* is significantly more object-oriented than *Fixed Palette*. *Finger Palette* and *Fixed Palette* are equally tool-oriented. We discuss cognitive reasons for these differences in strategies specific.

## 2   Related Work

Appert et al. [1] and Mackay [7] define a strategy as the order of elementary actions on objects to solve a task. Both works studied performance of interaction techniques in different contexts and identify which kind of strategy is best suited for each. With the *Complexity of Interaction Sequences* model (CIS), Appert et al. take the analyzed structure of an interaction technique and predict its performance time for a given strategy. The strategy should therefore be determined in advance. Mackay did not impose a strategy. Instead she observed interaction sequences and labeled them. Labeling is a tedious task, subjective and error prone considering sequences of actions scarcely belong to one category or the other. Appert et al. and Mackay's results concurred: fixed palettes are command-oriented, meaning that users repeatedly re-issue the same command to perform the task while marking menus and toolglasses are object-oriented, meaning that users issue multiple commands with respect to a single graphical object on screen.

Bhavnani and John [3, 4] studied higher level strategies (*i.e.* strategies that differentiate novices from expert users) and how users gain expert knowledge. They argue that users need to learn strategies: knowledge of a task and knowledge of tools are not sufficient to make users more efficient with a complex computer application. Cockburn et al. [6] discuss in their review paper various systems that help users to learn better strategies. *Skillometer* [8] is one of these systems helping users to use keyboard shortcuts instead of time-consuming menu navigation. Our metrics are intended to measure lower level strategies as Appert, Beaudouin-Lafon and Mackay studied.

Mackay [7] also measured the average number of identical actions performed before switching to another command: a high score indicates a command-oriented pattern while a low score suggests an object-oriented pattern. Besides being a subjective choice, switching a lot between commands does not necessarily involve being objectoriented (*e.g.* drawing a circle, then a triangle, then filling the circle in blue and finally filling the triangle in red is neither object- nor command-oriented). *Object-oriented* and *command-oriented* strategies are orthogonal to each other. The metrics we introduce are intended to measure automatically the degree of which an interaction sequence is object-oriented and command-oriented. Furthermore, our metrics also allow us to be more ecological since we do not impose users to follow any strategy.

# 3  Metrics

With a given interaction technique, users might optimize efficiency and perform a compound task using strategies varying between strictly *command-oriented* or *object-oriented*. A strategy (S) can be decomposed in $n$ elementary actions ($a_i$) performed on interactive objects $Obj(a_i)$ (the object modified during action $a_i$). For example, drawing two blue rectangles can be decomposed in the actions of *creating rectangle* ($c_{rect}$), and *blue-filling* ($f_{blue}$) performed on two rectangle objects $R_1$ and $R_2$: with a *command-oriented* strategy, users are reluctant to switch commands which would result in, *e.g.*, the following sequence: $(c_{rect})_{R1}\ (c_{rect})_{R2}\ (f_{blue})_{R1}\ (f_{blue})_{R2}$; with an *object-oriented* strategy, users favor completing an object before continuing with the next one, which would result in, *e.g.*, $(c_{rect})_{R1}\ (f_{blue})_{R1}\ (c_{rect})_{R2}\ (f_{blue})_{R2}$.

## 3.1  Quantifying Object-Oriented Strategy

With an object-oriented strategy, users finish all their actions on an object before moving to the next one. Therefore we penalize any action occurring on objects previously edited or created. For a Strategy $S = (a_1)_{Obj(a1)}, \ldots (a_n)_{Obj(an)}$ of $n$ actions, we measure the *ObjectOriented(S)* ratio as follows:

$$p(S) = \sum_{i=3}^{n} \begin{cases} 1 & \text{if } Obj(a_i) \neq Obj(a_{i-1}) \\ & \text{and } \exists j \in [\![1; i-2]\!] \text{ such as } Obj(a_i) \neq Obj(a_j) \\ 0 & \text{otherwise} \end{cases} \qquad (1)$$

$$ObjectOriented(S) = ObjOri(S) = 1 - \frac{P(S)}{n - m} \qquad (2)$$

If users complete their actions on an object before moving to the next one, $P(S) = 0$ and $ObjOri(S) = 1$. At the opposite if they switch to a different object for each of their action $P(S) = n\text{-}m$ (with $m$ the number of objects on the canvas) and $ObjOri(S) = 0$.

## 3.2   Quantifying Command-Oriented Strategy

With a command-oriented strategy, users keep using the same command as long as they can before switching to another one. As a result we penalize any switch to a command previously used. For a strategy $S = (a_1)_{Obj(a1)}, \ldots (a_n)_{Obj(an)}$ of $n$ actions, we measure the *CommandOriented(S)* ratio as follows:

$$p(S) = \sum_{i=3}^{n} \begin{cases} 1 & \text{if } a_i \neq a_{i-1} \\ & \text{and } \exists j \in [\![1; i-2]\!] \text{such as } a_i = a_j \\ 0 & \text{otherwise} \end{cases} \tag{3}$$

$$CommandOriented(S) = CmdOri(S) = 1 - \frac{P(S)}{n-c} \tag{4}$$

If users keep using the same command before switching to the next one, $P(S) = 0$ and $CmdOri(S) = 1$. At the opposite, if they keep switching from a command to another at each action, $P(S) = n\text{-}c$ (with $c$ the total number of commands used on objects) and $CmdOri(S) = 0$.

# 4   Experiment

To evaluate our metrics, we compared two novel interaction techniques, *Fixed Palette using Finger Identification* and *Finger Palette*, with *Fixed Palette* and *Toolglass*.

## 4.1   Participants

12 volunteers (3 female, mean age 26) participated in our study. Four reported their hand dexterity as 'good' and height as 'normal'. All were familiar with touch-screen technology and drawing applications.

## 4.2   Procedure and Tasks

We ran a 4 TECHNIQUE × 3 TASK within-subject design counter-balanced by TECHNIQUE. Unique conditions were repeated 7 times ($4 \times 3 \times 7 = 84$ data points per participant) and the order of TASK x REPETITION was pseudo-random. Participants were instructed to optimize time and TASK was to match the position, shape and color of several shapes displayed full-sized with light transparency on the canvas. Figure 1 illustrates the 3 TASKS: each contained 6 objects arranged in a two rows and three columns grid. TASKS contained either objects of same shape and fill color (T1), three shapes and colors spatially grouped (T2) and ungrouped (T3). All TASKS required the same number of actions in order to complete. All techniques provided access to *square*, *circle*, and *triangle* tools and *red*, *green*, *blue* coloring tools. We added an 'erase' tool to correct errors. We intentionally left out logical tools such as 'copy' + 'paste' or 'select group' to avoid noisy data.

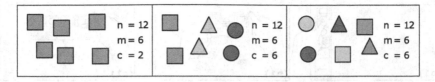

**Fig. 1.** Examples of instances for TASKS T1, T2 and T3 (Color figure online).

We displayed visual cues in the background image that enabled participants to draw all objects without the need for positioning them: the shapes were created by dragging a bounding box; a 15 mm (approximately the width of a finger) tolerance area at each corner of a shape indicated where each drag should start and end; the shape's stroke color turned red when it overshot the tolerated area. Newly created shapes did not have a fill color. When the right color was applied, the shape's stroke color turned green indicating successful completion of the object.

We implemented two techniques from the literature: *Fixed Palette*— expected to favor command-oriented strategies, and *Toolglass*— expected to favor object-oriented strategies [1, 7]. In addition, we implemented two novel techniques (*Fixed Palette using Finger Identification* and the *Finger Palette*) that we expected would favor object-oriented strategies.

TECHNIQUE 1: Fixed Palette *Fixed Palette, a.k.a.* tool palette, is a single-pointer widespread technique (Fig. 2a) [1]. It contains a set of commands that users select by pressing the appropriate button. Users conceptually hold the selected tool until they select another one. Since tool-switching requires large movements between canvas and palette, we expect users to follow a command-oriented strategy. We implemented the *Fixed Palette* to remain fixed at the right side of the display.

TECHNIQUE 2: Fixed Palette using Finger Identification We extended *Fixed Palette* to a single-handed multi-pointer technique. The onscreen representation remains the same. Users can temporarily assign tools to each finger of their dominant hand: by touching *e.g.* 'rectangle' with the index and 'circle' with the middle finger, both tools can be instantly operated using the corresponding finger. Since switching between a limited number of tools (5 fingers max) is quicker than for *Fixed Palette*, we expect to find object-oriented strategies.

TECHNIQUE 3: Toolglass The *Toolglass* is a bimanual dual-pointer technique: a widget containing a set of *semi-transparent* buttons [5] is positioned onscreen using the non-dominant hand. Command selection is performed using the dominant hand (Fig. 2b). The non-dominant hand's index finger positions the main *Toolglass* containing the six tools, the middle finger positions a second *Toolglass* containing the eraser. Since applying the same tool twice or switching tools requires equal 'effort', we expect to find object-oriented user strategies.

TECHNIQUE 4: Finger Palette The *Finger Palette* is a bimanual multi-pointer technique. The non-dominant hand controls the temporal but fixed assignment of tools to fingers of the dominant hand: for a right-handed person, *e.g.*, holding the left index finger down assigns rectangle, triangle and ellipse to the right index, middle and ring fingers (Fig. 2c). Tools are applied by the right hand's fingers independent of the left-hand's position. To reveal finger-command mappings, we display a cheat sheet

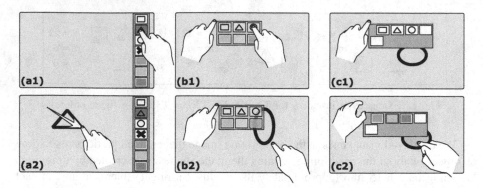

**Fig. 2.** Illustrating: *Fixed Palette*, the user selects the triangle tool (a1) and creates a triangle by dragging (a2); *Toolglass*, user positions semi-transparent widget using the non-dominant hand (b1) and starts drawing by press-and-drag through the ellipse button the dominant index (b2); *Finger Palette*, the left hand controls the assignment of tools to the right fingers (c1), user invokes color tools using the left thumb and colors an ellipse green using the middle finger (c2) (Color figure online).

next to the left index finger. We organized color and drawing tools into thumb and index finger palette; we placed the eraser into the middle finger palette. Again, we expect this technique to favor object-oriented strategies, since all commands are directly available from anywhere on the canvas.

### 4.3 Apparatus

We used an horizontal 32" 3 M touchscreen[1] (Fig. 3 left). We merged fingers' onscreen touch position with the 3D position reported by 5 GameTrak[2] devices (Fig. 3 right) attached to each fingertip via cords. We wrote a C ++ software using the *libgametrak*[33] library, that establishes a correspondence between the tracked finger positions and multiple touch points registered on the multi-touch surface. It uses a homography for each finger. The homographies are determined by a calibration procedure in which 3D points are sampled at known positions in the display reference frame. Once the system is calibrated, the software associates to an onscreen touch the identification of the closest finger.

### 4.4 Results and Discussion

The dependent variables were the *CmdOri* and *ObjOri* ratios. A one-way ANOVA showed no effect of REPETITION on *CmdOri* and *ObjOri* ratios suggesting there was

---

[1] http://www.3m.com

[2] http://en.wikipedia.org/wiki/Gametrak

[3] https://github.com/casiez/libgametrak/

**Fig. 3.** Experimental setup: (left) participant completing TASK T1 using the *Finger Palette*; (right) the 5 GameTrak devices located above the 32" 3 M touchscreen.

no learning effect. A repeated-measures MANOVA showed a significant main effect of TECHNIQUE ($F_{6,66} = 10.561$, $p < 0.0001$) and a significant TECHNIQUE x TASK interaction ($F_{12,132} = 5.201$, $p < 0.0001$) on *CmdOri* and *ObjOri* ratios (Fig. 4).

**Metric Evaluation.** Post-hoc analysis showed significant differences ($p < 0.03$) between all techniques except *Fixed Palette* and *Toolglass*. Figure 4 shows the distribution of both ratios per TECHNIQUE. Analog to previous findings [1, 7], participants performed identical tasks either command-oriented when using *Fixed Palette* (*CmdOri* ratio: $\bar{m} = 0.99$, *CI[0.99,1.00]* and *ObjOri* ratio: $\bar{m} = 0.05$, *CI[0.04,0.07]*, $\bar{m}$ is the mean) or object-oriented using *Toolglass* (*CmdOri* ratio: $\bar{m} = 0.51$, *CI[0.46,0.55]* and *ObjOri* ratio: $\bar{m} = 0.68$, *CI[0.63,0.74]*). This result provides a first validation of our metric.

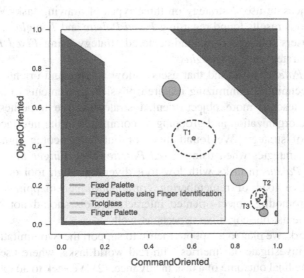

**Fig. 4.** Mean *ObjOri* and *CmdOri* ratios for each TECHNIQUE. Ellipses represent the 95 % confidence interval for the means. The gray areas represent the unreachable areas for the tasks we considered. The yellow dot corresponds to the mean strategy used in T1 using *Fixed Palette using Finger Identification* and the yellow square and diamond correspond to the mean values for T2 and T3, illustrating the interaction effect (Color figure online).

**Command-Oriented Strategies with *Finger Palette*.** *CmdOri* and *ObjOri* ratios are not significantly different for *Finger Palette* (*CmdOri* ratio: $\bar{m}$ = 0.93, CI[0.91,0.96] and *ObjOri* ratio: $\bar{m}$ = 0.06, CI[0.04,0.08]) and *Fixed Palette*: the smaller physical movement required to switch tools using *Finger Palette* did not affect users' choice to adopt an object-centered strategy. We hypothesize that this is due to the tool grouping of this technique that might encourage a command-centered strategy.

**Task-Dependent Strategy with *Fixed Palette Using Finger ID*.** For *Fixed Palette using Finger Identification*, we found significant differences (*p < 0.05*) between TASK: users adopted a significantly more object-oriented strategy with T1 (*CmdOri* ratio: $\bar{m}$ = 0.61, CI[0.51,0.71] and *ObjOri* ratio: $\bar{m}$ = 0.44, CI[0.35,0.53], see yellow dot in Fig. 4) than in both other tasks: T2 and T3 (*CmdOri* ratio: $\bar{m}$ = 0.92, CI[0.90,0.95] and *ObjOri* ratio: $\bar{m}$ = 0.14, CI[0.10,0.18], little yellow circle in Fig. 4). In T1, that consisted in drawing only red rectangles, participants reported that the personalization of command-finger mappings facilitated memorization. With increasing diversity of shapes and colors, memorizing the mappings became more difficult leading to a command-oriented strategy.

## 5   Conclusion and Future Work

We introduced two novel measurements that, combined together, can help researchersin quantifying the effects of interaction techniques on interaction sequences (users' strategy) when solving a task. Our metrics together penalize both the number of tool switches and switching the focus between on-screen objects. We compared four techniques to measure users' strategy on three types of drawing tasks.We empirically replicated previous results found regarding *Fixed Palette* and *Toolglass*, validating our metric [1, 7]: users follow a command-centered strategy using *Fixed Palette* and an objectcentered strategy using *Toolglass*.

For *Finger Palette*, we found that users follow a command-oriented strategy. We conclude that techniques minimizing required physical movements to switch tools do not necessarily lead to more object-oriented strategies. We hypothesize for future research that the organization and grouping of commands in the interface has an effect on the choice of strategy. We found that, for our task, people significantly favor object-oriented strategies when using *Fixed Palette using Finger Identification* compared to *Fixed Palette* in tasks with low tool diversity. High tool diversity leads to reported cognitive load of remembering command-finger mappings. This finding suggests that promoting object-oriented interaction tools should not only minimize physical movements, but cognitive aspects as well.

As future work, we plan to adapt our metric to support the two limitations at present: (1) We seek to investigate our metrics with real-world tasks, where users do not necessarily know the final outcome of a task in advance. (2) We seek to adapt our metrics to higher-level tool concepts. We applied our metric to investigate the effect of interaction techniques on interaction sequences. Tasks could also be solved using higher-level logical tool concepts, *e.g.* copy-and-paste, as investigated by Bhavnani et al. [4].

# References

1. Appert, C., Beaudouin-Lafon, M., Mackay, W.: Context matters: evaluating interaction techniques with the cis model. In: Fincher, S., Markopoulos, P., Moore, D., Ruddle, R. (eds.) People and Computers XVIII — Design for Life, pp. 279–295. Springer, London (2005). http://dx.doi.org/10.1007/1-84628-062-1_18
2. Beaudouin-Lafon, M.: Instrumental interaction: an interaction model for designing postwimp user interfaces. In: Proceedings of CHI 2000, pp. 446–453. ACM (2000). http://doi.acm.org/10.1145/332040.332473
3. Bhavnani, S.K., John, B.E.: Delegation and circumvention: two faces of efficiency. In: Proceedings. of CHI 1998, pp. 273–280 (1998). http://dx.doi.org/10.1145/274644.274683
4. Bhavnani, S.K., John, B.E.: The strategic use of complex computer systems. Hum.-Comput. Interact. 15(2), 107–137 (2000). http://dx.doi.org/10.1207/S15327051HCI1523_3
5. Bier, E.A., Stone, M.C., Pier, K., Buxton, W., DeRose, T.D.: Toolglass and magic lenses: the see-through interface. In: Proceedings of SIGGRAPH 1993, pp. 73–80. ACM (1993). http://doi.acm.org/10.1145/166117.166126
6. Cockburn, A., Gutwin, C., Scarr, J., Malacria, S.: Supporting novice to expert transitions in user interfaces. ACM Comput. Surv. (CSUR) 47(2), 31 (2014). http://doi.acm.org/10.1145/2658850.2659796
7. Mackay, W.: Which interaction technique works when? floating palettes, marking menus and toolglasses support different task strategies. In: Proceedings of AVI 2002, pp. 203–208. ACM. http://doi.acm.org/10.1145/1556262.1556294
8. Malacria, S., Scarr, J., Cockburn, A., Gutwin, C., Grossman, T.: Skillometers: reflective widgets that motivate and help users to improve performance. In: Proceedings of UIST 2013, pp. 321–330. ACM (2013). http://doi.acm.org/10.1145/2501988.2501996

# Users, Bystanders and Agents: Participation Roles in Human-Agent Interaction

Antonia L. Krummheuer[⊠]

Aalborg University, Aalborg, Denmark
antonia@hum.aau.dk

**Abstract.** Human-agent interaction (HAI), especially in the field of embodied conversational agents (ECA), is mainly construed as dyadic communication between a human user and a virtual agent. This is despite the fact that many application scenarios for future ECAs involve the presence of others. This paper critiques the view of an 'isolated user' and proposes a micro-sociological perspective on the participation roles in HAI. Two examples of an HAI in a public setting point out (1) the ways a variety of participants take part in the interaction, (2) how the construction of the participation roles influences the construction of the agent's identity, and (3) how HAI, as a mediated interaction, is framed by an asymmetric participation framework. The paper concludes by suggesting various participation roles, which may inform development of ECAs.

**Keywords:** Embodied conversational agent · Human-agent interaction · Participation role

## 1 Introduction

An embodied conversational agent is a computer interface in the form of a "virtual human" ([4], p. 39). ECAs are said to have social, embodied and linguistic abilities so that they can engage in 'human-like' face-to-face interaction with the aim of developing "computers that untrained users can interact with naturally" ([4], p. 60). Core studies have conceptualized the ECA interaction as a dyadic conversation between one agent and one user (e.g. [2, 5]) and do not address how to include several human participants simultaneously. This is a striking omission, as standard application scenarios tend to be settings in which other people are likely to be present and thus influence the interaction, as in a museum or clinical settings ([13, 18]). One exception is the anti-bullying system in [23], in which several agents with different participation roles were created. The system, however, is designed for individual use, even though it is tested in a school setting. The scenario in [20] is the only study in which an agent addresses two users at the same time.

This paper sheds light on situations in which many participants are present during the HAI and shows how the identities of the participants (users, bystanders and the

I am grateful to the Artificial Intelligence Group (Bielefeld University) and the participants of the recorded data for their cooperation. I also want to thank the reviewers for their constructive comments. This research has been supported by the German Research Foundation.

© IFIP International Federation for Information Processing 2015
J. Abascal et al. (Eds.): INTERACT 2015, Part IV, LNCS 9299, pp. 240–247, 2015.
DOI: 10.1007/978-3-319-22723-8_19

agent) shape and are shaped by the ways the parties take part in the ongoing production and interpretation of the HAI. This paper adds to the discussion of the term 'user' in HCI, which is often criticized for its simplistic perspective on the human relationship with the computational machine. While the term 'user' evokes the idea of a 'typical user' often conceptualised as interacting in isolation, [10, 12] point out that systems are used by several users with different background knowledge – such as experts and novices, developers and test-persons, or 'marginal' people, such as those maintaining the machine. Furthermore, the different practices of the individual's usage, the routines and practices of a task and the social-material context of e.g. the company shape the understanding of the user [1].

This paper understands 'user' and 'agent' as categories that describe participation roles within the participation framework of an HAI. These concepts stem from an ethnomethodological point of view, taking the perspective of participants who mutually negotiate their own and each other's action and identity in the ongoing production and interpretation of interaction, as in Suchman's classical study on the user's situated interpretation of an interactive copying machine [22]. A micro-sociological concept of participation ([7, 9]) is applied to two video recordings of a HAI in a public setting. While in both examples a communication problem is solved successfully, the encounter is framed by an asymmetric and mediated participation framework, in which different kinds of participants align in different ways to the production and interpretation of the event. In one, the user solves a communication problem together with the agent. In this case the agent is treated as an equal communication partner. In the other, the user solves the problem involving bystanders as helpers, while the agent is excluded from the interaction and treated as an unequal partner. On the basis of these examples, this paper emphasises that the construction of categories such as 'user' and 'agent' is situated, dynamic and reflexive, and suggests a variety of participation roles in HAI that may inform the development of ECA in social settings.

## 2 Participation Framework and Participation Status

Goffman stresses that interactions are *socially situated* [8], as many interactions take place in the presence of others, who are taken into account. In his paper on *footing*, Goffman deconstructs traditional linguistic concepts of hearer and speaker. He differentiates between the *participation status*, or *participation role* ([17], p. 162), that concerns the relation between the participants, what is said, and their understanding of their self, and the *participation framework* defined as the relations of all those present at a given moment of the encounter.

Goffman's model not only suggests the perspective of interaction as a *social* encounter, but also defines a nonexclusive list of participation roles as dynamic concepts that affect each other and can change during the interaction. Participants can, for example, be involved in an interaction as *ratified* or *unratified* participants, *addressed* or *unaddressed* hearers, and *eavesdroppers* or *bystanders*. This also has consequences for the status of communication. Goffman identifies different kinds of *subordinate communication* in relation to a dominating communication, such as *byplay*, a conversation of a subset of ratified participants (e.g. two people whispering to each other during multiparty conversation), or a *crossplay*, a communication between a ratified participant and a bystander across the boundaries of the dominant communication (e.g. calling the waitress during a conversation with a friend at a restaurant) ([7], p. 134). Furthermore, Goffman offers a complex understanding of a speaker, as he distinguishes for example between the *animator* producing the talk, the *author* who is responsible for the production of the words, and the *principal* who is socially responsible for what is said ([7], p. 144).

Goffman's work is often criticized for not being empirical [17] and offering only a "static set of categories" ([9], p. 225) that cannot account for the situated dynamics of interaction. Goodwin and Goodwin adjust Goffman's ideas for interactional analysis and define participation as "actions demonstrating forms of involvement performed by parties within evolving structures of talk" ([9], p. 222). In a detailed analysis of *talk-in-interaction*, they show the situated and interactive "practices through which different kinds of parties build actions together by *participating* in structured ways in the events" ([9], p. 225). Participation status and the ongoing interaction are thereby reflexively intertwined as they shape and reshape each other. From this theoretical basis, this paper will demonstrate how participants in a HAI in a public setting take part in different ways and how this influences their participation status, the participation framework and the actions themselves.

## 3   Data Collection

The data derives from an ethnographic study of recorded video, naturally occurring (not experimental) interactions between users and the ECA, Max, during a public presentation of the agent in a shopping centre where people could volunteer to communicate with Max ([15, 16]). The data were transcribed and analyzed according to the principles of conversation analysis, including embodied and material aspects [6]. Max is a human-sized agent who can be seen on a large screen. To communicate with Max, users send messages to the agent by typing text on a keyboard in front of the screen. The actual production of the text can be seen and corrected in the white space at the bottom of the screen. After the users press Enter, the text is sent to the system and can be seen in the grey space above the white one. The dialogue system searches the user's text for key symbols and grammatical phrases, assigns a single functional purpose to the message and selects a pre-programmed utterance combined with a bodily reaction performed by the agent (movement of lips, facial expression, gestures, etc.) ([13, 14]). During the presentation at the shopping centre, Max was constructed as a presenter. He could inform the user about certain topics (e.g. AI or the event), take part in small-talk or play a game, for example.

## 4   The Participation Framework of a Human-Agent Interaction

The recorded HAIs can be described as mediated interactions between two different entities located in two different situations and with different abilities to access each other's situation. Max's presence was mediated by screen and loudspeakers to the user, and the user's presence was mediated to Max by written text. Furthermore, the programmed structures that form the agent's understanding of actions differ fundamentally from the user's situated interpretations of the technology during the course of interaction (see [15, 16, 22]).

As the user accesses the virtual world from the keyboard and text-production, he is present in two situations: his physical situation in front of the screen and his engagement (as text-message) in the virtual world. Thus, the HAI is situated in a participation framework that is asymmetrically assessed by user and agent. While Max is programmed to engage in communication with a single user, the user is a participant of a larger social encounter in which various parties are involved in constructing meaning from the HAI. The following analysis demonstrates how this asymmetric participation framework affects the construction of participation roles and activities.

## 4.1 Solving a Communication Problem with the Agent

Figure 1 shows a sequence in which Max and the user, Dave, are playing a game. The agent tries to guess an animal the user has in mind. The agent asks questions and the user answers with yes or no.[1] In line 1, Max asks the user if the animal he has in mind has a mane. Dave does not answer the question but pauses briefly before he types and sends the text "pardon?" (line 3), which marks a problem of understanding. Dave leans forward (lines 4–5) as if he wants to listen closely to Max's next utterance. Max announces that he will repeat his former utterance and does so word by word (line 6). Dave slowly straightens up, puts his hands on the keyboard and eventually says "no" to Max's former question (line 12). Max treats the problem as solved. He asks his next question and continues the game (line 13). In this sequence, Max and Dave mark and *repair* [21] a communicative problem in understanding so the game can continue.[2]

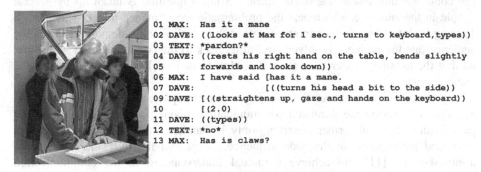

```
01 MAX:   Has it a mane
02 DAVE:  ((looks at Max for 1 sec., turns to keyboard,types))
03 TEXT:  *pardon?*
04 DAVE:  ((rests his right hand on the table, bends slightly
05         forwards and looks down))
06 MAX:   I have said [has it a mane.
07 DAVE:                [((turns his head a bit to the side))
09 DAVE:  [((straightens up, gaze and hands on the keyboard))
10        [(2.0)
11 DAVE:  ((types))
12 TEXT:  *no*
13 MAX:   Has is claws?
```

**Fig. 1.** Repair: solving a problem with Max

[1] The transcripts are simplified and translated form German [16]. Pauses are shown in brackets. Double brackets indicate nonverbal communication. Square brackets mark overlapping actions. Capital letters indicate stress and text within ** is the message sent to the agent.

[2] The pause in line 9–10 indicates that Dave still might not have understood Max. However, Dave produces the relevant answer to Max's question (line 12), which gives the communicative basis for continuing the game. On an interactional level, the problem is solved.

```
01 MAX:    Has it a mane?
02 SONJA:  [((looking at the keyboard))
03         [(0.75)
04 SONJA:  ((turns to the audience)) Has it WHAT?
05 ?:      [Ma:ne                 ]
06 CARL:   [((turns to Sonja))] MAne
07 CS:     Ma:ne
08 SONJA:     [((turns to the keyboard))
09 SONJA:  No [it does not ((typing))
10 TEXT:   *no*
11 MAX:    Has it claws?
```

**Fig. 2.** Troubleshooting: solving a problem without Max

Dave and Max treat each other as ratified and directly-addressed communication partners and are engaged in a focused interaction.

## 4.2  Solving a Communication Problem Without the Agent

In contrast to Dave, who solved the problem *with* Max, Fig. 2 shows how the user, Sonja, excludes Max from the problem-solving activity. Sonja came to the stand with her friend, Carl. He is standing in the background and observes the interaction with the computer scientist who programmed Max (indicated by the initials "CS" in the transcript), as well as other people observing the interaction. In common with Dave, Sonja experiences the same problem of understanding during the guessing game.

After Max asks if the animal has a mane (line 1), Sonja pauses and looks down at the keyboard, before she turns to the audience and asks, "has it what?" (line 2–4). Emphasising the word "what", she identifies the communication problem as specific – she could not understand the word "mane". Sonja's question is taken up by several people in the audience who repeat the problematic term "mane" for her (lines 5–7). Turning back to Max, Sonja announces "no it does not" (line 9), demonstrating to the audience that the problem is solved, and turns back to the communication with Max, writing the missing answer "no" (line 10). Max formulates his next question and the game continues.

By turning to the audience Sonja engages in a crossplay, a side-sequence with the bystanders to inform the dominant communication (playing a game with Max). The participation status of former observing-only bystanders changes to that of directly addressed participants. In this side sequence, Sonja and the bystanders engage in troubleshooting [11] and achieve a mutual understanding of the communication problem and its remedy. While the observers become addressed helpers, the agent is no longer treated as an addressed participant. Max is excluded from parts of the communication and part of the HAI becomes an object of a subordinate communication. Sonja seems to assume that Max is not able to repair her problem (at least not in the way she might hope) and thus treats Max as an unequal or inexperienced communication partner. At this point, the consequences of the asymmetric participation are evident – from Max's perspective, the crossplay did not happen. He is engaged in conversation with one person only.

# 5 Conclusion and Discussion

This paper described a HAI as an asymmetric, mediated and social encounter in which different kinds of participants take up different participation roles in producing and interpreting a HAI. User and agent have different abilities in accessing the situation of the other and are, as such, involved in different participation frameworks. The agent's actions are designed on the basis of a dialog with one single user, while the user is situated in a larger social encounter with other participants. While example 1 showed how Max could be constructed as a quasi-equal conversation partner in an interaction, example 2 highlighted the impact of the asymmetric participation framework – while the user was engaged in a crossplay with the bystanders, Max was not aware of it. The agent's participation status changed to that of an unequal or inexperienced communication partner.

Considering the whole event at the public presentation of the agent, it is possible to differentiate various kinds of participation roles that could inform other studies of HAIs in public or multiparty settings. The *user* was a person who left the audience and went to the table to write a message to the agent. Becoming a user included a change of footing as they 'took the stage' and performed the interaction with Max in front of an observing audience. Sometimes another person (e.g. a friend or the computer scientist helping out) joined the user at the keyboard, construing himself or herself as *co-user*. Other participation roles included those of *by-passers* who glimpsed or more or less ignored the HAI on their way through the shopping centre. *Observers* or *bystanders* formed the audience that surrounded the table and the screen. Most of the bystanders were observing silently, sometimes laughing, commenting on the performance or engaging in subordinated conversation. Some parts of the audience became *helpers* during the course of the interaction, as in example 2, suggesting how to solve a problem or what to write to the agent. People helping out the user often became *authors* or *co-authors* of the text that was written to Max, which also affected the role of the user who became the *animator* of another person's text. Some helpers demonstrated themselves as *experts* in this case, showing a familiar knowledge of the agent-system and how it worked. These were often, but not always, the computer scientist who developed the agent. They often became *principals* of the agent, as they spoke in favour of the agent or explained why it was doing what it did.

This is not a closed list of participation roles in HAI, but it does indicate that the view of an isolated and standardised user is a reductionist way of conceptualizing HAI. Users engage in HAI in various ways and often together with others. Different participation roles have also been found by other authors. Blomberg already has mentioned the special role of advanced users [3] and Woolgar observes *commentators* and *observers* during usability trials. He and argues that people take different roles towards the technology as "they can speak as insiders who know the machine and who can dispense advice to outsiders" ([24], p. 88).

Studies of ECA aiming for applications in social encounters where several parties are present therefore need a theoretical framework that accounts for the different participation roles. This is already done in other areas of interactive technologies. In [19], for example, Goffman's concepts are taken for developing a robot that shapes participation roles by gazing differently at addressees, bystanders and eavesdroppers of the human-robot interaction. However, more work needs to be done to understand the complex and situated ways in which people engage with technologies, so that interaction can be made more effective.

# References

1. Agre, P.E.: Conceptions of the user in computer system design. In: Thomas, P.J. (ed.) The Social and Interactional Dimensions of Human-Computer Interfaces, pp. 67–106. Cambridge University Press, Cambridge (1995)
2. Aylett, R., Krenn, B., Pelachaud, C., Shimodaira, H. (eds.): Intelligent Virtual Agents. Springer, Berlin (2013)
3. Blomberg, J.L.: Social interaction and office communication: effects on user's evaluation of new technologies. In: Kraut, R.E. (ed.) Technology and the Transformation of White-Collar Work, pp. 195–210. Lawrence Erlbaum, Hillsdale (1987)
4. Cassell, J., Bickmore, T., Campbell, L., Vilhjálmsson, H., Yan, H.: Human conversation as a system framework: designing embodied conversational agents. In: Cassell, J., et al. (eds.) Embodied Conversational Agents, pp. 29–63. MIT Press, Cambridge, Mass. (2000)
5. Cassell, J., Sullivan, J., Prevost, S., Churchill, E. (eds.): Embodied Conversational Agents. MIT Press, Cambridge (2000)
6. Heath, C., Hindmarsh, J., Luff, P.: Video in Qualitative Research: Analysing Social Interaction in Everyday Life. Sage, London (2010)
7. Goffman, E.: Footing. In: Goffman, E. (ed.) Forms of Talk, pp. 124–159. Blackwell, Oxford (1981)
8. Goffman, E.: The interaction order. Am. Sociol. Rev. **48**, 1–17 (1983)
9. Goodwin, C., Goodwin, M.H.: Participation. In: Duranti, A. (ed.) A Companion to Linguistic Anthropology, pp. 222–244. Blackwell, Malden (2004)
10. Grudin, J.: Interface: an evolving concept. Commun. ACM **36**(4), 110–119 (1993)
11. Haase, J.: Computer aus Nutzerperspektive von der Nutzeranalyse zum Interface-Design. DUV, Wiesbaden (2005)
12. Hyysalo, S., Johnson, M.: The user as relational entity. Options that deeper insight into user representations opens for human-centered design. Inf. Technol. People **28**(1), 72–89 (2015)
13. Kopp, S., Gesellensetter, L., Krämer, N.C., Wachsmuth, I.: A conversational agent as museum guide – design and evaluation of a real-world application. In: Panayiotopoulos, T., Gratch, J., Aylett, R.S., Ballin, D., Olivier, P., Rist, T. (eds.) IVA 2005. LNCS (LNAI), vol. 3661, pp. 329–343. Springer, Heidelberg (2005)
14. Kopp, S., Jung, B., Lemann, N., Wachsmuth, I.: Max – a multimodal assistant in virtual reality construction. Künstliche Intelligenz **4**, 11–17 (2003)
15. Krummheuer, A.: Conversation analysis, video recordings, and human-computer interchanges. In: Kissmann, U.T. (ed.) Video Interaction Analysis. Methods and Methodology, pp. 59–83. Peter Lang, Frankfurt am Main (2009)
16. Krummheuer, A.: Interaktion mit virtuellen Agenten? Zur Aneignung eines ungewohnten Artefakts. Lucius & Lucius, Stuttgart (2010)
17. Levinson, S.C.: Putting linguistics on a proper footing: explorations in Goffman's concepts of participation. In: Drew, P., Wootton, A. (eds.) Erving Goffman. Exploring the Interaction Order, pp. 161–227. Polity Press, Cambridge (1988)

18. Moosaei, M., Gonzales, M.J., Riek, L.D.: Naturalistic pain synthesis for virtual patients. In: Bickmore, T., Marsella, S., Sidner, C. (eds.) IVA 2014. LNCS, vol. 8637, pp. 295–309. Springer, Heidelberg (2014)
19. Mutlu, B., Shiwa,T., Kanda, T., Ishiguro, H., Hagita, N.: Footing in Human-Robot conversation: how robots might shape participant role using gaze cues. In: HRI 2009, March 11–13, La Jolla California, USA (2009)
20. Rehm, M.: 'She is just stupid' – analyzing user-agent interactions in emotional game situations. Interact. Comput. **20**, 311–325 (2008)
21. Schegloff, E.A., Jefferson, G., Sacks, H.: The preference for self-correction in the organization of repair in conversation. Language **53**(2), 361–382 (1977)
22. Suchman, L.: Human-Machine Reconfigurations Plans and Situated Actions. Cambridge University Press, Cambridge (2007)
23. Vannini, N., Enz, S., Sapouna, M., Wolke, D., Watson, S., Woods, S., Dautenhahn, K., Hall, L., Paiva, A., André, E.: "Fearnot!": a computer-based anti-bullying-programme designed to foster peer intervention. Eur. J. Psychol. Educ. **26**(1), 21–44 (2011)
24. Woolgar, S.: Configuring the user: the case of usability trials. In: Law, J. (ed.) A Sociology of Monsters: Essays on Power, Technology and Domination, pp. 58–99. Routledge, London (1991)

# Augmented Happiness: Simple Color Changes Influence Users' Conceptual Choices

Diana Löffler[1(✉)], Wolfgang Paier[2], Takashi Toriizuka[3], Mio Ikeda[3],
and Jörn Hurtienne[1]

[1] Chair of Psychological Ergonomics,
University of Würzburg, Würzburg, Germany
{diana.loeffler,joern.hurtienne}@uni-wuerzburg.de
[2] Fraunhofer HHI, Computer Vision and Graphics, Berlin, Germany
wolfgang.paier@hhi.fraunhofer.de
[3] College of Industrial Technology, Nihon University, Chiba, Japan
toriiduka.takashi@nihon-u.ac.jp,
mio.ikeda1220@gmail.com

**Abstract.** Color is a powerful visual property and is used to make interferences about the world. However, no theoretical framework is available that explains precisely where color associations come from and how they affect psychological functioning, making it difficult to predict how color affects human-computer interaction. This paper aims at closing this gap by suggesting an Embodied Cognition view on color, which assumes that the aggregate of our perceptual color experiences is part of the mental representation of tactile object attributes and thus systematically influences our abstract thinking via the process of metaphorical mapping. An empirical study is presented in which hues and saturation of objects were manipulated via Augmented Reality. Participants matched objects to abstract concepts, e.g., happiness. 83 % of the participants' choices were correctly predicted, suggesting that color information is considered during the processing of abstract information. Eight color-to-abstract-concept mappings are recommended and possible areas of application are discussed.

**Keywords:** Augmented reality · Color · Embodied cognition · Conceptual metaphor

## 1 Introduction

Color is a ubiquitous perceptual experience that influences perception, cognition and behavior. However, color research mainly focuses on establishing relations between color and psychological functioning and often lacks a rigorous theoretical understanding of why these relations occur [7]. This might be a main reason why findings on the impact of color on psychological functioning are largely inconsistent, unreliable and inconclusive [e.g., 13, 22]. In the field of human-computer interaction (HCI), design recommendations on color are usually restricted to issues of readability, aesthetics or color preferences [3]. This paper aims to advance our theoretical understanding of how and why color affects psychological functioning to leverage

© IFIP International Federation for Information Processing 2015
J. Abascal et al. (Eds.): INTERACT 2015, Part IV, LNCS 9299, pp. 248–255, 2015.
DOI: 10.1007/978-3-319-22723-8_20

a systematic application of color in the design of human-computer interaction. To achieve this, the framework of embodied cognition, which holds the promise of providing a unifying perspective for psychological research in general [8], is briefly reviewed and then applied to the field of color.

In recent years the predominant views of the human mind, such as the computational theories of information processing, have been increasingly challenged by findings that cognition is embodied (cf. [6]). Embodied cognition grants the body a central role in cognitive processing. Physical experiences we have, moving through the material world, scaffold the development of our conceptual knowledge. Many of such embodied experiences are manifested in language [15]. Expressions such as "the heavy burden of guilt" or "that warmed my spirits" reflect how the mental representations of guilt and happiness are metaphorically conceptualized. These conceptual metaphors involve a mapping from a physical source domain (weight, temperature) to another, more abstract, target domain (guilt, happiness) [15]. Being equipped with conceptual metaphors in our embodied minds, even seemingly unrelated visual or haptic properties of objects or technical devices influence our perception, feeling, and behavior (cf. [12]), in a way predicted by the framework of embodied cognition.

## 2   An Embodied Cognition View on Color

Color is an important perceptual feature and in natural environments often diagnostic for other perceptual properties [4], like edibility and taste [19], weight [1, 21] or temperature [10]. Thus, it is likely that color affects psychological functioning in a similar way than related perceptual properties via the process of metaphorical mapping [16, 20].

Many studies already investigated associations between color and other perceptual attributes like weight, size and temperature. For example, according to [5], temperature attributes are solely related to hue (red is warm, blue is cold). Increasing weight is related to decreasing brightness and an increase in saturation [1], while when the size of a stimulus is increased, it is perceived as brighter and more saturated [23].

In recent years, a few studies have been conducted to empirically test these associations between colors and perceptual properties. For example, in an HCI relevant application, Ban and colleagues [2] proposed an Augmented Reality (AR) system to manipulate weight perception through an increase in object brightness. They demonstrated that this facilitated the lifting of medium-weight objects. However, as with most of the research on relations between color and psychological functioning [7], no theoretical background is provided on how and why this association is shaped, making it difficult to transfer the results into other situations and contexts. An embodied cognition view on color may close this theoretical gap, as it explains that the association between weight and brightness arises through the repeated experience that heavier objects appear to be darker than light objects (e.g., when a shirt gets wet it will be heavier and darker, [21]). Thus, the perception of brightness and weight mutually influence each other. In addition, this association between brightness and weight might be extended to more abstract concepts via metaphorical mapping [17, 20]. For example, weight is metaphorically linked to psychological significance, or, in other words, weight is conceptualized as an embodiment of importance [14]. Therefore, it can be assumed that the perception of the color property brightness will bias information processing in contexts where psychological significance plays a role. This prediction can now be put to direct empirical test.

In this paper, we aim to experimentally test the embodied cognition view on color and investigate whether perceiving certain color characteristics will influence the cognitive processing of more abstract information (like happiness, emotionality, or power), which is metaphorically linked to the tactile properties weight, size and temperature.

# 3   Method

## 3.1   Participants

Fourteen volunteers were recruited at the campus of Nihon University, Japan, (seven male, seven female) to participate in this study. The participants' ages ranged from 21 to 24 years (M = 22.7, SD = 0.8). All participants had Japanese as their mother tongue and had no reported defective color vision. They were all naïve as to the subject under investigation.

## 3.2   Procedure

The experimental procedure was adopted from a study by Hurtienne et al. [12]. Each participant was asked to complete a short demographic questionnaire. The participants were then told that they would wear AR glasses and, in each trial, would be presented with two colored objects (spheres) and an adjective describing an abstract property (e.g. difficulty). AR technology was utilized because it allows for a convenient manipulation of object colors in the viewers' sight.

The participants were instructed to touch the objects with their dominant hand that they felt corresponded most closely to the adjective (Fig. 1). Participants were told to decide quickly and instinctively in favor of one object. Each session consisted of 30 trials. To avoid sequence effects, the adjectives and colored objects were presented in random order. The whole experiment lasted about 15 min.

## 3.3   Apparatus and Material

Each of the two wooden spheres was 9 cm in diameter and weighed 250 g. They were colored in blue and green (controlled for saturation and brightness) in order to facilitate technical object recognition against the background and against the participants' hands and arms. These spheres were the target objects for the color changes, which did perfectly obscure the spheres. The spheres' position was counterbalanced across participants. The participants were seated in an experimental room; the table and wall in front of them were covered in gray cloth. The spheres were placed on the table within the reach of the participants, with 15 cm distance between them.

**Fig. 1.** A participant wearing AR-glasses that change the object colors in the participants' sight.

The AR system used in the study was composed of a video see-through realizing Head Mounted Display VUZIX Wrap1200AR (resolution 852 × 480, 35 degrees diagonal field of view) and a notebook (Intel Core i7 4×2.4 GHz 8.00 GB RAM, Windows 8.1 64 bit). The color manipulation software was based on OpenCV, which provides convenient interfaces for processing and capturing images from the stereo-webcam integrated in the AR glasses. Each pixel was classified in background, green sphere or blue sphere, using a histogram-based color-classifier. The classifier was trained beforehand using six images with proper fore/background masks to fill the color-histograms for each pixel-class. The masks were generated using a semi-automatic approach for foreground extraction [18]. To guarantee the realtime-capability of the system, a static look-up table, containing the color-transform (RGBin to RGBout) for each camera was calculated after the color classifiers were trained.

Three HCI-relevant tactile properties with well-documented metaphorical extensions were selected for the experiment: weight (heavy-light), size (big-small) and temperature (warm-cold) [12]. A pre-study was conducted to determine the relationship between these tactile properties and color characteristics (hue, saturation and brightness). In an online questionnaire, 80 Japanese subjects rated how well 35 different colors (varying in hue, saturation and brightness) matched the properties weight, size and temperature. The results showed that weight and size were mainly associated with the color properties of saturation and brightness, and the temperature is almost solely associated with hue (red vs. blue). These results confirmed those of previous research [5, 23]. The tactile properties of weight, size and temperature were therefore operationalized through their associated color properties in the following way (numbers depict HSB values): heavy, big vs. light, small: violet (270/100/100) vs. (270/60/100), green (140/100/100) vs. (140/60/100), red (360/100/100) vs. (360/60/100), yellow (60/100/100) vs. (60/60/100), orange (40/100/100) vs. (40/60/100); cold: blue (200/100/100), cyan (180/100/100); warm: red (360/100/100), orange (20/100/100). Note that, although both, saturation and brightness, influence the perception of weight, size and strength, the brightness of the objects in the experiment was not altered. This would have led to a loss in texture and surface shading, thereby negatively affecting the three-dimensional impression of the objects. Hues in the weight and size condition were randomly chosen to create some variation and should, according to theory, have no effect, because hue is not diagnostic for these tactile properties.

For each condition, well-documented metaphorically linked abstract concepts were taken from literature [12, 17] (Table 1). Two lists of adjectives were prepared. One word from each adjective pair was placed on list A (e.g., important), and its opposite was placed on list B (e.g., unimportant). Both groups were balanced with regard to the number of positive and negative words they contained. Half of the participants were presented with adjectives from list A, and the other half with adjectives from list B.

The hypothesis for this experiment was that since specific color characteristics are diagnostic for certain tactile properties, viewing these color characteristics will trigger choices consistent with metaphorically related abstract concepts. If the color

**Table 1.** Tactile properties, conceptual metaphors, stimulus adjectives and results of color-to-abstract-concept mappings; all mappings with str < 0.60 have been grayed.

| Tactile Property | Conceptual metaphor with linguistic examples | Stimulus adjectives | Related color property | % | str |
|---|---|---|---|---|---|
| Weight is.. | Difficulty: heavy reading; light duties | difficult, easy | Saturation | 93 | 0.86 |
| | Importance: heavy matters of state; light, idle chatter | important, unimportant | Saturation | 91 | 0.82 |
| | Guilt: the heavy burden of guilt; easing conscience | guilty, innocent | Saturation | 61 | 0.21 |
| | Sadness: heavy news; light-hearted girls | sad, happy | Saturation | 61 | 0.21 |
| Size is.. | Significance: he is a big man in industry; only a small crime | significant, insignificant | Saturation | 96 | 0.93 |
| | Quantity: I only have a small amount of money | much, less | Saturation | 95 | 0.90 |
| | Education: he expanded his horizons | educated, uneducated | Saturation | 75 | 0.50 |
| Temperature is.. | Activity: a hot debate; frozen accounts | active, inactive | Hue | 93 | 0.86 |
| | Emotionality: a warm smile; cold logic | emotional, unemotional | Hue | 93 | 0.86 |
| | Difficulty: a smoldering conflict; the debate cooled down | problematic, unproblematic | Hue | 86 | 0.71 |
| | Happiness: that warmed my spirits; a deep cold sadness | happy, sad | Hue | 82 | 0.64 |
| | Intimacy: giving the cold shoulder; warm feelings | intimate, distant | Hue | 75 | 0.50 |

characteristics are not associated with the abstract concepts, participants will choose one of the two objects by chance.

## 4 Results and Discussion

The results are depicted in Table 1. The columns show the percentage of answers that were consistent with the metaphorically related concept (averaged over all color samples) and Cohen's kappa values are used as an index for associative strength (str) that takes into account the agreement occurring by chance (50 %). According to [16] 's categories of agreement, negative str values indicate "poor" agreement, $0 <$ str $\leq 0.19$ indicate "slight" agreement, $0.20 \leq$ str $\leq 0.39$ "fair" agreement, $0.40 \leq$ str $\leq 0.59$ "moderate" agreement, $0.60 \leq$ str $\leq 0.79$ "substantial" agreement, and str $\geq 0.80$ "almost perfect" agreement. Because of the limited and non-representative sample size we only interpreted strength values of above 0.60 as supportive of the color-to-abstract-concept mappings (8 of 12). However, across all 12 color-to-abstract-concept mappings, the mean value of str was 0.67 (SD = 0.26), suggesting that at least 83 % of the participants' choices were consistent with the conceptual metaphor. This value differs significantly from a chance str of zero, $t(11) = 8.94$, $p < .001$, Cohen's $d = 3.64$, and indicates non-randomness in the choices of the participants.

Overall, the results are interpreted in favor of an embodied cognition view on color: 8 out of 12 evaluated abstract concepts showed on average "almost perfect" agreement, while the remaining four concepts showed on average "fair" agreement [16]. These results were predicted by associations between color attributes and tactile properties: because heavier objects tend to be darker and less saturated [1, 21], darker and less saturated hues are assumed to bias our thinking about metaphorically related abstract concepts, like psychological significance, because weight is an embodiment of psychological significance. The link between brightness, saturation and size can be explained by the bodily constraint of a nonuniform distribution of photoreceptors across the retina, resulting in different color vision in the periphery compared to vision in the fovea [24]. The association between physical temperature and hue can be explained by the internalization of correlations between stimuli that are present in the environment (like fire, sun, water) and our bodies (blood circulation) [9]. As predicted, multiple McNemar tests (Bonferroni corrected) revealed no difference between the different hues tested across the weight and size conditions.

## 5 Conclusion and Future Work

With the help of the AR system it could be demonstrated that simple color changes in the users' sight resulted in a bias in decision-making in favor of metaphorically related abstract concepts. This is explained by an embodied cognition view of cognition on colors: because abstract concepts are grounded in observables in the world, we automatically consider perceived physical properties, such as color and tactile properties, during reasoning about these abstract concepts. The value of this embodied cognition view on colors lies in its ability to explain and predict why and which effects of color on psychological functioning occur, taking the guesswork out of color theory and design.

Moreover, this research has shown that not only hue but also saturation plays a great role in conveying abstract content [7]. Three abstract concepts were identified that can be influenced by a change in saturation: difficulty, importance, significance and quantity. Three concepts were influenced by hue: emotionality, activity and happiness. The concept of difficulty was influenced by both saturation and hue. We expect that the effects would have been even stronger had the brightness parameter been manipulated as well. Although selected well above chance level, four color-to-abstract mappings were weaker than expected and require further investigation.

By extending this approach to applied contexts, the validity and effectiveness of predictions derived from an embodied cognition view on colors is an area for future research. Changes in saturation, for example, could be used to indicate the most significant, or most-often used objects or functions (significance is saturation); they could be used to express priority among different items, such as the most valued menu option in a restaurant, or the best selling products in an online shop (importance is saturation). Reddish vs. bluish hues could be used to communicate or visualize subtle mood changes in social networks, online games or in real life situations (happiness is redness). Changing font or background color could influence the perceived difficulty of a computerized cognitive training (difficulty is saturation) – and this should also work for people with cognitive impairment, since embodied cognition effects are assumed to be rather independent of higher cognitive processing [11].

Although the results of this pilot study are promising, the sample size of the study reported here is very small (n = 14). Larger scale empirical studies have yet to be conducted in order to validate the results obtained here, also with regard to different cultures. Since color and also, to some extent, conceptual metaphors are subject to cultural influences, studies on the applicability of the results within and across countries and cultures are required.

**Acknowledgements.** We thank the Japan Society for the Promotion of Science for funding this research (grant ID PE14746).

# References

1. Alexander, K.R., Shansky, M.S.: Influence of hue, value, and chroma on the perceived heaviness of colors. Percept. Psychophys. **19**(1), 72–74 (1976)
2. Ban, Y., Narumi, T., Fujii, T., Sakurai, S., Imura, J., Tanikawa, T., and Hirose, M. Augmented Endurance: Controlling Fatigue while Handling Objects by Affecting Weight Perception using Augmented Reality. In Proceedings of CHI 2013, pp. 69–77. ACM Press (2013)
3. Bonnardel, N., Piolat, A., Le Bigot, L.: The impact of colour on Website appeal and users' cognitive processes. Displays **32**(2), 69–80 (2011)
4. Cant, J.S., Large, M.E., McCall, L., Goodale, M.A.: Independent processing of form, color and texture in object perception. Perception **37**, 57–78 (2008)

5. Cheng, K.M.: Quantitative evaluation of colour emotions (Doctoral dissertation, The Hong Kong Polytechnic University) (2002)
6. Clark, A.: Being There: Putting Brain, Body and World Together Again. Bradford Books, MIT Press, Cambridge (2007)
7. Elliot, A.J., Maier, M.A.: Color and psychological functioning. Curr. Dir. Psychol. Sci. **16** (5), 250–254 (2007)
8. Glenberg, A.M.: Embodiment as a unifying perspective for psychology. Wiley Interdisc. Rev. Cogn. Sci. **1**(4), 586–596 (2010)
9. Ho, H.N., Iwai, D., Yoshikawa, Y., Watanabe, J., Nishida, S.Y.: Combining colour and temperature: a blue object is more likely to be judged as warm than a red object. Scientific reports, 4 (2014)
10. Ho, H.N., Van Doorn, G.H., Kawabe, T., Watanabe, J., Spence, C.: Colour-temperature correspondences: when reactions to thermal stimuli are influenced by colour. PLoS ONE **9** (3), e91854 (2014)
11. Hurtienne, J., Horn, A.-M., Langdon, P.M., Clarkson, P.J.: Facets of prior experience and the effectiveness of inclusive design. Univ. Access Inf. Soc. **12**, 3 (2013)
12. Hurtienne, J., Stößel, C. and Weber, K. Sad is Heavy and Happy is Light – Population Stereotypes of Tangible Object Attributes. In: Proceedings of TEI 2009, pp. 61–68. ACM Press (2009)
13. Jalil, N.A., Yunus, R.M., Said, N.S.: Environmental colour impact upon human behaviour: a review. Procedia Soc. Behav. Sci. **35**, 54–62 (2012)
14. Jostmann, N.B., Lakens, D., Schubert, T.W.: Weight as an embodiment of importance. Psychol. Sci. **20**(9), 1169–1174 (2009)
15. Lakoff, G., Johnson, M.: Metaphors We Live By. University of Chicago Press, Chicago (1980)
16. Landis, J.R., Koch, G.G.: The Measurement of Observer Agreement for Categorical Data. Biometrics **33**, 159–174 (1977)
17. Löffler, D.: Population stereotypes of color attributes for tangible interaction design. In: Proceedings of the 8th International Conference on Tangible, Embedded and Embodied Interaction, pp. 285–288. ACM (2014)
18. Rother, C., Kolmogorov, V., Blake, A.: "GrabCut": interactive foreground extraction using iterated graph cuts. In: SIGGRAPH 2004, pp. 309–314. ACM Press (2004)
19. Shankar, M.U., Levitan, C.A., Spence, C.: Grape expectations the role of cognitive influences in color-flavor interactions. Conscious Cogn. **19**(1), 380–390 (2010)
20. Valdez, P., Mehrabian, A.: Effects of color on emotions. J. Exp. Psychol. Gen. **123**(4), 394–409 (1994)
21. Walker, P., Francis, B.J., Walker, L.: The brightness-weight illusion: darker objects look heavier but feel lighter. Exp. Psychol. **57**(6), 462 (2010)
22. Whitfield, T.W., Whiltshire, T.J.: Color psychology: a critical review. Genet. Soc. Gen. Psychol. Monogr. **116**(4), 385–411 (1990)
23. Xiao, K., Li, C.J., Luo, M.R., Taylor, C.: Colour appearance for dissimilar sizes. Conf. Colour Graph. Imaging Vis. **20**(1), 12–16 (2004). Society for Imaging Science and Technology
24. Xiao, K., Luo, M.R., Li, C., Cui, G., Park, D.: Investigation of colour size effect for colour appearance assessment. Color Res. Appl. **36**(3), 201–209 (2011)

# Investigating Representation Alternatives
# for Communicating Uncertainty
# to Non-experts

Miriam Greis[✉], Thorsten Ohler, Niels Henze, and Albrecht Schmidt

VIS, University of Stuttgart, Stuttgart, Germany
{miriam.greis,thorsten.ohler,niels.henze,
albrecht.schmidt}@vis.uni-stuttgart.de

**Abstract.** Non-experts are confronted with uncertainty of predictions everyday when, e.g., using a navigation device or looking at the weather forecast. However, there are no standards for representing uncertain information and representations could be easily misleading. Thus, we selected twelve representations that provide different levels of uncertainty information. We compared the representations in an online survey with 90 participants where we asked participants to judge their support in decision-making, familiarity, easiness to understand, and visual appeal. We further evaluated the four most promising representations in a turn-based online game. Players had to make decisions in a farming scenario based on a displayed weather forecast. The results of the survey and the game indicate that a function graph of a probability distribution function is the best way to communicate uncertain information. Nevertheless, our results also show that presenting more uncertainty information does not necessarily lead to better decisions.

**Keywords:** Uncertainty · Representations · Visualizations · Non-experts

## 1 Introduction

Simulation is a very powerful technique used in different fields to explore the behavior of complex systems as, e.g., the flow of ground water, the human walking behavior, and the world's climate. Due to its applicability to many problems, simulation is one of the most used techniques in research and management sciences [4].

The results of simulations are uncertain due to, e.g., assumptions made in the modeling process or the parameter choice. Non-experts, who have no specialized knowledge about simulations, are confronted with simulation results and uncertain data everyday, e.g., when looking at the weather forecast that shows the possible temperature for the next day. They rely on uncertain data to implicitly predict the future, plan activities, and make decisions. These decisions could be even unintentionally manipulated by choosing a specific representation.

Although several aspects of the communication and visualization of uncertain data were examined before, still work has to be done to get more insights in how different representations influence decision-making. From existing work, we selected twelve

© IFIP International Federation for Information Processing 2015
J. Abascal et al. (Eds.): INTERACT 2015, Part IV, LNCS 9299, pp. 256–263, 2015.
DOI: 10.1007/978-3-319-22723-8_21

representations (three textual and nine graphical representations) used for uncertainty communication for experts and non-experts. This leads to a wide range of used representations with different degrees of included uncertainty information.

First, we present the results of an online survey where participants had to rate the representations according to the perceived help for decision support in a farming scenario, familiarity, easiness to understand, and visual appeal. We found significant differences in the rating of the representations and also correlations between ratings. Surprisingly, we did not find any strong correlations between subjective ratings and the degree of uncertainty information included in a representation.

Second, we present the results of a small experiment with a turn-based online game. The four representations that performed best in the online survey were used to display a weather forecast. Decisions of players were analyzed on the basis of optimal decisions. The function graph of a probability distribution function performed best, but the representation with no information about the included uncertainty did not perform dramatically worse.

The contribution of our work is twofold. First, we show that people do not judge representations for the degree of uncertainty information they show. Other factors are more important for their judgment. Second, we show that a higher degree of uncertainty information does not necessarily lead to better decisions and that people are able to make good decisions with the help of a probability density function.

## 2 Related Work

The topic of uncertainty visualization is well explored for experts. Multiple areas such as vector field, surface and glyph visualizations are for example explored by Pang et al. [9] and Zuk and Carpendale [15]. Additionally, new versions of basic representations (e.g., box plots) are for example developed by Potter et al. [11]. In our paper, we do not take into account such visualizations and focus on basic representations developed for experts and non-experts.

For communicating uncertainty to non-experts, usually quantitative information, especially probabilities are used. One problem when using quantitative information is the inability of even well-educated adults to solve easy numeracy probability questions [5]. But also qualitative information, e.g., labels such as low uncertainty or low risk, could be misleading, as already examined by Wallsten et al. [14]. Additionally, the formulation of a risk or uncertainty, whether negative or positive, has a huge influence on decision-making [6].

One strand of work investigated uncertainty information in weather forecasts. Morss et al. [7] found that most people are aware of the uncertainty in deterministic weather forecasts, although the range of this uncertainty was perceived very differently. Additionally, 70 % of the people preferred forecasts that contained information about the uncertainty of the forecast. Studies by Roulston et al. [12] and Joslyn et al. [3] showed that people make better decisions when having information about the uncertainty of a forecast and that information about the uncertainty also increases the trust in a forecast. They used a small number of alternative representations in a decision task.

Another strand of work investigated and compared visualizations including uncertainty information. Ibrekk et al. [2] compared nine visualizations for uncertainty by giving non-experts specific tasks (e.g., finding the mean). They suggest displaying a normal probability distribution function together with a cumulative probability distribution function. Pappenberger et al. [10] made a study with experts in meteorology and asked them about their preferred representation for a probabilistic forecast. The most used representation were quantiles.

Additional studies focus on one specific visualization or aspect. Olston et al. [8] examined visualizations for presenting bounded uncertainty by adjusting the visual elements and including transparency in the visualizations and Tak et al. [13] used seven variations of a line graph to investigate the perceived certainty. Correll and Gleicher [1] proposed a redesign of bar charts and found that less well-known visualizations improve performance for interferential tasks.

Previous work mainly focused either on a small number or representations, variations of one representation, or a very specific task (e.g., finding the mean). They found that uncertainty information leads to better decisions, but it is not clear how this conclusion relates to different degrees of uncertainty information and how aggregated uncertainty information influence decision-making. In contrast to previous work, we decided to take a wide range of basic representations and concentrate our research on the degree of uncertainty information that is included in these representations.

## 3   Online Survey

To understand if the presented degree of uncertainty changes the perceived value of a representation for decision support and the easiness to understand the representation, we conducted an online survey. Building upon prior research, we selected twelve representations (see Fig. 1) with different properties for communicating uncertainty information. All representations show the expected rainfall for the next three days. Three representations use a textual representation of the information, whilst the other nine representations are graphical. We use a line chart, a box-and-whisker plot, bar charts, stacked bar charts, stacked area diagrams, shaded bars, and function graphs. The representations also communicate different degrees of uncertainty information, from no information about uncertainty at all up to detailed information. The displayed degree of uncertainty information for each representation is depicted in Table 1.

### 3.1   Questionnaire

On the first page of the questionnaire, we asked participants for demographic information: age, gender, their highest degree, and their field of work.

We then displayed a scenario description that told participants to imagine that they are a farmer and want to grow plants. The plants need a certain amount of water to grow and survive. A weather forecast will be available to support participants in making a decision, but it will be uncertain.

Participants then had to navigate through twelve pages with one representation on each page. The order of the representations was randomized across participants. For each representation, participants had to indicate their level of agreement on a five-level Likert scale from totally disagree to totally agree with four statements:

1. The representation supports me in making a decision.
2. I am familiar with the representation.
3. The representation is easy to understand.
4. The representation is visually appealing.

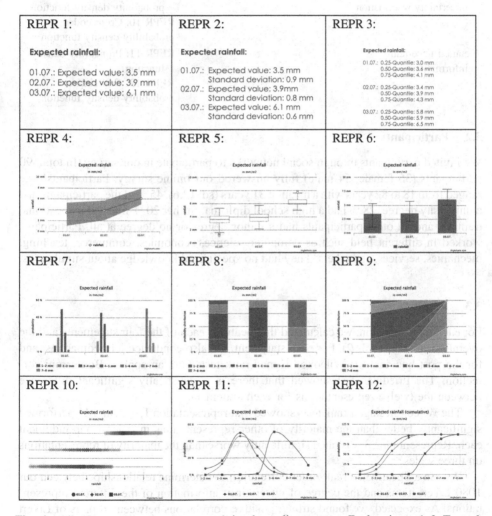

**Fig. 1.** All 12 representations compared in the online survey. Explanations: 1–3 Textual representations, 4 – Line chart with area diagram, 5 – Box-and-whisker plot, 6–7 Bar charts, 8 – Stacked bar charts, 9 – Area chart, 10 – Shaded horizontal bars, 11–12 Function graph

**Table 1.** Degree of uncertainty information included in the representations.

|  | Textual representation | Graphical representation |
|---|---|---|
| No uncertainty information | REPR 1: Expected values | / |
| Aggregated uncertainty information | REPR 2: Expected values and standard deviation<br>REPR 3: Quantiles | REPR 4: Expected values and confidence interval<br>REPR 5: Quantiles<br>REPR 6: Expected values and standard deviation |
| Detailed aggregated uncertainty information | / | REPR 7–9: Aggregated probability density function<br>REPR 10: Color-coded probability density function |
| Detailed uncertainty information | / | REPR 11: Probability density function<br>REPR 12: Cumulative probability density function |

## 3.2 Participants

We invited participants through social networks to participate in our survey. In total, 90 participants (36 female, 54 male) fully answered our online survey. Participants' age ranged from 18 to 82 years with a mean of 31 years (sd: 12.6). 45 % of the participants had a university degree, 28 % had a high school diploma, further 20 % finished a vocational training, and all other participants had a minor degree or no degree at all. Participants worked in different field such as computer science, economics, commerce, teaching, mechanics, services, and others. They had no specialized knowledge about simulations.

## 3.3 Results

For each representation, we calculated the mean for each of the four statements and the overall mean (see Table 2). For each statement, we also conducted a Friedman test and for the post hoc analysis Wilcoxon signed-rank tests with an applied Bonferroni correction. The Friedman test showed that there is a statistically significant difference between the twelve representations for each statement.

The Wilcoxon singed-rank tests showed that representation 1, 4, 7, and 11 performed significantly better than the majority of other representations in at least one judgment each. Representation 3 was rated significantly worse than the majority of representations on three scales.

We ran a Spearman's rank-order correlation to determine relationships between our 1080 Likert items and the degree of uncertainty information of the different representations. As expected, we found strong, positive correlations between all pairs of Likert items, which were all statistically significant ($p < 0.0005$), see Table 3 for detailed values. Surprisingly, we did not find any significant positive or negative correlation between the Likert items and the degree of uncertainty information of the representations, except one

**Table 2.** Calculated mean values for the level of agreement on a five-level Likert scale from totally disagree (1) to totally agree (5) with the statements: S1 – The representation supports me in making a decision., S2 – I am familiar with the representation., S3 – The representation is easy to understand., S4 – The representation is visually appealing., and O – the overall mean values for all 12 representations.

| REPR | S1 | S2 | S3 | S4 | O |
|---|---|---|---|---|---|
| 1: Expected values | 3.63 | 4.29 | 4.28 | 2.30 | 3.63 |
| 2: Expected values and standard deviation | 3.68 | 3.90 | 3.34 | 2.13 | 3.26 |
| 3: Quantiles | 2.86 | 2.79 | 2.37 | 1.70 | 2.43 |
| 4: Line chart with confidence interval | 4.12 | 3.74 | 4.12 | 4.01 | 4.00 |
| 5: Boxplot | 3.22 | 2.73 | 2.52 | 2.48 | 2.74 |
| 6: Bar chart with error bars | 3.48 | 3.11 | 3.08 | 2.98 | 3.16 |
| 7: Histograms as bar charts | 3.93 | 4.21 | 3.67 | 3.67 | 3.87 |
| 8: Histograms as stacked bar charts | 3.47 | 3.49 | 3.16 | 3.52 | 3.41 |
| 9: Histograms as area chart | 3.16 | 2.84 | 2.74 | 3.42 | 3.04 |
| 10: Shaded horizontal bars | 3.73 | 2.31 | 3.59 | 3.59 | 3.31 |
| 11: Probability distribution function | 3.89 | 3.88 | 3.46 | 3.60 | 3.71 |
| 12: Cum. probability distribution function | 3.44 | 3.50 | 2.88 | 3.52 | 3.34 |

**Table 3.** Spearmen's rho for a Spearman's rank-order correlation between Likert scale items of the online survey and the degree of uncertainty information of the presented representations. Statistically significant values are marked with asterisk(s). $**p < 0.01$, $*p > 0.0005$

| | Decision support | Familiarity | Easiness to understand | Visual appeal |
|---|---|---|---|---|
| Degree of uncertainty | 0.048 | −0.040 | −0.084** | 0.365* |
| Decision support | – | 0.505* | 0.670* | 0.527* |
| Familiarity | – | – | 0.609* | 0.530* |
| Easiness to understand | – | – | – | 0.530* |

moderate positive correlation with the Likert items for visual appeal (see Table 3). We assume that this correlation occurred because we used textual representations with low degrees of uncertainty information.

# 4 Experiment

Based on the results of the online survey, we implemented a turn-based online game that displayed a weather forecast using the four representations that performed best in our online survey. With the help of the weather forecast for the next three days, players had to decide which crops they want to plant. Crops needed specific values for rainfall, wind, and sun that were always displayed and gave different amounts of money when fully grown and harvested. Players had the goal to get as much money as possible. If one weather condition for a planted crop was violated, it withered and it gave no money at all.

We conducted a controlled experiment with 12 participants (4 female, 8 male), recruited with the help of social networks, who had to play the game with each of the four representations. The order of the representations was changed for each participant and randomly assigned to them. Each game lasted for 10 rounds. Participants were not trained and did not have any specialized knowledge about simulations. For the analysis, we logged all relevant information, which included the forecasted weather, the real weather, and all crops that were planted.

Participants played in total 480 rounds of the game, 120 rounds with each representation. For our analysis, we only considered rounds in which the players at least clicked on the button to open the weather forecasts once. This resulted in 442 rounds.

For each round, we calculated the optimal decision based on the weather forecast displayed and compared it with players' decisions. With representation 11, participants made the most optimal decisions, in 69 % of the rounds, with representation 7 in 64 % of the rounds, with representation 1 in 60 % of the round and with representation 4 in 57 % of the rounds.

At the end, we asked participants which representation they liked most. 8 participants selected representation 11, three participants selected representation 7, 1 participant selected representation 4, and no participant selected representation 1.

## 5   Discussion & Conclusion

The results of our online survey show that the representations were judged very differently. Surprisingly, the four best-rated representations taking the overall mean show a different degree of uncertainty information each. Correlating the judgments and the degree of uncertainty information provided by the representations, we found that there are no significant correlations between the perceived support in decision-making and the degree of uncertainty information. Thus, we showed that participants do not judge the perceived support of decision making for a representation in regard to the degree of uncertainty information presented. In contrast, factors such as familiarity, easiness to understand, and visual appeal have a huge influence on the judgment. Our work indicates that other factors besides the presented degree of uncertainty information have to be considered when displaying uncertain data.

Comparing results from the online survey and the experiment, we found that the line chart with the highest rating in the survey performed worse than the other representations in the experiment. Although other studies showed that participants make better decision when having uncertainty information, our experiment suggests that aggregated uncertainty information do not provide enough details to make better decisions than only information about the expected values. We assume that the aggregated uncertainty information, the confidence interval, was not enough information to make a better decision but instead alienated participants. Nevertheless, most participants in our experiment preferred using the representation of the probability distribution function. Additionally, participants made very good decisions using this probability density function although earlier studies suggest that people are not very good at intuitively interpreting statistical information. This indicates that a probability function should be used to communicate uncertain data for non-experts and that too much aggregation of uncertainty information should be avoided.

Our experiment is clearly limited by the small number of participants and the scenario, but nevertheless shows interesting factors that are relevant for uncertainty communication. Future work on different scenarios with more participants will help to generalize the findings.

**Acknowledgements.** The authors would like to thank the German Research Foundation (DFG) for financial support of the project within the Cluster of Excellence in Simulation Technology (EXC 310/2) at the University of Stuttgart.

# References

1. Correll, M., Gleicher, M.: Error bars considered harmful: exploring alternate encodings for mean and error. IEEE Trans. Vis. Comput. Graph. **20**(12), 2142–2151 (2014)
2. Ibrekk, H., Morgan, M.G.: Graphical communication of uncertain quantities to nontechnical people. Risk Anal. **7**(4), 519–529 (1987)
3. Joslyn, S.L., LeClerc, J.E.: Uncertainty forecasts improve weather-related decisions and attenuate the effects of forecast error. J. Exp. Psychol. Appl. **18**(1), 126–140 (2012)
4. Law, A.M., Kelton, W.D., Kelton, W.D.: Simulation modeling and analysis (1991)
5. Lipkus, I.M., Samsa, G., Rimer, B.K.: General performance on a numeracy scale among highly educated samples. Med. Decis. Mak. **21**(1), 37–44 (2001)
6. McNeil, B.J., Pauker, S.G., Sox Jr, H.C., Tversky, A.: On the elicitation of preferences for alternative therapies. N. Engl. J. Med. **306**(21), 1259–1262 (1982)
9. Morss, R.E., Demuth, J.L., Lazo, J.K.: Communicating uncertainty in weather forecasts: a survey of the US public. Weather Forecast. **23**(5), 974–991 (2008)
8. Olston, C., Mackinlay, J.: Visualizing data with bounded uncertainty. In: IEEE Symposium on Information Visualization (INFOVIS 2002) (2002)
9. Pang, A., Wittenbrink, C., Lodha, S.: Approaches to uncertainty visualization. Vis. Comput. **13**(8), 370–390 (1997)
10. Pappenberger, F., Stephens, E., Thielen, J., Salamon, P., Demeritt, D., Andel, S.J., Wetterhall, F., Alfieri, L.: Visualizing probabilistic flood forecast information: expert preferences and perceptions of best practice in uncertainty communication. Hydrol. Process. **27**(1), 132–146 (2013)
11. Potter, K., Kniss, J., Riesenfeld, R., Johnson, C.R.: Visualizing summary statistics and uncertainty. Comput. Graph. Forum **29**(3), 823–832 (2010)
12. Roulston, M.S., Bolton, G.E., Kleit, A.N., Sears-Collins, A.L.: A laboratory study of the benefits of including uncertainty information in weather forecasts. Weather Forecast. **21**(1), 116–122 (2006)
13. Tak, S., Toet, A., Van Erp, J.: The perception of visual uncertainty representation by non-experts. IEEE Trans. Vis. Comput. Graph. **20**(6), 935–943 (2014)
14. Wallsten, T.S., Budescu, D.V., Rapoport, A., Zwick, R., Forsyth, B.: Measuring the vague meanings of probability terms. J. Exp. Psychol. Gen. **115**(4), 348 (1986)
15. Zuk, T., Carpendale, S.: Theoretical analysis of uncertainty visualizations. In: Proceedings of IS&T/SPIE Electronic Imaging, vol. 6060 (2006)

# Proxemic Flow: Dynamic Peripheral Floor Visualizations for Revealing and Mediating Large Surface Interactions

Jo Vermeulen[1(✉)], Kris Luyten[2], Karin Coninx[2],
Nicolai Marquardt[3], and Jon Bird[4]

[1] HCI Centre, University of Birmingham, Birmingham, UK
j.vermeulen@cs.bham.ac.uk
[2] Hasselt University – tUL – iMinds, Expertise Centre for Digital Media,
Diepenbeek, Belgium
[3] UCL Interaction Centre/ICRI Cities, University College London, London, UK
[4] City University London, London, UK

**Abstract.** Interactive large surfaces have recently become commonplace for interactions in public settings. The fact that people can engage with them and the spectrum of possible interactions, however, often remain invisible and can be confusing or ambiguous to passersby. In this paper, we explore the design of dynamic peripheral floor visualizations for revealing and mediating large surface interactions. Extending earlier work on interactive illuminated floors, we introduce a novel approach for leveraging floor displays in a secondary, assisting role to aid users in interacting with the primary display. We illustrate a series of visualizations with the illuminated floor of the Proxemic Flow system. In particular, we contribute a *design space for peripheral floor visualizations* that (a) provides peripheral information about tracking fidelity with personal halos, (b) makes interaction zones and borders explicit for easy opt-in and opt-out, and (c) gives cues inviting for spatial movement or possible next interaction steps through wave, trail, and footstep animations. We demonstrate our proposed techniques in the context of a large surface application and discuss important design considerations for assistive floor visualizations.

**Keywords:** Feedback · Proxemic interactions · Implicit interaction · Discoverability · Intelligibility · Spatial feedback

## 1 Introduction

Large interactive surfaces, such as interactive vertical displays or tabletops, have become commonplace in many public settings. These displays often react to the presence and proximity of people [1] or support other interaction modalities such as mid-air gestures, body posture or touch [2].

Several studies, however, report on problems encountered by users while interacting with these large surfaces. People can be prevented from engaging in interactions with displays because they tend to ignore them (*display blindness* [3, 4]) or fail to recognize that they are interactive (*interaction blindness* [5]). Additionally, people

© IFIP International Federation for Information Processing 2015
J. Abascal et al. (Eds.): INTERACT 2015, Part IV, LNCS 9299, pp. 264–281, 2015.
DOI: 10.1007/978-3-319-22723-8_22

could be uncertain about the available possibilities for interaction [4, 6], or be hesitant to interact due to social embarrassment [2, 5, 7]. Finally, people are often unaware of ways to recover from mistakes such as accidental interactions [5, 7]. It is difficult for people to know how to address (or how *not* to address) displays and what they can do when the surface is reacting to their input, as these displays typically rely on implicit interaction using sensors [8]. These problems—users abandoning the surface or not interacting with it because of confusion, frustration or fear of being embarrassed—pose important challenges for designers of applications on large interactive surfaces.

In this paper, we explore the design of *dynamic, peripheral floor visualizations* to help address interaction challenges with large interactive surfaces. The core of our work is combining vertical interactive displays with a *secondary, peripheral floor display*. We apply the term 'peripheral' similar to its use for public ambient displays [9], as defined by Weiser and Brown [10] to describe, *"what we are attuned to without attending to explicitly"*. Information shown in the periphery can seamlessly become the center of the attention and move back to the periphery in fluent transitions [10]. Extending the foundations of existing work on interactive illuminated floors (e.g., [11, 12]), the floor display is not used as a primary interaction space, but serves a *secondary, assisting role* to aid users in interacting with the main display. The floor display can be used to inform users about the tracking status, indicate action possibilities, show interaction zones, and invite and guide users throughout their interaction with the primary interactive display. In the future, we imagine these floor displays being integrated in public spaces to accompany vertical public displays. Due to their relatively low cost, LED floor displays can be frequently found in urban spaces, such as the flashing LED lights in Washington DC metro stations to show arriving trains (Fig. 1).

**Fig. 1.** An LED floor display used in the Washington metro (You-Tube ID: DppgBi0ZMc8).

We illustrate how floor displays can provide additional feedback and guidance through a series of visualizations on the illuminated floor of the *Proxemic Flow* system. As shown in Fig. 2, we focus on leveraging floor visualizations to mitigate interactions with a proxemic-aware vertical display [1] that reacts to people's presence, approach, and movements (inspired by Ballendat et al. [1]). For example, the floor shows personal halos indicating when people are sensed by the system (circles in Fig. 2) and provides information about the quality of tracking. Furthermore, the floor reveals the boundaries of the interaction area (red line at the bottom of Fig. 2) and invites moving closer to interact (footsteps at the top of Fig. 2).

Our aim with this work is a *design space exploration*, and in the remainder of this paper we provide the following contributions:

- We propose an assistive role for floor displays, where they serve as secondary, peripheral displays that help users in interacting with the primary proxemic-aware surface.
- We demonstrate the expressive power of this new design space with a vocabulary of in situ floor visualization strategies, and explain in detail how we implemented these visualizations for a low-resolution large floor display.

## 2  Related Work

### 2.1  Feedback, Discoverability and Guidance for Large Interactive Surfaces

Earlier work has explored techniques to address interaction challenges for large interactive surfaces. We provide a brief overview of related techniques, categorized by the challenges that they address.

**Attracting Attention to Overcome Display Blindness and Interaction Blindness.**
Displays can be designed to attract attention and motivate users to interact with a display, and thus overcome *display blindness* [4] and *interaction blindness* [5]. Earlier work identified barriers that prevent people from engaging with a large display when passing by (e.g., [7, 13]). With a few exceptions (e.g., [14]), most techniques attempt to convey interactivity and attract users by using visualizations on the interactive display (e.g., [13, 15, 16]). In contrast, with Proxemic Flow we primarily focus on the floor display to convey interactivity. One of the advantages of providing visualizations on a secondary display is that they do not occlude or distract from existing content on the primary display. The floor can reveal the interaction area through borders and zones, and show halos when people are recognized by the display. Our floor visualizations are designed to indicate to passersby that they *can* interact, making them aware that they are tracked, and also allowing people to avoid interacting with the display.

**Fig. 2.** Proxemic Flow providing awareness of tracking and fidelity, zones of interaction, and invitations for interactions (Color figure online).

This addresses a common issue with interactive surfaces in semi-public settings, i.e., that they lack opt-in and opt-out choices [17].

**Revealing Action Possibilities and Providing Guidance.** Commonly used interaction modalities for public displays (e.g., proximity, body posture, mid-air gestures) are often hard to understand by passersby at first glance [2]. A number of systems suggest *action possibilities* and input gestures by visualizing sensor data, such as depth camera images, detected user skeletons [18, 19] or mirrored images [9, 20]. Early work by Vogel and Balakrishnan [9] included a self-revealing help feature using a mirror image video sequence. Walter et al. [6] studied different visualizations to reveal a 'teapot gesture' that allows users to indicate that they would like to start interacting with the display.

These techniques work well in particular for revealing action possibilities (e.g., mid-air gestures and body postures) on the display itself. Our in situ techniques introduce a new vocabulary of visualizations potentially more appropriate for proxemic-aware surfaces that often use people's and devices' spatial movements as implicit input. Such implicit application input might be surprising and possibly disturbing in walk-up-and use scenarios, as in the Proxemic Media Player [1] where videos are automatically paused when users are not facing the display. Techniques that reveal action possibilities on the primary display often focus on particular proxemic dimensions [1]. For example, cross-device interaction techniques typically use *orientation* to show possible targets around the user's device, as in the Gradual Engagement pattern [21] or the RELATE interaction model [22].

**Providing Tracking Feedback.** A common problem users experience while interacting with public displays is a lack of feedback about how the system is currently recognizing and interpreting their input, and also how reliably this input is being sensed. In crowded spaces, people can be unsure about the level of control they have over the display [19]. A number of systems reveal tracking feedback for proxemic interactions to convey what the system sees of the user, e.g., by visualizing detected skeletons [18] or mirror images [20]. With their interactive whiteboard, Ju et al. [8] showed a dot pattern to indicate in which proximity zone the user was recognized. In the Medusa proximity-aware tabletop [23], the user's proximity is shown using an orb visualization. Both in the Proxemic Media Player [1] and the Gradual Engagement pattern [21], tracked devices are visualized on the large surface with their relative size mapped to their proximity to the large display.

With Proxemic Flow we provide in-place tracking feedback on the floor, in the space where users are tracked. A number of earlier systems provided projected tracking feedback on the floor in the form of halos such as the Solstice LAMP [24] and Proximity Lab [25].

**In Situ Feedback and Guidance.** Proxemic-aware systems typically take different actions based on the interaction zone in which the user is located [1, 8, 9], which may be unintelligible to users. Rehman et al. [26] used augmented reality to visualize interaction zones in-place, but this technique required users to wear head-mounted displays. Researchers have also explored the possibilities of providing in situ feedback and guidance using spatial augmented reality, which uses a combination of projectors and depth cameras and thus eliminates the need for users to wear additional apparel. For example, LightSpace [27] shows when users are tracked by the system by projecting colored higlights on the user's body. LightGuide [28] uses a projector and depth cameras to project visualizations on the user's body that provide movement guidance. In a public art context, Ozturk et al. [29] explored people's reactions to projections of their 'future footsteps' in an airport terminal.

Although the use of projectors allows for high-resolution visualizations and more flexibility, projectors often require low-lighting conditions, which makes these techniques less suitable for large interactive surfaces in urban spaces (especially during daytime). Regarding guidance using LED floors, Rogers et al. [30] explored the use of LEDs embedded in carpet tiles to motivate people to use the stairs more often. They observed that the LED lights had a significant effect on people's behavior, which illustrates the power of in situ visualizations and guidance.

## 2.2 Related Work on Interactive Illuminated Floors

With Proxemic Flow, we propose the use of graphical information shown directly on the floor of the interactive space, around the people who are engaging in the interaction, for providing feedback about the system status or informing users of action possibilities and consequences.

Interactive illuminated floors have been used in different contexts, such as interactive art [24, 25] or games [31], and have recently seen increasing exploration as a primary interaction space [11, 12]. A variety of input and output technologies have been used for these interactive floors, such as tracking users through computer vision techniques [31] or pressure sensing [12], and showing output using projectors [12, 31], LED illumination [32] or vibrotactile feedback [33].

Our work extends this earlier research by (a) proposing the use of the floor as a peripheral/secondary output device that can help to mediate interactions with a different, primary interaction device, and (b) providing a vocabulary of strategies to provide in situ feedback about current and future interactions with the system.

## 3    In Situ Floor Visualization Strategies

In order to mitigate the previously mentioned interaction challenges, we introduce a series of interaction techniques and in situ visualizations on the floor. These are categorized into three phases, progressing from:

- (a) *in situ tracking feedback* (answering the questions: What does the system see? How well does the tracking work?), and
- (b) *revealing interaction possibilities* (answering: What possible interactions are available?), to
- (c) *inviting for and guiding interactions* (answering: What can I do next?).

## 3.1 Walkthrough with Photo Gallery Application

We will illustrate all our in situ visualization strategies with a running example application, inspired by the design of the Proxemic Media Player [1]. Our photo gallery application shows photos collections on a large public display. A series of interactions are possible with this gallery application: it shows photo thumbnails when in idle mode (Fig. 3a), reveals more content when a person approaches the display (Fig. 3b), shows full screen photos when people stand directly in front of the display (or sit down), and allows mid-air gestures to navigate the photo collection (e.g., waving left or right to browse through the timeline of photos). While limited in scope, we believe this example application captures the essence of many proxemic interactions applications and works best for demonstrating our in situ floor visualization strategies. Throughout this paper, however, we will also refer to the use of our visualization strategies in other application contexts.

**Fig. 3.** Walkthrough photo gallery application: photo thumbnails at a distance (a), revealing more content when moving closer (b).

## 3.2 Design Space for Floor Visualization Strategies

Our visualization strategies can be categorized in a design space for in situ floor visualizations. Table 1 shows an overview of the different strategies and indicates to which of the three phases (tracking feedback, action possibilities or guidance) they correspond. The table compares our floor visualization strategies based on three different aspects: *perspective*, *position*, and *temporal relevance*. Regarding perspective, we distinguish between *egocentric* and *exocentric* visualizations. For example, tracking halos are targeted towards being viewed from the user's own perspective (*egocentric*), while zones and borders are mostly useful from an external perspective (*exocentric*).

**Table 1.** An overview of the design space for in situ floor visualization strategies.

|          | Phase | Purpose | Perspective | | Position | | Temporal Relevance | | |
|----------|-------|---------|-------------|------------|--------|---------|------|---------|--------|
|          |       |         | Egocentric  | Exocentric | Static | Dynamic | Past | Present | Future |
| Halos    | 1     | Tracking feedback | ✔ | | | ✔ | | ✔ | |
| Trails   | 1, 3  | Historic traces of action | ✔ | ✔ | | ✔ | ✔ | ✔ (a) | ✔ (b) |
| Zones    | 2     | Interaction zones Action possibilities | ✔ (c) | ✔ | ✔ | | | ✔ | ✔ (d) |
| Borders  | 2     | Opt-in & opt-out | | ✔ | ✔ | | | ✔ | ✔ (e) |
| Waves    | 3     | Inviting for interaction | | ✔ | ✔ | | | | ✔ |
| Steps    | 3     | Guiding spatial movement | ✔ | | | ✔ | | | ✔ |

Additionally, a few visualizations have a *static* position on the floor, while others can move *dynamically* (e.g., together with the user). Finally, visualizations can be relevant to the user's current (or *present*) interactions with the primary display (e.g., quality of tracking), or can alternatively provide clues about *past* or *future* actions.

We see this design space as a starting point for characterizing in situ floor visualizations for mediating large surface interactions, and foresee possible future extensions. It also functions as an analytical tool to reflect on the set of floor visualization strategies that we propose in this paper, and can help to further explore alternative floor visualizations. We will now go over the three phases, and will later come back to these different aspects while discussing our floor visualization strategies.

### 3.3    Phase 1. In Situ Personal Tracking Feedback with Halos

A fundamental challenge for interaction with large surfaces is providing a person with immediate feedback about how the system is currently recognizing and interpreting gestures or other input from the user. In this section, we introduce visualization strategies to provide this feedback directly in the physical space where the person is moving in front of the display.

**Personal Halos.** The personal halo provides immediate feedback on the floor display about the tracking of a person in space. When the person enters the area in front of the public display, a green halo (an area of approximately 1 m diameter) appears underneath the person's feet (Fig. 4a). The halo moves with them when moving in the tracking area, and therefore gives continuous feedback about the fact that the person is being recognized and tracked by the system.

**Fig. 4.** Halos: (a) providing feedback about active tracking and (b) the tracking quality (Color figure online).

Another important part of information (besides information about the fact that a person *is* tracked) is the actual *quality* of tracking. Most computer vision based tracking systems (RGB, depth, or other tracking) have situations where tracking works well, where it does not work well, or where it does not work at all (e.g., due to lighting conditions, occlusion, limited field of view). Therefore, our personal halo visualization encodes the quality of tracking in the color of the halo. To indicate tracking quality, we use three different colors (Fig. 4b). A green halo indicates optimal tracking of the person in space. Its color changes to yellow when the quality of tracking decreases, for example when the person moves to the limits of the field of view or when partially occluded by another person or furniture. Finally, a red halo color is shown when the tracking of the person is lost, such as when moving too far away from the camera, or if the occlusion is hiding the person completely. For this last case, since the person is now not tracked anymore, the red halo visualization remains static at the last known location of the person, fades in and out twice, and then disappears (the duration of that animation is approximately 4 s). If the person moves back into the field of view of the camera and the tracked region, the halo color changes back accordingly to green or yellow.

The immediate feedback of tracking through halos can provide people with more control over their interaction with the system. For example, when noticing that they are being tracked, the user could decide to opt out of interaction with the system by moving back out of the active tracking area.

**Alternative Halo Visualization Strategies.** Although this is a crude mapping of tracking accuracy to different colors, we found it to be an effective in situ form of feedback about tracking activity *and* fidelity. Other applications might require different levels of granularity. For example, for interactive proxemic game experiences [34], tracking accuracy per body part could be helpful information for players, which could be visualized using more fine-grained halos. Tracking accuracy of different body parts could be mapped to different areas of the halo; e.g., front left corresponds to left arm, back left to the left leg. Alternatively, halos could change their size depending on the area covered by the player. There is a limit to the amount of information that can be conveyed using our low-resolution floor display. Revealing precise details about the tracking quality for different body parts (or showing text for instructions) would require higher-resolution floor displays. For the remainder of this paper, however, we focus on the expressive potential of low-resolution peripheral floor visualizations.

**Multi-User Halos.** Interaction around interactive surfaces is often not limited to a single person, but can involve multiple people present in the space and interacting with the display. With multiple people, information about active tracking and its fidelity becomes even more important, because tracking problems increase with the likelihood for occlusions.

**Fig. 5.** Halos for multi-user interaction: (a) both people are visible to the system; (b) one person is occluding the camera's view of the other person, indicated by the red halo (Color figure online).

If multiple people are present in front of the screen, each person's individual position that the system currently tracks is shown with a colored halo (Fig. 5a). Color changes indicate a change in how well the user is tracked. For example, in case another person walking in interrupts the tracking camera's view of a person, the changing color of the halo from yellow to red tells the person that they are not tracked anymore (Fig. 5b). Similarly, if two people stand very close to another, making it difficult for the computer vision algorithm to separate the two, the halo color changes to yellow.

**Trails: Revealing Interaction History.** As a variation of the halo technique, the *spatial trail* feedback visualizes the past spatial

**Fig. 6.** Trails, visualizing the history of spatial movements of a person (Color figure online).

movements of a person in the interaction area. The trails are shown as illuminated lines on the floor that light up when a person passes that particular area (Fig. 6). The illumination fades out after a given time (in our application after five seconds), thus giving the impression of a comet-like trail. The colors that are used to light up the floor are identical to those of the person's halo (i.e., green, yellow, red), and therefore still provide information about the tracking quality. Because the trail visualization remains visible for a longer time, it provides information about the past movements of the people interacting with the system. Potentially, the trails could help to amplify the *honeypot effect* [7] by showing the past trails of other people moving towards the interactive display, and thus inviting other bystanders and passersby to approach the display as well —which is why they are categorized in both phase 1 and 3 (Table 1).

**Reflecting on Phase 1 in the Design Space.** Halos are an example of an *egocentric* strategy (Table 1). They are primarily designed to be viewed from the user's perspective, providing feedback about the tracking status. The trails variation, however, is a mostly *exocentric* technique that shows information about past interactions from the perspective of other users. However, since the trails are still shown underneath the user's feet, and change color depending on the user's tracking accuracy, they are simultaneously *egocentric* and inform the user about their *present* interactions (Table 1a). In addition, as they potentially invite bystanders to interact with the display, the trails can serve as an invitation for *future* interactions (Table 1b). We can also imagine other *exocentric* halo visualizations. For example, pulsating exocentric halos could indicate open spots where users could move towards, e.g., to form teams in proxemic gaming scenarios [34].

## 3.4 Phase 2. Zones and Borders: Entries and Exits for Interaction

As mentioned earlier, people often have difficulties knowing when and how they can interact with a large public display [2, 19]. To mitigate this problem and to reveal interaction possibilities, we explicitly visualize the spatial zones for interaction and the borders of the interaction space (Fig. 7).

**Opting-in: Proxemic Interaction Zones.** Many designs of large interactive displays use spatial zones around the display to allow different kinds of interaction [9] or change the displayed content depending on which zone a person is currently in. These zones, however, are not always immediately understandable or perceivable by a person interacting with the display. Our floor-visualizations explicitly reveal zones of inter-action, allowing a person to see where interaction is possible, and make deliberate decisions about opting in for an interaction with the display by entering any of the zones.

We demonstrate the use of zone visualizations with the Proxemic Flow photo gallery application. Similar to earlier examples of proxemic-aware displays [1, 9], our application uses discrete spatial zones around the display that are mapped to the interactive behavior of the application on the large display. When no users are inter-acting with the system, a large red rectangular zone indicates the area furthest away from the display that triggers the initial interaction with the display (Fig. 7a). This serves as an entry zone for interaction, i.e., an area to opt-in for interaction with the system. In our current implementation, we use a 3 s pulsating luminosity animation, fading the color in and out, in our approach of balancing the goal of attracting attention while not being too intrusive. While a static color would be possible, identifying it as part of an interactive system is potentially more difficult. Once a person enters this zone, the large display recognizes the presence of the person, tracks the person's move-ment, and their halo is shown. The first zone now disappears and a sec-ond zone appears—an area to interact with the display when in front of is (visible as the blue rectangle in Fig. 7b). When the person begins approaching the display, the content gradually reveals more of the photo collection on the display. The closer the person gets, the more images become revealed (this is a behavior identical to the Proxemic Media Player [1]). Once entering the second

**Fig. 7.** The interaction areas in front of the display represented as (a) red and (b) blue rectangular zones; (c) borders indicate thresholds to cross for (d) leaving the interaction space in front of the display (Color figure online).

zone, the person can now use hand gestures in front of the display to more precisely navigate the temporally ordered photo gallery (e.g., grabbing photos, sliding left or right to move forward or back in time). Again, once the person entered that close-interaction zone in front of the display, the visualization disappears.

**Opting-out and Exit Interaction: Borders.** While we envision zones primarily as explicit visualizations of the zones to interact, and for allowing a person to deliberately engage and "opt-in" for an interaction with the system, we can also consider visualizations that help a person to leave the interaction area (i.e., opting out). We illustrate this concept with borders shown in the Proxemic Flow application. In continuation of the application example from before, once the person entered the interaction zone (blue) directly in front of the display and interacts with the display content through explicit gestures, a red border around the actively tracked interaction area surrounding the display is shown to make the boundaries of that interaction space explicit and visible (Fig. 7c). While we decided to dynamically show the border only in situations when a person engaged with the system, alternatively it could remain a fixed feature of the visualizations shown on the floor. A reason for showing a fixed visualization of the interaction boundaries with borders could be to always clearly indicate where a person can both enter but also leave the interaction area (Fig. 7d).

**Using Zones and Borders with Multiple Users.** We can consider alternative design aspects when using zone and border visualizations with multiple users. For example, we can consider whether area visualizations are only shown to the first user entering the space and disappear once that person entered the zone, or whether the visualizations remain persistent. Showing visualizations for the first person entering a space seem most critical, and hiding the zone visualizations after the person enters a particular zone has the advantage of a floor that is less visually cluttered and therefore can help emphasizing certain parts of the visualizations (for example, make the halos stand out).

**Reflecting on Phase 2 in the Design Space.** In contrast to halos and trails, zones and borders are *static* visualizations. They are fixed at a certain position, and although they might only be shown at certain times, they do not follow the user. Zones and borders are also mostly *exocentric*, as they are designed for observations from an external point of view. Nevertheless, zones can also be used from an *egocentric* perspective, when the user is inside the interaction zone (Table 1c). Finally, they convey cues relevant to the user's current interactions (*present*), such as borders around the actively tracked interaction area. However, zones and borders can also provide cues for *future* interactions, such as possible next areas to move to, or where to go to opt-out of the interaction (Table 1d–e).

### 3.5    Phase 3. Waves and Footsteps: Inviting for Approach, Spatial Movement, or Next Interaction Steps

The last set of floor visualization strategies we introduce is designed to invite for approach, encourage a person's movement to a new location, and suggest possible next interaction steps. In particular, in this category of visualizations we introduce two strategies: waves and footsteps.

**Waves: Encouraging Approach.** Our first strategy is intended for inviting people to move closer to the large display for interaction. Several strategies for encour-

**Fig. 8.** (a) Waves inviting for interaction and (b) footsteps suggesting action possibilities (Color figure online).

aging approach of people have been proposed in the past, including showing text labels, animations, graphic icon representations or using sound (e.g., strategies in [15]). With our waves technique, we leverage the output capabilities of the illuminated floor for showing looped animations of lights fading in and out, with the effect of a wave of light going towards the large screen (Fig. 8a). Alternatively, different visual designs of the wave effect are possible, for example a circular wave effect with the large display at the center, starting with circles having a large radius and continuously decreasing the circle radius.

**Footsteps: Suggesting Next Action Possibilities.** The footsteps visualization is designed to offer a person clues about possible next interaction steps (directly addressing *discoverability*), in particular for encouraging spatial movements in the environment. The visualization shows animated footsteps (in our case these are represented through glowing circles) beginning at one location on the floor and leading to another location. This technique is inspired by earlier work of the *Follow-the-light* [30] design that uses animated patterns of lights embedded in a carpet to encourage different movement behaviors by luring people away from an elevator towards the stairs.

To illustrate this technique, we again revisit our Proxemic Flow example application with the large display photo gallery viewer. When a person entered the interactive (i.e., tracked) space in front of the display and stands still for over 5 s, the floor begins the footstep animation (Fig. 8b) to invite the person to move closer to the display—in particular, moving to the interaction zone in front of the display allowing the person to use mid-air gestures to further explore the image collection. The footstep animation begins directly in front of the person and leads towards the blue rectangular area highlighted in front of the display (Fig. 8b). The footsteps visualization strategy can be used to reveal interaction possibilities—in particular those involving spatial movements of the person. The strategy can be used in many other contexts for guiding or directing a user in the environment, and for encouraging movements in space.

**Reflecting on Phase 3 in the Design Space.** The visualization strategies for phase three provide cues that invite users to *future* interactions. The waves strategy is *exocentric*, as it invites bystanders to interact with the primary display. It is a *static* visualization, as people's movements do not influence its position. The waves pattern could be shown across the full floor display or be centralized around the primary display. The steps strategy, on the other hand, is a *dynamic* and *egocentric* visualization that starts from underneath the person's feet, and guides them towards a certain position.

### 3.6    Reflection on In Situ Visualization Strategies

We discussed and demonstrated a set of in situ floor visualizations that provide peripheral tracking and fidelity information with *personal halos*, make interaction *zones and borders* explicit for easy opt-in and opt-out, and provide cues inviting for spatial movement or possible next interaction steps through *wave*, *trail*, and *footstep* animations. This set of floor visualization strategies targets important interaction issues with large interactive surfaces that were identified in earlier research. During informal observations of people interacting with our floor display, we noticed that essential concepts such as halos and zones were easy to understand. Future studies are necessary, however, to confirm these early observations. The strategies we presented here are a starting point for a collection of building blocks for how to provide in situ visual feedback on the floor to mediate spatial interactions. In the next section, we present the Proxemic Flow software architecture and explain how we implemented the floor visualizations.

## 4    Implementation

The Proxemic Flow architecture consists of three major technical components: (1) the *hardware setup* of the illuminated floor, (2) the *user tracker* and (3) the *floor renderer*. The user tracker is responsible for tracking users in the space in front of the display, and for mapping these positions to positions on the floor. The floor renderer consists of a .NET client that draws visuals to a bitmap and sends display updates over the network to a Processing sketch connected to the Arduino board controlling the different light units. We will now explain these components in more detail.

### 4.1    Hardware Setup of the Interactive Floor Display

The foyer floor that we use for our setup comprises 288 light wells set in concrete, of which 216 of these wells are fitted with a custom light unit [35]. The custom light units in each of the 216 light wells consist of four RGB LEDs cut from an LPD8806 LED strip, joined together and mounted onto a plastic cap which fits neatly into the concrete surface from the floor below. The light units are connected in series, with three modified ATX power supplies providing power. A single Arduino Mega with the ATmega1280 microcontroller is controlling the floor display. Each of the light units can be set to one of around 2 million colors and the whole array can be updated at a rate of up to 25 fps—effectively turning the floor into a large display with a resolution of $12 \times 18$ pixels.

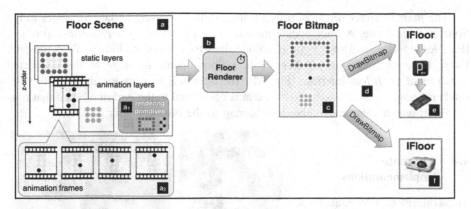

**Fig. 9.** The Proxemic Flow rendering pipeline: Visualizations on the floor display are abstracted in a floor scene (a). This floor scene is processed by the floor renderer (b), resulting in (c) a floor bitmap (an abstraction of a floor display update) that is sent over the network to the connected floor displays that implement the IFloor interface (d). We also implemented a projected floor display (f) (Color figure online).

## 4.2 Tracking Users

Users are tracked across the floor using a single Microsoft Kinect depth camera and the Kinect SDK, which allows us to track up to six simultaneous users (with skeleton data available for two users). As users positions can be represented in a 2D $(x, z)$ plane (we ignore the user's vertical position), a simple affine matrix transformation suffices to map the $(x, z)$ coordinates as given by the Kinect camera to a position on the floor. To set up the system, a four-point calibration is performed to map positions seen by the Kinect to the corresponding floor positions, after which the corresponding transformation matrix is calculated.

Each user's tracking accuracy—as used for determining the color of their personal halo—is specified as a value in the range [0,1]. We calculate the tracking accuracy by performing an arithmetic average over the accuracy of the skeleton joints. Skeleton joints have one of three states: *tracked*, *inferred*, or *not tracked*. We currently assign the value 1.0 to *tracked* joints, 0.3 to *inferred* joints and 0.0 to joints that are *not tracked*. Green halos are shown for accuracies over 0.7; yellow halos for accuracies between 0.3 and 0.7; and halos turn red when the accuracy drops below 0.3. These specific thresholds have been selected based on empirical observations, but can be easily changed.

## 4.3 Floor Renderer

The Proxemic Flow renderer provides a set of reusable rendering primitives that react to user tracking updates. All graphics and animations can be translated into a *floor bitmap*, which allows the *rendering pipeline* to be agnostic to the specifics of the graphics being shown on the floor. This *rendering pipeline* is the central hub of the architecture and handles updates to the floor display (Fig. 9).

The *floor renderer* (Fig. 9b) uses a timer to allow sending update messages to the floor at a fixed rate. A floor update message is represented by a *FloorBitmap* object (Fig. 9c), which is an 18 × 12 grid of color values for each of the light wells in the grid. Every tick, the rendering pipeline sends a floor update message to the connected instances of the *IFloor* interface (Fig. 9d). The default IFloor implementation (Fig. 9e) sends messages to a Processing sketch that is connected to the Arduino board that runs the floor, which then renders the floor bitmap to the physical floor display.

### 4.4 Alternative Implementations

The concept of Proxemic Flow goes beyond the specifics of our floor setup. The illuminated floor could be implemented using different floor displays (e.g., using projectors or FTIR floor displays [11]) and tracking solutions (e.g., 2D cameras with markers, other depth cameras, or optical trackers

**Fig. 10.** Alternative floor display using a ceiling-mounted short-throw projector (Color figure online).

such as VICON). Figure 10 shows an alternative rendering solution we implemented in order to show visuals on arbitrary surfaces, based on an overhead projector mounted to the ceiling. It connects another IFloor instance to the same rendering pipeline (Fig. 9f), so that applications written once run without modification. In this implementation, a separate Windows Presentation Foundation (WPF) window that renders the floor grid is projected onto the floor. Our projection-based floor responds to floor update messages by changing an internal model of the floor grid, which is then also updated in the WPF view. Higher resolution floor displays (e.g., with a circular halo visualization) would be possible by making rendering primitives adapt to different resolution floor bitmaps, specific to each IFloor instance.

## 5 Discussion

We presented Proxemic Flow, dynamic in situ floor visualizations for revealing and mediating large surface interactions. Based on previously identified interaction challenges with large interactive surfaces, we demonstrate the expressive potential of the floor as a peripheral/secondary output device for showing in situ feedback using three categories of visualizations: (1) personal halos and trails that provide peripheral information about current tracking and tracking fidelity; (2) interaction zones and borders for easy opt-in and opt-out; and (3) wave and footstep cues that invite users for movement across the space or possible next interaction steps.

Our approach is intentionally minimalistic: we reduced the visualizations to essential *cues* that require minimal visual bandwidth. These can be extended—for example with more fine-grained spatial movements cues—but we believe it is important to avoid a visually cluttered floor with (perhaps even animated) visualizations that distract the user. Ideally, the visualizations should be shown when needed, but not unnecessarily draw the user's attention and detract from interacting with the primary display, as the floor serves a secondary, assisting role. We plan studies further investigating the balancing of showing information while avoiding distractions.

During initial observations, we noticed that people became aware of the floor being a display as they approached the tracking zone. Users noticed their personal tracking halos when they entered space in front of the display. Due to their low visual complexity, a quick glance at the visualizations is often sufficient, e.g., when users are unsure about action possibilities. An interesting opportunity for future work is to investigate how user's peripheral view, which is very sensitive to motion [36], can be used to draw their attention when needed.

**Acknowledgements.** This work was supported by ICRI Cities.

# References

1. Ballendat, T., Marquardt, N., Greenberg, S.: Proxemic interaction: designing for a proximity and orientation-aware environment. In: Proceedings ITS 2010, pp. 121–130. ACM, New York (2010)
2. Müller, J., Alt, F., Michelis, D., Schmidt, A.: Requirements and design space for interactive public displays. In: Proceedings of MM 2010, pp. 1285–1294. ACM (2010)
3. Huang, E.M., Koster, A., Borchers, J.: Overcoming assumptions and uncovering practices: when does the public really look at public displays? In: Indulska, J., Patterson, D.J., Rodden, T., Ott, M. (eds.) PERVASIVE 2008. LNCS, vol. 5013, pp. 228–243. Springer, Heidelberg (2008)
4. Müller, J., Wilmsmann, D., Exeler, J., Buzeck, M., Schmidt, A., Jay, T., Krüger, A.: Display blindness: the effect of expectations on attention towards digital signage. In: Tokuda, H., Beigl, M., Friday, A., Brush, A., Tobe, Y. (eds.) Pervasive 2009. LNCS, vol. 5538, pp. 1–8. Springer, Heidelberg (2009)
5. Ojala, T., Kostakos, V., Kukka, H., Heikkinen, T., Linden, T., Jurmu, M., Hosio, S., Kruger, F., Zanni, D.: Multipurpose interactive public displays in the wild: three years later. Computer **45**, 42–49 (2012)
6. Walter, R., Bailly, G., Müller, J.: StrikeAPose: revealing mid-air gestures on public displays. In: Proceedings of CHI 2013, pp. 841–850. ACM, New York (2013)
7. Brignull, H., Rogers, Y.: Enticing people to interact with large public displays in public spaces. In: Proceedings of INTERACT 2003 (2003)
8. Ju, W., Lee, B.A., Klemmer, S.R.: Range: exploring implicit interaction through electronic whiteboard design. In: Proceedings of CSCW 2008, pp. 17–26. ACM (2008)
9. Vogel, D., Balakrishnan, R.: Interactive public ambient displays: transitioning from implicit to explicit, public to personal, interaction with multiple users. In: Proceedings of UIST 2004, pp. 137–146. ACM, New York (2004)
10. Weiser, M., Brown, J.S.: Designing calm technology. PowerGrid J. **1**, 75–85 (1996)

11. Augsten, T., Kaefer, K., Meusel, R., Fetzer, C., Kanitz, D., Stoff, T., Becker, T., Holz, C., Baudisch, P.: Multitoe: high-precision Interaction with back-projected floors based on high-resolution multi-touch input. Proc. UIST 2010, pp. 209–218. ACM, New York (2010)
12. Schmidt, D., Ramakers, R., Pedersen, E.W., Jasper, J., Köhler, S., Pohl, A., Rantzsch, H., Rau, A., Schmidt, P., Sterz, C., Yurchenko, Y., Baudisch, P.: Kickables: tangibles for feet. In: Proceedings of CHI 2014, pp. 3143–3152. ACM, USA (2014)
13. Michelis, D., Müller, J.: The audience funnel: observations of gesture based interaction with multiple large displays in a city center. Int. J. Hum.-Comput. Interact. 27, 562–579 (2011)
14. Houben, S., Weichel, C.: Overcoming interaction blindness through curiosity objects. In: Proceedings of CHI EA 2013, pp. 1539–1544. ACM, New York (2013)
15. Cheung, V., Scott, S.D.: Investigating attraction and engagement of animation on large interactive walls in public settings. In: Proceedings of ITS 2013, pp. 381–384. ACM, New York (2013)
16. Wang, M., Boring, S., Greenberg, S.: Proxemic Peddler: A public advertising display that captures and preserves the attention of a passerby. In: Proceedings of PerDis 2012, pp. 3:1–3:6. ACM, New York (2012)
17. Greenberg, S., Boring, S., Vermeulen, J., Dostal, J.: Dark patterns in proxemic interactions: a critical perspective. In: Proceedings of DIS 2014, pp. 523–532. ACM, New York (2014)
18. Beyer, G., Binder, V., Jäger, N., Butz, A.: The puppeteer display: attracting and actively shaping the audience with an interactive public banner display. In: Proceedings of DIS 2014, pp. 935–944. ACM, New York (2014)
19. Jurmu, M., Ogawa, M., Boring, S., Riekki, J., Tokuda, H.: Waving to a touch interface: descriptive field study of a multipurpose multimodal public display. In: Proceedings of PerDis 2013, pp. 7–12. ACM, New York (2013)
20. Müller, J., Walter, R., Bailly, G., Nischt, M., Alt, F.: Looking glass: a field study on noticing interactivity of a shop window. In: Proceedings of CHI 2012, pp. 297–306. ACM, New York (2012)
21. Marquardt, N., Ballendat, T., Boring, S., Greenberg, S., Hinckley, K.: Gradual engagement: facilitating information exchange between digital devices as a function of proximity. In: Proceedings of ITS 2012, pp. 31–40. ACM, New York (2012)
22. Gellersen, H., Fischer, C., Guinard, D., Gostner, R., Kortuem, G., Kray, C., Rukzio, E., Streng, S.: Supporting device discovery and spontaneous interaction with spatial references. Pers. Ubiquitous Comput. 13, 255–264 (2009)
23. Annett, M., Grossman, T., Wigdor, D., Fitzmaurice, G.: Medusa: a proximity-aware multi-touch tabletop. In: Proceedings of UIST 2011, pp. 337–346. ACM, USA (2011)
24. Hespanhol, L., Tomitsch, M., Bown, O., Young, M.: Using embodied audio-visual interaction to promote social encounters around large media façades. In: Proceedings of DIS 2014, pp. 945–954. ACM, New York (2014)
25. Karatzas, E.: Proximity Lab: Studies in Physical-Computational Interface and Self-Directed User Experience (2005)
26. Rehman, K., Stajano, F., Coulouris, G.: Visually interactive location-aware computing. In: Beigl, M., Intille, S.S., Rekimoto, J., Tokuda, H. (eds.) UbiComp 2005. LNCS, vol. 3660, pp. 177–194. Springer, Heidelberg (2005)
27. Wilson, A.D., Benko, H.: Combining multiple depth cameras and projectors for interactions on, above and between surfaces. In: Proceedings of UIST 2010, pp. 273–282. ACM, New York (2010)
28. Sodhi, R., Benko, H., Wilson, A.: LightGuide: projected visualizations for hand movement guidance. In: Proceedings of CHI 2012, pp. 179–188. ACM (2012)

29. Ozturk, O., Matsunami, T., Suzuki, Y., Yamasaki, T., Aizawa, K.: Real-time tracking of humans and visualization of their future footsteps in public indoor environments. Multimed. Tools Appl. **59**, 65–88 (2012)
30. Rogers, Y., Hazlewood, W.R., Marshall, P., Dalton, N., Hertrich, S.: Ambient influence: can twinkly lights lure and abstract representations trigger behavioral change? In: Proceedings of Ubicomp 2010, pp. 261–270. ACM, New York (2010)
31. Grønbæk, K., Iversen, O.S., Kortbek, K.J., Nielsen, K.R., Aagaard, L.: IGameFloor: a platform for co-located collaborative games. In: Proceedings of ACE 2007, pp. 64–71. ACM, New York (2007)
32. Dalton, N.S.: TapTiles: LED-based floor interaction. In: Proceedings of ITS 2013, pp. 165–174. ACM, New York (2013)
33. Visell, Y., Law, A., Cooperstock, J.R.: Touch is everywhere: floor surfaces as ambient haptic interfaces. IEEE Trans. Haptics **2**, 148–159 (2009)
34. Mueller, F., Stellmach, S., Greenberg, S., Dippon, A., Boll, S., Garner, J., Khot, R., Naseem, A., Altimira, D.: Proxemics play: understanding proxemics for designing digital play experiences. In: Proceedings of DIS 2014, pp. 533–542. ACM (2014)
35. Bird, J., Harrison, D., Marshall, P.: The Challenge of Maintaining Interest in a Large-Scale Public Floor Display. In: Proceedings of EIPS 2013 workshop (2013)
36. Heun, V., von Kapri, A., Maes, P.: Perifoveal display: combining foveal and peripheral vision in one visualization. In: Proceedings of Ubicomp 2012, pp. 1150–1155. ACM, New York (2012)

# Self-Actuated Displays for Vertical Surfaces

Patrick Bader[1,2(✉)], Valentin Schwind[1,2], Norman Pohl[1,2],
Niels Henze[1], Katrin Wolf[1], Stefan Schneegass[1],
and Albrecht Schmidt[1]

[1] VIS, University of Stuttgart, Stuttgart, Germany
{baderp, schwindv, pohl}@hdm-stuttgart.de,
{niels.henze, katrin.wolf, stefan.schneegass,
albrecht.schmidt}@vis.uni-stuttgart.de
[2] Stuttgart Media University, Stuttgart, Germany

**Abstract.** Most current devices are passive regarding their locations by being integrated in the environment or require to be carried when used in mobile scenarios. In this paper we present a novel type of self-actuated devices, which can be placed on vertical surfaces like whiteboards or walls. This enables vertical tangible interaction as well as the device interacting with the user through self-actuated movements. In this paper, we explore the application space for such devices by aggregating user-defined application ideas gathered in focus groups. Moreover, we implement and evaluate four interaction scenarios, discuss their usability and identify promising future use cases and improvements.

**Keywords:** Self-actuated · Display · Vertical surface · Mobile

## 1 Introduction

The variety of input and output devices that can be used to interact with computing systems is steadily increasing. Traditionally we can discriminate interaction devices into two groups.

The first group covers stationary devices, including desktop computers, TVs, and public displays. These are not mobile while in use. In many cases they are installed and become part of the environment. Notebook computers, even though they are often carried and used in different settings fall in this group, too, as they are stationary while in use. The second group describes mobile devices including, smart phones, tablets, and interactive glasses that are carried or worn by the user. Interaction with these devices takes place while the user is mobile. These two groups of devices are well explored and the design space is well understood (e.g., for input devices [2]). In recent years a third group of devices is emerging: devices which can move themselves and act autonomously, called self-actuated devices.

Interactive self-actuated devices combine the advantages of stationary devices – as the user does not have to carry them – with the advantages of mobile devices – as the device can always be with the user. Prominent examples of this device category are known from robotics. Domestic robots, such as Wakamaru [26] which provides companionship to elderly and disabled people, can autonomously serve the user. In

© IFIP International Federation for Information Processing 2015
J. Abascal et al. (Eds.): INTERACT 2015, Part IV, LNCS 9299, pp. 282–299, 2015.
DOI: 10.1007/978-3-319-22723-8_23

recent conferences attendees participated through a robotic device, e.g. using the Beam remote presence system[1]. Besides systems that are designed for a specific application domain recent work in HCI proposed interactive self-actuated general purpose devices (e.g. [24, 25, 29]). These works introduce devices that move freely, while providing rich input and output possibilities which is similar to state-of-the-art mobile devices, but without restricting the application purpose.

**Fig. 1.** Some exemplary use cases for self-actuated displays. They can (1) guide a person in using a coffee machine (2) write formulas on whiteboards with an attached pen (3) guide a user through an exhibition and give additional information by being placed besides an exhibit (4) change the display size according to in situ needs by joining multiple devices when multiple persons join a video conference.

Much like current stationary and mobile devices, interactive self-actuated devices can conceptually facilitate a large range of applications by combining different device behaviors and fitting several user roles. In this paper we explore an application space of how interactive self-actuated displays can be used from a human-centered perspective. Based on the idea that devices can move on any vertical surface, we implemented a prototype that can freely move on ferromagnetic planes. With the size and abilities of a standard tablet computer it can easily be carried and moved by the user while it has the additional abilities of a self-actuated device. Thus, the device combines the advantages of mobile, tangible, and self-actuated devices, which allows to support a broad set of use cases (see Fig. 1). Steerable projector systems [22] or display walls can provide visual output across large spaces, however, a free-moving device enriches the Every-where Display with a tangible dimension. In contrast to flying devices like *Midair Displays* [24] less power is consumed during operation. Furthermore unlike self-actuated devices for vertical surfaces flying and floor based devices share a movement space with users and thus may get in the user's way.

Using the interactive self-actuated prototype as a stimulus, we conducted a series of focus groups to explore the space of promising applications. Participants were asked to envision and discuss potential use cases. They proposed a truly broad range of corresponding ideas which we grouped in four categories: *role*, *context*, *application*, and *device behavior*. Using these categories, we identified four promising application scenarios that were implemented as cinematic showcases. Through a survey we further investigated the usability and emotional impact of the presented scenarios.

---

[1] https://www.suitabletech.com/.

After revising the related work on interactive self-actuated devices, we investigate the concept and implementation of the self-actuated display device. This implies its use cases and application scenarios that we investigated by different focus groups. Afterwards, we present four exemplary scenarios, their implementation, and the results of their evaluation that lead to a promising conclusion about the potential of self-actuated displays. The contribution of this paper is as follows:

- The concept and implementation of a novel self-actuated display device.
- An application space for the self-actuated displays for vertical surfaces.
- An evaluation of promising application scenarios for these devices.


## 2 Related Work

Before self-actuated user interfaces were proposed, user-actuated interfaces were used to manipulate digital information through manually moving physical representations of virtual information. This concept of tangible user interfaces (TUIs) has been explored as passive physical user interface and advanced towards self-actuated physical user interfaces. Nowadays, a wide range of autonomous or semi-autonomous moving user interfaces has been proposed and built, including self-actuated TUIs, devices, and robots.


### 2.1 Physical User-Actuated Interfaces

Even before coining the notion Tangible User Interface, Fitzmaurice, Ishii, and Buxton introduced *Graspable Interface* [4] that allow direct control and manipulation of digital objects through moving physical wooden bricks. Ishii and Ullmer later introduced *Tangible Bits* [10], a vision to use the whole real world as medium for manipulation of the virtual world. One of these prototypes was *transBOARD*, a digitally-enhanced whiteboard system that monitors the activity of physical objects on its vertical surface and has the capability of storing pen strokes. Another example was *Urp* [30], a TUI for collaborative urban planning using physical models of buildings on a tabletop system. Video projection and electromagnetic tagged wireless mice were used as pucks on the *Sensetable* [21], while the music interface *reacTable* [11] works with optical markers that are placed underneath the tangibles are moved on a tabletop system to play music. *Geckos* [17], *Magnetic Appcessories* [1], and *GaussBits* [18] use magnets to attach passive tangible elements on vertical surfaces and thus demonstrate that interaction with TUIs is not limited to horizontal planes. In addition to magnetic solutions, vacuum adhesion forces for sticking tangible objects on vertical surfaces were used in *Vertibles* [9].


### 2.2 Physical Self-Actuated Interfaces

Technologies proposed for actuating tangibles were for instance merged arrays of electromagnetic coils embedded in a tabletop system [20, 31], the six-legged Hexbug™ [27], and vibrating bristles [19]. Moreover, tabletop systems were using robots instead of TUIs (*Touch and Toys* [7], *RoboTable* [14], *RoboTable2* [28], *Remote-Bunnies* [6], and *TabletopCars* [3]). *PhyBots* [12] introduced a prototyping toolkit for adding locomotion on floors to everyday objects. *Curlybot* [5] was a driving educational toy robot that allows to be equipped with a pen extension. The *PMD* system uses tracked physical objects, whereby physical elements are moved by both, users and computers [23]. Self-actuated devices have also been developed for vertical surfaces. *WallBots* [15] are magnetic as well as self-actuated, autonomous wall-crawling robots equipped with a tri-colored LED and used in street art. Interactive self-actuated objects can also move in a three-dimensional space. *ZeroN* [16], a magnetic-controlled volume with a levitating tangible element tracked by a Kinect demonstrates a physical computer-actuated 3D interface. The *Midair Displays* [24], a display mounted to a quad-copter, is conceptually a spatially unlimited levitating and moving interface. Similarly, Seifert et al., developed *Hover Pad*, a tablet that is attached to a static crane construction and can thereby freely move within a 3D space [25].

### 2.3  Summary

Previous works on self-actuated interactive devices mainly focused on the technical aspects to realize novel types of devices, and mostly the device was build for one single application to demonstrate the technical concept. In contrast, our aim is to explore the application space of self-actuated interactive displays for vertical surfaces. Considering self-actuated devices as a new class of devices in this paper we explore potential applications of such devices from a human-centered perspective.

## 3  Self-Actuated Displays for Vertical Surfaces

In this section, we introduce the concept of self-actuated displays for vertical surfaces. Additionally we describe our prototypical implementation which realizes the main aspects of the concept using currently available technology.

### 3.1  Concept

In this work, we explore the possibilities of self-actuated displays that are able to move on horizontal as well as vertical surfaces. We present a device that can be grabbed and placed on surfaces (similar to tangible user interfaces [10]) and freely moved on these surfaces. This enables the usage of vertical surfaces such as walls, whiteboards, or ceilings. In contrast to most prior work, we thereby focus on devices that are actuated by the user as well as self-actuated depending on context and task.

To cover a broad range of interactions possibilities, we envision several input and output modalities. As input modality we mainly focus on touch screen, camera, and further sensors such as an accelerometer. The primary output modalities are visual and auditory. Since we envision a self-actuated device, we take the movement of the display itself into account as well. Moreover, the device can be equipped with traditional tools. For example, a pen can be attached to it, serving as an additional output means.

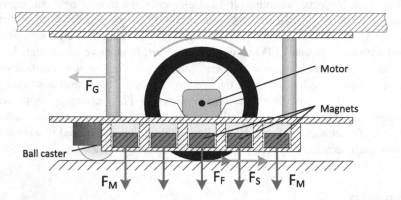

**Fig. 2.** Section view of the prototype showing main components relevant to vertical movement. Gravity $F_G$, stiction $F_S$ and magnetic forces $F_M$ are also shown.

Embedded sensors which are integrated in the device not only enable user tracking, they also facilitate coordination with other devices since we envision an active communication between multiple devices, so they can interact with each other and/or create a unified display space. Thus, the maximum display size is only limited by the number of devices used.

Whereas most current self-actuated interfaces are limited to horizontal surfaces, like interactive tables, our approach focuses on vertical surfaces. Therefore the device is also attachable to walls and whiteboards for example.

## 3.2    Prototype Implementation

We transferred the concept of our self-actuated display into two working prototypes (see Fig. 3).

Both are based on the commercially available 3pi robot platform by Pololu[2] with the 3pi expansion kit without cutouts[3] attached. We added support for external LiPo-battery usage and charging to compensate for increased battery drainage caused by vertical movement. For wireless communication with external and attached devices a Bluetooth enabled microcontroller was used.

We enabled the prototype to move on ferromagnetic vertical surfaces by attaching a 3D printed frame[4] to its bottom that holds up to 22 neodymium magnets.

---

[2] http://www.pololu.com/product/975.

[3] http://www.pololu.com/product/978.

[4] 3D-models to reproduce the robot are available at: https://github.com/patrigg/WallDisplay.

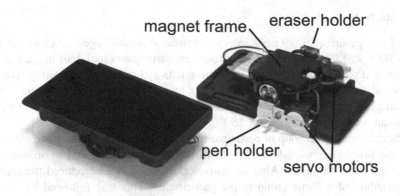

magnet frame    eraser holder

pen holder    servo motors

**Fig. 3.** A self-actuated display prototype without any extensions attached (left) and a bottom view of another prototype with pen and eraser holder attached (right). Both extensions are driven by servo motors.

To allow upwards movement on vertical surfaces, the motors have to generate enough torque to overcome both gravity $F_G$ and rolling resistance $F_F$ as depicted in Fig. 2. Thus, we replaced the default 30:1 gear motors with 298:1 gear motors. Furthermore, wheel slippage has to be prevented by generating enough stiction $F_S$. In our case this is done by increasing magnetic force $F_M$ and contact pressure by adding magnets. However, increasing contact pressure also increases rolling resistance and reduces acceleration and maximum speed. We empirically determined the number and locations of the magnets needed to enable stable operation and ended up using 15 magnets with some bias towards the ball caster.

To expand the robot's input and output modalities, we attached a 3D printed frame that encloses a Google Nexus 7 tablet[5]. Besides its display, the tablet also provides the robot with additional peripherals like cameras, inertial sensors, Wi-Fi, and speakers. The tablet frame may also be extended with additional tools. As examples for such tools (see Fig. 3) we built servo motor actuated pen and eraser holders to draw on whiteboards. Each prototype is approximately *205 × 117 × 49* mm in size and weighs *495* g.

## 4  Creating Potential Use-Cases

To increase our understanding of the application space and to explore potential use cases for the device we conducted a series of focus groups [13] and evaluated the results. We first presented the developed prototype to the focus groups to create a common understanding of the possibilities and interaction modalities. In the following, we first describe the design of the focus groups and afterwards, we present the results and a discussion.

---

[5] http://www.google.com/nexus/7/.

## 4.1  Study Method

Three focus groups with 19 participants (15 male, 4 female) aged 22 to 41 ($M = 26.9$ years, $SD = 4.3$) were conducted – six to seven participants took part in each of them. We recruited participants through our mailing lists and from our peer group. We strove for a broad cultural background and, thus, we invited participants originating from five different countries, namely the U.S., Germany, Egypt, Belgium and Argentina. Each participant was compensated with 15 €.

After welcoming a group of participants and providing them with basic information about the procedure, we asked them to fill in a consent form and to answer a brief demographic questionnaire. After an introduction round, we introduced the main goal and procedure of a focus group to the participants. This was followed by a demonstration of the prototype (see Fig. 4) on a whiteboard and its capabilities as a stimulus for participants. We also highlighted the ability to control a pen and an eraser to show its potential for further extension. Directly after the presentation, we asked participants to write down their initial reactions (Result R1). We asked them to discuss them afterwards, and we took notes during the discussion (R2).

**Fig. 4.** Photo of the prototype demonstration we showed participants as stimulus. Some lines were drawn with the pen that is attached to the device.

After the discussion of the participants' initial reactions, we asked them to write down potential use cases on large post-it notes (R3). This was followed by a discussion about the most promising and the most controversial cases, which were recorded in a written protocol for post hoc analysis (R4). During this discussion participants could write down additional ideas on post-its (R3). After the discussion, we closed the respective session.

## 4.2  Results

Participants' first impression (R1) and their discussion (R2) were mainly positive. Answers can be categorized in three main categories. (1) Participants were impressed by the overall idea. They, for example, stated that *"it looks impressive"* (P5), *"opens a new space"* (P6) and is a *"pretty interesting technology"* (P16). (2) Participants also imagined applications for similar devices. They stated that it would be *"useful if you have hands full"* (P18) and could be used *"in the kitchen"* (P17). Finally, (3) two participants expressed concerns about the presented technology. One asked *"For what?"* (P13) and another participants wondered if it *"must be able to move?"* (P19).

In total, participants created 137 potential use cases (R3) for the presented technology. Using a bottom-up analysis and open coding, we identified 49 groups of ideas in total that again could be grouped into four main categories. An emerging group, for example, contains 31 ideas that propose to use the device in home environments and another group with 25 ideas proposed ideas where the device follows the user's position. The groups were categorized by their *Role, Context, Application*, and *Device Behavior* (see Table 1). *Role* can be further divided in ownership, audience, and controlling subject. The device can, for example, be autonomous, part of the infrastructure, and with a single person as audience. *Context* was mostly provided in the form of description of a location, such as an office or a classroom but also through specific situations such as emergencies. Participants' ideas provide diverse *applications*.

**Table 1.** Aggregation of participants' ideas along the four dimensions. The numbers in the *n* columns denote the number of ideas that fit a particular group. Groups which are implemented by a specific scenario are highlighted using color coding. Blue groups are implemented by the kitchen scenario, green represents the classroom scenario. The museum scenario is highlighted with a yellow background, and the office scenario is red.

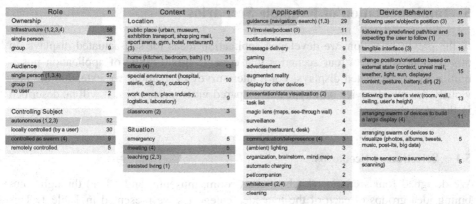

| Role | n | Context | n | Application | n | Device Behavior | n |
|---|---|---|---|---|---|---|---|
| Ownership | | Location | | guidance (navigation, search) (1,3) | 29 | following user's/object's position (3) | 25 |
| infrastructure (1,2,3,4) | 56 | public place (urban, museum, exhibition transport, shopping mall, sport arena, gym, hotel, restaurant) (3) | 36 | TV/movies/podcast (3) | 11 | following a predefined path/tour and expecting the user to follow (1) | 19 |
| single person | 25 | | | notifications/alarms | 11 | | |
| group | 9 | | | message delivery | 9 | tangible interface (3) | 16 |
| | | home (kitchen, bedroom, bath) (1) | 31 | gaming | 8 | change position/orientation based on external state (context, unreal mail, weather, light, sun, displayed content, gesture, battery, dirt) (2) | 15 |
| Audience | | office (4) | 13 | advertisement | 8 | | |
| single person (1,3,4) | 57 | special environment (hospital, sterile, old, outdoor) | 10 | augmented reality | 8 | | |
| group (2) | 29 | | | display for other devices | 7 | | |
| no user | 2 | work (bench, place industry, logistics, laboratory) | 9 | presentation/data visualization (2) | 6 | following the user's view (room, wall, ceiling, user's height) | 13 |
| | | | | task list | 5 | | |
| Controlling Subject | | classroom (2) | 3 | magic lens (maps, see-through wall) | 5 | arranging swarm of devices to build a large display (4) | 11 |
| autonomous (1,2,3) | 52 | | | surveillance | 4 | | |
| locally controlled (by a user) | 30 | Situation | | services (restaurant, desk) | 4 | arranging swarm of devices to visualize (photos, albums, tweets, music, post-its, big data) | 5 |
| controlled as swarm (4) | 9 | emergency | 5 | communication/telepresence (4) | 3 | | |
| remotely controlled | 5 | meeting (4) | 5 | (ambient) lighting | 3 | remote sensor (measurements, scanning) | 5 |
| | | teaching (2,3) | 1 | organization, brainstorm, mind maps | 2 | | |
| | | assisted living (1) | 1 | automatic charging | 2 | | |
| | | | | pet/companion | 2 | | |
| | | | | whiteboard (2,4) | 2 | | |
| | | | | cleaning | 1 | | |

Exemplary applications include navigation and route guidance, sending messages, as well as providing alarms and notifications or using the device as smart companion. The fourth category describes *device behaviors*. For example, arranging multiple devices in a grid generates a large display. Another example proposes that the device follows a predefined path and expects the user to follow for delivering location – and situation-based information to the user.

For a final improvement of the category consistency, we revised all ideas by going through the individual post-it notes and categorized them using the identified four idea categories. This procedure ensured that all ideas are covered by the four identified categories. During that process, we determined how often particular ideas appear in each group.

### 4.3 Discussion

The three focus groups identify a wide range of use cases for self-actuated displays on vertical surfaces (see Table 1). Using a bottom-up analysis we identified 76 groups to structure the ideas that can further be fused into the four categories *Role*, *Context*, *Application*, and *Device Behavior*. Moreover, these categories can be used to generate new application scenarios, which were not explicitly envisioned by one of our participants. Cells of Table 1, for example, can be fused to the following scenario: multiple devices that are part of an office's infrastructure (*Role*, *Context*), can build a large display (*Device Behavior*), to form a window by enabling the user to see through walls (*Application*). Whereas this particular scenario was not envisioned by one of our participants, it could be derived by combining idea groups across the four categories. However neither the results of the focus group can be generalized nor the amount of design ideas per group should be over interpreted. That means that ideas mentioned the most are not necessarily the most interesting ones. Yet we were able to cover a broad range of potential application scenarios.

## 5    Implementation of Example Scenarios

In the previous section, we developed application ideas for self-actuated displays. In this section, we select four scenarios that cover a broad range of application possibilities for self-actuated displays. For a later survey evaluation, we extended the previously described device prototype and prepared video prototypes. It will be described in the next chapter.

### 5.1    Selection of Scenarios

We designed four scenarios (kitchen, class room, museum, and office) through combining idea groups of each of the four idea categories we presented in Table 1. This allowed us to cover a broad variety of different application types. During that process, we aimed for covering diverse scenarios that are well represented through the ideas generated by the focus groups.

As shown by color coding in Table 1 the scenarios cover each sub-category of the *role* dimension: *ownership*, *audience*, and *controlling subject*. Moreover, we consider diverse *context* types as well as combinations of them: *home (kitchen), classroom and teaching*, *public space (museum)*, as well as *office* and *meeting*. Afterwards, we selected *applications* that suit the selected *contexts*, while also representing a good coverage of the idea groups: *guidance (task)*, *teaching* and *presentation/data visualization*, *guidance (navigation)* and *podcast* as well as *communication/telepresence*. Finally, we chose a *device behavior* for each scenario which fitted the combination of *role*, *context*, and *application* best.

## 5.2 Video Prototype

To evaluate the scenarios we created videos of the prototypes being used for each scenario. We present these videos to participants in an online survey. Thus, four storyboards, one for each scenario, were designed which describe how a user interacts with the self-actuated display during the four scenarios (see Fig. 5). The storyboards explain the context the scenario takes place in (e.g., museum or kitchen), the interaction sequence when a user is using the device in a specific application, and the content that is displayed on the device's screen during the interaction.

**Fig. 5.** Stills of the four video prototypes presenting the scenarios. (1) Device gives directions for preparing coffee. (2) Graph is visualized using a whiteboard marker attached to the device. (3) Device follows a user through an exhibition. (4) Remote participant joins a conversation during a video conference.

**Scenario 1 – Kitchen.** A person is in an unknown environment, for instance she just started to work in a new office. In the kitchen of this office is a commonly used coffee machine. She would like to have a coffee but she neither knows how the machine works nor where the cups and ingredients are. This video shows how a self-actuated display guides the person to find the cups and the ingredients as well as how to use the coffee machine.

**Scenario 2 - Class Room.** The teacher is teaching trigonometry and explains a new formula. The self-actuated display assists through being an interactive display where the teacher can write any formula on. The self-actuated display draws the formula on the whiteboard to present it to the class.

**Scenario 3 – Museum.** Visitors may want some kind of additional information about the exhibits, but some of them want to follow their own path and not being guided in a tour. A self-actuated – and at the same time tangible display – can follow the visitor in an exhibition and provides further information about exhibits of interest. Furthermore, placing the device manually (like TUIs) enables the user to gain further background information about an exhibit of interest.

**Scenario 4 – Office.** In this scenario the display can increase its size if that is necessary, for example, if additional people join an ongoing video conference meeting. For communicating with a single person, the display is sufficiently large enough to show that person. However, when another person joins the conversation, the display may be too small and, thus, one cannot see all conversation parties at once. In the video prototype we show how self-actuated displays allow to change their size through automatically gathering together and extend the display size similar to puzzle pieces.

The content displayed on the device during the video (text, images, and video) was pre-produced and presented in a remotely controlled slideshow while the video prototypes were recorded. The device has been remotely controlled in scenarios 1, 3 and 4 using a Microsoft Xbox360 game controller. For scenario 2 the predefined curve has been drawn autonomously using the control scheme described below. In summary, we developed four video prototypes with an average duration of 69 s.

### 5.3    Device Prototype

To realize the video prototypes we implemented two control schemes – remote control and autonomous behavior. For remote control we used a commercially available game pad connected to a laptop. Motor speeds were calculated according to the direction of the analogue sticks and sent to the prototype via Bluetooth.

The whiteboard task also requires the display to move autonomously so the position and orientation needs to be detected. As the prototype has a tablet attached, we exploited its gravity sensor to determine the orientation. This orientation data is send to a laptop using Wi-Fi. To obtain the position of the device, we used an external Asus Xtion depth camera[6] which was oriented perpendicular towards the prototype. The device position is obtained by segmenting depth values in a short distance to the surface (2 to 7 cm). After filtering out small segments we determined the exact position on the surface by calculating the center of mass for each segment in screen space. We chose this method for its simplicity. In future versions the position could also be obtained by the prototype without an external sensor using the built in camera and feature tracking, for example.

---

[6] http://www.asus.com/Multimedia/Xtion_PRO_LIVE/.

Based on the position and orientation data we implemented a control scheme using a proportional-integral-derivative controller which allowed us to implement two simple movement commands:

- **look at:** rotates the robot around its center until it is heading towards a target point.
- **move to:** reaches a specific point by following a straight line to the target.

We used these simple commands to build scripts for drawing axes and plotting simple mathematical functions such as a sine curve by linear approximation. The autonomous behavior is, for instance, used in the *classroom scenario* in which the self-actuated display draws mathematical functions to assist the professor.

# 6  Scenario Evaluation

## 6.1  Method

For evaluating the four scenarios, we conducted an online survey, which we distributed via mailing lists and social networks. The survey started with an introduction about its purpose and a questionnaire that records the age and the gender of the participants. Then the scenarios were presented in randomized order. At the beginning, a brief introduction was given, then the video was shown, and afterwards we asked (using a 5 item Likert scale) if the presented scenario was liked. Moreover, we used the AttrakDiff mini questionnaire [8] to collect opinions about the scenarios. Finally, in two open questions the participants were asked to report positive (e.g., strengths or possibilities) and negative (e.g., weaknesses or risks) aspects of the scenario.

## 6.2  Results

In total, 57 participants (13 female, 44 male) aged 20 to 58 years ($M = 33.7$, $SD = 9.6$) completed our online survey. Thus, we collected 57 completed AttrakDiff questionnaires for each scenario as quantitative results and 269 (64.9 %) out of 456 possible qualitative answers to open questions regarding positive or negative aspects.

**Quantitative Results.** The user perception of the emotional impact was evaluated according to the AttrakDiff scheme (based on a 1–7 Likert scale). Table 2 compares the mean values of the scores of each presented scenario. The hedonic quality (HQ) consists of the HQ-Identity (HQ-I) and HQ-Stimulation (HQ-S). In terms of pragmatic quality Scenario 1 performs slightly better than the others. Relating to attractiveness Scenario 4 performs best. Also in terms of hedonic quality Scenario 4 achieves the highest scores. The small and overlapping confidence intervals indicate that the participants generally assess the presented scenarios similarly.

We further analyzed the data using a Friedman Analysis of Variance. However, the Friedman ANOVA yielded no significant differences for the AttrakDiff scales of hedonic qualities (HQ-I: $\chi^2(3) = 0.587, p = .899$, HQ-S: $\chi^2(3) = 3.322, p = .345$) as well as for attractiveness (ATT: $\chi^2(3) = 5.818, p = .121$), we found a statistically significant difference in the pragmatic qualities (PQ: $\chi^2(3) = 8.051, p = .045$). Post hoc analysis with Wilcoxon signed-rank tests was conducted with a Bonferroni correction applied, resulting in a significance level set at .008. However, we did not find any statistically significant differences for the perceived pragmatic qualities between the four scenarios ($p > .008$).

**Table 2.** Results from the AttrakDiff evaluation ($N = 57$) of the four scenarios show the mean of the pragmatic quality (PQ), hedonic quality (HQ) and attractiveness (ATT). Confidence interval at 95 percent probability level.

| Scenario | PQ Mean (CI95) | HQ Mean (CI95) | ATT Mean (CI95) |
|---|---|---|---|
| 1. Kitchen | 4.619 (0.329) | 4.149 (0.277) | 3.930 (0.354) |
| 2. Classroom | 4.127 (0.310) | 4.184 (0.288) | 3.816 (0.380) |
| 3. Museum | 4.408 (0.335) | 4.136 (0.289) | 3.702 (0.393) |
| 4. Office | 4.338 (0.279) | 4.272 (0.236) | 4.272 (0.326) |

**Qualitative Results.** We analyzed the 269 qualitative answers of the questionnaire by manual assessment. Analysis was done in two iterations: derivation of a categorization and answer reassignment afterwards.

In the first iteration two researchers independently derived categories for each scenario based on the answers and counted their occurrences. Then both categorizations were discussed and merged into unified categorization schemes. Analysis revealed seven scenario independent categories, which we then separated from the scenario specific ones.

In the second iteration we went through the answers once again, reassigned them to the previously derived categorization and counted the occurrence of each category. Furthermore, occurrences of independent categories were also summed up over the scenarios.

*Concept.* We assigned 24 answers to the concept category, which deals with the device being attached to walls. This property has been mostly commented on in the *kitchen* and *office* scenarios. One answer stated that the *"contents of the [kitchen] drawer may be changed without having to tell someone"* (P96) and another one wrote *"it's nice to have additional screen space as needed and helpful that the screen aligns itself with the one already there."* (P86) or simply that the system is *"cool and universally applicable"* (P97). Whereas others mentioned *"the device seems to be limited to a 2d-region. If the procedure extends beyond this region (e.g., throwing the coffee filter into the wastebin at the door), the display is not usable adequately"* (P40), and *"is it able to move around corners or does it have to be detached?"* (P97).

*Usefulness.* In total 82 answers directly addressed the usefulness of the device. It *"fulfills its tasks"* (P59), gives a *"simple and lucid explanation, useful for complex tasks"* (P90), and *"might help some physically limited people"* (P73). Likely due to the simplistic scenarios some users asked *"what is its purpose?"* (P76), and regarded the device a *"gimmick"* (P48).

*Attention.* Another set of 35 answers addressed the attention of users. The system was described to have a *"good entertainment value"* (P72) and it *"attracts attention to itself"* (P90). Although some of them noted that the *"show-off & wow effect (works probably just once)"* (P73). In the *museum* scenario there were concerns that *"the device may attract negative attention from the viewer or disturbs him from viewing artworks since movement of the device automatically attracts attention to itself"* (P100), as stated by one answer.

*Alternatives.* Sixty eight answers compared the prototype with various alternative products including mobile phone applications (*"better [realized] with indoor-navigation app"* (P105)), camera projection systems (*"[I] think projector + software are clearly better suited for this [kitchen scenario]."* (P14)), or head mounted displays (*"I'd rather consider this [museum] a scenario for Google Glass or CastAR."* (P16)). These approaches, however, have additional drawbacks that need to be taken into account as well (e.g., stationary setup for projection, challenges in augmented reality). Others mentioned advantages like (e.g. *" "pointing" [at something] is easier than using static displays."* (P79)). This was especially the case in the *museum* scenario where there is *"no need for one's own tablet/smartphone"* (P36), and it also *"replaces guide, [and has] individuality"* (P42).

*Complexity.* In total 39 answers dealt with the influence of task complexity in the scenarios. The devices are a *"very nice possibility to maintain eye contact with many participants at video conferences"* (P10), *"It is quite easy for students, they can write the formula and the machine draws for them"* (P98), and *"managing new situations is definitively simplified"* (P87).We chose simple tasks that were easy to implement, like drawing simple functions. On such tasks there is a risk that it *"complexes a simple process"* (P16). Also when preparing coffee one participant found that it *"looks way too inconvenient for something such simple to me"* (P17).

*Multiple users.* Multi-user support has been identified as another category which was mentioned in 30 answers. In the *office* scenario *"the number of participants involved in the conversation may be easily varied"* (P87) using multiple devices. In public spaces like a *museum* where many people act in a quite limited space questions regarding the use of multiple displays that need to be addressed arose. For example: *"What happens when multiple people are looking at the same piece of art or passing each other?"* (P86) and *"how should probably dozens of displays be controlled and be distinguished from each other?"* (P45).

*Technical characteristics.* We categorized 102 comments into technical characteristics which describe particular aspects of the prototype. Our prototype is driven by two gear motors with relatively high gear transmission ratios, so *"the device is slow and noisy"* (P3). Especially one participant said *"it is too noisy to hear that this machine follows you. I need quiet and silence to visit the art exhibition."* (P98) In contrast, in the *office* the device was *"quiet-running"* (P59).

In the *kitchen* one answer remarked *"it is good that I don't need to ask anyone or spend more time to find out"* (P98) how to prepare coffee, whereas *"the teacher probably would have manually drawn the curve faster"* (P87) in the *classroom*.

Asthetics were also subject to potential improvement in future versions, especially in the museum scenario the *"metal driving plates around the exhibits are little aesthetic"* (P35).

*Scenario specific categories.* Besides the independent categories described above, we identified some categories that applied to specific scenarios only:

- **kitchen:** Nine answers dealt with the social aspect of preparing coffee. As with other technology that was introduced before (e.g. smart phones), some participants saw the risk that *"communication between colleagues is lost"* (P64).
- **classroom:** We identified two more categories with sixteen participants commenting on the precision and seven on the didactic meaning. The prototype used for the video clearly lacks precision and is *"quite scrawly, [and] surely problematic for more complex functions"* (P14), but future versions may as well produce a *"potentially better/more exact drawing of functions than quickly sketched hand drawings"* (P57) can. Thus some answers were skeptic about *"what is the didactic meaning and learning success?"* (P65).
- **museum:** Five answers saw the device as a *"personalized guide"* (P52) that is *"more personal than fixed video installations"* (P14). Additionally three answers emphasized the self-actuated aspect, for example *"further multimedia information [is available] at any time without having me to carry something with me"* (P61).
- **office:** Dynamically scaling the display with multiple devices was mentioned in ten answers. One participant found *"it's nice to have additional screen space as needed and helpful that the screen aligns itself with the one already there"* (P86), and another wrote *"having multiple displays merge into a single large one is fantastic"* (P3). Six participants were not sure *"where did the second display come from?"* (P14) since the scenario looked somewhat constructed with only a whiteboard and two devices.

## 6.3   Discussion

We evaluated four scenarios that have been derived from the application ideas that resulted from the focus groups. For each scenario, we collected qualitative comments as well as the scenarios' pragmatic and hedonic qualities. Participants' quantitative assessment was similar for the four scenarios. Despite the limitation of the concrete prototype used, the overall reaction is positive in terms of hedonic and pragmatic qualities with a tendency towards being desired.

Comments regarding the scenarios' usefulness were mainly positive, describing specific use cases. Some participants, however, also wondered about the additional value the device could provide. Accordingly, participants compared the device with existing devices that can support similar tasks. In this sense the self-actuated display is similar to devices that fill a position complementary to existing devices, such as tablets that fill a position between large static displays and small mobile smart phones. Participants also highlighted unique aspects of self-actuated displays and that in certain situation they could replace static but also mobile displays.

Participants widely addressed the technical characteristics of the concrete prototype. Comments suggest that self-actuated displays must be fast enough to draw or to follow a walking user. Furthermore, participants criticized the noise level. These technical limitations can be tackled by using more powerful gear motors with reduced noise emission. Concerns about the margin of the display's border could be addressed by further developments in display technologies that reduce the frame thickness. This would allow seamless display connections with several devices.

Challenge might emerge if a large number of self-actuated devices are used at the same time. On the one hand, devices might interfere with each other and on the other hand it might become difficult for a user to identify his or her devices.

Participants appreciated the general concept of a device that is attached to and can move on walls. They envisioned a general purpose device that can provide additional screen space. A limitation of the current prototype is the restriction to a single 2D surface. For the device to be more general purpose, the device must be able to change surfaces itself.

It was appreciated that the device attracts attention. Participants partially assigned this to the device's novelty but also to its ability to move into the users' field-of-view. While this can be seen as an advantage it can also distract users from other tasks or content.

Participants discussed the potential benefit of the developed scenarios. They agreed on using the device could reduce the complexity of new tasks through being a support, for instance by providing in situ information (assistance when acting in an unknown environment, e.g. *kitchen scenario* or *museum scenario*).

# 7 Conclusion

In this paper, we explored the space of applications for self-actuated displays. Assuming that self-actuated devices are a third class of devices that fill a space between mobile and static devices we developed the concept for a novel type of self-actuated display device. We implemented this concept through a prototype that is able to autonomously move vertically on ferromagnetic surfaces. Based on the results of a series of focus groups we derived a categorization for applications of self-actuated displays. To further explore this space we derived four application scenarios and implemented them as video prototypes showing interactive self-actuated displays in four application domains. Evaluating the video prototypes revealed that participants see advantages but also limitations of self-actuated displays. In particular, it is important that self-actuated devices are quiet and sufficiently fast to follow or guide a moving user. If this is the case, the device's physical position and movement provides a way to attract users' attention and can also encode information.

In this work, we used a particular self-actuated display to explore use-cases and to further explore them through concrete scenarios. Therefore, we are interested in extending the work through the use of other self-actuated devices [24, 25, 29]. On a technical level we are interested in approaches that extend the mobility of self-actuated displays for vertical surfaces. In particular, ferromagnetic wall paint could be used to make existing surfaces accessible for the current prototype. Further options are adding moveable suction cups and adhesive pads that could either be used to get over non-ferromagnetic spaces or to enable free movement on arbitrary surfaces.

**Acknowledgements.** This work was supported by the graduate program Digital Media of the Universities of Stuttgart and Tübingen, and the Stuttgart Media University.

# References

1. Bianchi, A., Oakley, I.: Designing tangible magnetic appcessories. In: Proceedings of TEI 2013, pp. 255–258 (2013)
2. Card, S.K., Mackinlay, J.D., Robertson, G.G.: A morphological analysis of the design space of input devices. ACM Trans. Inf. Syst. **9**(2), 99–122 (1991)
3. Dang, C.T., André, E.: Tabletopcars: Interaction with active tangible remote controlled cars. In: Proceedings of TEI 2013, pp. 33–40 (2013)
4. Fitzmaurice, G.W., Ishii, H., Buxton, W.A.S.: Bricks: Laying the foundations for graspable user interfaces. In: Proceedings of CHI 1995, pp. 442–449 (1995)
5. Frei, P., Su, V., Mikhak, B., Ishii, H.: Curlybot: Designing a new class of computational toys. In: Proceedings of CHI 2000, pp. 129–136 (2000)
6. Guerra, P.: Remotebunnies: Multi-agent phenomena mapping between physical environments. In: Proceedings of TEI 2013, pp. 347–348 (2013)
7. Guo, C., Young, J.E., Sharlin, E.: Touch and toys: New techniques for interaction with a remote group of robots. In: Proceedings of CHI 2009, pp. 491–500 (2009)
8. Hassenzahl, M., Monk, A.: The inference of perceived usability from beauty. Hum. Comput. Interact. **25**(3), 235–260 (2010)
9. Hennecke, F., Wimmer, R., Vodicka, E., Butz, A.: Vertibles: Using vacuum self-adhesion to create a tangible user interface for arbitrary interactive surfaces. In: Proceedings of TEI 2012, pp. 303–306 (2012)
10. Ishii, H., Ullmer, B.: Tangible bits: Towards seamless interfaces between people, bits and atoms. In: Proceedings of CHI 1997, pp. 234–241 (1997)
11. Jordà, S., Geiger, G., Alonso, M., Kaltenbrunner, M.: The reactable: Exploring the synergy between live music performance and tabletop tangible interfaces. In: Proceedings of TEI 2007, pp. 139–146 (2007)
12. Kato, J., Sakamoto, D., Igarashi, T.: Phybots: A toolkit for making robotic things. In: Proceedings of DIS 2012, pp. 248–257 (2012)
13. Kitzinger, J.: The methodology of focus groups: the importance of interaction between research participants. Sociol. Health Illn. **16**(1), 103–121 (1994)
14. Krzywinski, A., Mi, H., Chen, W., Sugimoto, M.: Robotable: A tabletop framework for tangible interaction with robots in a mixed reality. In: Proceedings of ACE 2009, pp. 107–114 (2009)
15. Kuznetsov, S., Paulos, E., Gross, M.D.: Wallbots: Interactive wall-crawling robots in the hands of public artists and political activists. In: Proceedings of DIS 2010, pp. 208–217 (2010)
16. Lee, J., Post, R., Ishii, H.: Zeron: Mid-air tangible interaction enabled by computer controlled magnetic levitation. In: Proceedings of UIST 2011, pp. 327–336 (2011)
17. Leitner, J., Haller, M.: Geckos: Combining magnets and pressure images to enable new tangible-object design and interaction. In: Proceedings of CHI 2011, pp. 2985–2994 (2011)
18. Liang, R.H., Cheng, K.Y., Chan, L., Peng, C.X., Chen, M.Y., Liang, R.H., Yang, D.N., Chen, B.Y.: Gaussbits: Magnetic tangible bits for portable and occlusion-free near-surface interactions. In: CHI EA 2013, pp. 2837–2838 (2013)

19. Nowacka, D., Ladha, K., Hammerla, N.Y., Jackson, D., Ladha, C., Rukzio, E., Olivier, P.: Touchbugs: Actuated tangibles on multi-touch tables. In: Proceedings of CHI 2013, pp. 759–762 (2013)
20. Pangaro, G., Maynes-Aminzade, D., Ishii, H.: The actuated workbench: Computer-controlled actuation in tabletop tangible interfaces. In: Proceedings of UIST 2002, pp. 181–190 (2002)
21. Patten, J., Ishii, H., Hines, J., Pangaro, G.: Sensetable: A wireless object tracking platform for tangible user interfaces. In: Proceedings of CHI 2001, pp. 253–260 (2001)
22. Pinhanez, C.: The everywhere displays projector: a device to create ubiquitous graphical interfaces. In: Abowd, G.D., Brumitt, B., Shafer, S. (eds.) UbiComp 2001. LNCS, vol. 2201, pp. 315–331. Springer, Heidelberg (2001)
23. Rosenfeld, D., Zawadzki, M., Sudol, J., Perlin, K.: Physical objects as bidirectional user interface elements. IEEE Comput. Graph. Appl. 24(1), 44–49 (2004)
24. Schneegass, S., Alt, F., Scheible, J., Schmidt, A.: Midair displays: Concept and first experiences with free-floating pervasive displays. In: Proceedings of PerDis 2014, pp. 27:27–27:31 (2014)
25. Seifert, J., Boring, S., Winkler, C., et al.: Hover pad: Interacting with autonomous and self-actuated displays in space. In: Proceedings of UIST 2014, pp. 139–147 (2014)
26. Shiotani, S., Tomonaka, T., Kemmotsu, K., Asano, S., Oonishi, K., Hiura, R.: World's first full-fledged communication robot "wakamaru" capable of living with family and supporting persons. Mitsubishi Juko Giho 43(1), 44–45 (2006)
27. Somanath, S., Sharlin, E., Sousa, M.: Integrating a robot in a tabletop reservoir engineering application. In: Proceedings of HRI 2013, pp. 229–230, March 2013
28. Sugimoto, M., Fujita, T., Mi, H., Krzywinski, A.: Robotable2: A novel programming environment using physical robots on a tabletop platform. In: Proceedings of ACE 2011, pp. 10:1–10:8 (2011)
29. Tominaga, J., Kawauchi, K., Rekimoto, J.: Around me: A system with an escort robot providing a sports player's self-images. In: Proceedings of AH 2014, pp. 43:1–43:8 (2014)
30. Underkoffler, J., Ishii, H.: Urp: A luminous-tangible workbench for urban planning and design. In: Proceedings of CHI 1999, pp. 386–393 (1999)
31. Weiss, M., Schwarz, F., Jakubowski, S., Borchers, J.: Madgets: Actuating widgets on interactive tabletops. In: Proceedings of UIST 2010, pp. 293–302 (2010)

# 3D-HUDD – Developing a Prototyping Tool for 3D Head-Up Displays

Nora Broy[1]([✉]), Matthias Nefzger[2], Florian Alt[2], Mariam Hassib[2], and Albrecht Schmidt[3]

[1] BMW Research and Technology, Munich, Germany
Nora.NB.Broy@bmw.de
[2] Group for Media Informatics, University of Munich, Munich, Germany
{matthias.nefzger,florian.alt,mariam.hassib}@ifi.lmu.de
[3] VIS, University of Stuttgart, Stuttgart, Germany
albrecht.schmidt@vis.uni-stuttgart.de

**Abstract.** The ability of head-up displays (HUDs) to present information within the usual viewpoint of the user has led to a quick adoption in domains where attention is crucial, such as in the car. As HUDs employ 3D technology, further opportunities emerge: information can be structured and positioned in 3D space thus allowing important information to be perceived more easily and information can be registered with objects in the visual scene to communicate a relationship. This allows novel user interfaces to be built. As of today, however, no prototyping tools exist, that allow 3D UIs for HUDs to be sketched and tested prior to development. To close this gap, we report on the design and development of the *3D Head-Up Display Designer (3D-HUDD)*. In addition, we present an evaluation of the tool with 24 participants, comparing different input modalities and depth management modes.

## 1 Introduction

Head-up displays (HUDs) allow information to be presented to users without requiring them to look away from their usual viewpoint. This property made them a popular asset in vehicles, since it allows the eyes-off-the-road time to be minimized as drivers attend to information such as speed or navigation cues [31].

More recently, 3D HUDs, allowing information to be presented at an arbitrary position within the 3D space of the user's viewpoint, received considerable attention. For example, Toyota and Lexus are currently developing 3D HUDs with the particular aim to show navigation cues at the very location users need to take a turn [27].

Furthermore, stereoscopic 3D (S3D) output can support the spatial character of the 3D HUD. Registering information both with the car and the environment is an obvious strength of this technology – yet, we see further potential as HUDs exploit the 3D-space to structure and present information. For example, information that is currently of particular interest to the driver, i.e. a warning about the malfunction of adaptive cruise control due to dirty sensors, can be presented

© IFIP International Federation for Information Processing 2015
J. Abascal et al. (Eds.): INTERACT 2015, Part IV, LNCS 9299, pp. 300–318, 2015.
DOI: 10.1007/978-3-319-22723-8_24

more prominently by displaying it closer to the driver while other information stays unobtrusively in the background but could still be perceived easily.

As 3D display technology improves, additional data becomes available, for example from new sensors or from Car-2-Car networks, and enables novel interfaces, there is an inherent need to prototype these interfaces prior to development. Currently, no tools exist that allow interfaces for 3D HUDs to be easily prototyped. To bridge this gap and encourage research in this particular field, this work presents a 3D HUD prototyping tool. We report on the design and development of the *3D Head-Up Display Designer*. In addition, we present an evaluation, investigating (1) how easily interface elements can be positioned, rotated, and scaled in 3D space, using different input modalities (mouse vs. gestures) and (2) how depth management modes can support the user in the design process. Our results show that the mouse outperforms gesture-based interaction and that users can position objects more accurately in 3D space if not constrained to distinct depth layers. However, the fact that precision was better in some cases using gesture control is promising.

Though anchored in the automotive domain, our work is not limited to this particular domain. A multitude of application areas for HUDs, particularly in the form of augmented reality (AR) glasses, have been identified in the past and commercial products exist, many of which could certainly benefit from 3D technology. Examples include motorcycles [34], sports goggles (scuba diving [8] and skiing [21]), personal HUDs [2] and virtual retina displays [10,16].

The contribution of this work is threefold. First, we provide detailed insights into the design process of the prototyping tool by means of an expert workshop. Second, we present a detailed description of the tool and how we implemented it. Third, we report on a controlled experiment, assessing task completion time and accuracy as well as usability and user experience as users prototype interfaces by means of different input devices and different design modes.

## 2    Related Work

In this section we cover previous work that is relevant to our research. First we introduce prototyping and tools commonly used. Then we discuss head-up displays and their integration with 3D technology. Finally, we present previous influential work in the area of gestural interaction with 3D displays.

### 2.1    Prototyping

Designing and building usable graphical UIs involves several stages. An iterative activity present at different stages of UI development is prototyping. Prototyping ranges from early sketching on paper to high-fidelity prototypes of the almost finished product [22]. In many cases, prototyping does not require any programming or development experience, particularly during the early stages in which prototyping is often done by sketching ideas on paper. In an early phase, sketching is especially important for communication and discussion among different stakeholders [1]. Although pen and paper prototypes are fast to create and powerful in communicating ideas, they can also hinder people's expression as they may be afraid of drawing ugly interfaces [1]. Comparing digital and paper prototypes with the same fidelity, Sefelin et al. found digital prototyping tools to be preferred over paper prototyping ones [26]. As reported by Schlachtbauer et al. [25] users tend to equally criticize both types of prototypes. Prototyping can not only be used in brainstorming and designing, but also for testing UIs to identify interaction issues [29].

There are many digital prototyping solutions that allow low, medium, and high fidelity prototypes to be rapidly created. These tools tackle a variety of use cases: desktop and mobile settings, context-aware applications, and hardware devices. They also try to overcome the classical drawbacks of paper prototyping by focusing on interaction. Tools like "Balsamiq"[1] provide an environment where the designer/developer can produce a rapid, sketch-like interface which allows to focus on the interaction rather than on the appearance. Another tool, "Antetype"[2] produces very high fidelity prototypes resembling the final product. In the domain of mobile prototyping, Weigel et al. developed a tool used for creating prototypes for mobile projection applications [33]. Additionally, tools that consider the aspects of context [30] or location [19] have been developed. Prototyping for interactive physical devices has been explored and various hardware toolkits were developed [11].

Prototyping tools are also available in the automotive domain. An example is the "Distract-R" project, which provides a prototyping environment for car interfaces and predicts the driver's behavior due to its underlying cognitive model [23]. It considers the special requirements of interaction while driving as well as parameters such as the driver's age and driving style. Also in the context of automotive interfaces, Lauber et al. introduced the paper prototyping tool, PapAR, which is designed to suit the requirements of mixed and augmented reality applications. PapAR was used to create a prototype during the early design phase of a HMD driven in-vehicle infotainment system [18].

Although prototyping tools for various contexts have been developed, tools for stereoscopic 3D interfaces are scarce. Broy et al. developed two physical prototyping tools, the "FrameBox" and the "MirrorBox". They allow to arrange visualisations on foil in the 3D space [7]. The integration of digital content is not supported by these tools. In our work we aim to bridge this gap by enabling digital content prototyping in S3D.

## 2.2    3D Head-Up Displays

Head-up displays (HUDs) are a type of display originally developed for military use. However, they have been adopted by other domains, most notably the car industry. In contrast to a traditional instrument cluster, they provide information to drivers without diverting attention from the road. In-vehicle HUDs use

---

[1] Balsamiq Studios: http://balsamiq.com/.

[2] Ergosign Technologies GmbH. Antetype: http://www.antetype.com/.15.07.2014.

the front windshield as a partly reflecting mirror. A virtual image is presented approximately 2 m in front of the driver [20]. HUDs decrease the stress of the driver, thus providing more safety and focus [31]. HUDs increase secondary task performance and driving performance compared to traditional head-down displays [20]. Currently, AR HUDs which project information at a larger distance (approximately 10 m) are being developed. This type of AR HUD was utilized by Toennes et al. for exploring arrow-based navigation [32].

Integrating stereoscopic 3D technology in HUDs allows the depth information to be used to enhance the driver's perception of the displayed content [6]. Judging distance during navigation, referencing real world objects, and highlighting urgent information are all cases that could use the depth aspect of 3D displays to communicate the urgency or spatial relations to the driver. Critical information is displayed closer to the driver, while less important notifications remain further in the back. Broy et al. showed that using 3D display technology in cars increases the usability and attractiveness as well as helps users understand the status of the system [5].

While automotive S3D HUDs provide many advantages, such displays can evoke discomfort and fatigue [17]. Current research explores the "comfort zone" which describes the depth range where image content can be displayed without causing discomfort to the user [28]. Broy et al. analyzed the use of stereoscopic 3D HUDs and found out that increasing the projection distance increases the comfort zone while decreasing depth judgment accuracy [6].

### 2.3   Gestures for 3D Displays

Gesture-based interaction with 3D environments has been subject to prior research. Kim et al. explored gesture control of a 3D scene on a non-stereoscopic display. They concluded that freehand gestures have the potential to replace traditional mouse and keyboard interaction in virtual environments [15]. Hilliges et al. created Holodesk, an interactive system made from a see-through glass and a Kinect camera. It provides users the illusion of interacting with objects via gestures [13]. The Leap Motion controller was used by [9] for an experiment in which users were required to position an object inside a target area in a monoscopic 3D scene. They showed that using gestures achieved good results only in simple tasks.

Few studies have explored gesture interaction on stereoscopic 3D displays. Yoshida et al. developed a system in which users can interact via finger movement using a haptic feedback device on their finger [35]. Otherwise, to the best of our knowledge, no prior work studied gestures for placing objects on a stereoscopic display as we do for our prototyping tool.

## 3   Informing the Design

When it comes to prototyping UIs for 3D HUDs, state-of-the-art prototyping or mockup tools, such as Balsamiq or Photoshop, are unsuitable for several reasons.

Firstly, they neither allow UI elements to be positioned in 3D space nor do they allow the registration of these UI elements with objects in the environment. Secondly, with the aforementioned tools it is in general not possible to render the UI and environment stereoscopically, making it difficult to understand the depth layout and thus identifying strengths and weaknesses of the design.

With our work we support the creation of low-fidelity prototypes that allow concept layouts to be created rapidly and early insights to be gathered through qualitative and quantitative evaluation. One focus of our work is providing means for the person creating the prototype to easily position and manipulate objects in 3D space. Since 2D devices, such as keyboard and mouse, lack intuitiveness when it comes to manipulating 3D objects [15], we opted to investigate technologies that enable mid-air gestures to better support the person creating the prototype.

To understand the requirements and inform the design of our tool, we conducted an expert workshop at the outset of our research, focusing on two objectives: (1) Identifying and prioritizing functions of a prototyping tool for a 3D HUD and (2) Collecting ideas for a suitable interaction concept in 3D space.

### 3.1 Procedure

For the expert workshop we recruited 7 people with backgrounds in computer science and HCI from our institute and invited them to a workshop at our lab.

We started the workshop with a short introduction on 3D HUDs by showing participants a stereoscopic picture of a 3D HUD in front of a street scene on a shutter notebook. We briefly discussed several use cases for such display. After that, we explained to the participants our motivation and ideas behind creating a 3D HUD prototyping tool. The rest of the workshop was split into two parts.

In the first part, participants had to come up with features a 3D prototyping tool should include and write them down on post-it notes. After the brainstorming, ideas were presented by participants to the plenum who discussed, grouped, and prioritized the ideas. In the second part, the participants were divided in two groups. The task for each group was to sketch the interface of the prototyping tool and to think about how would they interact with the interface. Participants were encouraged to consider reasonable gestural interactions as input modality.

### 3.2 Results

Results from the first part of the workshop are depicted in Table 1. Participants felt suitable means for positioning objects to be of utmost importance. In addition, the importing of graphics and objects was considered to be important. Presets for 3D objects and graphics were considered less important.

Regarding part two, the groups came up with fundamentally different concepts (Fig. 1). While group A designed the interaction using gestures as single interaction modality, group B suggested mid-air gestures to be used optionally.

Group A focused on the storyboard and the gesture input: Using the left hand for pointing gestures selects a function of a menu, for example, adding

**Table 1.** Results from the first part of the workshop. Participants came up with a list of features and prioritized them.

| Features | Priority |
|---|---|
| Altering position, orientation, scale | high |
| Positioning the layer with 0 parallax | high |
| Import graphics and objects | high |
| Insert text | high |
| Save and load prototypes | high |
| Drag & Drop | medium |
| Change background 3D scene | medium |
| Change color settings | low |
| Change font | low |
| Preset of 3D objects | low |
| Preset of HUD graphics | low |
| Visualization of depth positions | low |

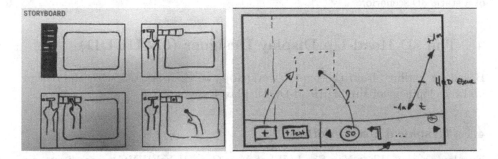

**Fig. 1.** Left: Storyboard of Group A - Right: Interface Sketch of Group B.

an element from an available object list to the 3D scene. The right hand is responsible for object manipulation, for example positioning and scaling.

Group B focused on sketching the user interface: The interface consists of a panel in the left and lower part of the display. The panel in the lower part allows different elements to be added to the scenery displayed in the remaining display space. The group suggested that graphics should be designed in an external program, such as Adobe Photoshop, and subsequently be important to the tool. The panel to the left offers functions for manipulating the objects in the scenery, as well as for clustering and registering them with different depth layers. Interaction is based on mouse and keyboard. Gesture input can be optionally included for object manipulation. As an important feature, group B presented a visualization of the z-axis representing the depth position of the objects.

**Fig. 2.** The 3D-HUDD allows to create the visual layout of an head up display in front of a static 3D scenario.

## 4    The 3D Head-Up Display Designer (3D-HUDD)

Based on findings from the expert workshop, we then started with the design and development of the 3D Head-Up Display Designer.

### 4.1    Graphical User Interface

Employing the What-You-See-Is-What-You-Get (WYSIWYG) paradigm, we designed the graphical user interface of the tool to allow users to immediately perceive the look-and-feel of the UI. Following recommendations from Schild et al., all UI elements are positioned on screen level (zero parallax) [24]. Main functionality controls are grouped at the bottom and the left side (Fig. 2). This allows the HUD representation in front of the scene (in this case a driving scenario) to be the central element of the UI. The borders of the virtual HUD are visualized by a light gray line. New elements can be added to this area. All control panels are rendered semi-transparent to better support the orientation in the 3D space.

3D-HUDD supports working with elements on separate depth layers. On the left side, an overview of the existing layers is provided alongside the options to hide or rename layers. Below, the user can find a list of elements currently active on the selected layer. As an alternative, users can work in what we call the'free mode'. In this mode, elements can easily be moved also across layers.

At the bottom part of the UI there are the available elements which can be added to the HUD scene by means of a simple click. There are three different kinds of elements: 3D shapes, images, and text elements. The former are displayed as actual 3D representation, which helps the user to easily differentiate between the options. The 3D-HUDD is bundled with a set of graphics often used in HUDs, like traffic signs and location markers. However, our software is also able to load user defined images that can then be added to the HUD scene. The text tool allows textual information to be created, such as speed indicators or menu structures for infotainment purposes (e.g. a music player).

By using the color panel on the left side, objects and text can be assigned a specific color and transparency. The'Setting' control allows the created HUD to be observed in front of different scenes. This functionality is helpful in checking HUD arrangements in multiple scenarios in the automotive context, for example, driving by night or driving on a freeway.

While the driving scenes in the background can be mere 2D images, we provide means to include 3D photographs specifically shot to fit the desired environment. We created several 3D photographs, using a 3D casing for two GoPro cameras. The casing keeps the cameras at a distance similar to the interocular distance of the human eyes. To solve the problem of different parallaxes in the rendered output and the photographs, we apply a technique called "horizontal image translation" [3]. This is crucial because the human vision system is very sensitive to stereoscopic distortions [17]. In our setup in *Unity 3D* we work with layer masks to hide the left image for the right camera and vice versa. The result is a 3D environment that appears in the correct distance to the HUD.

## 4.2 Depth Management

Our tool implements multiple controls for depth management. It allows the organization of UI elements on layers. On startup, the 3D-HUDD has three default layers activated. They are placed at a virtual distance of 0 m, 3 m, and 6 m, where 0 m is the projection distance (zero parallax). Users can add up to seven layers to be placed in the range of 2 m in front and 15 m behind the projection plane. This range was found to be comfortable for 3D HUDs [6].

To position a layer at a particular depth, users are provided with a *Depth Controller* (cf. Fig. 3). The currently active layer is highlighted and can be moved in z direction by adjusting the depth controller. The depth controller can be deactivated for working in free mode. Here, elements can be freely positioned

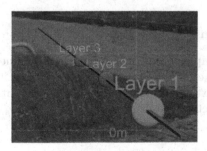

**Fig. 3.** A dedicated control allows to precisely manage and overview current depth positions.

on all three axes. The depth of an object can be adjusted by either using the mouse wheel, the hand tracking sensor, or the depth controller. If the free mode is active, the depth controller only visualizes the currently selected objects.

Additionally, we added means to control monocular cues in free mode. It allows dynamic size (objects appear smaller when distance is increased) and transparency (to simulate atmospheric haze) to be enabled or disabled.

### 4.3   Interaction

The standard form of interaction with the 3D-HUDD is input using mouse and keyboard, following group B's suggestion. After defining the HUD's size, the user can add elements by clicking on its representation. The new element appears at the center of the HUD on the selected layer. To edit and transform an element, it must first be selected via mouse click. Multiple objects can be selected at the same time. The selected elements are highlighted with a green border (Fig. 2).

Elements can be translated in x and y direction (z is restricted by the layer's position). For rotation and scaling, we included a *Transform* control panel. The user can select the operation (scaling or rotation) as well as the axes (x, y, z) to which this transformation should apply. If a cube is to be doubled in size, all axes must be selected to preserve the aspect ratio. Rotation in the 3D-HUDD was realized as a relative transformation: the current mouse position is regarded as starting point. The larger the distance to this point, the faster the rotation.

The alternative to mouse/keyboard interaction is gestural input using the "Leap Motion" sensor. It can be used for the three operations: translation, rotation and scaling. We implement dedicated keys to start the hand tracking so that it can not be activated accidentally. With one hand, users can press the activation key while the other hand is operating above the Leap Motion sensor.

Interaction with the virtual elements is designed to match real world interactions (cf. Fig. 4). To change the position of an element, the hand can simply be moved into the desired direction. The selected object in the 3D-HUDD is translated as if connected to that hand. Scaling is achieved by moving the hand along the y axis: a movement away from the sensor increases the element's size, while a movement towards the sensor decreases its size. Rotation is realized by rotating the hand around the according axis.

### 4.4   Implementation

The 3D-HUDD was implemented using the game engine *Unity 3D* and *C#*. We decoupled basic functionality, data storage, and user input. In this way, the software can be easily extended to support additional input devices in the future, such as Microsoft Kinect or eye trackers.

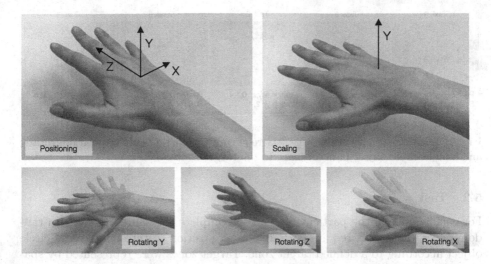

**Fig. 4.** Gesture interactions for positioning, rotating, and scaling objects.

To process the raw data from the Leap Motion Controller, we use a script provided by Leap Motion Inc[3]. For generating the necessary side-by-side output, we used another script which arranges two separate cameras in a predefined inter-axial distance and renders the image with a horizontal compression of 50 %[4].

## 5    Evaluation

To evaluate the usability of the presented 3D-HUDD and to understand how well users perform, we conducted a user study with 24 participants. In particular, we were interested if the tool allows to comfortably and quickly prototype 3D depth layout concepts. Since the 3D-HUDD offers the user to interact with the mouse as well as 3D gestures, we investigate which interaction method leads to better performance in positioning, scaling, and rotation of objects in 3D space. More-over, we evaluated if the management of the depth structure (freely positioning objects vs. organizing objects on depth layers) has an impact on the usability.

### 5.1    Study Design

The study is based on two independent variables with two levels each:

1. Interaction Technique: Mouse vs. Gesture
2. Depth Management: Free vs. Layered

We use a within subjects design resulting in four conditions per participant. To avoid sequence effects we divided our test sample ($N = 24$) in four groups (each $N = 6$), counterbalancing the order of the conditions applying latin square.

---

[3] https://www.assetstore.unity3d.com/en/#!/content/15677.
[4] http://forum.unity3d.com/threads/stereo-3d-in-unity-3d.63874/#post-416458.

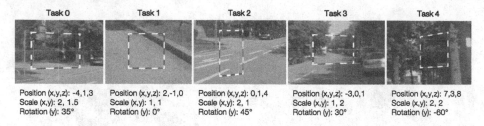

**Fig. 5.** The target zones of the five tasks requiring the participants to position, rotate, and scale a circle object in accordance to the target zones.

## 5.2 Task

For each condition the participants had to complete the same five tasks in random order. The tasks require participants to position, rotate and scale a circle object according to a defined target zone. Target zones were represented by spatially arranged rectangles. The circle and target were 2D objects since, first, we aimed at decreasing the complexity of the task and, second, automotive HUDs typically use 2D texts and graphics for unambiguous and simple visual feedback.

Figure 5 shows the position, rotation, and size of the target zones. To solve the task it was necessary to insert the circle into the 3D-HUDD scene, first, and then to arrange it in accordance to the target. The initial position of the circle is the middle of the screen at zero parallax and the same for all five tasks. If the user was satisfied with the entered position of the circle, she/he finishes the task by pressing the space key of the keyboard. After that, the participant could start the next task by pressing the space key once again.

## 5.3 Measures

We collected objective as well as subjective data during the study. For the objective data we measured for each task the task completion time (TCT) in ms and the accuracy for positioning, rotating, and scaling the circle. The start and end point of the TCT is marked by hitting the space key. Regarding accuracy, we calculated three scores depending on the end transformation of the circle and the target properties as follows:

- The position score ($score_{pos}$) defines the length of the vector between the center of the target object ($x', y', z'$) and the positioned circle (x,y,z):

$$score_{pos} = \sqrt{(x - x')^2 + (y - y')^2 + (z - z')^2} \qquad (1)$$

Note, that $score_{pos}$ cannot provide the accuracy of single axes but the total positioning accuracy in unity units.

- The rotation score ($score_{rot}$) calculates the difference of the rotation around the y-axis for the end rotation of the circle $rot_y(c)$ and the target $rot_y(t)$ in Euler angles (degrees):

$$score_{rot} = |rot_y(t) - rot_y(c)| \qquad (2)$$

– The scale score ($score_{scale}$) is the difference between the areas of the end scale of the circle ($a * b$) and the target object ($a' * b'$) in (unity units)$^2$:

$$score_{scale} = |(a * b) - (a' * b')| \tag{3}$$

For all accuracy measures, a lower score indicates higher accuracy. Besides the objective measures we used subjective methods to evaluate the user experience (UX) and usability of the system, in particular the questionnaires *mini AttrakDiff* [12] and *System Usability Scale* (SUS) [4]. Moreover, we conducted interviews with the participants while exploring the tool and its functions. In addition, the participants had to rank the four interaction techniques offered by the system.

### 5.4   Study Setup

Figure 6 shows the study setup. The study took place in a closed room at our lab to avoid any distraction. Participants were seated approximately three meters in front of a 3D TV (Samsung UE55ES6300) visualizing the 3D-HUDD using shutter technology. On the table in front of them we positioned the input devices (keyboard, mouse, Leap). The Leap was placed in an *interaction box* (Fig. 7a) showing the user in which range the device worked most accurately. Participants were allowed to arrange the devices in accordance to their preferences.

The software of the 3D-HUDD ran on a ASUS G52Jw notebook which transferred its graphical output to the 3D TV. The 3D TV received a side-by-side image and translated this picture to a stereoscopic image with a resolution of 1920x1080 using shutter technology. The shutter method required the participants to wear shutter glasses to perceive the stereoscopic effect properly. All participants that wore glasses confirmed that putting the shutter glasses on top of their glasses was not cumbersome or uncomfortable.

**Fig. 6.** Setup of the user study.

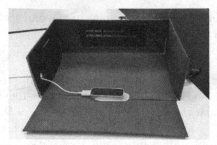

(a) The *interaction box* informs the user about the area which allows an accurate gesture interaction.

(b) The participants interacted with the system using mouse or gestures.

**Fig. 7.** Details of the study.

## 5.5 Participants

In total, 24 participants (6 female, 18 male, P1-P24) aged between 21 and 53 (M = 30.0, SD = 8.7) took part in this study. All of them are working in the automotive domain and are familiar with HUDs. Their backgrounds range from psychology, interaction design to computer science. One participant stated to have no experience with 3D displays while five use stereoscopic displays several times per week or have intensive background on stereoscopic displays. The remaining 18 participants are acquainted with the stereoscopic effect by being exposed to it occasionally, for example in the cinema.

## 5.6 Procedure

As participants arrived we introduced the study to them by giving a short introduction to stereoscopic 3D. Afterward, participants were seated in front of the 3D TV and conducted a stereo vision test using random-dot-stereograms (RDS) [14]. All participants passed the test and qualified for the study. Before introducing the 3D-HUDD, the different input devices were presented with focus on the leap motion since not all participants were familiar with the device.

The first part of the study consisted of an exploration of the tool's features and interaction modalities. Therefore, the participants had to solve simple tasks like inserting objects and text into the scene and manipulating its properties like position, rotation, scale, and color. Moreover, they explored the layered and the free mode. While exploring the features of the system, the participants were motivated to think aloud and to reflect on their thoughts and impressions.

In the second part of the study, participants compared the two different interaction techniques as well as the depth management variants. For each of the four conditions the following procedure applies: First, participants were acquainted by completing a sample task. We instructed participants to solve the task as fast and as accurate as possible. The participants initiated each task by pressing the space key on the keyboard. After completing each of the four test tasks the participants completed the mini AttrakDiff and SUS. Subsequently, the next test condition started including the example (Task 0) and test tasks (Task 1-4).

After participants completed all four test conditions they were asked to rank the conditions according to their preference. An interview about the tool offered the possibility to reflect on its functions. Finally, a demographic questionnaire was filled in by the participants. One session lasted about 60 min.

### 5.7    Results

For statistical analyses we used the Kolmogorov-Smirnov test to prove whether data is normally distributed. If the data shows a normal distribution we used a two-way Analysis of Variance (ANOVA). In case of a non-normal distribution we applied a Friedman-test and pairwise Wilcoxon tests with Bonferroni corrections.

**Subjective Results.** Figure 8 shows the descriptive statistics of the mini AttrakDiff, the SUS, and the ranking. Regarding the AttrakDiff, the ANOVA shows statistical significances for all dimensions: pragmatic quality (PQ), hedonic quality (HQ), and attractiveness (ATTR). In detail, testing for PQ is statistically significant for the main effects interaction technique, $F(1, 23) = 18.774$, $p < .001$, and depth management, $F(1, 23) = 12.470$, $p = .002$, as well as for interaction technique $\times$ depth management, $F(1, 23) = 11.918$, $p = .002$. In contrast, the dimension HQ solely shows a significant effect for the depth management, $F(1, 23) = 9.365$, $p = .006$. The dimension ATTR reveals statistical significances for the interaction technique, $F(1, 23) = 5.808$, $p = .024$, the depth management, $F(1, 23) = 15.755$, $p = .001$, and their interaction, $F(1, 23) = 4.832$, $p = .038$.

Analyzing the total score of the SUS yields similar results. Mouse interaction significantly outperforms gestures, $F(1, 23) = 22.139$, $p < .001$, and the depth management is improved for the free mode compared to the organization in layers, $F(1, 23) = 17,310$, $p < .001$. A Friedman test reveals that the ranking is statistically significant $\chi^2(3) = 50.950$, $p < .001$. Post-hoc Wilcoxon tests with Bonferroni corrections show that all pairwise comparisons are significant,

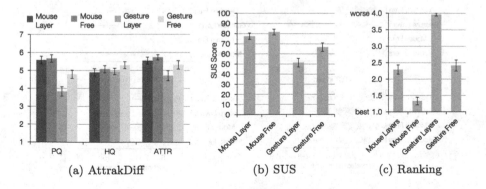

(a) AttrakDiff          (b) SUS          (c) Ranking

**Fig. 8.** Means and standard errors as error bars for the subjective measures.

$p < .007$, excluding the comparison of gesture interaction in free mode and mouse interaction with layers, $p = .640$.

Regarding the tool in general, the interviews revealed that the tool is "useful"(P8) and allows to "easily generate spatial layouts" (P24). Seven participants stated that the user interface is clearly structured (P1, P2, P9, P19, P20, P21, P24). Especially, the design meets the requirements of simulating a HUD in the real world, as it provides the feeling of "looking through a window" (P2). However, some participants missed well known features of familiar prototyping and graphic programs. For instance, seven participants noticed the lack of an undo function and ten participants asked for a drag &drop function for adding elements to the scene. Moreover, one participant suggested to add a dialogue box for object settings to directly enter position, rotation, and scale values.

At the beginning of the study, the participants welcomed the gesture interaction. Ten participants described the interaction as "cool" and "surprisingly easy". After the second part, most participants revised that impression, because the interaction was not always ergonomic, especially for rotating objects around the y-axis (P2, P3, P6, P10, P11, P12, P14, P17). Moreover, the gesture interaction required a lot switches between the mouse and the leap controller, for example, to activate scaling instead of rotating (P1, P9, P11, P15, P24). As an improvement, three participant suggested gestures to define the axes to which the object transformation should be applied. In contrast, the participants described the mouse interaction as "better controllable", "familiar", and "precise".

**Objective Results.** For all four tasks we measured task completion time as well as the accuracy of the object transformations. For analyzing the data we aggregated the TCT as well as the accuracy scores for the test tasks per condition for each participant. Figure 9 shows the descriptive statistics for TCT, $score_{pos}$, $score_{rot}$, and $score_{scale}$.

Analyzing the TCT, the ANOVA shows significant main effects for interaction technique, $F(1, 23) = 30.466, p < .001$, and depth management $F(1, 23) = 21.518$, $p < .001$. Regarding $score_{pos}$, positioning the objects with the mouse is significantly

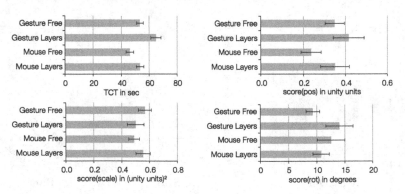

**Fig. 9.** Means and standard errors as error bars for the objective measures.

more accurate than using gesture interaction, $F(1,23) = 8.113, p = .009$, while the variable depth management has no significant influence, $F(1,23) = 2.660, p = .117$. Testing data of $score_{rot}$ shows no significant effect, neither for interaction technique, $F(1,23) = .001, p = .993$, nor for depth management, $F(1,23) = 1.276, p = .270$, nor for the interaction of both variables, $F(1,23) = 3.461, p = .076$. Also $score_{scale}$ shows no effects, $p > .155$.

## 5.8   Limitations

Our study has the following limitations. First, we only tested a limited number of tasks to decrease the complexity of the study. Hence, no conclusion can be drawn with regard to other tasks (such as alignment or grouping of objects) and their combinations. The tasks aimed at the evaluation of the interaction in 3D space rather than creating sophisticated UIs. Investigating such tasks could be subject to future work. Second, not all tasks were performed in all directions. For example, scaling was only done in the x- and y-dimension and rotation was only required around the y-axis. Future work could comprehensively assess all operations for all axes. Third, though we present findings on interaction with different depth management modes (i.e., the free and the layered mode), future studies could investigate how performance changes as users interact with more but one element at a time. In particular for multiple objects, the layered mode may at some point outperform the free mode.

## 5.9   Discussion

In summary, the qualitative and quantitative findings suggest that the 3D-HUDD is well accepted and allows S3D HUD prototypes to be created quickly and easily. This is particularly supported by the high SUS score.

With regard to the input modality, mouse interaction was significantly faster than gesture interaction. Using gesture input required to use the mouse as well to toggle between the transformation mode (positioning, rotating, scaling) and to toggle between the dimensions (x, y, z). These modality switches between the leap sensor and the mouse not only impacted on task completion time but also frustrated some of the users, resulting also in lower subjective ratings. At the same time, gesture interaction tends to increase the accuracy for rotating the objects in the free mode although participants stated that movements of the hand around the y-axis are uncomfortable and unergonomic. In future work, we plan to also investigate gesture-based rotations around x- and z-axis, to reveal improvements in accuracy. To address the challenge of switching between mode and dimension in the future, we plan to incorporating further modalities, such as speech or gaze to avoid moving the hand away from the controller.

With regard to the mode we found that participants performed tasks more accurately in the free mode and also reported on higher usability. Note, that a reason for this could be the fact that users worked with single objects only. The layered mode may unfold its potential as the user interface becomes more complex. In such cases, users may want to move a number of objects from one layer to another, which is well supported by the layered mode. An interesting question in this context is also, whether clusters of elements with a relationship should be structured according to their depth position (depth layers) or based on proximity (i.e., they could also be distributed over several depth layers). While for the first case, the layered mode seems to be more appropriate, the free mode may better support the latter strategy.

## 6    Conclusion

In this paper we presented the 3D Head-Up Display Designer. The tool is meant for designers who want to quickly and easily create early user interface prototypes for S3D head-up displays. An expert workshop in the early phase of the design process served two purposes. First, important features were identified, discussed, and prioritized; second, specific design suggestions were provided that we realized during the development process. Finally, we evaluated the tool with regard to two aspects: we compared user performance for different input modalities as well as for different depth management strategies. We found that (1) users were faster when using the mouse compared to gesture-based interaction, and (2) that allowing users to freely position elements compared to providing pre-defined depth layers led to increased accuracy and higher usability.

In the future we will use the tool for the creation of more complex user interfaces. In this way we aim to gather a comprehensive understanding of how the different input modalities support concurrent working with a large number of objects on multiple depth layers.

## References

1. Baskinger, M.: Pencils before pixels: a primer in hand-generated sketching. Interactions **15**(2), 28–36 (2008)
2. Bercovich, I.A., Ivan, R., Little, J., Vilas-Boas, F.: Personal head-up display. University of Massachusetts Amherst (2012). http://www.ecs.umass.edu/ece/sdp/sdp09/wolf/media.html
3. Broberg, D.K.: Guidance for horizontal image translation (hit) of high definition stereoscopic video production. In: Proceedings of the SPIE 2011. International Society for Optics and Photonics (2011)
4. Brooke, J.: Sus-a quick and dirty usability scale. Usability Eval. Ind. **189**, 194 (1996)
5. Broy, N., Alt, F., Schneegass, S., Pfleging, B.: 3d displays in cars: exploring the user performance for a stereoscopic instrument cluster. In: Proceedings of the 6th International Conference on Automotive User Interfaces and Interactive Vehicular Applications, Proceedings of the AutoUI 2014, pp. 2:1–2:9. ACM, New York (2014)
6. Broy, N., Höckh, S., Frederiksen, A., Gilowski, M., Eichhorn, J., Naser, F., Jung, H., Niemann, J., Schell, M., Schmid, A., Alt, F.: Exploring design parameters for a 3D head-up display. In: Proceedings of the PerDis 2014. ACM, New York (2014)
7. Broy, N., Schneegass, S., Alt, F., Schmidt, A.: Framebox and mirrorbox: Toolsand guidelines to support designers in prototyping interfaces for 3D displays. In: Proceedings of the CHI 2014. ACM, New York (2014)

8. Clothier, J.: Smart goggles easy on the eyes. CNN.com (2005). http://edition.cnn.com/2005/TECH/06/23/spark.goggle/index.html?section=cnn_tech
9. Coelho, J.C., Verbeek, F.J.: Pointing task evaluation of leap motion controller in 3D virtual environment. In: Creating the Difference, p. 78 (2014)
10. Fiambolis, P.: Virtual retinal display (vrd) technology. Virtual Retinal Display Technology. Naval Postgraduate School (2008). http://web.archive.org/web/20080413063727/www.cs.nps.navy.mil/people/faculty/capps/4473/projects/fiambolis/vrd/vrd_full.html
11. Gellersen, H., Kortuem, G., Schmidt, A., Beigl, M.: Physical prototyping with smart-its. IEEE Pervasive Comput. **3**(3), 74–82 (2004)
12. Hassenzahl, M., Monk, A.: The inference of perceived usability from beauty. Hum.-Comput. Interact. **25**(3), 235–260 (2010)
13. Hilliges, O., Kim, D., Izadi, S., Weiss, M., Wilson, A.: Holodesk: direct 3D interactions with a situated see-through display. In: Proceedings of the CHI 2012. pp. 2421–2430. ACM (2012)
14. Julesz, B.: Foundations of Cyclopean Perception. University of Chicago Press, Chicago (1971)
15. Kim, J.O., Kim, M., Yoo, K.H.: Real-time hand gesture-based interaction with objects in 3D virtual environments. Int. J. Multimedia Ubiquit. Eng. **8**(6), 339–348 (2013)
16. Lake, M.: How it works: Retinal displays add a second data layer. New York Times (2006). http://www.nytimes.com/2001/04/26/technology/26HOWW.html
17. Lambooij, M., Fortuin, M., Heynderickx, I., Ijsselsteijn, W.: Visual discomfort and visual fatigue of stereoscopic displays: a review. J. Imaging Sci. Technol. **53**(3), 030201-1–030201-14 (2009)
18. Lauber, F., Böttcher, C., Butz, A.: Papar: paper prototyping for augmented reality. In: Proceedings of the AutomotiveUI 2014, pp. 1–6. ACM (2014)
19. Li, Y., Hong, J., Landay, J.: Topiary: a tool for prototyping location-enhanced apps. In: Proceedings of the UIST 2004. ACM, New York (2004)
20. Milicic, N., Lindberg, T.: Menu interaction in head-up displays. In: Human Factors and Ergonomic Society, Annual Meeting, Soesterberg, The Netherlands (2008)
21. Mogg, T.: High-tech airwave ski goggles from oakley bring augmented reality to the slopes (2012). DigitalTrends.com
22. Rogers, Y., Sharp, H., Preece, J.: Interaction Design: Beyond Human-Computer Interaction. Wiley, New York (2011)
23. Salvucci, D., Zuber, M., Beregovaia, E., Markley, D.: Distract-r: rapid prototyping and evaluation of in-vehicle interfaces. In: Proceedings of the CHI 2005, pp. 581–589. ACM (2005)
24. Schild, J., Bölicke, L., LaViola, J., Masuch, M.: Creating and analyzingstereoscopic 3D graphical uis in digital games. In: Proceedings of the CHI 2013. ACM, New York (2013)
25. Schlachtbauer, T., Schermann, M., Krcmar, H.: Do prototypes hamper innovative behavior in developing it-based services? (2013)
26. Sefelin, R., Tscheligi, M., Giller, V.: Paper prototyping - what is it goodfor? In: Proceedings of the CHI EA 2003. ACM, New York (2003)
27. Sherman, D.: Toyota developing radical 3-d head-up display for production. Car and Driver (2014). http://blog.caranddriver.com/toyota-developing-radical-3-d-head-up-display-for-production/
28. Shibata, T., Kim, J., Hoffman, D.M., Banks, M.S.: The zone of comfort: predicting visual discomfort with stereo displays. J. Vis. **11**(8), 11 (2011)

29. Snyder, C.: Paper prototyping: the fast and easy way to design and refine user interfaces. Morgan Kaufmann, San Francisco (2003)
30. Sohn, T., Dey, A.: icap: an informal tool for interactive prototyping of context-aware applications. In: Proceedings of the CHI EA 2003. ACM (2003)
31. Tonnis, M., Broy, V., Klinker, G.: A survey of challenges related to the design of 3D user interfaces for car drivers. In: Proceedings of the 3DUI 2006, pp. 127–134. IEEE (2006)
32. Tonnis, M., Klein, L., Klinker, G.: Perception thresholds for augmented reality navigation schemes in large distances. In: Proceedings of the ISMAR 2008, pp. 189–190. IEEE (2008)
33. Weigel, M., Boring, S., Steimle, J., Marquardt, N., Greenberg, S., Tang, A.: Projectorkit: easing rapid prototyping of interactive applications for mobile projectors. In: Proceedings of the MobileHCI 2013. ACM, New York (2013)
34. Werner, M.: Test driving the sportvue motorcycle hud. News.motorbiker.org (2005). http://news.motorbiker.org/blogs.nsf/dx/SportVue.htm
35. Yoshida, T., Kamuro, S., Minamizawa, K., Nii, H., Tachi, S.: Repro3d: full-parallax 3D display using retro-reflective projection technology. In: ACM SIGGRAPH 2010 Emerging Technologies, p. 20. ACM (2010)

# Design and Evaluation of Mirror Interface MIOSS to Overlay Remote 3D Spaces

Ryo Ishii[1(✉)], Shiro Ozawa[2], Akira Kojima[2], Kazuhiro Otsuka[1],
Yuki Hayashi[3], and Yukiko I. Nakano[4]

[1] NTT Communication Science Laboratories, NTT Corporation, Atsugi,
Kanagawa, Japan
{ishii.ryo, otsuka.kazuhiro}@lab.ntt.co.jp
[2] NTT Media Intelligence Laboratories, NTT Corporation, Yokosuka,
Kanagawa, Japan
{ozawa.shiro, kojima.akira}@lab.ntt.co.jp
[3] Colleage of Sustainable System Sciences, Osaka Prefecture University,
Habikino, Osaka, Japan
hayashi@kis.osakafu-u.ac.jp
[4] Faculty of Science and Technology, Seikei University,
Musashino, Tokyo, Japan
y.nakano@st.seikei.ac.jp

**Abstract.** The MIOSS mirror interface can overlay two remote spaces, enabling users to feel as if they are in the same room and thereby to share 3D objects in the spaces. MIOSS imparts motion parallax through a mirror that adjusts to the viewpoint of the user, in addition to providing geometrical consistency in the occlusion, size, and positional relationships in the two remote spaces. Experimental evaluations of an implemented MIOSS system show that users can recognize the exact positions of shared objects in the partner's space via the mirror video.

**Keywords:** Mirror interface · Motion parallax · 3D modeling · Overlaid space

## 1 Introduction

One of the big challenges in creating media spaces is how to achieve the sharing of remote spaces containing people and objects. If this can be achieved, we will be able to work closely together while sharing our respective spaces, to discuss things, and to smoothly perform collaborative work with the shared objects. Several studies have made attempts to create systems to share two remote spaces as one shared space [1–3]. These systems make it possible to share objects in a narrow area but do not permit complete sharing of the whole space. We aim to achieve an advanced media space that provides a seamless overlay between two remote spaces containing users and objects. This will enable users to share the objects in the two spaces and work closely together while sharing their respective spaces, to discuss things, such as furniture layouts, and to smoothly perform collaborative work with the shared objects. The enormous challenge in realizing such a media space is how to share two remote spaces with real objects and display the video to users naturally.

© IFIP International Federation for Information Processing 2015
J. Abascal et al. (Eds.): INTERACT 2015, Part IV, LNCS 9299, pp. 319–326, 2015.
DOI: 10.1007/978-3-319-22723-8_25

To meet this challenge, we have developed a method, called MIOSS, for overlaying two remote spaces through a mirror video. The MIOSS enables users to feel as if they are in the same room and to share objects in their respective spaces. Figure 1 shows images of perspectives with a real mirror and MIOSS. The real mirror reflects the spaces of both user A and user B. With MIOSS, the display reflects the video of one space overlaid on the other space, and the users feel as if their space is overlaid on their partner's space. As an example of motion parallax, the yellow columnar object in user A's space is located behind user B on the display. The blue triangular object is located in front of user A on the display.

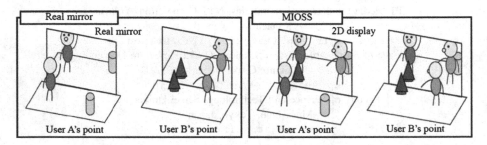

**Fig. 1.** Illustrations of real mirror and MIOSS.

The MIOSS system constructs 3D models of two remote spaces and displays the mirror video of a 3D model generated by overlaying the 3D models of the two spaces on a 2D display. The video provides geometrical consistency in occlusion, size, and positional relationships in the two remote spaces. Moreover, MIOSS imparts motion parallax through a mirror that adjusts to the viewpoint of the users. In this paper, we describe an implementation tool of MIOSS with a minimal setup as a first attempt to develop a MIOSS prototype. The setup comprises multiple Kinects and a 2D display in each user's space. We evaluated whether the implemented MIOSS enables users to recognize the exact positions of shared objects in the partner's space. The results show that the advanced functions of MIOSS— construction of 3D models of two remote spaces; reproduction of geometrical consistency in the position, size, and occlusion relationships among objects in the two spaces: and motion parallax to adjust to a user's viewpoint—enable users to recognize the exact positions of shared objects in the partner's space via the mirror video.

## 2    Related Work

Several studies have proposed systems for sharing two remote spaces as one shared space. Agora [1] provides the shared space on a desk, and users can share real objects in each space on the desk. In t-Room [2], each space has a 2D display. Video of users and objects in front of one of the displays is projected and displayed on the 2D display in the other remote space. Users and objects directly in front of the 2D displays can be shared, but those not directly in front of them cannot be. HyperMirror [3] overlays the

2D image of a space on the 2D image of another space. It doesn't construct a 3D model of the remote spaces and doesn't reproduce the geometrical consistency in the position, size, and shielding relationships of real objects in two remote spaces. In addition, it doesn't impart motion parallax to adjust to a user's viewpoint.

On the other hand, 3D modeling of users and objects with multiple depth sensors, such as Kinect, has been attracting attention lately [4–8]. In addition, media spaces that display a 3D model of a remote space on a 3D display have been developed [6–8]. These systems aimed to connect the two spaces via the display as a bonded surface and join the two remote spaces.

Holoflector [9], which has a half-silvered mirror three feet in front of a large LCD screen, can superimpose 3D modeling data on an image reflected on the mirror. This lets the system create some interesting interactive effects, such as turning the user into a pixelated mannequin generated by 3D modeling, displaying a floating "hologram" above the user's outstretched palm, or raining little bouncing balls all around you. However, this system cannot overlay two remote spaces reconstructed by 3D modeling.

MIOSS, the system proposed here, expands the functions of HyperMirror [3] to construct 3D models of two remote spaces and reproduce geometrical consistency in the position, size, and occlusion relationships among the objects in two spaces. In addition, it imparts motion parallax to adjust to a user's viewpoint. This research is the first attempt to create a system that can display a mirror video that reproduces geometrical consistency with motion parallax.

## 3  Mioss

### 3.1  System Summary

Figure 2 shows the system architecture of MIOSS for user A (the architecture for user B is the same). In each space, there are two Kinect cameras, which capture RGB and depth images, and a 2D display or projector screen. The processing steps for presenting a mirror video on user A's 2D display are as follows:

- Measure user A's viewpoint position: The 3D position of the center of the user's eyes in a world coordinate system is measured as the user's viewpoint by using robust face-tracking technology with a memory-based particle filter [10].
- Construct a 3D model of user A and user B: To construct the 3D model of the spaces of users A and B, the system uses the RGB and depth images from the Kinects and combines the 3D models of the spaces of users A and B in the same way as in previous research [4–8]. To construct a 3D model of a space, the system captures the RGB and depth images from the two Kinect sensors in each space. The system generates the two sets of 3D point cloud data from data captured from each Kinect using the of Point Cloud Library (PCL) function [11] for each space. The two sets of 3D point cloud data are combined with calibration data generated by a preprocessing for calibration by Zhang's method [12] between the two Kinects for each space. Finally, the two sets of 3D point cloud data for the spaces of users A and B are combined. At this time, the actual geometric consistency between the two

spaces is realized in consideration of the positional relationship between the position and mounting posture of the Kinects in the spaces.

- Generate the mirror image: With a 2D display used as a projection surface, the generated 3D model is projected in perspective to match the measured user's viewpoint. At this time, the world coordinate systems of the 3D position of the user's viewpoint and the 3D model are converted into the same coordinate system. Thus, mirror video on the display is implemented.

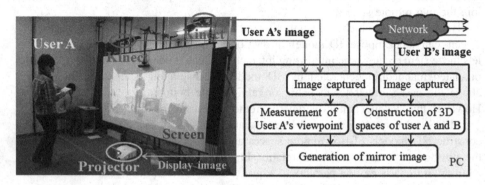

**Fig. 2.** System architecture of MIOSS.

### 3.2 Implementation

Using the above-described methods, we implemented a prototype of the MIOSS mirror interface. The development environment comprised two Kinects with VGA level resolution (640 × 480) of the RGB and depth images in each space, a computer with an Intel Core i7-3960X CPU and 16 GB of memory, and a NVIDIA GeForce GTX580 graphics board. The implementation results are summarized in Table 1, where "delay time of viewpoint movement" is the time from the user's viewpoint position's moving to the time the motion parallax appears in the video and "delay time of camera image" is the time until the captured video appears. In this regard, the prototype sends the RGB and depth image data from the Kinects to the partner's system directly via a non-computer network. The "delay time of camera image" has no network delay time for sending the data in this case.

**Table 1.** Performance of prototype of MIOSS

|  | Frame rate | Delay time |
| --- | --- | --- |
| Camera image | About 15 fps | About 500 ms |
| Viewpoint movement | About 15 fps | About 500 ms |

## 4    Evaluation of Recognition of Object's Position

### 4.1    Experimental Method

MIOSS expands HyperMirror [3] with two new functions. First, it constructs 3D models of two remote spaces and reproduces geometrical consistency in the position, size, and occlusion relationships among the objects in two spaces. Second, it imparts motion parallax to adjust to a user's viewpoint. We conducted experiments to examine whether the new two functions in MIOSS contribute to the user's recognition of the precise positions of objects in the partner's space. We set the following three experimental conditions as within-subject factors.

- **2D condition:** Mirror video of overlay of the 2D image of a space on the 2D image of another room (same as HyperMirror [3]). The video doesn't reproduce the geometrical consistency and doesn't impart motion parallax to adjust to a user's viewpoint. The setting of a user's viewpoint is where the image is displayed when the user is in the center of the room. As a method to generate the video for the condition, only the user and the objects in the space are extracted from the RGB image using depth information. The extracted user and objects are overlaid on the partner's RGB image.
- **3D condition:** Motion parallax is excluded from MIOSS. The mirror video realizes the actual geometric consistency. The setting of the user's viewpoint position is where the image is displayed when the user is in the center of the room.
- **MIOSS condition:** MIOSS is used. The mirror video realizes actual geometric consistency and motion parallax.

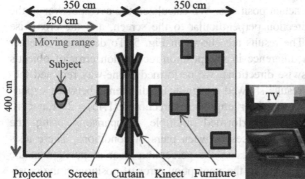

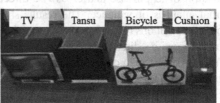

**Fig. 3.** Experimental equipment.

**Fig. 4.** Examples of objects used in the experiment.

We evaluated the effect of the repetition of the geometric consistency in the occlusion, size, and positional relationships in the two remote spaces by comparing the 2D condition with the 3D condition. We evaluated the effect of the repetition of the motion parallax by comparing the 3D condition with the MIOSS condition. Moreover, we evaluated the multiple effects of the repetition of the geometric consistency and the motion parallax by comparing the 2D condition with the MIOSS condition.

The experimental setup is shown in Fig. 3. The participants entered adjacent rooms (400 cm × 350 cm) divided by a curtain. They were allowed to move freely within the area (400 cm × 250 cm) 100 cm away from the screen. There were 100-in. (125 cm × 221 cm) screens placed 60 cm above the floor in front of the curtain in each room. The mirror video, which is 80 in. (108 cm × 172 cm), was projected onto the screens from the projector. Two Kinects were installed at the top of the screen on either side. Five objects were positioned randomly in the space where there was no partici- pant. The objects were photographs of real furniture and a bicycle of actual scale pasted to cardboard boxes (Fig. 4). There were three different combinations of five pieces of furniture (the total number of the pieces of furniture was fifteen). They were used as the objects for each condition randomly. The experiment began with the subject standing in the center of the space. At a signal to begin, the mirror video was output. The subject was given three minutes to write down the positions and sizes of the five objects in the room plan. The room plan has lines that indicate intervals of 5 cm. To minimize order effects, the three experimental conditions were used randomly. Each pair of participants used a different set of objects in each condition. After executing the experiment in each condition, the participants filled in a questionnaire for subjective evaluation (six-point Likert Scale) of their impression of the ease of recognizing the objects' positions. Sixteen persons (12 males and four females in their 20 s) participated in the experiments.

## 4.2  Results of Recognition of Position

To evaluate how accurately the subjects were able to recognize the positions of the objects, we calculated the average error for all subjects between the center position reported by the subjects and the actual positions. We calculated the average error in the lengthwise direction, i.e., the direction perpendicular to the screen, and the crosswise direction parallel to the screen. The results are shown in Fig. 5. To determine whether experimental conditions made a difference in the position-recognition error of object's position of lengthwise and crosswise directions, we performed a one-way repeated fac- torial analysis of variance. The results showed a significant difference between experi- mental conditions ($F(1,45) = 3.55$, $p < .05$ for lengthwise direction; $F(1,45) = 2.51$, $p < .10$ for crosswise direction). Next, we performed multiple comparisons using the Tukey-Kramer method to identify differences between pairs of conditions. These tests showed that there are significant differences in the perception error of position in the lengthwise direction and that differences in the perception error of position in the cross- wise direction trended to appear only between the 2D and MIOSS conditions ($p < .05$ for lengthwise direction; $p < .10$ for crosswise direction). The results demonstrate that position-recognition error was smaller for the MIOSS condition than for the 2D condition.

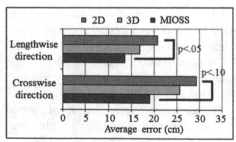

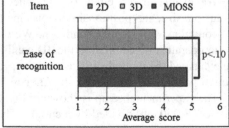

**Fig. 5.**  Average perception error of position.    **Fig. 6.**  Average score of subjective evaluations reported by subjects and the actual positions.

### 4.3  Results of Subjective Evaluation

The average score of participants' subjective evaluations for "ease of recognition" is shown in Fig. 6. We performed a one-way repeated factorial analysis of variance for the item to determine whether experimental conditions affected the values. Since the analysis showed a marginally significant effect of experimental conditions on the evaluation ($F(1,45) = 2.57$, $p < .10$), we performed multiple comparisons using the Tukey-Kramer method. A difference trend was found for the "ease of recognition" between the 2D and MIOSS conditions ($p < .10$). The average subjective score of the item of "ease of recognition" in the MIOSS condition is very high (4.8) and 1.2 score higher than in the 2D condition.

## 5  Discussion

In the results of the experiment, there was no difference in the average error of recognition of the object's position and subjective evaluation values between the 2D and 3D conditions. In contrast, the result showed that the average error of recognition of the object's position in the MIOSS condition is smaller than in 2D condition. The subjective evaluation of "ease of recognition" in the MIOSS condition was higher than in the 2D condition. The motion parallax, in addition to the reproduction of geometric consistency, is effective for enabling users to recognize an object's precise position. In the MIOSS condition, the average error of the recognition in the lengthwise direction was about 13.5 cm and that in crosswise direction was about 19 cm. The errors are very small. When a person observes an object that is directly in front of his/her eyes and writes the position on a sketch of the room, a little error is likely. In addition, the average subjective score of the item of "ease of recognition" in the MIOSS condition was very high (4.8). From the above, it is believed that users can recognize the position of an object accurately with MIOSS. Therefore, these results suggest that the reproduction of geometric consistency in video is, by itself, not sufficient for recognition of the precise position of objects in the partner's space. The motion parallax, in addition to the reproduction of geometric consistency implemented in MIOSS contributes to user's recognition of the precise position of objects in the partner's space. In this research, the prototype of MIOSS was implemented with a minimal setup with a 2D display (screen); it does not impart stereoscopic indications by means of monocular parallax with a 3D display. However, the results suggested that the motion parallax alone is quite sufficient for users to be able to recognize the position of objects in the mirror image.

## 6  Conclusion

We aim to create a media space that can overlay two remote spaces. We presented MIOSS, which enables users to feel as if they are in same room through the mirror and thereby to naturally share objects in two spaces. We developed a prototype of MIOSS that imparts motion parallax through a mirror that adjusts to the viewpoint of the user, in addition to providing geometrical consistency in the occlusion, size, and positional relationships in the two remote spaces. Experimental evaluations with the implemented MIOSS showed that the video expression of the geometric consistency in the video and motion parallax enables users to recognize the exact positions of shared objects in the partner's space via the mirror video. In future work, we plan to evaluate the effect of MIOSS in terms of the smoothness of remote cooperative work in detail with a conversation analysis.

# References

1. Kuzuoka, H., et al.: Agora: a remote collaboration system that enables mutual monitoring. In: CHI Extended Abstracts, pp. 190–191 (1999)
2. Hirata, K., et al.: t-Room: remote collaboration apparatus enhancing spatio-temporal experiences. In: Proceedings of CSCW (2008)
3. Morikawa, et al.: HyperMirror: toward pleasant-to-use video mediated communication system. In: Proceedings of CSCW, pp. 149–158 (1998)
4. Newcombe, E., et al.: KinectFusion: real-time dense surface mapping and tracking. In: Proceedings of ISMAR, pp. 127–136 (2011)
5. Kainz, B., et al.: OmniKinect: real-time dense volumetric data acquisition and applications. In: Proceedings of VRST, pp. 25–32 (2012)
6. Maimone, A., et al.: Encumbrance-free telepresence system with real-time 3D capture and display using commodity depth cameras. In: Proceedings of ISMAR (2011)
7. Maimone, A., et al.: A first look at a telepresence system with room-sized real-time 3D capture and large tracked display. In: Proceedings of ICAT, vol. 1 (2011)
8. Beck, S., et al.: Immersive group-to-group telepresence. IEEE Trans. Visual. Comput. Graphics 19(4), 616–625 (2013)
9. Holoflector. http://research.microsoft.com/apps/video/default.aspx?id=159487&r=1
10. Mikami, D., Otsuka, K., Yamato, J.: Memory-based particle filter for tracking objects with large variation in pose and appearance. In: Daniilidis, K., Maragos, P., Paragios, N. (eds.) ECCV 2010, Part III. LNCS, vol. 6313, pp. 215–228. Springer, Heidelberg (2010)
11. PCL (The point cloud library). http://pointclouds.org/
12. Zhang, Z.: A flexible new technique for camera calibration. IEEE Trans. Pattern Anal. Mach. Intell. 22(11), 1330–1334 (2000)

# Improving Spatial Awareness for Human Trajectory Visualization in Space-Time Cubes

Tiago Gonçalves[1,2(✉)], Ana Paula Afonso[1], and Bruno Martins[2]

[1] LaSIGE, Faculdade de Ciências, Universidade de Lisboa, Lisbon, Portugal
tgoncalves@lasige.di.fc.ul.pt, apa@di.fc.ul.pt
[2] INESC-ID, Instituto Superior Técnico,
Universidade de Lisboa, Lisbon, Portugal
bruno.g.martins@ist.utl.pt

**Abstract.** With the increasing evolution of computer graphics, 3D visualizations have become more common and are nowadays seen as a promising way to represent complex types of information. In particular, space-time cubes (STC) have been proposed as an alternative to 2D maps for the visualization of spatio-temporal data, and they have become increasingly used to explore the dynamics and patterns of human movement. However, previous research has pointed out perceptual limitations that can condition the use of 3D views for decoding locations and spatial properties. We aim to address those issues by presenting a comparative study between three variants of the STC technique, with different methods to improve spatial awareness. Our results support that the use of a movable plane or an additional 2D map view improve users' accuracy when performing common tasks, and are preferred over simpler, yet less cluttered approaches. Additionally, it also supports the possible advantages of combining 2D and 3D views for human trajectory visualization.

**Keywords:** Spatio-temporal data · Trajectories · Information visualization · Visual analytics · Space-time cube · Usability

## 1 Introduction

Throughout the years, researchers have tried to understand the dynamics associated with human movement and possible mobility patterns, e.g., in the context of urbanism studies and to improve the lives of citizens [3]. Nowadays, with the increasing popularity and accuracy of mobile computing technologies and navigational systems, large volumes of spatio-temporal data, representing human trajectories, have become available [3]. A trajectory can be defined as the evolution of an object's position through time, and represented as a time-stamped sequence of location points that may contain other types of *thematic* attributes, derived from the spatio-temporal locations or associated from other datasets.

Due to the critical role that spatial, temporal, and thematic attributes play in understanding trajectory data [2, 13] several challenges remain unsolved, in particular in areas related with visualization and human-computer interaction for the exploration of these data [2]. Considering the spatial properties of trajectories, maps are often seen

© IFIP International Federation for Information Processing 2015
J. Abascal et al. (Eds.): INTERACT 2015, Part IV, LNCS 9299, pp. 327–334, 2015.
DOI: 10.1007/978-3-319-22723-8_26

as important tools for their visualization [12]. In particular, 2D maps are among the most used techniques to represent georeferenced information. These take advantage of the manipulation of several visual variables (e.g., colour or size) from different graphical elements, such as points, lines, or areas, to display various types of information, as present in trajectories, over a geographical plane [6]. However, although excelling in the representation of the spatial component of trajectories, 2D maps tend to undermine the representation of the data's temporal component, thus often requiring the combination of additional visualizations (e.g., time graphs) [3].

With the increasing advancements of computer graphics, 3D maps, and in particular space-time cubes (STCs) [8], have been proposed as viable options for the visualization of trajectories [10, 12]. STCs represent both spatial and temporal information within a cube, where the $x$-$y$ axes usually represent spatial information (e.g., latitude/longitude), while the $z$-axis represents time [8]. Typically, time increases along the $z$-axis, implying that the higher the information is within the cube, the most recent it is [1, 10]. Similarly to 2D maps, trajectories can be displayed as a sequence of symbols, graphically encoded to represent variations in the thematic attributes. However, since time is represented as a spatial position, other visual variables are *available* to represent the thematic attributes, when compared with traditional 2D maps [10]. STCs also allow the representation of various layers of information, each one defined as a plane in the $z$-axis [15], representing the state of an object in different moments in time.

Some studies have been conducted in order to show that 3D visualizations, and STCs by extension, can be more effective than 2D visualizations in helping users understanding shapes and finding patterns/relations in the displayed data [7, 9]. However, due to their 3D characteristics, the interaction with STCs can be affected by human perceptual limitations. Previous studies have shown that 3D views are not as effective as 2D alternatives in location/positioning based tasks [7, 9]. To minimize these problems, previous studies suggested the use of interactive features, such as changing the point of view within the cube [10] or moving the plane representing spatial information up/downwards to facilitate locating objects in space and time [11]. As a result, while STCs can be considered as relevant tools for trajectory visualization, it is important to: (i) understand how to improve these techniques for spatially-related tasks; and (ii) empirically validate the proposed features to help the interaction with STCs, taking into account the types of tasks a user might perform to achieve a given goal [14].

In this paper, we aim to address those issues. We present a comparative user study between three variants of the STC technique, aiming to understand: (i) methods that non-expert users apply to acquire spatial information with STCs, as these increasingly have to deal with spatio-temporal analysis issues [2]; (ii) features that may improve spatial-information awareness in STCs; and, (iii) if there exist significant differences, in terms of performance and preferences, between those features. The remainder of this paper is organized as follows: the next section presents the three variants of the STC technique. Then, the paper describes the user study and results obtained with prototypes. The paper concludes with a discussion on the results, and with ideas for future work.

## 2  Compared Visualizations

We developed three prototypes integrating variants of the STC technique (Fig. 1), which allowed the visualization of pickup/dropoff locations of taxis, based on data provided by the Taxi and Limousine Commission of New York City.

The prototypes involved five main components. The first is the control panel (Fig. 1a), which allows the selection of which data to visualize according to various filters, including the dates of movement and several thematic attributes, like number of passengers or payment type. The second component (Fig. 1b) allows selecting the information to be represented by the visual variables of colour, shape, and size, supporting several combinations between the data attributes. Each colour and shape can be used to represent location types (pickup/dropoff), payment types and the periods of the day. Colour can also be used to represent the identification of the moving objects. Size can be used to display quantitative information, including the number of passengers or trip fares (larger icons representing larger values). The third component (Fig. 1c) displays all data associated with any point highlighted in the STC. The fourth component (Fig. 1d) describes the meaning of each visual variable illustrated in the STC, and allows un/viewing sub-sets of the data, based on those variables.

The last component consists of a STC visualization, as depicted in Figs. 1e, f, and g, respectively depending on the prototype. In all three prototypes, the STC is composed by a 2D map plane, at the bottom of the cube, providing spatial information, and by several labels along the cube's height, providing temporal information. Trajectories are depicted as a sequence of points connected with lines, and coloured/sized according to the attributes selected in the representation panel. All prototypes support common interactive features such as panning and zooming, for the entire 3D view or just the 2D map displayed at the bottom. Each visualization also allows the user to rotate the cube along any of its axes and to rescale its height enabling analysts to, respectively, change the point of view and manipulate the temporal granularity of the data.

As emphasized in Fig. 1, the differences between the three prototypes focus on this component, namely in how the spatial-component of the data is represented. In the first prototype (Fig. 1f - *P1*), representing the most simple STC variant, selecting an object will display the time moment in which the object was detected, with a thick line pointing at the object's location in the map plane. In the second prototype (Fig. 1g - *P2*), based on the most common (yet not validated) proposal to improve spatial awareness on STCs [11], in addition to the previous methods we have that a copy of the map plane is displayed at the same height as the selected object. Although this approach should provide, more easily, spatial context regarding the selected object, adding a plane to a certain height will, necessarily, occlude all data located bellow the selected object. Finally, the third prototype (Fig. 1e - *P3*) aims to combine the advantages of 2D and 3D views by displaying, at the right-bottom of the visualization, a 2D map overview. Although this alternative may lead users to divide their attention between views, also providing information with less detail [5], it will continuously provide some spatial context to the user.

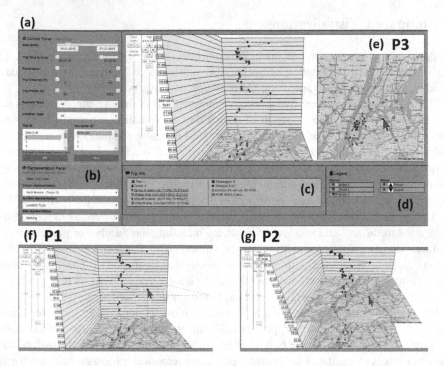

**Fig. 1.** Components of the prototypes used in the experiment: (a) Control Panel; (b) Representation Panel; (c) Information Panel; (d) Legend; (e) *P3* STC with overview; (f) *P1* basic STC; (g) *P2* STC with moveable spatial plane

## 3 User Study

This section describes the comparative user study conducted with the described prototypes. In this study we aimed at: (i) identifying strategies that analysts may adopt to obtain spatial information when using a STC; (ii) identifying possible interactive techniques to help obtaining spatial information; and (iii) assessing the users' experience with those methods, and empirically compare them.

Based on the features of each prototype, our hypotheses were the following: (*H1*) participants will prefer the interfaces with complementary spatial information (*P2* and *P3*), due to the additional maps displayed; (*H2*) participants will have a better performance and a lower number of interactive actions with *P2* and *P3*, due to spatial-context aids that are provided; and (*H3*) in elementary tasks, i.e. tasks that focus in just one object or time moment, users will have a better performance, due to the smaller number of points/lines displayed.

A total of 20 participants volunteered to the study, aged between 19 and 34 (Av: 24.6, SD: 4.1). Although, all participants were knowledgeable with computer applications and geographic information systems for the search of directions towards specific points of interest (e.g., Google Maps), none of them were familiar with trajectory data analysis, nor familiarized with New York's geography.

## 3.1   Experimental Design

To test our hypotheses, the participants performed two tasks, affected by the spatial components of trajectory data. These tasks are based on the most common types of cartographic visualization objectives described in the literature [14]. The first, identify, required users to locate taxis according to some spatio-temporal and thematic constraints (e.g., *which taxis dropped passengers at the Laguardia Airport? where was taxi n°1 by 3 pm?*). The second, compare, required the analysis of similarity/difference relations between data elements in the STCs (e.g., *which driver served, more frequently, over a larger geographical area? in which periods of the day did driver 1 serve over a larger area?*).

We considered two independent variables: Visualization technique ($Vt$), with three levels, corresponding to the three prototypes, $P1$, $P2$, and $P3$; and Query category ($Qc$), with four levels adapted from the spatio-temporal data queries identified by [4]: (i) *elementary what + where, elementary when* ($EE$); (ii) *elementary what + where, general when* ($EG$); (iii) *general what + where, elementary when* ($GE$); and (iv) *general what + where, general when* ($GG$). These categories determine whether the focus of the task is in just one (*elementary*) moving object (*what + where?*) and/or in a specific time moment (*when?*), or if the focus of the task is instead in several (*general*) objects and/or across a time period.

The experiment followed a within subjects design and all participants carried out each task individually, in a controlled environment. At the beginning of the study, subjects were briefed about the objectives of the experiment, and they viewed a demonstration of the prototypes. Before carrying out the tasks, they were asked to interact with the applications, and were encouraged to clarify any doubts. After the training phase, the participants performed the two tasks, taking into account the different visualizations and query categories. To mitigate sequence effects, the order in which the independent variables were presented was counterbalanced using a *latin-square* design. However, since comparison tasks require necessarily more than one data item (either from the same, or from different trajectories), the level *elementary what + where* elementary when (*Qc(EE)*) was not considered for these tasks. Consequently, each participant performed a total of 21 trials: (3 $Vt$) x (4 identify + 3 compare).

To assess our hypotheses, we considered the following dependent variables: (i) subjective preferences (i.e., participants were asked to rate the ease of use of each prototype on 10-Likert scale); (ii) task accuracy (i.e., each task was rated between 0 and 10, depending on the detail given by the participants - e.g. saying that a taxi dropped a passenger in *New York* is less detailed than *Manhattan*, which is less detailed than *Central Park*); (iii) task completion time; and (iv) number of actions performed, including panning and zooming operations, and rescaling the STC's height. During the study, participants were encouraged to *think aloud*, and share their opinions about the techniques.

## 3.2   Results

This section overviews the results obtained in the study, with a focus on the most statistically significant ones.

We applied Friedman's test, followed by a Wilcoxon Signed Rank test with a Bonferroni correction for pairwise comparisons, to compare the differences between the **participants' opinions** after each set of tasks. In the **identify** task, participants have shown a higher preference $(X^2(2) = 14.8, p = 0.001)$ for $Vt(P3)$ $(7.3/10)$ and $Vt(P2)$ $(6.5/10)$ over $Vt(P1)$ $(5.5/10)$ $(Z = -3.42, p = 0.001$ and $Z = -2.98, p = 0.001$, respectively). In the **compare** task, participants have also shown a significant higher preference $(X^2(2) = 11.7, p = 0.003)$ for $Vt(P3)$ $(7.2/10)$ over $Vt(P1)$ $(6/10)$ and $Vt(P2)$ $(6.5/10)$ $(Z = -2.96, p = 0.003$ and $Z = -2.56, p = 0.01$, respectively). These results, in turn, support our first hypothesis (*H1: participants would prefer P2 and P3 over P1*).

A similar procedure was used to compare the **participants' accuracy**, with the visualizations and in the different categories. Table 1a) shows the average scores obtained in the various tasks. The tests revealed significant differences in $Vt$ $(X^2(2) = 9.796, p = 0.007)$ and $Qc$ $(X^2(3) = 26.154, p < 0.001)$, in the **identify task**. Pairwise comparison tests revealed significantly less accurate results with $Vt(P1)$ comparatively to the other two $(Z = -2,72, p = 0.006$ and $Z = -2.54, p = 0.011$, for $Vt$ $(P2)$ and $Vt(P3)$ respectively). Participants were also significantly less accurate in $Qc$ $(GE)$ tasks, comparatively to all others $(Z = -3.57, p < 0.001; Z = -4.81, p < 0.001$; and $Z = -2.787, p = 0.005$ for $Qc(EE)$, $Qc(EG)$, and $Qc(GG)$ respectively). Similarly, in **comparison** tasks, participants were significant less accurate in $Qc(GE)$ tasks $(X^2(2) = 8.54, p = 0.014)$ comparatively to $Qc(EG)$ tasks $(Z = -2.83, p = 0.005)$. These results were somewhat expected, as in this category of tasks $(GE)$ users need to focus in several objects in one specific time moment. This implies focusing user attention on a single temporal plane, having to ignore/filter others, thus resulting in a higher visual noise and/or cognitive workload.

On the other hand, we applied a repeated measures ANOVA, followed by Bonferroni tests for pairwise comparisons, for the comparative analysis of the participants' **task completion times** and the **number of interactive actions**. Table 1 (b and c) shows the participants' mean results for all tasks, with all combinations of the two

**Table 1.** Mean results to the different participants' in terms of a) task accuracy (acc), b) task competion time, and c) number of interactive actions

| | | Identify | | | | Compare | | |
|---|---|---|---|---|---|---|---|---|
| | | EE | GE | EG | GG | GE | EG | GG |
| a) Acc [0-10] | P1 | 8,05 | 8.30 | 6.40 | 7.50 | 7.45 | 8.05 | 8.13 |
| | P2 | 8.40 | **9.20** | **7.55** | 8.35 | 7.75 | 8.83 | 8.13 |
| | P3 | **8.65** | 8.70 | 7.45 | **8.63** | **8.25** | **9.50** | **8.85** |
| b) Time (sec) | P1 | **122.90** | 166.55 | 203.71 | 176.33 | 141.40 | 116.26 | 122.38 |
| | P2 | **126.24** | 168.55 | 193.24 | 174.36 | 152.48 | 123.10 | 146.52 |
| | P3 | **127.93** | 180.05 | 178.81 | 142.64 | 156.17 | 121.57 | 107.07 |
| c) Nº Actions | P1 | 26.65 | 31.95 | 41.80 | 51.25 | 35.20 | 38.80 | 46.65 |
| | P2 | **22.85** | **28.10** | **35.90** | **40.15** | **34.55** | **32.95** | 46.55 |
| | P3 | **22.55** | 45.65 | 41.45 | 44.55 | **34.80** | 35.35 | **38.00** |

independent variables. Regarding **task completion times**, the tests revealed a significant effect from $Qc$ $(F(2.5) = 6.671, p = 0.001)$ in the **identify** task. The pairwise comparison tests revealed significant lower times in the less demanding type of task $(Qc(EE))$, comparatively to the remaining three (with $p \leq 0.05$ in all cases). Regarding the **number of actions**, significant effects were detected from $Qc$ and $Vt$ in the identify task $(F(2.57) = 10.464, p < 0.001$ and $F(1.68) = 3.260, p = 0.05$, respectively). Pairwise comparison tests revealed also a significantly lower number of actions in $Qc(EE)$ tasks $(p \leq 0.013$, comparing to all cases), and a generally significantly lower number of actions of $Vt(P2)$ comparatively to $Vt(P1)$ $(p = 0.046)$. As such, these results go in agreement with our second (*H2: better performance with P2 and P3*) and third hypothesis (*H3: better performance in 'simpler' tasks*).

Overall, participants commented that using a moveable plane, or a 2D map overview on the STC, indeed helped them to acquire spatially-related information more easily. They said that the 2D map overview helped them to have a better overall perception of the geographical space, and that the map allowed them to see spatial and temporal information simultaneously. The moveable plane, on the other hand, was considered more helpful to find the locations of specific points, or to analyse the evolution of locations over time from a given taxi. Some participants, however, commented that, sometimes, the moveable plane would occlude information, conditioning the interaction. Some users also expressed an interest in having more control over the 2D map overview on *P3*, possibly due to their familiarity with interactive 2D maps.

## 4 Conclusions and Future Work

This paper presented a comparative study between three variants of space-time cubes for the visualization of human trajectories, combining general types of visualization tasks with the main categories of spatio-temporal queries. The results point out that the use of a moveable plane with spatial information and/or the use of a 2D map overview significantly improves users' performance in tasks for the identification of locations and objects, even though sometimes these techniques can occlude information. Moreover, users have shown a significantly higher preference towards a variant that combines 2D and 3D views. This further supports the importance of studying the advantages of combining both types of techniques [1, 7], which may, in turn, be useful for developers and analysts needing to decide which features to use on a given technique for trajectory visualization.

Nevertheless, further studies should still be conducted. As future work, we propose to continue studying these issues, in particular, the combination of 2D maps and 3D STCs within the same visualization, and assessing their advantages and disadvantages comparatively to the individual use of 2D maps and 3D STCs.

**Acknowledgements.** This work was supported by national funds through by FCT (Portuguese Science and Technology Foundation) with the following references: *SFRH/BD/78837/2011, UID/CEC/00408/2013* and *UID/CEC/50021/2013*, and through the KD-LBSN project, with reference *EXPL/EEI-ESS/0427/2013*.

# References

1. Amini, F., Rufiange, S., Hossain, Z., Ventura, Q., Irani, P., McGuffin, M.: Theimpact of interactivity on comprehending 2d and 3d visualizations of movementdata. IEEE Trans. Vis. Comput. Graph. **21**(1), 122–135 (2015)
2. Andrienko, G., Andrienko, N., Demsar, U., Dransch, D., Dykes, J., Fabrikant, S.I., Jern, M., Kraak, M.J., Schumann, H., Tominski, C.: Space, time and visualanalytics. Int. J. Geogr. Inf. Sci. **24**(10), 1577–1600 (2010)
3. Andrienko, N., Andrienko, G., Bak, P., Keim, D., Stefan, W.: Visual Analytics ofMovement, 1st edn. Springer, Heidelberg (2013)
4. Andrienko, N., Andrienko, G., Gatalsky, P.: Exploratory spatio-temporal visualization: an analytical review. J. Vis. Lang. Comput. **14**(6), 503–541 (2003)
5. Baudisch, P., Good, N., Bellotti, V., Schraedley, P.: Keeping things in context: a comparative evaluation of focus plus context screens, overviews, and zooming. In: Proceedings of CHI 2002, pp. 259–266 (2002)
6. Bertin, J.: Semiology of Graphics: Diagrams, Networks, Maps. University of Wisconsin Press, Madison (1967)
7. Gonçalves, T., Afonso, A.P., Martins, B.: Visualizing human trajectories: comparing space-time cubes and static maps. In: Proceedings of HCI 2014, pp. 207–212 (2014)
8. Hägerstrand, T.: What about people in regional science? Pap. Reg. Sci. Assoc. **24**(1), 6–21 (1970)
9. John, M.S., Cowen, M.B., Smallman, H.S., Oonk, H.M.: The use of 2D and 3D displays for shape-understanding versus relative-position tasks. Hum. Factors: J. Hum. Factors Ergon. Soci. **43**(1), 79–98 (2001)
10. Kjellin, A., Pettersson, L.W., Seipel, S., Lind, M.: Evaluating 2D and 3D visualizations of spatiotemporal information. ACM Trans. Appl. Percept. **7**(3), 19:1–19:23 (2010)
11. Kraak, M.J.: The space-time cube revisited from a geovisualization perspective. In: Proceedings of ICC 2003, pp. 1988–1995 (2003)
12. Kraak, M.J.: Geovisualization and time new opportunities for the space-time cube. In: Dodge, M., McDerby, M., Turner, M. (eds.) Geographic Visualization Concepts, Tools and Applications, chap. 15, pp. 294–306. Wiley (2008)
13. Peuquet, D.J.: It's about time: A conceptual framework for the representation of temporal dynamics in geographic information systems. Assoc. Am. Geogr. **84**(3), 441–461 (1994)
14. Roth, R.E.: Cartographic interaction: what we know and what we need to know. J. Spat. Inf. Sci. **6**, 59–115 (2013)
15. Thakur, S., Hanson, A.: A 3D visualization of multiple time series on maps. In: Proceedings of IV 2010, pp. 336–343 (2010)

# MStoryG: Exploring Serendipitous Storytelling Within High Anxiety Public Spaces

Clinton Jorge[✉], Valentina Nisi, Julian Hanna, Nuno Nunes,
Miguel Caldeira, and Amanda Marinho

Madeira-Interactive Technologies Institute, University of Madeira,
Funchal, Portugal
{clinton.jorge,julian.hanna,miguel.caldeira,
amanda.marinho}@m-iti.org, {valentina,njn}@uma.pt

**Abstract.** The proliferation of interactive displays within public spaces has steered research towards exploring situated engagement, user interaction and user-generated content on public displays. However, user behaviors such as *display blindness* and *display avoidance*, *social embarrassment* and *participation inequality* are just some of the limiting factors restricting user commitment to interaction and participation. So-called "non-places", which include transportation terminals, are homogenized public spaces that seem to exist outside conventional notions of time and identity. These anonymous, fast-paced, high-anxiety spaces provide a significant challenge for designers hoping to engage the attention of passersby. Our study proposes to go beyond a traditional technology-centered approach and examine the relationship between individual, object, and space. We attempt to engage airport travelers in serendipitous interactive storytelling through reminiscence and nostalgia. We present our "in-the-wild" study at the baggage claim area of an international airport where 26 h of observations and 49 semi-structured interviews were collected.

**Keywords:** Pervasive display · Interactive storytelling · Airport installations · Public installations · Participation inequality

## 1 Introduction

Modern society is becoming increasingly mediated through (and dependent on) technology. People are governed more and more by hectic routines and tight deadlines, leading to increased stress and anxiety [9]. In an attempt to escape the limits of mundane reality, people look for a sense of wonder in their lives [41], more often than not through immersion in the imaginary world of fictional stories [40].

Storytelling is pervasive and ubiquitous; it was considered central to society long before humans could read and write, and represents a fundamental component of human experience. Stories perform a critical function in society, allowing for dialogue between people, culture, and time (c.f. Madej [31]). The telling of stories is an intrinsic part of people's lives, a creative process through which people share and reflect on life experiences, solve problems, or teach lessons [25, 45]. Storytelling began as an oral

© IFIP International Federation for Information Processing 2015
J. Abascal et al. (Eds.): INTERACT 2015, Part IV, LNCS 9299, pp. 335–353, 2015.
DOI: 10.1007/978-3-319-22723-8_27

technique, matured as a written form and in recent decades has worked its way into the complexity of digital media and devices.

Nowadays, as digital displays become pervasive and the underlying technology becomes ubiquitous, these displays present both opportunities and challenges as a new storytelling medium and means of bringing a sense of wonder to public spaces. This profusion of digital interactive displays within public spaces is of rising importance for the field of Human-Computer Interaction (HCI), as designers are faced with new challenges such as attracting glances of passersby towards public displays or installations, enticing interaction, and obtaining user-generated content. However, this shift from consumer culture to the culture of participation is not without its challenges [21]. Multiple studies have shown that designers are often plagued with lower than expected acceptance and attention towards pervasive displays [36]. This difference in participation may be compared to its counterpart in online communities: participation inequality. As defined by Nielsen [38], his 90-9-1 principle (also known as the power law distribution) describes the broad discrepancy between those who contribute and create, and those who view and consume content (or information). Two other common user reactions towards public displays are *display blindness* [35], when people have a preconceived expectation of uninteresting content and hence ignore the display, and *display avoidance* [28], where passersby notice the display but then quickly look away, actively avoiding the display in order to escape information overload.

When tailoring situated experiences, place plays a particularly crucial role. In the example of transportation terminals, these "supermodern" globalized spaces have been theorized as existing outside normal definitions of history, identity, and relations, and thus labeled "non-places" [5]. These so-called non-places may nevertheless instill feelings of nostalgia—arriving in a new country, starting a new experience or adventure, or watching loved ones arrive or depart. On the other hand, terminal spaces (especially airport terminals) are notoriously complex ecosystems that are known to stress, frustrate, and confuse consumers of their services [6]. These anonymous, fast-paced, high-anxiety spaces present an interesting challenge in engaging passersby.

This paper goes beyond a traditional technology-centered approach to examine the relationship between individual, object and space. Building on this premise, we explored the use of an obsolete, mechanical split-flap display—traditionally used in airports and other transportation terminals to convey flight information—as our storytelling medium and attempted to create a culture of story generation and participation in different environments.

In the following sections, we start by reviewing location-based storytelling, public displays and situated engagement, and cultures of participation. Next we introduce a series of deployments and lessons learnt leading to MStoryG, an interactive storytelling installation deployed at the baggage claim area of the Madeira International Airport as an "in-the-wild" study. We then present our synthesis of 26 h of observations and 49 semi-structured interviews, collected over a two-week period. Finally, we discuss the experiences the system provided in engaging serendipitous storytelling, or chance-based storytelling encounters, and our experience deploying an interactive installation inside an airport terminal.

# 2 Related Work

With large-scale electronic displays increasingly found in public spaces such as subway stations, airport terminals, and shopping centers, public spaces are experiencing a shift from traditional analogue to digital displays, enabling interaction and dynamic multimedia presentation [36]. This has led researchers to examine topics such as participation and engagement [19]. However, designing pervasive interactive public displays comes with a particular set of challenges that must be acknowledged. Designers may be overconfident, leading to lower than expected levels of user interaction, for example by creating embarrassing situations for users [7, 20].

In the following sub-sections we begin by reviewing prior work within the scope of public displays and public installations, focusing on situated engagement and location-based narrative and storytelling.

## 2.1 Public Displays

Public participation in public spaces has been a topic of considerable interest in the HCI community. Memarovic et al. [33] argue that public displays may stimulate essential human needs within public spaces. Müller and colleagues present a taxonomy for public displays and argue that interaction with public displays actually begins as early as the moment of passing by or glancing [36]. A significant amount of work has been performed to aid designers and researchers in designing and evaluating public displays, such as: analytical frameworks that evaluate public interaction [32, 34], public display design guidelines [20], guidelines for locating screens within public spaces [44], and techniques for enticing interaction [7, 14, 28].

People often resist interacting with displays in public spaces due to feelings of social embarrassment and awkwardness [7], or to maintain a social role [36]. Furthermore, people may avoid interaction due to the unclear immediate purpose (or benefit) of interacting with the display or simply avoid interaction because they assume the content is irrelevant or uninteresting [28]. When passing through public spaces, interacting with public displays is not our primary objective. Rather, a person will pass by a public display and become motivated or persuaded to interact by certain external factors. If the display fails to attract users it may not be used at all; catching the attention of passersby, alongside engagement and motivation, is therefore a central design issue [36]. In sum, Huang found that glancing at pervasive public displays is complex and depends on many factors [20].

## 2.2 User-Generated Content

Online communities such as blogs, forums, and wiki-sites rely heavily on user-generated content. Nielsen identified that a minority of users (as low as 0.003 % in Wikipedia's case) contribute the majority of content, while the majority of users ("lurkers") never contribute at all. This participation inequality, also coined the "90-9-1 principle" [38], is further explored by Muller et al. [37], who compiled some extensive literature on lurkers ("non-public participants") for online communities and organizations. Muller identifies lurkers as the modal class of users. However, Muller also notes that "active lurkers" might decide not to actively contribute, preferring not to clutter information areas, or feeling that they lack the standing or authority to make relevant contributions, but they still contribute by disseminating ideas within their communities. "Active lurkers" have been described as an important asset, adding to the effectiveness and "reach" of the content created by the main contributors [46].

The rise of social computing has facilitated a shift from consumer cultures to cultures of participation [12]. However, displaying user-generated content in public spaces raises an issue of moderation. Others could perceive content as explicit or troublesome, or inappropriate for a particular location. Miriam Greis et al. [17], chose to explore the use of pre-moderation of content for public spaces, and discovered how moderation delay would decrease the number of user-generated posts. The authors found 10 min to be an acceptable delay for over 70 % of users. However, the authors also noted that even delays of 90 s were enough to confuse some users.

Claude Fortin et al. [13] explored community bulletin boards as participatory non-digital display (as acts such as posting). Their results revealed how cultures of participation are dependent on type of context and how tangibility, flexibility, access and control play an important role in enabling posting.

### 2.3 Community-Based Storytelling and Location-Centric Narratives

Story diffusion has come a long way since its early oral and written forms. With the arrival of the Internet and blogs, webcasts, and social networks it has become increasingly possible to reach a broad, diverse audience. Projects such as Tim Burton's Exquisite Corpse and The Novel Iowa City Project [29, 49], for example, have employed Twitter for community-based writing projects, to gather or "crowdsource" story segments from public contributions in order to collectively author a story.

Storytelling innovation depends both on the medium and the story being told [24], as well as the cues embedded in physical surroundings [27]. In an attempt to increase immersion and utilize the inherent personality of physical spaces, research has looked into location-aware media stories [39], location-based pervasive games [18, 43], augmented stories and narratives linked to physical locations through digital devices [10, 26], immersive storytelling rooms [1, 8], and other innovations, which in turn has led to a closer rapport between storytelling and the HCI field.

## 3  Design Space

Studies show that airlines rank lowest in the American Customer Satisfaction Index in terms of accommodation and food services and the transportation sector [3]. Airport authorities recognize the issues that lead customers to rate their experiences as less than optimal. For example, one report stated that 72 % of passengers "cited inefficient streamlining of the core passenger journey from check-in to boarding" as a source of "stress and unhappiness", and suggested streamlining services to mitigate waiting times and increase task efficiency [2]. Takakuwa [47] found that passengers spent an average of 25 % of their time waiting during their airport experience. The Amadeus report [2] presented a "leisure timeline" foreseeing that pioneers should be adopting interactive artistic installations and immersive experiences by 2015.

Meanwhile, HCI research is looking at improving passenger experience by using mobile services to ease navigation and journey time through airport terminals, for example with smartphone applications that use social media to better connect travelers and enhance air travel experiences [6], as well as mobile pervasive games that passengers play while waiting in security lines [30]. Art installations are increasingly deployed at airport terminals with the goal of improving customer experience [15]. Moreover, artists such as Jenny Holzer have specifically chosen airport terminals to deploy their exhibitions. In 2004, Holzer repurposed LED departures screens in the disused TWA Flight Center at New York's JFK as part of the exhibition *Terminal 5*.

Furthermore, in their studies Fortin et al. [13] reveal how transportation terminals are without any sort of bulletin boards or other posting areas, and postulated that the deficit of cultures of participation in these spaces may be related to the postmodern theory describing how such globalized, anonymous, futuristic spaces, often described as "non-places", lack any sense of normal human relations or identity [5]. The renowned designer David Rockwell, who recently redesigned Newark Airport's United Airlines terminal, summed up the disorienting anonymity of most airport terminals. "The way airports are, it's like a Kubrick movie," Rockwell stated, referring to the horror film *The Shining*: "every hall you turn down looks the same." He worked specifically against this dynamic to create a less disconnected, more "grounded" environment with a greater sense of time and place: the terminal appearance changes from day to night, for example, and the food court includes "a cluster of clam shacks" to create the illusion of place, in this case the Jersey Shore [48].

## 3.1 Motivation

Storytelling is pervasive and ubiquitous in society [31] and inherent to our daily activities. However, we postulate that "non-places", such as airport terminals, may not support this medium for expression. MStoryG was ideated as a platform for telling stories in public spaces. The installation concept was driven by people's creativity and inspiration, and the hypothesis was whether, given the opportunity, users would draw cues from the surrounding physical space to produce fictitious stories, and whether they would feel compelled to share their stories with the public.

Initial exploration for a medium to support storytelling in public spaces steered us away from digital screens or video projectors. These were judged as too common and thus likely to be ignored by passersby, or they might also suffer from issues such as lighting conditions [28, 35]. Gaver et al. [14] suggest using ambiguity as something intriguing, mysterious, and delightful. This led to the exploration of traditional, subverted displays, such as large mechanical split-flap display (mainly seen in transportation terminals). Its characteristic sound should attract peoples' attention to updated information. We were able to secure one such display through a donation from the local airport. This large Solari Udine display (3.5 m by 2 m and 800 kg) had been in use for nearly 30 years and was highly recognizable to the local population. We aimed to use it as a medium to share stories and build upon its inherent history and nostalgia.

# 4 Concept Validation

In order to rapidly prototype, deploy, and test storytelling techniques and the mechanical display layout, a high fidelity software replica of the physical Solari Udine display was built in Adobe Flash and iterated during two deployments.

The deployments were non-concurrent and ran independently within semi-public spaces. Each deployment was built upon the results, observations, findings and user comments of the previous installment. In an attempt to maintain a higher degree of consistency, each deployment followed a similar evaluation protocol (defined in the MStoryG/Evaluation Protocol and Methodology section).

Our objective with the initial deployments was to discover a feasible and interesting storytelling technique and to help us understand how the installation was perceived by the public; providing some indication of the most adequate public space contexts that would best suite a storytelling installation resorting to and old mechanical airport flight information display.

## 4.1    Deployment One: The Exquisite Corpse Installation

User feedback from an initial pilot study performed within the researchers' office space led to the identification of the Surrealist parlor game Exquisite Corpse (Cadavre Exquis (Breton et al. 1925)) as a possible collaborative storytelling technique to drive the installation. In this game participants build upon the last story shared, while remaining blind to either the earlier contributions or the overall story.

The installation consisted of a retro-projection of a high fidelity software prototype of the physical Solari display, set up in the entrance of a science facility over four afternoons (1–5 pm). Sixty passersby were observed lurking (peripheral and focal awareness threshold [c.f. 6]), while 35 passersby interacted directly and contributed to the story. Passersby could interact through an adjacent laptop with dedicated web interface or through the Twitter social network by mentioning "@mstoryg".

During our case studies we found no evidence of the "honey pot" [7] effect and attributed it to the sporadic public flow within the public space. A collocated researcher was required to entice passerby interaction with the installation and to explain its purpose. We noted a difficulty for the majority of users in contributing with a story, even if only to continue a previous sentence (or a very short story segment). For an installation that relies heavily on user-generated content, location and public flow were also found to be key to the uptake of the installation and a constant feed of contributions.

We found that the repurposing of the display attracted glances and generated curiosity. People immediately recognized the display as "the one from the airport" and the ambiguity of its usage was beneficial in generating curiosity. However, the lack of a clear purpose could have intimidated users' exploration, thus hindering interaction.

In sum, the Exquisite Corpse storytelling concept was well received but was found to be too dependent on public interaction to be a sustainable source of content.

## 4.2 Deployment Two: The FNC0313 Installation

A second design iteration was performed targeting two previously identified key issues: installation location and public flow, and user-generated content sustainability.

Previously, we observed that a sustainable (user-generated) storytelling installation would be better suited to a high public flow space, in order to engage as many passersby as possible. The location chosen to deploy the second case study was at the local university's main entrance due to its combination of high people flow and a leisure space (student bar). We noted that initial story contributions revolved around travelling, and that soon afterward they began to include meta-references to real events (such as the approaching holidays). This led to the adoption of a travel theme to help guide contributors and strengthen the rapport between medium and content.

Experienced authors were invited to contribute travel-related stories to the installation, rather than relying solely on user-generated content. This provided quality stories displayed randomly during times of inactivity in order to maintain fresh content.

The FNC0313 installation was a five-week deployment at the main entrance of the university and involved approximately 15 h of observation and 119 interviewed passersby. The software prototype was used for rapid prototyping and easy deployment. Our attempt to reduce embarrassment by replacing the collocated interface with remote contributions via Twitter may in fact have hindered interaction by limiting opportunities for socializing [7]. Passersby did not see others interact and may therefore have perceived the installation as not being directed at them or without relevance. However, the waiting time afforded by the waiting line for the university bar provided an optimal viewing position of the installation and allowed enough time for passersby to discover, read, post and comment (amongst themselves) on the story or installation.

Overall, our invited authors produced compelling "micro-stories" and felt challenged by the new storytelling media. One author described the experiment as "a fascinating intersection between technology and the humanities".

## 4.3 Deployment Three: MStoryG

During our research we found that the vast majority of passersby recognized the display as "the one from the airport". This generated curiosity and the repurposed and re-contextualized display did attract attention. We noted that passerby contributions accounted for a minimal percentage of the overall stories created, with the larger body of content produced by our invited experienced authors. When feeding a storytelling installation we found it is best to rely on users who are confident in providing story content, while still leaving open the possibility of user interaction and contribution.

The objective for this study was to deploy MStoryG on the (physical) Solari Udine split-flap airport display, and to explore how receptive the public was to serendipitous storytelling activity and whether or not it was possible to create a culture of participation within high anxiety "non-places" such as airport terminals.

**Fig. 1.** The MStoryG installation deployed at the airport's baggage claim area.

In the next sections we describe MStoryG's final case study at the regional (international) airport (see Fig. 1), including the installation, design process, and implementation.

### 4.4 A Space Within a Place

Earlier results [22, 23] introduced the idea of an airport terminal as a possible location for deployment of the MStoryG installation. We envisioned a stronger relationship between travel-themed storytelling, the airport display, and the airport environment. The latter affords long waiting times and a variety of leisure spaces available for discretionary activities [42]—also noted in deployment two. We built upon this premise to explore airport (transportation) terminals and storytelling installations.

MStoryG was deployed at an international airport. According to the airport's statistics [4], in May 2013 the airport handled 1,688 flights (domestic and international) accounting for a total of 181,413 passengers. International airports are large and complex ecosystems. Elaborate social interactions, complicated navigation, strict security procedures, long wait times, anxiety, stress, frustration and confusion are common pitfalls of the airport experience for many travellers. At the same time, these are spaces tightly governed by security and thus access to these spaces is limited and highly controlled.

MStoryG's target audiences were passengers (visiting tourists), which could share a story about their stay at the island. Initially, the installation was going to be deployed near the boarding gates. Here passengers generally have the greatest amount of free time, and we hypothesized more availability and openness to explore the space and interact with installations. Unfortunately, this is a high security area and given the short time frame another location had to be chosen.

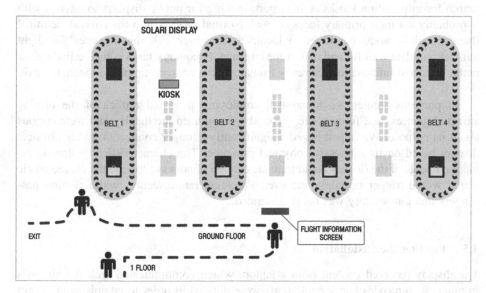

**Fig. 2.** Placement of the Solari display and kiosk within the baggage claim area.

The Arrivals terminal, and more specifically the baggage claim area, seemed like the most interesting (available) option due with similar conditions to the boarding gates, with wait times that would allow passengers to contribute. Their flight, possibly the most anxious part of the travel experience, would be over, and the experience of their journey could provide material and motivation for a story. The target audience was maintained, while the installation's "voice" took on a more greeting role rather than the initially ideated.

**The Design Space.** Free space is limited within baggage claim areas. Moreover, the best locations to deploy a public display or installation are occupied by paying advertisements. In terms of identifying the optimal position for MStoryG, initial observations of passenger flow led us to choose the back wall of the baggage claim area (see Fig. 2), between baggage carousels one and two (out of four). The proximity to the baggage carousels guaranteed a supply of stationary passengers (people waiting for their bags) with enough time to lurk and possibly contribute. A support pillar near the display was repurposed as a canvas to display information about MStoryG and information on how to interact through social networks, SMS, and using the kiosk (standard airport kiosk with a touchscreen and with full size keyboard). The kiosk was located in front of the pillar, allowing passengers access to project information, the interface, and a view of the display (see Fig. 1).

**Competing for Passenger Attention.** The baggage claim area represents one of the first contacts passengers may have with the airport and/or a city or country. It is overloaded with information and this required MStoryG to compete for passengers' attention with a profusion of publicity panels, airport information signage and tourist information, customer desks and information kiosks. While some travellers might search for information kiosks at an airport, looking for public displays to interact with is probably not their primary focus or goal. Normal tasks within the Arrivals terminal (baggage claim area) would be to locate the baggage belt that matches the flight number and then wait for and collect the baggage. Secondary tasks could be finding car rental or tourist information, currency exchange, customs, or simply to locate the exit.

In previous studies we found that employing a virtual replica of the display attracted glances, and furthermore, passersby recognized the display and were curious about its purpose. We hypothesized a significantly stronger connection to the physical display based on its impressive physical presence. The characteristically slow information update of the display could mitigate change blindness [36] and the characteristic sound would trigger nostalgia and even Proustian reminiscence, while alerting passengers that a new story was being generated.

### 4.5  Feeding the Installation

The display received content from a laptop, which communicated with the airport's Intranet. Web proxies and specific ports were defined in order to comply with airport Internet security policies and measures. The web server was implemented in Python using the CherryPy framework that employed a long-polling mechanism to keep all connected clients synchronized. Contributions are stored in a MySQL database and are pulled and served by the webserver as individual XML files.

Stories could be sent to the installation through SMS, Twitter and Facebook—allowing for our invited international writers, remote contributors, or passersby that prefer this more private interaction through mobile phones—or through an authoring platform developed in Adobe Flash. This interface was created to deploy on an airport touch-screen kiosk (also available online) and functions as an attempt to lower the entry interaction barrier that would otherwise arise from complicated airport Wi-Fi connections and international mobile data plans. The application emulated the look and feel of the physical Solari Udine display. Here users could control all modules available on the physical Solari display (including lights) through direct interaction, choosing precisely where and how to display their story.

The airport management required that all content displayed on the installation be pre-monitored and filtered. Twitter (and SMS) contributions were filtered by "favorite" or "retweeting" through the Twitter MStoryG account. Only favorited or retweeted tweets were stored in the database and displayed. Facebook posts followed a similar process by "liking" posts through the MStoryG account. Contributions from the kiosk were filtered through a webpage. This human-filtering method seemed the most reliable due to the ability of users to write horizontally, vertically and obliquely (through the kiosk interface). Moreover, the airport required filtering of content for offensive comments, prank messages, and negative passenger experiences.

While pre-monitoring content introduced delays of several minutes between interaction and viewing the story on the display, research has shown that the majority (70 %) of users display a tolerance of up to 10 min [17].

## 5 Evaluation Protocol and Methodology

People perceive art installations differently than they would more task-specific or unequivocal installations. Evaluating these installations through traditional HCI models, such as stressed quantitative methods, tells us little about the relationship resulting from the interaction between users and the installation [11, 16]. In order to measure passerby engagement with MStoryG we built upon work by Mathew et al., Brignull and Rogers, and Müller et al. [7, 32, 36]. The work performed by these authors employs the notion of engagement trajectories, defined by interaction phases, activities and thresholds, to evaluate the level of user engagement and curiosity.

The evaluation protocol was performed as follows: in-field observations and semi-structured interviews with passengers and passersby (performed by a single researcher), focusing on evaluation during two key phases, and textual analysis of the user-generated content.

- Perception Phase: At this phase it is possible to understand how users perceive and react to MStoryG upon first contact (glance). Using Brignull's "thresholds of activity" [7] we should be able to measure social engagement with MStoryG by measuring the peripheral awareness threshold (people are peripherally aware of the installation but at the time do not intend to interact with it), the focal awareness threshold (people in this activity zone are engaged in social activities relating to the installation), and direct interaction (here users are in direct interaction with the installation and formulate a deeper understanding of the installation). Finally, we should be able to evaluate the level of social apprehension.
- Interaction/Engagement Phase: Our objective during this phase is to observe the spectator experience and the "honey pot" effect [7]. Semi-structured interviews should allow us to identify if there is any social buzz around the installation and to ascertain whether bystanders are engaged with the installation.

Categorization and a textual analysis of the content created at the airport kiosk for the installation was performed in order to understand how users approached the storytelling concept and if they repurposed and subverted the airport display in other ways.

## 6 Findings

In this section we present 26 h of observations covering the arrival of 86 (domestic and international) flights distributed over four weeks. All stories were displayed in English. We conducted 49 short semi-structured interviews (97 people) to complement the observations. Due to passengers' anxiety in retrieving their bags, interviews were usually short, allowing on average two to three questions.

The number of passengers present at the baggage claim area varied from an estimate of 90 for a single flight, up to three concurrent flights resulting in an estimate of over 300 passengers—all of whom take the same route to the baggage claim area. Upon arrival the primary task for the majority of passengers is to search the space for digital screens containing their flight information that tells them which baggage carousel their bags will be delivered on. Passengers then search the area for the correct carousel, place themselves nearby, and wait. The baggage carousel rotates clockwise, thus passengers normally locate themselves to the front left side of the carousel. Average wait time for baggage was relatively short, between 5 and 10 min.

The airport distributes use of the baggage carousels. For flights with baggage at belts three and four (the furthest), passengers were largely unaware of the installation.

Even at belts one and two, MStoryG was often overlooked by passengers due to their location to the front left of the carousel, where they were out of sight of the installation—blocked by pillars and the belt carousel mechanism—or were too far away to hear the sound of the display's mechanical flaps. Passengers moving through the area, i.e., walking straight out of the baggage claim area, would rarely notice the installation on the back wall (to their right side) between the two baggage carousels.

## 6.1     Attracting Passerby Glances Using Sound

One of the most noticeable benefits of the mechanical display was the sound it produced when refreshing content and how recognizable that sound was to travellers. We observed 157 travellers waiting for their bags at belts one and two that turned their attention toward the display while it changed stories (producing the characteristic mechanical flaps sound). Three travellers standing on the right side of belt two heard the sound of the display and looked around to find the source. Due to the awkward placement of the board, however, they could not discover where the sound was coming from, so they did not glance at or move toward the board.

On the other hand, nine of the 157 travellers, as well as reacting to the noise by glancing back and reading the content, actually left the belt carousel to approach and explore the installation by observing and reading the kiosk and adjacent information.

## 6.2     Passerby Perception: Installation and Stories

A family of three standing near belt two did notice the display due to the sound. They glanced back and read the story. When asked about what they perceived the installation to be, one of the travellers commented: "This is about famous authors, quotes and stories", while another said: "I think it's for small stories." A family of four looked at the display while passing by, commenting and laughing together. One said: "When I heard the noise I knew it was an old fashioned display. I haven't seen one of those in a long time. Then I looked and saw no information but a story I really liked." Another traveller who was observed reading the stories responded: "Well, I looked first because

I'm not doing anything while I wait for my bags and the noise is attractive. When I read the story it was unexpected and I thought it was a great idea. I liked to watch because the stories are funny and a good way to kill the waiting time for bags."

Overall, 23 (of 97) of the travellers approached commented positively on how "unexpected", "funny", and "great" the stories were, and how surprised they were to discover the installation. Certain expectations relating to the purpose of the display were also found, relating to its original use in displaying flight information.

## 6.3    Traveller Focus, Goals and Objectives

Fifty-two, of 96 travellers interviewed, commented on how they were solely interested in their baggage and were not able to pay attention to the installation. ("I am only worried about getting my bags. Nothing else.") Other travellers said they preferred to focus on subsequent activities ("I want to get the bags quickly so I can go to the car rental desk"). Travellers intent on retrieving bags would glance at the display apparently in the hope of finding relevant information but quickly lost interest when they saw it did not.

## 6.4    Reading Stories and Authoring Stories

Twenty-six, of the 157 observed travellers, were noted reading more than one story on the display. Thirteen travellers were observed engaging in discussions about the installation and the stories being presented. Three travellers were observed taking photos of the display and kiosk. A 60-year-old female traveller heard the noise of the Solari display changing and went to find its origin and read the story, immediately returning to belt three once it started rotating. Expectedly, children were among the most curious often approaching the display to examine its mechanics.

Three travellers were observed interacting with the kiosk (the authoring interface). All three approached the kiosk, read the information, and then typed and submitted their messages. They waited near the kiosk for their story to appear, and when it was not immediately displayed, they returned to their belt. One of the three was observed repeatedly checking the display every time new content was displayed.

**Content Created.**   Over a four-week period, 88 "micro-fiction" stories were authored and displayed at MStoryG. Collaborators and invited authors contributed with 60 tweets and 28 Facebook posts. These users took on the storytelling role easily and were self-motivated to continue authoring stories during the initial weeks.

A total of 87 unique interactions with the authoring platform were received at the kiosk adjacent to the Solari display. After filtering out empty submissions, 64 individual submissions remained. A frequency analysis was performed with mean, standard deviation and a 95 % confidence. Three gibberish messages were received from children playing with the kiosk keyboard. The majority of contributions through the kiosk interface were categorized as "messages" (e.g. "We are waiting for our luggage") representing nearly 43.8 %. Greeting messages such as "Happy holidays the Browns" represented 15.6 % of all contributions. Stories accounted for 6.3 % while flight references, e.g. "22.30 TAP", accounted for 7.8 %.

# 7  Discussion

The interviews led us to acknowledge an improvement in traveller experience through the serendipitous discovery of "funny" stories, as some users described them. Additional comments supported the initiative, declaring that reading stories from others was a good way to pass the time. This reaction was most noticeable among those who were perceived, through observations and interviews, as being less anxious—about retrieving baggage or what to do after retrieving their bags—and thus free to explore and consume (or contribute to) the installation. Those who were mainly focused on their primary task (baggage retrieval), or were anxious, lost, or in a hurry, avoided or ignored the installation and displayed little or no interest in MStoryG, or in anything else that did not actively contribute toward their task.

Repurposing the mechanical airport display succeeded in attracting travellers' attention mainly due to its recognizable and distinguishable sound. This led travellers to expect specific information (baggage or flight information), but at the same time it also helped to emphasize the serendipitous story discovery. Playing with the nostalgia and familiarity of the display in its original context surprised travellers with an unexpected new media channel for storytelling. On the other hand, a certain type of traveller expected relevant, airport-related information to be displayed, and when they perceived the content as stories, they lost interest in the installation.

Location is key within these spaces, especially because in most cases users will not go out of their way to interact with or explore displays or installations that do not seem to offer airport specific information. The chosen location, between belts 1 and 2, did not expose the installation to the majority of passersby within the space; rather it focused on a small subset of specifically placed passengers. We argue that the characteristics of this location—an affordance of spare time to indulge in exploration even if still focused on their primary goal—justify its use in the installation, in comparison for example with the main foot path on the way to the exit. We found no noticeable "honey pot" effect, and would argue that this is due to passengers being primarily concerned with their baggage. Even with up to 15 min of waiting time, passengers were found to remain static at or near the baggage retrieval belt. As indicated by Brignull et al. [7], public displays and installations should be located near to leisure spaces in order to nurture this type of social behavior.

In terms of subverting the authoritative voice of the traditional airport display we observed passengers writing their names for display to the public. This was more noticeable than in the previous case studies. In previous studies we found a stronger connection to flight and travel topics, and meta-references to real events, while at the airport terminal (with the physical display) a stronger, more personal connection was observed: greeting messages, writing messages to loved ones, or writing one's own name were more prevalent. It might seem that the physical space would not influence the type of content being displayed, but the context where the installation is located (e.g. being located at the Arrivals terminal) might influence the display in favor of taking on more of a welcoming or greeting role.

We found that users had strong preconceived notions about the airport display: that it is regulated by an authority, is non-interactive, or displays only airport-related information. This could have hindered interaction by raising doubts that it would be possible to write on the "airport's board". Moreover, because of spatial constraints the kiosk and the installation information were located at some distance from the display. The connection was visible for those passengers that viewed the display from the front (right side of belt 1 and left side of belt 2), where the kiosk and information are located to the front of the display between the belts. For those passengers that viewed the display from an angle, however, the kiosk and information were not in their field of view and thus did not perceive the display as interactive. We attempted to guide people towards the installation through signage on the floor and overhead, but without observable success. It is crucial to keep the information and interaction together, as most passengers will not go far in exploring the space to search for it.

Local contributors (through the kiosk) expected the content they introduced to appear immediately on the display. This occurred despite our efforts to mitigate the assumption by indicating that the stories would be moderated. For asynchronous interaction clear feedback should be provided to the user in terms of an estimate of how long it might take to view their story. The kiosk was the preferred method for collocated interaction. Airports are notoriously difficult places to get Internet access, limiting the reach of Facebook and Twitter. SMS interaction was mainly targeted to locals, being unattractive for those with restrictive overseas cellular data plans.

The airport terminal provided a broad spectrum of travellers from a wide variety of backgrounds and demographics. The continuous supply of new passengers allowed smaller amounts of content to remain fresh for longer periods of time. However, limited exposure and competing goals and activities set limitations on user interaction and thus did not afford a culture of participation.

## 7.1  Viability of the Evaluation Protocol

We encountered a number of difficulties in employing the frameworks of Mathew et al., Brignull and Rogers, and Müller et al. [7, 32, 36] in this space due to the large number of individuals rushing toward the baggage carousels. Furthermore, the majority of individuals only discovered the installation after placing themselves near the baggage carousel, and at that point they were already waiting for their bags. Moreover, due to the distance between the installation and the baggage carousel, it was difficult to understand whether individuals were engaged with the installation or their baggage-retrieving task. Interviews were essential in disambiguating these cases.

# 8 Conclusion

This paper presented MStoryG, an "in-the-wild" public display based storytelling installation located inside an international airport's baggage claim area. The iterative design and deployment process allowed for continuous refinement of the concept and installation up to the final deployment. This unique installation surprised travellers by repurposing an old-fashioned mechanical airport display as a storytelling medium where travellers could share stories. However, the very nature of so-called "non-places" such as airport terminals limits the culture of participation, not only due to their alienating effect and lack of a normal sense of place and time but due to being such distracting, fast-paced, anxiety-filled spaces. As in previous studies, we did find a strong connection between individual, object (the airport display) and space (airport terminal), with curiosity triggered by the display's distinctive sound, and users seeming pleased to learn that a project was repurposing such a familiar, nostalgic object. We hypothesize that such a connection could not have been achieved, for example, with an ordinary television screen.

Nevertheless, our objective was to actively engage passers by and create a storytelling community around a physical space, and in this experiment we found minimal evidence of the participation of passersby in authoring coherent stories. On the other hand the experienced authors who participated in our project were intrigued and felt challenged by this new medium for storytelling. The restricted number of characters permitted and the connection between social networks and analogue displays within public spaces seemed compelling on both sides, with readers responding positively to the stories provided.

# References

1. Alborzi, H., et al.: Designing StoryRooms: interactive storytelling spaces for children. In: Proceedings of the Conference on Designing Interactive Systems Processes, Practices, Methods, and Techniques - DIS 2000, pp. 95–104. ACM Press, New York (2000)
2. Amadeus: Reinventing the Airport Ecosystem (2012)
3. American Customer Satisfaction Index, A.: June 2013 and Historical ACSI Benchmarks. http://www.theacsi.org/?option=com_content&view=article&id=213&catid=14&Itemid=262&q=M06&sort=Y2013
4. ANAM: Indicadores de Tráfego - Traffic Indicators. http://www.anam.pt/Media/Default/DocGalleries/AMPTIndicadores2013/IG_TrafegoPT_2013-03_Fnc.pdf
5. Augé, M.: Non-Places: Introduction to an Anthropology of Supermodernity. Verso, London (1995)
6. Awori, K., et al.: Flytalk: social media to meet the needs of air travelers. In: Proceedings of the 2012 ACM Annual Conference Extended Abstracts on Human Factors in Computing Systems Extended Abstracts - CHI EA 2012, p. 1769. ACM Press, New York (2012)
7. Brignull, H., Rogers, Y.: Enticing people to interact with large public displays in public spaces. In: Proceedings of INTERACT (2003)

8. Cavazza, M., et al.: Madame bovary on the holodeck : immersive interactive storytelling. In: Proceedings of the 15th International Conference on Multimedia - MULTIMEDIA 2007, p. 651. ACM Press, New York (2007)

9. Cohen, S., Janicki-Deverts, D.: Who's stressed? Distributions of psychological stress in the United States in probability samples from 1983, 2006, and 2009. J. Appl. Soc. Psychol. **42**(6), 1320–1334 (2012)

10. Dow, S., et al.: Exploring spatial narratives and mixed reality experiences in Oakland Cemetery. In: Proceedings of the 2005 ACM SIGCHI International Conference on Advances in Computer Entertainment Technology - ACE 2005, pp. 51–60. ACM Press, New York (2005)

11. England, D., et al.: Digital art: evaluation, appreciation, critique (invited SIG). In: Proceedings of the 2012 ACM Annual Conference Extended Abstracts on Human Factors in Computing Systems Extended Abstracts - CHI EA 2012, p. 1213. ACM Press, New York (2012)

12. Fischer, G.: Understanding, fostering, and supporting cultures of participation. Interactions **18**(3), 42 (2011)

13. Fortin, C., et al.: Posting for community and culture: considerations for the design of interactive digital bulletin boards. In: Proceedings of the 32nd Annual ACM Conference on Human Factors in Computing Systems - CHI 2014, pp. 1425–1434. ACM Press, New York (2014)

14. Gaver, W.W., et al.: Ambiguity as a resource for design. In: Proceedings of the Conference on Human Factors in Computing Systems - CHI 2003, p. 233. ACM Press, New York (2003)

15. Gorbet, M., et al.: Collaboration with the future: an infrastructure for Art + Technology at the San José International Airport. Leonardo **44**(4), 334–345 (2011)

16. Greenberg, S., Buxton, B.: Usability evaluation considered harmful (some of the time). In: Proceeding of the Twenty-Sixth Annual CHI Conference on Human Factors in Computing Systems - CHI 2008, p. 111. ACM Press, New York (2008)

17. Greis, M., et al.: I can wait a minute: uncovering the optimal delay time for pre-moderated user-generated content on public displays. In: Proceedings of the 32nd Annual ACM Conference on Human Factors in Computing Systems - CHI 2014, pp. 1435–1438. ACM Press, New York (2014)

18. Gustafsson, A., et al.: Believable environments – generating interactive storytelling in vast location-based pervasive games. In: Proceedings of the 2006 ACM SIGCHI International Conference on Advances in Computer Entertainment Technology - ACE 2006, p. 24. ACM Press, New York (2006)

19. Hinrichs, U., et al.: Interactive public displays. IEEE Comput. Graph. Appl. **33**(2), 25–27 (2013)

20. Huang, E.M., Koster, A., Borchers, J.: Overcoming assumptions and uncovering practices: when does the public really look at public displays? In: Indulska, J., Patterson, D.J., Rodden, T., Ott, M. (eds.) PERVASIVE 2008. LNCS, vol. 5013, pp. 228–243. Springer, Heidelberg (2008)

21. Jenkins, H.: Confronting the Challenges of Participatory Culture: Media Education for the 21st Century. MIT Press, Cambridge (2009)

22. Jorge, C., et al.: Fostering ambiguity: decontextualizing and repurposing a familiar public display. In: Proceedings of the Biannual Conference of the Italian Chapter of SIGCHI on - CHItaly 2013, pp. 1–10. ACM Press, New York (2013)

23. Jorge, C., Hanna, J., Nisi, V., Nunes, N., Caldeira, M., Innela, G., Marinho, A.: Storytelling and the use of social media in digital art installations. In: Koenitz, H., Sezen, T.I., Ferri, G., Haahr, M., Sezen, D., Çatak, G. (eds.) ICIDS 2013. LNCS, vol. 8230, pp. 233–244. Springer, Heidelberg (2013)
24. Kearney, R.: On Stories. Routledge, London/NY. 156 (2002)
25. Kelliher, A., Slaney, M.: Tell Me a Story. IEEE Multimed. 19(1), 4 (2012)
26. Khaled, R., et al.: StoryTrek : experiencing stories in the real World. In: Proceedings of the 15th International Academic MindTrek Conference on Envisioning Future Media Environments - MindTrek 2011, p. 125. ACM Press, New York (2011)
27. Kjeldskov, J., Paay, J.: Public pervasive computing: making the invisible visible. Computer (Long. Beach. Calif) 39(9), 60–65 (2006)
28. Kukka, H., et al.: What makes you click: exploring visual signals to entice interaction on public displays. In: Proceedings of the SIGCHI Conference on Human Factors in Computing Systems - CHI 2013, p. 1699. ACM Press, New York (2013)
29. Likarish, P., Winet, J.: Exquisite corpse 2.0. In: Proceedings of the Designing Interactive Systems Conference on - DIS 2012, p. 564. ACM Press, New York (2012)
30. Linehan, C., et al.: Blowtooth: pervasive gaming in unique and challenging environments. In: Proceedings of the 28th of the International Conference Extended Abstracts on Human Factors in Computing Systems - CHI EA 2010, p. 2695. ACM Press, New York (2010)
31. Madej, K.: Towards digital narrative for children: from education to entertainment, a historical perspective. Comput. Entertain. 1(1), 1–17 (2003)
32. Mathew, A., et al.: Post-it note art. In: Proceedings of the 8th ACM Conference on Creativity and Cognition - C&C 2011, p. 61. ACM Press, New York (2011)
33. Memarovic, N., et al.: Using public displays to stimulate passive engagement, active engagement, and discovery in public spaces. In: Proceedings of the 4th Media Architecture Biennale Conference on Participation - MAB 2012, pp. 55–64. ACM Press, New York (2012)
34. Michelis, D., Müller, J.: The audience funnel: observations of gesture based interaction with multiple large displays in a City Center. Int. J. Hum. Comput. Interact. 27(6), 562–579 (2011)
35. Müller, J., Wilmsmann, D., Exeler, J., Buzeck, M., Schmidt, A., Jay, T., Krüger, A.: Display blindness: the effect of expectations on attention towards digital signage. In: Tokuda, H., Beigl, M., Friday, A., Brush, A.J.B., Tobe, Y. (eds.) Pervasive 2009. LNCS, vol. 5538, pp. 1–8. Springer, Heidelberg (2009)
36. Müller, J., et al.: Requirements and design space for interactive public displays. In: Proceedings of the International Conference on Multimedia - MM 2010, p. 1285. ACM Press, New York (2010)
37. Muller, M., et al.: We are all lurkers: consuming behaviors among authors and readers in an enterprise file-sharing service. In: Proceedings of the 16th ACM International Conference on Supporting Group Work - GROUP 2010, p. 201. ACM Press, New York (2010)
38. Nielsen, J.: Participation Inequality: Encouraging More User to Contribute. http://www.nngroup.com/articles/participation-inequality/
39. Nisi, V., et al.: Location-Aware Multimedia Stories: Turning Spaces into Places. Universidade Católica, Port (2008)
40. Paay, J., et al.: Location-based storytelling in the urban environment. In: Proceedings of the 20th Australasian Conference on Computer-Human Interaction Designing for Habitus and Habitat - OZCHI 2008, p. 122. ACM Press, New York (2008)
41. Paulos, E., Beckmann, C.: Sashay: designing for wonderment. In: Proceedings of the SIGCHI Conference on Human Factors in Computing Systems - CHI 2006, p. 881. ACM Press, New York (2006)

42. Popovic, V., et al.: Passenger experience in an airport : an activity-centred approach. In: IASDR 2009 Proceedings, 18–22 September 2009
43. Rashid, O., et al.: Extending cyberspace: location based games using cellular phones. Comput. Entertain. 4(1), 4 (2006)
44. Schroeter, R., et al.: People, content, location: sweet spotting urban screens for situated engagement. In: Proceedings of the Designing Interactive Systems Conference on - DIS 2012, p. 146. ACM Press, New York (2012)
45. Smith, J.: GrandChair: conversational collection of grandparents' stories (2000)
46. Takahashi, M., et al.: The active lurker: influence of an in-house online community on its outside environment. In: 2003 International Conference on ACM, pp. 1–10 (2003)
47. Takakuwa, S., Oyama, T.: Simulation analysis of international-departure passenger flows in an airport terminal. In: 2003 International Conference on Machine Learning & Cybernetics (IEEE Cat. No.03EX693), pp. 1627–1634 (2003)
48. Weiner, S.: Newark Airport's New United Terminal Looks Like a Foodie Theme Park. http://www.fastcodesign.com/3038636/newark-airports-new-united-terminal-looks-like-a-foodie-theme-park
49. Tim Burton's Cadavre Exquis. http://burtonstory.com/connect.php

# Estimating Visual Comfort in Stereoscopic Displays Using Electroencephalography: A Proof-of-Concept

Jérémy Frey[1,2(✉)], Aurélien Appriou[1], Fabien Lotte[1],
and Martin Hachet[1]

[1] Inria Bordeaux Sud-Ouest/LaBRI, Bordeaux, France
{Jeremy.Frey,Aurelien.Appriou,Fabien.Lotte,
Martin.Hachet}@inria.fr
[2] University Bordeaux, Bordeaux, France

**Abstract.** With stereoscopic displays, a too strong depth sensation could impede visual comfort and result in fatigue or pain. We used Electroencephalography (EEG), which records brain activity, to develop a novel brain-computer interface that monitors users' states in order to reduce visual strain. We present the first proof-of-concept system that discriminates comfortable conditions from uncomfortable ones during stereoscopic vision using EEG. It reacts within 1 s to depth variations, achieving 63 % accuracy on average and 74 % when 7 consecutive variations are measured. This study could lead to adaptive systems that automatically suit stereoscopic displays to users and viewing conditions.

**Keywords:** Stereoscopy · Comfort · EEG · Adaptive system · Evaluation

## 1 Introduction

Stereoscopic displays have been developed and used for years in computer science, for example to improve data visualization or to better manipulate virtual objects [5]. However, only recently did they begin to reach users beyond experts, at home, with "3D" movies or game consoles. Yet, whenever devices use shutter or polarized glasses, parallax barrier or head-mounted displays (as with the Oculus Rift) to produce pairs of images, visual discomfort could occur when the stereoscopic effect is too strong. Some viewers could even suffer pain [10]. To mitigate those symptoms and adapt the viewing experience to each user, we propose an innovative method which can discriminate uncomfortable situations from comfortable ones. It reacts quickly (within 1 s), without calling upon users, so it does not disrupt the viewing. Our solution is versatile because all stereoscopic displays use the same mechanism to give the illusion of depth. They send a different image to the left and right eyes. As with natural vision, the visual fields of our eyes overlap and the difference between the two images helps our brain to estimate objects' distance.

To facilitate images merge, observers rely on two mechanisms. First, they need to maintain the point of interest at the same place on both their retinas. Thus, the closer an

© IFIP International Federation for Information Processing 2015
J. Abascal et al. (Eds.): INTERACT 2015, Part IV, LNCS 9299, pp. 354–362, 2015.
DOI: 10.1007/978-3-319-22723-8_28

object gets, the more eyeballs rotate inward. This is called "vergence", which also happens with stereoscopic displays. Second, in a way similar to how camera lenses operate, crystalline lenses need to focus light beams. They deform accordingly to objects' position in order to obtain a clear picture. This other physiological phenomenon is called "accommodation" and is *not* replicated with stereoscopic displays. In a natural environment, vergence and accommodation are locked to objects' positions and occur altogether. But since the focal plane in stereoscopic displays is fixed, accommodation will not change. The discrepancy between vergence and accommodation is called the "vergence-accommodation conflict" (VAC). When it is too strong or lasts too long, visual discomfort occurs [10]. VAC is one of the major causes of visual discomfort and fatigue in stereoscopic displays [10]. Guidelines exist to limit the VAC and prevent such negative effects. In particular, Shibata et al. [15] established a "zone of comfort" using questionnaires, a zone within which the apparent depth of objects should remain to avoid discomfort. It takes into account the distance between viewers and displays. Unfortunately, screen settings, viewing angle or individual differences [10] make it hard to generalize such recommendations and use them as is.

Complementary to qualitative questionnaires, as used in [15], brain activity recordings enable to monitor users' states [6, 17]. One of the main advantages of such a technology to assess human-computer interaction (HCI) comes from the real-time insights that it could give. Electroencephalography (EEG) is among the cheapest and most lightweight devices that sense brain signals. Even though EEG has been used to investigate visual fatigue induced by stereoscopic display [1, 3, 11], those studies only compared flat images with stereoscopy. They do not control for objects virtual positions, hence they cannot account for different comfort conditions. Furthermore, most EEG studies related to stereoscopic display and comfort analyzed stimuli which last several minutes. Such protocols could not lead to adaptive systems that react quickly; they focus more on the overall fatigue induced by a prolonged exposition to stereoscopy rather than discomfort. In [7], we conducted a preliminary investigation that compared short appearances of virtual objects. We showed that the average brain activity induced by stereoscopic displays was different whether objects were presented within the zone of comfort or not. However, the study involved only 3 participants, and only investigated the averaged EEG signal, with no classification of the events.

Inspired by these works, we designed and tested a system that classifies EEG data to measure visual comfort. This system is a *passive* brain-computer interface (BCI, [17]). Our main contribution is to prove the feasibility of an EEG system that could estimate in near real-time (1 s delay) the visual comfort viewers are experiencing as they watch stereoscopic displays. It could be adapted to real-case scenarios by controlling the discrepancy between left and right images depending on the output of the classifier. It could be employed in different settings to improve HCI by easing users' comfort, for example when they manipulate 3D contents during prolonged periods of time – e.g., remote design or video games – or when people are watching 3D movies – especially when there are many rapid depth variations, e.g., in action sequences.

## 2 Experiment

### 2.1 Overview

Virtual objects were presented to participants at different apparent depths for a few seconds (see Fig. 1). Objects appeared either at a comfortable position ("C" condition) or at an uncomfortable one ("NC" condition). We displayed three kinds of grey objects over a black background: cube, cylinder and icosphere. Objects' orientations were randomized along the three axes to create various stimuli. Rotations were controlled so as the objects faces could not be orthogonal to the camera plane, thus preventing the appearance of artificial 2D shapes. There were no distracting elements and no variables besides the VAC were manipulated. We deprived the depth cues to control for VAC. For example, shadows would have helped to differentiate close objects from far ones without the need of binocular fusion [12].

We defined ranges inside and outside the zone of comfort according to [15]. Related to the location of participants sitting 1 m away from the display, in "C" condition virtual objects were positioned within [0.75 m; 0.85 m] (comfortable close) or within [1.3 m; 1.6 m] (comfortable far). In "NC" conditions, ranges were [0.35 m; 0.45 m] (uncomfortable close) or [4 m; 6 m] (uncomfortable far). During one-third of the trials, objects appeared "flat" (no stereoscopic effect, 1 m away, as far as the screen).

To assess their capacity to situate virtual objects in space and to maintain their vigilance high during the whole experiment, participants had to perform a task. When a question mark was shown on screen, "down", "space" or "up" keys were pressed to indicate whether objects appeared "in front of", "as far as" or "behind" the screen. With both hands on the keyboard, those keys ensured that participants' gaze was not leaving the screen and that participants' movements would not pollute EEG signals.

A trial started with a neutral stimulus, a 2D cross appearing on-screen for 1 to 1.5 s (Fig. 1). Then the virtual object appeared for 2.5 to 3 s. Finally, a question mark appeared for 1.5 s, a period during which participants had to perform the task. After that a new trial began. The first two time intervals, which randomly varied by 0.5 s, prevented participants to anticipate objects appearance and the moment they had to respond to the task. On average a trial took 5.5 s. There were 160 trials per C and NC conditions, randomly distributed. Trials were also equally split across 4 sub-sessions to let participants rest during the investigation and avoid a too tedious experiment.

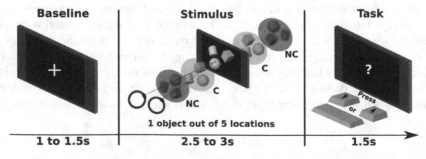

**Fig. 1.** One trial: cross (baseline), object at random depth, task.

## 2.2    Apparatus

Stereoscopic images were shown in 1080p resolution on a 65 inches Panasonic TX-P65VT20E active display – participants wore shuttered glasses. No matter the apparent depths of displayed objects, their sizes on screen remained identical. In combination with a diffuse illumination of the scene, this made it impossible to discriminate conditions without stereoscopy. The interpupillary distance used to compose stereoscopic images was set at 6 cm, an average value across population [4]. EEG signals were acquired at a 512 Hz sampling rate with 2 g.tec g.USBamp amplifiers. We used 4 electrodes to record electrooculographic (EOG) activity and 28 to record EEG. In the international 10-20 system, EOG electrodes were placed at LO1, LO2, IO1 and FP1 sites; EEG electrodes were placed at AF{3, 4}, F{7, 3, z, 4, 8}, FC{5, 1, 2, 6}, C {3, z, 4}, CP{5, 1, 2, 6}, P{7, 3, z, 4, 8}, PO{3, 4}, and O{1, z, 2} sites.

## 2.3    Participants

12 participants took part in the experiment: 5 females, 7 males, mean age 22.33 (SD = 1.15). They reported little use of stereoscopic displays: 1.91 (SD = 0.54) on a 5-point Likert scale (1: never; 2, 3, 4, 5: several times a year/month/week/day respectively). If needed, participants wore their optical corrections – there was enough space beneath the shutter glasses for regular glasses not to disrupt user experience. We made sure that no participant suffered from stereo blindness by using a TNO test [13].

## 2.4    Measures

Beside EEG measures, task scores were computed from participants' assessment of objects' virtual position in space – whether they appeared "in front of", "as far as" or "behind" the screen. During the 1.5 s time window when question marks appeared, the first key pressed, if any, was taken into account. A correct answer resulted in 1 point, an incorrect in -1 point and none in 0 point. Final scores were normalized from [-480;480] to [-1;1] intervals. A questionnaire inquiring the symptoms associated with the different apparent depths preceded first trials and followed each sub-session. There were 2 items, one asking about participants' vision clarity and the other about eyes tiredness. The corresponding 5-point Likert scales were adapted from [15], "1" representing no negative symptoms and "5" severe symptoms. We measured respectively how well participants saw the stereoscopic images and how comfortable they felt, averaging in total 10 answers for each C/NC conditions.

## 2.5    Procedure

The experiment occurred in a quiet environment, with a dimmed ambient light and was approximately 90 min long. It comprised the following steps:

1: Participants were seated 1 m away from the stereoscopic screen (distance from their eyes) and filled an informed consent form and a demographic questionnaire.

2: Participants' stereoscopic vision was assessed with a TNO test.

3: An EEG cap was installed onto participants' heads.

4: The "symptoms" questionnaire was given orally, experimenter manually triggering objects appearances and waiting for participants' answers during this phase. There was 1 object per virtual depth range (C close/far, NC close/far) and 2 flat objects; making 6 randomized objects per questionnaire.

5: A training session occurred. During this session participants had the opportunity to get familiar with the trials and with the task.

6: The 4 sub-sessions, described previously, occurred. When a sub-session ended, participants were given again the questionnaire of step 4 before they could rest, drink and eat. Once they felt ready, we pursued with the next sub-session.

# 3   Analyses

Data gathered from the 4 sub-sessions were concatenated. We applied a 0.5 Hz high-pass filter to correct DC drift and a 25 Hz low-pass filter to remove from our study signal frequencies that were more likely to be polluted by muscle activity. We extracted the 320 epochs – "slices" of EEG – around C and NC stimuli onsets, from -1 s to +2.5 s. Due to the substantial amount of data (3840 trials in total), we chose automated methods to clean the signals. The EEGLAB (http://sccn.ucsd.edu/eeglab/) function pop_autorej removed epochs that contained muscular artifacts ($\approx$ 10 %). Following the results from [8], EOG activity was suppressed using the ADJUST toolbox 1.1. After an Infomax independent component analysis (ICA), we removed from the original signal components that ADJUST labeled as eye blinks or eye movements (vertical and horizontal).

An event-related potential (ERP) corresponds to one or more "peaks" in EEG signals, associated with an event, here the appearance of stereoscopic images. Averaged ERPs across participants indicated that ERPs had a higher positive peak in C (see Fig. 2). Note that there were also some differences in EEG oscillations (not reported here due to space limitations), although less salient. Thus, in this study we only used ERP, as using EEG oscillations did not lead to any substantial improvement.

For classification, we first split the EEG dataset of each participant in two. The first half of the trials was used as a training set, to calibrate the classifier. The second half was used as a testing set, to test the classifier performances on unseen data, which simulates a real-case application. Feature extraction relied on the spatial filter from [9], which was specifically designed for ERPs classification, and reduced signals dimension from 28 EEG channels to 5 "virtual" channels whose signal is more discriminant between conditions. We selected a time window of 1 s. In order to reduce the number of features, we decimated the signal by a factor 16. As a result, there was 160 features by epoch (5 channels $\times$ 512 Hz $\times$ 1 s /16). We used shrinkage Linear Discriminant Analysis as a classifier, as recommended in [2] for ERP classification.

Although we used 1 s time windows as a basis for our analyses, we tested longer stimuli by clustering trials with Monte Carlo simulations. The principle is as follows: studying 3 presentations, we cluster 3 similar trials drawn from the testing set (e.g., "no-comfort", 3xNC). Then we look at individual classification results from the system

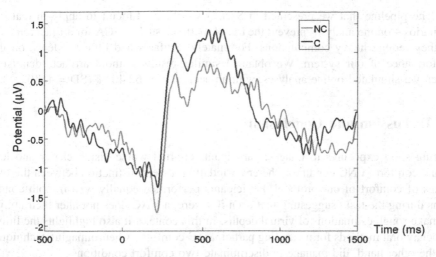

**Fig. 2.** Average ERP across 28 EEG electrodes and 12 participants. Blue: comfort condition; green: no-comfort condition ($\approx$ 160 trials each). The stereoscopic object appears at t = 0 ms (Color figure online).

(e.g., NC-NC-C) and keep the label which has the majority – in this case NC, the resulting classification is correct for this cluster. Had the classifier labelled trials as "C-C-C", the cluster would have been erroneously labeled as "C". Different combinations of trials were drawn from the testing set to compute the scores for n = 3,5,7.

## 4 Results

We used a Wilcoxon Signed-rank test to compare task scores between C and NC conditions. There was no significant effect (p = 0.78). There was a significant effect of the C/NC conditions on both symptoms items (p < 0.01). Participants reported more eye comfort (means: 2.41 *vs* 3.46) and more vision clarity (means: 2.10 *vs* 3.13) in C than in NC. We were able to predict with an average classification accuracy of 63.30 % (SD = 7.64) the visual comfort experienced by viewers (see Table 1).

**Table 1.** Classifier accuracy (in percentage) for each user. Mean: 63.30 %, SD: 7.64.

| User | 1 | 2 | 3 | 4 | 5 | 6 | 7 | 8 | 9 | 10 | 11 | 12 |
|------|------|------|------|------|------|------|------|------|------|------|------|------|
| Accuracy | 54.2 | 59.2 | 58.2 | 70.3 | 60.5 | 64.2 | 62.9 | 76.1 | 72.5 | 71.5 | 53.2 | 56.7 |

With Monte Carlo simulations, we investigated how the system would perform with the appearance of several images from the same condition. Classifier accuracy reached 68.91 % (SD = 10.32) over 3 trials. Over 5 trials the classification reached 90 % for some users, resulting in a 71.83 % average (SD = 12.28). With n = 7, one-third of the participants reached 90 % or more (74.08 % on average, SD = 13.39).

The pipeline that we presented in Sect. 3 would be difficult to apply in real-life scenarios – online analyses prevent the use of methods such as ICA for artifact removal as they require heavy computations. Fortunately, artifacts had little incidence on the performance of our system. We obtained similar results without artifacts denoising when we simulated online analyses, with an accuracy of 62.40 % (SD = 4.80).

# 5 Discussion and Conclusion

During short exposures to images, participant reported worse vision clarity and less visual comfort in NC condition, thereby validating a clear distinction between the two zones of comfort of our protocol. Participants performed equally well in both conditions during the task, suggesting that even if severe, a VAC does not alter their ability to make rough estimations of virtual depths. In this context, it also highlights the limits of behavioral methods for measuring participants' comfort. A neuroimaging technique, on the other hand, did manage to discriminate two comfort conditions.

EEG signals reflected the disparities in visual comfort. It was possible to build a classifier that achieved an accuracy greater than 63 %, with several participants exceeding 70 %. The system scored above chance level in all our analyses ($p < 0.01$) [14]. This score of 63 % accuracy, while not as high as some other established BCI systems, may be already sufficient to improve users' comfort. Indeed, on-the-fly correction of uncomfortable images can be seen as error correction. In such settings, detection rates from 65 % are acceptable to improve interactions [16]. These findings depend on the nature of the task; this is why we proposed a mechanism to increase the performance of the classifier by taking into account more than one object appearance. The system score improved by 6 points when we clustered trials by 3. During our simulations, the accuracy reached 90 % for some users with 5 trials, and for one-third of the participants over 7 trials. Therefore, this tool can estimate how many presentations are needed to reach a specific accuracy and suit the desired application. Interestingly enough, when using less EEG channels (only 14) we obtained similar classification accuracies – results not reported here due to space limitations – which suggests that our approach might be used with entry-level devices such as the Emotiv EPOC (https://emotiv.com/) or the OpenBCI system (http://www.openbci.com/).

We described an innovative system that can distinguish uncomfortable stereoscopic viewing conditions from comfortable ones by relying on EEG signals. We controlled the experimental conditions with questionnaires, founding significant differences in visual comfort between short exposures of images. Visual *comfort* was assessed, whereas existing studies focused on visual *fatigue* – a component that appears on the long term and that we propose to prevent beforehand.

Using short time windows (features were extracted over 1 s), we set the basis of a tool capable of monitoring user experience with stereoscopic displays in near real-time. Our offline analysis demonstrated the feasibility of such a method with clean EEG signals. We obtained a similar classification accuracy without computationally demanding artifacts filtering, demonstrating also that our approach could perfectly be applied online. Ongoing evaluations include considering additional EEG features such as EEG band power to further boost performances. The code that we used to generate the images and to process signals will be released in order to ease replication, in the hope that this combination of EEG and HCI evaluation will benefit end users.

Such a passive BCI can adapt the parameters to users' state (e.g., mental fatigue is likely to relate to visual fatigue) throughout the viewing. Moreover, a passive BCI does not disrupt work or the narrative of the stereoscopic environment. A passive stereoscopic comfort detector could potentially be useful for multiple applications, as a tool to: (1) objectively compare (possibly offline) different stereoscopic displays, (2) dynamically enhance stereoscopic effects, by increasing discrepancy without causing discomfort, (3) quickly calibrate stereoscopic displays, (4) dynamically adapt discrepancy to avoid discomfort (e.g., during 3D movies) or voluntarily cause discomfort (e.g., for basic science studies about perception), among many others.

We documented a novel solution to a famous issue – i.e., estimating stereoscopic discomfort – thus increasing fundamental knowledge. Besides 3D scenes control, by giving access in real-time to users' inner states, EEG will help to modulate more closely the viewing experience according to the effect one wants to achieve.

# References

1. Bang, J.W., Heo, H., Choi, J.-S., Park, K.R.: Assessment of eye fatigue caused by 3D displays based on multimodal measurements. Sensors **14**, 16467–16485 (2014)
2. Blankertz, B., Lemm, S., Treder, M., Haufe, S., Müller, K.-R.: Single-trial analysis and classification of ERP components–a tutorial. NeuroImage **56**, 814–825 (2011)
3. Cho, H., Kang, M.-K., Yoon, K.-J., Jun, S.C.: Feasibility study for visual discomfort assessment on stereo images using EEG. In: IC3D 2012 (2012)
4. Dodgson, N.A.: Variation and extrema of human interpupillary distance. In: SPIE 2004 (2004)
5. Drossis, G., Grammenos, D., Adami, I., Stephanidis, C.: 3D visualization and multimodal interaction with temporal information using timelines. In: Kotzé, P., Marsden, G., Lindgaard, G., Wesson, J., Winckler, M. (eds.) INTERACT 2013, Part III. LNCS, vol. 8119, pp. 214–231. Springer, Heidelberg (2013)
6. Frey, J., Mühl, C., Lotte, F., Hachet, M.: Review of the use of electroencephalography as an evaluation method for human-computer interaction. In: PhyCS 2014 (2014)
7. Frey, J., Pommereau, L., Lotte, F., Hachet, M.: Assessing the zone of comfort in stereoscopic displays using EEG. In: CHI EA 2014 (2014)
8. Ghaderi, F., Kim, S.K., Kirchner, E.A.: Effects of eye artifact removal methods on single trial P300 detection, a comparative study. J Neurosci Meth. **221C**, 41–47 (2013)
9. Hoffmann, U., Vesin, J., Ebrahimi, T.: Spatial filters for the classification of event-related potentials. In: ESANN 2006 (2006)
10. Lambooij, M.: IJsselsteijn, W., Fortuin, M., Heynderickx, I.: Visual discomfort and visual fatigue of stereoscopic displays: a review. J. Imaging Sci. Technol. **53**, 030201 (2009)
11. Li, H.-C.O., Seo, J., Kham, K., Lee, S.: Measurement of 3D visual fatigue using event-related potential (ERP): 3D oddball paradigm. In: 3DTV-CON 2008 (2008)
12. Mikkola, M., Boev, A., Gotchev, A.: Relative importance of depth cues on portable autostereoscopic display. In: MoViD 2010 (2010)

13. Momeni-Moghadam, H., Kundart, J., Ehsani, M., Gholami, K.: Stereopsis with TNO and titmus tests in symptomatic and asymptomatic university students. J. Behav. Optom. **23**(2), 35–39 (2012). http://www.oepf.org/journal/pdf/jbo-volume-23-issue-2-stereopsis-tno-and-titmus-testssymptomatic-and-asymptomatic-unive
14. Müller-Putz, G., Scherer, R., Brunner, C., Leeb, R., Pfurtscheller, G.: Better than random? a closer look on BCI results. Int. J Bioelectromagnetism **10**, 52–55 (2008)
15. Shibata, T., Kim, J., Hoffman, D.M., Banks, M.S.: The zone of comfort: predicting visual discomfort with stereo displays. J Vis. **11**, 1–29 (2011). doi:10.1167/11.8.11
16. Vi, C., Subramanian, S.: Detecting error-related negativity for interaction design. In: CHI 2012 (2012)
17. Zander, T.O., Kothe, C.: Towards passive brain-computer interfaces: applying brain-computer interface technology to human-machine systems in general. J. Neural. Eng. **8**(2), 025005 (2011). doi:10.1088/1741-2560/8/2/025005

# Exploring the Use of Virtual Environments in an Industrial Site Design Process

Ashley Colley[1(✉)], Jani Väyrynen[1], and Jonna Häkkilä[2]

[1] CIE, University of Oulu, Oulu, Finland
{ashley.colley, jani.vayrynen}@cie.fi
[2] Faculty of Art and Design, University of Lapland, Rovaniemi, Finland
jonna.hakkila@ulapland.fi

**Abstract.** Virtual environments are becoming more commonly used in urban planning and the construction industry. In this paper, we investigate whether exploring a 3D model of a factory site can identify design problems related to human perception, such as exposing users to heights without sufficient protection. Problems of height and space are not easily identified during the normal design process, and are costly to correct. We present a user study (n = 30) in which three different presentation formats, (1) CAVE, (2) Head Mounted Display (HMD), and (3) monitor display, are compared as methods to explore a virtual factory site. Our results indicate that HMD provides the most immersive experience and e.g. that the CAVE approach is problematic in cases where detailed navigation is required. We also identify that the use of heart rate monitoring when exploring the virtual environment can provide a useful indication of possible issues related to perceptions of the design.

**Keywords:** User studies · Virtual words · Head mounted displays · Immersion

## 1 Introduction

In today's world, Virtual Reality (VR) technologies have become more and more common due to increases in computing performance as well as advances in input and output technologies. Probably the most commonly known use of VR is in computer games, which have brought interaction with VR environments in to the reach of large audiences. While the VR industry is heavily driven by entertainment based use cases, especially in the gaming industry, the use of VR for professional purposes is also increasing. When building cities, factories and other large industrial sites, the role of simulation technologies can be essential in enabling cost-efficient exploration of different solutions in the design and planning phases. When exploring 3D models of industrial site architectural plans, it is important to gain a realistic perception of the environment in order to assess different construction designs. On the other hand, for sales purposes, the experiental factors may play a role when communicating with potential customers. For these reasons, it is interesting to explore different interaction technologies and immersion in this context.

Whereas 3D virtual worlds have traditionally been accessed via a PC with a monitor display screen, other interaction technologies are becoming more common, not

© IFIP International Federation for Information Processing 2015
J. Abascal et al. (Eds.): INTERACT 2015, Part IV, LNCS 9299, pp. 363–380, 2015.
DOI: 10.1007/978-3-319-22723-8_29

only for researchers but also for other audiences. Immersive environments such as CAVEs have become less expensive to set up, and HMDs such as the Oculus Rift and Google Glass have caught the attention of developers as well as consumers. In this paper, we describe our work on utilizing HMD and CAVE presentations, rather than a conventional PC set-up to explore an industrial site simulation utilizing 3D models of the physical world, see Fig. 1.

**Fig. 1.** Test participant exploring the virtual factory environment with Oculus Rift head mounted display Paths taken by users are shown as blue trails.

The contribution of this paper lies in:

- Providing user study based information on the relative benefits of CAVE and HMD visualizations in identifying human perception issues in the factory site design process.
- Demonstrating that heart rate monitoring can be used as a useful source of data on user perception when exploring a virtual industrial site environment.

## 2  Related Work

### 2.1  User Experience with 3D Virtual Worlds

User experience (UX) research covers both utilitarian and hedonic aspects related to the user a product, service or user interface [1]. Whereas a unified definition for UX has not yet emerged [2], it is generally agreed that it goes beyond the instrumental means and measures relevant for usability research. User experience research expands the traditional perspective of usability oriented user research by including hedonic values associated with the interaction, and investigating the system use in a more holistic manner. Whereas UX research on 3D virtual worlds has so far been altogether rather scarce, prior art has addressed selected topics UI design and users' perceptions on such systems.

Research on the UI design of virtual worlds (VWs) has typically focused on quite narrow topics, such as text readability in 3D games [3], avatars [4], or collaborative and shared space aspects [5]. However, it has been identified that the ability to create realistic visualizations is one of the advantages of using 3D virtual worlds, especially when compared to conventional textual or 2D graphical user interface (GUI) presentations. User perceptions of the use of 3D virtual worlds has been charted e.g. in the context of home health care professionals. One identified strength in the approach was the patient activity monitoring, which could be visualized in a realistic yet in anonymous manner by using activity tracking combined with a 3D virtual world presentation and avatars [6]. When investigating different visualization techniques, Vatjus-Anttila et al. conclude that when 3D models of the physical world are considered, a better user experience is achieved when the VW design matches people's mental expectations of the physical space [7]. Contrary to our research, in prior art the research focus has been on the GUI design elements, and not in comparing user perceptions when different technology platforms are used to interact with the virtual worlds.

Considering the perception of height in both real and virtual representations, Emmelkamp et al. [8] have presented work focused on the treatment of those with acrophobia, concluding that exposure to the virtual condition was as effective as real exposure in treating the condition. Here, the participants' heart rate was used as one measure of their response to real and virtual height. In other studies on the treatment of phobias using virtual reality [9] identified galvanic skin resistance as a more useful measurement technique than heart rate. The use of heart rate monitors in exploring user experience in general has been reported on by [10]. Changes in heart rate caused by playing conventional video games has also been studied e.g. Segal and Dietz [11], who identified a significant increase in heart rates caused by playing video games.

Prior art has compared different presentation formats of VR from the point of view of the symptoms induced during its use, e.g. Sharples et al. [12] compare the use of a Head Mounted Display, projection screen and desktop display. Here, the main conclusion being the large variation between subjects. In our study we compare a similar set of display formats, but rather focusing on differences in the utility of each to provide inputs to the architectural design process.

## 2.2  Immersive Environments and Human Perception

**CAVEs.** Immersive environments have received much attention in research. One of the most common technologies used being CAVEs [13], which typically surround the user with three large projected walls, and even ceiling and floor, creating an immersive display environment that can be used either in a 2D or stereoscopic 3D mode. As application domains for CAVE type immersive environments, game, architecture and cultural heritage related topic are often considered, see e.g. [14]. CAVE environments have been employed in professional use when investigating and assessing architectural plans both in research [15] and in commercial design studios [16]. Frost et al. [17] present a building design process that incorporated the use of a VR CAVE environment. In their work, future users of the space being designed virtually visited the environment during the design phase and provided feedback to the architects.

Related to our research, earlier work related to human perception is of particular interest. Prior art has investigated what kind of effect the use of immersive environment has on the perception of walking distance [18]. Here, it was found that test participants' distance estimates were almost identical between real world and 3D virtual world representations. When comparing a projected CAVE with a fish tank type display on a monitor, Demiralp et al. [19] found the different displays had an effect on how suitable they were for VR applications. Also, the effect of the field of view and peripheral vision on the level of immersion experienced by users has been reported in several studies [20, 21]. With desktop virtual reality, the use of Peripheral Lenses has been proposed as a way to increase the level of immersion [21]. Here, these kinds of additional screens next to the main display can be seen as a step towards a CAVE type setup.

**HMDs.** Head Mounted Displays (HMDs) are proposed as one method to provide the user with a deeper level of immersion in a virtual environment [22]. Since the early work of e.g. Chung in late 1980's, we have witnessed the evolution from bulky and heavy HMD equipment towards lightweight and truly mobile systems. In the scope of architectural design, Thomas' early work on using HMDs as an augmented reality tool allowing a building design to be viewed in its physical surroundings [23], providing an interesting base to build upon. Earlier work [24] has discussed the increased immersion provided by HMDs compared to monitors, but has however not included detailed evaluation of the differences.

Together with other development trends, such as display miniaturization and increases in computing power, we now have equipment that can be easily adopted to different kinds of use cases and customized for industrial applications. Recent research using the Oculus Rift HMD has demonstrated e.g. a simulation that enables the user to experience flying like a bird [25]. Related to the domain used in our study, i.e. construction sites, previous research has examined the role of HMDs in building renovation and construction, e.g. [26]. However, their use has been considered rather for Augmented Reality applications instead of Virtual Reality. Comparison of different interactive technologies and charting user perceptions of using them, remains so far unexplored.

## 3 Study Design

### 3.1 Industrial Site Virtual World

To evaluate the suitability of HMD and CAVE solutions for our defined use case, we implemented a prototype application that enabled a test user to move around a virtual 3D industrial site (Fig. 2) with HMD, CAVE and a normal PC monitor screen as the output device. In each case a Microsoft Xbox controller was used as the interaction method. The HMD used was an Oculus Rift, Developer Kit 1 version [27]. The CAVE environment used consisted of a 180° stereoscopic 3D projection screen that did not include floor or ceiling projected surfaces. In the CAVE environment users were required to wear polarized glasses to see the stereoscopic effect.

**Fig. 2.** 3D model used in the virtual world

Our virtual industrial site used a 3D model that was supplied by R-Taso ltd. [28], a company that specializes in creating stair and walkway solutions for large industrial complexes. The model represented a typical installation for their products and included stairs, walkways and vertical ladders, see Fig. 2. Thus, the evaluation was done with the models that are actually used for professional purposes, neglecting some of the details of high fidelity architectural models. Additionally, we added scenery and other elements to the virtual world to increase the level of realism.

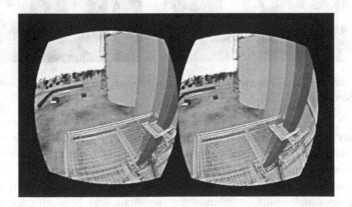

**Fig. 3.** View seen by the user through the Head Mounted Display

Our application was implemented using the Unity 3D environment, with a first-person camera controller to enable the user to move around the virtual industrial site. An example view of the 3D virtual world provided through the HMD is illustrated in Fig. 3. Physics objects were added to the model to enable the user to climb stairs and walk on the elevated walkways. Ladder climbing was enabled by use of a script such that forward motion when in the vicinity of the ladder would create upward motion, and vice versa. Walking and running speed in the virtual world was 3.8 km/h and

7.8 km/h respectively. The highest walkway in the model was 12.4 m above ground. To further increase the level of immersion we added sounds, such as different footstep sounds when walking on different surfaces.

To enable analysis of differences in users navigation routes in the 3 different presentation formats of the application, we included a logging functionality, so that the path taken around the model and the time taken to reach certain waypoints were logged. Additionally, some specific events, such as falling down or starting and finishing a mini task were logged. As prior art had highlighted the effect of virtual world conditions on heart rates, we included heart rate monitoring in our study. Participants put on a heart rate monitoring chest belt at the beginning of the study before completing the initial questionnaire, and wore it for the full duration of the study. The heart rate data was logged by an Android based application for later analysis.

### 3.2   User Study Set-up

**Study Set-up.** The three visualization modes compared in the study are shown in Figs. 4, 5 and 6. In each case the virtual world model and the navigation mechanism were identical.

**Fig. 4.** The three visualization modes compared in the study. Left to right: PC screen Oculus Rift HMD, Stereoscopic CAVE

The study was set up in one room; in one corner of the room there was the fixed CAVE system, additional equipment consisted of a laptop to run the simulation, a large flat screen display, an Oculus Rift and an Xbox gamepad. A camcorder was used to film the test sessions. In addition to video recording, users' heart rates were monitored both during tests and whilst completing the questionnaires between each test mode. During tests and while filling questionnaires users' comments and reactions were observed and notes made by a test moderator.

Each user was welcomed to the test and was asked to put on the heart rate monitor. Then the user completed a background information form. The user was told about the general phases of the test. The order in which users completed the three test modes was counterbalanced to avoid learning effects.

The user was guided to each test environment in turn and instructed on the use of the gamepad to navigate the virtual environment. The user was then briefly instructed on the tasks to be completed in the virtual environment. The user had to climb either the ladders or the stairs to the top of the silo structure. On the top of the silos there were two task checkpoints that were identified with a red glow, which the user had to find and move to. The location of the checkpoints was randomized. When arriving to a checkpoint, the simulation entered 'targeting mode' in which the user was required to find a target object on the ground below the silo towers and mark it by pointing it with a cursor and pressing a button on the controller. After finishing the two tasks, the user had to return to the starting point, either by ladder or stairs (Figs. 2 and 7).

**Fig. 5.** User using the HMD version of the application. Note the Xbox controller.

When the user had finished the test for one presentation format, s/he was given a questionnaire related to the experienced realism during the test. After filling the questionnaire the user carried out the tests in the other visualization environments. After the final test the user removed the heart rate monitor and completed a final questionnaire where s/he chose the favorite presentation format and gave reasons for their choice. Users then completed a word selection task, choosing five words from a grid of 52 adjectives to represent each experience. This method was a customized version of the Microsoft Research Product Reaction cards method [29]. Finally, the user was thanked for their participation and a cinema ticket was given as a reward.

**Fig. 6.** User navigating the CAVE version of the application using the Xbox controller.

**Participants.** Altogether, 30 participants took part in the user study. The participants were between the ages of 20 and 51 (M = 26.4, SD = 4.8), and 8 of them were women and 22 men. As a background, 71 % of the participants had not used any kind of HMD earlier, but 56 % had used 3D glasses once and 41 % more than once. In total 38 % of the participants played console games about once a year, 25 % every month.

## 4   Results

### 4.1   Paths Taken by Test Participants

Inspired by the work on visual presentations of real world user flows presented by Williamson and Williamson [30], we aimed to present similar visualizations for a virtual environment. Figure 7 presents a top-down view of the virtual environment indicating the paths taken by users.

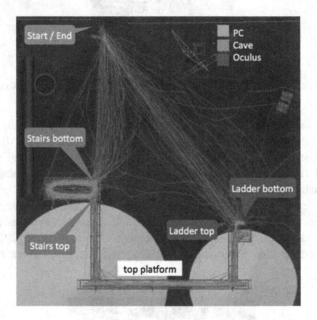

**Fig. 7.**  Top down view of our virtual factory environment, showing the paths taken by all users when exploring the space.

Considering the overall paths taken by participants (see Fig. 7) it appeared that with the PC participants took a straightforward, goal orientated path, compared to a more exploratory approach with the Oculus and CAVE. This is also reflected in the mean total time taken for users to complete the task with the PC (M = 3 m 45 s, SD = 76 s) being notably faster that either the CAVE (M = 5 m 8 s, SD = 123 s) or Oculus (M = 5 m 6 s, SD = 91 s). By visual inspection of the detailed navigation paths (e.g. Figure 8), the paths taken when using the CAVE were observed to be generally more spread and less consistent between users than either PC or Oculus conditions.

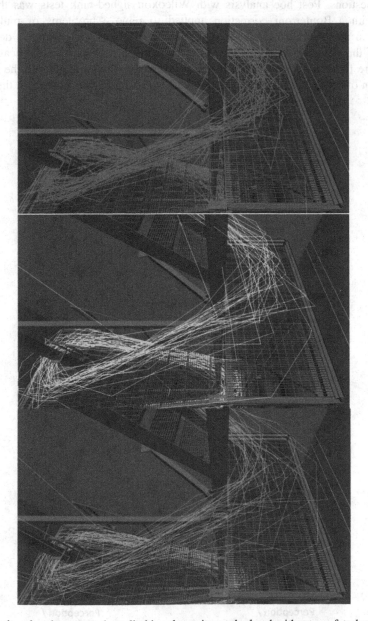

**Fig. 8.** Paths taken by users when climbing the stairs, at the level without a safety barrier. Top: Oculus, Middle: PC, Bottom: CAVE.

## 4.2  Subjective Ratings

The users' subjective ratings comparing each condition are presented in Fig. 9. To examine the significance of differences in the median subjective measures for each display condition, Friedman's tests were conducted on the responses to each of the Likert questions. Post hoc analysis with Wilcoxon signed-rank tests was then conducted with a Bonferroni correction applied to remove problems of multiplicity, resulting in a significance level set at $p < 0.016$ (.05/3 = .016). Table 1 details the results of the statistical analysis. For all of the criteria, statistically significant differences were found between the Oculus and both other conditions. Hence the reported perception of space and the feelings of height, motion, control and realism the feeling

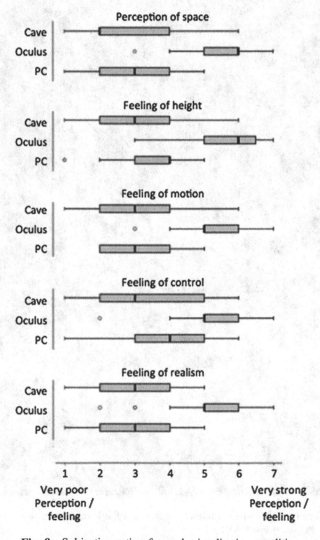

**Fig. 9.** Subjective rating for each visualisation condition.

of space provided by the Oculus were better than either the CAVE or the PC screen case. No significant differences were found between the CAVE and PC conditions.

Related to the feeling of space, half (15/30) of the users commented on the wide field of view provided by the CAVE. However, there seemed to be some disagreement as to whether it was a positive or negative issue, user #7 summing up the general responses "The field of view was too big. But on the other hand it was better than with a small screen, however orientation was hard to achieve" (User #7). In the case of the Oculus, 8/30 users mentioned the effect of moving their head as contributing to the feeling of space. Almost half of the users (13/30) felt that the feeling of height when climbing the stairs or ladders was realistic, with some comments about feeling dizzy, or keeping away from the edge, e.g. "Especially when I was at the top of the ladders and glanced down, I felt like being somewhere high. It felt horrible and frightening" (User #11) and "...I was more aware of edges in the staircase." (User #12).

**Table 1.** Analysis of significance of differences in median subjective ratings for each display condition. For the Wilcoxon signed rank tests a Bonferonni correction results in a significance level criteria of p < .016.

| | Friedman's test | Wilcoxon signed-rank | | |
| --- | --- | --- | --- | --- |
| | Oculus - Cave – PC | Oculus - Cave | PC - Cave | PC – Oculus |
| Perception of space | $\chi2(2) = 45.5$, p < 0.001 | Z = −4.73, p < .001 | Z = −.031, p = .975 | Z = −4.75, p < .001 |
| Feeling of height | $\chi2(2) = 44.7$, p < 0.001 | Z = −4.73, p < .001 | Z = −1.42, p = .157 | Z = −4.66, p < .001 |
| Feeling of motion | $\chi2(2) = 42.4$, p < 0.001 | Z = −4.68, p < .001 | Z = −1.01, p = .313 | Z = −4.71, p < .001 |
| Feeling of control | $\chi2(2) = 17.3$, p < 0.001 | Z = −3.82, p < .001 | Z = −1.15, p = .250 | Z = −3.04, p = .002 |
| Feeling of realism | $\chi2(2) = 51.0$, p < 0.001 | Z = −4.85, p < .001 | Z = −.511, p = .609 | Z = −4.82, p < .001 |

Issues related to the poor image quality, lag or low frame rate were mentioned by 8/30 users in relation to the feeling of motion when using the Oculus, e.g. "It was somewhat choppy when you turned your head." (User #3). One user (User #21) suggested that adding head swaying when walking or running would have improved the feeling of motion.

Users commented on difficulties controlling the movement in the CAVE visualization, with 6/30 users giving comments in this direction e.g. "Not so easy to control as the Oculus and normal screen." (User #6). In the Oculus case, the control of the camera rotation by both rotating the head and by using the left stick on the joystick was commented negatively by 6/30 users, however 2/30 users gave positive comments related to this functionality, e.g. "Mildly confusing because the view turned with both controller and head." (User #13).

Considering the overall realism of exploring the virtual world, 15/30 users commented on the low resolution of the Oculus image as on factor limiting the reality of the experience. When asked for their favorite of the three visualization conditions 27 participants selected the Oculus, 2 the Cave and 1 the PC. The reasons given for selecting the Oculus mostly related to the experience being fun or immersive in nature e.g. "The Oculus offered the best immersion, and naturally controlling your view was effortless." (User #20).

## 4.3 Product Reaction Cards

The adjectives chosen most frequently by test participants to reflect their experiences with each visualization condition are presented in Table 2. Generally the adjectives selected to describe the Cave were somewhat negative about both its visualization and ease of interaction with it. This corresponded with the descriptive comments given by the participants that described some discomfort with the wide field of view and relatively inaccurate control of the CAVE.

**Table 2.** Adjectives most frequently selected by users to describe the experience of each visualization mode. Bracketed numbers indicate the number of users selecting each adjective.

| Cave | Oculus | PC |
|---|---|---|
| Rigid (9) | Entertaining (12) | Ordinary (18) |
| Visually unpleasant (8) | Empowering (11) | Dated (13) |
| Difficult to use (7) | Inspiring (10) | Controllable (9) |
| Frustrating (7) | Fun + (9) | Familiar + (9) |
| Unclear (6) | Novel (8) | Rigid (9) |
| Easy to use (6) | Easy to use (7) | Approachable (8) |
| Simple + (6) | Responsive (7) | Clear (7) |
| Approachable (5) | Approachable (6) | Easy to use (7) |
| Fast + (5) | Innovative (6) | Poor quality (6) |

The majority of the words selected to describe the Oculus were hedonistic in nature, with entertaining, empowering, inspiring and fun being the most chosen adjectives. The PC interface was considered somewhat dull and old fashioned. However, in its favour, the users considered the PC interface controllable, clear and easy to use.

## 4.4 Heart Rate Analysis

The data logged by the Android application was transferred to Microsoft Excel where analysis was made. When reviewing the logged heart rate data there were many cases where the data was considered invalid. This was for example where the chest belt sensor had poor contact with the participant's skin during the test. Thus, test data that included heart rates above 180 bpm or heart rate jumps of more than 20 bpm were deemed erroneous. To enable within subjects analysis, participants whose test data included erroneous data for one or more test conditions were excluded from further analysis. Hence, the data from 17 participants was included in the heart rate based analysis (Fig. 10).

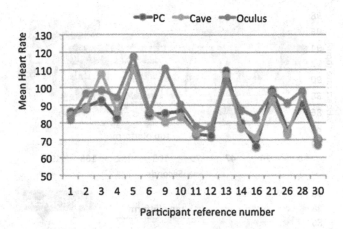

**Fig. 10.** Mean heart rates for each condition. Values for participants with invalid readings have been removed from the analysis.

To identify the significance of differences between the participant's mean heart rates in each condition A one-way within subjects ANOVA was conducted. There was a significant effect of the output modality, Wilks' Lambda = 0.606, F (2,15) = 4.88, p = .023. Three paired samples t-tests were used to make post hoc comparisons between the conditions with a target criteria of p < .05. However, due to the multiple comparisons a Bonferroni adjusted significance criteria of p < .016 was applied.

A first paired samples t-test indicated that there was no significant difference in the values for PC (M = 85.5, SD = 12.5) and Cave (M = 86.4, SD = 12.8) conditions; t (16) = −0.715, p = .485. A second paired samples t-test indicated that there was a significant difference in the scores for PC (M = 85.5, SD = 12.5) and Oculus (M = 91.7, SD = 12.7) conditions; t (16) = −3.81, p = .006. A third paired samples t-test indicated that there was no significant difference in the scores for Cave (M = 86.4, SD = 12.8) and Oculus (M = 91.7, SD = 12.7) conditions; t(16) = −2.326, p = .033. It may be noted that the latter comparison of Cave against Oculus conditions would have been considered significant if we had not applied the conservative Bonferroni correction. Hence, we consider that there is a borderline significant difference between the heart rates whilst using the Cave and Oculus.

When reviewing the heart rate of individual participants there is some evidence that changes in heart rate correspond to experiences in the virtual environment (Fig. 11). Although taken in isolation no conclusions can be drawn from variations in heart rate, as it is affected by many other factors beyond the experience of the virtual word, it may prove valuable when combined with other data sources. For example, peaks in heart rate at a certain point in the virtual environment could provide the trigger for qualitative interview questions related to that point.

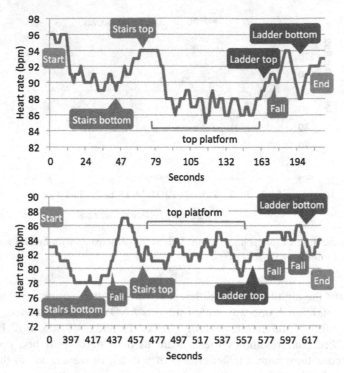

**Fig. 11.** Example heart rate of participants whilst exploring the virtual world (Top: user #10, Oculus. Bottom: User #1, Oculus).

## 5   Discussion

### 5.1   Experiental Aspects

Overall the Oculus was the clearly preferred visualization/interaction approach. The playful aspects of the Oculus based interaction identified by the users in both the product reaction cards and free form comments, highlights that playfulness in a key factor in user engagement.

In general our study had strong internal validity, the data obtained from Likert scale questions, and free form comments pointed to similar conclusions. Additionally, the heart rate data supported the findings, with the Oculus based exploration resulting in significantly higher mean heart rates than other methods, suggesting a higher level of immersion.

### 5.2   Control and Immersion

Although the three visualization approaches we compared were based on exactly the same model and used the identical control method of the Xbox controller, the test participants judged the feeling of control to be different. Specifically, the level of control with the Oculus case was considered to give a significantly stronger feeling of control than either the PC or cave cases. The Oculus' interaction based on the natural head movement was clearly appreciated, and our duplication of camera direction control with the handheld controller joystick was not positively received.

There was also indication that the PC based solution was perceived as being more controllable than the CAVE solution. Although the Likert responses did not alone indicate a significant difference, the direction was suggested and was supported by the large variance in the navigation paths taken by different users (Fig. 8) and the many free form comments related to the lack of controllability of the CAVE. This is perhaps not surprising, as although all users stood at exactly the same position when using the CAVE, we speculate that their perception of their own position in the 3D space was rather personal, depending on a variety of factors. This suggests that the CAVE type environments may not be suitable for tasks investigating precise navigation in a virtual world with a first-person camera viewpoint, as the user's exact location in the scene is not apparent. Rather the CAVE environment is more suited to presenting a relatively static view of a virtual world, and has other benefits compared to the head mounted display, for example being viewable by a number of people simultaneously without the need for additional hardware.

One interesting aspect relates to differences in perception caused by the visibility of the user's own body. While wearing the HMD, users cannot see their own hands and body, whilst in the CAVE presentation these are visible which may act to improve the level of reality, for example by providing a size benchmark.

## 5.3  Use of Heart Rate

We acknowledge that our use of heart rate is not rigorous in the medical sense, and the large number of results we had to discard due to operational issues was not ideal. However, we believe we have demonstrated that a simple heart rate monitoring set-up can provide useful information on the design of spaces that are being evaluated in a virtual reality environment. In this respect we have shown that, as well as for users with acrophobia as reported by [8], heart rate can be used as an indication of emotional state also for normal users in a virtual world.

## 5.4  Interaction Technologies as Tools

Our target was the creation of tools and methods to enable industrial site designs to be evaluated, potential problem issues identified and designs corrected before any site construction commences. Of particular interest are safety and psychological issues, for example the perception of height and feeling of personal security when working at height. Based on our user study results we have identified that in particular feelings of discomfort due to height can be well identified by this approach, particularly when experienced via a HMD such as the Oculus used in our study.

## 5.5    Limitations of the Study

By making a comparison between the three different presentation formats we hope to identify particular pros and cons of each solution. Here, we acknowledge the novelty effect may have influenced the users' perceptions. However, as few participants had experience of either both the Oculus or CAVE based solutions we feel our comparison of the two is valid. As noted in the users' free form comments each solution had some level of technical limitations e.g. the limited resolution of the Oculus and the field of view of the CAVE, however we feel that these limitations represent the state of the mainstream of the currently available technology in each case.

As we only used one virtual world model in our study that places a potential limitation on the applicability of our case. In addition, it should be noted that we explored a one-time use, and user's perceptions may change in the long term when the novelty effect wears off. However, in many situations, such as when presenting the construction site to costumers, management or marketing department, the interaction and the exploration within the 3D virtual world models is of a short duration. Thus, we believe that despite of the limitations, our study offers interesting insights on using different interaction technologies.

## 6    Conclusion

In our user research (n = 30) we have compared three different access methods for exploring a 3D model of an industrial site design, CAVE, Oculus HMD, and PC monitor. The main target of our work was to identify approaches that could provide user feedback to the architects and designers of the site installation. Our results show that the Oculus HMD was the clearly preferred method, especially for the experiental aspects it provided, but also because of the feeling of control in usage.

We have concluded that CAVE type environments are not ideal for first-person presentation of a virtual environment in cases where precise navigation is needed, e.g. exploring a factory building. We have demonstrated that the use of a commercial heart rate monitor can be used to give useful information on user perceptions when exploring a virtual environment.

**Acknowledgments.** The authors would like to thank Ville Törmänen of R-Taso ltd. who supplied the 3D models used and gave valuable insights into the practical problems associated with industrial site design.

## References

1. Hassenzahl, M., Tractinsky, N.: User experience - a research agenda. Behav. Inf. Technol. **25**(2), 91–97 (2006)
2. Law, E.L.-C., Roto, V., Hassenzahl, M., Vermeeren, A.P., Kort, J.: Understanding, scoping and defining user experience: a survey approach. In: Proceedings of the SIGCHI Conference on Human Factors in Computing Systems, CHI 2009, pp. 719–728. ACM, New York (2009)

3. Jankowski, J., Samp, K., Irzynska, I., Jozwowicz, M., Decker, S.: Integrating text with video and 3D graphics: the effect of text drawing styles on text readability. In: Proceedings of CHI 2010, pp. 1321–1330. ACM, New York (2010)
4. Wagner, D., Billinghurst, M., Schmalstieg, D.: How real should virtual characters be? In: Proceedings of ACE 2006. ACM, New York (2006)
5. Liu, H., Bowman, M., Chang, F.: Survey of State melding in virtual Worlds. ACM Comput. Surv. 44(4), 1–25 (2012). Article 21
6. Pouke, M., Häkkilä, J.: Elderly healthcare monitoring using an avatar-based 3D virtual environment. Int. J. Environ. Res. Public Health 10(2013), 7283–7298 (2013). doi:10.3390/ijerph10127283
7. Vatjus-Anttila, J., Ventä-Olkkonen, L., Häkkilä, J.: On the edge of a virtual World – investigating users' preferences and different visualization techniques. In: Augusto, J.C., Wichert, R., Collier, R., Keyson, D., Salah, A.A., Tan, A.H. (eds.) AmI 2013. LNCS, vol. 8309, pp. 198–203. Springer, Heidelberg (2013)
8. Emmelkamp, P.M., Bruynzeel, M., Drost, L., van der Mast, C.A.G.: Virtual reality treatment in acrophobia: a comparison with exposure in vivo. CyberPsychology Behav. 4(3), 335–339 (2001)
9. Wiederhold, B.K., Jang, D.P., Kim, S.I., Wiederhold, M.D.: Physiological monitoring as an objective tool in virtual reality therapy. CyberPsychology Behav. 5(1), 77–82 (2002)
10. Anttonen, J., Surakka, V.: Emotions and heart rate while sitting on a chair. In: Proceedings of the SIGCHI Conference on Human Factors in Computing Systems, pp. 491–499. ACM, April 2005
11. Segal, K.R., Dietz, W.H.: Physiologic responses to playing a video game. Am. J. Dis. Child. 145(9), 1034–1036 (1991)
12. Sharples, S., Cobb, S., Moody, A., Wilson, J.R.: Virtual reality induced symptoms and effects (VRISE): comparison of head mounted display (HMD), desktop and projection display systems. Displays 29(2), 58–69 (2008)
13. Cruz-Neira, C., Sandin, D., DeFanti, T., Kenyon, R., Hart, J.: The CAVE: audio visual experience automatic virtual environment. Commun. ACM 35(6), 64–72 (1992)
14. Cabral, M., Zuffo, M., Ghirotti, S., Belloc, O., Nomura, L., Nagamura, M., Andrade, F., Faria, R., Ferraz, L.: An experience using X3D for virtual cultural heritage. In: Proceedings of Web3D 2007, pp. 161–164. ACM (2007)
15. Mobach, M.: Do virtual worlds create better real worlds? Virtual Reality 12, 163–179 (2008)
16. Uki-arkkitehdit. https://www.youtube.com/watch?v=smC-rvzSph4. Accessed 21 September 2014
17. Frost, P., Warren, P.: Virtual reality used in a collaborative architectural design process. In: 2000 Proceedings of IEEE International Conference on Information Visualization, pp. 568–573. IEEE (2000)
18. Plumert, J.M., Kearney, J., Cremer, J.F., Recker, K.: Distance perception in real and virtual environments. ACM Trans. Appl. Percept. 2(3), 216–233 (2005)
19. Demiralp, C., Jackson, C., Karelitz, D., Zhang, S., Laidlaw, D.: CAVE and fishtank virtual-reality displays: a qualitative and quantitative comparison. IEEE Trans. Vis. Comput. Graph. 12(3), 323–330 (2006)
20. Lin, J.J.W., Duh, H., Abi-Rached, H., Parker, D., Furness, T.: Effect of field of view on presence, enjoyment, memory, and simulator sickness in a virtual environment. In: Proceedings of VR, pp. 164–171. IEEE (2002)
21. Robertson, G., Czerwinski, M., van Dantzich, M.: Immersion in desktop virtual reality. In: Proceedings of UIST 1997, pp. 11–19. ACM (1997)

22. Chung, J., Harris, M., Brooks, F., Fuchs, H., Kelley, M., Hughes, J., Ouh-young, M., Cheung, C., Holloway, R.L., Pique, M.: Exploring virtual Worlds with head-mounted displays. In: Proceedings of SPIE 1989, vol. 1083 (1989)
23. Thomas, B., Piekarski, W., Gunther, B.: Using augmented reality to visualise architecture designs in an outdoor environment. Int. J. Des. Comput. **2**, 1329–7147 (1999). Special Issue on Design Computing on the Net (dcnet'99)
24. Pausch, R., Proffitt, D., Williams, G.: Quantifying immersion in virtual reality. In: Proceedings of the 24th Annual Conference on Computer Graphics and Interactive Techniques, pp. 13–18. ACM Press/Addison-Wesley Publishing Co., August 1997
25. Ikeuchi, K., Otsuka, T., Yoshii, A., Sakamoto, M., Nakajima, T.: KinecDrone: enhancing somatic sensation to fly in the sky with Kinect and AR.Drone. In: Proceedings of Augmented Human 2014, Article No. 53. ACM (2014)
26. Webster, A., Feiner, S., MacIntyre, B., Massie, W., et al.: Augmented reality in architectural construction, inspection and renovation. In: Proceedings of ASCE 1996 (1996)
27. Oculus VR. http://www.oculusvr.com. Last visited 22 October 2014
28. R-Taso. http://www.r-taso.fi. Last visited 8 April 2014
29. Benedek, J., Miner, T.: Measuring desirability: new methods for measuring desirability in the usability lab setting (2002). http://www.microsoft.com/usability/UEPostings/DesirabilityToolkit.doc. Accessed 1 March 2014
30. Williamson, J.R., Williamson, J.: Analysing pedestrian traffic around public displays. In: Proceedings of PerDis 2014. ACM (2014)

# Pointing in Spatial Augmented Reality from 2D Pointing Devices

Renaud Gervais[1,2(✉)], Jérémy Frey[1,2,3], and Martin Hachet[1,2]

[1] INRIA, 33400 Talence, France
{renaud.gervais,jeremy.frey,martin.hachet}@inria.fr
[2] University Bordeaux, LaBRI, UMR 5800, 33400 Talence, France
[3] CNRS, LaBRI, UMR 5800, 33400 Talence, France

**Abstract.** Spatial Augmented Reality (SAR) opens interesting perspectives for new generations of mixed reality applications. Compared to traditional human-computer interaction contexts, there is little work that studies user performance in SAR. In this paper, we present an experiment that compares pointing in SAR versus pointing in front of a screen, from standard pointing devices (mouse and graphics tablet). The results showed that the participants tend to interact in SAR in a way that is similar to the screen condition, without a big loss of performance.

**Keywords:** Spatial augmented reality · Pointing devices

## 1 Introduction

Spatial Augmented Reality (SAR) consists in projecting digital information directly onto physical objects. Beyond conventional display methods based on monitor screens or planar projections, this approach opens new perspectives in numerous fields including design, education and mediation. Since the pioneering work of Raskar et al. [7], inherent problems of computer vision and computer graphics are being solved today. On the other hand, the problems related to interaction remain largely unexplored. In this work, we have investigated the question of pointing in SAR.

Several strategies to point at augmented objects exist. One is to touch directly the area of interest. This approach is very straightforward and, consequently, it may be valuable in many contexts. However, direct touch suffers from many drawbacks. In particular, anatomical issues including the "fat finger" problem and the fatigue that is linked to mid-air interaction make direct touch little adapted as soon as accurate and prolonged actions are required (e.g. professional object design). In addition, direct touch is not possible when dealing with very fragile objects (e.g. relics in museums) or as soon as the objects are out of reach. For distant interaction, laser pointers or virtual rays can be good alternatives, but they still suffer from similar accuracy and fatigue issues. In our approach, we have explored the use of standard pointing devices (see Fig. 1), namely mice and graphics tablets, to point at augmented objects. Years of human-computer interaction (HCI) have shown that these devices are decidedly well suited to point at visual objects displayed on 2D screens. Our assumption is that they can benefit to SAR as well, as soon as precision and prolonged work is required.

© IFIP International Federation for Information Processing 2015
J. Abascal et al. (Eds.): INTERACT 2015, Part IV, LNCS 9299, pp. 381–389, 2015.
DOI: 10.1007/978-3-319-22723-8_30

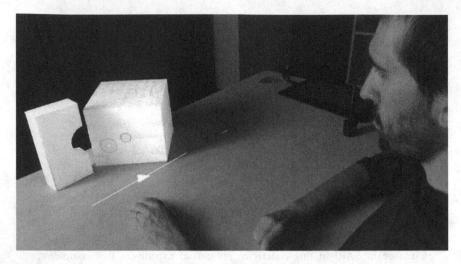

**Fig. 1.** A user moving a cursor (represented in blue) to a target (represented in red) on an augmented object by way of a standard mouse (Color figure online).

As an example, we can imagine an inspection scenario where an engineer points at an augmented circuit board with a mouse to highlight defects on small components. Another example is a design scenario where the artist draws by way of a tablet on a physical object, e.g. a 3D-printed one, to give it a specific appearance. For these two scenarios, it is interesting to note that the user equipped with a standard pointing device is still able to interact efficiently with standard GUI components displayed on a traditional screen, opening the way to true hybrid applications.

Pointing from mice and tablets has been extensively studied in traditional HCI contexts. In particular, Fitts' law [4] is able to predict the speed at which a user will be able to select a target depending on its distance and its size. Other works have been dedicated to pointing in 3D stereoscopic contexts [10, 11]. The current work is the first one that studies the question of pointing in SAR, from standard pointing devices. In this work, we are interested in a setup where the user is sitting at a desk (desktop environment) and is interacting with objects located in front of him or her, as illustrated in Fig. 1. Our contribution is the evaluation of the performance of pointing in a SAR environment using a standard pointing device compared to a traditional screen-based setup.

## 2 Related Work

Since SAR has been introduced [7, 8], there have been some research projects exploring interaction with projected content. Bandyopadhyay *et al.* [1] proposed the first interactive SAR prototype allowing users to "paint" physical objects with projected light using a six degrees of freedom tracked stylus. Physical-virtual tools [5] is a refinement of this concept, introducing more flexible editing tools inspired by real physical tools (e.g. an airbrush). Benko *et al.* [3] interacted with stereoscopic SAR using a mix of tangibles and gestures. These systems aimed for interaction modalities close to real-world metaphors. However, while perhaps more natural, they might prove to be less suited for precise and prolonged work than traditional 2D input devices.

The concept of pointing in SAR is similar to pointing in other contexts, namely multi-display environments (MDEs) and stereoscopic displays. In some ways, SAR can be compared to MDEs in that the physical world acts like a continuous space comprised of small display surfaces. As with MDEs, SAR might have some blind spots where the cursor will disappear because of a lack of projection support. Mouse Ether [2] and Perspective Cursor [6] are both systems that were developed to circumvent problems related to switching from one screen to another. The work of Xiao *et al.* [12] consists in projecting a cursor that can slide on any surface of the environment (which has been modeled in 3D beforehand). However, the system has been designed as a way to give feedback on the cursor's position when transitioning between screens and no targets were located in the environment itself in their evaluation. Pointing on a stereoscopic display has been studied by Teather and Stuerzlinger [11]. They studied different cursor types in what is effectively a "2.5D", or projected pointing task using a 3D Fitts' law pointing task. We also used projected pointing in this study. However, working on a real-world canvas is different from working on a screen since the real-world does not provide any reference frame for the 2D interaction. Moreover, a SAR installation does not suffer from the vergence-accommodation conflict present when using stereoscopic screens. Closer to a SAR setup, Reikimoto and Saitoh [9] proposed a spatially continuous workspace, allowing users to drag and drop content across different surfaces and objects. However, the pointing activity was not studied.

## 3 Pointing in SAR

Our SAR environment is comprised of a static scene laid out on a table in front of the user. A projector is then used to augment the objects.

On a standard screen configuration, the mouse cursor is generally represented as an arrow moving on the screen plane. When a 3D scene is displayed, the user is able to select any visible part of this virtual scene by picking the rendered result at the cursor location. Since most people are already experienced with this way of pointing, we wanted to know if this technique could be ported to a SAR environment albeit the lack of a physical screen support. Therefore, we used exactly the same metaphor in SAR, with the difference that the 3D scene is physically there, while the screen plane becomes virtual. The user moves the cursor on this virtual plane as he or she would do with a physical screen, as illustrated in Fig. 2. A line representing the intersection between the virtual plane and the table is projected onto the table, and an arrow indicates the horizontal position of the cursor (see Fig. 1). Contrary to standard screen configurations where the cursor is displayed on the screen plane, our SAR cursor is displayed directly on the physical objects. This cursor is represented as a cross within a 2D circle that is aligned with the underlying surface. Technically, we cast a ray formed by the eye and cursor position on the virtual plane towards the scene. We then position

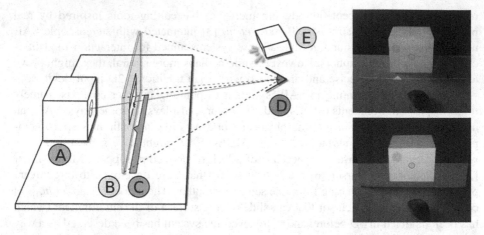

**Fig. 2.** LEFT: Drawing of the experimental setup. (A) Objects composing the scene to be augmented on which the cursor is displayed (light blue halo). (B) Plane on which the cursor is projected. This plane is either virtual in the SAR condition or physical (white wooden panel) in the Screen condition. (C) Feedback used in the SAR condition indicating the position of the virtual plane with the tip of the triangle indicating the horizontal position of the cursor. (D) The position at which the user is viewing the scene. (E) Projector. RIGHT: Scene in SAR (top) and SCREEN (bottom) conditions, with the same viewing angle (Color figure online).

the cursor perpendicularly to the normal of the picked point. The visual feedback (line and arrows) helps to know where the cursor is as soon as the latter does not project onto an object.

## 4    User Study

We conducted a user study to assess the performance of the pointing technique described in the previous section (SAR) in comparison to a screen-based baseline (SCREEN). Our research question was the following: What is the difference in performance of a pointing task realized on a screen compared to one realized with a SAR installation given that all other conditions are constant? Does pointing in SAR follows Fitts' law?

### 4.1    Participants

Sixteen participants took part in the study (12 males, 4 females, mean age 28.75, SD 4.71). All of them obtained a university degree. Six participants were left-handed (the mouse used during the experiment was adapted to both left- and right-handed users). All the participants were familiar with mice, whereas they had very little experience with tablets. None of them had previous experience with SAR systems.

## 4.2   Apparatus

The scene to be augmented was laid out on a table in front of the user. Each object of the scene was manually measured and modeled in 3D. A projector was located above and behind the user pointing at the scene. The projector was calibrated using OpenCV's camera calibration functions. We used a 3.6 GHz Core i7 PC with Windows 8 equipped with two GeForce GTX690 graphic boards. The videoprojector was a ViewSonic Pro9000 with a resolution of $1920 \times 1080$ pixels. The same setup was used for both SAR and SCREEN conditions. In SAR, the virtual scene was projected directly onto the physical objects whereas a white wooden surface located at the same position was used in the SCREEN condition. This ensured a similar frame rate (50 FPS), colorimetric configuration (color, brightness, contrast) and approximately same pixel size in both conditions. The focus of the videoprojector was set on the screen plane. On this plane, the resolution was effectively of $915 \times 904$ pixels.

In the SAR condition, the objects were augmented by reprojecting the virtual scene from the point of view of the projector. In the SCREEN condition, the viewpoint of the user on the scene was virtually reproduced and reprojected on the virtual counterpart of the physical screen. Then, this reprojection was rendered from the point-of-view of the projector, effectively making the viewed scene in both conditions identical (see Fig. 2 (right)). We did not use real-time head tracking but the user head's position was measured manually and thus accounted for. The whole installation has been created using the creative coding framework vvvv.

For the input device, we used both a mouse (MOUSE) and a Wacom Cintiq 13HD tablet (TABLET). The screen of the tablet was not used for the experiment and therefore was displaying a black viewport. The button located on the pen was used for the selection action. The mouse was used in a relative mode while an absolute mapping was associated with the tablet. The acceleration transfer function of the mouse was disabled.

The 3D scene was composed of a $21 \times 18 \times 21$ cm cube, as well as a more complex shape with comparable dimensions (see Fig. 1). The scene onto which the targets to acquire were laid out varied by rotating the cube by an angle of $45°$ to provide more depth changes between trials. The participants sat at a distance of 1 m from the screen or physical objects, and the height of the chair was set in order for the participants' head to be located at the ideal observer position.

## 4.3   Procedure

We followed the procedure described in [4]. The participants had first to position the cursor in a home area represented by a red circle. After one second, this circle moved from red to green and a target appeared in the scene. The participants were instructed to select this target as quickly and accurately as possible. The start time was recorded when the cursor left the home area and stopped when the users clicked on the target. The targets were spread on a circle centered on the home area.

## 4.4  Design

We used a 2 × 2 within-subjects design. The independent variables were the output modality (SCREEN, SAR) and the input modality (MOUSE, TABLET). The dependent variables were the completion time, the inefficiency defined as $\frac{Path_{actual} - Path_{optimal}}{Path_{optimal}}$ [13] and the number of errors, defined as the number of selections outside the target area. For each condition, the participants had to acquire 40 targets, resulting in 160 target acquisitions by participant, and 2560 records in total. The order for the input and output were counter balanced following a latin square to avoid any learning effects.

## 5  Results and Discussion

**Table 1.**  Statistical results. Marks: **for $p < .01$, *for $p < 0.05$; · for $p < 0.1$; ns: not significant; –: not applicable.

| Factors | | Time (ms) | Inefficiency | Errors | Throughput (bits/sec) |
|---|---|---|---|---|---|
| *Input* | Mouse / Tablet | ns | 0.16 / 0.22 (SD: 0.05 / 0.08) * | ns | ns |
| *Output* | Screen / SAR | 846 / 959 (SD: 154 / 119) ** | 0.17 / 0.21 (SD: 0.07 / 0.07) · | ns | 5.75 / 3.84 ** |
| | *Grand average* | 902 (SD: 404) | 0.19 (SD: 0.30) | 0.05 (SD: 0) | – |

Because the homogeneity of variance couldn't be verified according to Levene's test ($p < 0.001$), we analyzed our data with non-parametric statistics, using multiple Wilcoxon signed-rank tests and false rate discovery correction. We retained trials which did not comprise errors to study time and inefficiency across our factors. Statistical results are reported in Table 1.

**Time.** There was no significant effect of the input device on completion time. However, output modality had a significant impact. Users were 11 % faster in the SCREEN condition compared to the SAR condition. While having higher completion time, the drop in performance is relatively low, especially considering that the cursor reference frame was virtual.

**Inefficiency.** Inefficiency is a measure of "wasted" cursor movement by the user. Input modality had a significant effect, the tablet being more inefficient than the mouse. This difference can be explained by the lack of experience of almost all participants with such a tablet. Output did not have a clear significant effect on the inefficiency of the movements of the users.

**Error Rate.** There was no significant effect of either input modality or output on the error rate. On average, the error rate was 5 %.

**Throughput.** The target condition is reflected by the Index of Difficulty (ID), which indicates the overall pointing task difficulty. $ID = \log_2(\frac{D}{W} + 1)$ [4]. D is the projected target distance in the virtual screen and W is the perceived target size. W varied according to the location and orientation of the target in the scene. ID was discretised from [1.91; 4.92] to [2; 5] by steps of 0.5. We averaged the completion time across ID and conditions (input × output). We modeled the movement time (MT) with a linear regression. We obtained an adjusted $R^2$ value of 0.8479 which shows that the completion time of pointing tasks in SAR using mice and tablets still follows the Fitts' law (see Fig. 3), and consequently remains predictable. We also computed associated measures of performance, also known as "throughput", using the slope of the regression lines. Throughput $= \frac{1}{b}$ [13].

There was no significant effect of the input device on the throughput, whereas output device did have an effect. The screen condition was significantly more efficient than the SAR condition although, as it was the case for the completion time, the difference is relatively low.

Overall, the participants were slightly less efficient in the SAR condition than the SCREEN one. This difference could be explained by the years of experience of the participants with pointing in front of a screen whereas they were exposed to a SAR setup for the first time. Also, it is interesting that removing the physical reference frame (screen) of the cursor does not prevent users to interact in the same way they are used to, i.e. as if a physical screen was there. We can thus presume that with additional experience, participants may improve their performance with SAR. Another possible cause for the drop of performance is the presence of blind spots where the cursor disappear because of a lack of projection support (such zones were involved in about 1/4 of the trials). It could be interesting to compare the effect of these gaps in MDEs vs SAR to evaluate the impact of the frame of reference provided by the screen. Additionally, possible extensions of this work include studying the performance when moving the viewpoint of the user while using the Perspective Cursor [6] and evaluating

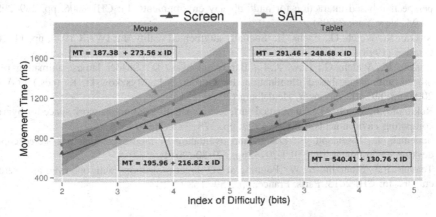

**Fig. 3.** Fitts' law models. $R^2 = 0.8479$.

if the performance drop observed in the SAR condition can be reproduced with other interaction techniques such as laser-pointer.

## 6 Conclusion

We presented an approach for interacting with desktop SAR, i.e. when the user interacts with physical objects in front of him/her by way of standard pointing devices. A user study has shown that Fitts' law remains valid even if no physical screen is present. Users are able to point at targets displayed on the augmented objects in a manner that is comparable to what they used to do in front of a standard screen. This finding opens interesting perspectives, allowing desktop SAR applications to be used to extend the current desktop setup with augmented physical objects. Beyond pointing tasks, interaction in SAR is still a domain that has been little explored and, consequently, a large variety of HCI work is still to be conducted.

**Acknowledgements.** This work was supported by the ISAR project ANR-14-CE24-0013.

## References

1. Bandyopadhyay, D., Raskar, R., Fuchs, H.: Dynamic shader lamps : painting on movable objects. In: ISAR 2001, pp. 207−216 (2001). doi:10.1109/ISAR.2001.970539
2. Baudisch, P., Cutrell, E., Hinckley, K., Gruen, R.: Mouse ether: accelerating the acquisition of targets across multi-monitor displays. In: CHI 2004 eA, pp. 1379−1382 (2004)
3. Benko, H., Jota, R., Wilson, A.: Miragetable: freehand interaction on a projected augmented reality tabletop. In: CHI 2012, pp. 199−208 (2012)
4. MacKenzie, I.S.: Movement time prediction in human-computer interfaces. In: Readings Human-Computer Interaction, pp. 483−493 (1992)
5. Marner, M.R., Thomas, B.H., Sandor, C.: Physical-virtual tools for spatial augmented reality user interfaces. In: ISMAR 2009, pp. 205−206 (2009). doi:10.1109/ISMAR.2009.5336458
6. Nacenta, M.A., Sallam, S., Champoux, B., Subramanian, S., Gutwin, C.: Perspective cursor: perspective-based interaction for multi-display environments. In: CHI 2006, pp. 289–298. ACM, New York (2006)
7. Raskar, R., Welch, G., Fuchs, H.: Spatially augmented reality. In: IWAR 1998, pp. 11–20. Citeseer (1998)
8. Raskar, R., Welch, G., Low, K.-L., Bandyopadhyay, D.: Shader lamps: animating real objects with image-based illumination. In: Gortler, S.J., Myszkowski, K. (eds.) EGWR 2001, pp. 89−102. Springer, Heidelberg (2001)
9. Rekimoto, J., Saitoh, M.: Augmented surfaces: a spatially continuous work space for hybrid computing environments. In: CHI 1999, pp. 378−385 (1999)
10. Schemali, L., Eisemann, E.: Design and evaluation of mouse cursors in a stereoscopic desktop environment. In: 3DUI 2014, pp. 67−70 (2014)
11. Teather, R.J., Stuerzlinger, W.: Pointing at 3D target projections with one-eyed and stereo cursors. In: CHI 2013, Paris, France, pp. 159−168 (2013)

12. Xiao, R., Nacenta. M.A., Mandryk, R.L., Cockburn, A., Gutwin, C.: Ubiquitous cursor: a comparison of direct and indirect pointing feedback in multi-display environments. In: GI 2011, pp. 135–142 (2011)
13. Zhai, S.: Characterizing computer input with Fitts' law parameters – the information and non-information aspects of pointing. Int. J. Hum.-Comput. St. **61**, 1–17 (2004)

# The Comparison of Performance, Efficiency, and Task Solution Strategies in Real, Virtual and Dual Reality Environments

Frederic Raber[✉], Antonio Krüger, and Gerrit Kahl

DFKI GmbH, Saarbrücken, Germany
{frederic.raber,krueger,gerrit.kahl}@dfki.de

**Abstract.** Using virtual models of a real environment to improve performance and design effective and efficient user interfaces has always been a matter of choice to provide control of complex environments. The concept of Dual Reality has gone one step further in synchronizing a real environment with its virtualization. So far, little is known about the design of effective Dual Reality interfaces. With this paper we want to shed light on this topic by comparing the strategies, performance and efficiency in a real, virtualized and a DR setting given a complex task. We propose a cost and efficiency measure for complex tasks, and have conducted an experiment based on a complex shelf planning task. Our results show that for certain tasks interacting with the virtual world yields better results, whereas the best effectivity can be observed in a Dual Reality setup. We discuss these results and present design guidelines for future Dual Reality interfaces.

**Keywords:** Immersion · Dual reality · Efficiency · Performance differences in real and virtual environments

## 1 Introduction

More and more tasks that were previously successfully conducted in a real-world environment are now being virtualized. For example, car design, which was previously done using miniature models, is now done on a PC using a CAD tool. Cars are designed and tested virtually, and architectural design and structural engineering calculation is done completely on virtual models, replacing their real counterparts. Both virtualization and a real environment have their advantages: On the one hand, virtual tools are fast and easy to use, as the physical demand is reduced. The virtual interface can be enriched by additional visual clues, using coloring of parts of the scene, lighting or textual information. For example, in [16], the work piece is visualized so it cannot be occluded, and additional textural information in the form of process data is displayed. On the other hand, a real-world environment with real objects has better haptic feedback. Size, height and distance estimation is easier in the real world, as we will discuss in the next section. The concept of *Mirror Worlds*, first mentioned by David Gelernter [9] and later by Lifton and Paradiso under the term *Dual Reality* [12], describes a

© IFIP International Federation for Information Processing 2015
J. Abascal et al. (Eds.): INTERACT 2015, Part IV, LNCS 9299, pp. 390–408, 2015.
DOI: 10.1007/978-3-319-22723-8_31

setting where both worlds, a real and a virtual world, are connected together and influence each other. Lifton and Paradiso define it as follows:

**Dual Reality** is an environment resulting from the interplay between the real world and the virtual world, as mediated by networks of sensors and actuators. While both worlds are complete unto themselves, they are also enriched by their ability to mutually reflect, influence, and merge into one another [12].

In Dual Reality, an event in one world can, but does not have to, cause a corresponding action in the other world. The users can act either with the real environment or with its virtual counterpart. Every action can be reflected in the corresponding counterpart. Although not directly stated in their paper, a mechanical entity is implicitly needed, which synchronizes both worlds. Consider the model of a virtual apartment in Dual Reality: The user can turn on a lamp in the virtual environment. In the real counterpart, the light is also turned on remotely by the software. In turn, if the user turns on the light in the real world, this is recognized by the software, which then turns on the light in the visualization. Our goal is to understand how people interact with a Dual Reality setup, whether they take advantage of the possibilities of this concept, which possible problems arise and how this interaction can be improved. We are interested in questions such as "Are the users acting the same way in a virtual replica and in the physical environment?", "How efficient is a Dual Reality setup compared to the real and virtual world?", and "Which interface type should I use to meet my requirements?"

In order to investigate these questions, we have created an experimental setting, consisting of a real and a virtual environment, representing the same setup and influencing each other. Subjects were asked to perform a complex task requiring both strategic planning and physical actions. We propose a cost function, which allows us to judge and compare the efficiency of each task. As an initial step we were interested to learn more about the differences in terms of performance and behavior between real-world, virtual-world, and Dual Reality interaction. Dan Montello argues in his work [14] that the definition of space is a perceptual problem, and gives the definitions of four different sizes of space. The space that can be seen by the user without loco-motion is called the *vista space*. A bigger space that can only be apprehended with a significant amount of locomotion is called the *environmental space*. Most of the related work that compares the task solution strategies between a virtual and real environment does not take Dual Reality settings into account, and uses only a small space (such as the size of a table), meaning it is clearly limited to a vista space. The Dual Reality systems that are known from the literature, but which are not evaluated in terms of performance and efficiency, are situated in the environmental space. Our experimental setting, which evaluates a real, virtual, and a Dual Reality interface, resides somewhere between the vista and environmental space: The scene can be viewed as a whole from a single point, but the detailed information and actions needed for the task can only be performed with significant locomotion. The remainder of this paper is organized as follows: The next section will first discuss related work and provide some background information on the topic of Dual Reality. Then we will present the experimental setup and how we designed the task to be performed in a real, a virtual, and a Dual Reality world. We then discuss the experiment, including a pilot study, and its results. Finally, a discussion and conclusion complete the paper.

## 2 Related Work

For our work, three different aspects are of importance: first, the differences in *perception* of a virtual world or object compared to a real environment; second, the research field of *Dual Reality*; and third, comparisons between *interaction in a real and in a virtual* environment. Research in the field of visual perception has shown that users perceive a virtual world significantly differently than the real world. A first problem is the perception of rotation, orientation and shape of a three-dimensional object. Dobbins and Grossmann [7] showed that orientation can be perceived differently, depending on the position of the object in relation to the beholder. Mistakes in the perception of the metric structure of 3D objects from multiple cues were previously discovered by Todd and Norman [17]. We expect that differences in visual perception will influence performance and behavior in real and virtual worlds.

There exist several examples of such a setup of complex worlds in the Dual Reality paradigm: Back et al. [4] present a Dual Reality chocolate factory, consisting of a real factory and a virtual model. The applications of this project are, first, to allow a virtual trip through the factory, as well as the remote control of the machines inside the factory for authorized persons. In addition, the states of the machines in the real world, as well as interactions with them, are reflected inside the visualization. Davies and Callaghan [6] examined how human behavior can be captured and learned by sensors. Their goal is to create an autonomous virtual avatar, whose behavior seems natural. They instrumented an apartment with motion sensors, and created a corresponding virtual world in 3D. The behavior of the user in the real world is perceived and also visualized in the virtual component. Conversely, interactions with the virtual world (e.g. turning on the light), will also affect the illumination of the real apartment. Khan et al. [11] created a virtual supermarket, displayed on a CAVE (Cave Automated Virtual Environment). The interaction is realized by a "human joystick" principle: The camera is moved with respect to the user's position in relation to the center of the CAVE. Their objective was to evaluate the user's experience of pervasive applications within a virtual environment, and to show the potential of evaluating location-based services, especially location-based advertisements in a virtual supermarket. They claim that a virtual world has the advantage of being fully controllable and adaptable to the researchers' needs, but they did not investigate the differences between their simulated and a real environment. In contrast to the chocolate factory and the virtual avatar mentioned before in this subsection, this visualization has no real counterpart, so it does not form a Dual Reality system. Still, it is the virtualization of an environment as it can exist in the real world. Therefore, the interaction and visualization techniques are related to our experiment.

The design of the two Dual Reality worlds (or the virtualized world), and especially the interaction possibilities, are of interest for our work. We designed our real and virtual environment similarly to these systems in terms of visualization as well as interaction possibilities and techniques, to discover the differences in interaction and behavior between the two environments, as well as a DR setup containing both environments at the same time. In the following we will discuss several studies which compare the performance and behavior of a digitalized 2D representation (e.g. controlled via mouse or touch) with a physical or tangible version for the same task and domain. Kozak et al. [1] observed in the past that training in the virtual world does not necessarily lead to an improved performance in the real world. In their study, subjects had to place a set of cans on a table according to given positions. The first test group was able to train in advance using the real cans and table. A second group used a virtual reproduction of the setup, using a data glove and a head-mounted display. A third group had no training at all. Only the first test group was able to perform significantly better; the group using the virtual version did not perform better than the group without training. A simple task where a ruler or several simple geometric objects have to be aligned to fit a template is presented in [18]. The results show that subjects needed significantly more time on the touch-based system. In contrast to our experiment, the tasks here are tasks which are easy to perform, like aligning a ruler to a given shape. Lucchi et al. [13] compared actions like selection, scaling, rotation and positioning using a touch-based version or tangible objects. Here as well, the tangible version outperformed the touch version in terms of time, precision and number of translations needed to reach the desired goal. Still, a comparison of complex tasks is absent from this paper; only easy rotation and scaling tasks are performed there. More complex tasks are presented in [2, 3]. The participants were asked to solve a puzzle by using either an interactive surface (based on touch input), or real puzzle pieces lying on top of the surface. The results show that the virtual version was outperformed by its tangible counterpart. The behavior and the percentage of time devoted to each sub-task were significantly different. While this is similar to our setup, the task itself can be considered rather simplistic in terms of strategy and behavior, if for example compared to a more complex control task in a factory or when finding a solution to a spatial configuration task.

In summary, several studies have been carried out comparing the performance between a virtual and a real condition for simple tasks, involving simple actions. We will extend this work for a more complex task, which requires a strategy, as well as more complex actions including locomotion. We will introduce a new test condition, namely the Dual Reality condition, which is also compared against the virtual and real conditions. An efficiency measure for all three conditions will be proposed. We will observe and discuss differences in terms of performance, efficiency, as well as the number and duration of actions conducted in order to complete the task, in order to give guidelines on the optimal interface for a given environment and task.

# 3   Experimental Setup

We decided to take a pick-and-place task, which had to be extended to form a more complex task, requiring strategic planning as well as a higher amount of locomotion as stated in the introduction. Instead of giving the user a specific target location, we gave him a complex formula which scores the placement of the object, depending on its position and which other objects are situated in its surroundings. To form a meaningful task, we decided to replicate a realistic task from the retail domain, namely that of "shelf planning": Retailers have to plan their shelf layouts (i.e. the order and position of product placements in a shelf) to optimize their profit. We have designed a real and a virtual environment where real and virtual products could be placed at arbitrary positions on the respective shelves in a shelf unit. In the Dual Reality condition of our experiment, both environments can influence each other, and are always "synchronized". Each product placement or movement which is done in the virtual environment will also be applied automatically to the real shelf, and vice versa. Normally, in a Dual Reality system, the "synchronization" of the real world is done by machines, such as a robot. Details on how this robot was emulated for our experiment will be given later. For our efficiency calculation, we will assume that this task is done by a robot or an automated process.

Each product is assigned to a price category. Depending on the price and the placement within the shelf unit, the overall profit is calculated. Profit is influenced by the placement (some positions in the shelf unit are more profitable than others) and on which other products have been placed nearby (products of the same price category reduce each other's profit). Details on the profit calculation will be given below. The main task consists of maximizing the profit of the shelf unit as a whole.

## 3.1 Efficiency Calculation

To be able to compare the efficiency of the tasks, an efficiency function is essential. In this subsection, we give a general formula which has to be refined for a specific task. We will create a specific formula for our shelf planning task in the next section. We define efficiency as the fraction of the performance $P$ (in terms of score reached for the task) and the cost $C$ needed to achieve this result:

$$Efficiency = \frac{P}{C}$$

The shelf planning task can be divided into several types of *sub-tasks*. We will denote this type-set of sub-tasks as $ST$, their elements as $ST_i$ and the number of times this sub-task type was executed during the experiment task as $|ST_i|$. The cost depends on the number of times each sub-task $ST_i$ in $ST$ is conducted, as well as the cost for each of them ($C(ST_i)$):

$$C = \sum_{ST_i \in ST} (|ST_i| * C(ST_i))$$

Each subtask is conducted by an *entity*, which can either be a real person, or a machine such as a robot. Each entity has a different cost for operating over a certain period of time. For a human this would be his salary; for a machine, the operating cost. The cost of a given subtask is therefore calculated by multiplying the cost per hour $C_{hour}(E)$ of the entity $E$ that conducts the sub-task by the time needed to complete it ($Time(ST_i)$):

$$C(ST_i) = C_{hour}(E) * Time(ST_i)$$

The efficiency formula then is calculated as follows:

$$Efficiency = \frac{P}{\sum_{ST_i \in ST} (|ST_i| * (C_{hour}(E) * Time(ST_i)))}$$

This formula needs to be refined in the next step according to the given experiment task that should be measured. There are three domain-specific variables: *Time on average* needed to complete each individual Subtask *ST* (Time(ST$_i$)), *Cost per hour* of the entities that fulfill these subtasks (C$_{hour}$(E)) and *Measure of the performance* P. It is not our primary goal to show which of the interfaces is most efficient, but to see how changes in different parameters, such as cost per hour/salary of a worker or time needed for a subtask, can influence the efficiency and make another interface concept become the most efficient one. This should give the reader an idea of whether he should prefer a real, virtual or DR interface for his specific task. Calculating the measures is rather straightforward: for example for a pick-and-place task, the performance P could be the number of placed objects divided by the sum of offsets of each object compared to its target position. There is only one sub-task, namely the pick-and-place subtask, whose average time can be computed in a short trial. The cost per hour is the hourly wage of the human performing the task. In the experiment section, we will determine these variables according to our shelf planning task. The next section will give an overview of the schematic setup of the real environment, followed by the design of the virtual environment, and the Dual Reality system which is a linkage of these two environments.

## 3.2 Schematic Setup

The schematic setup is shown in Fig. 2 and is the same for all three conditions. The worlds are designed in exactly the same way, illustrated in Fig. 1. For the virtual version, we used a 3D scene displayed on a 2D touchscreen for representing a virtual version of the real world.

**Fig. 1.** Environment in the real, virtual and Dual Reality conditions

The products are initially placed in the right shelf unit ("start shelf"), and have to be placed inside the left one ("target shelf"). The touch display running the virtual environment is placed on a table in between the two shelf units. The user stands in front of these two shelf units ("interaction zone"), so he has access to both the real shelves as well as the virtual environment on the display. Behind the shelves is an assistant zone, where the experimenter as well as an assistant can observe the experiment.

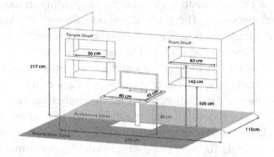

**Fig. 2.** Schematic setup of the experiment (all measures in cm)

### 3.3 Interaction Design

**Real Environment.** The subject uses real products and shelves to accomplish the task. We implemented several assistance systems, which should help the subject in achieving a good score, without reducing the cognitive effort too much. We displayed the actual score as well as the change with respect to the last step on the screen between the shelves, giving the subject an idea of whether his actions were going in the right direction. Additionally, we installed LED lights in different colors on each shelf of the left shelf unit (target shelf). As soon as the subject touches a product or holds it in his hands, the LEDs are turned on, indicating if there is not enough space to place the product (red light); there is enough space, but the score would decrease (yellow light); or there is enough space and the score would increase (green light) after placing the product (see Fig. 3).

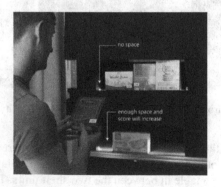

**Fig. 3.** Lights indicate available space and score

**Virtual Environment.** We designed the virtual world to be as similar as possible to the real world in order to ensure comparability. Therefore we decided against a 2D representation and used a 3D view instead. A screenshot of the virtual model is shown in Fig. 4. For additional functions such as switching views between shelves or zooming, several command buttons are displayed in the lower left corner of the interface.

**Fig. 4.** Setup in the virtual world condition

Several interaction techniques are provided, based on single-touch input:

- **Selection of a product:** For selecting a product, a single tap on the product is sufficient. Tapping the product again, or selecting another product, deselects it again. The currently selected object is highlighted by a red overlay on the product.
- **Placement of a product:** A selected product can be placed by tapping on the exact position on the shelf where the product should be placed. The program automatically moves the adjacent products aside if the selected space is not sufficient, as long as there is enough space on the shelf. If no space is left on the shelf, a corresponding message appears in the upper right corner of the screen as feedback to the user. The product remains selected and can be placed at some other location.
- **Moving a product:** A product inside the shelf unit can be moved simply by dragging and dropping it. A move is possible only on the same shelf; moving it to another shelf is not allowed using this technique. In that case, a placement action has to be performed.
- **Shelf views:** When clicking on one of the two rightmost buttons, the user gets an overview perspective of the contents inside the left or right shelf unit. This facilitates a better identification and selection of products. In the new visualization, an additional button appears to get back to the shelf view.
- **Zoom:** We implemented a zoom functionality, allowing the user to zoom in or out in the current perspective, to have a more detailed view of a shelf unit or product desk. This corresponds to the action of walking towards the shelf unit.

Users were not forced nor encouraged to use zooming or view switching, if they did not want to. We implemented the assistance functions from the real environment (see last section) in the virtual environment as well: Whenever a product is selected, the shelves inside the target shelf are colored according to available space and possible score after the placement of the selected product. The score is displayed in the upper left corner of the screen.

**Dual Reality Environment.** In this environment, both the real products and visual cues of the real environment, as well as the virtual system using the touchscreen, can be used. The subject should always have the possibility to switch between the two environments at will. Therefore, both environments always have to be synchronous: Whenever an action is conducted in one of the two worlds, it will be mimicked in the other world. If the subject places a real product on a shelf, the product is also automatically placed in the virtual environment. When the subject uses the touchscreen to place a product in the virtual environment, the real product also has to be transported to its new location.

### 3.4 Pilot Study

Prior to our experiment, we conducted a pilot study with a slightly different setup in order to find first differences in people's behavior and performance in a real and in a virtual environment, and to decide which measures might be interesting to observe in our main experiment. Twenty-seven students volunteered to take part in the pilot study. We tested only a real and a virtual condition without any assistance functions. The products were initially placed on two product tables, and had to be placed inside two target shelves, which were standing opposite each other. All subjects were asked to optimize the product placement in the two shelf units in order to maximize the profit of products from three different price ranges (high, medium, low). For more detail on how the profit was calculated, see the later section on the main experiment.

The results reveal that the profit was significantly higher for the real condition ($M_{real} = 0.943$, $M_{virtual} = 0.909$, $p = 0.02$). We observed a higher number of interactions, especially product movements ($M_{real} = 16.62$, $M_{virtual} = 24.35$, $p = 0.04$), in the virtual condition. Most participants used only one hand to interact with the real world and never picked up two products at once. Two-handed interactions were conducted by only 50 % of all participants. Those subjects performed on average four two-handed interactions per session. The time needed for placing a product was significantly higher for the real environment ($M_{real} = 4371$, $M_{virtual} = 3362$, $p = 0.02$).

## 4 Main Experiment

### 4.1 Hypotheses

Although there are small differences in the experimental setup, we expect a similar outcome in terms of performance in the main experiment, as all conditions have the same assistance functions guiding the user to get an optimal profit. Therefore we expect the real condition to perform better than the virtual one (**H 1**). We did not calculate the efficiency for our pilot experiment, but observed a significantly higher number of interactions and a lower performance in the virtual condition. As the Dual Reality interface should combine the advantages of both worlds, we expect the best efficiency to be in this condition, and the second best for the real setup (**H 2**), as the latter already outperformed the virtual version in our pilot study. Relatedly, we expect the most interaction with the virtual interface and the least within the real condition. The number of interactions in the Dual Reality setup should lie in between (**H 3**). As interacting with a virtual interface should be easier in terms of physical demand, we assume more interaction and less workload in that condition (**H 4**). Regarding the Dual Reality condition, we assume that most people switch between the virtual and real environment either in their physical interactions (**H 5**) or by switching the view focus (**H 6**).

## 4.2 Apparatus

Within each shelf unit, one shelf is at eye level and one below. For calculating the "eye level", we first retrieved the current average body height from the German Federal Bureau of Statistics (DESTATIS),[1] which is 171 cm. From this value, we subtracted 15 cm (a value derived from a pre-test) to arrive at an eye level of about 155 cm. We then designed the shelf to be at eye level, so the placed products can be seen best from that height. We arrived at a shelf height of 142 cm. The second shelf is placed below this, at 105 cm. Shelves in the starting shelf unit had a width of 82 cm, whereas the ones in the target unit were only 56 cm wide. We designed the latter to be smaller so not all the products inside the start shelf unit can be placed in the target; the subjects had to make a selection. The table between the shelves has a squared shape with a width of 90 cm, where only half of the table is visible to the subject. The monitor is placed on the table at a height of 90 cm. On the other side of the shelf is an "assistance zone" for the experimenter and an assistant; this is completely covered by cloth, so it is hidden from the experiment participant. The shelves of both shelf units are accessible from the back as in a puppet theater, so that the assistant can grab and place products undetected by the participants, simulating the "robot" which synchronizes the real world in a Dual Reality environment. The experimenter has a second screen inside the assistance zone, which shows a duplicate screen of the participant's touch display. It allows the experimenter to "synchronize" the virtual world in a Wizard of Oz style, whenever an action is done in the real environment by the participant.

The experiment was designed in a within-subject design: Each participant performed the task in the real, virtual and Dual Reality conditions, one after another. Additionally, we had three sets of products, A, B and C. Each set contained different products, although some of the products appeared in several sets. Each participant had the possibility to become familiar with each interface in advance, so we did not expect any influence on the experiment results, neither from the order of conditions, nor the order of product sets. Nevertheless, we balanced the order in which conditions and product sets were used. The products of a set are placed in the same style and ordering for each experiment. In order to capture eye movements, subjects use a mobile eye tracker in the Dual Reality condition.

---

[1] https://www.destatis.de/DE/Publikationen/Thematisch/Gesundheit/Gesundheitszustand/ Koerpermasse5239003099004.pdf.

## 4.3    Participants

We recruited 17 participants over several university mailing lists. Their ages ranged from 21 to 44 years (average 27.5). We had 10 male and 7 female subjects. Each was paid 10 Euro for the experiment.

## 4.4    Task

The subjects were given a set of products and one empty shelf unit. Every product placement contributed to an overall profit, as we will describe in the next section. The main task was to place the products in the shelves so that the overall profit was maximized. In the DR condition, subjects were free to make use of only the real, only the virtual or both worlds. We set no time limit, and the subjects could change the placement of the products as often as they wanted. The test run was marked as finished once the subject reported being satisfied with the current shelf layout.

The formula to derive the profit for the placements was based on related work from economics [5, 10, 15]. To enable subjects to better estimate the profit of their shelves, we based the formula on a few simplistic assumptions. The first aspect taken into account was the effect of the inventory level on the product demand, as proposed by Drèze et al. [8] and implemented by Hwang et al. [10] and Murray et al. [15]. It reflects the fact that products at eye level receive a significantly higher demand than products located below or above. In our formula, we modeled this effect by a deduction of 10 % for products below eye level. The second aspect is the space and cross-space elasticity as described by Corstjens and Doyle [5]. This earlier theory says, on an abstract level, that if two products of the same price and product category are next to each other, or on the same level in neighboring shelves, the profit of both is reduced.

In detail, the total profit was calculated as follows: Each product has a different price, which is printed on the real product or the 3D model of the product in the virtual interface. We divided the products into three price categories: low-priced products (price < 0.50€), medium-priced products (price between 0.50€ and 1€) and high-priced products (price > 1€). The profit of the target shelf unit is the sum of the profits of its contained products. If a product is placed on a shelf below eye level, its profit is the product price reduced by 10 %. If more than one product from the same price category is placed at the same eye level, the profit is again reduced. We call such a group of products (on the same level and in the same price category) "colliding products". For every collision, the profit of each colliding product is reduced by an additional 20 %. The reduction can be at most 100 %.

More formally, let $C(p) = collisions$ for a given product p (e.g. the products in the same price level and placed at the same shelf height as p), $Pr(p) = price$ of a product, as printed on the product, and $H(b) = handicap$ of a shelf, respecting its height level. It is 0 for the shelf at eye level and 0.1 for the shelf below. Then the overall profit $P$ is inductively defined as follows:

Profit of a product p:

$$P_p = Pr(p) * (Max(0; 1 - (|C(p)| * 0.2)))$$

Profit of a single shelf b:

$$p_b = (1 - H(b)) * \sum_{product\ p\ on\ b} (P_p)$$

The profit of the target shelf unit is then the sum of the profit of all of its shelves. The setup included more products than could be placed into the shelves. The subjects had to decide which products they wanted to use, and which would remain in the starting shelf. Participants were informed in advance of this effect by the experimenter. Apart from the assistant systems described earlier, we gave no further advice or strategy on how they could best complete the task.

## 4.5  Procedure

First, the participants were given written instructions. After possible questions were answered, a training phase started where first a short introduction to the interface was given. The introduction was done in a live demo by the experimenter. Following this, the subjects were given time to familiarize themselves with the interface. Once they stated they were comfortable with it, the main experiment phase started, where the users executed the given task in one of the three conditions. The starting condition was selected in a balanced way, as described in section *Apparatus*. This step was repeated with the second and third conditions. Each condition ended with a short two-page questionnaire, consisting of a NASA-TLX, and an additional page where users could explain their feelings towards efficiency, learnability and enjoyability of the respective condition, and what differences between conditions they perceived.

## 4.6  Efficiency Formula Refinement for the Experiment Task

The interface allows two sub-tasks: The *placement* task, e.g. picking up the product, transporting it to the desired location and dropping it off, and the *movement* task, which is moving the product inside the shelf without picking it up. In our example, let us assume that we have three different entities that can conduct this task: **The expert** has the highest qualification and salary. His part in the task is to design the layout for the shelf. **The assistant** has a lower qualification. He can place the products according to a given layout, but cannot design a shelf layout himself. **The robot** is the cheapest entity, but can only reproduce an interaction in the real environment if it was done in the virtual environment, as described in our definition of Dual Reality. In our three conditions, we then have the following sub-tasks that have to be conducted, in order to get a shelf layout using real products:

– **Real Environment:** The placement of the real products is done directly by the expert; we have only the cost of his placement and movement tasks. Our set of sub-tasks *ST* therefore consists solely of sub-tasks done by the expert: $ST = \{ST_{plc\_r\_exp}; ST_{mv\_r\_exp}\}$

– **Virtual Environment:** All actions by the expert are done virtually. Therefore, an assistant needs to fill in the real products after the design is finished (sub-task $ST_{plc\_ass}$): $ST = \{ST_{plc\_v\_exp}; ST_{mv\_v\_exp}; ST_{plc\_r\_ass}\}$

– **Dual Reality Environment:** Some of the expert's actions are done using the real shelf ($ST_{plc\_r\_exp}; ST_{mv\_r\_exp}$), some virtually ($ST_{plc\_v\_exp}; ST_{mv\_v\_exp}$). The expert's virtual manipulations are executed in the real world by the robot entity ($ST_{plc\_rob}; ST_{mv\_rob}$):
$ST = \{ST_{plc\_r\_exp}; ST_{mv\_r\_exp}; ST_{plc\_v\_exp}; ST_{mv\_v\_exp}; ST_{plc\_rob}; ST_{mv\_rob}\}$

The interaction times needed for each of the subtasks are calculated based on the results of our experiment, which will be given in the next sections. We found the following average interaction times: human placement in the real environment: 4130 ms; human placement in the virtual environment: 1698 ms.

Our experimental setup did not allow us to measure the time needed for a movement, as this action is too fast to be annotated correctly by the experimenter. We estimated the times in a short trial, using a stopwatch: human movement in the real environment: 1933 ms; human movement in the virtual environment: 1633 ms.

To allow a fair comparison, we designed both conditions, the virtual and the real one, as it is typically done by (software) engineers, using a screen for the virtual version, and a physical environment for the real one. Because the real environment typically involves a higher amount of locomotion, it requires more interaction time than the virtual environment. For the Dual Reality condition, we did not have a robot for our experiment, but there are industrial robots like the KUKA KR-16 which can conduct the placement/movement tasks. We estimated the time needed for those tasks using the datasheet[2] as follows:

– Grabbing/releasing the product: max. 90° rotation by axis 5, 45° by axis 6 $\rightarrow$ 316 ms
– Pull back/forward to shelf: max. 45° rotation by axes 2/3 $\rightarrow$ 288 ms
– Swivel between start/target shelf: max. 90° by axis 1 $\rightarrow$ 577 ms
– Movement inside shelf: max 45° rotation by axes 1/2/3 $\rightarrow$ 288 ms

  – Time(plcmt.) = grab + pull back + swivel + pull forward + release = 1785 ms
  – Time(movemt.) = grab + movement inside shelf + release = 920 ms

### 4.7 Measures—Dependent Variables

We divide our measures into two categories: task and sub-task measures. A task measure is taken during the whole test-run, and scores the overall result of the complex task. A sub-task measure is taken in relation to a specific sub-task that is conducted during the overall task. For the task, we recorded for all three conditions: **Profit** of the

---

[2] http://www.kuka-robotics.com/res/sps/e6c77545-9030-49b1-93f5-4d17c92173aa_Spez_KR_16_en.pdf.

target shelf unit with the user's solution, compared to the optimum solution; **Efficiency** of the task for each condition, according to our efficiency measure; and **Workload** according to the NASA-TLX. In the Dual Reality condition, we additionally documented: **Number of context switches** the user performs within his physical actions and **Number of visual context switches** in terms of visual attention switches between the two environments.

The idea of the *profit* measure is to compare how successful the participants were in accomplishing the given task. The *profit* is a percentual value, comparing the overall profit reached by the subject against an optimum shelf arrangement with the highest possible profit. We calculated this optimum on the given products and space using a brute-force algorithm. Measuring the profit helps us to investigate hypothesis 1. For us, *visual context switches* are only switches where the user looked at the main part of the screen containing the 3D model. Only looking at the score is not a context switch for us. We used the results from our eye tracker to discriminate between those two cases.

For each sub-task, such as placement or movement of a product, we recorded the **number** of times the sub-task was conducted during the task as well as the **time** on average that the user needed to complete the sub-task. The analysis of the measures was done automatically for actions in the *virtual* environment by the software. For activities in the *real* environment, the subject's actions were duplicated in this software by the experimenter on his display inside the assistance zone.

## 5 Results

The total time for the whole experiment varied from 15 to 30 min, as we set no time limit. On average, each participant needed about 20 min. All measures were pairwise compared using a paired t-test. The answers from the questionnaire were evaluated using chi-square.

### 5.1 Task Measures

In contrast to our initial hypothesis H 1, the overall profit in the real-world condition was significantly lower than for the virtual condition ($M_{real} = 0.93$, $M_{virtual} = 0.96$, $SD = 0.04$, $t = 3.51$, $p < 0.005$), as shown in Table 1. The Dual Reality score lay between the two, but without any significant difference from each of the other conditions ($M_{dr} = 0.945$). Although this profit was best for the virtual condition, the efficiency, according to our efficiency measure, was highest for the Dual Reality setup. The real setup was significantly less efficient ($M_{real} = 0.67$, $M_{dr} = 1.09$, $SD = 0.64$, $t = 2.72$, $p < 0.05$), as was the virtual condition ($M_{virtual} = 0.63$, $SD = 0.59$, $t = 3.2$, $p < 0.05$). We could not find any significant difference between the efficiency of the real and virtual interfaces.

We measured a significantly higher workload for the real compared to the virtual ($M_{real} = 4.95$, $M_{virtual} = 2.94$, $SD = 1.01$, $t = 8.2$, $p < 0.005$) and Dual Reality ($M_{dr} = 3.02$, $SD = 1.12$, $t = 7.12$, $p < 0.005$) conditions. Regarding the DR condition, we observed 7 of 17 participants switching between the real and virtual environments within their physical actions, for example placing a first product on the real shelf and then another product inside the virtual environment on the screen, or vice versa. Those who did such a context switch did it twice on average during the experiment. 15 of the subjects switched their eye focus between the two environments (26 times on average). We recorded the time users spent in both conditions of the DR setup, but could not find any significance. Some users acted mainly in the real environment, whereas others used the virtual environment all the time. Differences in terms of performance or efficiency could not be shown between those two groups. We evaluated the questionnaire using a chi-square test. Only one of the questions was of high significance in favor of the real environment, all others being insignificant: Users stated that the real interface made it easier to solve the task ($X^2 = 24.93$, $p < 0.005$).

**Table 1.** Results of the experimental task: real, virtual and dual reality (DR)

| Measure | Real | SD-real | Virtual | SD-virt. | DR | SD-DR |
|---|---|---|---|---|---|---|
| Profit | 0.926 | 0.06 | 0.963 | 0.04 | 0.941 | 0.06 |
| Efficiency | 0.67 | 0.24 | 0.63 | 0.22 | 1.09 | 0.62 |
| Workload | 4.95 | 0.77 | 2.94 | 0.49 | 3.02 | 0.65 |

Table 2 shows the results for the sub-tasks, regarding the number of times the task was conducted during an experiment for both conditions, as well as the average time needed for the task. As the logging of the experiment was done by an annotation tool used by the experimenter, we could not record the time needed for a movement: a movement task is completed too quickly to be annotated correctly.

**Table 2.** Sub-tasks measure results

| Measure | Real | SD-real | Virtual | SD-virt. | DR | SD-DR |
|---|---|---|---|---|---|---|
| Placemts. | 13.59 | 4.73 | 21.65 | 9.2 | 14.88 | 5.3 |
| Plc. time | 4130 | 2260 | 1698 | 736 | 2817 | 1861 |
| Movemts. | 0.18 | 0.53 | 4.35 | 5.6 | 1.18 | 1.67 |

In the virtual condition, products were moved significantly more often than in the Dual Reality setup ($M_{virtual} = 4.35$, $M_{DR} = 1.18$, $t = 2.26$, $p < 0.05$). The DR condition again had significantly more movements than the real condition ($M_{real} = 0.18$, $t = 2.2$, $p < 0.05$). We observed a similar result for the number of placements for each condition, where the participants positioned products at a new location more frequently in the virtual condition than in the DR setup ($M_{virtual} = 21.65$, $M_{DR} = 14.88$, $t = 3.12$, $p < 0.05$) and the real condition ($M_{real} = 13.59$, $t = 3.64$, $p < 0.005$). The number of placements between the real and Dual Reality conditions remains insignificant. For the placement times, the real condition was slowest, followed by the DR system ($M_{real} = 4130$, $M_{DR} = 2816$, $t = 3.29$, $p < 0.005$), which itself was significantly slower than the virtual condition ($M_{virtual} = 1898$, $t = 2.85$, $p < 0.05$).

# 6  Discussion

Hypothesis *H 1* is rejected, as it implies that the performance is lower for the virtual than the real condition. Contrary to this hypothesis, and although the assistance systems are the same in both conditions, the overall profit in the virtual world condition was significantly higher (p < 0.005). It seems like an "instrumented" system, e.g. a system that is enriched with assistance functions, works better in a virtual environment. There might be two possible causes of that effect: First, people are used to getting additional information in a virtual system, and are therefore more accustomed to using it. Real environments usually have no assistance functions. Second, we observed a significantly higher amount of interaction within the virtual system, and a smaller workload, as predicted by *H 4* and confirmed by our results. The virtual system, which requires less body movement in order to complete tasks, seems to enable users to explore the solution space more than the real environment, which could be a cause of the increased performance. Although the workload is highest for the real condition, subjects stated that this condition made it easiest to solve the task.

Our efficiency measure could only partly confirm *H 2*, given for the example cost setting of our main experiment: We assigned the expert a reference cost of $C_{hour}$(expert) = 100€. For the other entities we set cheaper costs of $C_{hour}$(assistant) = 50€ and $C_{hour}$(robot) = 1€. Within this example setting, the real condition was not as efficient as the virtual one. Dual Reality outperformed them both. If we change these entity costs, the results can also change significantly: If we reduce the expert cost by a half, so it is equal to the assistant cost, the real interface becomes significantly more efficient than the virtual condition ($M_{real}$ = 1.33, $M_{virtual}$ = 0.93, SD = 0.47, t = 3,56, p < 0.005). Dual Reality again outperforms them both. Every interface has its own drawbacks: In the real environment, the user needs extra time for the task, as he has to carry and handle the products, whereas the design on a desktop screen requires an additional person to fill in the shelf afterwards. The Dual Reality setup allows a virtual or a real-world design, but always has to synchronize with the real world using a machine entity. Our formula makes it possible to find an equilibrium, based on entity cost, at which the efficiency of two interfaces is equal. A designer can then investigate which changes in the cost of a specific entity give one interface an advantage over the other. To do so, two simple steps are required: First we need to equate the efficiency formulas of both conditions. In the second step, we resolve the equation to the specific entity cost that we want to modify to achieve our equilibrium. This gives us the entity cost at which both conditions have an equal efficiency. As an example, if we want to find the equilibrium for the virtual and DR conditions, using the cost of the robot entity as a modifier, we set $Efficiency_V$ = $Efficiency_{DR}$ and resolve the equation by $C_{hour}$(robot). We then get $C_{hour}$(robot) = 111.114€ as an equilibrium value. In this example, reducing the robot cost gives the DR condition an advantage, whereas increasing the cost raises the efficiency of the virtual condition.

*H 3* has been confirmed: the number of interactions was least for the real and greatest for the virtual condition. This effect can also be based on the workload of the different conditions, which is highest for the real condition, lower for the Dual Reality condition and lowest for the virtual condition. Most of the subjects switched between the virtual and real environment in our Dual Reality condition: About half of the subjects (7 of 17) did such a context switch within their physical actions ("hard" context switch), while nearly every subject (15 of 17) changed at least their eye focus between the two environments. This leads to the assumption that the concept of Dual Reality and the design of our DR condition works, as people took advantage of the possibilities such a system offers. *H 5* and *H 6*, claiming that people switch between the environments within their actions as well as within their visual attention, have also been confirmed. Interestingly, the participants always used the same problem-solving strategy in all three conditions: First they placed high-priced products, then medium- and low-priced products, until the score did not increase anymore, although this mostly does not yield optimal results.

## 7    Design Principles

Based on the results of the user study and the cost/efficiency function that we propose, we give guidelines on which interface type fits best for given preconditions. The guidelines presented here mainly apply to our experimental setting. Whether or not the rules can hold for other complex Dual Reality setups has to be confirmed in future research. We designed our generic efficiency formula so that it can be translated to an arbitrary composed task.

Regarding the *performance* of the task, as we observed in the pilot study, a real interface works best when the user has to interact without additional information or support functionality. The average user is most accustomed to the real world and can therefore achieve the best results under those circumstances. That changes if an additional instrumentation is done, like highlighting parts of the scene, or adding a capability to view the current score. Virtual environments will outperform their real counterparts in that case, although the number of interactions is likely to be higher within that environment.

If the focus is on the *efficiency* of the interface, e.g. the cost that is incurred in relation to the result, it depends on the actual cost for each entity. With the settings from our experiment, DR mostly outperformed the other two conditions. But as we have shown in the discussion, a general answer is not possible. The efficiency formula has to be modeled first according to the task, in order to compute the most efficient solution. Using our efficiency formula, it is possible to calculate the point from which one or the other interface type should be preferred, in relation to the cost of the entities involved.

Apart from these analyses, another important aspect is the setup effort of a Dual Reality environment. Whereas the effort is rather low for a real or virtual setup, a Dual Reality setup involves a significantly higher effort, especially for the realization of the synchronization of the real and virtual environment by machines. Our experiment has provided evidence that most people actually use the advantages of the DR environment and can achieve better results with it. Therefore, a Dual Reality setup should always be considered, in addition to a conventional real or virtual setting.

# 8   Conclusion

More and more tasks are being virtualized, such that users can perform them in the virtual world instead of the real world. Several studies have researched differences between real and virtual environments using rather simple tasks. Our experiment investigated a setup with a complex task, involving complex actions with a significant amount of locomotion, in real, virtual, and Dual Reality settings. We proposed an efficiency function, and compared the performance, efficiency, and number and timing of sub-tasks within the three conditions. In contrast to the hypothesis and our pilot study, the performance in maximizing the profit was significantly better in the virtual version, although the efficiency is best for the Dual Reality setting. We explored the impact of entity cost on the efficiency, and identified guidelines which guide the developer in selecting the right interface for his purpose, depending on the task that has to be fulfilled as well as the subtasks and entities involved.

# References

1. Kozak, J.J., Hancock, P.A., Arthur, E., Chrysler, S.: Transfer of training from virtual reality. Ergonomics **36**(7), 777–784 (1993)
2. Antle, A.N., Droumeva, M., Ha, D.: Hands on what?: comparing children's mouse-based and tangible-based interaction. In: Proceedings of the 8th International Conference on Interaction Design and Children, pp. 80–88. IDC 2009. ACM (2009)
3. Antle, A.N., Wang, S. Comparing motor-cognitive strategies for spatial problem solving with tangible and multi-touch interfaces. In: Proceedings of the 7th International Conference on Tangible, Embedded and Embodied Interaction, pp. 65–72. TEI 2013. ACM (2013)
4. Back, M., Kimber, D., Rieffel, E., Dunnigan, A., Liew, B., Gattepally, S., Foote, J., Shingu, J., Vaughan, J.: The virtual chocolate factory: mixed reality industrial collaboration and control. In: Proceedings of the International Conference on Multimedia, pp. 1505–1506. MM 2010. ACM (2010)
5. Corstjens, M., Doyle, P.: A model for optimizing retail space allocations. Manage. Sci. **27** (7), 822–833 (1981)
6. Davies, M., Callaghan, V.: iWorlds: Generating artificial control systems for simulated humans using virtual worlds and intelligent environments. JAISE **4**(1), 5–27 (2012)
7. Dobbins, A.C., Grossmann, J.K.: Asymmetries in perception of 3D orientation. PLoS ONE **5**(3), e9553 (2010)
8. Drèze, X., Hoch, S.J., Purk, M.E.: Shelf management and space elasticity. J. Retail. **70**(4), 301–326 (1994)
9. Gelernter, D.: Mirror Worlds: or the Day Software Puts the Universe in a Shoebox… How it Will Happen and What it Will Mean. Oxford University Press, New York (1992)
10. Hwang, H., Choi, B., Lee, M.-J.: A model for shelf space allocation and inventory control considering location and inventory level effects on demand. Int. J. Prod. Econ. **97**(2), 185–195 (2005)
11. Khan, V.-J., Nuijten, K., Deslé, N.: Pervasive application evaluation within virtual environments. In: Benavente-Peces, C., Filipe, J. (eds.) PECCS, pp. 261–264. SciTePress (2011)

12. Lifton, J., Paradiso, J.A.: Dual reality: merging the real and virtual. In: Lehmann-Grube, F., Sablatnig, J. (eds.) FaVE 2009. LNICST, vol. 33, pp. 12–28. Springer, Heidelberg (2010)

13. Lucchi, A., Jermann, P., Zufferey, G., Dillenbourg, P.: An empirical evaluation of touch and tangible interfaces for tabletop displays. In: Proceedings of the Fourth International Conference on Tangible, Embedded, and Embodied Interaction, pp. 177–184. TEI 2010. ACM (2010)

14. Montello, D.: Scale and multiple psychologies of space. In: Campari, I., Frank, A.U. (eds.) COSIT 1993. LNCS, vol. 716. Springer, Heidelberg (1993)

15. Murray, C.C., Talukdar, D., Gosavi, A.: Joint optimization of product price, display orientation and shelf-space allocation in retail category management. J. Retail. **86**(2), 125–136 (2010)

16. Olwal, A., Gustafsson, J., Lindfors, C.: Spatial augmented reality on industrial CNC-machines. Proc. SPIE **6804**, 680409–680409-9 (2008). doi:10.1117/12.760960

17. Todd, J., Norman, J.: The visual perception of 3-D shape from multiple cues: are observers capable of perceiving metric structure? Percept. Psychophys. **65**(1), 31–47 (2003)

18. Tuddenham, P., Kirk, D., Izadi, S.: Graspables revisited: multi-touch vs. tangible input for tabletop displays in acquisition and manipulation tasks. In: Proceedings of the SIGCHI Conference on Human Factors in Computing Systems, pp. 2223–2232. CHI 2010. ACM (2010)

# Hard-to-Get-at Data from Difficult-to-Access Users

Bob Fields[✉], Andy Bardill, Lisa Marzano, and Kate Herd

Middlesex University, London, UK
{b.fields,a.bardill,l.marzano,k.herd}@mdx.ac.uk

**Abstract.** This paper reports on the development of a suite of tools to collect, analyze and visualize a diverse range of data from sufferers of mental ill health. The aim is to allow researchers and ultimately sufferers and clinicians to better understand 'individual signatures' of factors that indicate or identify episodes of ill health. The tools have been applied in a study working with clients of a mental health service that demonstrates their applicability and acceptability in developing a better understanding of the factors surrounding self-harm behavior.

**Keywords:** Apps · Wearable technology · Mental health · Visualization

## 1 Introduction

The importance of context on behaviors and experiences has long been recognized, and many attempts by the HCI community have been made to devise methods for understanding what people do, in the settings they do it. Approaches to collecting data in-situ have yielded tools for mobile 'experience sampling' [2], that regularly collect data from the user, for example to gauge emotional responses to specific locations.

This paper reports an approach to collecting 'live' data 'in the field' from users who often fall outside of the 'standard' population, and in situations that are not typically the focus of more traditional user research methods such as evaluations, diary studies etc. An array of technologies are employed: mobile devices, wearable computing, web applications, to allow participants to engage in a data collection process that is both autonomous and active, providing an enriched understanding of the way that physical, physiological, emotional and environmental factors can influence mal-adaptive behaviors, in this instance, that of self-harm. Qualitative and quantitative approaches are combined to construct an understanding of both the perception of activity, behavior and context as well a quantitative underpinning of what is actually occurring.

## 2 Background

This research project sought to create an 'ecological model of self harm', by better understanding the lives and actions of young men who have a history of self-harm. The literature on self-harm has identified a number of factors that may be implicated in the changes in mental state leading to self-harm episodes. However, such studies have tended to rely heavily on self-reports that require after-the-fact recollection. The case

© IFIP International Federation for Information Processing 2015
J. Abascal et al. (Eds.): INTERACT 2015, Part IV, LNCS 9299, pp. 409–416, 2015.
DOI: 10.1007/978-3-319-22723-8_32

for reliably monitoring symptoms and signs, and the potential for novel mobile technology is made forcefully in a recent report of the Chief Medical Officer [3].

Several experimental attempts have been made to collect and analyze data that can afford a patient or clinician a better understanding of relevant contextual factors. Typically, however, such projects have been quite narrow in scope – either focusing only on a single condition, or employing only limited sensing, monitoring and analysis technologies. In some cases, projects have been unable to engage with actual patients – an important class of users – and have relied instead on experts and proxy test users.

The Trajectories of Depression project focused on the effects of mobility (as a proxy for activity) on depression [12]. In addition to subjective self-reports, only a single type of more objective data was captured (GPS location). Darzi and others [4] propose a similar approach – using data that can be readily collected by modern smartphone sensors (physical activity and location) to build up a picture of peoples' lifestyle to support better weight loss strategies. Mappiness [10] demonstrates similar ideas in an attempt to study the effects of place and location on happiness and well-being. Again, a range of subjective data and GPS location is collected, and again, the capabilities of a smartphone provide a convenient platform, but also limit what data is available. The unCUT app [9] is similar in spirit to Insight, though it focuses only on self reporting, rather than the broader range of sensing and data collection used in the initial Insight prototype, and has not, as yet been tested with real patients.

In the current study, we recognized the need for a methodological approach and appropriate tools to collect a diverse range of data from real patients, allowing us to build up an understanding of both the broad context in which self-injury takes place and the individual perspective of experience and personal history on the behaviors taking place.

## 3    Design Objectives

Difficulties in affect regulation, poor sleep and lack of physical activity are all markers of poor physical and mental health. Accurate assessment and monitoring of these and other key variables (e.g. compulsive and impulsive behaviors) have long been recognized as important, particularly for relapsing psychological problems. They can help us to understand individual symptom trajectories and potentially identify personalized relapse signatures. To collect a broad range of multi-dimensional data that are not reliant only on self-report, a suite of smartphone apps and other devices were brought together. The system (Fig. 1) includes a combination of off-the-shelf and bespoke hardware and software, and supports the collection of digital diary content, location, and activity and physiological data, that is uploaded to a secure server, and made accessible to the research team via a web-based interface.

### 3.1    Digital Diary

Participants are prompted twice-daily to complete a multi-media diary (*'My Diary'*) on moods and activities; intensity, duration and contextual features of any self-injurious

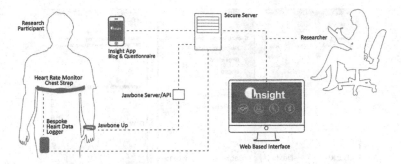

**Fig. 1.** Insight system structure

thoughts and behavior; other risk-taking and impulsive behaviors (e.g. binge eating and drinking); flashbacks; and nightmares. Diary entries include closed questions consisting of check-boxes, rating scale sliders or free text entry fields (Fig. 2).

Participants conclude the diary entry with a free text account of events, thoughts and feelings that can incorporate audio, photographs and video. This content is uploaded to a private 'blog' that can be used for personal recollection and reflection. Participants are also encouraged to post about their broader life histories and experiences ('*My Story*'). The blog-diary and questionnaire responses are also available, via the web server, to project researchers for later analysis.

Important ethical questions surrounds the effect that using an app like this may have on users. Several studies have shown that individuals participating in research about suicide and self-harm (including qualitative interview studies such as the one used here) do not appear to be negatively affected, and many derive benefit from participation [e.g., see 11]. In addition, previous research has shown that maintaining contact with those who self-harm (through letters, postcards, text messaging, etc.) does not increase their risk of suicide and has potential to reduce repetition. For example, studies have suggested that suicide attempters who receive a follow-up letter or postcard including a simple message of concern are less likely to engage in further self-harm than those who do not receive such contact [8].

### 3.2 Location Tracking

Location and physical mobility have been implicated as factors affecting mental state [e.g. see 12], and there is evidence that specific locations may have a causal effect on self-harm behavior (e.g. because of memories triggered in a particular place).

The Insight app tracks location, and uploads location data to the secure server each time the participant completes a diary entry. To manage the desire for privacy, location tracking can be disabled or the tracking accuracy adjusted by the user.

### 3.3 Activity and Physiological Data

Research suggests heart rate variability (HRV) is a reliable biomarker for stress [e.g. 1, 7]. Obtaining reliable data for assessing HRV over an extended period (around 3 weeks

**Fig. 2.** The Insight app: open and closed diary question entries

in this project), outside of the laboratory in naturalistic settings using non-invasive methods is a non-trivial task. Many commercial heart rate measurement products exist, either as 'lifestyle devices', sports training aids, or medical monitoring devices (e.g. cardiological diagnostic tools). However, none (at the time of this study) was intended to unobtrusively capture heart data over a prolonged period: many do not monitor continuously, and those that do tend to be bulky and uncomfortable.

A bespoke heart beat data logger was developed to collect data wirelessly from a commercial chest strap heart sensor. The inter-beat intervals are used to calculate heart rate and HRV. Many ways exist of calculating HRV [e.g. see 5], and the one employed here was the commonly-used approach of using standard deviation of inter-beat intervals over fixed time windows. This sensing method enables reliable data to be collected in a relatively non-invasive and power efficient way.

While collecting continuous heart beat data required bespoke hardware, the measurement of other indicators of behavior was made simpler by the range of readily available activity tracking devices. The project made use of Jawbone UP wristbands (http://jawbone.com), to sense physical activity, and sleep quality and duration (see Fig. 3).

**Fig. 3.** Data collection using Jawbone UP, chest-strap heart monitor, data-logger and app

## 4 Making Sense

A key aim has been to provide a means of analyzing data so researchers can gain insights into factors and variables influencing a person's mental state. Of particular interest is the identification of *individual signatures*, indicative of a person's mental state, and which may be connected with recurrence of self-harming behavior. The aim is therefore not (only) to make data amenable to statistical analysis across a cohort of participants. Rather the aim is to support investigations in which patterns, possibly highly individual in nature, may be discerned.

Key questions for a researcher concern the events leading up to an instance of self harm. For instance, was the person in a particular location? Was the person's sleep of poor quality? Were there indications of stress? Do subjective reports of affective state appear to correlate with physiological and environmental data?

To this end, the Insight system provides two main visualization tools: a map and a timeline, which are linked so that selections in one view (e.g. to select only a portion of the timeline data) filters data displayed in the other view (e.g. to show only locations logged during the selected time window). This approach has proved successful in other contexts where an analyst attempts to make sense of related temporal and geographical data [13]. The Geo-view (Fig. 4) shows the locations logged by the smartphone app, overlaid on a map.

**Fig. 4.** Geo-view showing user's movement

The second visualization is a timeline that plots a broad range of data over time, including measured variables (e.g. activity, sleep quality, heart rate and variability) and subjective reports (e.g. responses to questions about affective state) as well as discrete events (e.g. reports of self harm). Data in this fairly raw form presents a confusing and complex picture, and is likely to be of limited use in discerning any pattern. However, the view provides filtering and zooming, allowing the user to interact with the data to investigate more specific patterns and relationships (e.g., see Fig. 5). Currently, data visualizations are at a prototype stage, and suitable for researchers rather than patients.

Future development will create visualizations that enable patients to explore and better understand their own behavioral signatures.

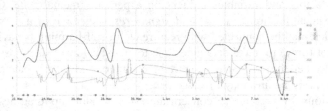

**Fig. 5.** Data zoomed and filtered to explore link between HRV and thoughts of self-harm

# 5   An Ecological Study of Self-harm

The technology setup was trialed with 5 users who had a history of self-injury, and who were recruited through a mental health service of which they were clients. People who self-injure may feel uncomfortable discussing their feelings and behavior in a one-to-one interview situation, or find it difficult to verbalize what triggers self-harming behavior. They can however be more willing to engage with a well-designed digital diary or blogging study (for example, 'Day in the Life' Projects – see https://dayinthelifemh.org.uk/).

The research was approved by the Middlesex University Psychology Department's Ethics Committee, which is subject to the University research governance and the code of conduct of the British Psychological Society and Health and Care Professions Council. Participant were asked to take part in the study for around 3 weeks, though two participants chose to take part for considerably longer. Table 1 summarizes participation in the study, indicating the volume and variety of data collected.

**Table 1.** Summary study data

| Participant no. | Days in study | No days made *My Diary* entries | Total no. *My Diary* entries | Total no. *My Story* entries | Thoughts of self harm | Self harm |
|---|---|---|---|---|---|---|
| 1 | 79 | 65 | 99 | 128 (+4 videos/photos) | 36 | 15 |
| 2 | 21 | 21 | 43 | 60 (+30 videos/photos) | 13 | 0 |
| 3 | 21 | 13 | 15 | 4 (text) | 6 | 0 |
| 4 | 21 | 18 | 36 | 12 (+1 photo) | 8 | 1 |
| 5 | 49 | 35 | 37 | 5 (text) | 29 | 5 |

A thorough analysis of the data, and presentation of a 'model of self harm' is beyond the scope of the current paper. However, it is worth noting that all participants continued in the study for the expected duration, persisting in making diary entries throughout (averaging around 1.3 entries per day). No significant drop-off was observed, with participants continuing to contribute throughout the study. The aim here is not to evaluate usability or study the participants' experience directly, but to explore issues such as participants' motivation and willingness to engage, as a way of understanding the potential of the approach as an effective research tool.

Post-study, participants were de-briefed in an interview that explored, among other things, the experience of participation and use of the tools. Reactions to the technology, its usability, and reflections on the value of participation, were generally positive. For example, one participant (P5) reported that the study had helped him "*express some of what I'm going through that's in my head down as data. So it has, yeah, I've found it beneficial. [especially] after I've self-harmed because...*". Another participant reported using the digital diary app to vent frustrations in a safe way, "*I'm alone but I got my diary to keep me company. I can rant on here and not get told off or nicked...*" (P1); whilst P2 told us that he planned to invest in his own Jawbone wristband at the end of the research, as this had helped him with "*...keeping me in touch with my sleep patterns and when to go to bed, which is fantastic*". The same participant also reported watching his own video-diaries back and then showing them to his therapist "*so they can see what I am actually like when I'm feeling depressed and down .... So again doing the research is helping me again.*"

# 6   Conclusions

This research-in-progress has developed a novel suite of software and hardware tools to support the collection, analysis and visualization of a range of self reports and sensed data from people with a history of self-harming behavior. The approach has been trialed on a small but substantial study in which data was collected over a period of more than 3 weeks from 5 users. Initial analysis of the data, as well as post-study interviews suggest a very positive response to the approach, with the experience of the technology being generally positive, and the ability to record and reflect being regarded as highly beneficial.

Work is progressing in several areas. The analysis process, and the interactive visual analytic tools needed to make sense of a mass of complex, heterogeneous data is progressing towards the original aim of informing a model of self-harm, that explores links between contextual variables and behavior.

The aim of this project was certainly not to develop a therapeutic tool (although the study indicated a positive effect in taking part and in reflection and gathering of personal commentary). Indeed, the intended users of the data and visualizations of it are mental health researchers, rather than patients or clinicians (and, apart from the blog elements, users don't have access to the recorded data other than through the project team). However, giving patients easy access to their data, and exploring the use of such data in personal and clinical settings is a natural direction for the project to take.

A further set of developments under active investigation concern making the technology more configurable (e.g. to easily create bespoke content for a particular study), personal (e.g. identifying data relevant to an 'individual signature' of a particular patient), and general (e.g. allowing a range of sensors and visualization tools to be incorporated). On this latter point we are exploring the use of extensions of quite general 'm-health' frameworks such as *Open mHealth* [6].

**Acknowledgements.** The work described in this paper was supported by the Richard Benjamin Trust, to whom the authors are grateful. We would also like to thank our study participants for their participation, and the service through which they were recruited for their support.

# References

1. Brosschot, J.F., et al.: Daily worry is related to low heart rate variability during waking and the subsequent nocturnal sleep period. Int. J. Psychophysiol. **63**(1), 39–47 (2007)
2. Cherubini, M., Oliver, N.: A refined experience sampling method to capture mobile user experience. In: Workshop on Mobile User Experience Research – CHI 2009 (2009)
3. Chief Medical Officer: Annual Report of the Chief Medical Officer 2013, Public Mental Health Priorities: Investing in the Evidence (2013). https://www.gov.uk/government/uploads/system/uploads/attachment_data/file/351629/Annual_report_2013_1.pdf
4. Darzi, A.: Quantified-self for obesity: physical activity behaviour sensing to improve health outcomes from surgery for severe obesity. EPSRC project EP/L023814/1. http://gow.epsrc.ac.uk/NGBOViewGrant.aspx?GrantRef=EP/L023814/1
5. Electrophysiology, Task Force of the European Society of Cardiology and the North American Society of Pacing: Heart rate variability: standards of measurement, physiological interpretation, and clinical use. Circulation **93**(5), 1043–1065 (1996)
6. Estrin, D., Sim, I.: Open mHealth architecture: an engine for health care innovation. Science **330**(6005), 759–760 (2010)
7. Horsten, M., et al.: Psychosocial factors and heart rate variability in healthy women. Psychosom. Med. **61**, 1 (1999)
8. Kapur, N., et al.: Postcards, green cards and telephone calls: therapeutic contact with individuals following self-harm. Br. J. Psychiatry **197**(1), 5–7 (2010)
9. Lederer, N., et al.: unCUT: bridging the gap from paper diary cards towards mobile electronic monitoring solutions in borderline and self-injury. In: 3rd International Conference on Serious Games and Applications for Health. IEEE (2014)
10. MacKerron, G., Mourato, S.: Happiness is greater in natural environments. Glob. Environ. Change **23**(5), 992–1000 (2013)
11. Muehlenkamp, J.J., et al.: Emotional and behavioral effects of participating in an online study of nonsuicidal self-injury: an experimental analysis. Clin. Psychol. Sci. **3**(1), 26–37 (2014)
12. Musolesi, M.: Trajectories of Depression: Investigating the Correlation between Human Mobility Patterns and Mental Health Problems by means of Smartphones. EPSRC project EP/L006340/1. http://www.cs.bham.ac.uk/research/projects/tod
13. Xu, K., et al.: Visual analysis of streaming data with SAVI and SenseMAP. In: 2014 IEEE Conference on Visual Analytics Science and Technology (VAST), pp. 389–390 (2014)

# Oh, What a Night!
# Effortless Sleep Monitoring at Home

Bert Vandenberghe[✉] and David Geerts

Centre for User Experience Research (CUO),
iMinds – KU Leuven, Leuven, Belgium
{bert.vandenberghe,david.geerts}@soc.kuleuven.be

**Abstract.** As sleep is considered an important aspect of our health, a range of products that would benefit our sleep is brought to market. Like many of these products, smart wristbands or fitness trackers make promises to improve the user's quality of life by improving sleep quality. We performed a sensitizing diary study followed by a user experience evaluation comparing sleep-tracking features of the Fitbit Flex, Jawbone Up, Misfit Shine, and Polar Loop products with six users. We summarize their findings in three recommendations for sleep-tracking functionalities: find the right balance between automation and control, make data intelligible for users, and acknowledge the role of emotions. These design recommendations should make sleep trackers more transparent, and thus more usable and useful to the users in their endeavor to sleep well.

**Keywords:** Activity trackers · Sleep monitoring · User experience · Wearables

## 1 Introduction

For both scientists and the public, sleep is hot topic nowadays. Medical literature is pointing towards disturbed sleep as underlying cause for health related issues that challenge modern society. In hospitals, there are long waiting lists for people who want or need their sleep to be studied in a sleep center, leaving a growing group of people undiagnosed. As these specialized centers use traditional and expensive techniques, hospitals face some challenges to make use of the available capacity in the most efficient way. In addition to the increased medical attention to sleep related problems, with initiatives like the Sleep Awareness Week or the international World Sleep Day, the debate on disturbed sleep is brought to the attention of the broad public as well. Topics like sleep, sleep related disorders, and solutions to improve your sleep are also attracting increased attention from newspapers, magazines, and public broadcasting.

Along with this increased attention for sleep, we see a growing market for products that are meant to improve sleep quality: from intelligent alarm clocks for smartphones that wake the sleeper in light sleep to state-of-the-art sleep monitoring devices to be used at home. One type of products that has the purpose to assist people in monitoring or improving their sleep is the smart wristband. These wearables track activity 24/7, counting steps during the day and measuring sleep patterns at night, and make promises

© IFIP International Federation for Information Processing 2015
J. Abascal et al. (Eds.): INTERACT 2015, Part IV, LNCS 9299, pp. 417–424, 2015.
DOI: 10.1007/978-3-319-22723-8_33

to improve the quality of the user's sleep. For example, the Fitbit Flex product website states: "Flex never sleeps, even when you do. Continue to wear it all night and it'll measure your sleep quality. Your dashboard will reveal how long you slept and the number of times you woke up to help you learn how to sleep more soundly" [3]. As we find similar statements on the websites and product packaging of the Jawbone Up, Misfit Shine, and Polar Loop, it is clear that these tools make big promises and set high expectations for buyers regarding sleep. In 2015, with the launch of the Apple Watch, the success of smart watches is expected to be at the expense of smart wristbands [4]. And although neither of the two is widely adopted, this new wave of wearables comes with new technology, so we can expect even more extensive features related to sleep in the near future.

Prior evaluations of wearables focus on the fitness and activity tracking features, e.g. [6]. From a technical point of view, alternatives for existing sleep monitoring techniques are suggested, e.g. using smartphones [1]. And from a medical point of view, the effectiveness of popular activity tracking products has been evaluated [7]. The social impact of wearables is also being studied, mainly concerning privacy aspects [8]. But despite Choe's call for work on sleep in the HCI community [2], to our knowledge, no work on these sleep-tracking tools exists from the user's perspective.

The present study looks at the user experience when monitoring sleep at home through smart wristbands. We don't make a verdict on the accuracy, effectiveness, or the sense or nonsense of these products from a technical or medical perspective. We contribute to the research on sleep-tracking by sharing experiences of users using popular tools and summarizing design recommendations for sleep monitoring features and tools to be used at home from a user's perspective.

## 2   The Study

We performed a diary study to sensitize the participants to their own sleep patterns and habits. After the diary study, we asked the participants to use two different smart wristbands to track their sleep, and then asked them to report on their experiences with these products by comparing them. We recruited six participants via a call that was shared on Facebook. The participants were between 21 to 60 years old, and five of the six participants were female. The participants had a moderate to advanced knowledge of technology. They all used (laptop) computers and smartphones daily, and two participants used a tablet regularly. Some of the participants were familiar with the selected tools, but no one had actually used one before. All participants received a gift card of €50 as incentive after the concluding interview.

Inspired by cultural probes [5], we composed a niary – a diary to record the night – for the participants. As with the original probes, the niary wasn't meant for extensive analysis in the first place. Our niary had the purpose to sensitize the participants about their own sleep patterns. By completing the niary, people were made more conscious about their evening rituals, their sleep, and the night, before they started using sleep-tracking tools. This made the evaluation of the activity trackers more focused on sleep-tracking features of the tools.

The niary (see Fig. 1) consisted of a booklet to record each night for one week, three postcards with a question related to sleep, and a to-do list. In the booklet, participants were asked to write down when they went to sleep and when they woke up, and how they were feeling (as in how tired they were, and their mood). Also, we asked them to use a metaphor for their sleep and for waking up (e.g. a song, movie, or object). Finally, we also asked them to sketch the night (this could be a drawing, a graph, a written text, or a collage). The cards listed the questions: "The most important thing in my bedroom is…", "Sometimes, I can't sleep because…", and "I prefer to get awakened…". On the to-do list, people could write down their evening ritual.

**Fig. 1.** An impression of the niary as given to the participants (left), and completed (right).

After the diary study, we evaluated the user experience when using a smart wristband. We selected four popular wristbands with sleep-tracking functionalities: the Fitbit Flex, Jawbone Up, Misfit Shine, and Polar Loop (see Fig. 2).

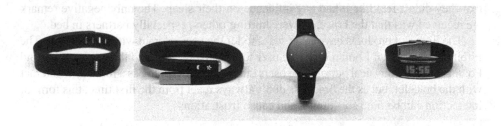

**Fig. 2.** From left to right: the Fitbit Flex, Jawbone Up, Misfit Shine, and Polar Loop.

These four products have the same working principle and offer similar functionality regarding sleep-tracking. Although other, more specific sleep-tracking devices exist, these are more expensive and require the latest smartphones. In order to keep the study feasible, we decided to limit our set of devices to those with a higher compatibility with computers or smartphones.

We visited our participants three times in two weeks. During the first visit we explained the overall course of our study. After signing an informed consent, we handed over the niary, and explained every aspect of it in detail with the participant.

Then, the participants completed the niary in one week, after which we had a second conversation to discuss the completed niary. These conversations were not analyzed, but it allowed the participants to formulate their story and to give thought to their sleep and sleep habits once again, in order to become more conscious of it. We then gave the participants two wristbands for a pairwise comparison, and explained how they could use the devices. We chose the wristbands for each participant based on the available technology (e.g. only a few participants had access to an iPhone or iPad required for the Misfit Shine, while all participants had a computer that could be used for the Fitbit Flex). We also distributed the devices to have them equally used among the participants. We limited our instructions to the bare minimum (how to install, how to synchronize, and how to view the data). Afterwards, we also sent the instructions to the participant by e-mail. Then, the participants could use the two trackers for one week, after which we had a third and final encounter. We interviewed the participants and focused on their experiences with the products, and we asked them to compare the two systems. This interview was recorded for further analysis. We transcribed the recorded interviews, and made an affinity diagram from the experiences people reported to identify recurring patterns.

## 3   Results

The interviews with participants of our study gave interesting insight in the user experience of the sleep-tracking features, which we bundled in five themes: the bracelet, night mode, synchronization, viewing results, and value.

### 3.1   The Bracelet

The participants reported that wearing the bracelet did not bother them. They also said that they didn't feel like it had any influence on their sleep. The only negative remark we received was that the bracelets were hurting others, especially partners in bed.

The different products have other ways to let the user interact with the bracelet. The Fitbit Flex and Polar Loop require the user to tap the bracelet, and the Jawbone Up and Polar Loop have physical button. The users did regard the tapping as a fun way to interact with the bracelet, but as the bracelets don't always react from the first time, this form of interaction can be time consuming and cause frustrations.

> "When I had to tap the bracelet to get the lights, it didn't always respond in the way I wanted it. I knew that I should have two, so I kept tapping until I saw the two lights. Sometimes, this could take a while." – U02

Confusing situations where the bracelet did not respond as expected are enforced by unclear or missing feedback. Figure 2 shows the different displays: 5 small lights on the Fitbit Flex, a sun and moon icon on the Jawbone Up, 12 lights as a clock on the Misfit Shine, and digits (which can also show text) on the Polar Loop. During the study, two participants switched day and night mode (for counting steps and measuring sleep) on the Fitbit Flex for some days because they misinterpreted the displayed patterns of lights, which resulted in no data and caused frustration. On the Jawbone Up, the feedback was clearer, but people were wondering why day mode is shown as a flower. As one of the participants noted, the bracelets are useless until they are synchronized with the app or website.

## 3.2  Night Mode

The bracelets have two modes: day mode for counting steps and night mode for measuring sleep. Some devices require a manual action to switch modes. The participants thought it was nice that they could indicate "now I go to sleep", but they didn't understand there was no data recorded if they forgot this. And our study showed that people do forget to put the bracelet in night mode. As some devices are able to switch day and night mode automatically, the participants expected this behavior from all products.

> "I forgot to put it in night mode a few times. The bracelet could detect it automatically, or measure both in case you forget to change it. [...] If you forget it now, all data is lost and you can not retrieve it anymore." – U03

People found a fully automatic switch not ideal, as they thought that the device was not always right. The Misfit Shine detects sleep automatically and allows people to correct the data, but then all measured data is removed so the user only has the manually entered times left, which is not better than having slightly incorrect data.

## 3.3  Synchronization

To view the measured nights, people first have to synchronize the data. Some bracelets have small extras to do this: dongles, cables, ... Participants didn't bother using these extras, but were afraid to lose them, as they are quite small. People did have a clear preference to synchronize the data via their smartphone to their computer, especially in the morning after waking up.

> "I always have my smartphone with me, as well as my tracker, so synchronizing goes much smoother. With the dongle and the computer it was more cumbersome." – U04

Some products provide automatic synchronization, but our participants didn't regard this as a necessary function. As people have the goal of looking at their data, they do take time for it and take their smartphone or computer with them. As opposed to switching day and night mode, people are unlikely to forget synchronizing before viewing the results.

> "Manual sync may make it less handy, but it's not bad either. You know you have to log in on the website so you can not forget to sync, as opposed to put the tracker in night mode manually." – U06

Also, participants did perform a manual sync every time before looking at the results even with an automatic synchronizing product, just to be sure to have the most recent data, especially in the morning when they were curious about their night.

### 3.4   Viewing Results

As with synchronization, people preferred viewing results on their smartphone to their computer.

> *"The phone is really interesting. It was quicker to take a look at my phone more regularly. With the computer, you have to start it every time." –* U05

Regarding data visualization, people preferred linear graphs to circular graphs, as 24 h circles were confused with 12 h clocks. The use of color could also be improved, as some websites used colors with very little difference (e.g. different shades of blue, which makes it hard to distinguish restful and restless sleep). People did expect a more detailed view on their night, and were disappointed by the lack of details.

When viewing the results, people were wondering whether the measurements were correct. People were missing explanation on how the bracelets decide whether the user was awake or sleeping.

> *"It is not clear how they make up their conclusions. How does the band know when I'm sleeping? Maybe I'm watching television in the sofa. If you look at the results the day after, you immediately see the error. But if I don't look at the results for over a week, I don't remember this anymore. I would like to know how they define when I am sleeping, and how they calculate the 'time to sleep'." –* U06

We also got a lot of questions on how people should interpret the data. People want to know what the data means, and what is normal.

> *"I would like to have some tips that help me to interpret the data, what is good and what is bad. Maybe some more explanation would be better, what is sound sleep and light sleep." –* U01

People were missing tips and advice to improve their sleep, based on the measurements.

### 3.5   Value

During our interviews, the participants said the trackers were fun to use, and we did not see any differences between trackers on this aspect. People liked to have an overview of the times they went to bed, the times they woke up, and how long it took before they actually fell asleep. Our participants said it was nice to see the difference between light and deep sleep. However, most participants found the activity trackers very basic. The information was found descriptive and rather limited. People were not convinced of the value of the trackers, because the devices gave too little information and the explanation was too brief. People had the impression that you cannot do much with these devices.

> *"You can tell that sleep is not the company's core business. But it is good it is included next to steps and food, as sleep has an impact on your health." –* U04

People told us they learned that a good night doesn't necessarily mean a long night, and a short night can be very restful.

> *"I noticed that sleep is very subjective. You can have a very bad night, while the graph is good." –* U05

People also felt that there is more than numbers when talking about sleep. Having an app that tells your night was good, while you feel terrible, is damaging for the credibility of the system. So where these products offer very little guidance to make interpretations and meaning from the data, they do make simplistic statements based on numbers. People do feel that emotions play a big role as well.

## 4 Discussion

Based on the experiences from the users in our study, we formulate three recommendations for sleep-tracking tools: find a good balance between automation and control, make data intelligible, and don't ignore the role of emotions.

People want control, they want to be able to tell the system when they're going to sleep. But, we must take into account that people do forget to push the button to do this, so an automatic fallback is no luxury. This ensures that there is data in the morning. However, if the automatic fallback would be incorrect, the user should be able to fine-tune the data without losing valuable data. On the other hand, synchronization can be manual, as this doesn't seem to bother users. We should keep in mind that people don't have a computer nearby while waking up, so it is more convenient to use a smartphone or tablet to synchronize the data.

It's obvious that graphs should be clear. By using distinct colors, the users can easily spot disturbances and patterns in their measured sleep. Users will want to compare nights, so the interface should facilitate this. Providing an overview of multiple days, or at least by using the same timescale for each graph can do this. It is important to inform people how the data was measured, and on what ground statements were made. Also, we need to teach users how to make meaning from the measured data, so how they should interpret the signals.

People feel that numbers are not everything, that emotions play a big role as well in sleep quality. Therefore, tools should be more careful when judging how sleep was. Judging a night as long enough is better than saying the night was perfect, purely based on numbers.

As with every study, there are some limitations that should be taken into account when discussing these results. We only had six participants, who tested two devices in a pairwise comparison, for the duration of one week. Of course, a longer study with more participants would be very interesting. Then, a more quantitative approach could be taken as well, using standardized questionnaires to assess the usability of these systems. Also, by having a more correct gender balance, the importance of emotions might be nuanced or new themes might arise.

## 5 Conclusion

While the existing sleep trackers can help people to assess their sleep and improve their sleep quality, the users experienced some frustration while using these tools. We think that the tools should be more transparent. By finding the right balance between automation and control, trackers can be more effortless to use and forgiving to the user.

By telling users what they see, and teaching them what they could do with this information, data can be more intelligible. Then, people can take the next step beyond measuring, and actually improve their sleep. And to conclude, trackers should also broaden their view on sleep by including emotions. Numbers are valuable to quantify sleep, but there is more. By giving room to emotions, users can get a more nuanced view on their sleep. With these small efforts, which are feasible, existing tools and technology can address user needs in a more regarding sleep-tracking at home.

**Acknowledgements.** The research described is part of the NXT_SLEEP project co-founded by iMinds (Interdisciplinary Institute for Technology), a research institute founded by the Flemish Government. Companies and organizations involved in the project are IMEC, Sensotiss, University Hospital Antwerp, Custom8, Fifthplay, and NXP Semiconductors, with project support of IWT for the latter three. Academic partners are VUB-SMIT, KU Leuven-STADIUS, and KU Leuven-CUO.

# References

1. Chen, Z., Lin, M., Chen, F., Lane, N.D., Cardone, G., Wang, R., Li, T., Chen, Y., Choudhury, T., Campbell, A.T.: Unobtrusive sleep monitoring using smartphones. In: Proceedings of the 7th International Conference on Pervasive Computing Technologies for Healthcare, pp. 145–152. ICST, Brussels (2013)
2. Choe, E.K., Consolvo, S., Watson, N.F., Kientz, J.A.: Opportunities for computing technologies to support healthy sleep behaviors. In: Proceedings of the SIGCHI Conference on Human Factors in Computing Systems, pp. 3053–3062. ACM, New York (2011)
3. Fitbit: Fitbit Flex. http://www.fitbit.com/flex. Accessed 13 March 2015
4. Gartner: Gartner Says in 2015, 50 Percent of People Considering Buying a Smart Wristband Will Choose a Smartwatch Instead. http://www.gartner.com/newsroom/id/2913318. Accessed 13 March 2015
5. Gaver, B., Dunne, T., Pacenti, E.: Design: cultural probes. Interactions 6(1), 21–29 (1999)
6. Guo, F., Li, Y., Kankanhalli, M.S., Brown, M.S.: An evaluation of wearable activity monitoring devices. In: Proceedings of the 1st ACM International Workshop on Personal Data Meets Distributed Multimedia, pp. 31–34. ACM, New York (2013)
7. Marino, M., Li, Y., Rueschman, M.N., Winkelman, J.W., Ellenbogen, J.M., Solet, J.M., Dulin, H., Berkman, L.F., Buxton, O.M.: Measuring sleep: accuracy, sensitivity, and specificity of wrist actigraphy compared to polysomnography. Sleep 36(11), 1747–1755 (2013)
8. Paul, G., Irvine, J.: Privacy implications of wearable health devices. In: Proceedings of the 7th International Conference on Security of Information and Networks, pp. 117:117–117:121. ACM, New York (2014)

# SkInteract: An On-body Interaction System Based on Skin-Texture Recognition

Manuel Prätorius[✉], Aaron Scherzinger, and Klaus Hinrichs

Visualization and Computer Graphics Research Group (VisCG),
University of Münster, Einsteinstraße 62, 48149 Münster, Germany
{manuelpraetorius,scherzinger,khh}@uni-muenster.de

**Abstract.** In this paper we propose *SkInteract*, a system for on-body interaction utilizing the diverse texture of the human skin. We use an area fingerprint sensor to capture images and locate the corresponding area within a previously created map of the skin surface. In addition to the location of the sensor it is possible to calculate its orientation with respect to the reference map. This allows to assign arbitrary semantics to areas of the user's skin and to use the rotation as an additional input modality. In order to evaluate the feasibility of *SkInteract* a user study with a preliminary prototype was conducted. We propose two different interaction concepts which are based on either attaching a fixed sensor to a wearable device or using a moveable sensor, for instance attached to a pen, to perform on-body input.

**Keywords:** Mobile · Input · Sensors · Fingerprint · Skin · On-body · Smartring · Smartwatch · Biometrics

## 1 Introduction

Miniaturization has fostered the research and development of small mobile and wearable interaction devices. The diminishing interaction space of these devices, which comes at the cost of their mobility, has become a major challenge in the field of human computer interaction.

Recently an increasing number of mobile devices have integrated small fingerprint sensors as a means of user authentication. In this paper we propose the *SkInteract* system which utilizes those sensors to expand the limited interaction space of wearables to the skin surface. With our approach especially area type sensors provide the opportunity to design novel interaction techniques based on biometric features of the skin texture by creating a map of the skin surface and recognizing the position and orientation of sensor images within the mapped regions. Specific user interfaces can then be realized by assigning semantics to distinct areas of the map and utilizing the rotation as an additional modality. Because of a user's proprioception the interaction on the skin can be performed eyes-free which is advantageous especially in a mobile context.

© IFIP International Federation for Information Processing 2015
J. Abascal et al. (Eds.): INTERACT 2015, Part IV, LNCS 9299, pp. 425–432, 2015.
DOI: 10.1007/978-3-319-22723-8_34

## 2    Related Work

Several input systems have been proposed which are based on recognizing the body part that is used for interaction. This allows to perform user authentication, map different semantics to the body parts, select sets of input metaphors, or increase the precision of the interaction [1–3].

Harrison et al. [4] have presented a system which is able to recognize different objects and parts of the finger such as the pad, tip, knuckle, and nail by analyzing the acoustic signal produced while tapping on a touch surface. Another system by Harrison et al. [5] appropriates the forearm and the hand as an input surface by analyzing the vibrations caused by finger taps on those areas. The enhancement of expressiveness in multi-touch interaction by utilizing fiduciary-tagged gloves is presented in [6]. A finger-worn device which is equipped with a camera to recognize the texture the user is touching is presented in [7]. The device is able to distinguish 22 different materials, e.g., wood, jeans, and skin.

The first user interface based on fingerprint recognition has been proposed by Sugiura and Koseki [8]. Their approach is to assign commands to the user's fingertips and perform the corresponding action once a fingerprint is recognized.

The user performance in a scenario where a push button is able to identify the user's fingers was evaluated in the work of Wang and Canny [9]. In order to recognize the fingers they used colored markers attached to the fingertips. They compared several input situations considering input speed between multi-finger and single finger tapping.

In contrast to previous work on user interaction on the human skin we propose the novel approach to create a map of the skin texture which enables us to recognize the location and orientation of a sensor. This technique appropriates the skin for both discrete and continuous input.

## 3    Prototype System Outline

To evaluate the capabilities of the *SkInteract* approach we have created a simple hardware prototype and software implementation which is capable of both generating maps of specific skin texture areas and detecting the position and rotation of input images within those areas.

### 3.1    Hardware Setup

Since capacitive area sensors have already been integrated into mobile devices such as Apple's iPhone we have chosen to use this type of sensor for our first prototype. We use an FPC1011F3 model which has a resolution of 363 dpi. The resulting size of the recorded images is $152 \times 200$ pixels for an area of $10.64 \times 14.00$ mm. We read data from the sensor using the SPI interface of a RaspberryPi and transfer each complete image via Ethernet to a standard laptop with an Intel Core i7-2670QM CPU which performs the expensive image processing and recognition tasks. Using this setup, which is shown in Fig. 1a, we are able to retrieve four images per second from the sensor.

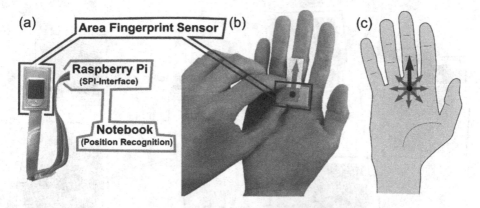

**Fig. 1.** (a) Preliminary *SkInteract* prototype setup. (b) A user capturing images of the skin with the area fingerprint sensor. (c) An example of a position and orientation as indicated during the user study. The arrows depict the eight orientations of the sensor which were tested for each position.

### 3.2 Scanning and Mapping the Hand

To create a map of a region of the skin surface a simplified version of the image stitching method proposed in [10] is applied to the images captured by the sensor. For both the image stitching as well as the later recognition and classification of the input images our method utilizes scale-invariant feature transform (SIFT) without the need for any preprocessing [11]. Although more sophisticated feature extraction and image enhance-ment methods have been proposed for the use of fingerprint images in user authentication applications, SIFT features work well in our context as they provide a more generalized method which is also applicable to regions of the palm and the wrist.

In the stitching process new images are added sequentially to an intermediate stitching result by computing matches between the SIFT features of the two images and calculating a homography matrix using random sample consensus (RANSAC) [12]. For robustness we perform several checks regarding the determinant of the matrix as well as the transformed bounding box of the input image.

For the prototype system evaluation presented in Sect. 4 we have focused on creating separate sub-maps of the skin surface as shown in Fig. 2 instead of a single global map, since the stitching of larger numbers of images can lead to accumulated distortion effects caused by the projection of non-planar soft tissue into two-dimensional space, depending on the particular region of the skin. Although this problem could be alleviated to a certain degree by applying an additional global optimization to minimize the accumulated errors, continuous interaction could be realized more efficiently by specifying transitions between the separate sub-maps, thus narrowing down the recognition to such areas.

### 3.3 Region Detection

For a new input image we first compute the SIFT features. We then iterate over the list of previously recorded areas of the fingers, palm, and the wrist (which are each

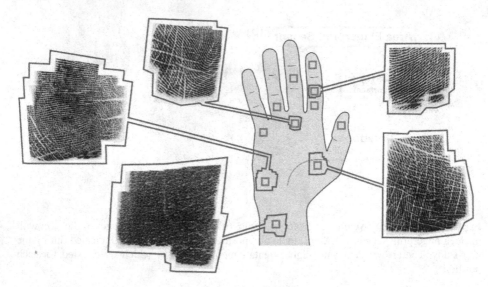

**Fig. 2.** Several examples of stitched skin textures. The green squares mark the areas that were used for the user study (Color figure online).

represented by a stitched reference image) and match the features of the input image and the reference image. Feature matching is performed using an exhaustive brute-force approach in order to obtain the best matching results. For each feature we compute the two best matches and only keep matches where the ratio of the distance between the best and the second-best match is better than a threshold $t$. Our experiments have shown that $t = 0.8$ generally seems to be a good value for our prototype implementation.

For the region with the largest number of good matches we perform RANSAC to calculate a homography matrix $H$ that transforms our input image with respect to the reference image. If we cannot find enough good matches or the determinant of $H$ is near zero we reject the input image. Otherwise we apply $H$ to transform the bounding box of the input image, and use the vertices and edges of the transformed image to compute the rotation and translation with respect to the reference image (see Fig. 3). This allows us to not only recognize the region of the finger or palm but also to determine the orientation of the sensor which can be used as an additional interaction modality.

## 4   System Evaluation

To evaluate the feasibility of *SkInteract* we have conducted a user study and performed some additional tests to characterize the system parameters. We have focused on three main aspects of the system which are the recognition rate, runtime duration of the recognition, and the required size of the sensor for use in a potential user interface.

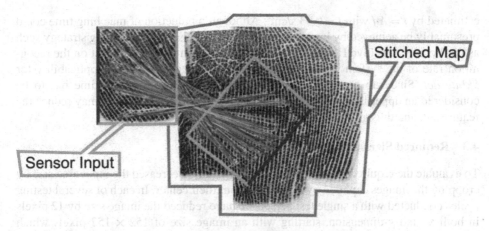

**Fig. 3.** Transformation of the sensor image

## 4.1 Recognition Rate

In order to quantify the recognition rate of our prototype system we have conducted a user study with a total of 8 participants from our department, 7 male and one female. For each participant we have captured reference images for 11 different skin regions (green squares in Fig. 2) with the stitching method outlined in Sect. 3.2. Examples for the stitched reference images are given in Fig. 2. For each of the reference regions we have captured 8 test images with different orientations of the sensor (gray arrows in Fig. 1c). Image capturing has been triggered manually once the sensor was placed appropriately and the preview of the image did not show significant artifacts caused by the oiliness and the moisture of the skin (see Sect. 4.4). The acquisition of test images was randomized regarding both region and orientation. Each test image was then matched using the algorithms described in Sect. 3.3. From the total of 704 test images 698 were classified correctly, resulting in a recognition rate of 99.15 %. From the total of 6 recognition failures 5 were rejected as non-matchable. One test image was captured at the wrong position but has correctly been recognized and thus resulted in a false positive. Other than that no false positive matches occurred in the user study.

## 4.2 Computational Cost of the Area Recognition

We have tested the duration of the area recognition and homography matrix calculation using OpenCV's standard implementations of SIFT, brute force feature matching, and RANSAC. For a small number of reference regions (corresponding to a small area of the skin surface) the computation of the SIFT features for the input image limits the processing speed, while for larger areas the matching of the features becomes the limiting factor. For our tests we have gradually increased the area $A$ of the scanned reference region in each testing cycle by adding an additional image of the sensor, each corresponding to an area of 1.49 cm$^2$ and not overlapping with any of the other reference images. For $A > 12$ cm$^2$ the influence of the feature computation step becomes negligible and the required processing time $t$ for the matching step and homography can be estimated by $t = A \cdot f$ with $f = 0.03$ s/cm$^2$. Although a reduction of matching time could presumably be achieved by implementing a more sophisticated matching strategy such as the Locally Sensitive Hashing algorithm proposed in [13], the impact on the recognition rate of the system would have to be evaluated to consider its applicability for *SkInteract*. Since no optimization has been applied, the processing time has to be considered an upper limit. More adapted features and feature selection may reduce the feature set, and thus give a significant speed-up.

### 4.3    Required Size of the Input Region

To evaluate the required sensor size we have gradually decreased the input area size by cropping the images captured by our sensor from their center. In each of several testing cycles conducted with a single test person we have reduced the image size by 12 pixels in both x- and y-dimension, starting with an image size of 152 × 152 pixels which corresponds to a surface area of 10.64 × 10.64 mm$^2$. In each testing cycle we have tested 10 input images against the same set of 5 reference regions. The recognition rate in our tests remained constant at 100 % up to an input image size of 56 × 56 (which corresponds to a surface area of 3.92 × 3.92 mm$^2$) and decreased drastically afterwards. For an input image size below 32 × 32 pixels or 2.24 × 2.24 mm$^2$ the system could not perform the recognition at all. The minimum area size required for a robust recognition could potentially be decreased even further by using a fingerprint sensor with a higher resolution compared to our 363 dpi model.

### 4.4    Drawbacks of the Capacitive Fingerprint Sensor

During the user study we have observed that the moisture and oiliness of the skin have a considerable impact on the quality of the images captured by the sensor, making it necessary for some users to occasionally clean the sensor. While this was not necessary in most cases it may restrict a continuous interaction for some users. Other types of sensors like ultrasonic or optical sensors, however, may not be affected by this problem.

Additionally, capacitive fingerprint sensors have a short sensing range and therefore need a good contact to the skin to capture images of appropriate quality, which makes it difficult to sense areas around knuckles and joints.

## 5    Design Space and Applications

*SkInteract* can be used as a basic platform for several different user interface applications. These applications can be divided into two main categories, the first being a system with a fixed sensor and the second a system with a moveable sensor.

An example of a system with a fixed sensor is a smartwatch or a smartring which allows to interact with an integrated sensor using the fingers and palm of the other hand (see Fig. 4a). In addition to mapping different functions onto the selected interaction areas of the skin surface, rotating could be used as a gesture for additional functions, for instance controlling the volume in a music player. An alternative would be to map distinct functions to discrete states defined by the relative orientation between the user's hand and the sensor. However, it would be necessary to perform an in-depth user study to evaluate the usability and comfort of potential interaction areas on the hand under the constraints of a smartwatch or a smartring scenario.

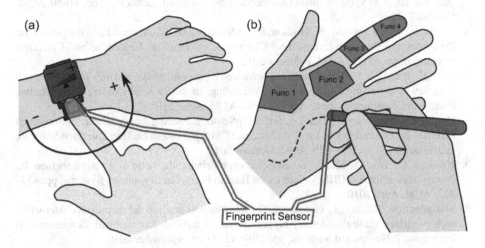

**Fig. 4.** (a) Fixed sensor setup integrated into a smartwatch. (b) Moveable sensor attached to the tip of a pen.

As the required size of the input area of the sensor in the current setup is only $3.92 \times 3.92 \text{ mm}^2$ we hypothesize that an appropriate sensor can be integrated into a small moveable device. Such a device could be a pen as shown in Fig. 4b or a thimble with the sensor attached to its tip. Besides the discrete selection of functions by tapping on the respective areas, the continuous motion of a moveable sensor on the skin surface could be used to provide gestural interaction.

To alleviate the cognitive load of remembering all of the input areas and the function mapping they could be visualized by an augmented reality head-mounted display.

Furthermore, privacy issues regarding both the potentially required data transfer as well as the storage of the captured images would have to be taken into account to avoid any exploitation of the biometric information included in the data.

## 6  Conclusion and Future Work

In this paper we have presented *SkInteract*, a novel system that appropriates the skin as an interaction surface. A device which can sense the texture of the skin can be utilized to generate maps of the skin which allows to recognize the position and the orientation of such a sensor. We have conducted a user study to evaluate the feasibility of the approach with a prototype which is based on a capacitive area fingerprint sensor.

In future work we plan to test several setups with different sensors and to design actual interfaces to explore the interaction space.

# References

1. Holz, C., Baudisch, P.: Fiberio: a touchscreen that senses fingerprints. In: Proceedings of the 26th Annual ACM Symposium on User Interface Software and Technology, pp. 41–50. ACM, October 2013
2. Harrison, C., Ramamurthy, S., Hudson, S.E.: On-body interaction: armed and dangerous. In: Proceedings of the Sixth International Conference on Tangible, Embedded and Embodied Interaction, pp. 69–76. ACM, February 2012
3. Holz, C., Baudisch, P.: The generalized perceived input point model and how to double touch accuracy by extracting fingerprints. In: Proceedings of the SIGCHI Conference on Human Factors in Computing Systems, pp. 581–590. ACM, April 2010
4. Harrison, C., Schwarz, J., Hudson, S.E.: TapSense: enhancing finger interaction on touch surfaces. In: Proceedings of the 24th Annual ACM Symposium on User Interface Software and Technology, pp. 627–636. ACM, October 2011
5. Harrison, C., Tan, D., Morris, D.: Skinput: appropriating the body as an input surface. In: Proceedings of the SIGCHI Conference on Human Factors in Computing Systems, pp. 453–462. ACM, April 2010
6. Marquardt, N., Kiemer, J., Greenberg, S.: What caused that touch?: expressive interaction with a surface through fiduciary-tagged gloves. In: ACM International Conference on Interactive Tabletops and Surfaces, pp. 139–142. ACM, November 2010
7. Yang, X.D., Grossman, T., Wigdor, D., Fitzmaurice, G.: Magic finger: always-available input through finger instrumentation. In: Proceedings of the 25th Annual ACM Symposium on User Interface Software and Technology, pp. 147–156. ACM, October 2012
8. Sugiura, A., Koseki, Y.: A user interface using fingerprint recognition: holding commands and data objects on fingers. In: Proceedings of the 11th Annual ACM Symposium on User Interface Software and Technology, pp. 71–79. ACM, November 1998
9. Wang, J., Canny, J.: FingerSense: augmenting expressiveness to physical pushing button by fingertip identification. In: CHI 2004 Extended Abstracts on Human Factors in Computing Systems, pp. 1267–1270. ACM, April 2004
10. Brown, M., Lowe, D.G.: Automatic panoramic image stitching using invariant features. Int. J. Comput. Vis. **74**(1), 59–73 (2007)
11. Lowe, D.G.: Distinctive image features from scale-invariant keypoints. Int. J. Comput. Vis. **60**(2), 91–110 (2004)
12. Fischler, M.A., Bolles, R.C.: Random sample consensus: a paradigm for model fitting with applications to image analysis and automated cartography. Commun. ACM **24**(6), 381–395 (1981)
13. Auclair, A., Cohen, L.D., Vincent, N.: How to use SIFT vectors to analyze an image with database templates. In: Boujemaa, N., Detyniecki, M., Nürnberger, A. (eds.) AMR 2007. LNCS, vol. 4918, pp. 224–236. Springer, Heidelberg (2008)

# Towards a Model of Virtual Proxemics for Wearables

Junia Anacleto[1(✉)] and Sidney Fels[2]

[1] Advanced Interaction Laboratory, Department of Computing, Federal University of São Carlos,
São Carlos, SP, Brazil
junia@dc.ufscar.br
[2] Human Communication Technologies Laboratory, Electrical and Computer Engineering
Department, University of British Columbia, Vancouver, BC, Canada
ssfels@ece.ubc.ca

**Abstract.** We present a Virtual Proxemics Model inspired by Hall's Proxemics Theory targeting wearable technology design and use. In Virtual Proxemics the degree of data control defines different levels of data spaces personal closeness including: Intimate, Personal, Social and Public in the same way Hall's proxemics defines these for physical distance from a person. This model is important for wearable technology design due to the design characteristics of wearables such as: attention-free, invisibility, closeness to the body, sensory linked, controllability and always-on that may compromise a wearer's ability to adequately control data either coming to them or being sent. We describe an experience with a wearable system, called 'The Cat in the Map.' In this system, when strangers accessed the wearer's Intimate data space, she became uncomfortable, consistent with the model. Likewise, when her intimate relations accessed the same data space, she enjoyed the experience. Thus, we see that Virtual Proxemics Model aligns with wearer's experience of data control that may be suitable for the design of auto-mated data access control mechanisms.

**Keywords:** Wearables · Proxemics · Virtual proxemics · Control-based spaces

## 1 Introduction

As wearable technologies promise benefits from invisibly sensing your body's state, providing unobtrusive, attention-free access to your digital world and providing an "always on, always connected" experience [19], these same features exaggerate the range of consequences due to unauthorized data access. The issue arises from the desire to minimize the amount of attention the wearer pays to the technology leading to a potential loss of control of who can send or access data from the wearer [26]. Attentional and use design categories of wearable technology, presented in (§2), include not being visible, close to the body, sensory linked and un-monopolizing and controllability. Some of these conflict with each other, greatly impacting actual and perceived levels of data control [26]. As the data becomes more sensitive, due to the types of application areas for wearables, the potential loss of control can lead to a sense of violation if inappropriate access behaviour occurs.

© IFIP International Federation for Information Processing 2015
J. Abascal et al. (Eds.): INTERACT 2015, Part IV, LNCS 9299, pp. 433–447, 2015.
DOI: 10.1007/978-3-319-22723-8_35

In the physical world, social and cultural protocol and physical proximity provide cues for appropriate behaviours with respect to a person's personal space [11]. To understand how the physical space around someone defines her/his comfort zones, Hall introduced the theory of proxemics [10]. In Hall's theory physical distance from a person provides comfort categories mapped as distance based zones. These zones then provide a sense of socially and culturally associated acceptable distances for different types of people based on familiarity. For example, from 0–45 cm is a person's intimate space reserved for people that are intimate with the person. Someone, say a colleague, who comes within this intimate space, may cause feelings of discomfort and violation due to the lack of control available at that distance.

The virtual world does not have a direct equivalent to physical distance, however we argue that the degree of control a person has over data can serve the same function when defining a *Virtual Proxemics*. Specifically, the *less control* of data a person has, the closer it is to his/her intimate data space, while the *more control* they have, the closer to their pubic data space as shown in Fig. 3. Then, similar to Hall's proxemics, the virtual proxemics determines the comfort level a person has from someone accessing or sending data into their data spaces depending on their relationship with them. So, data in a person's intimate data space can be comfortably sent to or accessed by a person's intimates, but a violation will be felt if it is from more distant relationships. We also argue, that virtual proxemics can be used in the same way that Greenberg [9] uses Hall's proxemics for technology to function when people (or technology) are physically close. That is, the virtual proxemics can provide cues for how a person's data space may be accessed based on the types of human relationships. Thus, virtual proxemics is a model for defining what level of control to provide for a user over their data space, as well as the possibility to automate this control to better allow attention free properties of wearables to be exploited.

In this paper, we describe how virtual proxemics applies to wearables and why the design criteria for wearables emphasize the need for a model based on Hall's proxemics. We begin with Related Work (Sect. 2) discussing wearable technology by describing some of the main factors that have been identified in the literature that impact virtual proxemics. We also present related work on the proxemics theory and how it has been explored in computer science. We present the details of Virtual Proxemics in (Sect. 3). We then present a wearable prototype in (Sect. 4) where we fixed the level of data control and experience two different community relationships with the wearer. We also discuss the observations from the experience in (Sect. 4). Finally we conclude and discuss future work in (Sect. 5).

## 2   Related Work

Wearable technologies have emerged as an important direction for the next wave of sensing, fabrication, computing and communication technologies. As the technologies are intended to be worn, key factors related to adoption and effectiveness of the technology have to be addressed. A number of the factors for each of the design characteristics can compromise a wearer's ability to control data flow. We highlight these particular factors as they relate to virtual proxemics.

## 2.1   Related Properties for Wearables

Wearable design characteristics, from hardware to software, from appearance to comfort, from body fitting to garment-technology integration, have been presented by: Mann [19] who defines attributes for wearables' behavior, Gemperle et al. [7] who define guidelines for wearability, and Todi and Luyten [25] who present design goals for wearables.

In particular, Mann describes a general framework for comparing and studying wearable technologies with six necessary attributes for a wearable computer in order to better serve wearers. These attributes are: it (a) must be *un-monopolizing* of wearer's attention, it (b) must be *unrestrictive* to the wearer's tasks, it should be (c) *observable* and (d) *controllable* by the wearer, it should be (e) *attentive* to the environment and, it should be (f) *communicative* to others. His framework is focused on how the wearable technology should behave when worn. However, considering the virtual proxemics perspective, some of the attributes conflict with each other when providing necessary data control in the virtual space, e.g. *un-monopolizing* wearer's attention and *controllable* by the wearer. By un-monopolizing the wearer's attention, the user may not be aware of state changes that would require his or her attention; thus, even if the system is controllable, the wearer wouldn't use those controls. Likewise, if the device is controllable, it may require too much attention for the wearer to use effectively. Thus, following these principles may make it more difficult for a wearer to exercise control of their data spaces leading to a higher likelihood that their data space could be violated.

Concerns about aesthetics and interaction are raised based on the design goals presented by Todi and Luyten [25]. Their first two design goals consider aesthetics problems and the last three consider interaction situations: (1) The wearable device can be *integrated* into existing clothing, preventing wearers from having to wear additional accessories to achieve the desired interactions; (2) The technology is *not* readily *visible* to the naked eye, allowing for inconspicuous interactions and does not compromise the aesthetics of the clothing; (3) Interactive elements should be *easily reachable*, and allow for eyes-free interactions; (4) Each entity has its own *dedicated* functions, to avoid mode-switching; and, (5) Individual elements should be *linked* together to form an automated workflow, what would guide us in our design. The inclination to hide the technology, provide an automated workflow and lack of mode switching may impede actively changing data space access; however, having each entity easily reachable may help the wearer; again providing potential design tradeoffs around data control for the wearer. Todi and Luyten included additional missing goals to support designing wearables, hence, Mann's attributes naturally combine with them. Together, these form a useful set of factors to attend to when developing wearables.

Considering the interaction between the wearer's body and the wearable, issues on wearability are brought forth by Gemperle et al. [7] as a concern when designing wearable computers. They describe 13 guidelines that cover wearability by discussing: (i) *Placement* determines where the application should go considering the dynamics of the human body. To guarantee a placement in unobtrusive locations the areas should: be relatively the same size across adults, have low movement/flexibility, and have large surfaces; (ii) *Form language* defines the shape of the application to ensure a comfortable and stable fit; (iii) *Human movement* takes into consideration the dynamic structure of the human body and suggests designing around the more active areas or creating spaces on the wearable to allow movement; (iv) *Proxemics* guideline relates to the human perception of space and dictates that forms should stay within the wearer's intimate space; (v) *Sizing* takes into consideration the different types of body that could use the wearable application; (vi) *Attachment* should also consider the different body sizes on top of offering a comfortable form of fixing the application to the body; (vii) *Containment* remembers the designers about the constraints brought by the components of the wearable application; (viii) *Distribution of the application's weight* and how it should not hinder the body's movement or balance has to be considered; (ix) *Accessibility* suggests testing to verify if the physical access to the wearable-wearer forms is adequate; (x) *Sensory interaction* states that the interaction should be kept simple and intuitive; (xi) *Thermal* issues can arise when placing processing intensive modules close to the body; and (xii) *Aesthetic* means the wearable should be seen as appropriate by the group of people wearing it; (xiii) *Long-term use* guideline is about the effect an application may have on the body and mind.

Gemperle et al. [7] sometimes refer the guidelines as suggestions, states, or definitions, suggesting that some of them have different impact into the design. However, from our perspective all of the guidelines seem relevant enough so that they should be considered for a successful design process for wearables.

Although the discussion of these properties are not stressed in here, they formed the basis for developing the wearable prototype and we are continuously investigating which and how these characteristics impacts the relationship between the wearers and the technology as well as the people they are interacting with, mainly focused on virtual interactions. In this paper, the considered context is the degree of controllability the wearer has and how this impacts his or her feelings of comfort when virtually communicating with a remote group that are either intimate or part of a public related group according to Hall's theory.

## 2.2 Proxemics Theory

The term *proxemics* is used by Gemperle et al. [7] to name their guideline *(iv)* in which the distance between the wearer and the wearable is determined as the wearable device being placed in contact with the wearer's body, using the concept of intimate space based on *Proxemics Theory* by Edward Hall [10], shown in Fig. 1. Hall's theory includes distance among people, not only between wearer and wearable, and describes a type of nonverbal communication based on distance and level of intimacy considering a body-centric perspective: close to a person is the intimate circle, and away becomes public space. Such terms were coined by Hall to explain the concept of social cohesion, describing how people behave and react in different types of culturally defined personal spaces. According to Hall, proxemics theory was defined as "the study of man's [sic] transactions as he perceives and uses in his *intimate, personal, social*, and *public* space in various setting" [11] mainly related to other people. Although Hall uses the term 'space' to discuss proxemics, we understand that, in fact, his discussions about spaces are more focused on one single dimension of space: a layer of horizontal distance from the central subject at the height would be as tall as the subject.

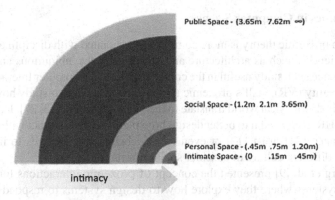

Public Space - (3.65m   7.62m ∞)

Social Space - (1.2m   2.1m  3.65m)

Personal Space - (.45m  .75m  1.20m)
Intimate Space - (0      .15m   .45m)

intimacy

**Fig. 1.** Four proxemic circles as defined by Hall [10]. In red: Intimate space; in yellow: Personal Space; in green: Social Space; and, in blue: Public Space. First and second numbers of each space represent the interval for the close state and second and third number, the far state (Color figure online).

In Hall, the *Intimate space* represents the distance for those allowed to touch and be touched by the subject; *Personal space* is reserved for friends and family; *Social space* is used for social and work interactions; and, *Public space* is used for public occasions (e.g.: distance kept from people in a market, plaza or a nightclub). Finally, each of these spaces has variations inside them according to cultural and individual values related to the perception of proximity. These spaces are interpreted and illustrated in Fig. 1. The image considers 2 axes: distance from the person's body versus degree of intimacy: the bigger the distance, the smaller the degree of intimacy, impacting on our behavior and interaction with others, as people transition from one circle to another. In the work reported here, our model uses the same names from Hall to relate physical space to perceived degree of control as well as the categories of relationship between the wearer and others they encounter. Likewise, we use the same names Hall gives to the level of intimacy between people. We use this mapping to suggest the type of behaviour that the wearable should evoke in the wearer when violations of their data space occur.

In our studies, we adapt this Proxemic Theory as a model to represent the concept of Virtual Proxemics for wearables as described in Sect. 3. For this, we interpret the different spaces Hall identified as relating to a person's need for control around their physical space as the distance between other people changes. However, in our adaptation to the virtual data space, we consider the degree of control over a data space to be the correspondence of distance. Thus, we map Intimate space to Intimate Data Space, Personal space to Personal Data Space and Public space to Public Data Space based on degree of control. In our mapping, the least control over data is considered intimate and the most control over data to be public. Thus, in the same manner as a stranger entering your intimate space is a violation, so would public access to your Intimate Data Space be. However, a close relation, such as a spouse, would have access. Note that we consider data space to be bidirectional where a wearer can be putting data or receiving data into their data spaces.

## 2.3 Proxemics in Computer Science

Even though proxemic theory is more commonly associated with disciplines other than computer sciences, such as architecture and social sciences, ubiquitous and pervasive computing made such study useful in the context of Human Computer Interaction (HCI). In Virtual Reality (VR), Hall's proxemic theory has been used to study how behaviors that happen in the physical world translate to the virtual world [2, 13, 27]. Human-Robot Interaction (HRI) has used it to better design how people could interact with robots [24], their acceptance [21], trust [12] or even robot's behavioral changes to interact with people from different culture to consider social norms [16].

Greenberg et al. [9] presented the concept of proxemic interactions for ubiquitous computing systems where they explore how to design systems to respond as a person would, adding four variables, besides distance, to correlate the human proxemics to 'smart' information and communication technology (ICT) proxemics, such as orientation, movement, identity and location. By doing so, they provide their ICT systems some human senses to give awareness about proximity beyond only a front camera to capture the presence of a user or other 'smart' technology.

In the ICT context, there are two main relationships involving interactions to which Greenberg applied Hall's proxemic circles in order to determine the technology's behavior: (A) the interaction between technological devices and user and, (B) the interaction between technological devices and technological devices, as shown in Fig. 2. However, the similarity in both contexts shows that Greenberg's main point is the proxemical behaviour of ICT related to users (with or without a device mobile mediation).

 (A)   (B)

**Fig. 2.** Greenberg et al. [9] definition for ICT proxemic interaction between (A) located technology and user and (B) located technology and users mediated by a mobile device (from [9]).

In the studies presented here, the proxemic theory and additional variables were combined and used to analyze and better define technology's automatic behavior so that it fits better with the user's expectations based on intimate space. This is particularly evident in Greenberg et al.'s work with proxemic interactions. From the wearable computer perspective, we consider Greenberg et al.'s work may also be applicable to how technology should mediate control of a wearer's data spaces to ensure that appropriate access is provided in situations where the wearer's attention, or the design of the garment, makes it difficult for the wearer to do so.

## 2.4  Control of Data Spaces and Wearable-Based Interactions

Additional complexities in data control with wearables have been identified by Viseu [26]. She makes the point that wearables, through connection with the digital world, augment the physical world where the wearer is the host for the technology. She identifies that some wearable researchers (i.e. Mann [19], Gershenfeld [8], Barfield [5] to name a few) believe that technology gives user more control over the environment while others like Lessig [18] argue it provides less, since the wearer can end up being controlled by the technology, such as an employee being monitored by an employer. She further makes the observation that this aspect of wearables transcends control and power to the realm of cultural biases. Hall's theory acknowledges how critical this aspect is. In adopting a model based on Hall's theory, we also encapsulate the elements of social protocol and cultural norms about what is appropriate for people to access within a person's data space.

In the literature on wearables, there are examples of virtual proxemics at play to support the view that people do have a sense of different levels of comfort based on different elements of how a wearable data is used. For example, Mann's work on a wearable technology allowing him to block out the world [19] is a form of complete control of his visual channel. By doing so, he keeps data outside his intimate data space to extent that people would need to pay him to enter it. Augmented reality with a head's up display that doesn't completely block the wearer's view provides filtering on what the wearer sees. Further along the continuum of control are wearables such as Google Glass that do not block the view, however provide opportunities for interpreting what is seen. In these examples, we can see that wearables provide differing levels of control over visual data that can be placed on the continuum of virtual proxemics.

The model of virtual proxemics can also be applied to establish appropriate access control responses by the technology, much as Greenberg et al. [9] uses Hall's theory to determine how technology should behave as discussed in the previous subsection. Even though, they are looking more at technology-human and technology-technology interactions rather than human-human mitigation, we believe their thinking extends to human-human interaction. Angelini et al. [1] proposed a combination of wearable technology to mediate sharing user information when two wearers hug. Using the technology to sense proximity, length of hug and history of hugging allowed the system to infer that those two wearers are intimate, thus, allowing access to each person's intimate data space.

A more direct interpretation of Hall's theory applied to control and wearables within a person's intimate space is the Spider Dress [17]. The dress senses when someone enters a wearer's personal space combined with the wearer's breathing pattern raising menacing spiderlike arms preventing close contact. If the system were to also know whether an approaching person is an intimate from understanding the breathing pattern related to fear or excitement, it could keep its arms lowered. Ideally, for an attention free wearable, the technology would know how to establish this relationship. In a sense, the virtual proxemics model should provide the wearer a sense of the spider arms over their data space when a non-intimate sends data or wants to read the wearer's data.

Puikkonen et al. [22] also represent a similar concept with a performative wearable technology to explore inappropriate attention. Though, Puikkonen et al.'s also expose how the proximity and intimacy of interaction between the wearer and the wearable can lead to the wearer not always being aware of what is happening, leading to a concern over one's right of privacy and a low level of acceptance of certain wearable devices, as shown in [23] and [28]. We argue this design characteristic of wearable technology leads to a lack of control of their data space, implying that all interactions with this data space should be treated as a person's intimate data space.

In contrast to collocated interactions between people, wearables also provide a means for communication between remote participants. Work such as Min and Nam [20] used wearable technology 'to bridge the communication gap between people in close relationships who have to live apart'. They collected one of the partner's bio-signals and reproduced them to their distant partner using wearable prototypes, so that this partner would feel more connected by physically feeling their partner's heartbeat and breathing rate. Differently from the work of Min and Nam, He and Schiphorst [14] explored the concept of mediated communication using wearables and presented a wearable prototype named Patches that allowed for two-way nonverbal communication. In this prototype, the wearer could be poked via a Facebook application by one of his/hers friends and receive the poke on the prototype by simulated feelings of warmth and pressure from one of the patches. In turn, the wearer could return the poke by pressing that patch. When the wearer and observer are physically distant from each other, the wearable becomes the sole channel of communication, effectively mediating the communication between the wearer and observer. In this situation, it may be difficult to know the relationship between the two actors as physical proximity cues are unavailable. Explicit representations are needed, such as using Facebook settings as done in He and Schiphorst [14]. However, these mechanisms then require attention from the wearer, conflicting with some of the desired wearable characteristics brought by Mann. We argue in these situations, where a wearer has not specified explicit control, that the data space has to be treated as their intimate data space.

In summary, many of the related wearable technology explorations have touched upon the challenges of how wearable technology provide channels of data to and from the user and that depending upon the control of the data, can lead to feelings of empowerment, disempowerment, comfort, discomfort. In next section, we describe how virtual proxemics is a suitable model for wearers to think about their data spaces and what degrees of control they have. This model also establishes a means to discuss the socio-cultural biases of power and control over people's data spaces in more structure fashion.

## 3   Virtual Proxemics

Our model of Virtual Proxemics derives from Hall's theory of physical proxemics. However, we use degree of control as the measure for the different categories of data space in contrast to physical distance for Hall's proxemics (shown in Fig. 1). In Fig. 3 we illustrate our mirrored representation of virtual proxemics with data space replacing physical space and the dimension of control replacing distance. As in Hall's proxemics,

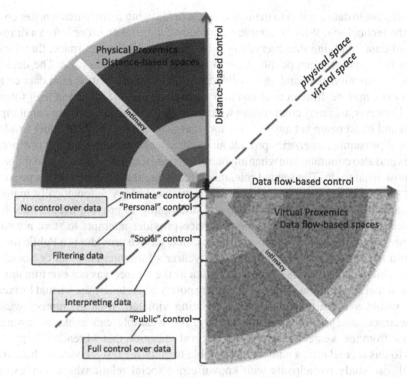

**Fig. 3.** Representation of virtual proxemics with Hall's physical proxemics from Fig. 1 included for comparison. In virtual proxemics, the higher the degree of control of the data space (i.e. data coming in or out) the lower the level of intimacy in the data space. For example, for data where the wearer has no control of the data, it would be considered in their Intimate data space.

we envision the virtual proxemics as a continuum with some useful categories that can be identified as related to the type of relationships between people.

As shown in Fig. 3, Intimate data space is one where the wearer has little or no control of the data (or doesn't need/want to have). The data may either be directed towards the wearer such as messages, images, voice etc. or coming from the wearer, such as sensor data, annotation, messages etc. For example, a text message appearing in a head's up display coming from someone that isn't filtered or blocked enters a wearer's intimate data space. Or, a heart rate sensor that sends its data to a third party cloud service is in the wearer's Intimate data space. As the amount of control increases over the data, the data space becomes further out to be Personal data space, then Social data space and finally Pubic data space. In the wearer's Public data space he or she has complete control of the data including being able to completely block all incoming or outgoing data. Social space may include filters or other manipulations that mask or block data such augmented reality glasses that filter out advertisements. The Personal data space is where controls provide interpretation of data but does not completely block or filter it such as aggregate data from sensors being sent to a third party.

Virtual proxemics for a wearer's data space serves two potential roles. First, for wearers, by providing this model they may more easily understand the type of exposure they will have to data coming to them or from them allowing them to make better choices about the technology. While wearable technology can be taken off or left in a drawer to block all data, implying that everything is in wearer's Public data space, this does not address the issue of when people want to use a wearable technology. The desire for always on, attention-free, and an invisible form factor imply that manual data controls that do exist may be difficult to attend to or need to be pre-specified and then forgotten about. However, this may compromise wearers' comfort when something unanticipated happen and wearers are not aware or do not want to stop what they are doing to address it. Virtual proxemics categories provide an explicit way to understand any prespecified settings and also communicate when anyone is entering a certain data space so the wearer will know what to do. The second role, much like Greenberg applies Hall's proxemics is that the categories can be used for having the technology automatically managing someone access to wearers' data space and attempting to provide access only to the appropriate data space. Thus, if a cloud service provider attempts to store a wearer's heart rate data, the system could infer that the cloud service provider is a Public member so would not have access to any data in the wearer's Intimate, Personal or Social data spaces, which would include the heart rate data as the wearer was not exerting any data control of that sensing data. Thus, such privacy policy provided by the Virtual Proxemics model would avoid a potential feeling of being violated, what guarantees wearers' empowerment and data control. Alternately, the wearable can evoke an awareness response from the wearer so they have a visceral sensation that a breach is happening.

As to this second role, a number of wearable technology researchers, such as, [6, 14, 15, 20], use study participants with known close social relationships. For example, Cercos and Muller [3] avoid privacy concerns by having participants who knew each other and worked closely together on a daily basis, i.e. would likely have been in the wearer's Personal or Social circle. Min and Nam [20] provide some insight that the sense of virtual proxemics is understood with their participants, as they noted that some users commented that they would feel considerably different depending on their relationship with the connected partner.

Finally, for this second role, we have not specified access control policies that could be applied to facilitate automatic mechanisms to alert wearers about potential transgressions, much like the spider dress tries to with real proxemics. With respect to confidentiality of data being read by members from different levels of intimacy, access policies such as Bell-Lapadula model [3], fit with the intuition for access we propose for virtual proxemics. The approach of "no read up, no write down" is consistent with the notion that if someone from a given comfort circle of the wearer tries to read data from a closer data space the wearer would be made aware of the transgression. Likewise, if data is being written from a close data space to a farther one, the wearer would be notified; would not be for the other way around. In this way, only potential data confidentiality breaches require attention from the wearer. With respect to integrity of the data, models such as Biba's [4] could also be applied. In this case, the "no read down, no write up" can be applied to alert the wearer of potential data integrity problems.

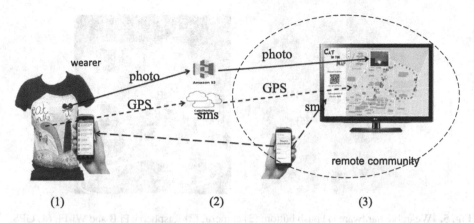

**Fig. 4.** 'The Cat in the Map' system with the three primary data paths: SMS, photo and GPS. The system has three main parts: (1) the wearable prototype that collects position data of the wearer and allows her to take pictures; (2) a REST API that creates the bridge between these two parts; and (3) the community shared display showing where the wearer has been, photos taken, messages sent and the send message widget.

## 4    The Cat in the Map Experience

The Cat in the Map is a wearable-based functional prototype designed to provide communication between the wearer and her community when she is out of the community, as shown in Fig. 4.

The wearable was designed to extend the wearer's senses by allowing her to send her location and photos taken while she walks. The location and photos she takes are presented on a shared display for the remote community. The community could also send real time messages or photo requests to the wearer; the wearer could then choose to do so or not. Together the wearer and community had bidirectional communication so that the community could see what she sees and where she is and send messages and requests.

Our wearable prototype had three main functionalities: taking a picture, collecting GPS data and uploading such information to the servers. These functionalities used the camera module and a push button; GPS module; and, Wi-Fi dongle, respectively; with the Raspberry Pi as the processing unit. In terms of controlling the data channels, the wearer could choose when to take a photo. However, she did not control sending GPS data to the shared display so anyone watching could see where she was. Using the phone, anyone in the remote community could send an SMS to the wearer. These messages would appear on her phone and she could choose to ignore or not after she read it; thus, she was not able to filter messages prior to receiving them, nor could she delete them. Figure 5 shows the hardware built in the wearable.

To see the effect of the data control on her feelings with respect to the data spaces created in this prototype, we had one wearer (female graduate student) and two communities in different relationships to her, i.e., co-workers and partner.

In the co-worker condition the wearer walked around a university campus for 4 h. During this period, she went about her regular activities (e.g. walked around the campus, stayed at the laboratory, had lunch, etc.). The shared display was put in the entrance

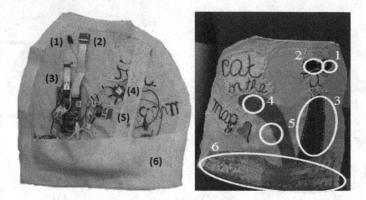

**Fig. 5.** Wearable hardware (1) push button; (2) camera; (3) Raspberry Pi B and Wi-Fi; (4) GPS; (5) LEDs for feedback; (6) battery pouch with two 1500 mAh batteries (GPS and Wi-Fi) and a USB charger (Raspberry Pi).

lobby of her department at the university. Many observers stopped to watch the photos and the path she was taking. She received ten messages: four were requests for photos (e.g. 'Take a picture of my house' – Ant Man), two were comments (e.g. 'Where's the cat now?' – V.), and four were jokes (e.g. 'A neutron walks into a bar […]' - Dr. Sheldon Cooper). The comments and anonymous jokes sometimes had content classified by the wearer as 'insulting', like 'Fresh meat – Hannibal'. These situations made the wearer feel uncomfortable and 'invaded by strangers'. She also commented that she didn't want them to know where she was. This observation suggests that the lack of control of the GPS data appearing on the shared display and the messages coming from the remote community make her uncomfortable. The violation made her feel powerless and 'deeply unmotivated' to continue the interaction, as reported.

In contrast, for the second condition with her partner at the shared display in his home, she used the Cat in the Map for a period of 2 h. During this period, twelve messages were received such as: comments (e.g. 'Wow, it's huge'), expressions of concern (e.g. Seems windy, did you bring your coat sweetie?) and requests (e.g. '[…] take some pictures of that World of Science place. […]'). Unlike in the co-worker case, the sender identity was known. The wearer reported to have a 'more pleasant experience' on sharing the photos and receiving requests of photos, comments and advice from her partner.

The prototype was designed to have the GPS and messages in the wearer's Intimate data space. Though, the photos were in her Public data space in that she could choose when to take a photo. As expected, her partner, being intimate, did not cause discomfort when he either sent or watched her moving on the shared display. In contrast, co-workers, not being intimates, caused discomfort accessing her Intimate data space. This is consistent with our view of Virtual Proxemics.

## 5   Conclusion

We presented a model of Virtual Proxemics derived from Hall's proxemic theory. In Virtual Proxemics the degree of control defines different levels of intimate data spaces from Intimate, Personal, Social and Public in the same way Hall's proxemics defines these for distance from a person. We argue that this model is important for wearable technology design due to the design characteristics of wearables often interfering with the ability for people to control data coming and going from their wearable device. Specifically, attention-free, invisibility, sensory linked, controllability and always-on characteristics in wearable design compromise a wearer's ability to control the data channels. Yet, people understand the social and culturally biased physical space around them as Hall pointed out. Thus, these same understandings can be applied to their data spaces as well. By doing this, it is easier for wearers to understand the complexities of data access policies. This is particularly important once data often associated with wearables is quite sensitive. The other advantage derived from this model is the possibility that technology can be used to infer a wearer's relationship to people that are entering different parts of their data spaces and can provide appropriate protection. We presented an example wearable system where we constructed an Intimate data space to see whether access to it by people in the wearer's Social circle made her uncomfortable, which it did. Likewise, we saw that people in her Intimate space did not make her uncomfortable, thus, suggesting that our approach is promising.

Future work entails exploring the continuum of control and how that relates to the different categories of Virtual Proxemics in the same way that Hall established ranges of distance. As well, if these become established, it will be possible to investigate how technology can use these rules in the same way as Greenberg et al. demonstrated how Hall's proxemics can be used to mitigate human-technology and technology-technology interactions. Though, as Hall noted, proxemics depends upon social and culturally constructed norms, thus, exploring how virtual proxemics are impacted by social and cultural norms seems appropriate as well.

**Acknowledgments.** We thank BRAVA, BOEING, CAPES, NSERC, DFAIT and PWAIS for their support. We thank Colnago, Gasques and Oliveira for the first steps on this project.

# References

1. Angelini, L., Khaled, O., Caon, M., Mugellini, E., Lalanne, D.: Hugginess: Encouraging Interpersonal Touch through Smart Clothes. In: Proceedings of the 2014 ACM International Symposium on Wearable Computers, pp. 155–162 (2014)
2. Bailenson, J., Blascovich, J., Beall, A., Loomis, J.: Equilibrium theory revisited: mutual gaze and personal space. Presence 10(6), 583–598 (1965)
3. Bell, D.E., LaPadula, L.J.: Secure computer systems: mathematical foundations. MITRE Corporation, p. 29 (1973)
4. Biba, K.J.: Integrity considerations for secure computer systems. Mitre Corporation, Bedford, Massachusetts, p. 61 (1975)
5. Barfield, W., Mann, S., Bair, K., Gemperle, F., Kasabach, C., Stivoric, J., Bauer, M., Martin, R., Cho, G.: Computational clothing and accessories. In: Barfield, W., Caudell, T. (eds.) Fundamentals of Wearable Computers and Augmented Reality. Lawrence Erlbaum Associates, Mahwan (2001)

6. Cercos, R., Mueller, F.: Watch your steps: designing a semi-public display to promote physical activity. In: Proceedings of the 9th Australasian Conference on Interactive Entertainment Matters of Life and Death. ACM Press (2013)
7. Gemperle, F., Kasabach, C., Stivoric, J., Bauer, M., Martin, R.: Design for Wearability. In: Proceedings of the 1998 International Symposium on Wearable Computers, p. 116. IEEE Computer Society (1998)
8. Gershenfeld, N.: When Things Start To Think. Henry Holt and Company, New York (1999)
9. Greenberg, S., Marquardt, N., Ballendat, T., Diaz-Marino, R., Wang, M.: Proxemic interactions: the new Ubicomp? Interactions 18(1), 42 (2011)
10. Hall, E.: The hidden dimension. Doubleday, New York (1966)
11. Hall, E.: Handbook for Proxemic Research. Society for the Anthropology of Visual Communications, Washington (1974)
12. Haring, K.S., Matsumoto, Y., Watanabe, K.: How Do People Perceive and Trust a Lifelike Robot. In: Proceedings of the World Congress on Engineering and Computer Science, vol. I (2013)
13. Hasler, B., Friedman, D.: Sociocultural conventions in avatar-mediated nonverbal communication: a cross-cultural analysis of virtual proxemics. J. Intercultural Commun. Res. 41(3), 238–259 (2012)
14. He, Y., Schiphorst, T.: Designing a wearable social network. In: CHI 2009 Extended Abstracts on Human Factors in Computing Systems, Boston, pp. 3353–3358 (2009)
15. Hong, Y., Jo, J., Kim, Y., Nam, T.: "STEPS": Walking on the music, moving with light breathing. In: Proceedings of the 28th of the International Conference Extended Abstracts on Human Factors in Computing Systems, pp. 4799–4804. ACM Press, New York (2010)
16. Joosse, M., Evers, V.: Lost in proxemics: spatial behavior for cross-cultural HRI. In: HRI 2014 Workshop on Culture-Aware Robotics (2014)
17. Kaplan, K.: Is That a Spider on Your Dress or Are You Happy to See Me? Intel –Innovation Everywhere.        iq.intel.com/smart-spider-dress-by-dutch-designer-anouk-wipprecht/. Accessed on January 2015
18. Lessig, L.: Code and Other Laws of Cyberspace. Basic Books, New York (1999)
19. Mann, S.: Wearable computing as means for personal empowerment. In: Proceedings of the 1998 International Conference on Wearable Computers, pp. 12–13 (1998)
20. Min, H.C., Nam, T.: Biosignal Sharing for Affective Connectedness. In: Proceedings of the Extended Abstracts of the 32nd Annual ACM Conference on Human Factors in Computing Systems - CHI EA 2014, pp. 2191–2196. ACM Press, New York (2014)
21. Mumm, J., Mutlu, B.: Human-robot proxemics: physical and psychological distancing in human-robot interaction. In: Proceedings of the International Conference on Human-robot Interaction, pp. 331–338. ACM Press (2011)
22. Puikkonen, A., Lehtiö, A., Virolainen, A.: You can wear it, but do they want to share it or stare at it? In: Campos, P., Graham, N., Jorge, J., Nunes, N., Palanque, P., Winckler, M. (eds.) INTERACT 2011, Part I. LNCS, vol. 6946, pp. 497–504. Springer, Heidelberg (2011)
23. Schuster, D.: The revolt against Google 'Glassholes'. The New York Post. nypost.com/2014/07/14/is-google-glass-cool-or-just-plain-creepy/. Accessed on September 2015
24. Takayama, L., Pantofaru, C.: Influences on proxemic behaviors in human-robot interaction. In: International Conference on Intelligent Robots and Systems, pp. 5495–5502. IEEE (2009)
25. Todi, K., Luyten, K.: Suit up! enabling eyes-free interactions on jacket buttons. In: Extended Abstracts CHI 2014, pp. 1549–1554. ACM Press (2014)
26. Viseu, A.: Simulation and Augmentation: Issues of Wearable Computers. J. Ethics Inf. Technol. 5(1), 17–26 (2003)

27. Wilcox, L., Allison, R., Elfassy, S., Grelik, C.: Personal space in virtual reality. ACM Trans. Appl. Percept. **3**(4), 412–428 (2006)
28. Zennie, M.: Tech pioneer with augmented-reality glasses bolted to his head traps Paris McDonald's workers 'who tried to rip the device off his face'. Daily Mail (2012). www.dailymail.co.uk/news/article-2175062/EyeTap-augmented-reality-pioneer-Steve-Mann-assaulted-Paris-McDonalds-employees.html. Accessed on September 2014

# ZENse - Supporting Everyday Emotional Reflection

Christian Löw, Chalid Gad-El-Hak, Roman Ganhör[(✉)],
and Hilda Tellioglu

Multidisciplinary Design Group, Vienna University of Technology, Vienna,
Austria
christian.loew@me.com, chalid.gadelhak@gmail.com,
{roman.ganhoer,hilda.tellioglu}@tuwien.ac.at

**Abstract.** Healthcare benefited greatly from the trend of self-quantification. However, emotional states and psychological health are more elusive and defy description by simple sensor data. In this paper we show how a user oriented design process resulted in ZENse, a wearable prototype for digitally supporting ideas of *Positive Psychology*, a psychological approach to help patients with mental disorders. A conducted user study shows promising results on the idea and the design. Despite it being only a small explorative study with healthy participants, we found that the prototype triggers situations and interactions that are known to have a beneficial effect on mental well-being.

**Keywords:** Quantified-self · Wearable · Emotion · Tracking · Self-reflection

## 1 Introduction

A number of personal monitoring and feedback systems have been suggested for the management of a wide range of health-related conditions. These types of systems help users by enabling them to monitor and visualize their behavior, keeping them informed, reminding them to perform specific tasks, providing feedback and recommending healthier behavior or actions [2].

Sensors that are embedded in wearable devices such as smartphones, smart watches or jewelry are able to quantify, and thus monitor our physical activities and spatial locations. Reflecting on these data can change the way we organize and experience our daily life. In the context of health care, such wearable or ambient sensor systems may also help to bridge the gap between care-giving institutions and patients by actively involving the patient, monitoring multiple conditions in a long-term or continuous manner and providing real time information and timely feedback about a patients health condition [15]. Physical data are not only easy to collect, they are also quite meaningful, e.g., the amount of physical activity will assumingly correlate with the physical fitness of a person.

In contrast, emotional states and psychological health in general are more elusive and defy description by simple quantification of sensor data. As an example, mental diseases like depression or generalized anxiety spectrum disorders (GAD) exhibit very heterogeneous etiology [12]. However hard it is to collect appropriate data, patients

© IFIP International Federation for Information Processing 2015
J. Abascal et al. (Eds.): INTERACT 2015, Part IV, LNCS 9299, pp. 448–455, 2015.
DOI: 10.1007/978-3-319-22723-8_36

suffering from above mentioned mental diseases can regain and improve their quality of life by quantifying their positive everyday experiences [14]. Such *Positive Psychology* emphasizes on the positive aspects in someone's life and thus, helps patients to develop and nurture resilience, identity and optimism among other beneficial psychosocial effects [7, 18]. As negative experiences can lose their depressing and dreadful component, people, especially patients, are more willing to accept both emotional states as equivalent parts of a normal life.

Collecting experiences is only a first step, whereas reflecting on these experiences complements the procedure. Reflecting on someone's own experiences can offer insight to patterns and dynamics interweaved in a bigger picture. Self-reflection is an activity closely related to learning and can be seen as a form of processing and responding to experiences of any kind [3]. In psychological therapy, self-reflection is used as an intervention to gain influence over pathological patterns and eventually break these patterns [1, 4].

Researchers have proposed various approaches for collecting experiences and to reflect on them. Hall et al. implemented a game-like Facebook application for the measurement of emotional states and concluded both, the underuse of social features as well as the rejection of comparative and evaluative features [10, 11]. Lindström et al. proposed the Affective Diary allowing users to augment sensor data with pictures and comments. The user study showed that users value and log negative experiences as well as positive experiences [17]. Imbe et al. presented a service visualizing the users geo referenced points of interest and/or frequently visited places over a certain period of time [13]. This visualization allows the user to contemplate on past activities from a different and unusual perspective. However, as today's sensor technology is not able to record the users' emotional state unambiguously and adequately, Eichhorn argues for devices that allow users to record them manually [6].

A number of smartphone applications for tracking the emotional state have been designed such as *My Mood Tracker* [21] and *Emotionsense* [19]. Both applications aim at capturing mood and emotional experience by prompting the user with regular surveys throughout the day. In contrast, we suggest several design decisions currently not reflected in existing applications. First, applying a wearable wristband instead of a smartphone lessens the burden to pull out the latter repeatedly. Second, instead of a repetitive survey a pro-active, however facile user engagement is proposed. And third, location data for every recorded positive or negative experience is tracked and visualized in order to utilize the structuring power of location memory.

In this paper we present ZENse, an application that facilitates reflection on everyday emotional experiences supporting users to maintain a balanced lifestyle. It is based on the work of the aforementioned research and incorporates their findings and suggestions. ZENse consists of two components: a wristband for manually collecting experiences throughout a day and a web-based visualization to retrospectively reflect on these experiences.

ZENse was designed with a likeable and motivating interface and interaction design in mind. To reach this goal the ideas of gamification [5, 16] and user oriented design were utilized. Thus, making the act of collecting the right data easy and playful for the users should support them to remain engaged in the activity.

## 1.1  How to Gather Data?

The first step when designing ZENse was interviewing a human computer interaction researcher focusing on wearable sensors and a psychotherapist with expertise in *Positive Psychology*. While the psychotherapist described her daily practice, she highlighted the constructive nature of emphasizing positive aspects of everyday life: "Everything I focus on, I enlarge, like with a magnifying glass. When you focus on something positive, the rest takes a back seat. The positive becomes augmented". However, the ability to reflect on experiences needs cultivation and training and usually is underdeveloped among people, according to her experience. At the end, when she was asked how to collect positive aspects, she suggested a conscious interaction. This was in line with the statements of the human computer interaction researcher who recommended manual interaction techniques as he considered automatic biological feedback as not very reliable. Thus, focusing on positive experiences seems like a first obvious choice. However, *Positive Psychology* also argues for the multifaceted relevance of negative experiences in the activity of self-reflection. Negative experiences can serve as learning for future improvement, and ultimately, help to attribute relative value to their positive counterparts.

The heterogeneous etiology of mental diseases includes numerous possible physical causes identifiable by physiological data like the amount of sweat or the eye movement. Therapy, on the other hand, builds upon the person and the context in which the therapy unfolds. Biological data implies extrinsic evaluation or even classification in healthy and unhealthy, which clashes with the subjective nature of psychotherapy. A different approach is collecting and analyzing nonverbal communication as a source for honest human expression such as gestures, postures, face and eye behavior [8, 20].

As the automatic collection of data is not reliable and the interpretation of such data is ambiguous we focused on collecting data manually for the support of personal wellbeing. This implicates an active involvement of the user in both, collecting good and bad experiences in their daily life and analyzing the collected data at a later point in time.

## 1.2  What Data to Gather?

To foster design ideas for ZENse a package with a cultural probe [9] (Fig. 1) was prepared. The cultural probe consisted of a city map, a set of blue and red mark stickers, two handheld counters, several emotion diary-postcards and an instruction manual. We invited four healthy persons with various backgrounds to use the cultural probes for six consecutive days to document their emotional daily life. Whenever the test-persons experience a positive or negative situation they were asked to mark these situations on the map using a colored sticker.

If participants felt the need to describe a situation in more detail they could do so by using emotion postcards. While the "emotion diary"-postcards were only used rarely the average map counted 38 markers after a six-day period. As the markers represent place and mood the interviews conducted afterwards revealed that the time, when the marker was set, also played a significant role for the participants. These results led to the design decision to focus on place, time and mood.

**Fig. 1.** Cultural Probe (Counter, Emotion-Diary, etc.) [9]

### 1.3    What Interface?

The requirements for the interface were usability, wearability and compactness. After initial sketches we decided on the form factor of a wristband for the reasons mentioned above: it is wearable and compact and offers enough space to implement unambiguous interfaces. However, the interaction is reduced to two buttons in the shape of a plus sign and a minus sign. The design was to reflect the question of "How are you feeling"?

The design ideas were implemented iteratively as mock-ups and the interaction was developed and deployed as a technology probe. The early implementations were given to participants for three days. When we invited the users for de-briefing, we showed them their loggings on a map and asked for their general opinion. Feedback and suggestions from the users were incorporated into the final prototype.

## 2    ZENse Prototype

In general, the prototype should help users by enabling them to monitor and visualize their daily emotional life. To keep the costs low only standardized hardware components and open web techniques are used. To gather viable data in a user-study the portable part of the prototype must work for a whole day without the need for recharging. The visualization, used for self-reflection should be generated automatically.

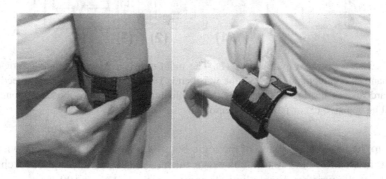

**Fig. 2.** Using the ZENse wristband

To fulfill these requirements the prototype consists of a wearable wristband, an Android smartphone application and a web backend. The wristband (Fig. 2) is made of comfortable fabric to ensure wearing comfort. All electronic parts are mounted in the wristband, however, the battery can be removed for charging. The wristband allows users to self-monitor their positive and negative experiences by pressing the corresponding button. Whenever a button is pressed the wristband sends a signal to the smartphone via Bluetooth. The smartphone application then acquires the current location, associates it with the experience and uploads the record to the web backend.

**Fig. 3.** Representations of experiences (circles) fade out over time

The web application is designed to enable users to visualize their experiences on a web-based map and reflect upon them in hindsight (Fig. 3). Green dots represent positive experiences whereas red dots mark negative experiences. The web application has been developed utilizing Ruby on Rails and OpenStreetMap API. Any user input is sent to a smartphone utilizing the Bluetooth capability of the logic board (Fig. 4).

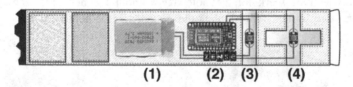

    **(1)**        **(2) (3)**     **(4)**

**Fig. 4.** ZENse is powered by a battery (1). The main unit is a Bluetooth enabled logic board (2) that handles all input and output of the wristband. Two buttons are connected directly to the logic board and as the logic board can track both buttons separately the user input can be identified as negative (3) or positive (4) emotion.

Due to the low power design of the logic board a standard Li-Ion battery with 3.7 V and 1000 mAh allows the continuous usage for more than one day without recharging. The costs of the wristband including all components are below 100 Euro.

# 3    User Study

To gather feedback on the interaction and the representation graphics a small user study was conducted. As the aim was gaining a first insight on the design and on the reflection the prototype had triggered, the selection of the participants was not based on their specific medical records but rather on general diversity.

## 3.1    Study Setup

The user study consisted of five persons in the age of 17 to 59 years. The participants had diverse backgrounds (pupils, university student, school teacher, IT expert) and the sample featured mixed genders (three male, two female). Each user received one ZENse prototype in the morning and was briefed to use it throughout the day to document emotional experiences. When the users brought back the prototype after 12 h, an individual visualization of their collected emotions was generated and shown to them. Finally, a semi-structured interview was conducted regarding the perception of the physical properties of the device and the overall experience.

## 3.2    Findings

In the interview three participants described the wristband as visually appealing and one described it as being "elegant". However, the positive reactions were intermingled with critical comments. One participant mentioned the faint "click" sound as too loud during a visit in a library. While one participant felt no discomfort wearing the wristband four participants mentioned some issues like the weight (2 participants), the size (2 participants) and the fabric of the sleeve (1 participant).

However, all participants used the wristband for a whole day and collected their emotional experiences. The amount of recorded experiences ranged from 8 to 40 per person resulting in an average of 18.4 experiences per person. The average number of positive emotional reflections was 13.2 (72 %) whereas the number of negative emotional reflections was 5.2 (28 %).

When talking about the feeling the participants had during the day using ZENse we received a variety of reactions. One participant felt influenced by the wristband stating that he "[walked] around more consciously, [taking] a closer look at people and their faces". He felt the need to constantly interpret his surroundings to log the situation appropriately. A second participant described his loggings intensifying his emotional experiences, positive or negative. The third participant described her daily life as rather stressful at the moment. Thus, ZENse invoked a quite active stance on her otherwise unquestioned and unreflected emotional experiences. The fourth participant described ZENse as "exciting", however, she reported little activity of self-reflection. She missed a "neutral"-button in addition to + and − and would prefer ZENse o be "more like a regular diary". The last participant was mainly impressed by the GPS-positioning functionality of ZENse and used it to satisfy his curiosity on seeing what route he'd follow all day. The visualization was positively commented as a useful source for recording daily activities and as tool for reconstructing past loggings.

During the user study ZENse invoked self-reflection in three of five participants, while the two noted the potential value of this technology as a tangible diary. The result shows the potential of tangible devices to support people in their everyday self-reflection. In contrast to existing wristbands like *fitbit*, ZENse prompts a user intervention linking a specific place and time with an emotional state. This active involvement of the user exhibited different approaches to and strategies of self-reflection during our study. While some users rely on the visualization others reflect more "in-situ". This ambiguity of usage patterns is consistent with the empowering effect of a setting open to personal adaption argued for in [16].

## 4  Discussion and Future Work

Personal health technologies hold promises for improvements in medical healthcare. Even though this study did not provide clinical evidence the prototype has shown that it is feasible for everyday use with minor adaptations. A successful system must be easy to use and perceived as useful by the patients. Thus, beside the technical implementation the design of such personal health technologies is an important topic [2].

ZENse was designed to support the ideas of *Positive Psychology*, encouraging people to reflect on their daily lives in a playful, unobtrusive way. It can be worn on the wrist and therefore is easily accessible for interaction. With only minimal efforts from the user ZENse can provide beneficial insight through additional data that is automatically collected such as place and time.

However, encouraging participants to reflect on their daily emotional events could possibly lead to a situation where participants focus only on their negative incidents. This would be in strong opposition to the desired effect of juxtaposing negative and positive events. In an upcoming design this possible progress during an intervention should be anticipated.

The device and the study presented in this paper were focusing on the technology and the interaction. To gain more insight on various forms of self-reflection a larger study with more participants and longer duration - in conjunction with a hospital - is planned. This long-term study can provide more specific insights in the usage, practices and needs of patients suffering from mental diseases. The physical characteristics of the device should be advanced to get a smaller and lighter appliance. Future work had also to involve psychological researchers and therapists to built an interdisciplinary approach for a better understanding on *Positive Psychology*.

## References

1. Arditte, K., Joormann, J.: Emotion regulation in depression: reflection predicts recovery from a major depressive episode. J. Cogn. Ther. Res. **35**(6), 536–543 (2011). doi:10.1007/s10608-011-9389-4
2. Bardram, J.E., Frost, M., Szanto, K., et al.: Designing mobile health technology for bipolar disorder: a field trial of the MONARCA system. In: Proceedings of SIGCHI Conference on Human Factors in Computing Systems, pp. 2627–2636. ACM (2013)

3. Boud, D., et al.: Reflection: Turning Experience Into Learning. Routledge Chapman & Hall, London (1985)
4. Burwell, A., Shirk, S.R.: Subtypes of rumination in adolescence: associations between brooding, reflection, depressive symptoms, and coping. J. Clin. Child Adolesc. Psychol. **36**(1), 56–65 (2007)
5. Deterding, S., Khaled, R., Nacke, L., Dixon, D.: Gamification: towards a definition. In: Proceedings of CHI 2011, pp. 1–4. ACM Press (2011)
6. Eichhorn, E.: Recording inner life. In: Proceedings of 4th Tangible and Embedded Interaction Conference, pp. 313–314 (2010)
7. Fredrickson, B.L.: The value of positive emotions. Am. Sci. **91**(4), 330–335 (2003)
8. Gaver, W., Boucher, A., Law, A., et al.: Threshold devices: looking out from the home. In: Proceedings of CHI 2008, pp. 1429–1438. ACM Press (2008)
9. Gaver, W., Boucher, A., Pennington, S., Walker, B.: Cultural probes and the value of uncertainty. Interactions **11**(5), 53–56 (2004). doi:10.1145/1015530.1015555. ACM Press
10. Hall, M., Glanz, S., Caton, S., et al.: Measuring your best you: a gamification framework for well-being measurement. In: Proceedings of 3rd International Conference on Cloud and Green Computing (CGC), pp. 277–282 (2013). doi:10.1109/CGC.2013.51
11. Hall, M., Kimbrough, S., Haas, C., et al.: Towards the gamification of well-being measures. In: Proceedings of IEEE 8th International Conference on E-Science, pp. 1–8 (2012). doi:10.1109/eScience.2012.6404457
12. Hasler, G.: Pathophysiology of depression: do we have any solid evidence of interest to clinicians? World Psychiatry **9**(3), 155–161 (2010). doi:10.1002/j.2051-5545.2010.tb00298.x
13. Imbe, T., Ozaki, F., Kiyasu, S., et al.: Myglobe: a navigation service based on cognitive maps. In: Proceedings of 4th Tangible and Embedded Interaction Conference, pp. 189–192 (2010)
14. Isaacs, E., Konrad, A., Walendowski, A., et al.: Echoes from the past: how technology mediated reflection improves well-being. In: Proceedings of SIGCHI Conference on Human Factors in Computing Systems, pp. 1071–1080. ACM (2013)
15. Khan, I.A.: Personalized electronic health record system for monitoring patients with chronic disease. In: Proceedings of 2013 IEEE Systems and IE Design Symposium, pp. 121–126 (2013)
16. Kirman, B.: Emergence and playfulness in social games. In: Proceedings of 14th Int. Academic MindTrek Conference: Envisioning Future Media Environments, pp. 71–77 (2010)
17. Lindström, M., Ståhl, A., Höök, K., et al.: Affective diary: designing for bodily expressiveness and self-reflection. In: Proceedings of CHI 2006, pp. 1037–1042. ACM Press (2006). Quoted after: [6]
18. Seligman, M.E.P.: Authentic Happiness: Using the New Positive Psychology to Realize Your Potential for Lasting Fulfillment. Atria Books, New York (2003)
19. University of Cambridge. Ubhave Project (2011–2014). http://www.emotionsense.org/faqs.html. Accessed 13 March 2015
20. Vinciarelli, A., Pantic, M., Bourland, H., Pentland, A.: Social signals, their function, and automatic analysis: a survey. In: 10th International Conference on Multimodal Interfaces, pp. 61–68 (2008)
21. My Mood Tracker. http://aspyreapps.com/project/my-mood-tracker/. Accessed 13 March 2015

# BlurtLine: A Design Exploration to Support Children with ADHD in Classrooms

Dorothé Smit[✉] and Saskia Bakker

Industrial Design Department, Eindhoven University of Technology,
Eindhoven, The Netherlands
g.d.smit@student.tue.nl, s.bakker@tue.nl

**Abstract.** This paper presents BlurtLine, an interactive belt designed to support children with ADHD in regaining control over their impulsive speaking in class. Two exploratory evaluations of BlurtLine indicate that the design can indeed identify indicators of blurting and was experienced positively by a boy with ADHD and his mother and teachers.

**Keywords:** Research-through-design · ADHD · Blurting · Classroom · Interaction

## 1 Introduction

The number of students with extra needs in regular primary schools is increasing. The largest subgroup of these students is diagnosed with Attention Deficit Hyperactivity Disorder (ADHD) [4]. A symptom of ADHD is verbal impulsivity, or 'blurting' [1]: speaking in direct reaction to stimuli, without first considering the appropriateness to the situation. Supporting children with ADHD in regaining control over their blurting behaviour could potentially improve their learning situation in the classroom.

This paper presents the iterative design and evaluation of 'BlurtLine'; a belt that informs children when they are about to blurt through a softly vibrating signal (Fig. 1). BlurtLine monitors the wearer's breathing patterns. Since respiratory rate is changed extensively by emotional changes [2], rapid inhaling can be seen as a precursor for blurting. BlurtLine measures the chest circumference and constantly compares this to a baseline measurement. If BlurtLine is stretched beyond a certain set value, it sends out a signal to the wearer by vibrating, enabling him to consider his verbal actions.

This paper presents two exploratory studies using a prototype version of BlurtLine: a lab study in which the practical functionality of BlurtLine is explored and a field study to gain first insights in how BlurtLine is experienced in the classroom.

## 2 BlurtLine in the Lab

The lab study with BlurtLine served to assess both its most suitable placement on the body, and its suitability to recognize breathing patterns in adults. The test took place in a controlled setting with seven adults of 19–23 years old. The participants performed a reading exercise and a breathing exercise twice: once with the BlurtLine prototype

J. Abascal et al. (Eds.): INTERACT 2015, Part IV, LNCS 9299, pp. 456–460, 2015.
DOI: 10.1007/978-3-319-22723-8_37

**Fig. 1.** BlurtLine prototype

worn around the chest, at the height of the sternum, and once with BlurtLine worn around the abdominal area, at the height of the navel, as excited breathing often engages the chest while relaxed breathing engages the abdominal area [5]. Participants were asked to read three paragraphs of text in three different volumes: normal speaking volume, very low volume and very loudly. After reading, the participants were asked to breathe in deeply, first slowly, and then quickly. If they felt a vibration from BlurtLine during the exercise, they were to ring a bell. Afterwards, the BlurtLine was moved to the second location and the test was performed again.

The goal of this test was to determine whether BlurtLine can distinguish between different volumes of speech and to confirm that rapid breathing is more prevalent in the chest area than in the abdominal area. During reading at high volume, three out seven of participants set off the vibration motor with their chest breathing patterns when speaking loudly, while only one participant set off the vibration motor when speaking at high volume wearing the band around the abdominal area. The prototype did not vibrate for any participant during reading at normal and low volume. These findings indicate it is unlikely that a wearer will receive a false signal during normal speaking. When asked to take a quick, deep breath, all participants triggered the vibration motor when wearing BlurtLine around the chest, while four out of seven participants failed to trigger the vibration motor when wearing BlurtLine around the abdomen. This indicates that fast, impulsive breathing is mainly situated in the chest.

## 3    BlurtLine in the Field

Following the promising findings after exploring BlurtLine in the lab, a second study was set up at a primary school with an 8-year-old boy diagnosed with ADHD. The goal was to gain first insights into the child's experience of wearing BlurtLine to regain control of his blurting behaviour. Secondarily, we aimed to determine whether the child or teachers derived any benefit from it, and to gain insight in whether child, teachers or parents experienced moral concerns regarding the use of BlurtLine.

### 3.1    User Study Setup

The field study with BlurtLine spanned three consecutive mornings. The participating child wore the prototype during the last two mornings. The first morning was included for the child to get used to the presence of the researcher, and for the researcher to gain insight in the child's normal blurting behaviour. The second morning was used as a habituation period. During the third day, the participant was closely monitored to review the possible effects of BlurtLine on his behaviour in class. During the whole study, a webcam was set up in the classroom, directed towards the table of the participant. The first author monitored the participant's behaviour from a different room via a live stream. This video stream was also recorded for later analysis. To grasp the experience of using BlurtLine, interviews were conducted with the child, his mother and his teachers on the final day of the user study. Both teachers of the child were asked whether they had noticed any differences in the behaviour of the child. The participant and his mother were asked about their experiences during this user study.

## 3.2   Results

Throughout the study, the participant mentioned several times that the signals he received made him mindful of his behaviour, and encouraged him to think about the ways in which he could contribute to the class conversations. However, he also indicated that he did not always feel like he was about to blurt when he received a signal. As a result, the participant would sometimes ignore the signals and still speak out in class. The signals that the participant received from BlurtLine were described as clear, non-invasive, but sometimes too present due to their frequency.

During the interview, the participant disclosed that he did not mind wearing BlurtLine. It was clear that he was very excited about participating in the test. After initial enthusiastic interest from his peers, the children in the classroom went about their day without taking much notice of BlurtLine. One of the child's teachers said that she did not notice much difference in the participant's behaviour; the other teacher mentioned that he behaved very differently, though she remarked that this might have resulted from the presence of the camera. Overall, both of the teachers were positive towards the idea of using this tool, when its function has been proven.

The mother of the participant recounted that she did not notice any extraordinary behaviour in her child. None of the interviewees had any moral objections against the use of BlurtLine to support the child in gaining control of his blurting behaviour. The mother and teachers agreed that if it helps the child, there is no apparent problem.

## 4   Discussion

This paper presents a lab and a field study with BlurtLine, a belt designed to support children with ADHD to control speech impulsivity, in order to improve their learning environment. Both studies were exploratory, yielded a number of points for discussion and brought along a few limitations. Firstly, a limitation of the presented field study is the clear presence of the Hawthorne effect [4], indicating that a longer acclimatisation period may have been helpful. Secondly, since the user study was conducted with a first prototype version of BlurtLine, false positives have likely been present, affecting the participant's experience. Future work should therefore involve a more sophisticated, accurate prototype that can be used for an extended period of time. Despite these limitations, the performed explorations led to valuable insights into the possibilities to help children gain awareness of their blurting behaviour. During the field study, it became clear that the prototype performed well in a real life setting. However, the participant also mentioned that he wasn't always aware of his imminent blurting when he received a signal, which could either indicate false positives or unawareness of his blurting behaviour. This might pose a limitation of the study; we cannot be sure if signals were false or not. However, it may also indicate the potential value of BlurtLine: children indeed seem unaware of their blurting behaviour right before they are about to blurt. BlurtLine may thus assist them recognizing the signals that indicate impending blurting. A potential risk of using devices such as BlurtLine is that it may have a stigmatizing effect for the user. During the field study this did not seem the case, nor did the participant's mother or teachers observe negative effects. Despite the small scale and exploratory nature of the study, we believe this is a promising finding, which deserves more exploration in future work.

## 5   Conclusion

This paper presents BlurtLine, a belt designed to support children with ADHD, who show impulsive speaking behaviour (blurting), thereby unintentionally interrupting their own learning process in the classroom. BlurtLine provides tactile feedback at moments the wearer is about to blurt, potentially enabling them to regain control of their behaviour. Two exploratory studies with a prototype version of BlurtLine indicated that (1) BlurtLine can accurately measure rapid inhaling, a precursor for blurting, when worn around the chest, (2) the 8-year-old participant in our field-study positively experienced wearing the prototype and was encouraged to consciously think about his speaking intentions and (3) no stigmatizing effects were found. While exploratory, we believe these findings are encouraging future research in which BlurtLine would be used for a longer period, by a larger number of children in a classroom. Considering increasing diversity among students in classrooms, this paper contributes by laying out an opportunity to support children with ADHD to improve their learning experience and increase their ability to reach their full potential in regular education.

## References

1. Barkley, R.A.: ADHD and the Nature of Self-Control. Guilford Press, New York (1997)
2. Homma, I., Masaoka, Y.: Breathing rhythms and emotions. Exp. Physiol. **93**(9), 1011–1021 (2008)
3. Landsberger, H.A.: Hawthorne Revisited: A Plea for an Open City. Cornell University, Ithaca (1957)

4. Smeets, E., Ledoux, G., Blok, H., Felix, C., Heurter, A., van Kuijk, J., Vergeer, M.: Op de drempel van passend onderwijs. http://www.nwo.nl/over-nwo/voorlichting-en-communicatie/publicaties. Accessed 17 November 2014
5. Stevenson, I., Duncan, C.H.: Alterations in cardiac function and circulatory efficiency during periods of life stress as shown by changes in the rate, rhythm, electrocardiographic pattern and output of the heart in those with cardiovascular disease. Res. Publ. Assoc. Res. Nerv. Ment. Dis. 29, 799 (1949)

# Cooperation in Real-Time Using a Virtual Environment

Máté Köles[1]([✉]), Károly Hercegfi[1], Balázs Péter Hámornik[1],
Emma Lógó[1], Bálint Szabó[1], and Anita Komlódi[2]

[1] Department of Ergonomics and Psychology,
Budapest University of Technology and Economics, Budapest, Hungary
{kolesm,hercegfi,balazs.hamornik,emma,
szabobalint}@erg.bme.hu
[2] Department of Information Systems,
University of Maryland Baltimore County, Baltimore, MD, USA
komlodi@umbc.edu

**Abstract.** Effective team interaction over great distances are already supported by many digital tools. However, cooperative manipulation of common objects is limited and most non-verbal information (gaze direction, facial expressions) can be transmitted only partially or are missing completely. The inclusion of these additional information sources can enrich cooperative problems solving situations. In our demonstration we highlight the capabilities of the Virtual Collaboration Arena to support such interactions. With the help of a volunteer from the audience in Bamberg we will present parts of an information management task solved cooperatively with another user seated in Budapest.

**Keywords:** Virtual reality · Cooperation · Problem solving

## 1 Introduction

Non-verbal communication is just as important as verbally transmitted information in real world scenarios. If the social interaction takes place in a virtual world, the number of available non-verbal cues becomes limited. This is a problem, since partial or incomplete non-verbal signals can lead to misinterpretation and ultimately hinder cooperation [1]. The more sources available the easier it is to disambiguate what the other person was trying to communicate. Also having congruent signals from these different channels will increase percentage of recalled information [2] and create a more empathic feel towards the other person [3, 4].

Collaboration in virtual spaces is currently limited in conveying important non-verbal information. Since registering and virtually recreating whole body movement (including facial expression) of an individual is not cost effective at this time, compromises have to be made. A selection of easy to implement non-verbal channels should be selected to enhance communication in virtual environments. Head orientation is a powerful cue that can signal social attention [5].

Virtual environments may seem to be inherently inferior to real-life environments in case of cooperation, but that is not true for all aspects of the interaction. First of all,

© IFIP International Federation for Information Processing 2015
J. Abascal et al. (Eds.): INTERACT 2015, Part IV, LNCS 9299, pp. 461–464, 2015.
DOI: 10.1007/978-3-319-22723-8_38

the laws of physics can be changed according to the goals of the cooperators. Inspection and theoretical modification of a heavy object for example is much easier to do in virtual space. And if the virtual space supports it, changes are instantly visible compared to a drawing on a paper. Also, some suggest that people can feel more liberated in virtual environments and express their character better than in real-life [6]. And at last but not least, geographic distances are not a problem anymore. Virtual team meetings can be held even if the members are on different continents.

### 1.1 The Virtual Collaboration Arena (VirCA)

The demonstration will feature the Virtual Collaboration Arena (VirCA) as the system responsible for the virtual environment. It is a loosely coupled, modular system capable of supporting a wide array of tasks. From remote robot control [7] through virtual meetings to psychological experiments in spatial cognition [8]. It was developed by Cognitive Informatics Research Group of the Computer and Automation Research Institute of the Hungarian Academy of Sciences. Custom rooms and objects are easy to define and use. It support classic input devices as mouse and keyboard but also gaming controllers and motion tracking.

## 2 Demonstration

### 2.1 The Virtual Environment

The interaction will take place in a $3 \times 3$ m virtual room designed to represent a tourist office. It contains a map of Budapest, posters and flyers about different sights and activities and jointly editable documents (Fig. 1). It also has a few decorative items (a plant, a trash bin and a window) to create a more natural feel.

The posters contain information about the location of the given activity with opening hours and entry fees (if any). They are grouped into four different categories by symbols: sights, baths, clubs and restaurants. Both participants are able to move or highlight the posters.

The editable documents serve as notepad pages, where ideas can be written down. They can also be used to add activities not represented by the available posters.

Each participant is represented by a single colored head. The reason behind the simplicity of the avatars is the following. As established in the introduction earlier, the more detailed the avatar, the more equipment and resources are required. These simple avatars are able to convey head orientation which is a very important social cue [5], pointing gestures (for clarifying common attentional objects) and also intonations through real-time voice chat.

### 2.2 Brief Description of the Task

The demonstration aims to replicate the first part of an information management task. There will be two phases. The training will introduce the participant and the audience

**Fig. 1.** The virtual environment representing a tourist office with the avatars of the users in the middle.

in Bamberg to the virtual space and the possible forms of interaction. For the actual collaborative part of the task, we will connect live to another user situated in Budapest. From that point on, users will have to solve a task that simulates creating a holiday plan for a tourist group for a weekend at Budapest. We decided to include a few conditions that should be met by every successful solution.

The exact instructions are: "Create a holiday plan for two days for a foreign tourist group who are around your age. Make sure to include in your plan a trip to a bath and a pub. Also, both days should end at a club. Suggest places for lunch and dinner for both days; they receive breakfast at their hotel. Try to fill both days with classic tourist attractions. Create a plan that is varied, yet manageable. Display the final plan in the table located on the front wall."

The task requires participants to decide together on a plan that satisfies most criteria. The posters contain all the information required to solve the task. No existing knowledge of Budapest is required. However, there are some activities that are not available on weekends so they have to be mindful of their choices. All posters that become part of the plan should be placed in a timetable on the wall. The task will run until the plan is finished or time for the demonstration runs out. A brief evaluation of the solution is given at the end.

**Acknowledgements.** The present study was supported by the KTIA_AIK_12-1-2013-0037 project: Virtual NeuroCognitive Space for research and development of future immersive mediatechnologies (NeuroCogSpace). The project is supported by the Hungarian Government, managed by the National Development Agency/Ministry, and financed by the Research and Technology Innovation Fund. The authors thank Péter Baranyi and the 3DICC Lab of SZTAKI for organizing the project and supporting the VirCA virtual environment.

# References

1. Cheshin, A., Rafaeli, A., Bos, N.: Anger and happiness in virtual teams: emotional influences of text and behavior on others' affect in the absence of non-verbal cues. Organ. Behav. Hum. Decis. Process. **116**, 2–16 (2011). doi:10.1016/j.obhdp.2011.06.002
2. Buisine, S., Martin, J.-C.: The effects of speech–gesture cooperation in animated agents' behavior in multimedia presentations. Interact. Comput. **19**, 484–493 (2007). doi:10.1016/j.intcom.2007.04.002
3. Ang, C.S., Bobrowicz, A., Siriaraya, P., et al.: Effects of gesture-based avatar-mediated communication on brainstorming and negotiation tasks among younger users. Comput. Hum. Behav. **29**, 1204–1211 (2013). doi:10.1016/j.chb.2012.10.013
4. Bente, G., Rüggenberg, S., Krämer, N.C., Eschenburg, F.: Avatar-mediated networking: increasing social presence and interpersonal trust in net-based collaborations. Hum. Commun. Res. **34**, 287–318 (2008). doi:10.1111/j.1468-2958.2008.00322.x
5. Langton, S.R.H., Honeyman, H., Tessler, E.: The influence of head contour and nose angle on the perception of eye-gaze direction. Percept. Psychophys. **66**, 752–771 (2004). doi:10.3758/BF03194970
6. Stanilova, K.: Survey on verbal and non-verbal behaviors in real and virtual world. Procedia Soc. Behav. Sci. **114**, 311–316 (2014). doi:10.1016/j.sbspro.2013.12.703
7. Galambos, P., Baranyi, P.: VirCA as virtual intelligent space for RT-middleware. In: IEEE/ASME International Conference on Advanced Intelligent Mechatronics, Budapest, Hungary, pp. 140–145 (2011)
8. Persa, G., Torok, A., Galambos, P., et al.: Experimental framework for spatial cognition research in immersive virtual space. In: 2014 5th IEEE Conference on Cognitive Infocommunications, pp. 587–593. IEEE (2014)

# Diving into the Data Ocean

Dieter Meiller[✉]

Faculty of Electronic-Engineering, Media and Computer Science,
East Bavarian Technical University Amberg-Weiden, Amberg, Germany
d.meiller@oth-aw.de

**Abstract.** In this paper we present the concept for a novel user interface that simplifies the management of data and the search of information strongly: Instead of a reactive system, a proactive system is suggested. As a substitute of the desktop metaphor we propose to model data as active creatures that move inside the ecosystem computer: a Data Ocean. The concept can be used for different applications to manage objects with varying properties.

**Keywords:** Graphical user interface · Information visualization · Information retrieval · Internet of things

## 1 Background

The desktop metaphor nowadays is established as the dominant user interface for interaction with personal computers. Since its invention in the 1970s it is almost unchanged, the dominant metaphor for searching and managing data objects aka files. After Apple transferred the desktop invented by Xerox to Macintosh and Microsoft Windows was created as competing product afterwards, classical desktop has changed only marginally [1]. Other operating concepts were displaced or could not prevail. The pre-main interface with keyboard for text input on console was replaced by the WIMP-system with the mouse as primary input device. However, there have been some other interesting concepts, such as the Zoomable User Interface [2] or Life Streams [3]. Both systems do not have a folder structure for organizing data. There, structure results from spatial or temporal arrangement of objects.

## 2 Problem and Approach

Mobile devices increasingly replace traditional PCs and so the classic method of computer usage is put more and more into question; alternatives are wanted. Another pestering issue is the rapidly increasing number of data objects that must be managed by users. In previous systems, users usually had to search themselves and navigate to the location (folder) of a single data object. Therefore, search functions in modern operating systems are becoming increasingly popular. There, mechanisms are reversed: Files come, figuratively, to the users, when they initiate a search. So, the challenge is to find methods of file management, which satisfy new requirements and changed user behaviors. The presented approach is based on findings from different areas:

© IFIP International Federation for Information Processing 2015
J. Abascal et al. (Eds.): INTERACT 2015, Part IV, LNCS 9299, pp. 465–468, 2015.
DOI: 10.1007/978-3-319-22723-8_39

*Artificial Life (AL):* Formal description of behavior and simulation of living beings is an interdisciplinary area of research. A sub-area deals with simulation and description of swarm behavior and its wider effects, the emergence [4].

*Information Retrieval:* This area deals with the search in databases. Of particular interest is fuzzy retrieval, which weights search results and found documents by relevance [5].

# 3 Concept

The concept presented here provides no folder structure to manage data objects, like in Zoomable User Interfaces. Each object does have characteristics by which it could be identified. Files with textual content can be identified by terms that are part of their full text. Other existing attributes such as creation date or date of last modification, file size, place of production or other metadata stored in the files could also be used for identification. In addition, there should be the opportunity to mark data objects with tags (keywords). Objects should be able to move in a space (Data Ocean, $O$). The dimensionality and structure of this space could preferably be a 2½-D space. That means, objects are located in a two-dimensional space in which can be zoomed in and out. It would also be possible to arrange objects in a 3D space. Objects should behave like creatures in a swarm, such as fishes or birds, for example. They should behave in accordance with the following rule: objects are heading towards others with similar properties. Other objects with common characteristics should attract them. The more is in common, the greater the attraction. The attraction of two objects $o_1, o_2 \in O$ should be a function $attr : P \rightarrow [0, 1]$. P is defined as: $P = O \times O | (o_1, o_1) \notin P, (o_1, o_2) \in P \Rightarrow (o_2, o_1) \notin P$. This strength of attraction depends on specific criteria $C$ of an amount of $n = |C|$ criteria and the strength of accordance of objects with these criteria: $c_i^{o_1}, c_i^{o_2} \in [0, 1] (0 \leq i \leq n)$. In this way, the system is self-organizing itself in groups of related data. Since data do not fit into disjoint sets, groups will be interwoven. So, users can control this process, it is necessary that they can weight the criteria with a specific weight $w_i \in [0, 1]$ and determine which features lead to formations of groups. The strength of attraction of two objects in dependence of accordance with particular criteria then will be defined as follows:

$$attr((o_1, o_2)) = \frac{1}{n} \sum_{i=1}^{n} w_i (1 - |c_i^{o_1} - c_i^{o_2}|)$$

*Agility and Vitality:* Data objects should have a certain agility, which decreases with age. Old, slow objects could be removed from the space by being eaten up by certain other objects. These predator-objects should have a similar function like paper baskets from the desktop metaphor, but in a more active way. It is also conceivable that the user has the ability to open these predator-objects to restore deleted content. Users could be able to delete the objects finally by removing the predator-objects. Feeding data objects could increase their agility: users could feed them by viewing or editing them. Thus, unused files become obsolete and are removed automatically.

*Search and User Actions:* In traditional desktop systems, the user has to go towards the data objects by navigating through file trees. This principle is reversed here: Files will be attracted and come to the user. Files are lured by the prospect for food: the chance to be used or viewed. Attributes, which the desired files should have, can be scattered as "attractors". Specifying weights can change intensity of the attractors. Best matching files are most attracted to the attractors (Fig. 1). In addition, agile file objects, which are used more often, will be faster on target. Attractors could be temporarily spread for spontaneous search tasks or can serve as an anchor to organize data. Users could be able to look at this world from two perspectives: from the outside as observers, or from the inside, almost as a diver in the data ocean.

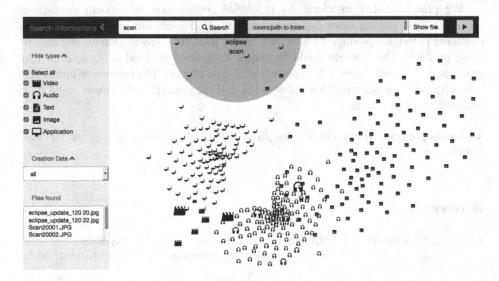

**Fig. 1.** Prototype of the concept

## 4 Implementation and Evaluation

The concept was implemented by a group of students. 26 participants of a subject "Information Visualization" had to solve the following task: They should implement the concept above. The prototypes should be able to visualize a part of the files of a file system. They should allow searching for files like mentioned. Teams with maximum three students released 13 different versions. These varying programs are useful for evaluating the capability of the concept. Furthermore, the best ways to implement the mentioned features could be identified. A screenshot of one of the best implementations is shown in Fig. 1 (Student: Johannes Wisneth). It has a web-based surface with responsive layout. The program allows filtering and finding all desired files in a specific folder very quickly. It provides a useful stop-button to freeze all movements. This helps to pick single objects.

## 5  Summary and Future Work

Due to the large amounts of data and the fact that many modern systems don't provide access to their file systems, users of today's devices are often no longer able to cope with them. Search functions are intuitive and fast, and so they are preferred for accessing files. Hence, a reversal of the usual concept would be suitable: In a modern system, users should not have to navigate towards the file, but the desired data should come to the user. This implies an active behavior of data objects. Therefore, a new metaphor as a replacement for the classic desktop is proposed: An ecosystem in which data behave like living things, which organizes themselves and can be lured by the user. The next step will be to find some practical applications for the concept.

We plan to realize interfaces for industrial applications. In modern production processes products are often highly customized. End users are increasingly able to configure individual products by their own. There must be a way to monitor and control these products. Our concept could be useful to control all kind of data, even real physical objects, which could be represented as data objects. The Internet of things and "Industry 4.0" are hot topics for industry [6] and the concept Data Ocean could be a building block to realize it.

**Acknowledgements.** We would like to acknowledge all participating students for their contribution.

## References

1. Reimer, J.: A history of the GUI. http://arstechnica.com. Accessed 5 May 2005
2. Bederson, B.B.: The promise of zoomable user interfaces. Behav. Inf. Technol. **30**(6), 853–866 (2011)
3. Freeman, E.T.: The Lifestreams Software Architecture. Yale University, New Heaven (1997)
4. Mataric, M.J.: Designing emergent behaviors: from local interactions to collective intelligence. In: Proceedings of the Second International Conference on Simulation of Adaptive Behavior, pp. 432–441 (1993)
5. Cross, V.: Fuzzy information retrieval. J. Intell. Inf. Syst. **3**(1), 29–56 (1994)
6. Atzori, L., Iera, A., Morabito, G.: The internet of things: a survey. Comput. Netw. **54**(15), 2787–2805 (2010)

# ETA Wizard App: Make Design and Evaluation of Accessible Electronic Travel Aids Easy

Limin Zeng[✉], Gerhard Weber, and Alexander Fickel

Human-Computer Interaction, Computer Science Department, TU Dresden
Nöthnitzer, Str. 46, 01187 Dresden, Germany
{limin.zeng,gerhard.weber,
alexander.fickel}@tu-dresden.de

**Abstract.** To support designers and researchers a touch-screen based Wizard-of-Oz application is demonstrated. It can be used to develop electronic travel aids for blind and visually impaired people and allows evaluating audio and haptic user interfaces in an early development stage. A scenario for presentation of obstacles combines sonification and feedback from vibration of a tactile belt.

**Keywords:** Electronic travel aids · User-centered design · Auditory and haptic user interface · Wizard of Oz

## 1 Introduction

More and more innovative electronic travel aids (ETAs) are proposed in order to overcome the disadvantages of traditional assistive mobility tools, like white canes and guide dogs. Both the larger and the narrower context are important to improve mobility. For example, users cannot use the white cane to detect obstacles above knee level, specifically for dangerous obstacles at head level (Manduchi and Kurniawan 2011). Besides numerous technologies studied for capturing contextual information, the design of multimodal output is crucial in order not to overload users in everyday scenarios.

Aiming at presenting spatial information about obstacles and hazards in an accessible way, ETAs employ auditory output, haptic/tactile output or a combination of them (Meijer 1992; Dakopoulos and Bourbakis 2009; Zeng et al. 2012). However, for the developers it is challenging to acquire users' feedback on their user interface design in an early stage of an ETA development (i.e., before the obstacle detector module is available), specifically when a user-centered design method is employed for designing an accessible user interface.

In this paper, we demonstrate a touch-screen based Wizard of Oz (WoZ) app (namely ETA Wizard App) for helping researchers and designers to evaluate their ETA's user interface design in an early development stage. In addition to setting up test environments (e.g., room size and distribution of obstacles) and importing virtual and

© IFIP International Federation for Information Processing 2015
J. Abascal et al. (Eds.): INTERACT 2015, Part IV, LNCS 9299, pp. 469–472, 2015.
DOI: 10.1007/978-3-319-22723-8_40

real obstacles, the ETA Wizard App offers an auditory and haptic interface which allows researchers and designers to implement their own design easily.

## 2    ETA Wizard App

When the user-centered design approach is adopted for designing and developing an ETA, in addition to collect user requirements at the beginning, it is important to acquire user feedback about the prototypes at an early stage. As illustrated in Fig. 1, the proposed ETA Wizard App supports developers and researchers to design two parts of an interactive demonstration:

- **WoZ Test Preparation:** the module helps researchers quickly setting up a test environment, consisting of obstacles and their spatial distribution. It supports augmenting the scene by adding real or virtual obstacles.
- **WoZ Field Test:** the module can simulate localizing the user by tapping and trigger actions from gestural input to perform researchers' user interface designs and deploy them in a WoZ field test easily.

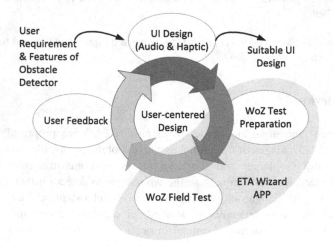

**Fig. 1.** EAT Wizard App in the life circle of a user-centered design

In the two modules, several features have been implemented:

### 1. WoZ Test Preparation Module

(a) *Test Room Setting:* Set the test room size, including the size of visual grid which is helpful to update subjects' position quickly and easily.

(b) *Real and Virtual Obstacle Setting:* In addition to specify different types of obstacles (e.g., doors and grounded obstacles), the feature allows to add virtual obstacles which might be dangerous in a real world, like drop-offs and descending stairs, and add special obstacles at fixed sites, such as a real hanging paper board.

2. **WoZ Field Test Module**

(c) *Update Subject's Position & Heading Orientation:* Touch-based interaction allows to update subject's position and heading orientation, see Fig. 2.

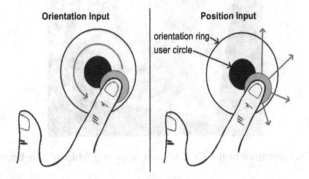

**Fig. 2.** The touch interaction to simulate subject's position and heading orientation

(d) *Support Auditory User Interfaces:* Regarding to the auditory output, in addition to playback basic sounds (e.g., WAV files) the ETA Wizard App also support playing spatial sounds, via the Open Audio Library (OpenAL)[1]. It is possible to extend by adding other auditory library, like Libpd[2].

(e) *Support Haptic User Interface:* Obstacles' spatial information is presented also by haptic (vibrotactile) output. In this App, a tactile belt with 8 vibrators[3] is supported, which is connected to the host tablet via a Bluetooth interface (see Fig. 3). It can be extended to support other haptic/tactile devices.

(f) *Experiment Log Data:* The main experimental data will be recorded in detail, including subject's position and heading orientation, and a time stamp.

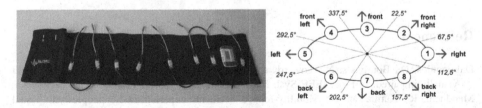

**Fig. 3.** The tactile belt with 8 vibrators (the interval angel of each vibrator is 45°)

---

[1] OpenAL Soft: http://kcat.strangesoft.net/openal.html.

[2] Libpd: http://puredata.info/downloads/libpd.

[3] Elitac Science Suit: http://elitac.nl/products/sciencesuit.html.

Figure 4 illustrates a screenshot of the ETA Wizard App. A red point indicates the subjects' position, and a black line leaving this point indicates the subject's heading orientation. Figure 5 shows a typical scenario where a wizard evaluates audio/haptic user interfaces in a real test environment, via the ETA Wizard App.

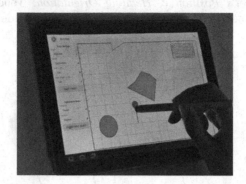

**Fig. 4.** The screenshot of the ETA Wizard App on a tablet (Color figure online)

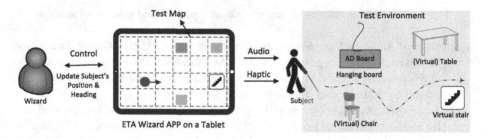

**Fig. 5.** A typical scenario about the ETA Wizard App for a WoZ field test

**Acknowledgement.** This study was supported by the Range-IT[4] project within the framework of EU FP7 SME Program (Grant no. 605998).

# References

Dakopoulos, D., Bourbakis, N.: Towards a 2D tactile vocabulary for navigation of blind and visually impaired. In Proc. IEEE Syst. Man Cybern. **2009**, 45–51 (2009)

Manduchi, R., Kurniawan, S.: Mobility-related accidents experienced by people with visual impairment. Res. Pract. Vis. Impairment Blindness **4**(2), 44–54 (2011)

Meijer, P.B.L.: An experimental system for auditory image representations. IEEE Trans. Biomed. Eng. **39**, 112–121 (1992)

Zeng, L., Pescher, D., Weber, G.: Exploration and avoidance of surrounding obstacles for the visually impaired. In: Proceedings of ACM ASSETS 2012, pp. 111–118 (2012)

---

[4] Range-IT project, http://www.range-it.eu/.

# Generating Narratives from Personal Digital Data: Using Sentiment, Themes, and Named Entities to Construct Stories

Elaine Farrow[1(✉)], Thomas Dickinson[2], and Matthew P. Aylett[1]

[1] School of Informatics, University of Edinburgh, Edinburgh, UK
Elaine.Farrow@ed.ac.uk, matthewa@inf.ed.ac.uk
[2] Knowledge Media Institute, The Open University, Milton Keynes, UK
thomas.dickinson@open.ac.uk

**Abstract.** As the quantity and variety of personal digital data shared on social media continues to grow, how can users make sense of it? There is growing interest among HCI researchers in using narrative techniques to support interpretation and understanding. This work describes our prototype application, ReelOut, which uses narrative techniques to allow users to understand their data as more than just a database. The online service extracts data from multiple social media sources and augments it with semantic information such as sentiment, themes, and named entities. The interactive editor automatically constructs a story by using unit selection to fit data units to a simple narrative structure. It allows the user to change the story interactively by rejecting certain units or selecting a new narrative target. Finally, images from the story can be exported as a video clip or a collage.

**Keywords:** Social media · Narrative · Triptych · Multi-media

## 1 Introduction

Social media use has led to such an explosion in personal digital data that users can easily become lost and overwhelmed, and a common challenge for HCI researchers is to help users cope. Selection and summarization tasks (such as identifying a list of hashtags which are currently popular or reporting which Facebook posts got the most 'likes') represent a typical approach to improving understanding – treating it as a database to be queried.

In contrast, we often interpret our own experiences, desires, and motivations using stories not statistics. Both in the commercial world and in academia, interest is growing in bridging the gap between viewing personal digital data as a database, and viewing the data as (elements of) personal narratives. The use of narrative to make sense of our everyday lives is considered to be a fundamental human behavior [2], and the exploration of narrative formats for data presentation can help HCI researchers understand how meaning is constructed through stories and how stories can be used to interpret data. There have been some recent popular examples of automatic narrative generation

J. Abascal et al. (Eds.): INTERACT 2015, Part IV, LNCS 9299, pp. 473–477, 2015.
DOI: 10.1007/978-3-319-22723-8_41

from social media data. For example, Facebook's *A Look Back*[1] compiles users' most popular posts into a short film. However, as noted in previous research [3–5], the resulting film is very much a finished product. Users can replace chosen posts with others from a limited selection, but have very little overall control.

The ReelOut application is part of a wider project in which we seek to build a novel text-driven software system that can automatically generate film-like life documentaries from personal digital data, and to explore the human experience and response to such systems. We aim to empower users by allowing them to interpret their data to suit their own vision of the narratives they see within their lives. ReelOut allows users to build stories from primitive units (such as tweets and Facebook posts) with reference to a particular narrative target: as a simple example for illustration, consider a story on the theme of 'food and drink' that starts with a negative sentiment and ends with a positive sentiment.

Our process is illustrated in Fig. 1. We extract text and metadata from a user's social media posts and augment it with semantic tags. Next, we employ a unit selection process borrowed from speech synthesis to fit the data to the desired narrative target. The user can change the story by rejecting certain units or selecting a new narrative target. Finally, the images associated with the generated story can be exported as a short movie clip or a collage of images.

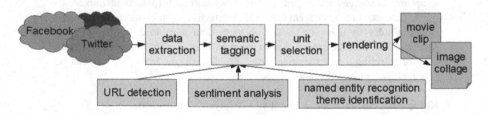

**Fig. 1.** The processing pipeline

## 2   Generating Narratives from Personal Digital Data

At the time of writing, our online service can extract data from Twitter and Facebook, with limited support for Instagram. We intend to add further platforms to this list in the near future. The sentiment of each post is calculated using Sentistrength,[2] a popular sentiment analysis tool for short web texts. Entities such as locations are extracted using AlchemyAPI's[3] entity extraction endpoint, while themes are identified using AlchemyAPI's taxonomy endpoint. Some social media posts, such as comments and replies, form a conversational thread. For these, we note which other units come before and after them in the thread. Finally, the data is passed to the interactive editor as a series of RLUnits, an XML format consisting of marked-up text and semantic tags (Fig. 2).

---

[1] facebook.com/lookback.

[2] sentistrength.wlv.ac.uk.

[3] www.alchemyapi.com.

The interactive editor (Fig. 3) provides a graphical user interface for story creation. By default, generated stories are sequences of three linked units (a *triptych*), corresponding to the classic 3-act structure of setup, confrontation, and resolution. The generated picture sequence can be exported as a short movie clip or saved as a collage of images.

```
<rlunit id="15028" src="facebook" time="20091101:190400">
  <image>...</image>
  <messagetext>Happy after dinner face</messagetext>
  <sentiment>positive</sentiment>
  <theme>food and drink</theme>
</rlunit>
```

**Fig. 2.** An RLUnit representing a Facebook post with a positive sentiment and a theme of 'food and drink' (the image URL is omitted due to space constraints).

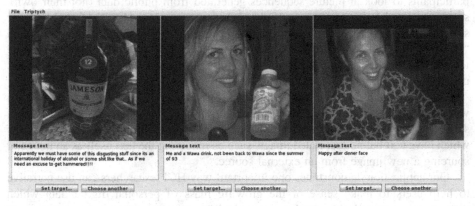

**Fig. 3.** The interactive editor, showing a story on the theme of 'food and drink' that starts with a negative sentiment and ends with a positive sentiment.

Our story generation algorithm is inspired by the unit selection process in speech synthesis, where many thousands of units are fitted to an utterance structure. We use dynamic programming to fit the marked-up data units (RLUnits) to a predefined narrative target, represented as an ordered collection of slots with associated semantic tags which constrain their contents.

Two cost functions are optimized to produce the output. The first, *target cost*, represents the fit with the narrative target: units which share semantic tags with the target slot will have a low target cost. The second, *join cost*, represents how connected two adjacent RLUnits are: units which have a similar set of semantic tags and appear in the correct order will have a low join cost.

The editor allows the user to set the target for each story slot interactively, using the semantic tags found in the extracted data. It also offers unit reselection – rejecting a particular unit and automatically selecting the next-best unit to fit that slot – a powerful method borrowed from speech synthesis, where it enables users to modify automatically synthesized utterances without requiring an understanding of the linguistic or phonetic structure of speech.

## 3   Conclusion and Future Work

Our novel end-to-end automatic narrative generation application, ReelOut, augments personal digital data from social media sites with semantic tags such as sentiment, themes, and named entities. It uses unit selection to build a story that fits a specified narrative target, and allows users to change the story interactively by rejecting particular units or selecting a new narrative target. It is extensible for further research and development.

We have run an initial evaluation of the story-generation algorithm by asking participants to look at picture sequences generated from public data (not their own), some generated by our system and others chosen at random [1]. We found that our system produced output which users rated significantly higher than random when asked "How much does this sequence of pictures tell a story?" We are currently working towards a user trial of the full system, allowing people to create and evaluate stories using their own personal digital data.

Our future plans include developing a data-driven event detection algorithm which will allow us to classify individual units as belonging to a larger event, such as 'starting school' or 'getting married'. We are also experimenting with ways to represent units which have text but no associated image, such as rendering the text itself as an image or sourcing a new image from an external source.

Our application demonstrates one important way HCI researchers can use narrative to help users to make sense of the growing mass of personal digital data which threatens to overwhelm them – by automatically constructing stories.

**Acknowledgments.**   This work was supported by EPSRC grant EP/L004062/1.

## References

1. Aylett, M.P., Farrow, E., Pschetz, L., Dickinson, T.: Generating narratives from personal digital data: Triptychs. In: CHI EA 2015. ACM, New York, NY, USA, pp. 1875–1880 (2015). http://doi.acm.org/10.1145/2702613.2732702
2. Sarbin, T.R.: Narrative Psychology: the Storied Nature of Human Conduct. Praeger Publishers/Greenwood Publishing Group, Westport (1986)
3. Schwanda Sosik, V., Zhao, X., Cosley, D.: See friendship, sort of: how conversation and digital traces might support reflection on friendships. In: CSCW 2012. ACM, New York, pp. 1145–1154 (2012). http://doi.acm.org/10.1145/2145204.2145374

4. Thiry, E., Lindley, S., Banks, R., Regan, T.: Authoring personal histories: exploring the timeline as a framework for meaning making. In: CHI 2013. ACM, New York, NY, USA, pp. 1619–1628 (2013). http://doi.acm.org/10.1145/2470654.2466215
5. Zhao, X., Lindley, S.E.: Curation through use: understanding the personal value of social media. In: CHI 2014. ACM, New York, pp. 2431–2440 (2014). http://doi.acm.org/10.1145/2556288.2557291

# Interactive Light Feedback: Illuminating Above-Device Gesture Interfaces

Euan Freeman[1]([⊠]), Stephen Brewster[1], and Vuokko Lantz[2]

[1] Glasgow Interactive Systems Group, University of Glasgow,
Glasgow, Scotland, UK
{euan.freeman,stephen.brewster}@glasgow.ac.uk
[2] Nokia Technologies, Espoo, Finland
vuokko.lantz@nokia.com

**Abstract.** In-air hand gestures allow users to interact with mobile phones without reaching out and touching them. Users need helpful and meaningful feedback while they gesture, although mobile phones have limited feedback capabilities because of their small screen sizes. *Interactive light feedback* illuminates the surface surrounding a mobile phone, giving users visual feedback over a larger area and without affecting on-screen content. We explore the design space for interactive light and our demonstration shows how we can use this output modality for gesture feedback.

**Keywords:** Above-device interaction · Gesture feedback · Gesture interaction · Interactive light feedback · Mobile devices

## 1 Introduction

Above-device interfaces allow users to interact with their mobile phones using in-air hand gestures over the device. Gestures can be used when touchscreen input is unavailable or inconvenient; for example, users could gesture to follow a recipe on their phone without getting the touchscreen messy or having to wash their hands between using the phone and handling food. Gestures also allow more expressive forms of input than touch, allowing users to do more than simply touch the screen.

Users need helpful feedback when gesturing to be able to interact confidently and effectively. However, mobile phones have limited display capabilities because of their small size. Giving visual feedback about gesture interaction would affect on-screen content and may require redesigning application interfaces for gesture and non-gesture use. Audio and tactile feedback have been considered instead, although lacks the expressive, spatial characteristics of visual feedback. We propose giving visual feedback in the space *surrounding* the device, using light to illuminate surrounding table surfaces while users gesture (as in Fig. 1). We call this *interactive light feedback*.

Mobile phones have already used light to illuminate table surfaces for other purposes. For example, Samsung's *Galaxy S6 Edge* [1] has a curved screen which

J. Abascal et al. (Eds.): INTERACT 2015, Part IV, LNCS 9299, pp. 478–481, 2015.
DOI: 10.1007/978-3-319-22723-8_42

**Fig. 1.** Interactive light feedback around a mobile phone. Here, brightness changes dynamically to show how users how well their hands can be sensed.

illuminates the table surface when placed face-down, glowing different colours to show who is calling. Some of Sony's *Xperia* phones feature an *Illumination Bar* [2] along one edge, which is used for visualisations during media playback. Research prototypes have also used lights embedded within the device bezel [8] and case [9] to visualise off-screen content. We build on these examples by looking at how interactive light can be used for dynamic gesture feedback instead.

In this paper we look at the design space for interactive light feedback. We share ideas about how light can be used to create gesture feedback and our demonstration allows others to experience these designs.

## 2    Related Work

Users require plentiful feedback when gesturing. However, mobile phones have small displays which limits the amount of feedback they can give. Others have suggested using other modalities instead for gesture feedback. Freeman *et al.* [4] looked at tactile feedback for in-air gestures. They evaluated a variety of methods of giving tactile feedback, including ultrasound haptics and vibration from smartwatches and other wearables. They found tactile feedback effective at enhancing visual feedback, although it lacked necessary bandwidth to replace it.

Others have used audio feedback for in-air interactions while phones are in a pocket, where visual feedback would go unnoticed. *Imaginary Phone* [6] and *Nenya* [3] read selected menu items aloud as users gestured, either in front of their body (for *Imaginary Phone*) or by moving a ring on their finger (for *Nenya*). In these cases, audio feedback came *after* gestures; users received no cues during interaction to help them. Our research looks at continuous interactive light feedback during gesture interaction, giving users cues as they interact.

In similar work to ours, Qin *et al.* [9] presented a prototype mobile phone which had LEDs embedded in its case. They presented an example application where users could respond to phone calls by touching the table on the left (illuminated red) or right (illuminated green) side of the phone. We build on this idea by using interactive light for dynamic feedback during gestures, rather than static feedforward before interaction. *Rainbowfish* [5] used a grid of LEDs to give feedback about gestures over a proximity-sensing surface, acting as a display. In our work, light is used to illuminate the area *around* a display, instead.

## 3   Interactive Light Feedback

Earlier we defined interactive light feedback as visual feedback given by illuminating the space surrounding a device. In our prototype (Fig. 1), we use LEDs around the device edge to present interactive light feedback, although light sources could be enclosed within the bezel itself, as in *Sparkle* [8]. We use LEDs as they are small, cheap and have low power requirements. Our prototype consists of a flexible strip of 60 LEDs[1] (approximately 7 mm apart) affixed to a mobile phone and controlled by an Arduino microcontroller. Each LED is independently controllable and can vary its own hue and brightness.

Each LED has two design properties: **brightness**, which is always variable, and **hue**, which is fixed in some LEDs. These basic properties of light become more expressive when varied over **time** and **location**. Harrison *et al.* [7] showed how expressive and informative a single LED can be when change in brightness is animated over time. They presented a set of "light behaviours" which could be used to communicate information from a single light.

We have found dynamic change in brightness to be especially effective for gesture feedback, as users immediately see a response to their hand movements. One of our feedback designs uses brightness to show how well users' hands and gestures can be sensed, using a visibility metaphor: when light is easier to see (that is, brightness is greater), it is because hands can be more easily seen (Fig. 1). If light is less visible, it is because users are not as easily sensed; for example, their hands may be too far from the sensor.

Brightness can also be varied at different locations to create spatial patterns. For example, lights could be illuminated (that is, brightness greater than zero) to show hand position relative to the mobile phone (as in Fig. 2). This is similar to the "shadow" feedback design in *Rainbowfish* [5], although feedback does not occlude on-screen content, since it is around the device instead. Spatial and temporal changes in brightness could also be combined to create rich feedback

**Fig. 2.** Varying brightness at different locations to show hand position.

---

[1] Adafruit NeoPixel LED Strip: http://www.adafruit.com/products/1506.

metaphors; for example, a progress bar could "fill up" over time as users dwell to make a selection (as with the gestures in [4]).

Hue can also be changed by some LEDs, allowing colourful feedback designs. Like brightness, hue can be varied over time and location to create expressive and informative feedback. Colours often have iconic meanings, making them useful for presenting state or static information. For example, green and red light could be used to show if a gesture was recognised or not. Hue could also be used for application-specific feedback metaphors; for example, using blue and red light to show temperature for thermostat control.

## 4    Summary

In this paper we described interactive light feedback, a technique which allows phones to give visual feedback about above-device gestures without affecting on-screen content. We discussed how brightness and hue allow rich information presentation and described how these could be used for gesture feedback. Our demonstration allows others to interact with a gesture interface and experience these designs themselves, to see how interactive light feedback can be used to informatively illuminate in-air interfaces.

**Acknowledgements.** This research was part-funded by Nokia Technologies, Finland.

## References

1. Samsung Galaxy S6 Edge. http://www.samsung.com/global/galaxy/galaxys6/galaxy-s6-edge/ Accessed March 10 2015
2. Sony Illumination Bar. http://developer.sonymobile.com/knowledge-base/experimental-apis/illumination-bar-api/ Accessed March 10 2015
3. Ashbrook, D., Baudisch, P., White, S.: Nenya: Subtle and eyes-free mobile input with a magnetically-tracked finger ring. In: Proceedings of CHI 2011, pp. 2043–2046. ACM Press (2011)
4. Freeman, E., Brewster, S., Lantz, V.: Tactile feedback for above-device gesture interfaces: adding touch to touchless interactions. In: Proceedings of ICMI 2014, pp. 419–426. ACM Press (2014)
5. Grosse-Puppendahl, T., Beck, S., Wilbers, D., Zeiß, S., von Wilmsdorff, J., Kuijper, A.: Ambient gesture-recognizing surfaces with visual feedback. In: Streitz, N., Markopoulos, P. (eds.) DAPI 2014. LNCS, vol. 8530, pp. 97–108. Springer, Heidelberg (2014)
6. Gustafson, S., Holz, C., Baudisch, P.: Imaginary Phone: Learning imaginary interfaces by transferring spatial memory from a familiar device. In: Proceedings of UIST 2011, pp. 283–292. ACM Press (2011)
7. Harrison, C., Horstman, J., Hsieh, G., Hudson, S.: Unlocking the expressivity of point lights. In: Proceedings of CHI 2012, pp. 1683–1692. ACM Press (2012)
8. Müller, H., Löcken, A., Heuten, W., Boll, S.: Sparkle: an ambient light display for dynamic off-screen points of interest. In: Proceedings of NordiCHI 2014, pp. 51–60. ACM Press (2014)
9. Qin, Q., Rohs, M., Kratz, S.: Dynamic ambient lighting for mobile devices. In: Proceedings of UIST 2011 Posters, pp. 51–52. ACM Press (2011)

# StoreAnt: A System to Support Finding Collaborative Systems Evaluation Methods

Marcella Leandro Costa de Souza, Lidia Silva Ferreira[✉],
Raquel Oiliveira Prates, and Marília Lyra Bergamo

Federal University of Minas Gerais, Belo Horizonte, MG, Brazil
{marcellasouza, lidiaferreira, rprates}@dcc.ufmg.br,
marilialb@eba.ufmg.br

**Abstract.** This paper presents StoreAnt, a virtual repository tool containing information about collaborative systems evaluation methods. It supports researchers and practitioners in finding and comparing information about methods, and identifying methods that comply to specific criteria (e.g. how the data is collected). The system is functional but has not yet been deployed publicly. Hopefully it will provide the HCI and CSCW communities with a valuable support regarding collaborative systems evaluation methods.

**Keywords:** Collaborative systems evaluation methods · Repository · Groupware

## 1 Introduction

Although collaborative systems are now integrated to people's everyday lives, designers of such systems still face challenges when developing them. One of the challenges involved is in evaluating these systems [2]. There have been many evaluation methods proposed specifically to or adapted to collaborative systems, however the great majority cannot be considered consolidated [5].

As a result, from time to time, researchers perform and publish a survey of existing methods (e.g. [4–6]). In these surveys, authors propose (usually based on the literature) criteria to classify and discuss existing collaborative methods. Antunes et al. [1] have gone a step further and proposed a framework to characterize collaborative evaluation methods that will support evaluators in comparing or choosing among them.

In spite of such efforts, identifying among the proposed methods which one would be (the most) appropriate in a given context may be a challenge. The surveys would allow evaluators to choose among the methods they have analyzed, but any updates – new methods or new empirical data about existing methods – would be left to the evaluators to identify and contrast to the work. In the case of the framework, although it supports evaluators in comparing methods of interest, the comparison would require the evaluator to identify the potential methods to be compared, as well as classify them according to the framework's proposed dimensions.

The goal of this work is to present StoreAnt, a tool developed to create a central repository in which information about collaborative evaluation methods can be stored, supporting researchers and practitioners in finding and comparing existing methods.

© IFIP International Federation for Information Processing 2015
J. Abascal et al. (Eds.): INTERACT 2015, Part IV, LNCS 9299, pp. 482–485, 2015.
DOI: 10.1007/978-3-319-22723-8_43

# 2    Goals and Requirements

StoreAnt was motivated by the challenge to identify and compare collaborative evaluation methods. To address this challenge, our solution was to create a collaborative information system that could be a repository for information for collaborative evaluation methods, as well as a tool that could support researchers or practitioners learn and compare about existing methods]. To achieve this goal, the requirements for StoreAnt were:

- Store information about each method: name, description, publications and tools;
- Provide a search tool according to different aspects of the methods;
- Allow the comparison of two methods;
- Allow researchers and practitioners to share their experience in applying a method;
- Maintain the method's base updated;

In order to search and compare methods it was necessary to classify methods in different dimensions. We chose to classify the methods using the dimensions used in dos Santos et al. [5] which adopted general terms usually known in the HCI field:

- **Source:** refers to the origin of the method, and each method can be classified as: *new* (new collaborative evaluation method proposed), *adapted* (the method exists for single-user applications but has been adapted to collaborative systems, or combines existing collaborative systems' methods); *existing* (the method has been proposed for single-user applications but can be directly applied to collaborative systems). Besides indicating the origin of the method, this criterion can also be an indicator of how consolidated it is.
- **Focus:** refers to what type of collaborative system the method is aimed at. Each method can be classified to *specific* (methods created for a specific domain or technology – e.g. collaborative learning) or *general* (apply to all collaborative systems independently of domain or technology).
- **Data collection method:** describes how the data is collected in the method: *inspection, observation in controlled environment, observation in natural setting, users' opinion* or *experiment measurements*. This information is useful for evaluators in considering the resources available, as well as application costs.
- **Moment of application:** refers to the moment of the systems development in which the method should be applied – *formative* (during the development), or *summative* (once the system is ready).
- **Type of analysis:** refers to what type of analysis the method yields - *quantitative* or *qualitative*. This dimension can be relevant for evaluators to identify methods that allow for generalization and comparison of data (quantitative) and those that explore motivations, experiences or interpretations (qualitative).

To support users in sharing their experiences and keeping the methods repositories updated, StoreAnt should be accessible from different locations, using different devices and operational systems. Therefore, the decision was to implement a web system.

## 3   StoreAnt

StoreAnt allows users to search for the methods by name or by choosing one or more of the classification dimensions. The resulting methods will be ranked and displayed according to how well rated it is by users (5 stars being the most well rated). For each method its name and short description will be displayed. The user can choose one of the methods to see its full description containing its name, a descriptive abstract, authors, resources (publications and links) and existing tools to support the method's application, as well as to have access to other user's comments. Figure 1 depicts StoreAnt's screen for a full method description.

**Fig. 1.** StoreAnt method description screen

The interface was designed to support users in identifying an appropriate method for the situation at hand. Therefore, the search tool and visual elements were chosen to convey an overall view of each evaluation method. The icons and graphics of visual interface elements were developed specifically for StoreAnt. The sketches were made using an open source application named Inkscape. As for the interfaces' implementation, front-end frameworks like Bootstrap and Jquery were used. The database structural organization and management was achieved using MySQL. Finally, the PHP language was used to develop the search engine and the system's data processing.

The system is currently functional, but not yet available for public use[1]. StoreAnt already allows the registration of users and methods. The user can evaluate the registered methods by rating stars. The possibility to post comments has not been

---

[1] Link: http://www.storeant.dcc.ufmg.br/.

implemented yet. Preliminary informal evaluations of the interface have been conducted. The next steps involve populating the database with the information about the methods described in the research surveys [4, 5] and evaluating the systems.

## 4 Final Remarks

StoreAnt has been developed as a curation system [2], that is a system that will allow members to identify, organize and assess collaborative systems evaluation methods As soon as StoreAnt is deployed to the scientific community, we hope that researchers will be interested in using it, as well as including the information about methods they have proposed or used in the system. The success of the system depends on it being adopted by the community (critical mass) which is crucial for it to be always updated. One of the factors that can positively influence its use is that members can benefit from StoreAnt for different reasons – evaluators can be supported in finding and comparing methods; researchers who have proposed methods will be able to have a unique repository to share information and collect feedback about their methods; students, practitioners, or those new to the field can easily learn about different methods. As people use StoreAnt more broadly, its interface and functionality may also evolve based on feedback and comments by users. Finally, StoreAnt has initially been developed for collaborative evaluation methods, but it could easily be used for other methods or models.

**Acknowledgments.** Authors thank CNPq and Fapemig for partially funding their research.

## References

1. Antunes, P., Herskovic, V., Ochoa, S.F., Pino, J.A.: Structuring dimensions for collaborative systems evaluation. ACM Comp. Surveys (CSUR) **44**(2), 8 (2012)
2. Duh, K., Hirao, T., Kimura, A., Ishiguro, K., Iwata, T., Yeung, C.-M.A.: Creating stories: social curation of twitter messages. In: Proceedings of ICWSM 2012
3. Grudin, J., Poltrock, S.: Computer supported cooperative work. In: Soegaard, M., Dam, R.F. (eds.) The Encyclopedia of Human-Computer Interaction, 2nd edn. The Interaction Design Foundation, Aarhus (2013)
4. Pinelle, D. Gutwin, C.: A review of groupware evaluations. In: Proceedings of 9th IEEE WETICE 2000 (2000)
5. Santos, N.S., Ferreira, L.S., Prates, R.O.: An overview of evaluation methods for collaborative systems. In: Proceedings of IX Brazilian Symposium in Collaborative Systems, pp. 127–135 (2012). (In Portuguese)
6. Wainer, J., Barsottini, C.: Empirical research in CSCW — a review of the ACM/CSCW conferences from 1998 to 2004. J. Braz. Comput. Soc. **13**(3), 27–35 (2007)

# TUIOFX—Toolkit Support
# for the Development of JavaFX Applications
# for Interactive Tabletops

Mirko Fetter[✉] and David Bimamisa

Human-Computer Interaction Group, University of Bamberg, Bamberg, Germany
{mirko.fetter, david.bimamisa}@uni-bamberg.de

**Abstract.** TUIOFX is a novel toolkit for developing multi-touch, multi-user applications for interactive tabletops and surfaces. By seamlessly integrating with JavaFX, TUIOFX provides a low entry barrier for developing state-of-the-art applications with multi-user, multi-touch capabilities and allows the cross-platform deployment on various interactive tabletop and surface hardware.

**Keywords:** Multi-touch · Interactive tabletop · Toolkit · SDK · JavaFX

## 1 Introduction

While the hardware for interactive tabletops and surfaces is getting more and more affordable, these technologies did not yet find a broad adoption in productive settings, beyond being an attention getter in exhibitions, showrooms and hotel lobbies. The absence of off-the-shelf applications for such systems can be considered as one barrier for technology adoption. An explanation for this absence is that the development for interactive surfaces often requires highly specialised knowledge and tools, and applications need to be tailored to specific hardware. With TUIOFX, a new toolkit that leverages on existing knowledge and standards aims to speed up the development of multi-user, multi-touch applications for a variety of hardware setups.

**Fig. 1.** Three demo apps realised with TUIOFX in a few lines of code (LOC): (1) a multi-user video viewer (∼100 LOC), (2) a drawing app (∼450 LOC), and (3) a 3D model viewer (∼400 LOC).

The TUIOFX toolkit was conceived to enable developers to easily develop appealing cross-platform applications (cf. Fig. 1). To achieve this, TUIOFX combines the strengths of multi-user, multi-touch toolkits by supporting the TUIO protocol [3] with an extensive and fully stylable library of standard widgets (i.e. JavaFX UI

© IFIP International Federation for Information Processing 2015
J. Abascal et al. (Eds.): INTERACT 2015, Part IV, LNCS 9299, pp. 486–489, 2015.
DOI: 10.1007/978-3-319-22723-8_44

controls). By building on JavaFX—and hence the Java programming language—TUIFOX builds on Java's cross-platform support and the wide-spread knowledge of one of the most widely used programming languages.

In the following we highlight the requirements that guided the design of TUIOFX. We look at structure and implementation of TUIOFX and how programmers can utilise its' possibilities. We conclude with a discussion in respect to the related work.

## 2 Requirements and Design Decisions

Besides the overall goal of platform independence, the design of the TUIOFX was lead by *three* main requirements:

The first requirement was to *build on existing technology* to minimise the learning effort and maximise the available support. From our own experience with various toolkits, we often learned that those can be niche solutions, with sparse documentation and support, and sometimes even a limited lifespan. By building up on JavaFX we leverage on a huge, active community and a well-documented base technology. Through the minimal invasive design of TUIOFX a great number of tools—like the JavaFX Scene Builder for visual editing (cf. Fig. 2)—seamlessly can be used for developing multi-user, multi-touch applications. By smoothly implementing everything beneath the surface, the documentation and support requirements for TUIOFX could be kept minimal. From our experience so far the transition effort— even for inexperienced JavaFX programmers—is negligible.

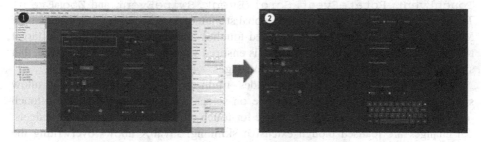

**Fig. 2.** A TUIOFX GUI visually edited in Scene Builder (1) and the resulting application (2) with a touch enabled widgets including a soft-keyboard.

The second requirement was to provide an *extensive widget toolkit out of the box*. A great drawback of many existing toolkits is the limited amount of widgets that are provided, as the toolkit designers often need to implement each widget from scratch. By building on JavaFX, we are able to leverage from the many existing widgets from simple buttons to complex UI controls like charts, HTML editor, color picker, etc. However, the realisation required a major effort to adapt and optimise all existing widgets for touch on large interactive surfaces—including adding the possibility for text-entry through soft-keyboards, etc. By utilising JavaFX's concepts of skins and behaviours, this could be achieved while keeping possibilities for reusability, extensibility and stylability of the widgets intact. For a programmer, using a TUIOFX widget is no different than using the standard JavaFX API—all adaptations are made transparent for the programmer by loading the TUIOFX styles in the background.

The last requirement was the *support of multi-user interaction*. While JavaFX basically supports multi-touch, the design of JavaFX departs from a perspective of a single user on a hand-held device. To support multiple users on large interactive surfaces, TUIOFX adds various modifications to the standard behaviour of widgets. This includes solutions for: handling simultaneous user actions; reducing multi-user conflicts resulting from JavaFX single-focus model; free orientation of widgets; etc.

In the following more details on the implementation of TUIOFX are provided, as well as a few insights on how the toolkit is utilised by developers.

## 3  The TUIOFX Toolkit

The TUIOFX Toolkit is composed out of two parts, the TUIOFX–Core and the TU-IOFX–WidgetToolkit. To migrate any existing JavaFX project into a multi-user, multi-touch TUIOFX project, both libraries can be easily added as JARs to a project.

TUIOFX–Core provides an abstraction from the raw TUIO messages and transforms them into standard JavaFX Touch- and Gesture-Events. TUIOFX core therefore uses JavaFX's multi-touch event handling infrastructure and its predefined Touch-Event and GestureEvent types in order to send events about recognised touches and gestures to the associated target Node (i.e. the UI element). TUIOFX's platform-independent touch and gesture recognizers are able to process TUIO messages into the corresponding event types for the JavaFX event platform, which are TouchEvent, RotateEvent, ScrollEvent, SwipeEvent and ZoomEvent. To achieve this TUIOFX analyses the global stream of TUIO touch events grouped per Node and sends events about recognised touches and gestures to the specific target Nodes. Additional support for tangibles is ensured via a custom listener-interface, that simply forwards TUIO tangible object messages.

The TUIOFX–WidgetToolkit provides multi-user (e.g., text-fields that allow simultaneous text-entry through multiple on-screen soft keyboards) and multi-touch (e.g., UI controls that are adjusted in size for touch on big screens) optimised widgets. All changes are realised though extensive skinning. JavaFX allows overwriting the default look-and-feel of a Control by implementing custom Skin and Behaviour classes. This allows for complex adaptations of a UI element—like adding our own soft-keyboard to the TextField component—without any changes for developers on how to use this component in their code. Accordingly, we were able to keep the API of TUIOFX very lightweight, allowing the toolkit to be minimally invasive to existing code. The TuioFX class with only seven methods is the main point of interaction with the API. Two further classes (Configuration and Configuration.Builder) allow tailoring parameters of the gesture recogniser to specific hardware with several presets. And finally the class TuioTangible and the TangibleListener provide possibilities to deal with Tangibles.

By adding the two lines TuioFX tuioFX = new TuioFX(stage) and tuioFX.start() to the code, any existing JavaFX application immediately is able to react to TUIO input. With the line tuioFX.enableMTWidgets(true) widgets will loose their default look-and-feel and gain capabilities like soft-keyboard input, etc. This already provides the developer with 99 % of TUIOFX's functionality for developing multi-user, multi-touch applications. Beyond that, only understandings of a few custom properties are needed, for further fine-tuning the TUIOFX behaviour.

## 4 Related Work and Discussion

While a variety of multi-user, multi-touch toolkits exists, (e.g., libTisch [1], DiamondSpin [5], PyMT [2])—some even Java-based (e.g., MT4j [4])—most of them only provide a few custom widgets (e.g., button, text field). TUIOFX leverages on the several dozen, standard UI controls of JavaFX (incl. charts, tables, HTML5 editor, etc.), which are all fully skinnable with CSS. This further allows using tools like Scene Builder for visually developing multi-touch, multi-user applications and removes the need to learn highly specialised APIs. So far, the only comparable extent of functionality can be found in the Microsoft Surface 2.0 SDK (in combination with Expression Blend). However, the resulting applications are lagging a cross-platform support and are only running under Windows and on PixelSense or Surface hardware. TUIOFX applications can be deployed on a variety of hardware and software combinations as long as they support the TUIO protocol and Java 8.

We provided insights in the TUIOFX toolkit, a novel toolkit for developing multi-touch, multi-user applications for interactive tabletops and surfaces with JavaFX. We were able to collect first feedback by handing out TUIOFX to a small number of developers, which were quickly able to develop their own small applications. In a next step we plan to publicly release a first version of the TUIOFX.

**Acknowledgments.** We thank the members of the Cooperative Media Lab, especially Tom Gross.

## References

1. Echtler, F., Klinker, G.: A multitouch software architecture. In: NordiCHI 2008, Lund, Sweden, pp. 463–466. ACM Press, New York (2008)
2. Hansen, T.E., Hourcade, J.P., Virbel, M., Patali, S., Serra, T.: PyMT: A post-WIMP multi-touch user interface toolkit. In: ITS 2009, November 23–25, Banff, Alberta, Canada, pp. 17–24. ACM Press, New York (2009)
3. Kaltenbrunner, M., Bovermann, T., Bencina, R., Costanza, E.: TUIO - A protocol for table-top tangible user interfaces. In: GW 2005, May 18–20, Ile de Berder, France (2005)
4. Laufs, U., Ruff, C., Zibuschka, J.: MT4j – a cross-platform multi-touch development framework. CoRR 2010
5. Shen, C., Vernier, F.D., Forlines, C., Ringel, M.: DiamondSpin: an extensible toolkit for around-the-table interaction. In: CHI 2004, April 24–29, Vienna, Austria, pp. 167–174. ACM Press, New York (2004)

# "I Was Here": Enabling Tourists to Leave Digital Graffiti or Marks on Historic Landmarks

Matjaž Kljun[✉] and Klen Čopič Pucihar

Department of Information Sciences and Technologies, University of Primorska,
Koper, Slovenia
matjaz.kljun@upr.si, klen.copic@famnit.upr.si

**Abstract.** Since ancient times travellers and tourists were carving or writing their names and messages on historic landmarks. This behaviour has prevailed to this day as tourists try to leave their marks at places they visit. Such behaviour, today often seen as vandalism, is particularly problematic since the society tries to preserve historic landmarks while graffiti often leave indelible markings. One solution to this problem is to allow tourists to write digital graffiti projected on historic landmarks and other public surfaces as an additional tourist offer. Projecting digital information on walls does not leave permanent marks while still allows authors to "physically" mark the place they visited. In this paper we frame our vision and highlight the approach we plan to pursue within the context of this topic.

**Keywords:** Digital graffiti · Tourism · Projections

## 1 Introduction

Graffiti are a form of expression that can be carved or painted on walls or other surfaces. They can take many forms from simple written messages to elaborate° drawings and are considered either as acts of vandalism [3] or admired as a from of art [4]. They exist since ancient times [1, 2] and can carry political, social, artistic or any other message. Graffiti are primarily associated with different subcultures such as hip-hop youth or street art movements. However, there is a group of graffiti makers that are often forgotten – tourists.

Since ancient times travellers and tourist were leaving marks and writings on sites they visited. This is manifested across cultures and covers simple inuksuit built by Inuit peoples for navigation and as a point of reference marking routes or sites, to scribbled messages on the walls of ancient buildings denoting ones presence and appreciation of the site. The later form can be seen for example on the walls of the Church of the Holy Sepulchre in Jerusalem scribbled by the crusaders and pilgrims (see left side of Fig. 1) or on the Mirror wall in an ancient village of Sigiriya in Sri Lanka (see right side of Fig. 1) featuring over 1800 pieces of prose, poetry and commentary written by ancient tourists between 600AD and 1400AD [2].

© IFIP International Federation for Information Processing 2015
J. Abascal et al. (Eds.): INTERACT 2015, Part IV, LNCS 9299, pp. 490–494, 2015.
DOI: 10.1007/978-3-319-22723-8_45

In a similar way, today's tourists also exhibit the tendencies to leave their mark in places they visit. For example the breast of the statue of Juliet in Verona is showing prominent signs of wear by years of groping. Even more personal example of expression is leaving D locks with declarations and messages on bridges in cities all over the globe. While these are "socially accepted" marks, some tourists also carry out unacceptable acts by today's standards. For example scribbling ones initials on a brick of the Roman Colosseum can result in a large fine [6] or signing one's name on an ancient Egyptian's statue can result in an outrage of masses on social media [7].

**Fig. 1.** Left: Crusader Graffiti on the walls of the Church of the Holy Supulchure in Jerusalem. (Courtesy of "Victor" by Victorgrigas. Licensed under CC BY-SA 3.0 via Wikimedia Commons) Right: graffiti on the Mirror Wall in Sigiriya in Sri Lanka. (Courtesy of RomeshD. Licensed under CC BY-SA 3.0 via Wikimedia Commons)

One possible solution to prevent premanent marks on historic landmarks is to allow tourists to create their mark in a digital form and project it on a desired location of the historic site. Our idea includes wraping segments of historic objects with projected beams of light using mounted projectors which can be controled by the user through their mobile devices.

## 2 Related Work

There are different ways of how digital technology can be incorporated into creation of digital content on a surface such as wall. The most common solutions include a dedicated large screen (digital wall) and a special input device of which location is tracked (as it moves in the air) and communicated to the system that produces the content on the screen. There are several commercial products available, such as Digital Graffiti Wall,[1] YrWall[2] and Air Graffiti.[3]

Another way of creating digital graffiti is by the means of augmented reality (AR). Cisco's mobile phone application called Digital Graffiti allows one to leave

---

[1] Digital Graffiti Wall: http://www.tangibleinteraction.com/rentals/digital-graffiti-wall.

[2] YrWall: http://thisisluma.com/yr/yrwall-digital-graffiti/.

[3] Air Graffiti: http://fotomasterltd.net/products/digital-graffiti-air-graffiti-wall/.

geo-positioned messages that other users can see only if they are physically present at that location and look through the camera lens of their smart phone. In a similar way DigiGraff allows "spraying" a geo located graffiti with a projector mounted on a mobile phone. Others can interact (with by using a projector) with a particular graffito only if physically present at that location [5].

Graffiti Research Lab developed so called LED Trowies, which are made of a coloured LED and a magnet that can be attached to a ferromagnetic surface; positioning many of such Trowies allows one to create a grafitto made of LEDs. They also created a system called L.A.S.E.R. Tag that tracks the laser beam with a web cam and in its trail projects the beam of light. The simplest method is to project existing artwork onto walls as done for example at the Digital Graffiti projection art festival.[4]

None of the presented solutions is particularly suitable for a system enabling a tourist to leave a digital graffito on a historic site because they either require special equipment (indoor screens, laser pointers, IR equipped input devices, pico projectors) or are visible just by means of a particular technology (i.e. AR).

## 3  Discussion

The basic principle of our proposal can be seen on Fig. 2. We are currently building the app that is sending the content to a networked projector, which is projecting the image on a historic site in a contextually sensitive way, hence, the projection is mapped to the shape of the 3D structure it augments.

**Fig. 2.** The principle of how our idea would work in the real context.

However, there are several technical and research questions that need to be considered and studied before we commence studying the interaction within public spaces.

**Technical questions:**

- *Locality of graffiti*. The digital technology allows drawing of graffiti from a remote location and anyone in the world could leave a mark in a place they have not

---

[4] Digital Graffiti at Alys Beach http://www.digitalgraffiti.com/.

visited. However, this may dilute the appeal of digital graffiti to audiences at the physical location. As it is possible to track geo location of users, one could limit graffiti creation to only those physically present.

- *Inappropriate content.* Although, the idea can be used to propagate any content, it is primarily intended for tourists who commonly do not write messages with political, social or other such connotation. There are several ways to moderate graffiti: e.g. up or down voting, registering users, restricting graffiti creation to only organized groups of tourists, or restricting the making of graffiti from dedicated locally placed devices (which would eliminate the need of public internet access, app installation, using ones own device, and would simplify moderation).

**Research questions:**

- *Multiple edits.* There are two implementing possibilities that need to be studied: allowing multiple users to draw at the same time (e.g. each one gets a piece of the canvas or draws on a dedicated layer) or reserving the time when one can draw the content.
- *Real time or commit based drawing.* One of the research questions is whether users would prefer creating the content on their devices first and only then submit it (e.g. after they preview it by the means of AR) or edit it in real time directly on the wall while others can watch it changing?
- *Time allocation.* There are different possibilities to implement time allocation: all graffiti get the same time slot, a graffito is shown while the author is nearby, a graffito fades with time, etc. However, as they can be intended for the broader audience, we should investigate a way to selectively print graffiti or devise a way to cleverly select desirable objects (e.g. up or down votes as with moderation).

## 4 Conclusion

Paradoxically, whilst ancient graffiti are seen as a valuable window into the lives of past generations, many current graffiti are considered acts of vandalism. In the later, we are not discussing paintings on an underpass, even if these are threated as such by some, but rather for example defiling a facade of a historic landmark. Digital graffiti may be able to provide sustainable means of fulfilling tourists' wish for marking a place they visited. In addition, transferring the graffiti in the digital domain can allow sharing them with others on social media, broaden the graffiti audience, and foster additional conversations online. This can provide indirect advertisement for local communities and promote touristic places to a wider public. In addition, the recorded history of changes could provide a database of tourists' graffiti of which content could be further studied.

## References

1. Balzani, M., et al.: Digital representation and multimodal presentation of archeological graffiti at Pompei. In: VAST 2004, Belgium, pp. 93–103 (2004)

2. Cooray, J.N.: The sigiriya royal gardens; analysis of the landscape architectonic composition. Archit. Built Environ. **6**, 1–286 (2012). TU Delft. http://abe.tudelft.nl/index.php/faculty-architecture/issue/view/12
3. Halsey, M.: 'Our desires are ungovernable': writing graffiti in urban space. Theor. Criminol. **10**(3), 275–306 (2006)
4. Von Joel, M.: Urbane Guerrillas: street art, graffiti & other vandalism. State Art **1**, 4 (2006)
5. McGookin, D.K., et al.: Studying digital graffiti as a location-based social network. In: CHI 2014. ACM (2014)
6. Neild, B.: Russian tourist fined $24,000 for Colosseum graffiti (2014). http://edition.cnn.com/2014/11/24/travel/italy-colosseum-graffiti/
7. Wong, H.: Netizen outrage after Chinese tourist defaces Egyptian temple (2013). http://edition.cnn.com/2013/05/27/travel/china-egypt/

# A Hybrid Approach for Visualizing Spatial and Non-spatial Data Types of Embedded Systems

Ragaad AlTarawneh, Shah Rukh Humayoun[(✉)], and Achim Ebert

Computer Graphics and HCI Group, University of Kaiserslautern, 67663
Kaiserslautern, Germany
{tarawneh, humayoun, ebert}@cs.uni-kl.de

**Abstract.** Due to the heterogeneity nature of embedded systems, visualizing them from different perspectives requires including different data sets about the underlying system. This opens the doors to think about integrating between the spatial and the non-spatial data sets in this domain. In this work, we present the SceneMan (Scene Manager) platform that integrates between the different data sets using a 2D*plus*3D style to reflect the system from different perspectives. In this context, we visualize the non-spatial data using the normal 2D representation, which can be converted to a 3D representation in some cases such that the stereoscopic depth cue is used to encode some aspects about this data set. Additionally, we visualize the spatial data using 3D visualization techniques. This hybrid solution provides the possibility to bridge the gap between the 2D representations and the 3D visualizations.

**Keywords:** 3D visualization · Graph visualization · Stereoscopic depth · Integrating spatial data · Non-spatial data

## 1 Introduction

Many techniques have been proposed to trace the possible failures in embedded systems. The Fault Tree Analysis (FTA) [3] and the Component Fault Tree (CFT) [5] are amongst the most usage techniques. These both mentioned techniques enable *safety experts* (who are responsible for detecting the failures) to model the possible failure and to trace the failure dependencies between the system components. The resulting fault tree representations model some possible failure scenarios in the system at certain times. However, in order to use such representations *system engineers* (who are responsible for maintaining all the system components) should be able to understand it and map it with the actual system structures. The collaboration between safety experts and system engineers is important in order to analyze the system behavior and to eliminate the possible critical situations during the system life [1]. However, this collaboration faces several challenges, e.g., the divergence between the interested perspectives. Further, there is a variation in data representations for both groups, e.g., the hardware model of the underlying system (normally used by system engineers) is mostly represented as a 3D data type while the safety scenario (normally used by safety

© IFIP International Federation for Information Processing 2015
J. Abascal et al. (Eds.): INTERACT 2015, Part IV, LNCS 9299, pp. 495–498, 2015.
DOI: 10.1007/978-3-319-22723-8_46

experts) is mostly modeled as a fault tree and is considered to be an abstract data type, which can easily be represented as a 2D graph representation.

In order to fill the above-mentioned gap, we propose a hybrid solution, called the **SceneMan** (**Scene Man**ager) platform, to visualize the two data types in a 2D*plus*3D world, such that the 2D graph representation is available to visualize the abstract fault tree structure while the 3D part is used to visualize the system hardware model. Further, we propose to visualize this 2D*plus*3D world using the stereoscopic displays such that the stereoscopic depth is utilized to encode some aspects about the nodes (e.g., to encode the structural relations) in the graph representation. In this case, the depth is used together with other visual cues to encode or convey some data aspects.

## 2   The SceneMan Platform

In Fig. 1, we show the overall hybrid approach behind the SceneMan platform. SceneMan is responsible for integrating the system 3D view with the graph representation of the abstract data. For this, it combines and synchronizes the system 3D view together with the abstract graph 2D view for creating a 2D*plus*3D environment. It supports these views' alignment in order to respect each other in the 3D world (see Fig. 2). It also gives the viewers the ability to control the positions of each view for getting more insight about the underlying data.

SceneMan offers different interaction techniques for interacting with each view individually without distorting the other view. This is achieved through the *scene-graph* concept. In this case, the root node represents the whole 3D space containing all

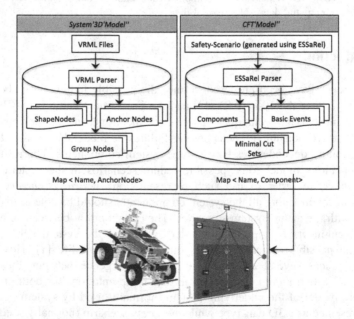

**Fig. 1.** The mapping operation in the SceneMan hybrid approach

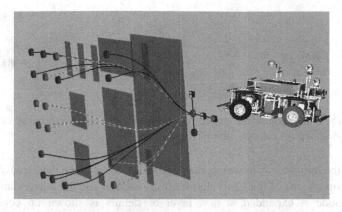

**Fig. 2.** An integrated *Layered* view showing the correlation between the two views (i.e., the 2D abstract view and the system 3D model view) using the stack metaphor.

the views while children of this root are the 2D abstract view using the graph representation of the component fault tree and the 3D model view of the system.

In order to minimize the occlusion effects, elements in the 3D space are arranged together especially when the size of any of the two views is changed. For this, the size of non-focused view is adapted consequently to guarantee a readability increment of the current focused view. The initial *side-by-side* configuration is changed when the viewer starts interacting with the 3D space. For example, both views can be arranged into a *layered* view where these views are stacked above each other, as shown in Fig. 2. In this case, the depth cue is used to show the importance degree of the view Moreover, viewers can also get more focus on the top-view by increasing the distance in depth between it and the lower view. Additionally, SceneMan provides the facility to adjust the size of the view based on the degree of interest in the required view.

## 3   Utilizing the Stereoscopic Depth

SceneMan visualizes the safety aspects of embedded systems using the compound graph representation, where these graphs represent the fault tree models to describe the possible critical situations. Because these models represent abstract non-spatial data; therefore, SceneMan visualizes them using 2D representations, as it is commonly accepted visual representation approach for this data type. However, in order to integrate it with the 3D environment of the platform, we designed it in a way that bridges the representation gap between the two data types. This is achieved by rendering the overall system in a stereoscopic platform, where the stereoscopic depth is used to encode some aspects about the nodes in the graph representation.

Based on our knowledge, this is the first approach that integrates between the 2D representations and the 3D technologies through encoding structural relations in compound graphs using the stereoscopic depth cue. SceneMan visualizes compound graphs using multi-level graph layout algorithms. In this context, it provides different levels of details inside the graph structure. For example, in Fig. 3 all the nodes are

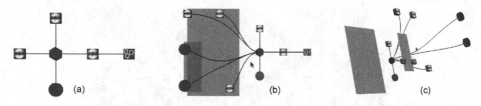

**Fig. 3.** (a) The initial compound graph, (b) the front view after expansion of two nested compound nodes; and (c) the side view of (b).

clustered in the initial view; however, they can be explored using the *expanding* and the *contracting* operations of the CluE algorithm [2] used inside the SceneMan. Once any compound node is expanded, a new level of details is shown up containing the expanded node's internal structure. This level is visualized using a new plane that is created closer to the viewer than the remaining graph parts that are not explored yet. The children of the expanded node are positioned in a depth value closer to the viewer than the other graph parts. This approach produces a layered graph representation. However, due to the stereoscopic effect these elements look sharper than the remaining graph parts, which gives a natural *focus* + *context* interaction technique, i.e., the closer elements are in focus while the unexplored parts are in the background of the scene to keep the context of the whole graph structure.

Additionally, SceneMan allows changing interactively other graph settings, e.g., the transparency of the depth layers in which the further layers look more transparent than the closer layers in the 3D world. The transparency effect was added as it was proposed by Eades and Feng [4] to show the hierarchical relations of clustered graphs. This parameter is useful in decreasing the occlusion ratio between the different visual objects at different depth layers. Naturally, this increases the emphasis to the closer objects reside in the closer layers.

In the future, we intend to evaluate our system with users from different background as well as to evaluate it in other 3D platforms like CAVE systems or power-wall screens.

# References

1. AlTarawneh, R., Bauer, J., Humayoun, S.R., Ebert, A., Liggesmeyer, P.: Enhancing understanding of safety aspects in embedded systems through an interactive visual tool. In: IUI Companion 2014, pp. 9–12. ACM, New York, NY, USA (2014)
2. AlTarawneh, R., Schultz, J., Humayoun, S.R.: CluE: an algorithm for expanding clustered graphs. In: PacificVis 2014, pp. 233–237. IEEE (2014)
3. Bozzano, M., Villafiorita, A.: Design and Safety Assessment of Critical Systems. CRC Press (Taylor and Francis), Boca Raton (2010). (An Auerbach Book)
4. Eades, P., Feng, Q.-W.: Multilevel visualization of clustered graphs. In: Proceedings of Graph Drawing, GD, no. 1190, pp. 101–112 (1996)
5. Kaiser, B., Liggesmeyer, P., Mckel, O.: A new component concept for fault trees. Reproduction **33**, 37–46 (2003)

# A Multi-modal System for Public Speaking

## Pilot Study on Evaluation of Real-Time Feedback

Fiona Dermody[1(✉)], Alistair Sutherland[2], and Margaret Farren[1]

[1] Faculty of Humanities, Dublin City University, Glasnevin, Dublin 9, Ireland
Fiona.Dermody3@mail.dcu.ie
[2] Faculty of Engineering and Computing, Dublin City University, Glasnevin,
Dublin 9, Ireland

**Abstract.** A prototype has been developed for a digital system and multi-modal user interface to analyze social signals displayed during public speaking. User testing on the prototype has commenced to evaluate the most effective way to display real-time feedback to users on their speaking performance.

**Keywords:** Affective computing · Multi-modal interfaces · Social signal recognition · Human computer interaction

## 1 Introduction

The fear of public speaking tops the list of human phobias. However, success in social, academic and occupational situations depends on the ability to communicate effectively to groups. A fear of public speaking thus limits achievement in social gatherings, education and enterprise [1]. However, the fear of public speaking can be so great that it can lead to avoidance of speaking in the public domain altogether [2]. The problem is a recursive one, how can an individual improve their speaking skills and reduce their fear of speaking in public if they avoid speaking in public?

Public speaking is not just about the words spoken. Effective speaking involves the use of gestures, facial expressions and vocal variety. All these social signals combine to give the appearance of self-confidence in a speaker. Research has found that anxious speakers do not engage the attention of an audience [3]. Rather the audience focuses on the speaker's nervous disposition instead of their words [4].

The solution, which we propose, is interdisciplinary. It incorporates theory from computing, psychology and communications. It is envisaged that this social signal recognition system will enable individuals to develop their competence in public speaking.

Using a combination of 3D video imaging, audio and social signal processing algorithms, this digital system analyses facial expressions, tone of voice and gestures. The system then provides feedback on the user's speaking performance. It will also deliver tutorial videos on good speaking practices. Exposure to these dynamic features will enable a speaker to systematically develop confidence and skill before speaking in front of a live audience.

© IFIP International Federation for Information Processing 2015
J. Abascal et al. (Eds.): INTERACT 2015, Part IV, LNCS 9299, pp. 499–501, 2015.
DOI: 10.1007/978-3-319-22723-8_47

Skilled human trainers in communication are scarce and expensive. This digital system incorporates experience from one such skilled human trainer to provide constructive feedback to users on their speaking performance. This digital experience will enable anxious speakers to develop their public speaking skills cost-effectively, in private and at their own pace.

### 1.1 Existing Research

There have been attempts to use social signal recognition for public speaking but not for instruction purposes [5]. This system is innovative because it will extend the field of human computer interaction:

- Combining all modalities – voice, gesture, facial expression and body pose into a multi-modal system for delivering instruction in public speaking
- Incorporating the knowledge of experts in public speaking ensures that the feedback provided on a user's speaking is based on a real-world, practice-based approach.

## 2  Research Question

Which form of real-time multi-modal feedback is most effective for users to develop skill in public speaking?

## 3  Proposed Multi-modal System for Public Speaking

The system will use a Microsoft Kinect connected to a computer. Social Signal Processing techniques will be used to recognize the speaker's body language, gestures, voice, and facial expressions

- Classify speaker's emotion, as perceived by the audience, from the combination of the above
- Perceived emotion is regarded as the primary component for analysis.
- Give feedback to user on speaking performance
- Provide examples of good and bad speaking practice
- Set tutorial exercises from beginners level to advanced level and will evaluate the user's performance.

## 4  Progress to Date

A prototype has been developed following a user survey on the features required in a multimodal system for public speaking. Initial user testing has commenced.

# 5    Expected Results

One of the technical challenges to be overcome during the development of the system is the optimal way to display feedback to the user in real time during their speaking task. The nature of the feedback is imperative, as our survey showed that some users prefer visual feedback while others prefer textual feedback. The system will be evaluated to ascertain what is the most effective way to display feedback to users on their speaking performance. Results of this user testing will be presented.

**Acknowledgement.** This material is based upon works supported by Dublin City University under the Daniel O'Hare Research Scholarship scheme.

# References

1. Dwyer, K., Davidson, M.: Is public speaking really more feared than death? Commun. Res. Rep. **29**(2), 99–107 (2012)
2. Feldman, P., Cohen, S., Hamrick, N.: Psychological stress, appraisal, emotion and cardiovascular response in a public speaking task. Psychol. Health **19**, 353–368 (2004)
3. Freeman, T., Sawyer, C.: Behavioral inhibition and the attribution of public speaking state anxiety. Commun. Educ. **46**, 37–41 (1997)
4. Winton, E., Clark, D., Edelmann, R.: Social anxiety, fear of negative evaluation and the detection of negative emotion in others. Behav. Res. Ther. **33**(2), 193–196 (1995)
5. Batrinca, L., Stratou, G., Shapiro, A., Morency, L.-P., Scherer, S.: Cicero - towards a multimodal virtual audience platform for public speaking training. In: Aylett, R., Krenn, B., Pelachaud, C., Shimodaira, H. (eds.) IVA 2013. LNCS, vol. 8108, pp. 116–128. Springer, Heidelberg (2013)

# A Study on How to Express Non-manual Markers in the Electronic Dictionary of Japanese Sign Language

Mina Terauchi[1(✉)] and Yuji Nagashima[2]

[1] Information Processing Engineering Unit,
Polytechnic University, Tokyo, Japan
terauchi@uitec.ac.jp
[2] Department of Information Design, Kogakuin University, Tokyo, Japan
nagasima@cc.kogakuin.ac.jp

**Abstract.** This paper reports on how we would express non-manual markers in NVSG element model. Sign language is a visual language for which there are no general methods of providing descriptions in text. That is why we are proposing a new NVSG element model that focuses on the linguistic structure of sign language. The NVSG element model defines four elements that describe sign language. Manual movements are expressed as N and V elements, and non-manual markers as S and G elements. We have mostly finalized the descriptive parameters for the N and V elements. Up until this point, we have described approximately 1,500 words using the NVSG element model. As a result of this process, we have achieved a greater visual understanding of the hierarchical structures of morphological elements per word. Such descriptions of non-manual markers also enable us to write sentences.

**Keywords:** Sign language · Morpheme · Non-manual markers · NVSG element model

## 1 Introduction

Sign language is a visual language for which there are no general methods of providing descriptions in text [1, 2]. When translating sign language, the system needs to understand its morphological structure. Using the NVSG element model that we propose, a system can express the morphological structure of sign language with ease [3]. We are currently developing a dictionary of the morphological elements of sign language using the NVSG element model. The NVSG element model defines the elements that comprise sign language using N for a hand shape, V for a hand movement, S for the sightline, and G for all non-manual markers other than the sightline. For this report, we discussed the details of how to express the non-manual S and G elements that were not yet determined. As a result, we are now able to express the detailed morphological structures of sign language at the individual word level. With this result, and by using the NVSG element model to express the structure of sign language words, we are now able to offer a new methodology of translating sign language.

© IFIP International Federation for Information Processing 2015
J. Abascal et al. (Eds.): INTERACT 2015, Part IV, LNCS 9299, pp. 502–505, 2015.
DOI: 10.1007/978-3-319-22723-8_48

## 2    NVSG Element Model

We defined the four elements of the NVSG element model: hand shape, movement, sight line and non-manual markers. Sign combines these four elements morphologically to form more than one word in some cases. In composing a sign, we need to analyze what kind of movement each element describes. The NVSG element model thus expresses each of these four elements independently. The N element describes items concerning hand shape, while the V element describes those concerning movement. Non-manual markers related to the sight line are written as S elements, and all other non-manual markers are written as G elements. The NVSG element model that we propose is able to express morphological elements in a combination of these four elements. This model is also able to form two or more morphological elements at the same time, thereby expressing multiple morphological structures simultaneously.

Below, we first offer a simple explanation of how we express the N and V elements. We then report on how we would write the non-manual S and G elements.

### 2.1    N Element and V Element

Of all the elements that comprise manual movements, those that concern hand shape (other than their general movements) are expressed as N elements. The dominant hand is expressed as Ns to mean the "strong" hand, and the non-dominant hand is expressed as Nw, or the "weak" hand. Internal values would describe the shape, position and direction of the hand. The description of the hand shape would consist of changes in the finger joint motion or the movement of a certain finger joint. We therefore assign each finger a number from 1 to 5.

Changes in finger joint motion largely break down to how a finger bends and how the fingers relate to one another. How a finger bends is expressed based on defining the closed hand as the original form and expressing the shape of bend with a specific code together with the finger number. We would express the relationship of the fingers by describing it for the fingers subject to the bend/change.

The general movements of the arms (rather than the local movements of the joints beyond the wrist) are expressed as V elements. We would write internal values using either Vs to define the strong arm or Vw to define the weak arm. Arm motion is complex, as sign language uses three-dimensional space. The parameters that serve as internal values are simplified classifications of sign movements to which we assigned codes. We classified the sign movements into four categories: Movement, Instruction, Presentation and Air Writing.

### 2.2    S Element

The S element would consist of non-manual markers descriptions that concern the eye line. The line of sight of the signer (speaker) may serve the role of pointing to something. Particularly in a sign language sentence, the eye line frequently replaces finger pointing (PT: Pointing) to refer to a person or pronoun using spatial expression.

The direction of sight may be the hand itself or where the hand moves, which are both N elements. The parameter in this case would take the value of N, Ns (strong hand) or Nw (weak hand). Take, for example, the sign for "Purpose", which is made by hitting the presented weak hand (Nw) with the strong hand (Ns). Since the eyes look at the target weak hand (Nw), the sign is described as below.

$$\text{Example:} \{\textit{mokuteki}(\text{target})\} = \left[ \text{Nw} \left( g_{(\text{UM})} @_{C2} \right) \left[ \text{Ns}_{(\text{H1})} \text{Vs}_{(\text{MV(contact)} \gg \text{WH}))} \right] \right] \text{S}_{(\text{Ns})}$$

There are cases where the eyes follow a hand in motion. In such cases, the parameter would take a V element target value. When the signer is "thinking of" something, his eyes will normally look up in most cases. In such cases, we assign an "r". The sign for "Think" as described in dictionary form would not include an S element indication to describe the sightline. But to indicate the sentence "Think of < something/someone>", we would need an S element description.

$$\text{Example:} \{\textit{wo omou}(\text{think of} < \text{something/someone} > )\} = \left[ \text{N}_{(\text{h1})} \text{V}_{(\text{PT} \gg \text{temple})} \right] \text{S}(\text{r})$$

A signer may refer to a person in a sentence by using his line of sight. When a sign refers to a particular person, the information on that person remains in effect until the next sign is presented. In such a case, the signer's eyes spatially express the person rather than looking at either one of the hands. The parameter for such a case would be per1, per2 or per3.

### 2.3    G Element

Considering the conversational nature of sign language, where its words connect and form a chain, we define non-manual markers (NMM) such as the facial expressions, nodding and mouth shapes necessary to expressing context and meaning as G elements, or the grammar elements of sign language. We substitute values for G elements using sIGNDEX V.2 [4]. sIGNDEX V.2 defines 91 types of NMS codes in 14 categories. Since we define finger pointing (PT) as a V element, we would not use it to describe G elements. The sightline, as mentioned in the preceding section, would be written as an

**Table 1.** sIGNDEX V.2 codes

| Non-Manual Markers | Code | Non-Manual Markers | Code |
|---|---|---|---|
| head | hD | mouthing | mO |
| eye brow | eB | Lips | iP |
| eye | eY | teeth | tH |
| tongue | tN | corner of lips | cL |
| shoulder | sH | jaw | jW |
| body posture | bP | cheek | cK |

independent S element, so it would also be excluded from our parameters for G elements. Thus, the NVSG element model that we propose would use 12 categories of codes as defined in sIGNDEX V.2. Table 1 lists the sIGNDEX V.2 codes that our NVSG element model would use.

## 3   Sign Description Using the NVSG Element Model

The NVSG element model indicates the hands separately as either the strong or weak hand. However, to better describe their motional relationship with one another, their motional relationship would determine whether the description would be in the form of an N element or a V element. An example is given below.

$$
\begin{aligned}
\text{Example:``I visit his house``} &= \{\text{his house}\} + \{\text{visit}\} \\
&= \left[ NN_{(CL:many(H0))} \, V_{(PR@PT3)} \right] S_{(PT3)} \\
&\quad + Ns_{(CL:one(H1))} \, V_{(MV(per1 > per3))} \right] S_{(Ns)}
\end{aligned}
$$

## 4   Conclusion

This paper has suggested methods of writing parameters for S and G element non-manual markers in the NVSG element model that describes sign language. By adding S and G element descriptions, we are now capable of expressing the detailed morphological structure of sign words. And with the capability to describe people and pronouns as expressed spatially using the sightline, the model can also describe sentence structures. We are currently using the sign language stored in our database to confirm the descriptive indications, and we will then refine and finalize the parameters. We will also increase our NVSG element model data and aim for efficient collaboration with the three-dimensional motion database.

**Acknowledgment.** Part of this study was subsidized by a Grant-in-Aid for Scientific Research (A) 23240087 and 2624402, a scientific research grant by the Ministry of Education, Culture, Sports, Science and Technology.

## References

1. Friedman, L.A. (ed.): On the Other Hand. Academic Press, New York (1977)
2. Fischer, S.D. (ed.): Theoretical Issues in Sign Language Research, vol.1: Linguistics. University of Chicago Press, Chicago (1990)
3. Watanabe, K., Terauchi, M., Nagashima, Y.: NVSG element model for analyzing morpheme in japanese sign language. IEICE Trans. Fundam. Electron. Commun. Comput. Sci. **J98-A**(1), 113–128 (2015). (Japanese Edition)
4. Kanda, K., Ichikawa, A., Nagashima, Y., et al.: Notation System and Statistical Analysis of NMS in JSL. In: Proceeding of Gesture and Sign Languages in Human-Computer Interaction, International Gesture Workshop, GW 2001, UK, pp. 181–192 (2001)

# Applying "Out of Body" Vibrotactile Illusion to Two-Finger Interaction for Perception of Object Dynamics

Jaedong Lee, Youngsun Kim, and Gerard J. Kim[✉]

Digital Experience Laboratory, Korea University, Seoul, Korea
{jdlee,zyoko85,gjkim}@korea.ac.kr

**Abstract.** Vibrotactile feedback is an effective and economical approach for enriching interactive feedback. However, its effects are mostly limited to providing supplementary alarms or conveying the sense of simple object presence or contact. We propose to apply the "out of body" tactile illusion for selecting and manipulating a virtual moving object while also being able to feel its dynamics using two fingers. We assessed the user experience (focusing on the perception of the dynamics of the selected object) of the proposed method by comparing it to the conventional contact-based method. Our results indicate that users were able to perceive the dynamic feedback, and preferred it over the conventional method.

**Keywords:** Out-of-body illusion · Illusory tactile sensation · Pinch interaction · Vibrotactile interaction

## 1 Introduction

Vibrotactile feedback is an effective and economical alternative to mechanically complex haptic devices. Despite its simplicity, it produces good results, especially when coordinated in a multimodal fashion with other associated feedback [1]. Still the effects are to mostly provide the sense of physical existence only. Therefore, it would be desirable for vibrotactile feedback to have the ability to express other aspects such as more dynamic interactions with objects (e.g., feeling a pulsating heart or holding on to a live animal). To achieve such a goal, we propose to apply an "out of body" tactile illusion. Funneling is one of the most notable illusory feedback techniques associated with vibrotactility [2]. Funneling can generate illusory tactile sensations by presenting two or more simultaneous tactile stimuli directly to two parts of the body. It is also possible to elicit a "moving" directional sensation by rendering successive funneling stimulations, which is also known as the "apparent movement" [3, 4]. Miyazaki et al. [5] discovered that a tactile illusion could be extended to "body connecting" objects and that it could create illusory sensations that from "out of the body," e.g. as if coming from an object that is external to the user's body.

 Based on these illusion phenomena, we propose a two finger interaction method where two fingers "pinch" an object, and two vibration motors attached to the two tips

© IFIP International Federation for Information Processing 2015
J. Abascal et al. (Eds.): INTERACT 2015, Part IV, LNCS 9299, pp. 506–509, 2015.
DOI: 10.1007/978-3-319-22723-8_49

of the fingers convey tactile touch/contact and directional object dynamics (see Fig. 1). The proposed method is comparatively assessed for its user experience (focusing on the perception of the dynamics of the object) through a user experiment.

## 2    Related Work

The mechanism most commonly used to generate hand-held tactile/haptic feedback has been employing small vibrating motors. These have been mostly used with mobile devices or hand-held game controllers to provide supplementary feedback for various interaction events (e.g., alarm, touch/key input, and virtual collision). Researchers have searched for ways to simulate other types of information by controlling the vibrating signal (e.g., texture simulation) [6] and by combining it with other modalities [7]. Nevertheless, vibrating motors are still inherently limited in terms of their ability to convey true haptic force, i.e., rigid contact as well as directional or inertial effects. Piezo-electric materials are another popular technology that is used for tactile feedback for mobile and hand-held devices [8, 9]. However, while this method is able to recreate static surface textures, e.g., protrusions and bumps, the devices lack features to provide more dynamic feedback.

A number of researchers have applied tactile illusion techniques to human interfaces [3, 4, 7, 10, 11] e.g. to minimize the number of tactile actuators (instead of using a comparable tactile array) [7] or to design vibrotactile feedback method that do not require direct contact to the fingers/hands. However, most of the prior tactile interactions have focused only on the providing feedback to indicate an existence of an object, the perception of texture patterns, and the outer shape of the object rather than its dynamics. In addition, illusion techniques have been usually applied to a continuous skin area rather than external to the body. Thus, applying the out of body tactile illusion seems one promising way to enrich the feedback while improving the general usability.

## 3    Experiment: Perception of Dynamics by Out of Body Tactile Illusion in Two-Finger Interaction

### 3.1    Experimental Set-up and Procedure

We demonstrate an application of "out of body" tactile illusion for two-finger object selection and manipulation and experimentally assesses whether the proposed method can bring about an improved user experience, when compared to conventional methods, by providing tangibility and sensation of the object and its interaction dynamics. Fourteen paid subjects, 10 men and 4 women with a mean age of 25, participated in the experiment.

An experiment with one-factor (3 feedback methods) within-subject with repeated measures was conducted. The task was to pick and hold a moving object (an animated fly) (Fig. 1). Both fingers were tracked using the Leap Motion sensor, and two conventional methods with no vibrotactile feedback (NF) and contact-only feedback (CF, nominal vibration given only for indicating contact with fingers) were compared to the proposed method (TI) where tactile illusion rendering was applied to the fingertips. No quantitative performance was measured, and only a questionnaire of the user's experience was filled out (for the questionnaire categories, see Fig. 2).

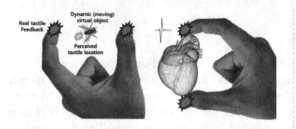

**Fig. 1.** The proposed vibrotactile illusion based interaction method for holding a moving object and feeling for its dynamics (left), and its experimental implementation (right).

### 3.2   Results

Figure 2 shows the average responses to the seven UX survey questions and the differences among the three feedback methods. In most categories (except for the "Fatigue" category), it is quite clear that the proposed method (TI) exhibited a much more positive user experience. Obviously, the NF condition scored the least in all UX categories. In fact, the Kruskal-Wallis test (non-parametric analysis) revealed that there existed statistically significant differences in all categories except for Q6 (Fatigue). A Tukey test using Ranks post hoc analysis showed that the proposed method had statistically significant effects over the NF and CF.

Note that to convey the feelings of object dynamics, providing only contact feedback (CF) at the respective fingertips would not be sufficient because the object may be moving at the mid-location without direct contact with the fingertips. The subjects also showed an overwhelming preference for the proposed method (TI) (out of 14 subjects, 13 for task). In summary, the experiment demonstrated that the interaction experience can be significantly improved through the proposed tactile illusion based rendering of the interaction object dynamics.

## 4   Discussion and Conclusion

In this paper, we have presented the possibility of applying an "out of body" tactile illusion to a two-finger object interaction in order to improve the user experience without causing significant fatigue. We strongly argue that the proposed tactile rendering of the object dynamics (and not just a multimodal fusion) was the contributing factor to the improvement in the interaction experience. The proposed method can be applied to many other interactive tasks, such as in tangible manipulation of augmented objects, interacting with holographic/stereoscopic virtual objects, surface computing, etc. Our future work will continue to develop and apply other illusion based techniques (including saltation) in a similar manner. One disadvantage of the proposed method is in its wearability. We are investigating whether the vibrators can be positioned and worn like a ring with similar effects.

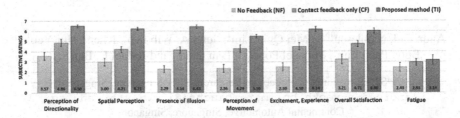

**Fig. 2.** Responses to the UX questionnaire for and differences among the three feedback methods (the error bars indicate the standard error of the mean).

**Acknowledgement.** This research was supported by Basic Science Research Program (No. 2011-0030079) and International Research & Development Program (Grant number: 2014K1A3A1A17073365) through the National Research Foundation of Korea (NRF) funded by the Ministry of Science, ICT & Future Planning

# References

1. Linjama, J., Kaaresoja, T.: Novel, minimalist haptic gesture interaction for mobile devices. In: Third Nordic conference on Human-computer interaction, pp. 457–458. ACM (2004)
2. Alles, D.S.: Information transmission by phantom sensations. IEEE Trans. Man Mach. Syst. **11**(1), 85–91 (1970)
3. Israr, A., Poupyrev, I.: Tactile brush: drawing on skin with a tactile grid display. In: SIGCHI Conference on Human Factors in Computing Systems, pp. 2019–2028 (2011)
4. Seo, J., Choi, S.: Initial study for creating linearly moving vibrotactile sensation on mobile device. In: Haptics Symposium, pp. 67–70. IEEE (2010)
5. Miyazaki, M., Hirashima, M., Nozaki, D.: The "cutaneous rabbit" hopping out of the body. J. Neurosci. **30**(5), 1856–1860 (2010)
6. Okamura, A.M., Dennerlein, J.T., Howe, R.D.: Vibration feedback models for virtual environments. In: IEEE International Conference on Robotics and Automation, pp. 674–679. IEEE (1998)
7. Hoggan, E., Anwar, S., Brewster, S.: Mobile multi-actuator tactile displays. In: Oakley, I., Brewster, S. (eds.) HAID 2007. LNCS, vol. 4813, pp. 22–33. Springer, Heidelberg (2007)
8. Poupyrev, I., Maruyama, S., Rekimoto, J.: Ambient touch: designing tactile interfaces for handheld devices. In: 15th Annual ACM symposium on User interface Software and Technology, pp. 51–60. ACM (2002)
9. Chubb, E.C., Colgate, J.E., Peshkin, M.A.: Shiverpad: a glass haptic surface that produces shear force on a bare finger. IEEE Trans. Haptics **3**(3), 189–198 (2010)
10. Mizukami, Y., Sawada, H.: Tactile information transmission by apparent movement phenomenon using shape-memory alloy device. Int. J. Disabil. Hum. Dev. **5**(3), 277–284 (2006)
11. Ooka, T., Fujita, K.: Virtual object manipulation system with substitutive display of tangential force and slip by control of vibrotactile phantom sensation. In: IEEE Haptics Symposium, pp. 215–218. IEEE (2010)

# Designing IDA - An Intelligent Driver Assistant for Smart City Parking in Singapore

Andreea I. Niculescu[1(✉)], Mei Quin Lim[2], Seno A. Wibowo[2], Kheng Hui Yeo[1], Boon Pang Lim[1], Michael Popow[3], and Dan Chia[2], and Rafael E. Banchs[1]

[1] A*STAR Institute for Infocomm Research (I2R), Singapore, Singapore
{andreea-n,yeokh,bplim,rembanchs}@i2r.a-star.edu.sg
[2] Continental Automotive, Singapore, Singapore
{Mei.Qing.Lim,Wibowo.Seno,
Wei.Ming.Chia}@continental-corporation.com
[3] TUM Create, Singapore, Singapore
michael.popow@umcreate.edu.sg

**Abstract.** A current problem modern cities are facing is the increased traffic flow and heavily congested parking places. To reduce the time and traffic caused by finding available parking we propose IDA, an **I**ntelligent **D**river **A**ssistant. The main objective of IDA is to help drivers to find suitable park places, to online monitor car park availability and to redirect drivers when the number of free available spots drops to a critical level. Unlike other parking applications, IDA uses speech to interact with the driver and becomes an active helper during the navigation process by adjusting dynamically the parking decisions based on the traffic situation. The paper presents the current work in progress, interaction design aspects, uses cases, as well as a first user feedback received during a public event where IDA was showcased.

**Keywords:** Multimodal interaction design · Speech recognition · Smart parking

## 1 Introduction

Urban traffic experts estimate that 30 % of vehicles on the road in downtown areas of major cities are searching for a parking place and spend in average 7.8 min to find one [1]. This increases the traffic congestion, fuel expenses and drivers' time waste. For the past two decades traffic authorities in many cities have been concerned with finding solutions to this problem and as a result, many intelligent transportation systems (ITS) and smart parking technologies have been developed.

Despite being ranked on the top for smooth traffic flow, efficient road network, road quality and public transportation [2], Singapore is confronted during peak hours with heavy traffic jams. To help drivers avoid such stressful situations we have started developing an interactive application for smart parking assistance. The paper presents the application work in progress and covers interaction design aspects, use cases, first feedback from public audience and future work directions.

© IFIP International Federation for Information Processing 2015
J. Abascal et al. (Eds.): INTERACT 2015, Part IV, LNCS 9299, pp. 510–513, 2015.
DOI: 10.1007/978-3-319-22723-8_50

## 2    IDA- An Intelligent Driver Assistant

IDA is a smart parking app that builds on the park guidance information systems[1] (PGI). However, IDA extends common PGI systems by offering suggestions based on parking fee or proximity to destination. Additionally, IDA' makes a new contribution to the existing parking systems by adding two novel features. These are:

1. *Use of natural language*: the interaction between the application and the driver is done using speech dialogues. This feature complies with current traffic regulations in Singapore enabling drivers to safely use the app while driving.
2. *Ability to react to changes in the car park occupancy* - unlike E-parking systems which reserve lots for a nominal fee, IDA takes a more sustainable approach: after a parking decision is taken IDA keeps monitoring the car park availability following a once-per-minute check-up routine. If the number of lots drops to critical level, i.e. less than 20, IDA redirects the driver to another parking place. In this way, drivers save costs and parking resources are optimal allocated - parking lots are not kept empty for reservations while drivers with no reservation are struggling to find an empty spot driving around and increasing the traffic. Furthermore, the app includes several interconnected modules responsible for:
   - **Collecting and managing parking availability** - the data is obtained from the Singapore Land Transport Authority (LTA); it is periodically updated and stored on a data base server
   - **Processing speech and dialogues**, as well as generating responses in natural language using a text-to-speech (TTS) module.
   - **Assigning parking lots on a floor map** - currently, the assignments are only simulated; this feature will be implemented in the second project milestone
   - **GPS and google maps** interfacing which enables the application to detect the driver location and calculate the nearest car park distance
   - **Keeping track of parking details** - the app can send on request the parking details per SMS

## 3    Interaction Design

The IDA's story board is depicted in Fig. 1. The app is designed to turn on once the driver starts the car engine. In a short dialogue IDA greets the driver and asks about the driving direction and parking intention (Fig. 2A). Upon driver's answer IDA starts searching the data base for suitable car parks and makes three suggestions. The information is spoken (only the first suggestion) and graphically displayed on the screen. The screen is divided in two parts (Fig. 2B): the left upper part shows the car park name, number of available lots, distance to target location and parking fee; the left lower part contains the dialogue history. On the right side, the screen displays the google map navigation to the car park.

---

[1] Park guidance information (PGI) systems are technologies that monitor car parks and direct drivers to available parking lots.

**Fig. 1.** IDA story board

The car parks are by default ranked on the distance proximity to the driving location. However, the driver can change this setting using speech or the touch screen, as shown in Fig. 2C. If the driver dislikes the suggestion, he/she can request other parking locations up to 3 times. After the third rejection IDA turns into manual mode. In the manual mode the driver can search by himself for available parking once the car is standing. If the number of available parking places is less than 20, the label designating the car park lots turns into red (Fig. 2B). The application warns the driver on the spot and offers parking alternatives. When the driver reaches the car park, IDA displays – on the right side of the screen - the floor map where the empty lots are marked in green. On the left side, the driver can request the application to send him/her an SMS with the exact parking location (Fig. 2D). The driver has the option to switch off the application at any moment in time by saying: "*Dismiss*".

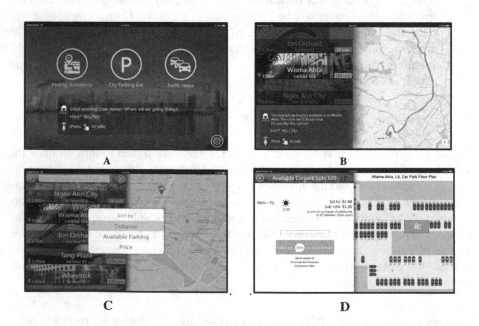

**Fig. 2.** Screen shots IDA

## 3.1   Ida's Personality

To shorten the dialogue and enhance the user experience we designed some personality features for IDA through the use of humor. When the driver keeps rejecting IDA's parking's suggestions as being *"too expensive"* the system shows disapproval: *"Expensive? This is cheap lah! If you want cheaper go Malaysia! Anyway, don't have cheaper! Sure you don't want?"*. The surprise effect is increased by the fact that IDA uses typical Singlish - a local colloquial English variant - words and expressions when she gets upset. IDA also gives similar responses to undecided drivers who keep asking for the *"next"* option: *"Again next? You drive me crazy! This place is nice and cheap! Why not taking?"*. IDA's dominant personality shows up each time the driver persists in rejecting her suggestions for more than 3 times in a row, i.e. just before turning into manual mode. In cases where the noise level reaches a critical level hindering the automatic speech recognition (ASR), IDA asks the driver to speak louder or to turn off the radio. While for native English speakers IDA's remarks might sound rude they are very common for local Singaporeans being used in the daily slang. As such, they do not hold negative connotations.

# 4   Demo at a Public Event and Future Work

The first IDA prototype was presented to the public during an official event. Due to the afflux of visitors and the short time allocated for demonstrations it was difficult to organize a more elaborate system evaluation. However, the demo allowed us to observe the visitors and gather some important observations. In general, the application received positive feedback and visitors seemed interested to test it; after the demo we received an overwhelming amount of questions regarding additional features, development process and future commercialization. When the ASR performed well, people tended to ask out of domain questions, probably in an attempt to test the application limits. This observation is important for the future dialogue development. On the other side, user expectations need to be kept at reasonable levels. Another observation refers to the fact that many visitors were foreigners living in Singapore. As such, they spoke well English, but had a different accent as the local one. This caused some ASR problems, as our system was initially trained using Singaporean speech data. In the future, we are planning to enhance the ASR module with additional English accents and enlarge the vocabulary to allow more complex dialogue structures. Additionally, an indoor navigation module will be integrated to guide drivers inside the car park. Also, two user studies are in preparation: one will evaluate the user experience while the other one will focus on sustainability effects achieved by daily application use.

# References

1. Geng, Y., Cassandras, C.: A new "smart parking" system infrastructure and implementation. Procedia Soc. Behav. Sci. **54**, 1278–1287 (2012)
2. Schwab, K. The Global Competitiveness Report 2012–2013. World Economic Forum. http://www3.weforum.org/docs/WEF_GlobalCompetitivenessReport_2012-13.pdf

# Development of Usability-Criteria for the Selection Process of Document Management Systems

Antje Heinicke[✉], Christina Bröhl, Ioannis Dokas, Katrin Walbaum, Jennifer Bützler, and Christopher Schlick

Chair and Institute of Industrial Engineering and Ergonomics
of RWTH Aachen University, Bergdriesch 27, 52062 Aachen, Germany
a.heinicke@iaw.rwth-aachen.de

**Abstract.** As the overload of digital information in the SMEs requires an adequate management, document management systems (DMS) increasingly gain significance since they enhance the automation of processes within documents' registration, classification, processing, archiving and forwarding. However, in current selection processes of DMS the usability aspect seems to be unconsidered. For this purpose criteria are developed that measure the usability of existing DMS and allow the selection of a DMS according to usability aspects.

**Keywords:** Document management · DMS · Usability · Software ergonomics · Selection criteria

## 1 Introduction

The current scientific methods for software selection are not capable of representing the differences in the usability of the DMSs. The methods largely consider functional system requirements [1]. Objective criteria concerning the usability of DMS do not exist. Consequently, usability problems usually become visible only after the implementation. This study introduces an approach to determine objectively measurable usability criteria which can be applied by non-usability-experts for the evaluation and selection of DMS with regard to usability.

The evaluation of whether a system has a good or bad usability depends largely on the product itself and as well on the user and the context of use [2]. Accordingly, the identification of usability weaknesses of the existing DMSs, as well as the characterization of the users and their requirements was carried out in a first step [3]. Based on the analysis of requirements, a user test was performed to detect the relevant usability criteria.

## 2 Method

The study included 22 subjects aged 27 to 60 years (M = 43.41, SD = 10.9). All Participants had experience in document management, yet little or no experience in dealing with document management systems. Only novices where included in the

© IFIP International Federation for Information Processing 2015
J. Abascal et al. (Eds.): INTERACT 2015, Part IV, LNCS 9299, pp. 514–517, 2015.
DOI: 10.1007/978-3-319-22723-8_51

analysis in order to find as many aspects as possible for the formulation of the criteria which may not be important for experienced DMS users and DMS experts. To make valid statements, two commercial DMS were exemplarily used for the tasks: A system with a graphic layout very similar to Microsoft Office and a system with an individual user interface design were used.

The requirement-analysis indicated that the invoice receipt, a frequently used process in many companies, is often supported by a DMS. Consequently, specific test tasks, which are associated with this process, have been developed and tested.

## 2.1 Procedure

A training video was presented at the beginning of the test, providing an introduction to the field of document-management and a description of DMS' aim. This ensured that also novice users of DMS gain a certain degree of knowledge about the features as well as the spectrum of uses and that all subjects had a similar knowledge about DMS. The training video was followed by the processing of the three tasks: Task type 1 included the searching and displaying of a filed document; task type 2 included the filing of a document in the DMS, while in task type 3 the participants were asked to share and comment on a document. To minimize sequence effects, both the sequence of task performance, as well as the sequence of the systems was permuted. While working on the tasks, the participants were encouraged to think aloud (Concurrent Thinking Aloud). After completing each task participants were asked to reflect their experience with the DMS in form of a structured interview.

## 2.2 Formulation of Criteria

With the aid of the comments made during the task execution and during the interviews, the formulation of the usability criteria took place. For this purpose the comments regarding the participants' subjective experience, were systematically analyzed, indexed and categorized with an expert evaluation. The first step hereto was the transcription of the comments into a list, sorted by subject, system and task type. In every comment, the key messages were highlighted and the comments were multiplied according to the number of key messages. Additionally, the key messages were compressed and assigned to the categories function, layout, wording, user guidance, system feedback, to the characteristics positive or negative system feature, and to the keywords depending on the type of task. Using the compressed key messages, the formulation of criteria was carried out starting with the first key message. If the further key messages could not be assigned to already existing criteria, a new criterion was formulated. Regarding the formulation of criteria it was ensured that the criteria can be evaluated with yes/no or available/not available.

# 3   Results

More than seventy usability criteria were formulated based on which the usability of a DMS can be evaluated. The usability criteria are to be considered as DMS-specific operating requirements that are related to the design of the entire user interface or to individual elements of the user interface and to the interaction with the system. The criteria show different characteristics, enabling various methods of evaluation and application.

## 3.1   Criteria Classification

For the specific use of the usability criteria in the DMS selection process, the criteria were separated in two categories. Criteria related to characteristics of the entire DMS user interface are of cross-functional nature (suitable for the specification sheet). Criteria, concerning specific controls or properties of the main functions "search", "import", "workflow" were correspondingly assigned as function related characteristics. In the following four examples of the most frequently mentioned criteria are listed (for the number of mentions, subjects were counted, whose comments a criterion could be assigned to at least once):

- Cross-functional: Is a graphical representation of the filing structure available (e.g. in form of a tree structure)?
- Functional reference to "Search": Do document details (nature/type of the document) are displayed in a search results?
- Functional reference to "Import": Does the user receive a visual feedback on the successful filing of a document into the DMS?
- Functional reference to "Workflow": Are high priority tasks graphically highlighted in the task list (e.g. by a special symbol or colored highlighting)?

In case of the comparison between an already reduced number of possible DMS solutions, the usability of the main functions can be considered separately based on the functional classifications. This allows, for example, the usability evaluation of the search function separately from the usability of the workflow function. Thus, at the DMS-selection it can be focused on the usability of the particularly relevant functions for the user enterprise. Furthermore, the criteria could be characterized regarding their affiliation to norm-based dialogue principles [4]. This allows a standardized evaluation of a system's operating requirements.

## 3.2   Criteria List

The developed criteria were listed in a catalog. A weighting of the criteria based on the number of mentions was not made. The relevance of a criterion cannot be inferred from the number of mentions. Moreover, frequent mentions could be caused by the obviousness of a deficiency or a positive feature. The identified criteria primary concern general system properties as well as the three main features search, import and workflow. This fact is due to the type of tasks that were carried out. Therefore, the catalog of criteria does not claim to be complete. With the help of project partners, both DMS users and DMS provider companies, the set of criteria could be validated in terms of relevance, practical application and comprehensibility. For this purpose, the categorized catalogue of criteria was given to the users, expanded by an evaluation option according to the specification sheet. Users should evaluate each criterion as to whether it is critical for them, required, optional, or not required. A note below each category intended to provide information on whether the review decision was easy to make or not. If not, the users could name the criteria which were difficult to evaluate. Furthermore, optional comments could be included. Providers also received an expanded catalogue including the evaluation of whether a criterion is met, not met or partially met by their own system. Furthermore, they were able to insert comments when understanding problems occurred. On the basis of the comments made by both the users and the providers, criteria were reformulated and redundancies as well as irrelevant criteria were removed from the catalogue.

## 4 Summary and Outlook

In the DMS selection process, established procedures are applied that often neglect usability aspects. With the aid of user tests, over seventy objectively measurable usability criteria were formulated, which can add the factor of usability to the future selection process. Due to the classification in cross-functional and function-related criteria, these can be used in different phases of the DMS selection process.

**Acknowledgements.** The joint research project uSelect DMS (01MU12018A) is supported by the Federal Ministry of Economics and Technology within the framework of the research program "SME-Digital" initiative "Simply intuitive - usability for SMEs" program.

## References

1. Naß, E., Scheibmayer, M.: 3-Phasen-Modell zur DMS-Auswahl, Unternehmen der Zukunft, FIR − Zeitschrift für Organisation und Arbeit in Produktion und Dienstleistung, Schwerpunkt "Informationsmanagement", 12 Jg. Ausgabe 2/2011
2. Herczeg, M.: Software-Ergonomie. Grundlagen der Mensch-Computer-Kommunikation, 2. Auflage, München: Oldenbourg (2005)
3. Heinicke, A., Bröhl, C.: Bützler, J., Schlick, C.: Usability of document management systems considering users' level of experience: a survey. In: Ahram, T., Karwowski, W., Marek, T. (eds.) Proceedings of the 6th International Conference on Applied Human Factors and Ergonomics 2014 (AHFE) Hrsg. The Printing House, Inc., Stoughton, FL, USA ISBN 978-1-4951-1572-1, S. 359-367 (2014)
4. ISO 9241 1999 − 2011, Ergonomics of human-system interaction, Part 8, Part 110, Part 129, Parts 11-17, Part 171, Part 210, Beuth Verlag, Berlin 1999 − 2011

# Digital Co-design Applied to Healthcare Environments: A Comparative Study

Lei Shi[✉], James MacKrill, Elisavet Dimitrokali, Carolyn Dawson, and Rebecca Cain

International Digital Laboratory, WMG, University of Warwick, Coventry, UK
{lei.shi, j.b.mackrill, e.dimitrokali, c.h.dawson, r.cain.1}@warwick.ac.uk

**Abstract.** Co-design approaches have been used by different sectors, to understand end-user perspectives. They have been diversified from traditional use in product development to sectors such as healthcare environments. They put emphasis on innovation with end-users where this is seen as a source of competitive advantage, and fits with the logic of end-user-led innovation. It does however ask the question of *how to enable such approaches* and if digital approaches are more useful than traditional paper-based methods. We propose a digital co-design tool for environment improvement that can potentially promote user involvement. This paper reports on a comparative study on co-designing a healthcare environment using the digital tool versus a traditional paper-based tool. Discussion centers on the benefits and drawbacks of proposed approach.

## 1 Introduction

Co-design approaches have been adopted by an array of different sectors to understand the end-user perspective. This diversified from traditional product development to sectors such as healthcare. Improving user experiences of healthcare services and environments via their involvement has become a central theme in health research [1] and strategic agendas [5]. This has involved different stakeholder groups including patients and hospital staffs in discussions about personal experiences of healthcare as well as how services and environments might be improved, often utilizing methods of co-design. It does however ask the question of *how to enable such approaches.*

As part of an ongoing research program "Participation in Healthcare Environment Engineering", in order to explore the use of technologies in the co-design process, we developed a digital tool having an interactive surface and can be positioned in hospital areas such as staff rooms on departments and wards. The rationale of the tool was to engage hospital users in participating in design and appraisal of hospital areas when having a spare moment to collect small amounts of relevant data [4]. This recognized that healthcare staffs do not have time during the working day to take large amounts of time out to participate in co-design activities for workplace improvement.

The digital tool has been used in situ within hospital spaces. The aim of this work is to discover deeper nuances of use and reports on a comparative study aimed to understand end-users' perceived engagement when using the developed digital tool verses a more traditional paper-based tool (questionnaire worksheets).

© IFIP International Federation for Information Processing 2015
J. Abascal et al. (Eds.): INTERACT 2015, Part IV, LNCS 9299, pp. 518–522, 2015.
DOI: 10.1007/978-3-319-22723-8_52

## 2  Experiment Setup

The experiment was conducted in the 3D Sound Room, as shown in Fig. 1 (left), in the International Digital Laboratory, at the University of Warwick. It consists of a 16-speaker system and 3 projector displays. It enables a 3D visual and aural simulation to a hospital environment. A cardiothoracic (CT) hospital ward environment was simulated using previously obtained sound recordings and images.

**Fig. 1.** The 3D Sound Room and the digital tool in simulated cardiothoracic ward environment

The digital tool, as shown in Fig. 1 (right), consists of a tablet computer attached to a stand. The tablet was fixed at a height suitable for use while sitting. A screen was positioned above the tablet and displayed questions, text and images. Participants responded to questions using the tablet. The questions, revealed bespoke tasks created to investigate a single healthcare environment. Other respondents' comments were displayed on the larger top screen once they had been completed. Presenting the views of other respondents was hoped to encourage mediated discourse amongst participants. A detailed discussion of the design and development is provided in [2].

## 3  A Comparative Study

15 computer science PhD students at the University of Warwick took part in the experiment (mean age 29 years; s.d. 4.2). The experiment was divided into 2 phases. In Phase I, the participants were asked to use the paper-based tool, to improve 4 areas in the CT hospital ward, including the patient bay area, the ward corridor, the view outside the ward and the entrance to the ward, as shown in Fig. 2. For each participant, it took approximately 15 min to complete the tasks. Following this each completed a questionnaire containing nine statements, as shown in Table 1, and a free comment space. The questionnaire was designed based on a pervious study [3]. It contained 3 dimensions including Satisfaction of Use (**SU**), Confidence of Use (**CU**), and Behavioral Intention (**BI**), aiming to investigate participants' perceived engagement of using the tool. Participants rated their agreement to each statement as −2 (strongly disagree), −1 (disagree), 0 (neither agree nor disagree), 1 (agree), and 2 (strongly

agree). One week after Phase I, in Phase II, the participants were asked to use the digital tool to perform the same tasks and completing the same questionnaire.

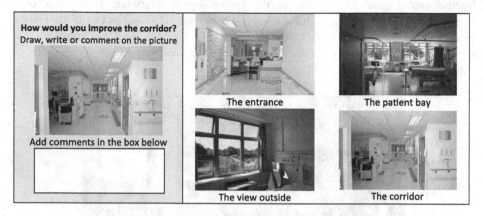

**Fig. 2.** The paper-based tool (on the left), and the four hospital areas to improve (on the right)

**Table 1.** The statements in the questionnaire and the results

| Statement (variable) | Phase I (n = 15) | | Phase II (n = 15) | |
|---|---|---|---|---|
| | Mean | SD | Mean | SD |
| **Satisfaction of Use (SU)** | | | | |
| SU1. The tool was attractive to use | 0.67 | 1.29 | 1.13 | 0.83 |
| SU2. The tool was fun to use | 0.33 | 1.40 | 1.27 | 0.88 |
| SU3. The tool was pleasant to use | 0.27 | 1.16 | 0.93 | 0.88 |
| **Confidence of Use (CU)** | | | | |
| CU1. I felt confident to interact with the tool | 0.93 | 0.88 | 1.00 | 0.85 |
| CU2. I felt confident to contribute to the design | 0.47 | 1.25 | 0.93 | 0.70 |
| CU3. I felt confident my contribution was recorded | 0.67 | 1.11 | 1.20 | 0.68 |
| **Behavioral Intention (BI)** | | | | |
| BI1. I would use the tool again for the design | 0.40 | 1.06 | 0.80 | 0.94 |
| BI2. I would use the tool frequently for the design | 1.13 | 0.83 | 0.93 | 0.70 |
| BI3. I would tell other people about the tool | 0.80 | 1.08 | 0.87 | 0.74 |

## 4    Results and Discussion

Table 1 shows the results of the comparative study. Overall, all the results, from both Phase I and Phase II, indicated a positive response to using both tools, i.e., mean ≥ 0 (the neutral value) suggesting that both were effective in eliciting response and comment on the healthcare CT environment. The Wilcoxon signed-rank test was performed to examine if and where differences in engagement may lic. The test results revealed no significant differences p > .05 between the paper-based tool and the digital tool in terms of the perceived engagement across all 9 statements. Yet, the digital tool did elicit a more positive response, as Table 1 shows that for the digital tool 4 out of 9 statements received scores greater than 1 i.e. the statements were 'agreed', whilst for the paper-based tool only 1 statement received a score greater than 1. Besides, only 1 statement for the digital tool received a lower score than that for the paper-based tool. This might be caused by usability issues, which is out of this paper's scope.

There were three main limitations in this pilot study. One was the low number of participants, although *Cronbach's Alpha* 0.883 suggested a high level of reliability. Another was that all the participants were generally familiar with technology, as they were computer science students. Thus, engagement with individuals not as familiar with technology might be different. The third limitation was that all the participants firstly performed the tasks using the paper-based tool then using the digital tool. This could potentially have led to order effects, as in Phase II the participants had already been familiar with the tasks that they had learnt from Phase I. However, the one-week break between the two phases might go some way to control for their familiarity.

## 5  Conclusion and Future Studies

In this paper, we have investigated the use of an innovative digital co-design tool for improving healthcare environments. In particular, the user engagement of adopting such an approach has been tested in a comparative study on using digital tool versus paper-based tool. Although the results indicated no significant difference, the digital tool did elicit a more positive response, thus warranting further investigation.

In the future, we aim to reduce the limitations discussed in Sect. 4: We will repeat the study and invite a larger and more diverse range of participants. We will reverse the condition order to avoid and account for order effects. In the future, we also aim to investigate how participants perform co-design tasks using such a digital tool, e.g., by analyzing the frequency and sequence of using functionalities provided by the digital tool. By understanding these nuances of interaction with co-design approaches we hope to be able to develop innovate ways for user participation in healthcare to help shape the future by their effective involvement.

**Acknowledgements.** This research was conducted as part of the EPSRC-funded project "Participation in Healthcare Environment Engineering" under the grant no: EP/H022031/1.

## References

1. Bate, P., Robert, G.: Experience-based design: from redesigning the system around the patient to co-designing services with the patient. Qual. Saf. Healthc. **15**(5), 307–310 (2006)
2. Marshall, P., et al.: Situated crowdsourcing: a pragmatic approach to encouraging participation in healthcare design. Pervasive Computer Technologies Healthcare, PervasiveHealth pp. 555–558 (2011)

3. Shi, L.: Defining and evaluating learner experience for social adaptive e-learning. In: 2014 Imperial College Computing Student Workshop, pp. 74–82 (2014)
4. Shi, L., Dawson, C., Mackrill, J., Dimitrokali, E., Cain, R.: Digital co-design: a future method? In: Proceedings of the 2015 British HCI Conference, British HCI 2015, pp. 295–296. ACM, New York (2015). doi:10.1145/2783446.2783618
5. The ebd approach (experience based design) – NHS Institute for Innovation and Improvement. http://ow.ly/KR0PG. Accessed 20 May 2015

# Dual Camera Magic Lens for Handheld AR Sketching

Klen Čopič Pucihar[1]([⊠]), Jens Grubert[2], and Matjaž Kljun[1]

[1] Computer Science Department, University of Primoraska, Koper, Slovenia
{klen.copic,matjaz.kljun}@famnit.upr.si
[2] Embedded Interactive Systems Laboratory (EISLab), University of Passau,
Passau, Germany
jg@jensgrubert.de

**Abstract.** One challenge of supporting in-situ sketching tasks with Magic Lenses on handheld Augmented Reality systems is to provide accurate and robust pose tracking without disrupting the sketching experience. Typical tracking approaches rely on the back-facing camera both for tracking and providing the view of the physical scene. This typically requires a fiducial to be in the scene which can disrupt the sketching experience on a blank sheet of paper. We address this challenge by proposing a Dual Camera Magic Lens approach. Specifically, we use the front facing camera for tracking while the back camera concurrently provides the view of the scene. Preliminary evaluation on a virtual tracing task with an off-the-shelf handheld device suggests that the Dual Camera Magic Lens approach has the potential to be both faster and lead to a higher perceived satisfaction compared to Magic Lens and Static Peephole interfaces.

**Keywords:** Magic-lens · Dual-camera · Sketching · Trace-drawing · Virtual-tracing

## 1 Introduction

Sketching is an important ancient human skill stimulating creative, visual and spatial thinking. Computer systems that support sketching have been studied since the early days of computer science [5]. Through the development of mobile computing devices, such as smartphones, Magic Lens (ML) became a popular interface to support user sketching (e.g. [2–4, 6, 7]). ML acts as filter augmenting the scene with additional digital content, for example, by adding 3D models based on a recognized paper sketch [2] or by allowing the creation of new 3D content [4, 7]. In this paper we explore how novice users can be supported in creating physical sketches through *virtual tracing,* i.e. creating a physical sketch on paper given a virtual image on the handheld device.

The core challenge for this (and other sketching) tasks, which involve a physical pen and paper, is to provide accurate and robust pose tracking without disrupting the sketching process. So far, AR sketching systems focused on authoring digital objects and relied on external tracking systems (e.g. [4]) or on marker based tracking (e.g. [6]). Here we focus on utilizing AR as a crafting tool for curtain of real objects (e.g. pen

© IFIP International Federation for Information Processing 2015
J. Abascal et al. (Eds.): INTERACT 2015, Part IV, LNCS 9299, pp. 523–527, 2015.
DOI: 10.1007/978-3-319-22723-8_53

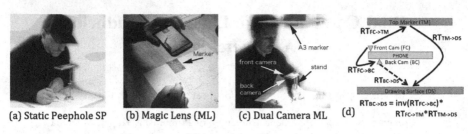

**Fig. 1.** (a)–(c) Mobile device sketching aid tools on the study; (d) D-ML transformations

drawings). While marker based tracking would allow in-situ sketching on physical paper in otherwise unprepared environments (Fig. 1b), it limits the sketching experience in a fundamental way: the marker has to be in the camera view taking away valuable space for sketching. While approaches, such as contour tracking [1, 2] circumvent the use of a marker, they are prone to failure as they cannot be occluded during interaction.

An alternative is to eliminate the need for pose tracking by placing the device and drawing surface at fixed position, such as in the case of a virtual mirror[1] or camera sketcher.[2] In both situations the user has to manually position the graphical content into the real world using traditional handheld interfaces such as static peephole (SP). Hence, if the drawing format does not fit into camera's field-of-view (FOV), the user is required to manually realign the graphic every time the device is moved.

In this paper we address the challenge of pose tracking while mitigating the effects on in-situ sketching experiences. Specifically, we evaluate how utilizing both front and back facing cameras concurrently could improve the utility of ML as a sketching aid tool. In order to do so, we: (i) design and build a Dual Camera Magic Lens (D-ML) system utilizing the front camera for pose tracking and the back camera for scene capture and rendering; (ii) evaluate the proposed solution on a commercially available handheld device by conducting a preliminary user study with 6 participants performing virtual tracing task. We compare 3 interaction methods: Static Peephole (SP), Magic Lens (ML) with fiducial marker and Dual Camera Magic Lens (D-ML).

## 2  Dual Camera Magic Lens

In contrast to using the back facing camera as in standard handheld AR applications we propose to utilize the front facing camera for pose tracking while providing the view of the scene through the back facing camera. We do this in order to mitigate the effects on in-situ sketching experiences.

In order to enable front camera pose tracking, a marker is placed above the drawing surface in parallel orientation (in our case ca. 60 cm, see Fig. 1c). As the tracking and rendering camera are not the same, a set of additional transformations (Fig. 1d) needs to

---

[1] https://www.playosmo.com/en/.

[2] https://play.google.com/store/apps/details?id=com.aku.drawissimo.

be added to the tracked pose result (on Fig. 2a denoted as $RT_{FC->TM}$). However, as the two cameras on the phone are fixed and the top marker is rigidly attached above the drawing area, the only two transformations that change are $RT_{FC->TM}$ and $RT_{BC->DS}$. Hence, as long as the front camera tracking is successful and the two constant transformations are known, $RT_{BC->DS}$ can be calculated (Fig. 1d).

# 3  User Study

The preliminary user study asked participants to perform a virtual tracing task on A3 paper. Participants were instructed to sit at a table and draw a cartoon character as quickly and as accurately as possible. To estimate participants' perceived satisfaction we are utilizing the "overall reactions" part of the Questionnaire for User Interaction Satisfaction (QUIS). In addition, we asked participants to rank interaction modes and to justify their choice. As objective measure we recorded task completion time.

We used a within-subjects design. Each participant drew three different contours with each interaction method: SP, ML, D-ML (see Fig. 1). In SP manual alignment is required each time the phone is moved. In ML the drawing is possible whilst holding the phone in hand, whereas in SP it is mandatory to place the phone on the stand. In case of the D-ML, the stand was included because contrary to the tracker used in ML implementation, the tracker used in D-ML did not provide sufficiently robust and accurate orientation tracking results. By placing the phone on stand, we locked two degrees of freedom (Rx and Ry) improving tracking quality. We recognize this as a limitation. However, this decision was mandatory as poor tracking quality is bound to undermine performance of the proposed interaction paradigm. Additionally, as it should be possible to improve tracking performance of future D-ML systems, this does not undermine the proposed interaction concept per say, but rather affects the direct comparability of captured results. Yet, within the context of this study which is of exploratory nature and predominantly based on qualitative data, we consider our study design as appropriate.

# 4  Results

The study was completed by six participants. All were male, aged between 24 and 45 years. Due to the small number of participants null-hypothesis significance testing would result in poor statistical power. Hence, we present solely descriptive statistics. By overlaying drawn contours with template contours, two researchers independently and subjectively compared the quality of all three drawings for each participant and ranked drawings from best to worst. As shown in Fig. 2e, the comparison did not highlight any obvious deviations in obtained rankings. The results in Fig. 2 also suggest that D-ML has the potential to (i) be the fastest mode; (ii) have the highest QUIS score across all properties; and (iii) have best rank. Again those results could not be reliably tested for statistical difference. Five participants that ranked D-ML as the best method justified their ranking choice by highlighting the advantage of automatic alignment and the fact that marker was not in their way.

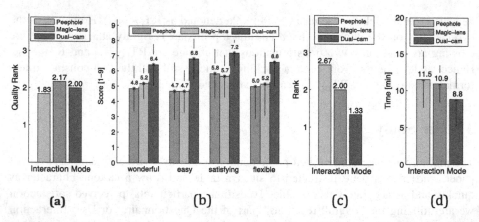

**Fig. 2.** (a) Drawing quality ranking results (smaller is better); (b) "Overall reactions" part of QUIS scores [1–9]. (c) Preference ranking results (smaller is better); (d) Task time in minutes

## 5  Discussion and Conclusion

The results show that the utility of handheld AR as an in-situ sketching tool has the potential to be improved utilizing the D-ML approach. The designed and implemented system demonstrates such a solution is feasible on commercially available mobile devices. The preliminary study indicated that whilst achieving comparable quality of drawing, compared to SP and ML, D-ML is: potentially faster, users perceived higher satisfaction, and is preferred by participants. We believe the main reason for such a results is the fact the camera tracking did not interfere with user sketching. As underlined by participants themselves, the main benefit is automatic alignment of virtual image with the real word. Even though, until the user moves the marker, automatic alignment is also present in case of ML, in D-ML the user did not have to put up with the marker and avoid occluding the marker whilst trace drawing onto the paper. Although one could argue that the stand ambiguity increased the divide between the ML and D-ML, none of participants highlighted the stand as the factor influencing their ranking choice, suggesting the importance of the stand might be limited. However, in future work we will explore the effects of stand vs. handheld mode in more detail. Additionally, due to the small sample size our results are of preliminary nature and hence should be verified with a larger number of users. Finally, future research should look at less intrusive ways of placing a marker above the user.

## References

1. Hagbi, N., Bergig, O., El-Sana, J., Billinghurst, M.: Shape recognition and pose estimation for mobile augmented reality. In: IEEE TVCG, pp. 65–71, October 2009
2. Hagbi, N., Grasset, R., Bergig, O., Billinghurst, M., El-Sana, J.: In-place sketching for content authoring in augmented reality games. In: CIE, vol. 12, issue 3, p. 3 (2015)

3. Čopič Pucihar, K., Coulton, P., Alexander, J.: The use of surrounding visual context in handheld AR: device vs. user perspective rendering. In: CHI, pp. 197–206 (2014)
4. Seichter, H.: Sketchand+. In: CAADRIA 2003, pp. 209–219 (2003)
5. Sutherland, I.E.: Sketchpad: a man-machine graphical communication system. Technical report No. 296, Lincoln Laboratory, Massachusetts Institute of Technology (1963)
6. Xin, M., Sharlin, E., Sousa, M.C.: Napkin sketch: handheld mixed reality 3D sketching. In: Proceedings VRST 2008, pp. 223–226. ACM (2008)
7. Yee, B., Ning, Y., Lipson, H.: augmented reality in-situ 3D sketching of physical objects. In: Proceeding of IUI 2009 (2009)

# Enabling Naturalness and Humanness
# in Mobile Voice Assistants

Sanjay Ghosh[(⊠)] and Jatin Pherwani

Samsung R&D Institute, Bangalore, India
{sanjay.ghosh, j.pherwani}@samsung.com

**Abstract.** Voice Assistant applications are preferred to be designed with some form of personalization to enhance user experience. However, the question remains that what is the kind of Voice Assistant that users would prefer. As part of this research we tried formalizing the notion of naturalness and humanlike in the context of voice assistants by defining its optimal personality, creating guidelines for natural dialogues and expressions. We decomposed the design problem into four aspects, communication style, personality, speech or dialogue, and appearance along with non-verbal gestures. To investigate on each of these four aspects, we performed four different user elicitation techniques.

**Keywords:** Voice interface · Natural language · Voice interactions

## 1 Introduction

Our research goal was not to introduce yet another new candidate into the world of Siri, Cortana, Google Now and various other Voice Agents. Instead our attempt was to design a very natural and humanlike Voice Assistant from scratch. With modulations in language styles, speech parameters, and visuals it is possible to impart quasi-human characteristics in new versions of voice assistant. Earlier research reported in this area includes explorations of the personality for a robotic assistant for television [1], robot for giving advice [2], including emotions in a conversational agent [3]. Beyond all the existing work in this area, our contributions lies in incorporating the user's perspective as an important element in formulating a personality for the voice avatar, creating dialogues and expressions for the voice agents. We decomposed the design problem into four, (i) Communication Style, (ii) Personality, (iii) Speech/Dialogue, (iv) Appearance and Non-verbal gestures. Contextual interviews, survey questionnaires and participatory design were conducted to get an insight into the problem from user's view point. We studied human personal assistants to understand their communication style and behavior with their boss. Then we used a personality elicitation survey to formulate the attributes of personality desired by the users. This followed by the study of linguistic, speech and characteristics of user created dialogue library for a voice assistant across different scenarios. Users' direct perception regarding these were taken into account through a co-creation activity. Overall scope of research has been illustrated in Fig. 1.

© IFIP International Federation for Information Processing 2015
J. Abascal et al. (Eds.): INTERACT 2015, Part IV, LNCS 9299, pp. 528–532, 2015.
DOI: 10.1007/978-3-319-22723-8_54

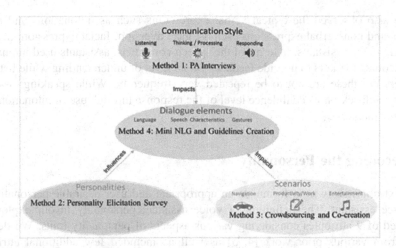

**Fig. 1.** Illustration of the scope of research

## 2 Defining the Communication Style

In the first phase, our interview sessions with seven professional assistants were focused mainly to identify various personality traits of the assistants, understand how they handle various situations and observe explicit cues that are exhibited during conversation. We formulated the social behavior of the assistants through our observations on emotional, behavioral and functional aspects. Outcome from the assistant interviews has been summarized in Fig. 2.

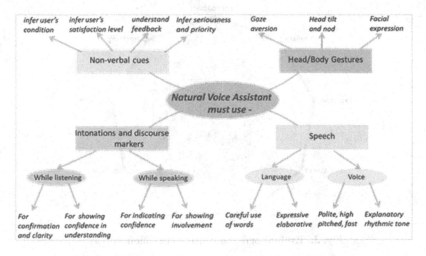

**Fig. 2.** Illustration of outcome from Assistant Interviews

We also observed the typical verbal expressions such as, intonations and exclamations and non-verbal expressions such as, gaze aversion, facial expression, head tilt and nod, on the assistants. In terms of the speech constructs, assistants used intonations and discourse markers to provide feedback on its level of understanding while listening to others but these are not to be repeated very frequently. While speaking, assistant provide feedback on its confidence level of the response through use of intonations and discourse markers.

## 3   Decoding the Personality

Our next objective was to formulate an appropriate and user desirable personality for the voice assistant. The definition of voice assistant personality in our exploration consisted of 9 attributes considering various aspects of personality traits. We derived these from various prior work [4, 5] as well as included few additional attributes relevant to the case of Voice Assistant like, Spontaneous, Inventiveness and Similarity based on our insights from the earlier personal assistant interviews. Next we performed the Personality Elicitation session through a brief questionnaire, a face to face survey discussion session with 30 participants to understand the importance and desirability of each of those attributes for a voice assistant. Our intent was to quantify, how much of each of these traits was desirable to a user. The evolved personality based on the 9 attributes is illustrated in Fig. 3. Interesting facts emerged out of the personality analysis; such as, users preferred their Voice Assistant to *Control* them to some extent, but they would prefer not be fully *Dependent* on it. Therefore, perhaps the users wish to see it as a Companion than as an Assistant.

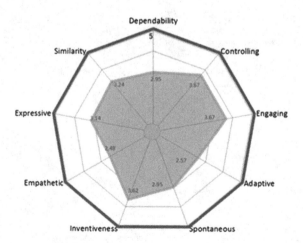

**Fig. 3.** Evolved personality from elicitation activity

## 4    Developing Speech and Dialogue

In the next phase we conducted crowdsourcing and co-creation sessions with 32 participants which included language enthusiasts and avid readers of literature in order to create natural dialogues for the voice assistant in various situations. The intent of this experiment was to extract the underlying common patterns in responses from the users. The participants were given a set of user queries and corresponding responses from an existing voice assistant application covering various usage scenarios. They were asked to frame the response of the voice assistant as natural and in the way they would prefer to hear. Participants could specify speech variables like pitch, speech rate and stress along with their language responses. Figure 4 lists all the goal parameters used for the co-creation activity.

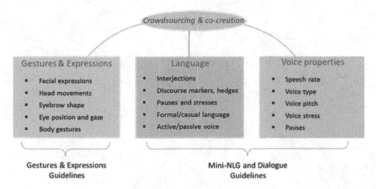

**Fig. 4.** Goals parameters for the co-creation activity

## 5    Creating Appearance and Gestures

As the next step, few of these raw dialogues from the participants in this earlier session were given to 6 animation designers with the intent of generating the visuals of the gestural aspects. This helped us formulate various gestural cues like smiles, frowns, eyebrow shapes, head nods, head positions, body postures, etc. [5].

## 6    Conclusions

The design guidelines, dialogues and personality definitions evolved from our research is being used as a framework for creating natural voice assistant avatar. Going forward, we plan to extend this research in exploring the notion of Voice as a Companion, beyond being an Assistant.

# References

1. Meerbeek, B., Hoonhout, J., Bingley, P., Terken, S.: Investigating the relationship between the personality of a robotic TV assistant and the level of user control. In: Robot and Human Interactive Communication, pp. 404–410 (2006)
2. Torrey, C., Fussell, S., Kiesler, S.: How a robot should give advice. In: 8th ACM/IEEE Human-Robot Interaction (HRI), pp. 275–282 (2013)
3. Ball, G., Breese, J.: Emotion and Personality in a Conversational Agent, Embodied conversational agents, pp. 189–219. MIT Press, Cambridge (2000)
4. Costa, P., Robert, M.: Revised NEO personality inventory and NEO five-factor inventory: professional manual. Psychological Assessment Resources (1992)
5. Breese, J., Ball, G.: Modeling emotional state and personality for conversational agents. Rapport technique MSR-TR-98-41, Microsoft research (1998)

# Estimation of Radius of Curvature of Lumbar Spine Using Bending Sensor for Low Back Pain Prevention

Takakuni Iituka[✉], Kyoko Shibata, and Yoshio Inoue

Kochi University of Technology, Miyanokuchi 185,
Tosayamada, Kami, Kochi, Japan
150003n@ugs.kochi-tech.ac.jp,
{shibata.kyoko,inoue.yoshio}@kochi-tech.ac.jp
http://www.kochi-tech.ac.jp

**Abstract.** Estimation of the disk load in order to prevent low back pain is useful. However, the conventional methods of measuring disc load are invasive and their use is limited due to measurement environments. This study proposes a new method of estimating the lumbar disc load to measure curvature of the lumbar portion and to estimate the lumbar disc load safely using a bending sensor. The radius curvature can be measured relatively easily and without damaging the body by using this method. The bending sensors are attached along vertebra end of five vertebras and the curvature of the lumbar portion is estimated by reading the change in output voltage. The lumbar disk load with static posture was estimated by proposed method. The result shows the same tendency as the previous method. The proposed method has a possibility of developing a new system using the biofeedback based on the lumbar disc load.

**Keywords:** Bending sensor · Herniated disk · Wearable sensing system · Radius of curvature

## 1 Introduction

In recent years, people suffering from low back pain increase by changes in labor environment and living environment. But the obvious way for preventing low back pain is not yet introduced. So it is useful to develop of wearable sensor system for preventing low back pain. Although there are various causes in low back pain, this study targets a herniated disk. Herniated disk works as cushioning material that exists between the vertebrae of the lumbar. Pain and numbness come out when excessive force is applied to herniated disk. Therefore we can make use for treatment, rehabilitation and prevention if it is possible to measure the load on the disk.

Useful method of measuring the load on the disk has been reported up to the present time. One of them is a method of inserting a direct pressure sensor into the disk by Nachemson an orthopedist in Sweden. This method is a highly accurate, and measurement can be done in various positions but it has a risk of damaging the body, sometimes putting a patient into surgical operation. The other previous research [1, 2] suggests that there is a way to measure the intervertebral disc load by using a non-linear

© IFIP International Federation for Information Processing 2015
J. Abascal et al. (Eds.): INTERACT 2015, Part IV, LNCS 9299, pp. 533–536, 2015.
DOI: 10.1007/978-3-319-22723-8_55

three-dimensional finite element model of the vertebrae disk based on the CTs and to estimate the joint moments and muscle tone by adapting the inverse kinematics. But it is difficult to measure the mechanical properties of the dynamic characteristics because it is a partial model links. To measure with high precision and the procedure of measurement is complicated because there are various factors to be considered. The present study group focuses on the vertebral edge which exists near skin surface of the back. Since lumbar system is curved due to the attitude change [3], a bending sensor is attached along the five vertebral edge portions that constitute the lumbar part and the curvature of the lumbar part is estimated by reading the change in the output voltage. With this method measurement can be done relatively easily without damaging the body. Since the bending sensor is thin, cheap and wearable, it can be worn in everyday life. The proposed method has a possibility of developing a new system using the biofeedback based on the lumbar disk load, and in the future, this system could be used for preventing low back pain and improving the posture. In this paper, the radius of curvature of lumbar spine is estimated using the same position that Nachemson did in his experiment. The validity of the proposed method is considered by comparing the intervertebral disc load estimation result of Nachemson and the proposed method.

## 2    Methods

Figure 1 shows a schematic diagram of spine, lumbar part and vertebrae. As the Fig. 1 indicates, disc exists between the vertebrae and has the role of cushioning material. Upper and lower vertebrae are connected with a pin at the facet joints. Vertebrae should be considered as a rigid body [3] because the Young's modulus is larger than the disc and the human body. The elastic deformation in the zygapophysial joint is contravened because it is very small. If attitude changes, the gap between the vertebral bodies changes as vertebrae move. That is to say, change of the disk load is caused by the gap change between the vertebral bodies. Let us consider that the lumbar spine moves uniformly, and that the internal pressure in the lumber disc is also uniform. The radius of curvature is obtained by the approximation by arc of the surface shape of body. The average intervertebral disk load is derived [3] by estimating the gap variation between

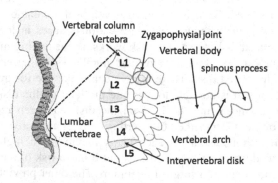

**Fig. 1.**  Lumbar vertebrae

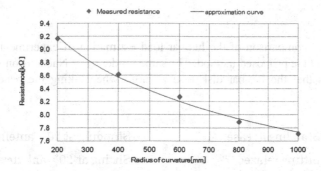

**Fig. 2.** Calibration curve

the average vertebrae using the changes of the radius of curvature in the lumbar system with the posture change.

Bending sensor is a variable resistance. Resistance value changes according to the force applied to it. The radius of curvature is estimated from the change in the resistance value of the bending sensor attached on the skin surface of lumbar. Bending sensors are attached along vertebral end from the first lumbar spine to the fifth lumbar spine (L1–L5). The resistance value is calculated from output voltage and the radius of curvature of the lumbar spine is estimated. Figure 2 shows calibration curve which represents the relationship between the known radius of curvature and the resistance value.

The resistance value obtained from the bending sensor is substituted into the calibration curve to estimate the radius of curvature when the bending sensor is attached to the lumbar part of the human body. The test is administered in four different positions, two standings and two sittings (Fig. 3). These are the same as Nachemson used in his experiment, where the electrodes were inserted directly [1]. A measurement was done four times with each position to all three subjects (Table 1).

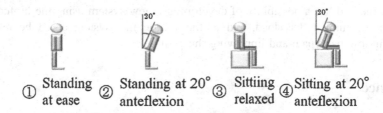

① Standing at ease  ② Standing at 20° anteflexion  ③ Sittiing relaxed  ④ Sitting at 20° anteflexion

**Fig. 3.** Measurement static postures

**Table 1.** Information of subjects

| Subject | Age | Height [m] | Weight [kg] | MBI |
|---------|-----|-----------|-------------|-------|
| A | 22 | 1.67 | 66 | 23.70 |
| B | 22 | 1.69 | 54 | 18.90 |
| C | 22 | 1.72 | 70 | 25.40 |

## 3  Results

Figure 4 shows comparison of the lumbar load estimation of experimental results by Nachemson and the proposed method. The same tendency as Nachemson was obtained in all subjects that the lumbar disk load is large when taking the bending forward positions.

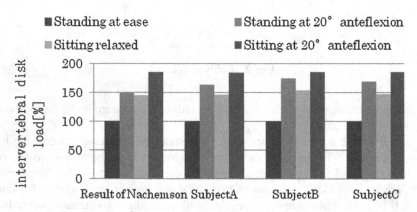

**Fig. 4.** Comparison of the lumbar load estimation of experimental results

## 4  Discussion

The some variations in intervertebral disk load are found. This is because body movements of the subjects were slightly different and also because a curve of the data sheet is approximated by a quadratic function. It could be considered that the estimating of the radius of curvature of lumbar spine is possible with static posture using the measurement method proposed in this study. The proposed sensing system can be applied to car seats and their use is not limited due to measurement environment. The proposed method has a possibility of developing a new system using the biofeedback based on the lumbar disk load, and in the future, this system could be used for preventing low back pain and improving the posture.

## Reference

1. Andersson, B.J.G., Örtengren, R., Nachemson, A., Elfström, G.: Lumbar disc pressure and myoelectric back muscle activity during sitting, I. Studies on an experimental chair. Scand. J. Rehabil. Med. **6**, 104–114 (1974)
2. Rohlman, A., Zander, T., Schmidt, H., Wilke, H.-J., Bergmann, G.: Analysis of the influence of disc degeneration on the mechanical behavior of a lumbar motion segment using the finite element method. J. Biomech. **39**, 2484–2490 (2006)
3. Shibata, K., Inoue, Y., Iwata, Y., Katagawa, J., Fujii, R.: Study on noninvasive estimate method for intervertebral disk load at lumbar vertebrae. Jpn. Soc. Mech. Eng. **78**(791), 2483–2495 (2012)

# Evaluation of Dispatcher Requirements on Automated Customer Feedback in Public Transport

Cindy Mayas[1(✉)], Stephan Hörold[1], Anselmo Stelzer[2],
Frank Englert[3], and Heidi Krömker[1]

[1] Media Production Group, Technische Universität Ilmenau, Ilmenau, Germany
{cindy.mayas,stephan.hoerold,
heidi.kroemker}@tu-ilmenau.de
[2] Railway Engineering, Technische Universität Darmstadt, Darmstadt, Germany
stelzer@bahn.tu-darmstadt.de
[3] Multimedia Communications Lab, Technische Universität Darmstadt,
Darmstadt, Germany
frank.englert@kom.tu-darmstadt.de

**Abstract.** This paper presents a study to analyze fundamental requirements for dispatching systems in public transport, integrating the new technical possibilities of automated customer feedback. Dispatchers in German transport companies are surveyed on their acceptance and expectations, regarding the integration of automated customer feedback in their dispatching decisions. The results serve as a basis for the user-oriented development of dispatching and mobile information systems in public transport with bi-directional communication.

**Keywords:** Dispatching systems · Public transport · User requirements

## 1 Introduction

Public transport is a widespread mobility service for the society, which is based on a network of defined stations and routes, that operate at defined times. In order to guarantee an optimal execution of the mobility services, dispatchers monitor and manage the actual situation within the mobility system and take measures to react on short-term interruptions. New possibilities of automated customer feedback, for instance via the "Travellers' Realtime Information and Advisory Standard" (TRIAS) [1], provide more precise real-time data about actual traveler flows and needs. By having timely access to feedback from travelers, the dispatchers are able to assess the actual situation more precisely and reach better decisions. Exemplarily, the information about actual and future traveler flows can support dispatchers in minimizing the total traveler delay in case of service interruptions or demand peaks [2].

By contrast, the increasing data volume might lead to a growing complexity of the dispatching systems and an information overload of the dispatchers. For this reason, the introduction of automated customer feedback has to be adapted to the dispatchers' workflow [3] and the dialogue principles [4]. However, there is a lack of research,

© IFIP International Federation for Information Processing 2015
J. Abascal et al. (Eds.): INTERACT 2015, Part IV, LNCS 9299, pp. 537–541, 2015.
DOI: 10.1007/978-3-319-22723-8_56

regarding the dispatchers' requirements on real-time customer data for dispatching systems. Thus, the aim of this study is to analyze these requirements, considering the dispatchers' expectations and the relevance of different data for dispatching decisions.

## 2 Method

A survey among dispatchers was conducted anonymously in November 2014 based on an online questionnaire. 34 dispatchers, who took the survey voluntarily, were acquired from nationwide and regional transport companies. These surveyed dispatchers represent the typical range of duties and roles in German transport companies. The majority of the dispatchers perform tasks for operational dispatching decisions or dispatching management. Additionally, some dispatchers also maintain the customer information service or conduct further activities, such as operational command. The standardized questionnaire included questions in regard to the individual assessment of influencing factors on operational decisions, the supply with actual data about customers, attitudes towards using automated customer feedback, and the relevance of customer feedback contents. While the influencing factors, attitudes, and relevance of contents were surveyed in single items on a five-point Likert scale, the participants had to quantify their demand of actual data by multiple selection.

## 3 Results

### 3.1 Supply with Actual Data About Customers

According to the statements of the dispatchers, dispatching decisions in transport companies are mainly influenced by the operational procedures. 97 % of the dispatchers assess the operational procedures as very relevant or relevant for their decisions. Nevertheless, other influencing factors, such as customer needs, personal experiences, and external situational factors, are also rated as very relevant or relevant by 77–85 % of the dispatchers. Furthermore, the dispatching decisions of regional companies are more oriented on the management of external situational influences than on customer needs. This might be caused by the higher frequency of vehicles per route and the resulting higher variety of route alternatives for customers in cities, in comparison to long-distance traffic. In contrast to these results, which indicate that customer needs are at least relevant factors for dispatching decisions, the answers about the actual data supply reveal that 83 % of dispatchers in regional transport companies do not have any actual data about customers available. Most customer data is available in nationwide transport companies, for instance regarding the number of travelers (73 %), who are affected by an interchange, and their destinations (36 %). This information is mainly provided by messages from the staff in the vehicles [3].

## 3.2  Attitudes Towards Using Automated Customer Feedback

The analysis of the attitudes towards the integration of automated customer feedback considers the need and the possible realization of such dispatching systems. While the assessment of the needs includes the improvement, support, and appraisal of decisions, the realization considers the workload, integration, and automation of the data [2]. The results reveal that half of the dispatchers confirm the need and realization of automated customer feedback for operational dispatching decisions with quite positive attitudes (cf. Fig. 1). However, nearly 24 % of the surveyed dispatchers associate quite negative opinions with the usage of automated customer feedback for dispatching decisions. The answers of the single items of the negative attitudes show that these opinions refer to an expected higher workload, in contrast to a suspected low added value.

## 3.3  Relevance of Different Contents of Automated Customer Feedback

The assessments of the relevance of customer information for dispatching decisions show considerable differences according to the type and content of information. For instance, the survey reveals that the real-time information about travelers is most relevant as an aggregation of the number of interchangers per connection (cf. Fig. 2). Furthermore, additional information, such as destinations and itineraries of travelers, can provide valuable information about travel alternatives and allow conclusions about the prioritization and the characteristics of the required decisions. Direct customer feedback can not only comprise the success of interchanges, but also the reasons and consequences of failures from the travelers' point of view. Due to the

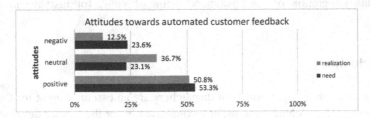

**Fig. 1.** Attitudes towards the need and realization of automated customer feedback

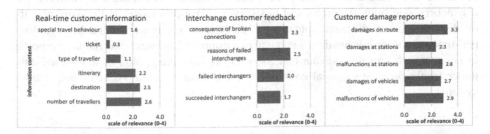

**Fig. 2.** Appraisals of the relevance of the content of automated customer feedback

fact, that this customer feedback could provide valuable data for the evaluation of the dispatching quality in retrospect, the relevance of this information is mainly rated moderately. In contrast to the previous customer information and feedback, the relevance of damage reports by customers is rated high and very high, especially by the dispatchers of regional transport companies. Due to the fact, that the regional dispatchers also often supervise the according infrastructure, such as tram wires and station facilities, these results indicate the highest acceptance and need of automated customer information.

## 4 Discussion

The evaluation reveals fundamental user requirements of dispatchers on the content, the processing, and the design of automated customer feedback. Due to the chosen methods, these results enable a representative overview of the situation within transport companies in Germany. In the following step, the results have to be linked to the individual tasks and working environments of different kinds of dispatchers. Therefore, additional methods are required, such as contextual inquiries, which include the individual context and extend the results to the context of use [4] of the dispatching interactions.

Some dispatchers are concerned about a suspected higher workload due to the higher system complexity with integrated automated customer feedback. In order to allay these concerns, the introduction of user-friendly and workflow-oriented dispatching systems is required to support the dispatching decisions and compensate for the higher amount of information.

In addition, the development of information systems for automated customer feedback is related to the functions of mobile applications for travelers and also requires the integration of the customers' point of view, for instance in usability tests.

## 5 Conclusion

The fundamental user requirements of dispatchers are an essential input for the further development of dispatching systems, and consequently for the further development of mobile information systems for travelers.

In general, dispatchers are open-minded about automated customer feedback, if the content actually has a direct reference to their tasks and is expected to improve the dispatchers' decisions. The results of this survey reveal differences in the requirements of dispatchers for different contents of automated customer feedback, regarding real-time customer information, interchange customer feedback, and damage reports. In summary, the results indicate that the user-oriented integration of automated customer feedback is an essential condition for the further development of dispatching systems.

# References

1. Verband Deutscher Verkehrsunternehmen: VDV 431-2, Echtzeitkommunikations- und Auskunftsplattform EKAP Teil 2: EKAP-Schnittstellenbeschreibung (2013)
2. Stelzer, A., Englert, F., Hörold, S., Mayas, C.: Using customer feedback in public transportation systems. In: Advanced Logistics and Transport (ICALT), pp. 29–34, 1–3 May 2014. doi:10.1109/ICAdLT.2014.6864077
3. DB Fernverkehr AG: Ril 61501, Transportleitung Personenverkehr, non-public (2010)
4. ISO-International Organization for Standardization: ISO 9241-110: Ergonomics of Human-System Interaction – Part 110: Dialogue Principles. ISO, Geneva (2006)

# Experiences of Teaching HCI to a Multidisciplinary Cohort of Computing and Design Students

Omar Mubin[1][✉], Abdullah Al Mahmud[2], and Suleman Shahid[3]

[1] University of Western Sydney, Parramatta, Australia
o.mubin@uws.edu.au
[2] Swinburne University of Technology, Hawthorn, Australia
[3] Tilburg Center for Cognition and Communication, Tilburg University,
Tilburg, Netherlands

**Abstract.** In this paper we present our initial insights on the redesign of an undergraduate unit on Human Computer Interaction to suit a mixed cohort of Computing and Design students. In order to address the diversity in student background we implemented an open brief project assessment. We summarise changes to the unit and present sample student projects that emerged from the unit as outcomes.

**Keywords:** HCI education · Design

## 1 Introduction

Pedagogical methodologies in the area of HCI follow numerous strategies, encouraged perhaps by the freedom provided by HCI as a discipline. These include a hands on studio approach [6] or a case study based assessment [5]. Researchers acknowledge that HCI education must be tailored to the background of the students. For example prior work has considered how the content, assessments and learning outcomes may be adapted to computing students [1]. Similar endeavors have been reported for engineering students [3] and for design students [2], where for the former the focus was on problem solved based learning and for the latter the emphasis was on the design and evaluation of tangible artifacts. HCI is a common and usual occurrence in most Computing undergraduate programs however it is slowly gaining ascendancy in Design, Arts and Interaction Design Programs, mainly due to the rise of innovative products such as those from Apple where aesthetics is an important design consideration. Upon analyzing prior work it is observed that there are not extensive insights on measures to employ if the student cohort is mixed in discipline. This is precisely the challenge that was confronted in coordinating the Human Computer Interaction unit at the University of — where both Computing and Design students were being offered the unit (with no pre-requisites) due to course restructures on both sides. The previous version of the unit was only offered to computing students and was

© IFIP International Federation for Information Processing 2015
J. Abascal et al. (Eds.): INTERACT 2015, Part IV, LNCS 9299, pp. 542–545, 2015.
DOI: 10.1007/978-3-319-22723-8_57

heavily focused on Graphical User Interface Design with a theoretical exam having 50 % contribution towards the final grade. It was evident that to facilitate the integration of both Design and Computing students of varying year levels (1–3), unit changes were required both in depth and in breadth, i.e. in content as well as in assessment offerings. Our approach in the reformed unit was along the lines of designed thinking with a hands on approach; developing empathy with a user group, finding inadequacies and thereby solutions for those problems.

## 2  Changed Unit Proposal for HCI

The following guidelines were proposed and approved by the university's administration via a changed unit proposal:

- Assessments must advocate a hands-on approach (i.e. practical and utilizing creative skills). This is has also been argued for in prior work in HCI education [7], where a constructivist ideology was proposed to support learning across disciplines.
- Assessments must have at least a half in half element of both Design and Computing aspects. For example have as much of a Design/Conceptualization phase as a Development/Implementation/Programming phase.
- Encourage group-based assessments allowing students to collaborate with each other and potentially endorse Design and Computing students to work together.
- Employ a relatively open brief, in order to allow students to explore their interests and a wide design space.
- Develop a marking criterion that takes into account the background of the student. One of the elements that were hence incorporated was that the base requirement of the assessments was standardized across the unit (i.e. all students had to design at least three scenarios and implement at least one of them). Consequently, students were then allowed to build upon the base requirements according to their own preferences.
- Build upon the assessments in the tutorials, allowing students to exchange ideas with their peers and their tutors.
- Lecture content was adapted so project ideas were facilitated and mediated. For example special guest lectures were arranged which showcased novel project ideas and upcoming state of the art techniques in HCI.

The freedom that was extended to the students in the project brief also extended to the choice of the tools that they could employ to create solutions. For each project assessment a minimum of three tools were discussed in lectures and tutorials therefore allowing a wide array of possibilities to the students. In addition to allow better integration of both disciplines of Design and Computing facilitation techniques were employed. For example, Interface Design was propagated to Computing Students via software based methodologies (such as wireframing software, for e.g. Balsamiq, Just in Mind Prototyper) and not paper, thereby allowing them to overcome any deficiencies in hand sketching. On the other hand strategies employed to instruct programming to students from non-technical background included script based and graphical programming languages (such as Arduino using Max/MSP), with the ultimate goal of reducing the learning curve. Content taught in lectures was supplemented in the tutorial sessions where students could practice using the tools under the supervision of the tutors. It is worth mentioning this unit was the only HCI unit being offered with no graduate options, therefore course content was generally delivered in breadth providing a flavour of all stages of a typical design process in HCI. The primary assessments for the unit were weekly tutorial exercises and one project that would run across the semester. The project was performed by a group of 2–4 students. Each project was evaluated at 3 checkpoints. These included: (1) a project brief proposal written in the form of a report; (2) low-fidelity prototype details (typically wireframe designs or product sketches) submitted in the form of a written report and (3) hi-fidelity semi-functional prototype showcased as a demo presentation in the last week of the semester in addition to an evaluation plan of their prototype.

## 3   Student Projects

We now discuss the impact of the changes in relation to some example projects. Total enrolment in the unit was more than 300, so we present 4 of the most exemplary projects in this paper.

1. Case Study 1: Design Students. A group of 3 Design students worked on the re-design of a TV remote control for the elderly. The students performed well in the conceptualization phase of the project, where an efficient low fidelity prototype was built using a 3D printer. They incorporated electronics in their prototype for the second phase of their project (see Fig. 1). However they could only implement one feature in their working concept.
2. Case Study 2: Computing Students. A group of 2 computing students created an online shopping website for home furniture. The solution allowed for real time three-dimensional visualization of a certain piece of furniture. Despite the novelty of this feature, the team was let down by aesthetics and layout chosen for their website.
3. Case Study 3: Design and Computing Students in collaboration; focusing on the design of a mobile app. A group comprised of 4 students (3 Computing and 1 Design) created a mobile application for the elderly that allowed the user to translate textual phone messages if they were written in slang (for e.g. acronyms such as lol, brb, etc.). The Design student took care of the layout, drawings and sketches of the application and the computing students implemented the functionality of it. The final solution was an almost market ready application for Android mobile phones.
4. Case Study 4: Design and Computing Students in collaboration; focusing on the design of a tangible artifact. A group of 3 students (2 Design and 1 Computing) took on a unique challenge of redesigning a gun as a gaming controller and providing tactile and real time feedback (see Fig. 1). The Design

**Fig. 1.** Examples of prototypes created by students

students took care of the physical casing and electronics of the prototype and the Computing student implemented the sensor technology inside the controller.

## 4 Conclusion

By reviewing student output in the unit of HCI, a trend seems to appear. Projects that involved both design and computing students collaborating together delivered the most complete, well-executed and well-motivated outcome. Expertise of each student was utilized in full and brought on board, with a complete chance to each student to express him/herself in areas that they were the most comfortable in. Similar findings w.r.t the benefits of collaborative learning in HCI have been reported [4]. In addition the uniqueness of our approach is the open brief adopted for the unit, which resulted in a wide array of projects with students taking the freedom to facilitate their creativity. Nevertheless, future work in continued restructuring of the unit must contemplate how to encourage enhanced cross disciplinary work regardless of, if the students are in cross disciplinary groups or not.

## References

1. Chan, S., Wolfe, R., Fang, X.: Teaching HCI in IS/EC curriculum. In: Americas Conference on Information Systems, pp. 1011–1020 (2002)
2. Ciolfi, L., Cooke, M.: HCI for interaction designers: communicating the bigger picture. In: Inventivity: Teaching Theory, Design and Innovation in HCI, vol. 1, pp. 47–51 (2006)
3. Larsen, L.B., Andersen, S.K., Fink, F.K., Granum, E.: Teaching HCI to engineering students using problem based learning (2009)
4. Lester, C.Y.: Advancing the multidisciplinary nature of human computer interaction in a newly developed undergraduate course. In: Conference on Advances in Computer-Human Interaction, pp. 177–182. IEEE (2008)
5. McCrickard, D.S., Chewar, C.M., Somervell, J.: Design, science, and engineering topics? Teaching HCI with a unified method. SIGCSE Bull. **36**(1), 31–35 (2004)
6. Reimer, Y.J., Douglas, S.A.: Teaching HCI design with the studio approach. Comput. Sci. Educ. **13**(3), 191–205 (2003)
7. Vat, K.H.: Teaching HCI with scenario-based design: the constructivist's synthesis. In: ACM SIGCSE Bulletin, vol. 33, pp. 9–12. ACM (2001)

# Experiencing a Home Energy Management System: Finding Opportunities for Design

Bingxin Ni[2], Abdullah Al Mahmud[1(✉)], and David V. Keyson[2]

[1] School of Design, Swinburne University of Technology,
Melbourne, Australia
Nibingxin1117@gmail.com, aalmahmud@swin.edu.au
[2] Department of Industrial Design, Delft University of Technology,
Delft, The Netherlands
d.v.keyson@tudelft.nl

**Abstract.** This paper reports a study, which examines how people experience a Home Energy Management System (HEM). We conducted a probe study with six families in China for two weeks. From our study, we found that people had difficulty in understanding energy data, which were shown as graphs. Families with teenage children showed more interest in using the Home-Energy Management System. Overall, all the participants were fascinated by the remote monitoring and controlling of the appliances offered by the probe. Based on the findings, opportunities for designing HEMs for the target groups are discussed.

**Keywords:** Smart home control system · Home energy management system · Chinese context · User experience

## 1 Introduction

Home Energy Management Systems (HEMs)/eco-feedback systems are defined as intermediary devices installed at home that can visualize, monitor and/or manage domestic gas and/or electricity consumption [1]. The end-goals of HEMs are to help homeowners to conserve energy, reduce cost of energy bills and improve comfort [3]. It is a fact that residential energy consumption has been increasing each year in China due to the rapid urbanization [1, 2, 4]. There exist a gap between an awareness of energy-conservation and behaviors, because it is difficult for users to link their various activities and develop a coherent, comprehensible, and concise cognitive frame of what energy conservation could mean in one's everyday life [2]. HEMs offer a worthy solution by providing timely feedback of daily energy usage. It is evident that some studies and experiments of implementing HEMS into people's life have been conducted in western countries [1, 7]. Several Chinese companies have already stepped into this field and have started developing solutions. However, it is not known how HEMs can be applied to existing Chinese families, which arouses great curiosity for further exploration.

© IFIP International Federation for Information Processing 2015
J. Abascal et al. (Eds.): INTERACT 2015, Part IV, LNCS 9299, pp. 546–549, 2015.
DOI: 10.1007/978-3-319-22723-8_58

## 2    Experiencing the Plugwise HEMS Package

To discover how people would feel using a home energy management system, user experiments were conducted in Chengdu, China. We used the Plugwise package [6] to assist participants to monitor in-home energy usage and take control of it. The Plugwise package contains four basic components such as one or more Circles, Circle+, USB Stick and Source Home Software. The Circle is plugged in between an appliance and the socket. It measures energy consumption of the connected appliances and can switch it on and off, and send the measured energy consumption data to the Plugwise software via Zigbee wireless network. The Circle+ has the same functionalities as a Circle, but also serves as the network coordinator to control and organize the network. The USB Stick is the connection between the Plugwise Source Home Software, the installed plugs (Circles) and other Plugwise products. After being connected to the USB port of the computer, the Stick receives data from and transmits commands to the installed Plugwise modules. Source Home is the Plugwise software for visualizing energy data and controlling appliances. Ten upper-middle class families responded to volunteer the experiments. However, four families did not install the Plugwise program (three families felt uninterested and bothered to install it, and one family was leaving for a vacation and found no time to experience the Plugwise package). Hence, in total, six families used the Plugwise package for two weeks.

### 2.1   Procedure

On the first day, the Plugwise PC program was installed by the first author. Later on, participants were asked to choose several household appliances to be connected with the Circles to measure electricity consumption (see Fig. 1). After the program was ready and all the hardware were well connected, the interface was shown to the participants with an explanation of each item. Then sensitizing cards were left to participants to fill in. People were asked to first explore the program and then answer a few questions, which would reflect their experience with the Plugwise system. Finally, they needed to fill out the task cards after each time they checked energy usage data. On the day when the Plugwise package was picked up after the study period, the participants completed an evaluation form and participated in short interview sessions. The sensitizing card

**Fig. 1.** Circle+ is connected to a television; circles is connected to a desktop and to a refrigerator (left to right)

consists of three parts: (1) collect first time user experience, (2) task card to understand why participant would like to use the probe, what kind of data they are concerned about and what is their emotion, and (3) an evaluation form, to get an overall opinion of the system. The interview data were analysed thematically.

## 2.2 Results

Test participants cared more about high-energy consumption appliances. They always chose what they thought were high energy consuming, such as television, water kettle, laptop and refrigerator. However, they did not choose air conditioners because it was not the right time to use them. They appreciated that it was easy to use the Plugwise hardware but some participants thought it was troublesome to install the plugs for the first time. Furthermore, they felt it was quite like magic that with just a small device, they could track energy consumption of their household products in a simple way. However, since it was only a test for a shorter period, participants did not feel a strong involvement with the system.

Families with teenage children showed more interest in HEMs. From the sensitizing booklet, some feedback were received, such as when asked what emotional feeling they might have when they checked energy information on the Plugwise dashboard. Participants reported that it was interesting to receive energy feedback. Participants had questions about energy consumption such as how much electricity it would consume if the computer was on for the whole night? How much electricity it would consume for one light and how much they could save? These detailed information were present however, participants did not know how to switch between different views in the Plugwise dashboard.

The energy feedback data were understandable, but they could not evoke a sense of caring of the participants because the data were found meaningless to them. Two of the participants mentioned that the reasons for causing the changes were not clear to them, which made them feel frustrated after seeing the graphs. Participants were not interested in seeing the numbers and information provided on the interface. They reported that the data in kWh and graphs are generally understandable but quite meaningless to them. "I know what this means, but I need energy forecast. Since I still have to consume this amount even I know its energy usage, I am not sure this system will make a difference on my family." (One person from family #5). "Those data are not hard to understand, but according to my knowledge, I cannot understand why the curve is shaped like this? I want to know the reason caused the changing which I cannot find in the program." (One person from family #1).

Participants were very interested in the turn on/off the appliance function provided by the Plugwise HEM package. Participants were quite surprised by remote control function when it was shown to them and later when they interacted with it. One participant even asked to set a schedule for their television because sometimes they fell asleep and left the TV on for a whole night.

## 3    Discussion and Design Implications

For some families, the program could only be installed on a desktop computer, which they used very often. Hence, it was not convenient to check the energy data now and then, which was the limitation of the Plugwise HEMS package. They treated the Plugwise system as a test rather than their own property, so they did not pay much attention and did not truly experience it, either. At this phase, by using the system, it is important to help users to cultivate their awareness of in-home energy management. Making energy more transparent to people proved to be a key insight for changing consumers' attitude and behaviour towards saving energy [5, 7]. Although it is argued that money is not a good stimulus to rise people's attention in the long run, it is still of great necessity in the early development phase when people start to experience any HEMS. Another remarkable finding was that participants were more attracted to the remote control of household appliances rather than the home energy management system. The reason was that the remote controlling of appliances at home provided them direct advantages when compared with the home energy management system. This also verifies that if users could be offered some benefits, they could pay more attention to HEMS. Besides cost-effectiveness it is an influential aspect to consider when designing HEMs for the target group. From the study, it has been revealed that the target groups are positive to accept the notion of controlling home appliances remotely, which can be considered part of HEMs. Therefore, it is assumed that integrating HEMS with smart home control system could be a good idea for the target group. Another key design issue is the visualization of the energy data, which should be more meaningful to the users and help users to get engaged. Though our study period was quite short and the Plugwise package had several limitations, it was helpful to gather valuable feedback, which provided directions for designing an adapted Home Energy Management System (HEMS) for the target group.

## References

1. Van Dam, S.S., Bakker, C.A., Van Hal, J.D.M.: Home energy monitors: impact over the medium-term. Build. Res. Inf. **38**(5), 458–469 (2010)
2. Fischer, C.: Feedback on household electricity consumption: a tool for saving energy? Energ. Effi. **1**, 79–104 (2008)
3. Wei, Y.-M., Liu, L.-C., et al.: The impact of lifestyle on energy use and $CO_2$ emission: an empirical analysis of China's residents. Energy Policy **35**, 247–257 (2007)
4. LaMarche, J., Cheney, L., Christian, S., Roth, K.: Home Energy Management Products and Trends. Fraunhofer Center for Sustainable Energy Systems, Cambridge, MA (2011)
5. Darby, S.: The Effectiveness of Feedback on Energy Consumption. A Review for DEFRA of the Literature on Metering. Environmental Change Institute, Oxford (2006)
6. Plugwise. https://www.plugwise.com
7. Petkov, P., Goswami, S., Köbler, F., Krcmar, H.: Personalised eco-feedback as a design technique for motivating energy saving behaviour at home. In: NordiCHI 2012, pp. 587–596 (2012)

# Eye Strain from Switching Focus in Optical See-Through Displays

Jaeun Yu and Gerard J. Kim[✉]

Digital Experience Laboratory, Korea University, Seoul, Korea
{yujaaa,gjkim}@korea.ac.kr

**Abstract.** The optical see-through (OST) display is one of the key enabling devices for augmented reality. Despite the latest craze such as with the Google Glass, there are still many ergonomic problems associated with the OST displays. One of the already well known such problem is the "refocusing" problem, in which the user has to switch one's focus between the distant real world and see-through display up front. Such refocusing, for one, is bound to cause significant strain and fatigue to the eyes. However, there are not many studies, nor guidelines devoted to this issue. In this preliminary work, we ran experiments to measure the degree for eye strain and its pattern at different refocusing distances and durations (or number of focused targets). The findings should serve as one guideline in designing OST glass based interaction and applications.

**Keywords:** Optical see-through displays · Eye strain/fatigue · Usability · Augmented reality · Focus

## 1 Introduction

The continued innovations and advances in computer vision, mobile/cloud computing and portable display devices have brought about a renewed interest in augmented reality (AR) as a prominent information visualization and interaction medium. In particular, since the recent introduction of the Google Glass [1], optical see-through (OST) displays are becoming more compact and fashionably designed, and thereby getting accepted to the mass users. Yet, there are some concerns as well [2, 3], and one such is the eye fatigue and even the potential to hurt the eye as the user has to make conscious effort to focus on the tiny display in the upper right corner of the glass (as in the case of Google Glass). More specifically, the use of OST displays unavoidably entails the frequent switch between looking into the real world and refocusing on the small display up front (or at distance to the virtual image plane).

While this refocusing problem (and fatigue) is unavoidable, its detailed ergonomic effects need to be studied and known to reflect it into the interaction design involving the use of OST displays. However, aside from general literatures on various factors that can cause different types of eye fatigue, not many studies have been made in the context of this AR specific problem. With such motivation, we ran experiments to measure the level of fatigue caused by the frequent refocusing between real and virtual objects, and its relation to the focusing duration.

© IFIP International Federation for Information Processing 2015
J. Abascal et al. (Eds.): INTERACT 2015, Part IV, LNCS 9299, pp. 550–554, 2015.
DOI: 10.1007/978-3-319-22723-8_59

## 2  Related Work

Usability problems with OST displays are not new, e.g. due to its cost, weight, size, image quality and lowered brightness, distorted depth perception, mismatch in the resolution of the augmentation with that of the real world imagery, registration and calibration errors, incomplete masking by the augmentation, etc. [4, 5]. The recent introduction of Google Glass made quite a stir with its sleek and light-weight design, and has much improved the wearability aspect, however, many ergonomic problems still remain. While there have been almost no formal studies on the Google Glass itself, there have been few media reports of the potential eye strain problem [2, 3]. Huckauf et al. compared the visual search and focus switching tasks on between computer screens and OST displays, and confirmed the lowered performance on the OST displays. Furthermore, they also found that users tended to misjudge the target object depth, namely closer than the actual [6].

## 3  Experiment 1: Fatigue Caused at Different Refocusing Lengths

Obviously, the fatigue from the refocusing task will be closely related and proportional to, among others, the refocusing distance. In this study, we are interested in the changing pattern of the fatigue level, e.g. whether it is approximately linear, exponential, saturating (e.g. log), step-like form and whether it is symmetric with respect to some nominal comfortable focusing distance. Based on the findings, we might limit the objects targeted for augmentation only to be within some nominal range of distance to minimize the eye strain.

Five paid subjects, 3 men and 2 women with a mean age of 23, participated in the experiment. An experiment with one-factor (4 different refocusing distances) within-subject with repeated measures was conducted. The task was to focus at an object in the real world and refocus to information displayed on the Google Glass in which the virtual image plane is formed at about 2.4 m away from the eyes. The objects were placed at 6 m, 3 m, 1 m and 30 cm from the user making the refocusing distances, 3.6 m, 0.6 m, 1.4 m and 2.1 m, respectively. The user had to state whether the object in the real world and the information displayed on the glass matched or not (see Fig. 1).

The fatigue level was measured indirectly by measuring the response time. (i.e. stating whether the information in the display matched or not) and through a survey. The task was repeated over four five-minute blocks after which a fatigue survey was completed. The level of eye fatigue can be measured in many ways, ideally through optometric measurements, physiological signals (e.g. EMG of eye muscles) or using eye tracking devices. However it is generally difficult to use such apparatus because the glass has to be worn. Instead eye strain can be indirectly assessed by other indicators such as degradation in task performance, immediate symptoms such as dryness or over-blinking, and after effects such as headaches and neck [7].

**Fig. 1.** The refocusing task using the Google Glass and measuring the associated fatigue level: (a) Experiment 1 (left), (b) Experiment 2.

Figures 2 shows the average response time (for total of successive 200 trials) and answers to the survey (about the perceived fatigue and eye strain). As expected, the fatigue level was proportional to the refocusing length, where the least amount of fatigue was felt at the refocusing distance of 0.6 m, and the most at 3.6 m. The fatigue levels actually slightly dropped after 5∼6 min but then rose sharply and steadily increased afterwards. No other clear trend of particular changing patterns, other than direct proportionality, was detected.

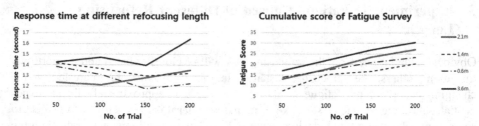

**Fig. 2.** Average response time (for total of successive 200 trials) and cumulative score of the fatigue survey about the perceived fatigue and eye strain.

## 4   Experiment 2: Refocusing Frequency vs. Duration

Through the first experiment, we were merely able to confirm an obvious fact that the eye fatigue and eye strain increased according to the extended refocusing distance. In the second experiment, we fixed the refocusing distance and varied the information amount at which to focus, namely one, three and five objects laid out vertically (similarly to the typical Google Glass menu). This way, we can compare the level of fatigue between when displaying little information but having to refocus several times vs. displaying more information at a time and focusing longer on them and having to refocus a less number of times.

Again 5 paid subjects, 3 men and 2 women with a mean age of 23, participated in the experiment. Again the experiment with one-factor (3 different information amounts) within-subject with repeated measures was conducted. In the three treatments (presented in a balanced order), the user had to look at one, three and five real world objects and placed at 2.4 m, refocus to the glass display and report if the objects matched to those in the glass display (see Fig. 1). The user was given 20 min and the user performance was recorded (i.e. how many refocusing tasks could be accomplished and how much pieces of visual information could be processed).

Figure 3 illustrates the results and among the three treatments, the best performance (per effort/fatigue) was achieved by managing the refocusing and focusing duration with a block of three objects (ANOVA, $F(2, 72) = 14.18$, Tukey tests with p-values $< 0.03$). The results shows the refocusing distance and amount of information displayed need to be carefully modulated to improve general usability of OST displays.

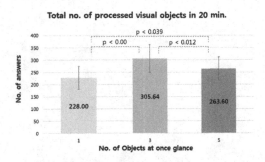

**Fig. 3.** Number of tasks accomplished (or amount of visual information processed) in unit time. Best performance per effort/fatigue was obtained with the block of three objects.

## 5   Conclusion and Future Work

In this poster, we have conducted pilot experiments assessing the nature of eye strain and fatigue as related to the refocusing distance and how it might relate to the amount of visual information that need to be focused at one time and processed. The findings are still only preliminary as it requires more subjects and experimental conditions to derive more definite conclusions. The contribution lies in taking the first step toward quantifying ergonomic problems of OST displays in the context of AR, and showing directions for the future full scale experiments.

**Acknowledgements.** This work (Grants No.C0239066) was supported by Business for Academic-industrial Cooperative establishments funded Korea Small and Medium Business Administration in 2014.

## References

1. Google, Inc., Google Glass. http://www.google.com/glass
2. Horn, L.: Is Google Glass Bad for Your Eyes? http://gizmodo.com/is-google-glass-bad-for-your-eyes-484466332
3. Ackerman, E.: Could Google glass hurt your eyes? A harvard vision scientist and project glass advisor responds. http://www.forbes.com/
4. Azuma, R.T.: A survey of augmented reality. Presence **6**(4), 355–385 (1997)
5. Rolland, J.P., Fuchs, H.: Optical versus video see-through head-mounted displays in medical visualization. Presence **9**(3), 287–309 (2000)

6. Huckauf, A., Urbina, M., Gruber, J., Bockerlmann, I., Doil, F., Schega, L., Tumler, J., Mechek, R.: Perceptual issues in optical-see-through displays. In: 7th Symposium on Applied Perception in Graphics and Visualization, pp. 41–48. ACM (2010)
7. Sheedy, J.: Visual fatigue in near vision: visual fatigue. In: Points de Vue 70th issue, pp. 4–7. Essilor International (2014)

# First Impression Matters: Exploring the Mediating Effect of Previous Experience on the Perception of Beauty and Usability

Suleman Shahid[1] and Omar Mubin[2(✉)]

[1] Tilburg Center for Cognition and Communication, Tilburg University,
Tilburg, The Netherlands
s.shahid@uvt.nl
[2] University of Western Sydney, Sydney, Australia
o.mubin@uws.edu.au

**Abstract.** This study investigated how the previous experience of a product possibly mediates the effect of beauty on usability. In an experiment 32 individuals, half with and half without experience, tested two different, but equally usable espresso machines. The results showed that previous experience had a considerable influence on the effect of beauty on usability.

**Keywords:** Usability · Beauty · Experience

## 1 Introduction

In the past decade the effect of beauty on perceived usability has been thoroughly researched with contradicting results [1]. Recent research on user experience has clearly shown that usability does not stand on its own and is just one attribute in the whole user experience of a product [2]. Hassenzhal's model [3] assumes that a product has certain features that are chosen by a designer to convey a certain intended product 'character'. When users come in contact with a product they first create a personal product character, this is based on their initial expectations and the products functions. On some occasions, users tend to infer attributes, features about their experiences with products. Beauty is an important starting point of the inference processes because it is one of the most immediately available attributes when judging a product [4]. Prior research has shown that that previous experience of the product could possibly mediate the effect of beauty on usability. A study by Lindgaard et al. [5] tried to further examine and clarify the strength and implications of the correlation between beauty and usability. The study however did not show any results of perceived beauty on usability. A suggestion was made that previous experience might be the cause of the lack of correlation between beauty and usability. If a user has no experience with a product, the goodness or usability of a product will be inferred from how beautiful it looks. Therefore the main focus of our research is centered around the question if previous experience mediates the effect of beauty on usability.

© IFIP International Federation for Information Processing 2015
J. Abascal et al. (Eds.): INTERACT 2015, Part IV, LNCS 9299, pp. 555–558, 2015.
DOI: 10.1007/978-3-319-22723-8_60

## 2    Method

A total of 32 users participated in this study. 16 participants were active users of automatic espresso machines daily and 16 participants had never used an espresso machine before. All participants were regular coffee drinkers and drank coffee once a day. To measure the previous experience the participants were asked what different ways they had used to make coffee. For choosing one more beautiful and one less beautiful but equally usable machines, we ran two pre-tests. In the pre-test for beauty four espresso machines were presented in an online survey (Fig. 1), two brand x (Siemens) espresso machines and two brand y (Saeco) espresso machines. 60 participants participated in the survey where they judged four machines for their beauty, 1 being very beautiful and 7 being very ugly (see Fig. 1 for results). In order to test the usability of both espresso machines another pre-test was conducted with 10 people who had no previous experience with such espresso machines. We choose two SAECO machines from the same brand because these two machines were significantly different (beautiful vs. ugly) from each other. Furthermore, user interfaces of both machines were exactly the same. By choosing the same brand, we also ensured that taste of the coffee would be the same (because the coffee making process of both machines was same). Each participant had to perform five tasks using both machines (the primary task was to make a coffee). After these tasks they were handed a usability questionnaire (1 for very usable and 7 for unusable), one after each machine and one at the end of the pre-tests. All participants agreed that both machines were equally easy to use and it was mentioned multiple times that the interfaces were 'exactly the same'.

**Fig. 1.**  The coffee machines used in the pre-test A = Saeco Incanto (Avg. beauty: 4.61, Avg. Usability = 2.00) Deluxe, B = Siemens 1 (Avg. beauty = 2.75), C = Saeco Royal Proferssional (Avg. beauty: 3.09, Avg. usability = 2.20) and D = Siemens 2 (Avg. beauty: 2.91)

## 3    Main Experiment

The 32 participants were asked to perform five tasks on each espresso machine after which they had to make a cup of coffee and taste it. The participants were divided into four groups, the first group was a group with experience and started with the beautiful espresso machine, the second group was a group with experience and started with the less beautiful espresso machine. The third group was a group without previous experience and started with the beautiful espresso machine, the fourth group was again a group without experience and started with the less beautiful espresso machine. The questionnaires were taken from an earlier experiment [5] about the effects of beauty on usability and modified with questions about previous experience with espresso machines. The questionnaires inquired about the taste of the coffee, the previous experience with the espresso machines, the usability of the espresso machines, the beauty of the espresso machines and the willingness to purchase the espresso machines. In order to measure the usability two questions about usability were asked, the first enquired about the ease of use (effectiveness and efficiency) and the second enquired about the satisfaction (pleasing to use). The first and second questionnaire were identical (one for each machine) and were given to the participants after they finished their coffee.

After performing 5 tasks and making a coffee participants were lead back into the main room where they were given time to drink their coffee. Once the participant had drunk the coffee they were asked to fill in questionnaire. They were given a neutralizer, in order to neutralize their taste. The procedure with the first espresso machine was repeated with the second espresso machine. This second machine was placed in a different room than the last espresso machine to make sure they would not see both of them together. While both machines used the same kind of coffee, the participants were asked to rate the coffee they just tasted (1 for very tasty and 5 for not tasty at all).

## 4 Results

There was no significant effect of order of the espresso machines for both groups and therefore we combined the results. The results of the t-tests (with Bonferroni correction) show that both the group with previous experience, $t(15) = 9.27$, $p < .05$, and the group without previous experience, $t(15) = 8.58$, $p < .05$, judged the beautiful espresso machine to be more beautiful than the less beautiful espresso machine. The results of the t-test showed that the group with previous experience did not perceive the usability of both machines to be different from each other, $t(15) = 1.95$, $p > .05$. However the group without previous experience judged the two machines to be different in usability $t(15) = 4.22$, $p < .01$. The comparison results show that the group without previous experience judged the beautiful espresso machine also to be the most usable espresso machine, $t(15) = 6.54$, $p < .01$. For the group without previous experience there is also a strong positive correlation between the machine they judged to be the most beautiful and the machine they judged to be the most usable $r = .734$, $n = 16$, $p < .01$. All results support the claim that previous experience has an effect on the way beauty affects the usability of a machine. Finally the results show that while the group with previous experience judged the taste of the coffee to be the same, $t(15) = .49$, $p = .63$, the group without previous experience judged the taste of the coffee made with the more beautiful espresso machine to be better (mean taste of beautiful machine = 1.87, mean taste of less beautiful machine = 2.62, $t(15) = 3.50$, $p < .05$.

## 5 Conclusion and Discussion

The results showed that previous experience mediated and even completely negated the effect beauty has on perceived usability. The group without previous experience judged the beautiful espresso machine to be more usable than the less beautiful espresso machine. The beautiful espresso machine has been found more beautiful than the less beautiful espresso machine by all participants of the experiment. Our results also showed that the group with previous experience did not judge the usability of both machines to be different, while they did judge the beautiful espresso machine to be more beautiful than the less beautiful espresso machine. These findings are in line with previous research [4, 6]. Our current research supports the claim that beauty has a direct effect on pragmatic quality, at least for individuals without previous experience with the product. This is contrary to prior work [3], where no strong direct correlation between beauty and usability was found. While there is a direct correlation between beauty and usability, a machine, which is perceived to be 'beautiful', is not necessarily usable. The less beautiful espresso machine was also in no way judged to be unusable, it was only judged to be less usable than it's beautiful counterpart. While Hassenzahl and Monk [4] mention that a brief amount of previous experience is enough to mediate or negate the effect of beauty on usability, this research speculates that a longer 'hands-on' experience is possibly needed before it negates the effect of beauty on usability. The focus of future research could be to control the amount of previous experience of users to make sure variances in experience and expertise do not affect the results obtained.

## References

1. De Angeli, A., Sutcliffe, A., Hartmann, J.: Interaction, usability and aesthetics: what influences users' preferences? In: Proceedings of the 6th ACM Conference on Designing interactive Systems (DIS 2006), pp. 271–280 (2006)
2. Hassenzahl, M.: The interplay of beauty, goodness and usability in interactive products. Hum. Comput. Interact. 19, 319–349 (2004)
3. Hassenzahl, M.: Aesthetics in interactive products: correlates and consequences of beauty. In: Schifferstein, H.N.J., Hekkert, P. (eds.) Product Experience. Elsevier, San Diego (2008)
4. Hassenzahl, M., Monk, A.: The inference of perceived usability from beauty. Hum. Comput. Interact. 25(3), 235–260 (2010)
5. Lindgaard, G., Fernandes, G., Dudek, C., Brown, J.: Attention web designers: you have 50 milliseconds to make a good first impression. Behav. Inf. Technol. 25, 115–126 (2006)
6. Hartmann, J., Sutcliffe, A., De Angeli, A.: Investigating attractiveness in web user interfaces. In: Proceedings of the CHI 2007 Conference on Human Factors in Computing Systems. ACM, New York (2007)

# Informing Costumers via Interactive Shelves

Peter Rogelj[✉]

University of Primorska, 6000 Koper, Slovenia
peter.rogelj@upr.si

**Abstract.** Consumers often need additional information to decide which products would best suit their needs. This information is in practice limited due to limited space, limits of human attention, large number of products, etc. On the other hand, any approach to provide any kind of information to the customer is effective only if it does not require excessive user involvement. As a solution to offer only relevant information with minimal customer engagement we propose our vision of interactive shelves. The general idea is to observe the customer interaction with the products in order to recognize and display relevant information. At the moment the observation of interaction is achieved by using passive infrared sensors (PIR) and ultrasound distance measuring sensors (US) to detect user grabbing or pointing to products. We are planning to enhance the current system with camera and gaze detection in the future.

**Keywords:** Interest recognition · Shopping shelves · Sensor integration

## 1 Introduction

In a process of selecting/buying products, customers need to take several decisions based on the information available. Traditionally they get support from shop assistants, which can advise them and provide additional information. Nevertheless, it is important that customers are able to get certain information of the products even without such assistance. One way of providing information is by writing it on declaration labels of products, which are usually limited due to space constraints. In addition, the process of informing is affected by the large number of products available and human ability to extract the required information. All these adds to the amount of effort required for the costumer to extract relevant information and reading product declarations often turns out to be too complex to be effective.

The described limitations can be solved with interactive shelves that would recognise costumers' information needs with minimal customer engagement. As a good shop assistant, the interactive shelves would need to provide only that much information the customers can bear and only the information that is relevant for the specific customer at the specific point in time. Information selection must be thus based on customer interaction with the environment. Our solution to recognise costumers' interaction include the detection of grabbed or pointed products as well as detection of their gaze.

J. Abascal et al. (Eds.): INTERACT 2015, Part IV, LNCS 9299, pp. 559–562, 2015.
DOI: 10.1007/978-3-319-22723-8_61

## 2 System Description

Interactive shelves offer customers additional information on display(s) mounted in the vicinity of the products, usually above or on the side of the shelves. The shelves are equipped with sensors that detect presence and position of customer hands when reaching towards the products. The combination of passive infrared sensors (PIR) used for presence detection and ultrasonic distance sensors for accurate hand position detection is proposed. The information of hand location is used to recognize customer's information requirements. We see additional possibilities of customer interest detection using camera(s) and gaze detection, omitting the need of any kind of active customer involvement. A possible configuration of shelves equipped with display and sensors is illustrated in Fig. 1. In practice, all the sensors are small and hidden. The detected interest/information requirements are used to select predefined information pages to be displayed on display(s). In the initial implementation each product is explained with one information page displayed at the time of detected customer attention to the product. In addition, product observation history could also be used to make recommendations of related products. Each information page may consist of any type of information, e.g., text, images, videos or their combination.

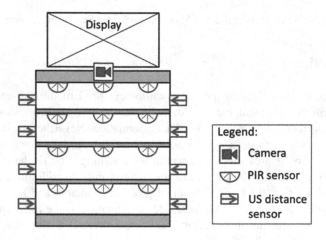

**Fig. 1.** A typical sensor configuration of interactive shelves. In practice, all the sensors are small and hidden to the customers.

## 3 System Design and Implementation

One of the primary goals of the system design was to make it modular, such that additional advanced functionality can be added to the initial basic functionality. Thus, the system is designed to be easy to upgrade and also easy to understand. The system architecture, consisting of five layers and a data storage, is illustrated in Fig. 2.

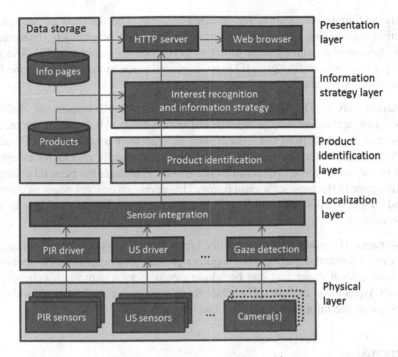

**Fig. 2.** Interactive shelves system architecture.

**Physical Layer.** Physical layer consists of hardware sensors. In our implementation they are all connected to the main processing unit, the Raspberry PI version 2. Due to relatively large number of PIR and US sensors they cannot all be directly connected to the GPIO port such that I2C IO extensions (using integrated circuit MCP23017) are planned. For future upgrades additional sensors are possible, e.g., camera(s) for gaze detection [1].

**Localization Layer.** It is used to process the signals from the sensors in order to obtain information of the location of interest, i.e., in the basic implementation the coordinates of detected customer hands reaching towards the shelves. This layer requires additional information of sensor geometric configuration, which depends on actual shelves geometry. For a typical sensor configuration see Fig. 1. Information from all the sensors is integrated into a single vector of interest location.

**Product Identification Layer.** It serves to identify which product is in focus of customer interest. It requires information of product locations on the shelves, which it gets from the system data storage. Typically the closest products are selected.

**Information Strategy Layer.** It is used to define a strategy of displaying additional product information on display(s). Its implementation is trivial for the basic functionality where only one page of additional information is planned for each item. Its advanced version may consist of two stages, i.e., interest recognition obtained from metadata of few latest products and definition of a sequence of information pages providing additional information for detected interest. The decision of sequence of information pages shall be defined according to metadata of products, interests and available information pages, similar as it was developed for e-shopping [2]. The result of this layer is an information page ID to be displayed at the moment (or multiple IDs if multiple displays are used).

**Presentation Layer.** The additional information regarding products on shelves is displayed using a standard web browser in full screen mode. All the pages are prepared in advance and passed from the system data storage over a standard HTTP server. A simple Javascript function running in a browser periodically checks for changes of page ID by calling a simple PHP script on the server. Whenever the page ID changes, it reloads the page in the browser's main frame. This approach enables pages to consist of any kind of information, not only static text and images, but also videos or other dynamic content.

**Data Storage.** There are two main entity types stored in system data storage, i.e., products and information pages. They together present all the information specific for the interactive shell usage and can be administered from a dedicated web interface. Both entity types have attributes that relate them with customers' interests and enable their linkage in the information strategy layer.

## 4   Conclusion

The interactive shelves are a step towards improved customer experience. The actual system is currently in the implementation stage. In addition to technical implementation issues explained here, other questions need to be considered before using such technology in practice. For example, the specifics of customer psychology and marketing issues shall be clarified in order to find the best positioning of displays, temporal specifics of interest recognition and sequence of information pages, recommend principles of product ordering, and to test different design issues of information pages. The concept could be extended to general information points, which could in addition to shelves have a form of interactive boards, posters or maps. As such the concept has a wide usage not limited to product shopping but also to tourism and services.

## References

1. Dostal, J., Hinrichs, U., Kristensson, P.O., Quigley, A.: SpiderEyes: designing attention- and proximity-aware collaborative interfaces for wall-sized displays. In: Proceedings of the IUI 2014
2. Kwon, O.B.: "I know what you need to buy": context-aware multimedia-based recommendation system. Expert Syst. Appl. **25**, 387–400 (2003)

# Intelligent Ankle-Foot Orthosis by Energy Regeneration for Controllable Damping During Gait in Real Time

Kyoko Shibata[1(✉)], Yoshio Inoue[1(✉)], and Hironobu Satoh[2]

[1] Kochi University of Technology, Tosayamada, Kami, Kochi, Japan
{shibata.kyoko, inoue.yoshio}@kochi-tech.ac.jp
[2] National Institute of Technology, Kochi College, Monobeotsu 200-1,
Nangoku, Kochi, Japan
satoh@ee.kochi-ct.ac.jp

**Abstract.** Many hemiplegia patients use the ankle-foot orthosis (AFO) to prevent foot-drop when they walk. However, it is difficult to walk smoothly because conventional AFOs have high rigidity. In order to support natural gait of hemiplegias, in this study, a technique to regenerate energy is applied, and a new self-powered semi-active AFO combining a DC motor and a step-up chopper circuit is developed. In this method, it is possible to drive a long time safely and the damping on an ankle joint can be controlled. From gait experiments, this study show that developed AFO can be rotated the ankle joint smoothly, be charged battery by regenerating energy loss during a gait, and prevent foot-drop. Hence developed AFO can be expected to have high gait improvement effect than the conventional type. Furthermore, developed AFO shows high electricity recovery (86.5 %).

**Keywords:** Medical and welfare assistance · Ankle-foot orthosis · Semi-active damper · Energy regeneration

## 1 Introduction

In natural normal gait, as shown in Fig. 1, with the appropriate braking force generated by working dorsal and planter flexors alternately, the rotation of the ankle joint changes. In view of energy, it is applied during toe-off timing, and it is consumed during other timing because the braking force is required. On the other hand, in the swing phase, hemiplegic patients cannot be taken the clearance between the foot and the ground (foot-drop), and be leading to stumble and fall, because they are difficult to generate a braking force by muscular weakness, etc. Therefore, conventionally, many hemiplegic patients mount ankle-foot orthosis (AFO) which are possible to suppress the movement by a fixed ankle joint. This braking force of plantar flexion is compensated, so foot-drop can be prevented. The use of conventional AFO is effective to improve their gait. These are clinically well known. However, since conventional AFOs have large rigidity, cannot be freely rotated ankle, appropriate braking force is not generated, in other words, the patient performs an unnatural and high energy consumption gait. This causes hyperextension of the knee joint during heel ground.

© IFIP International Federation for Information Processing 2015
J. Abascal et al. (Eds.): INTERACT 2015, Part IV, LNCS 9299, pp. 563–568, 2015.
DOI: 10.1007/978-3-319-22723-8_62

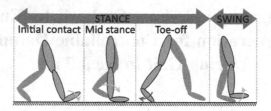

**Fig. 1.** Normal gait

So, because hemiplegic gait differ significantly from healthy gait, even using conventional AFO, rehabilitation effect cannot be obtained to reacquire a smooth gait.

Here, if an AFO that is intelligent that can variably control the resistance (damping) of the ankle joint according to the gait state, it is considered that the patient's gait motion becomes smoother, and more so that continue to use to lead to the restoration of gait function by learning the natural gait. However, when the function of the orthosis becomes higher, secure energy source is required. Therefore the increase in weight and size and the restriction of use time or space become new problems. For AFO with a variable damping ankle, so far, the orthosis with a passive non-linear hydraulic damper [1], semi-active orthosis by MR fluid [2], active orthosis by a servo motor [3], etc. are commercialized or studied. In these, effect of gait improvement have been reported, however, it is difficult to be satisfied both to ensure the natural gait and energy sources.

For these problems, in this study, new AFO system (iAFO) is developed by the semi-active damper using the DC motor and the energy regeneration with the step-up chopper circuit. It can be controlled the damping of rotated ankle joint depending on the gait state, and driven a long time. This iAFO allows for active rehabilitation of continuous long-term. A single iAFO can be applied for of course rehabilitation at hospital, home rehabilitation (Fig. 2) and life support. In Fig. 2, time-series data of the ankle joint angle are transmitted in real time to the server from the controller including iAFO. This data can be monitored to doctors or physical therapists in a hospital, and patient can be instructed in remote by them. Also, if necessary, it can be derived that the patient gait becomes more natural gait by automatic adjusting the strength of the controllable damping by real time remote feedback. Since this is become self-training, it is considered that effect of gait functional recovery is large. Further doctors or patients can check the progress of the recovery of gait ability at any time with cloud service.

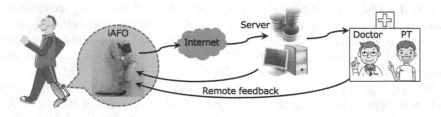

**Fig. 2.** Overview of remote feedback system including iAFO

In this report, first, the overview of iAFO is described. Then, from gait experiments using iAFO, the results of investigation is shown about the damping variable control, charging of a battery, gait improvement, and the power recovery ratio.

## 2  Basic Characteristics of the Prototype

In this study, the DC motor and the set-up chopper circuit are combined, whereby rotation damping is controllable and energy is regenerated.

The prototype iAFO is shown in Fig. 3. The controller which is consisted of the microcomputer and the set-up chopper circuit [4] is attached to the plastic AFO with an ankle joint can be rotated freely. The DC motor is rotated through links and gear (159:1) depending on the motion of the ankle joint. The gait state (Fig. 1) is determined by the output of the two pressure sensors attached to the foot, and the rotation damping ankle is controlled. Specifically, the damping magnitude is smaller in order to soften the movement of the ankle in the stance phase, and is larger in order to restrict the movement of the ankle in the swing phase. Depending on the gait state, ON circuit without battery and OFF including battery of the set-up chopper circuit is switched at high frequency by the controller. The average current per unit time flowing through the DC motor by controlling duty ratio of the PWM control is changed, therefore, the appropriate braking torque is generated. That is, it is possible to obtain the semi-active damping for plantar flexion or dorsiflexion. At this time, the energy due to the rotation of the DC motor is converted into electrical energy, it is charged in the battery by the step-up chopper circuit, and the driving force required for the control is obtained. The total weight of iAFO including the battery is 1.110 kg.

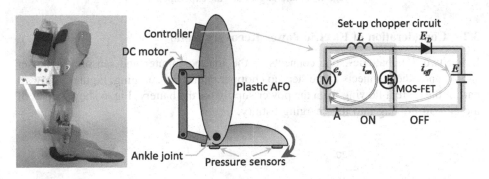

**Fig. 3.**  iAFO

## 3  Continuous Gait Experiments

### 3.1  Consideration of Gait Improvement

A healthy subject is wearing iAFO on his right leg, and imitates a hemiplegic gait. He is continuously gait at a velocity of 3 km/h using a treadmill. In this experiment, duty ratio is set to 0.4 to slightly soften the rotation damping of the ankle joint at the initial contact, 0.1 to soften at the mid-stance or 0.9 for tightly at the toe-off timing and swing phase.

Figure 4 is time history of the ankle angle per one gait cycle when (1) wearing the conventional AFO, (2) wearing iAFO, (3) normal gait (bare foot).

At results, since it is not open large ankle angles when fitted either AFOs, it can be seen that it is possible to prevent foot-drop. Also, because the ankle of iAFO can move freely, the range of ankle angle change of iAFO is larger than conventional AFO. In other words, it is considered that gait difficulty due to the rigidity of AFO has been improved by the proposed method. In addition, gait time is longer, that is, gait improvement is shown since the step length is increased.

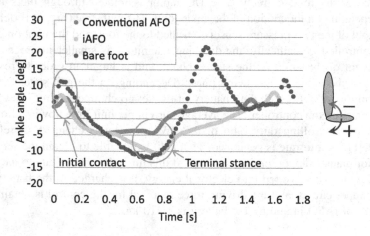

**Fig. 4.** Ankle angles at gait experiments

### 3.2    Consideration of Electric Power Recovery Ratio

Using two 5 V batteries, one connects to the microcomputer and sensors for power supply and other connects to the step-up chopper circuit for charging. Figure 5 shows a part of the current flowing from the power supply for the battery, Fig. 6 shows a part of the current flowing into the charging battery.

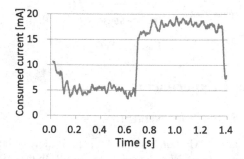

**Fig. 5.** Consumed current (One gait cycle)

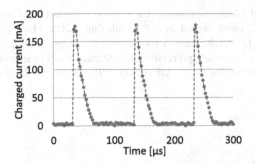

**Fig. 6.** Charged current

In this paper, power recovery ratio is defined the percentage of charging power to the power consumption. By an average value of five measurements, power consumption is 57.36 mW, charging power is 49.60 mW. Therefore the power recovery ratio in this gait is 86.5 %.

## 4  Conclusion

In this study, it is proposed to assist a hemiplegic gait using the AFO with the DC motor and the set-up chopper circuit. Developed iAFO can be controlled to the semi-active damping of ankle joint depending on the gait state. At the same time, iAFO is capable of driving long time using by regenerated energy that is absorbed by the ankle joint motion into the small battery.

In this paper, prototype iAFO are produced, and gait experiments with healthy person are performed using iAFO. As a result, it is confirmed that it is possible to charge the battery, it is possible to prevent foot-drop, further, it is possible to change the ankle joint smoothly compared to the conventional AFO, and the power recovery is high ratio. Thus, effectiveness of this proposed system is shown.

In the future, based on the ankle joint angle from the encoder of the DC motor, this study deploy to the cloud services, such as remote monitoring by orthopaedists or physical therapists and real-time damping adjustment.

## References

1. Yamamoto, S., et al.: Development of an ankle-foot orthosis with dorsiflexion assist, part 2: structure and evaluation. J. Prosthet. Orthot. **11**(2), 24–28 (1999). Spring
2. Kikuchi, T., et al.: Development of shear type compact MR brake for the intelligent ankle-foot orthosis and its control. In: IEEE 10th International Conference on Rehabilitation Robotics (2007)

3. Blaya, J.A., Herr, H.: Adaptive control of a variable-impedance ankle-foot orthosis to assist drop-foot gait. IEEE Trans. Neural Syst. Rehabil. Eng. **12**(1), 24–31 (2004)
4. Okada, Y., Kim, S., Ozawa, K.: Energy regenerative and active control suspension. In: ASME International Design Engineering Technical Conference and Computers and Information in Engineering Conference, vol. 5, No. DETC2003/VIB-48560, pp. 2135–2142 (2003)

# Interactive Check System for Facilitating Self-awareness of Dorm Students in Upper Secondary Education

Shigenori Akamatsu, Masanobu Yoshida, Hironobu Satoh,
and Takumi Yamaguchi[✉]

National Institute of Technology, Kochi College, 200-1 Monobe,
Nankoku, Kochi 783-8508, Japan
aka@me.kochi-ct.ac.jp,
{myoshida,satoh,yama}@ee.kochi-ct.ac.jp

**Abstract.** We describe a new interactive system using a social learning platform to provide dormitory students with the ability to communicate with teachers/advisors in a timely manner to promote self-active awareness of the dormitory environment. Our system comprises tablet PCs, cloud computing services, and application and server software to enable collaboration over a high-speed wireless local area network that covers the campus, dormitory, and teachers' homes. The purpose of this system is to facilitate the self-recognition of behavioral problems, raise awareness, and encourage student initiative in a natural manner.

**Keywords:** Mental health · Wellbeing · Upper secondary education

## 1 Introduction

In present-day society, encouraging the role of computers in schools is very important. It has been suggested that the primary challenge in our information-rich world is to use information specifically to say the right thing at the right time and in the right manner [1]. In particular, the fundamental pedagogical concern regarding information use is to provide learners with the right information at the right time and place in the right manner rather than merely enabling them to learn at any time and any place.

In our present study, we have developed a new collaborative learning system called Terakoya [2] for remedial education, which helps students actively study anywhere on a high-speed wireless local area network (WLAN) that is linked to multipoint remote users and covers the campus, dormitory, and student and teacher homes. Terakoya provides interactive lessons and a small private school environment similar to the 18th-century Japanese basic schools called Terakoya.

We propose a new interactive communication system with the use of a social learning platform to provide students housed in dormitories with the ability to communicate with teachers/advisors in a timely manner for promoting self-active awareness in the dormitory environment. The target dormitory houses over 400 students and is supported by 11 staff members. At least one staff member is present in the dormitory

© IFIP International Federation for Information Processing 2015
J. Abascal et al. (Eds.): INTERACT 2015, Part IV, LNCS 9299, pp. 569–572, 2015.
DOI: 10.1007/978-3-319-22723-8_63

at all times when it is occupied by students. Regularly scheduled transition briefings allow information sharing among staff members. Nevertheless, the staff members are a small group, and it is hard to provide instantaneous services for real-time information sharing.

Under such conditions, it is necessary to design and implement a new communication system for the students to create the environment required to build self-discipline by reflecting on their behavior. To enable the students to review their behavior in the dormitory, the staff records student activities, i.e., the five W's and the one H (who, where, when, why, what, and how), related to acceptable and unacceptable behavior using a tablet PC. Information that is difficult to quantify is recorded as objective information by obtaining the camera image on a tablet computer.

This information is stored as centralized time-series data on a cloud server using several front-end graphical user interface (GUI) tools via the dormitory WLAN. Thus, students can review their behavior in chronological order. The dormitory WLAN connects seamlessly to the campus WLAN. Multipurpose pocket size electronic devices are provided to all students; thus, each student can access the high-speed WLAN anytime and anywhere. The purpose of this system is to facilitate the self-recognition of behavioral problems, raise awareness, and encourage student initiative in a natural manner.

This paper describes how the proposed new interactive communication system assisted in student dormitory life, and the implementation of a prototype framework and its practical application. The test verified the feasibility of the system for helping the students to obtain advice actively and willingly. The feasibility of the system indicates that the proposed new interactive communication system has the ability to create an environment that facilitates the development of student socializing skills. Enhancing student sociality through dormitory life is an educational policy of our school.

## 2 Basic Configuration

Our prototype system comprised 10 iPad tablet PCs, cloud computing services, and application and server software to enable collaboration over the WLAN. The prototype system was applied to facilitate real-time counseling for a group of students in a dormitory. The tablets were used to record the evaluations of the acceptable and unacceptable behaviors of the students based on dormitory room inspections, which are then stored as secure centralized time-series data on a cloud server. Students can review their behavior by accessing the data on the cloud server using a multipurpose pocket-sized electronic device provided to each student. Individual data of the students on the cloud server is backed-up in order to secure data. Furthermore, the parent of a student can access that student's behavioral data on the cloud server via the Internet to monitor his/her child's activity.

As the cloud server, we adopted Edmodo, which is a social learning platform website for teachers and students, and some customized ICT tools running on Windows. Edmodo supports the Japanese language on the login screen—a portion of the "Invitations" page—and some menus and buttons. As such, it is accessible for teachers and schools in Japan.

## 3  Implementation and Practice

The proposed prototype system was implemented experimentally in a foreign student's dormitory. The conventional procedure employed in our dormitory required an inspection of each student room every weekday morning by a dormitory counselor to ensure that the door and the window were locked, the bedding was put away, and the curtains were opened. The inspection results were recorded on a checking list, and later manually entered into a computer. The dormitory staff provided only verbal commentary to a student in accordance with the records. It seems that it is difficult for many students to heed the staff's advice due to verbal advice alone. We have come to embrace the idea that to facilitate self-recognition, raise awareness, and encourage student initiative in a natural manner, it is necessary for students to review their actual behavior in the dormitory.

We required the new procedure incorporating the interactive communication system that additional procedures be kept down to the minimum necessary, and the conventional procedure used by the dormitory counselors employing non-exclusive equipment such as pens and paper were retained as much as possible. Doing so alleviated the need to require individuals unfamiliar with the usage of electronic devices such as smartphones, tablet PCs, and laptops to adopt complicated and non-intuitive procedures in order to provide digital records of review results. This also allowed students to obtain feedback easily and timely from the written record on the checking list, and the communication is recorded for students' subsequent use.

Figure 1 illustrates the prototype system and GUIs for viewing a result of the routine check. After the dormitory counselor inspects the condition of the room, the results are entered on the appraisal list as check marks for each condition, and the written record is then captured by the camera on the tablet PC and stored electronically. The written record remains on the wall outside the room as a message to students. The students are therefore provided timely information regarding their behavior when they return to their rooms.

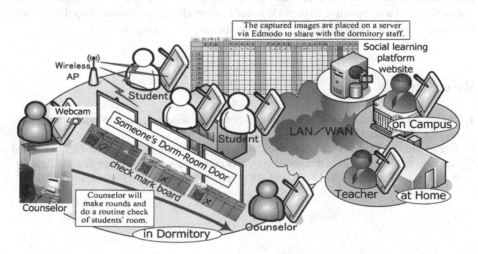

**Fig. 1.** Prototype systems and GUIs for viewing a result of the routine check.

The captured images were posted on our server made of the customized ICT tools through Edmodo to share with the dormitory staff. The on-campus teacher was capable to access Edmodo to clarify the conditions of each student's dormitory room, and the teachers were capable to engage in face-to-face and/or online contact with students as required. The student's parent would like to able to examine their child's conduct in the dormitory via Edmodo.

## 4   Conclusions

In this paper, we detailed how the proposed new interactive communication system assisted in student dormitory life. A prototype system was implemented experimentally in a foreign student's dormitory as a social learning platform to provide dormitory students with the ability to communicate with teachers/advisors in a timely manner for self-active awareness of the dormitory environment. The staff members, including student advisors, record acceptable and unacceptable behaviors using a tablet PC. This information is stored as centralized time-series data on a cloud server using several front-end GUI tools via high-speed WLAN in the dormitory in order to enable students review their behavior in the dormitory. The feasibility and practicality of the system in helping students to obtain advice actively and willingly was verified through observation and by evaluation of the assistance provided.

For our system, we considered the benefit of continuing the usage of conventional methods employing paper and pens owing to its simplicity and requirements for no exclusive equipment. The written records can be used by students, to review their behavior. Therefore, the new communication method requires no additional procedures, no complicated and non-intuitive actions, and no exclusive equipment. The captured images are located on our customized server via Edmodo to share with the dormitory staff. The campus teacher is able to access Edmodo to clarify the conditions in a student's room. The teachers can engage in face-to-face and/or online contact with the students as needed. The proposed system can also evolve to provide the necessary counseling and a perspective to provide relief from study stress, relationship difficulties, SNS-addiction, and serious mental health problems.

## References

1. Fischer, G.: User modeling in human-computer interaction. J. User Model. User-Adap. Interact. (UMUAI) **11**(1–2), 65–86 (2001)
2. Yamaguchi, T., Shiba, H., Yoshida, M., Nishiuchi, Y., Satoh, H., Mendori, T.: Posture and face detection with dynamic thumbnail views for collaborative distance learning. In: Zaphiris, P., Ioannou, A. (eds.) LCT. LNCS, vol. 8524, pp. 227–236. Springer, Heidelberg (2014)

# Interactive Toys in the Home:
# A Parents Perspective

Omar Mubin[1]([✉]), Duncan Rutishauser[1], Mauricio Novoa[1], Derek Wainohu[2],
and Suleman Shahid[3]

[1] University of Western Sydney, Parramatta, Australia
o.mubin@uws.edu.au
[2] InfaSecure Private Limited, Emu Plains, Australia
[3] Tilburg Center for Cognition and Communication, Tilburg University,
Tilburg, The Netherlands

**Abstract.** In our research we argue for the benefits of Learning through play. In this initial design case, we report on the general requirements of household educative and interactive toys and current usage practices via a focus group with parents. Our results indicate that the parents in our focus group held greatest importance to social and physical play and wished to reduce the dependency on electronic devices.

**Keywords:** Tangible interfaces · Learning through play

## 1 Introduction

In this paper we report on our early research efforts that contribute towards a larger venture that we term as *Learning by Interactive Play*. Learning by Interactive Play is the development of design intervention for better education, by integrating an enjoyable and recreational method of Play. Advances in technology have opened opportunities to create interfaces that promote conventional learning components (such as tangible interaction) complemented with a variety of interaction techniques, styles, modalities and tools [3]. Within Human Computer Interaction research, there are also significant new, post-digital developments, exemplified by the new surge of board games (including hybrids with digital elements), motion detection technology in console gaming (especially Wii) and location-based mobile and pervasive games.

However, touch screens and socially exclusive play have become common place with tablets and gaming consoles in the home and school. It is becoming too easy to produce a toy that fosters distraction without involving the essential components of learning; such as: social interaction, parent/peer involvement, physical manipulation/movement and experience based learning. Vygotsky [10] recognised the significance of adults and peers in extending a childs learning. Known as the Zone of proximal development, the belief that help provided to a child by parents/peers through stages of difficulty to ensure they do not get stuck allows them to continue to learn and eventually be able to complete the

© IFIP International Federation for Information Processing 2015
J. Abascal et al. (Eds.): INTERACT 2015, Part IV, LNCS 9299, pp. 573–577, 2015.
DOI: 10.1007/978-3-319-22723-8_64

task independently. The importance of parents in the development of learning abilities in children has been advocated [6] but the involvement of parents and their preferences/requirements in the design processes of interactive educative products has been limited in prior literature. One study which supports our view point of involving parents is [9], where the role of parents and teachers as expert users during the design process is strongly emphasized. Parents are the key peers/partners while the children interact with toys at home and hence need to be involved in the design process. In the initial phases of our research we have focused on interactive educative toys to be used at home by pre-schoolers (3–6 years old). In this paper we report on an initial elicitation of design requirements and current usage practices of interactive educational toys through a focus group with parents to ultimately drive concept development in the area of Learn through Play. In conclusion we synthesize our findings which we aim to feed back into our design process and to further drive the design of new concepts and prototypes.

## 2   Focus Group with Parents

A focus group with parents (N = 7 mothers; voluntarily recruited, each having at least one pre-schooler child) was conducted to firstly gain background information, preferences and requirements about the user group (pre-schoolers) through parents. Ethics clearances to conduct the focus group were attained from the host institution.

### 2.1   Procedure

After obtaining consent from the 7 mothers the facilitator gave a brief summary of the agenda of the focus group which was followed by a presentation about the project vision. In the focus group, questions were asked regarding the requirements of interactive educative toys at home.

### 2.2   Setup and Measurements

The participants were seated around a central table in a room. Opinion based qualitative data was recorded, via audio and notes by the facilitator. Open ended questions were used to facilitate the discussion. Themes that were addressed in the focus group included: goals when purchasing, child benefits, independent vs. combined learning, operation, aesthetics, size and shape.

### 2.3   Results

The majority of mothers in our focus group stated to have bought educational toys but more often that not they thought of the educational value as a bonus. When purchasing educative toys the features that the mothers would look for included: ease of use, allowances for motor skills development, uni-sex, animated through music or sound, not entirely an electronic/digital interface, possibilities to engage in social play with peers, etc. Discussion around tablets and iPads was interesting and figured fairly regularly in the focus group. Many mothers wished to see more physically open interfaces combining both digital and tactile components as Tablets were already being used regularly at pre-school. One mother was quoted to say: *I'll be honest, mine(iPad) is a babysitter for my X (name of son).* One of the key benefits of tablets that was presented by the mothers was minimal start up/set up; i.e. so simple that the children could do it themselves. Some mothers also commented that they preferred customisable toys/interfaces so that the younger children could jointly play with their younger or older siblings.

By synthesizing the discussion with the mothers we concluded that there were two types of play in a common household; namely 1. Toys/games that are used to entertain a child or busy them allowing a parent to do daily tasks freely; OR 2. Specifically set time where learning, imagination and exploration is encouraged. More often than not the first is used in a busy household, with tablets and games/apps, it is generally quick and easy, requires little space and minimal explanation/introduction to the child. While not ideal for learning it serves the purpose for most of the mothers day to day routine; as exemplified by the following quote: *we use ours in the morning, they have their breakfast and then they get their iPads for 20 min, while I run around cleaning up, and packing schools bags.* The second mode was said to be typically used at set aside times where open play by the children was encouraged, as evidenced by one mother's statement: *I like to create a space with a lot of toys, and they can just do a round robin, a little bit of drawing here some play doh here.*

All mothers in our focus group unanimously agreed that they would like to play a much more active role in any play sessions while maintaining the child's independence. The mothers believed that by playing an active role they could also introduce language in the game play; for e.g. *It is good for them to be independent, however I love having the option of doing something with them.* In the conclusion of Session 1 there were some discussions on aesthetics of educative toys, with terms such as sustainability popping up. Preference towards uni-sex but also monochrome colors was also put forward.

## 3    Discussion and Conclusion

Our experiences with the focus group indicated that the mothers whom we interviewed put forward an emphasis on attributes such as social play, supportive play, open and uninhibited play, endorsing physicality, avoiding a complete emphasis on digitization, etc. These attributes and the vision that they initiate are shared by our research team and we look forward to further advance our design ideas based on the feedback attained. Our results portray that parents realise the importance of joint play; i.e. using playtime as a connection pathway between parent and learning child, introducing language as a support tool and letting the child explore the play space independently. Examples of the role of parents in a supporting capacity during the learning process of the child can be found in prior work [5]. Other insights presented in prior work [7] support our assertion that parents should be at hand to facilitate setup/training and *guide interaction*. Eventually, social play can not only involve parents but also peers. Our findings also indicate the importance of physical play via tangible elements and consequently combining both digital and analog mediums to facilitate a move away from purely graphical or electronic interfaces such as tablets. The merge of digital and analog as two aspects in play and learning has been discussed in prior work [4]. Most of the mothers acknowledged the importance of tablets such as iPads however wished to see more of social and physical play. Tablets such as iPads are tailored to be used individually and the nature of the devices does not support the child to be easily observed or supported by peer or parent [8]. The mothers in our focus group also indicated that they preferred toys that would assist in open gameplay, minimizing rules and allowing for exploration and creativity; elements also advocated in prior research [1].

We acknowledge that our results are inferred from a single focus group with Australian mothers. Literature [2] informs us that culture and the personality of mothers will play a significant role in the interpretation of what constitutes learning by playing. Taking this into account, in the future we aim to run more user research sessions whilst developing our prototypes and concept ideas further within our project of learning through play.

# References

1. Bekker, T., Sturm, J., Wesselink, R., Groenendaal, B., Eggen, B.: Interactive play objects and the effects of open-ended play on social interaction and fun. In: Conference on Advances in Computer Entertainment Technology, pp. 389–392. ACM (2008)
2. Fisher, K.R., Hirsh-Pasek, K., Golinkoff, R.M., Gryfe, S.G.: Conceptual split? parents' and experts' perceptions of play in the 21st century. J. Appl. Dev. Psychol. **29**(4), 305–316 (2008)
3. Greener, S.: Smart toys and sophisticated learning tools. Interact. Learn. Env. **22**(5), 549–550 (2014)
4. Heibeck, F.: Cuboino: extending physical games. An example. In: CHI 2013 Extended Abstracts on Human Factors in Computing Systems, pp. 2935–2938. ACM (2013)
5. Horn, M.S., Solovey, E.T., Crouser, R.J., Jacob, R.J.: Comparing the use of tangible and graphical programming languages for informal science education. In: Conference on Human Factors in Computing Systems, pp. 975–984. ACM (2009)
6. O'Hara, M.: Young children's ICT experiences in the home: Some parental perspectives. J. Early Child. Res. **9**(3), 230–231 (2011). doi:10.1177/1476718X10389145
7. Plowman, L., McPake, J.: Seven myths about young children and technology. Child. Educ. **89**(1), 27–33 (2013)
8. Plowman, L., Stephen, C.: Guided interaction: exploring how adults can support children's learning with technology in preschool settings. Hong Kong J. Early Child **12**(1), 15–22 (2013)

9. Robins, B., Ferrari, E., Dautenhahn, K.: Developing scenarios for robot assisted play. In: Symposium on Robot and Human Interactive Communication, pp. 180–186. IEEE (2008)
10. Tudge, J.: Vygotsky, the zone of proximal development, and peer collaboration: Implications for classroom practice. In: Moll, L.C. (ed.) Vygotsky and Education: Instructional Implications and Applications of Socioistorical Psychology. Cambridge University Press, Cambridge (1992)

# Learning Lessons from Controlled Studies to Investigate Users' Resilience Strategies

Jonathan Day(✉), George Buchanan, and Stephann Makri

Centre for HCI Design, City University London,
Northampton Square, London EC1V 0HB, UK
{Jonathan.Day.2,George.Buchanan.1,
Stephann}@city.ac.uk

**Abstract.** This work describes the development and implementation of a controlled study into the way users form and utilise resilience strategies to overcome threats to performance. Despite a carefully considered design, participants demonstrated creative and unanticipated strategies to overcome deliberately 'designed-in' challenges in our task, thus circumventing the errors and responses we had predicted. We discuss the variety of unanticipated resilience strategies we observed during the course of this study, as well as methodological lessons learned as a result. Furthermore, we describe a forthcoming study which seeks to build upon the initial investigation, utilising a revised task paradigm to address and overcome its limitations.

**Keywords:** Resilience strategies · Workarounds · Cognitive resilience

## 1 Introduction

A key concern of HCI is the investigation of error:- how and why errors occur, and how they can be prevented in future interactions. An alternative, complimentary perspective however, is the investigation of Resilience Strategies, which constitute positive behavioural adaptations by users to reduce or mitigate threats to performance.

The study of resilience also presents new opportunities to improve systems and interactions, given that historically, it has largely been overlooked [1]. When errors or adverse events occur, the traditional model is to consider the frailties and causal factors that contributed to such, in an attempt to design interventions to reduce the likelihood of future occurrence. However, when resilient interventions pre-empt or neutralise a threat, thus avoiding an adverse event, analysis is seldom deemed necessary.

While the concept of resilience is primarily considered as a *property* of sociotechnical systems, an emerging reconceptualisation of the term considers 'cognitive resilience' or the resilience strategies of users interacting with systems. Such strategies include creating cues to assist memory, appropriating items, ensuring resource availability, and so fourth. This work addresses these phenomena, exploring how users develop and deploy tactics to mitigate risk, minimise error and improve performance.

© IFIP International Federation for Information Processing 2015
J. Abascal et al. (Eds.): INTERACT 2015, Part IV, LNCS 9299, pp. 578–581, 2015.
DOI: 10.1007/978-3-319-22723-8_65

## 2  Previous Work

As noted, the targeted investigation of users' resilience strategies in HCI is relatively lacking. There are some parallels between this topic and workarounds in a HCI context (e.g. [2]), however we draw distinctions based on both coverage and consequence. Resilience includes many prospective, anticipatory interventions, as opposed to the generally responsive nature of workarounds. Moreover, where (particularly in safety critical domains), workarounds are generally deemed to be unconducive to safe practice, resilience is inherently by its definition a positive contributor to outcome.

Furniss et al. have however described specific work in this area, and note that existing strategy-specific work largely constitutes anecdotal discussion, with little to frame or situate such accounts. This forms the rationale for their Resilience Markers Framework [3]. Furniss et al. also offer a categorisation scheme to collate and consider themes across strategies, serving to facilitate discussion and analysis [4].

While such work provides an insightful account of resilience as observed, efforts to empirically elicit examples of resilience or operationalise the concept in order to establish predictive power are seemingly not available to date. We present here an initial step towards achieving these objectives.

## 3  A Controlled Study into Cueing Strategies

As an early step toward isolating and investigating resilience strategies in a controlled setting, and owing to the apparent diversity of strategies, we initially opted to limit our scope to focus upon cueing-related strategies. Building on existing work [5, 6] that suggests users not only utilise, but in some cases develop or appropriate cues to assist prospective memory, we sought to investigate the effectiveness of user-configured cues in reducing placekeeping errors during a challenging and interrupted task.

### 3.1  Study Design and Hypotheses

We designed an independent samples study, with the dependent variable consisting of error rate across three independent variables; IV1: user-configured cues, IV2: system-incorporated cues, and IV3: no cue support. IV2 enabled comparisons against a baseline where cues had been designed into the interface, and IV3 was a control where no cues were intended to be available. Our primary one-tailed hypothesis was that user-configured cues (IV1) would reduce error rates compared to the absence of cues (IV3). As a secondary, two-tailed hypotheses, we also anticipated a performance different between user configured cues (IV1) and cues hard-coded into the system (IV3).

### 3.2  Task Paradigm

The task composed for the study was modelled on a common, interruption-prone and HCI-relevant task within the medical domain: setting up the delivery of multiple medications. The task involved performing a number of relatively simple calculations (of a [speed = distance/time] nature, but for values: rate, volume and duration) followed by data entry, transcribing data from paper to onscreen form. The different conditions were represented in this interface, with IV1 featuring unpopulated arbitrary checkboxes that users could appropriate as cues, IV2 consisting of automated visual cues of a similar size and nature, and IV3 featuring no such progress-tracking UI elements.

In an attempt to isolate engagement with and effectiveness of these cues, we attempted to 'design out' other implicit cues in the interface. For example, participants were trained to confirm each value immediately upon entering it, which cleared the corresponding field (so values left in fields couldn't be used as a progress tracking cue). We also removed the standard blinking text-field cursor from the interface after a few seconds upon each field being selected, so this wasn't available as a cue.

During the task, participants were interrupted with a paper-based distractor task (checking completed calculations). The points of interruption were predetermined, and as with the design of the onscreen form, increased the threat of place-keeping error. Data capture was via automated logging of input, remote screen monitoring and recording, collection of paper sheets, and brief informal ad hoc questioning upon completion. Finally, prior to the study proper, a limited pilot with users unfamiliar with the research was undertaken to elicit feedback on the task and instruction.

## 4    Findings and Observations

The task performance data did not reveal any relationships between condition (form of cue) and error rate, thus leading to the rejection of the experimental hypotheses. There were however two notable insights provided from this study, one regarding the conduct and resilience of our participants, and one related to setup and task paradigm.

*Participants Can Be Highly Resilient, Even When They're Not Expected to Be.* One key insight was that despite our best efforts to carefully control available cues, participants were very proactive in establishing alternative and additional cueing behaviours and other strategies. This enabled them to maintain performance and manage the threat presented by interruptions. Participants were, to put it simply, far more resilient than we had anticipated, and found novel and innovative ways of coping when critical threats to their cognitive working capacity were presented.

In terms of cueing, such strategies included utilising or marking paper sheets as external physical artefacts to track progress (n = 13), restructuring the sequence of data entry into the onscreen form (resulting in values serving as implicit visual cues) (n = 11), and using unanticipated digital artefacts as visual cues (e.g. the mouse pointer, or placing temporary and arbitrary values in fields; n = 3). We also observed other types of potential resilience strategy, including the momentary deferring of experimenter interruptions (n = 14), and intentional verbal rehearsal to assist memory (n = 6).

*Pitching the Complexity of the Task Paradigm is Key.* Another unanticipated insight was the significant level of individual variation of task performance between subjects, with total errors per participant ranging from 0 up to 13. This made it unfeasible, given the sample size available (n = 29), to establish a baseline level of performance for each of the three groups.

While there is insufficient information to determine why this significant variation in performance occurred, we postulate this was largely a reflection of natural variation in subjects' dexterity with figures. Both the primary and distractor tasks involved calculation, and it was noted that some participants completed such exercises with relative ease using mental arithmetic, while others relied heavily on the provided calculator and appeared to find this aspect of the task more challenging.

## 5 Lessons Learned and Revised Study

The study showed that users may be more resilient than we give them credit for. Even in a tightly constrained task, users coped well and deployed unanticipated resilience strategies, a finding which has implications for future work. In our next study we will strive not to exclude potential unforeseen resilience strategies, but will be better equipped to recognise and account for them, and potentially capture more information to enable more targeted and rigorous analysis, providing additional insights.

Another important consideration would be to ensure a stable baseline performance rate could be established in a revised task paradigm, by reducing the level of variance in terms of individual differences. We propose addressing this consideration in three ways: (i) We will avoid the use of a numerical task, and are instead moving towards a paradigm where cognitive load is introduced by workload structuring and interleaving, and subtask sequencing (ii) we will seek to establish and participants' abilities and baseline performance in a screening activity, enabling us to control for variance, and finally (iii) we will employ more stringent and extensive piloting to ensure such a baseline in performance can be established, and will adjust task parameters as necessary to achieve this prior to execution of the study phase.

**Acknowledgements.** This work was supported by UK EPSRC grant [EP/G059063/1], *CHI+MED*.

## References

1. Hollnagel, E.: A tale of two safeties. Nucl. Saf. Simul. **4**(1), 1–9 (2013)
2. Kobayashi, I.M., Fussell, S.R., Xiao, Y., Seagull, F.J.: Work co-ordination, workflow, and workarounds in a medical context. In: Proceedings of CHI 2005, Portland, Oregon, USA (2005)
3. Furniss, D., Back, J., Blandford, A., Hildebrandt, M., Broberg, H.: A resilience markers framework for small teams. Reliab. Eng. Syst. Saf. **96**(1), 2–10 (2011)
4. Furniss, D., Back, J., Blandford, A.: Cognitive resilience: can we use twitter to make strategies more tangible? In: Proceedings of ECCE 2012 (2012)
5. Back, J., Furniss, D., Hildebrandt, M., Blandford, A.: Resilience markers for safer systems and organisations. In: Proceedings of SAFECOMP 2008, pp. 99–112 (2008)
6. Dix, A.: Designing for appropriation. In: Proceedings of BCS HCI 2007, vol. 2, pp. 28–30 (2007)

# LightWatch: A Wearable Light Display for Personal Exertion

Jutta Fortmann[1(✉)], Janko Timmermann[2], Bengt Lüers[1],
Marius Wybrands[1], Wilko Heuten[2], and Susanne Boll[1]

[1] University of Oldenburg, Oldenburg, Germany
jutta.fortmann@uni-oldenburg.de
[2] OFFIS Institute for Information Technology, Oldenburg, Germany

**Abstract.** Wearable devices need to seamlessly integrate into everyday life and meet a user's aesthetic needs. In this paper, we present LightWatch, a wearable light display integrated into a common analogue wristwatch without interfering with the functionality of the watch itself. Input is enabled through a pressure-sensitive bezel mounted beneath the light display. LightWatch shall raise body awareness by enabling sensor-based measurement, adjustment and display of a user's personal exertion level. We see LightWatch as a promising approach for an unobtrusive everyday companion that can be used for various applications.

**Keywords:** Wristwatch · Digital jewellery · LED · Pressure sensitive · Heart rate

## 1 Introduction and Background

In the last years, wearable devices have been widely disseminated. A body-worn device needs to integrate seamlessly into everyday life and to meet a user's aesthetic needs. Thus, the latest trend on the wearable market is towards good-looking solutions, often referred to as digital jewellery.

In this work, we present a wearable light display for personal exertion. Our aim was to develop a wearable system that is integrated into a common wristwatch and seamlessly integrates into everyday life. We expanded an off-the-shelf analogue wristwatch by a pressure-sensitive light display and a heart rate sensor. LightWatch serves as a proof of concept that the integration of a pressure-sensitive light display into a common analogue watch is possible without interfering with the functionality of the watch itself. We see LightWatch as a promising approach for a useful everyday companion that meets a user's aesthetic needs and can be used for various use cases. One scenario is the raise of body awareness. We implemented this by enabling the user to measure her or his heart rate and to adjust a measured value whenever he or she thinks it does not match his or her perception. This way, a user is trained to assess his or her perceived exertion level.

Some research has investigated light displays that present information on wrist-worn digital jewellery, such as watches [1] or bracelets [2]. Besides, different input methods have been researched. These were e.g. mechanical pan, twist, tilt and click on the bezel [3], and touch gestures performed on the wristband [4]. In contrast to previous work, we integrate a point light display into a common analogue wristwatch without interfering

© IFIP International Federation for Information Processing 2015
J. Abascal et al. (Eds.): INTERACT 2015, Part IV, LNCS 9299, pp. 582–585, 2015.
DOI: 10.1007/978-3-319-22723-8_66

with the functionality of the watch itself. Further, our light display can be intuitively operated via pressure that a user applies directly to the surface of the light display.

## 2  LightWatch

The idea of LightWatch is to present information about a user's exertion level on a common wristwatch. It was developed in an iterative design process. During the process, we repeatedly tested the hardware elements in our lab, both, separately, and when integrated into the watch. We tested technical functionality and usability. In the following, we describe the conceptual design and the implementation of the final prototype of LightWatch.

### 2.1  Conceptual Design

The requirements on the system are, that, it must provide the function to measure, adjust, and display a user's exertion level. It must be integrated into a common wristwatch, everyday suitable, and easily usable while being worn. The conceptual design of Light Watch is as in the following. A user can measure his or her exertion level with a heart rate sensor. The exertion level is displayed by circular arranged LEDs on the bezel of the watch. The lowest exertion level is indicated by the first LED on the 12 o'clock position. The mapping of LEDs to exertion levels goes clockwise from low to high. The higher the exertion level, the more LEDs are illuminated clockwise. A user can adjust the measured value by pressing the LED that represents his or her perceived value.

In the following, we describe the interaction concept. After switched on, the watch is in idle state. The user can open the menu by pressing the bottom area of the LED ring, i.e. about the six o'clock position, for at least 2 s. Three different areas of 4 LEDs each light up in red, green, or blue (see Fig. 1). Within the next 7 s, the user can press one of the three areas to choose between the options *measure heart rate* (red), *show latest value* (green), or *quit menu* (blue). The system confirms a user input by switching off the LEDs in the not-chosen areas. After a user has chosen the red area, he or she can place a finger onto the heart rate sensor. For each measured pulse beat, an LED lights up red. If 12 pulse beats have been measured, the calculated exertion level is displayed in that the according LEDs light up white. Within the next 4 s, the user can adjust the value if he or she perceived the exertion differently. If he or she does not react, the value will be saved after 4 s. To adjust the value, the user presses the according LED. The input is confirmed in that the LEDs representing the entered value light up white. After 2 s the input is saved. If the user chooses the green area, the latest value that was captured will be displayed through white illuminated LEDs. Whenever a user does not react for 7 s after opening the menu, the watch will return to idle state. The blue option offers a quick exit in case the user does not want to wait for 7 s.

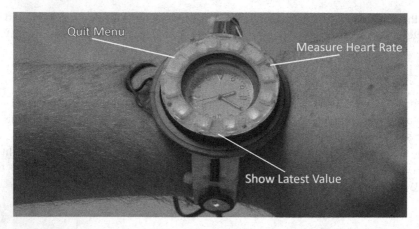

**Fig. 1.** A user wears LightWatch: Light menu is opened and heart rate sensor is enabled (Color figure online).

## 2.2 Implementation

For the implementation of LightWatch, we used an off-the-shelf analogue plastic wrist-watch. Following, we describe the design of LightWatch from top to bottom. On the top of the watch there is a cover made from a 6 mm thick pane of acrylic glass that we cut with a laser cutter. Indentations for the underlying LEDs and circuit board were laser etched and the glass was cut to round shape. It protects the underlying delicate electronics from forces of the user when he or she makes inputs by pressing the surface of the watch. Beneath the cover glass we mounted an Adafruit NeoPixel 12 RGB LED ring. It carries 12 serially addressable RGB LEDs on a common circuit board. When the LEDs are illuminated, the etched glass atop the LEDs diffuses their light. A ring of 2 mm thin foam rubber flexibly connects the LED ring to the underlying HotPot rotary potentiometer. It encodes the position of pressure that a user puts on the glass to an analogue resistance.

The rotary potentiometer is taped down to a ring of pressboard by double-sided adhesive tape. The pressboard was laser cut and glued to the watch case. The pressboard ring provides a stable base to the rotary potentiometer and transfers applied forces to the watch case. The watch case and watchstrap were modified from a common analogue plastic wristwatch. We drilled and grinded holes to fit a connector and to route cables to the outside. The watchstrap carries a 1000 mAh LiPo battery and a heart rate sensor, the Sparkfun Pulse Sensor Amped. In lab tests we found that the heart rate sensor does not provide reliable measurements on the wrist, but on fingers. Therefore, we mounted the sensor on the watchstrap. The heart rate sensor is attached to the lower watchstrap by a cable tie, and faces upwards. It measures the user's heart rate when a finger is applied (see Fig. 1).

The watch case houses the original clockwork and an ATtiny85V-10SU microcontroller. We soldered all connections directly or via stranded wire to the microcontroller. The microcontroller processes data provided by all sensors and drives the LED ring. Embedded into the side of the watch case is a female pin strip with 0.1 inch (2.54 mm) pitch. It leads out the connections needed for in system programming (ISP) the microcontroller. Via the pin strip the watch can be programmed and the collected data can be downloaded to a computer.

# 3 Discussion and Conclusion

In this paper, we presented LightWatch, a light information display for personal exertion that is integrated into a common analogue wristwatch. Our prototype serves as a proof of concept that the integration of a pressure-sensitive light display into a common wristwatch is possible without interfering with the functionality of the analogue watch itself. The major advantage is that a user can keep using his or her preferred watch, that is enhanced by further digital functionality. Wearing another device like a technically looking smart watch that does not meet the user's fashionable requirements is not needed. We think that a regular wristwatch that is expanded in a way like LightWatch is a promising approach for a useful everyday companion that can be used for various applications. These could e.g. be a display for physical activity, fluid intake, or medicine, as well as a reminder for dates.

The LightWatch prototype we presented in this paper is limited in that it is in an early development status. In the next step, we want to conduct user studies to investigate the user experience and practicality of LightWatch in real life. Therefore, we need to technically refine the prototype, i.e. to thin it, to hide all cables and the battery, and to improve its visual appeal.

# References

1. Xu, C., Lyons, K.: Shimmering smartwatches: exploring the smartwatch design space. In: Proceedings of TEI 2015, pp. 69–76. ACM (2015)
2. Fortmann, J., Cobus, V., Heuten, W., Boll, S.: WaterJewel: design and evaluation of a bracelet to promote a better drinking behaviour. In: Proceedings of MUM 2014, pp. 58–67. ACM (2014)
3. Xiao, R., Laput, G., Harrison, C.: Expanding the input expressivity of smartwatches with mechanical pan, twist, tilt and click. In Proceedings of CHI 2014, pp. 193–196. ACM (2014)
4. Perrault, S.T., Lecolinet, E., Eagan, J., Guiard, Y.: Watchit: simple gestures and eyes-free interaction for wristwatches and bracelets. In: Proceedings of CHI 2013, pp. 1451–1460. ACM (2013)

# Perceptive Media – Adaptive Storytelling for Digital Broadcast

Adrian Gradinar[1(✉)], Daniel Burnett[1], Paul Coulton[1], Ian Forrester[2],
Matt Watkins[3], Tom Scutt[3], and Emma Murphy[4]

[1] Lancaster Institute for the Contemporary Arts,
Lancaster University, Lancaster, UK
{a.gradinar,d.burnett,p.coulton}@lancaster.ac.uk
[2] BBC R&D North Lab, Mediacity, UK
ian.forrester1@bbc.co.uk
[3] Mudlark, Sheffield, UK
{matt.watkins,tom.scutt}@wearemudlark.com
[4] Institute of Design Innovation, School of Design,
Glasgow School of Art, Glasgow, UK
e.murphy@gsa.ac.uk

**Abstract.** Storytelling techniques within traditional broadcast media have not made major advances in recent years due to the linear and relatively rigid approach to narrative despite advances in the technology that delivers the content. This research proposes the concept of 'perceptive media' in which the content creators have at their disposal different tools and sensors to allow for the subtle adaption of the narrative without any direct interactions from the audience members. The concept is demonstrated through the creation of a 'perceptive radio' that is able to play specially designed content that adapts to the physical and social context in which the radio resides.

**Keywords:** Adaptive narrative · Digital storytelling · Context-aware media · Perceptive media · Perceptive radio

## 1 Introduction

The storyteller greets the group slowly easing them into a relaxed ambiance where everyone is preparing to enjoy a well-told tale. As the story progresses, the storyteller adapts it to the particularities of the location and the group, making use of specific expressions, sayings or habits, referencing landmarks and places in the local vicinity to ensure the story resonates with the audience. The narrator also provides a warm welcome as more listeners join in, as well as becoming more engaged with the audience if their attention is drawn away from the story. It is through the use of these refined techniques, a personalized, unobtrusive storytelling practice is achieved, one where the subtle changes used by the storyteller contribute to the overall immersion level of the audience. In a similar vein, a well-versed stand-up comedian adapts their show to the specifics of the location of the theatre where the performance is taking place, tailoring the jokes around the audience and own perception of how well the audience is

© IFIP International Federation for Information Processing 2015
J. Abascal et al. (Eds.): INTERACT 2015, Part IV, LNCS 9299, pp. 586–589, 2015.
DOI: 10.1007/978-3-319-22723-8_67

engaging with the show. Whilst the show is generally regarded as a performance, with an entertaining lead actor, the audience is experiencing a narrative given by a professional storyteller.

Despite the rapid pace of technological development across different mediums, broadcast storytelling content is still inflexible in comparison to these oral traditions. One medium that can adapt is digital games where game developers often create quite complex and twisting stories in which the player's actions, across diverse situations, directly influence the progression of the story as well as the evolution of the character and thus deliver a unique experience to each individual player (Mass Effect franchise,[1] TallTale: The Walking Dead,[2] Alpha Protocol[3]). Whilst this technique has also been adapted to theatre by companies such as Punchdrunk,[4] it has yet to be seen in traditional broadcast media.

The main advances we have witnessed recently in broadcast media have only affected the way that we consume the digital content (TV, stream box, mobile, laptop) or how it is being delivered (on-demand media versus traditional media). Whilst online voting can change the outcome of a TV episode or show, no real advances have been made around how program makers are looking at making their content more dynamic and adaptable. Therefore, this research explores different ways in which content creators can start thinking about how they may produce adaptable stories, by making subtle changes to the storyline based on the context in which the listeners are consuming the media. In doing so, the content creators are generating a new form of media that within this research we referred to as 'perceptive media'.

Since there is little direct experience of creating such media, a research through design methodology [1] has been used to facilitate an exploratory process in which different technologies are used independently and concurrently to gather contextual information about the current context of the audience in order to influence specially created media. To this end various physical and digital sensors have been encapsulated into a physical device that is able to deliver this dynamic radio content and which we refer to as 'perceptive radio'.

## 2 Perceptive Media

Unlike interactive narrative, "in which users create or influence a dramatic storyline through their actions" [2], 'perceptive media' looks at narrative from a different perspective; it adapts a story to the audience by using information about them, gathered through the use of a range of sensors and sensing technologies, whilst shaping the story within the predefined scope set by the storyteller. If the goal of the interactive narrative is "to immerse users in a virtual world such that they believe that they are an integral part of an unfolding story and that their actions can significantly alter the direction or

---

[1] http://masseffect.bioware.com/.

[2] https://www.telltalegames.com/.

[3] http://uk.ign.com/games/alpha-protocol/.

[4] http://punchdrunk.com/.

outcome of the story" [2], in the case of the *'perceptive media'*, the overall story arc does not change, it is simply varying the more ambient parts of the narrative to create an engaging experience for the listeners. Thus these changes may not be immediately apparent to the user and rather they are subtle and awareness may develop slowly during the course of the broadcast. Therefore, *'perceptive media'* attempts to bridge the gap between the 'flexibility' of the storyteller and the 'rigidness' of the broadcasted story delivered. The technologies employed take advantage of the implicit and explicit data the audience is generating and, in doing so, it redefines narrative as a set of logical attributes (variables), which could be moulded into different experiences. It is through the creation of adaptable stories and new experiences that the concept of *'perceptive media'* is achieved.

Since the story has to adapt to the contextual information gathered by the available sensors, new requirements are being placed on content creators. Whilst they have the unique opportunity to create new experiences, they are also required to generate the essential materials to cover all possible scenarios for a particular story. Each sensory output needs to be thoroughly considered before being used within a broadcast and it is within the responsibility of the content creators to ensure the correct usage of the sensors.

## 3   The Perceptive Radio

Currently, the *'perceptive media'* concept takes the shape of a radio, that expands on the capabilities and content of the original Perceptive Radio developed by the BBC R&D Department at MediCityUK in 2013.[5] Presently the range of sensors available consists of a microphone, used for noise cancellation, a camera, used to detect the number of people facing the radio, and a mobile phone, which is used to locate the radio. Based on the currently obtained information, extrapolated data is easily acquired, such as the weather, *'felt'* temperature, *'real-feel'* temperature or the time of day. Every piece of information could easily contribute to an even deeper personalisation level.

All the contextual information gathered through the sensors is passed to the radio, which employs a *node.js* server running on top of an *Ubuntu* distribution and delivering independent access to the sensors through an *application program interface* (API) built in *JavaScript*. The current setup was chosen to allow for the development of an easily expandable system, where other sensors could be effortlessly integrated. Furthermore, as the API is built using one of the most commonly used programming languages[6] it permits for the rapid prototyping of new ideas content creators could design.

The final aim of the *'perceptive radio'* is to demonstrate that the linear storytelling techniques developed within traditional broadcast media can be raised to a higher level, where contextual information can have a major contribution to the overall immersion level of the audience. The generated materials and concepts of this research will be made publicly available to encourage content creators to think of new ways in which digital stories are produced and delivered to the audience.

---

[5]  http://cubicgarden.com/2013/05/22/perceptive-radio/.

[6]  http://www.tiobe.com/index.php/content/paperinfo/tpci/index.html.

# 4  A Campfire Story

To demonstrate the notion of *'perceptive media'* to both audience and content producers, the current prototype uses a storytelling narrative in the form of a *'campfire story'*, in particular an adaptation of one of the most well known Aesop's fables: The Two Travellers and the Farmer. The first contextual information gathered by the radio is its own location, by using the GPS position provided by the mobile phone. Based on this location, data such as the current weather and *'felt'* temperature are obtained from online weather services. The time of day is also acquired from the internal clock alongside with the number of people currently within the sight of the camera. Based on this data, the story is dynamically generated. The *'campfire story'* starts by greeting the listeners acknowledging their numbers, the time of day and *'felt'* temperature. During the play, the radio monitors the activity of the listeners and the *'virtual storyteller'* greets the listeners as they walk in or out of the room.

Similar to the original Aesop's fable, the *'virtual storyteller'* asks each traveller about where they came from. Since the radio already has the contextual information about the location of the broadcast, the replies given by the travellers in the story reflect the current location. This is a subtle adaptation of the story, one that might not be perceived by all members of the audience; but, if registered by some of the listeners, it could enhance the overall experience.

# 5  Conclusion

The current iteration of this research introduces the concept of *'perceptive media'*, a new type of broadcast media, which makes use of contextual information provided through a range of different physical and digital sensors, to create a more engaging experience for the listeners by simply varying some of the ambient parts of the narrative. To demonstrate this concept a *'perceptive radio'* has been developed. Through the use of a revised fable, the radio delivers an adapted narrative based on the location of the play, number of people in the room, time of day and weather data collected through the available sensors. In future work, the *'perceptive radio'* will go under scrutiny from both content creators as well as the audience listening to the plays and conclusions will be drawn on the impact the *'perceptive media'* makes on both categories involved.

# References

1. Gaver, W.: What should we expect from research through design? In: CHI 2012, pp. 937–946. ACM, New York, NY, USA (2012)
2. Riedl, M.O., Bulitko, V.: Interactive narrative: an intelligent systems approach. AI Mag. **34**(1), 67 (2013)

# Redesigning Interaction in CODES

Elisa Leo de Oliveira, Evandro Manara Miletto, and Luciano Vargas Flores[✉]

Instituto Federal do Rio Grande do Sul (IFRS), Porto Alegre, Brazil
elisaleoo@gmail.com,
{evandro.miletto,luciano.flores}@poa.ifrs.edu.br

**Abstract.** Our research group is currently working on the user interface and interaction redesign of CODES, a system for collective music creation on the Web. Cooperative work over a piece of music in CODES follows a cyclic, proto-typing approach, which brings some challenges for interaction design. This poster summarizes our redesign concept guidelines, the problems we identified through evaluation of the previous version, and our proposed solutions. The main issues addressed were task conformance, site structure and navigation, aesthetics, and simplicity.

**Keywords:** Music-making · Prototyping · CSCW · HCI · UI evaluation

## 1 Introduction

Internet use has been growing every day, and so is its use as a means to foster human relationships. As a consequence, social networking systems are becoming increasingly present in people's lives. The basic idea behind CODES is to take advantage of such means in order to facilitate collective music creation.

CODES is the result of academic research, and is an interactive system that allows users to create musical compositions collaboratively and without needing any previous knowledge on music theory [1]. Collaboration happens over the Web and, therefore, contributors do not need to be in the same physical location.

Since CODES is in development for over ten years, some of the technologies used are outdated. The goal of the current research project is to reengineer the system based in Web Standards [2], considering their benefits for rich Web applications, such as: plugin independence; standardization (and a resulting multi-platform support); ease for responsive implementation.

## 2 CODES Overview

CODES is an RIA that aims at allowing novices in music to collaborate in the creation of music pieces. These songs are called "music prototypes" in CODES, because the system tries to facilitate music creation based on prototyping: a user posts an initial draft of the song and invites collaborators; everyone in the group provides their individual contributions – they may also discuss their ideas through the system's cooperation tools;

© IFIP International Federation for Information Processing 2015
J. Abascal et al. (Eds.): INTERACT 2015, Part IV, LNCS 9299, pp. 590–593, 2015.
DOI: 10.1007/978-3-319-22723-8_68

at some stages they can save different versions of the song; finally, this process of collaboratively creating versions, discussing ideas, assessing and refining versions of the song leads to a definitive version of the music piece, which may be published for the general public of the website [1].

The original (previous) design of CODES was organized into three levels: the Public level – when users are not logged in or, if logged in, where you can search for people and songs; the Intermediary level – when a user selects one song for editing (he/she will have access to versions and collaborators of that song); and finally the Prototyping level, which presents the collaborative editor.

## 3  Current Issues

Since we are reengineering the system, we also decided to redesign its UI and interaction. Therefore, initially, we carried out a simplified heuristic evaluation [3] with three members of the development team, just to identify any usability and UX problems that should be avoided already in the first versions of the new system (formative assessment).

We found a total of 27 different problems, mainly related to clarity (design, visual organization), feedback and efficiency issues. For instance, small problems like filling a field and pressing "Enter" on the keyboard not causing to trigger the desired action (you have to click a button on the screen), or more complex problems, such as the user not being able to identify where a collaborator made changes in a composition.

The main problems found during evaluation were how the versions of the song under work are listed for the user to choose from, and also the level of awareness about where changes have occurred and what was their context (why changes were made, in which order, etc.). For the user to edit a song in the original CODES, he/she must select a sequence of options that are progressively revealed through the tabs My Prototype > Version > Contribution (Fig. 1). The first problem with this approach is that the user takes a long time to reach his/her goal, that is to edit a song. Secondly, when contributions are listed they are very numerous, and it is not clear that you can combine them to open in the editor. It is also not clear which is the latest version and which are the latest contributions.

During heuristic assessment, evaluators have an experience that is similar to the user using the system. So, considering user's interaction with the system, and that the goal for that user is the editing task, the process described above was perceived as not being suited for the task. We assume that it would be more appropriate to quickly get to the edition of the latest version and, while at this task, to have access to previous versions and contributions from other users.

## 4  Proposed Solution and Concept Criteria

In addition to the problems encountered in the initial assessment, we have considered, for redesigning the system, some new criteria that we defined during the concept stage for the new version. Among the main proposed criteria, we may point out: minimalist design (only the necessary elements on the webpage); task-based page organization; and improvements in navigation (website structure), including simplified navigation. We have also considered the requirements for general mechanisms of the original CODES system: version control, argumentation/negotiation, modification requests, and support for the perception of actions and intentions of the group (awareness) [4].

We believe that the newly proposed design criteria already potentially solve many of the problems observed in the previous version, since they are based on the experience of our team in the field of HCI, and also on modern best practices of Web application usability.

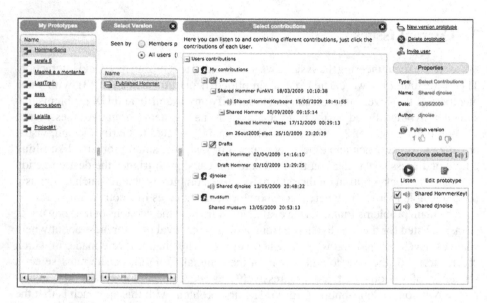

**Fig. 1.** Detail of the prototypes, versions and contributions screen.

The solution to the main problem, of the versions list presentation, is to bring this information to the task where it is needed: the editing task (Fig. 2). This means, during the composition the user will have access to the other versions for comparisons and to discuss them. In the original CODES, navigation and selection of versions was done in a previous step, and only then they were opened for edition (Fig. 1).

## 5    Final Considerations

A challenge that we still have in the design relates to compliance with the task of collective composition. We need to find a UI design solution that enables communication among collaborators during the task of musical composition, both synchronously and asynchronously. It is also necessary to be possible to refer to specific elements of the composition in these conversations.

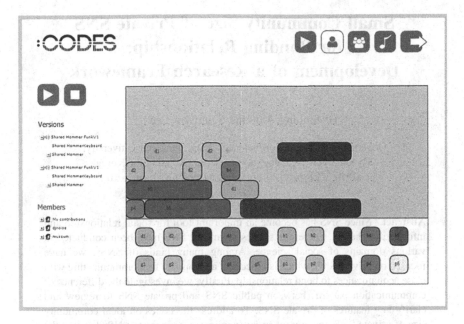

**Fig. 2.** Draft of the new editor screen, including versions and contributions.

One of the possibilities points out to the metaphors that are already familiar to current Web users, for the collaborative editing of texts and worksheets. Users work in a single version, and they can navigate through the history of changes and their respective authors, as well as restore these "checkpoints".

To test the validity of our hypotheses, regarding the efficiency, flexibility, clarity to the user and task conformance of the new design, will require testing with real users using a first prototype of the new version of CODES.

**Acknowledgements.** We thank CNPq and CAPES LIFE for funding this research, and IFRS – Campus Porto Alegre for the support provided to its development.

# References

1. Miletto, E.M.: CODES: an Interactive Novice-Oriented Web-Based Environment for Cooperative Musical Prototyping. Doctorate Thesis – PPGC, Universidade Federal do Rio Grande do Sul, Porto Alegre (2009)
2. W3C: Web Design and Applications. http://www.w3.org/standards/webdesign
3. Nielsen, J.: Heuristic evaluation. In: Nielsen, J., Mack, R.L. (eds.) Usability Inspection Methods. Wiley, New York (1994)
4. Hoppe, A.F., Miletto, E.M., Flores, L.V., Pimenta, M.S.: Cooperation in musical prototypes design. In: 13th International Conference on Computer Supported Cooperative Work in Design, pp. 698–703. IEEE Press, Los Alamitos (2009)

# Small Community Size of Private SNS
# for Bonding Relationship:
# Development of a Research Framework

Hyeonjung Ahn and Sangwon Lee[✉]

Department of Interaction Science, Sungkyunkwan University,
Myeongnyun 3-ga, Jongno-gu, Seoul, Republic of Korea
ahnhj77@gmail.com, upcircle@skku.edu

**Abstract.** Since SNS has become an important tool for social relationship and information sharing, numerous studies regarding SNS have been conducted in various domains of social science. Among many kinds of SNSs, we have focused on private SNS, which is especially appropriate for communicating with close acquaintances to bond relationship. Firstly, we investigate the difference of communication patterns between public SNS and private SNS to review and clarify key features of private SNS. To address the issues on ideal community size of private SNS, the present study examines some private SNSs limiting the number of friends. With these kinds of SNSs, we secondly clarify whether this function will be useful in managing the users' relationships for 'strong ties' with emotional closeness. As a preliminary study on private SNS, we suggest research framework based on other studies about research methods to analyze SNS usage patterns. Through online questionnaire survey, we expect to attain the results of the research questions regarding private SNS.

**Keywords:** Private SNS · Public SNS · Community size · Bonding relationship · Bridging relationship

## 1 Introduction

Nowadays, social network services (SNS) have become a major social media with much impact on individual's daily life. Numerous people are using SNS for various purposes, including social relationships and information sharing with others through computer-mediated communication. Facebook is one of the most popular SNS, with 1.3 billion users across the world. However, some problems including privacy risks, information overload, and uncountable online friends arose in using some types of SNSs [1]. In this paper, we call those SNSs, which are beneficial for bridging relationship and with no restrictions to be a friend online, to public SNS (e.g., Facebook, Twitter). Steinfield et al. (2008) regard the social networking in Facebook as diverse collection of "weak ties" [2] which are good for sharing new information [3]. In contrast, private SNS is designed to communicate with only the close friends such as family and close friends for bonding relationship. 'Path', 'Band', and 'Kakao Group' are the most representative examples of private SNS. 'Band' is the most popular private SNS launched by NAVER, a popular search portal company in Republic of Korea, and has over 12 million domestic

© IFIP International Federation for Information Processing 2015
J. Abascal et al. (Eds.): INTERACT 2015, Part IV, LNCS 9299, pp. 594–598, 2015.
DOI: 10.1007/978-3-319-22723-8_69

users [4]. 'Band' also planned to extend its service to the United States in 2014 because they noticed foreign users' needs of privacy on SNS arising from aforementioned problems. Similarly, Kakao Group's number of users has increased by over 4 million in six months with its linkage with Kakao Talk [4]. These figures imply that the SNS user's other needs that are hard to be satisfied by using public SNS.

In a few studies, researchers have raised a question about the community size for effective offline relationships and online relationships. Dunbar insisted that 150 people is the most desirable number of community size for individual's effective relationship with others, and 150 is well known for Dunbar's number [5]. Later, some other researchers suggested that Dunbar's number is only valid in offline relationships, and that it is possible to maintain a relationship with 200 to 300 people in social networks. This is dubbed a new magic number [6]. In the current study, we firstly aim to find out the difference of communication patterns between public SNS and private SNS to clarify key features of private SNS. We will mainly refer to the studies about SNS usage patterns on Facebook to compare them with that of private SNS. Additionally, we examine whether the intimacy between friends on private SNS is influenced by the constraints on community size of private SNS such as Path and Daybe. Therefore, we attempt to answer to the following research questions:

- RQ1. What is the difference of communication patterns between public SNS and private SNS?
- RQ2. Do constraints on community size of private SNS have an impact on the more emotionally close relationship?

As a preliminary study on private SNS, we focused on the key trait of the community size on the SNS. Through our suggestion of research framework, we expect to obtain the results of these research questions.

## 2 Background

### 2.1 Social Network Service

SNS is one of the most effective communication methods that allow the user to create his/her own profile online, and to share any information with other users in social networking sites [7]. Each of the social networking sites including 'Cyworld', 'Facebook', and 'Twitter' has its own targets and concept. The effect of these SNSs became much bigger with the emergence of smart phones in 2007 making our lives more accessible to the Internet anytime and anywhere. A large number of researchers have raised questions regarding how the SNS could be utilized to maintain individual social relationships.

Social capital theory is very essential in understanding and studying social networking to build and promote one's relationship in real or virtual environments. The social capital is the resources derived from social relationship [8] and it classifies the type of relationship into two types; bridging and bonding social relationship [9, 10]. Bridging social relationships is considered as a collection of "weak ties" [2] that do not show intimacy among people. On the contrary, bonding social capital is regarded as a collection of "strong ties" [2] and close social relationship among close friends or family. However, most of SNSs are still beneficial in maintaining weak ties rather than strong ties [11]. These SNS users can use their relatively big sized relationship to share any information that their friends and themselves do not have.

In the present paper, we have apparently divided types of SNS into public SNS and private SNS. Facebook and Twitter are public SNS, which are effective tools for bridging social capital online. On the contrast, Band and Path are private SNS, for they are mainly used to bond one's social capital online. Most of these private SNSs are designed to communicate with family, close friends, and even neighbors, according to their own concept of the services. Among these diverse private SNSs, we have mainly focus on the private SNSs which give constraint to the community size such as Path and Daybe to investigate RQ 2.

## 2.2  Community Size for Effective Relationship

Some researchers in the field of social science have studied about community size for effective relationship in real and virtual environments. Dunbar's number is one of the most popular theories demonstrating that a maximum of 150 people is the most appropriate number of group size to effectively maintain personal relationships with others [5]. Several social network services were designed based on this theory for bonding social capital. 'Path' and 'Daybe' have similar function of limiting the maximum number of friends up to 150 and 50, respectively. Path limits the size of social network up to 150 friends to promote relationship based on the Dunbar's number theory [5]. Even though 'Daybe' discontinued its service in the latter half of 2014, it limited the maximum number of friends to 50 people. If the number of members exceeds 50, the member who has communicated and interact the least with the user is eliminated automatically in order. This is a very simple function but differentiation strategy which is different from other private SNS in that it can grant the users some cognition to strengthen existing weak ties with members.

Other researchers insisted that Dunbar's number can be applied to social capital in real environments and suggested a new magic number ranging from 200 to 300, demonstrating individual sustainable social networking size online [6]. However, this result is valid in bridging relationships rather than bonding them online. In the current study, we focused on the purpose of forming solid relationship not bridging social capital on private SNS.

## 3  Development of a Research Framework

We target SNS users who are currently using Facebook and more than one private SNS together among the following private SNSs; Band, Kakao story, Kakao Group, and Path. As a research method, we suggested online questionnaire to be distributed to over 200 participants to collect the following data; demographic data, communication patterns of private SNS, and the degree of intimacy before and after using private SNS. We plan to design the questionnaire about private SNS usage by including the following contents with the reference of 'Facebook intensity scale' developed for measuring user's Facebook usage patterns [12] and 'Bonding Social Capital Scale' validated by Williams [13].

- Average private SNS usage time per day and per week
- The number of friends and groups on private SNS and public SNS, respectively
- Private SNS users' satisfaction regarding the aspects of bonding relationships
- The degree of intimacy before and after using private SNS
- The effectiveness of 'limiting the number of friends' function such as Path and Daybe
- Personal opinions regarding the ideal community size on private SNS for "strong ties"

For example, the following items are filled out based on 'Bonding Social Capital Scale' [13] to obtain data about 'the degree of intimacy before and after using private SNS' with the Likert scale ranging from 1(strongly disagree) to 5(strongly agree).

- There are several people on private SNS that I can trust to solve my problems.
- If I need an emergency loan of $100, I know someone on private SNS that I could turn to.
- There is someone on private SNS I could turn to receive advice about making very important decisions.
- The people I interact with on private SNS would be good jog references for me.
- I do not know people on private SNS well enough to get them to do anything important.
- I feel I am part of the private SNS community.

Prior to the online survey, we will conduct a pilot test to revise the contents in the questionnaire. After analyzing the collected data through SPSS, we expect to obtain results about different communication patterns between public SNS and private SNS and higher sense of closeness between friends after using private SNS.

## 4 Discussion and Conclusion

In the present study, we focus on private SNSs, which are designed to promote relationship online, unlike from the public SNS. We firstly compared public SNS and private SNS with regard to communication and usage patterns in order to clarify the different effect of communication between them. Among many kinds of private SNSs, we examine the private SNSs having the function of limiting the maximum number of friends. With this kind of SNSs, we raised a question about whether the function is beneficial for users in increasing their 'strong ties' in social networks. With this question by extension, we intend to find out desirable community size on private SNS in our future study.

Through this study, we expect to contribute private SNS service providers to innovate and improve their services for relationship promotion online. It will result in taking their relationship with others to next level most effectively with higher satisfaction levels. The results can be also utilized in social network services to develop easier way to expand and form solid social network.

**Acknowledgements.** This research was supported by the Ministry of Education, South Korea, under the Brain Korea 21 Plus Project (No. 10Z20130000013) and Basic Science Research Program (No. NRF-2014R 1A 1A2054531).

# References

1. Dwyer, C., Hiltz, S., Passerini, K.: Trust and privacy concern within social networking sites: a comparison of Facebook and MySpace. In: AMCIS 2007 Proceedings, 339 (2007)
2. Granovetter, M.S.: The strength of weak ties. Am. J. Sociol. **78**, 1360–1380 (1973)
3. Steinfield, C., Ellison, N.B., Lampe, C.: Social capital, self-esteem, and use of online social network sites: a longitudinal analysis. J. Appl. Dev. Psychol. **29**, 434–445 (2008)
4. http://www.digieco.co.kr/KTFront/dataroom/dataroom_weekly_view.action?board_seq=9185&board_id=weekly#
5. Hill, R.A., Dunbar, R.I.: Social network size in humans. Hum. Nat. **14**, 53–72 (2003)
6. Zhao, J., Wu, J., Liu, G., Tao, D., Xu, K., Liu, C.: Being rational or aggressive? A revisit to Dunbar's number in online social networks. Neurocomputing **142**, 343–353 (2014)
7. Ellison, N.B., Boyd, D.: Social network sites: definition, history, and scholarship. J. Comput. Mediated Commun. **13**, 210–230 (2007)
8. Portes, A.: Social capital: its origins and applications in modern sociology. In: Lesser, E.L. (ed.) Knowledge and Social Capital, pp. 43–67. Butterworth-Heinemann, Boston (2000)
9. Putnam, R.D.: Bowling alone: the Collapse and Revival of American Community. Simon and Schuster, New York (2001)
10. Woolcock, M., Narayan, D.: Social capital: implications for development theory, research, and policy. World Bank Res. Observer **15**, 225–249 (2000)
11. Donath, J., Boyd, D.: Public displays of connection. BT Technol. J. **22**, 71–82 (2004)
12. Ellison, N.B., Steinfield, C., Lampe, C.: The benefits of Facebook "friends:" social capital and college students' use of online social network sites. J. Comput. Mediated Commun. **12**, 1143–1168 (2007)
13. Williams, D.: On and off the'Net: scales for social capital in an online era. J. Comput. Mediated Commun. **11**, 593–628 (2006)

# Sushi Train Interface: Passive and Interactive Information Sharing

Tomomi Takashina(✉) and Yuji Kokumai

MS Research Section, Nikon Corporation, 471, Nagaodai-cho, Sakae-ku,
Yokohama, Kanagawa 244-8533, Japan
{Tomomi.Takashina,Yuji.Kokumai}@nikon.com

**Abstract.** We proposed sushi train interface as a novel information sharing method to have users notice everyday information in a natural manner. In the interface, information rails are projected on ceilings or walls, and information dishes go around on the rails. Users interact with the information rails using remote pointing devices. We constructed a prototype as a proof-of-concept and implemented pointing methods by a camera device and a smart laser pointer. The both methods are expected to be used for interacting information rails.

**Keywords:** Sushi train · Information sharing · Pointing method · Passive attitude · Smart laser pointer

## 1 Introduction

Up until a decade ago, physical bulletin boards had been a primary information sharing method for groups at offices, schools, and so on. Now it is changing to digital information sharing systems as their alternatives. Their primary advantage is that people can access information from everywhere. However, their chances are limited to the time when people operate computers or electric devices. Moreover, people must check them intentionally. This is disadvantage as compared to physical bulletin boards usually installed in such places that people naturally notice.

Therefore, there is the necessity of a new information sharing method which can be used by users with a passive attitude. Watanabe proposed a new visual interface focusing the advantage of passiveness [3]. It is intended to show useful information in idle times on a PC. However, it might be a small amount of time to look such information on PCs considering the whole time of their daily life.

Our proposal is to share information with the style of sushi train (or rotating sushi bar) in real space. One reason of sushi train's popularity is that people can find their favorite dishes easily in a passive attitude by watching moving showcase (i.e. sushi trains). So we applied the model of sushi train to information sharing and constructed a prototype as a proof-of-concept. In the prototype, information rails are projected on ceiling and walls, and information dishes go around there. People interact with the information rails using remote pointing devices.

© IFIP International Federation for Information Processing 2015
J. Abascal et al. (Eds.): INTERACT 2015, Part IV, LNCS 9299, pp. 599–602, 2015.
DOI: 10.1007/978-3-319-22723-8_70

## 2 Sushi Train Interface

The concept of sushi train interface is shown in Fig. 1. We assume the target environment is a typical office environment and there are some coworkers using PCs on their desks in the environment. Many dishes to carry information (=information dishes) on circular rails displayed on the ceiling using projectors (Fig. 1(a)). Such dishes might carry a schedule of the group, a circular notice, a task instruction, a menu of company cafeteria, a party information, and so on. As another form, information rails can span multiple planes as shown in Fig. 1(b). A user can notice dishes that the user might have interests from a distant place. Then, the user can see such a dish closely when they pass near the user. If the dish is really needed by the user, the user can pick the dish up to one's own environment by pointing with methods (finger gesture, some pointing device, and so on). Circular rails are suitable for information sharing with a passive manner because dishes appear again in a continuous manner even if the user missed to check them.

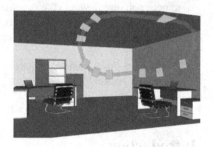

(a) Basic Concept of Sushi Train Interface        (b) Extension to Multiple Planes

**Fig. 1.**   Concept of sushi train interface

## 3 Prototype

We constructed the prototype of sushi train interface. The prototype consists of two projectors, two PCs, a digital still camera (Android-powered COOLPIX S800c), a high-speed camera (DITECT HAS-L2), and two smart laser pointers developed by us. As for the software modules of the prototype, SushiController displays information rails and dishes with projectors, InteractionManager deals with 'put' and 'get' interaction by exchanging messages using network, and RailEditor designs the rail layout based on 3D measurement of ceilings and walls.

Figure 2 shows the example of information rails projected by a single projector. Multiple projectors can also be utilized in the prototype. SushiControllers in different PCs cooperatively generate a single view by stitching images of multiple projectors. A user can get and put information dishes using some pointing methods. As for such methods, we employed a camera based interaction method and a laser pointer based interaction method.

**Fig. 2.** Sushi train interface: information dish go around on a ceiling

## 3.1 Interaction Using Cameras

This method is to point a location in information rails through a view finder of a camera. A user puts information onto the rails and gets information from the rails with a camera device. The location specified by the camera is calculated by homography between a live image camera and a corresponding internal image bitmap data in SushiContorller. This is the same method as described in [2]. As for the user experience, the user points a location in the information rails and press shutter button (Fig. 3). By this operation, the user places information on the rails in the "put mode" and gets information from the rails in the "get mode".

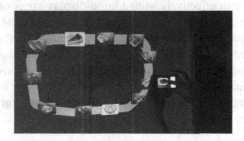

**Fig. 3.** Sushi train interface: choosing an information dish by a camera

## 3.2 Interaction Using Smart Laser Pointers

The interaction method with cameras is a little awkward because people usually don't aim cameras at ceilings. As a more intuitive pointing method, we employ smart laser pointers, which has the ability to encode ID with blinking pattern. A global high-speed camera recognizes the gesture and identifies the device. We combined some methodologies for laser pointer interaction proposed so far, such as [1].

By making a circular stroke, a user can select an information dish inside the circle. Then InteractionManager detects the gesture and the ID, and sends the selected dish to the digital device linked with the ID.

We constructed a smart laser pointer using an Arduino Micro and a LED laser module with a case fabricated by a 3D printer (Fig. 4(a)). The global camera captures the strokes of laser pointers with 100 FPS and the 3-bit ID encoded in blinking pattern and a gesture are recognized with in 240 ms. Figure 4(b) shows the selection of an information dish using a smart laser pointer.

(a) Prototype                              (b) A dish selected by a gesture

**Fig. 4.** Smart laser pointer

## 4  Conclusion

We proposed sushi train interface as a novel interaction method to share information in a group. The method can effectively utilize huge display areas of ceilings and walls. Users can feel a sense of unity of the environment by sharing same information presentation through real space. We also proposed two pointing methods to interact such information. We haven't any quantitative evaluation, but smart laser pointer has more natural style to point information and it is also advantageous to know which information others have interests in. As for future work, it is useful to employ some concepts of real sushi train and reflect them to the interface (e.g. changing contents color based on the freshness of information).

## References

1. Oh, J.Y., Stuerzlinger, W.: Laser pointers as collaborative pointing devices. In: Graphics Interface 2002, pp. 141–149. AK Peters and CHCCS, Natick (2002)
2. Takashina, T., Sasaki, H., Kokumai, Y., Iwasaki, Y.: Point, shoot, and paste: direct photo pasting from a digital still camera. In: Proceedings of the IEEE 2nd Global Conference on Consumer Electronics (2013)
3. Watanabe, K., Yasumura, M.: A proposal of persistent interface and its implementation for ubiquitous environment. IPSJ J. **49**(6), 1984–1992 (2008)

# Tangible Microscope with Intuitive
# Stage Control Interface

Tomomi Takashina[✉], Hitoshi Kawai, and Yuji Kokumai

MS Research Section, Nikon Corporation, 471, Nagaodai-cho,
Sakae-ku, Yokohama, Kanagawa 244-8533, Japan
{Tomomi.Takashina,Hitoshi.Kawai,Yuji.Kokumai}@nikon.com

**Abstract.** Control interfaces of microscope stage have been conservative because they historically precede compact mechanisms which can be used in dark rooms with the sense of fingertips. However, there is a trend of expanding frontier in microscope interaction. New kinds of interactions for microscope are proposed and the freedom of stage control increases by hexapod micropositioning. We propose a tangible microscope which has an intuitive stage control interface. The interface combines a tablet device and a hexapod stage. Because a stage is a plane, we virtually assume a stage is on one's palm. It is very intuitive that the stage moves in the same manner of palm's move. As a proof-of-concept, we constructed a prototype by regarding a tablet as a palm. We haven't any quantitative evaluation yet, but it is expected that the concept of tangible microscope brings a new sense of stage control to users.

**Keywords:** Microscope · Tangible interaction · Gesture by palm metaphor · Hexapod stage

## 1 Introduction

Control interfaces of microscope stage have been conservative because they historically precede compact mechanisms which can be used in dark rooms with the sense of fingertips. One of the traditional stage control interface is coaxial X-knob and Y-knob in the one side and Z-knob in the other side, which are convenient to control X, Y, Z direction with two hands. But it is against one's intuition that X-knob and Y-knob are located in a coaxial relation.

There is a trend of expanding frontier in microscope interaction. Boulanger developed a robotic microscope in cooperation with user's gazes [1]. It is useful when a user does some work such as soldering electric circuit with observing a microscope. However, the application is limited because the interaction is based on gaze angle and it is difficult to use in generic microscopes. On the other hand, the freedom of stage control improves in hexapod micropositioning [2]. By adjusting the length of six legs to support the stage, it has 5 stage movements; x, y, z, pan, and tilt. In order to utilize such stages, we need a new stage control interface as an alternative of traditional stage control interfaces.

© IFIP International Federation for Information Processing 2015
J. Abascal et al. (Eds.): INTERACT 2015, Part IV, LNCS 9299, pp. 603–606, 2015.
DOI: 10.1007/978-3-319-22723-8_71

We focus on how users feel a stage as an extension of the body. Because a stage is a plane, we virtually assume a stage is on one's palm. It is very intuitive that the stage moves in the same manner of palm's move. We constructed a prototype as a proof-of-concept and confirmed that such an interface brings new user experience to users in microscope imaging.

## 2    Tangible Interaction for Microscope

As for tangible interaction in microscopes, Lee et al. proposed tangible interaction from the viewpoint of subjects [4]. In the system, a user can interact euglena with light controlled by one's finger. Though their viewpoint is on subjects, our viewpoint is on view control in micro world.

In order to control the view of microscope, we employ a palm-based metaphor for the stage. We assume a stage is virtually on users's palm. As for palm-based metaphors, there are some researches on palm-based gestures. Dezfuli et al. proposed an interaction method to use palm as imaginary remote control for TV set, air conditioner, and so on [3]. They focus on convenience that users don't need to search any remote control devices. However, the reason we employ the palm is its intuitiveness. If one can move stage on one's palm, this can be said as tangible interaction for microscope.

In this research, we employ a small size tablet as a proxy of a palm instead of using palm directly. It is effective that we can deal with tablet just as a palm and we can utilize display and sensor at the same time.

The variations of tangible interactions are XY move, Z move, rotate, and tilt. They are so sensitive that user must push mode switch on the tablet screen. Figure 1 shows operations of tilt control and z control. In tilt control gesture, user must specify a pivot point which is the center of tilt movement.

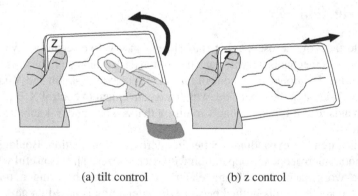

(a) tilt control                    (b) z control

**Fig. 1.**    Stage control by palm-metaphor gesture

## 3    Prototype

Our prototype consists of PI H811 (hexapod stage), Nikon SMZ25 (microscope), Prosillica GE1660 (camera), HP620 (computer), and Sony Xperia Z3 Tablet Compact (user interface). Figure 2 shows the partial appearance of the prototype; PI H811 and Nikon SMZ25. PI H811 and HP620 are connected by serial interface. Sony Xperia Z3 and HP620 are connected by WiFi. Prosillica GE1660 and HP620 are connected by ethernet.

**Fig. 2.** Microscope with Hexapod Stage

A host program is working on HP620 and communicates with Sony Xperia using WebSocket. User interface program is written in HTML5. Motion sensors in Sony Xperia detects the movement of the tablet and then sends control commands to HP620, which controls the hexapod stage.

## 4    User Experience

As for horizontal moves, a user can move the stage using strokes on the touch panel of the tablet. As for pan and tilt moves, the user can move the stage using tilting tablet with touching the surface. The stage moves quickly enough responding these gestures.

Examples of result images are shown in Fig. 3. Figure 3(a) shows the image captured in a initial position. If the user wants to observe the subject (a fruit fly) from the direction over the head of the fruit fly, the user moves the tablet to the side of the user. Then the desired image is captured as shown in Fig. 3(b).

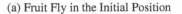

(a) Fruit Fly in the Initial Position        (b) Fruit Fly after Moving the Tablet

**Fig. 3.** Examples of Result Images

As for image display, the current prototype shows poor performance in speed (5 FPS). If a user moves the tablet quickly, the images don't follow the move. The weak point of the hexapod is that working area is not so large. If the stage is located apart from the center, it is impossible to control pan and tilt of the stage. In such a case, the tablet notifies the user of the limitation with vibration.

From this prototype, we identified the advantage and the disadvantage of intuitive stage control using gestures based on palm metaphor. The advantages are as follows.

- It is very intuitive to control stage by a tablet. This is a clear metaphor.
- By changing view angle, it is easy to understand 3D shape of a subject.
- It is so enjoyable to control a microscope just like a game.

The disadvantage is that the movement is sometimes very awkward because the range of working area is limited in the hexapod stage.

## 5   Conclusion

We proposed an intuitive stage controller for microscope and constructed a prototype as a proof-of-concept. Our contribution is the proposal of a novel gesture; tilt gesture with specifying a pivot point. This should enable new experience of imaging from the angle controlled in an intuitive and flexible manner.

## References

1. Boulanger, C., Dietz, P., Bathiche, S.: Scopemate: a robotic microscope. In: Proceedings of the 24th Annual ACM Symposium Adjunct on User Interface Software and Technology, UIST 2011 Adjunct, pp. 63–64. ACM, New York, NY, USA (2011)
2. Coulombe, J., Bonev, I.A.: A new rotary hexapod for micropositioning. In: Proceedings of 2013 IEEE International Conference on Robotics and Automation, pp. 877–880 (2013)
3. Dezfuli, N., Khalilbeigi, M., Huber, J., Muller, F., Muhlhauser, M.: Palmrc: imaginary palm-based remote control for eyes-free television interaction. In: Proceedings of the 10th European Conference on Interactive TV and Video, EuroiTV 2012, pp. 27–34. ACM, New York, NY, USA (2012)
4. Lee, S.A., Chung, A.M., Cira, N., Riedel-Kruse, I.H.: Tangible interactive microbiology for informal science education. In: Proceedings of the Ninth International Conference on Tangible, Embedded, and Embodied Interaction, TEI 2015, pp. 273–280. ACM, New York, NY, USA (2015)

# Touch Skin: Proprioceptive Input
# for Small Screen Devices

Changhyeon Lee, Jaedong Lee, and Gerard J. Kim[(✉)]

Digital Experience Laboratory, Korea University, Seoul, Korea
{ellypx,jdlee,gjkim}@korea.ac.kr

**Abstract.** The smart watch, increasingly gaining popularity, has limited input and output capabilities due to its size and thus mostly used as a surrogate device to the smart phone. In this poster, we propose "Touch Skin (TS)" that enlarges the interaction space of the smart watch using the hand (or skin) surface and proprioceptive sense. While the input interface is displayed on the small smart watch screen, the interaction is carried out by touching on the larger hand surface to which the input interface elements (e.g. graphical buttons and keys) are mapped. We hypothesize that even though the display and interaction surface are separated, the humans are nevertheless able to perform competently based on one's proprioceptive sense. While sensing for finger touch positions on the hand/skin surface remains to be a technical hurdle, we first explore whether our hypothesis is valid through an enactment study comparing the performance the Touch Skin input to that of the nominal smart phones.

**Keywords:** Touch screen · Proprioception · Smart watch

## 1 Introduction

The smart watch has limited input and output capabilities due to its form factor. As such they are used more as of a fashion item and a surrogate slave device to the larger smart phones. For example, the touch screen on the smart watch can only display about four to six easily touchable icons (e.g. on a $2 \times 2$ grid) and touching in letters or digits, selecting an application out of many menu items can be very difficult. Improving the interactivity of the smart watch can make it more independent and self-contained device. With this motivation, we propose in this poster the concept of "Touch Skin (TS)," that enlarges the interaction space of the smart watch using the large hand (or skin) surface area and proprioceptive sense. Proprioception refers to the human's capability of sensing of the relative position of neighboring parts of the body and strength of effort being employed in movement [1]. In humans, it is provided by proprioceptors in skeletal striated muscles and in joints. With the TS, while the input interface is displayed on the small smart watch screen, the interaction is carried out on the hand surface to which the input interface elements (e.g. graphical buttons and keys) are mapped. We hypothesize that even though the display and interaction surfaces are separated, the humans are projected to nevertheless perform very well based on the proprioceptive sense. For example a human user might be able to pinpoint (with one's finger) to a particular part

© IFIP International Federation for Information Processing 2015
J. Abascal et al. (Eds.): INTERACT 2015, Part IV, LNCS 9299, pp. 607–610, 2015.
DOI: 10.1007/978-3-319-22723-8_72

on the hand (e.g. palm, back, fingers) up to some accuracy and resolution, e.g. up to par with similar touch screen devices. The concept of TS is well illustrated in Fig. 1.

To realize "Touch Skin", sensing movement or position on skin surface and installing such a capability on the smart watch will be the major technical challenge. We believe that, for example, a smart watch equipped with a depth or ultrasonic sensor on its side can detect finger position on the palm at sufficient resolution to realize our proposal (see Fig. 1). In this study, however, as a first step, we explore whether the proposed interaction scheme will perform sufficiently or comparable to that of the smart phone (for certain major tasks) through an enactment study (i.e. pretending as if the finger/skin tracking is operational).

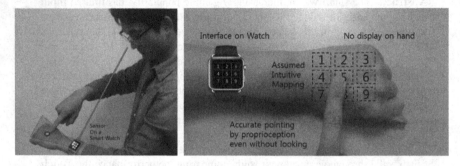

**Fig. 1.** The concept of the proprioception based "Touch Skin" input method for a small screen device.

## 2   Related Work

Proprioception has been applied to HCI in few occasions. Mine et al. introduced the concept of the "scale-down grab" in which a remote object manipulation was carried out by scaling down the entire scene and bringing the target object within reach and rely on the proprioceptive sense to manipulate it well [2]. Gustafson et al. presented the notion of "imaginary" interface in which one might interact on an arbitrary object well even a without display (e.g. on the palm) as a convenient substitute. While similar to our approach, theirs was not based on the notion of proprioception, but rather similarity in the physical mapping and familiarity [3]. Using the skin (e.g. palm of the hand) for interaction surface is an increasingly popular idea. In the context of wearable augmented reality, it is an attractive option where a interface elements can be augmented onto the hand using a projector or through a see-through display [4] and where the fingers/hands are tracked using a vision based approach. Skinput, on the other hand, by Harrison et al., sought to transform the skin into a touch screen like surface by analyzing the mechanical vibrations that propagate throughout the body [5]. Laput et al. presented an augmented input method for smart watches, by projecting icons on the nearby user skin and making them touch sensitive [6]. Our concept is similar except that we claim that the interaction surface can be relatively far from the small screen device (like the smart watch) without any display.

# 3 Experiment

## 3.1 Experimental Procedure

The purpose of the "enactment" pilot experiment was just to quickly and partially validate the feasibility of our approach, that is, whether the proposed proprioceptive interaction can produce input performance competitive to that of the usual smart phone. Five paid subjects, 4 men and 1 women with a mean age of 25 (one left handed), participated in the experiment. The experiment tested four input methods: (1) regular smartphone input, (2) TS with keys mapped to the palm, (3) TS with keys mapped to the back of the hand, and (4) TS with keys mapped to the fingers (see Fig. 2). The dependent variables were the input completion time, error, and answers to a usability questionnaire (omitted here for lack of space).

The task was to enter fifteen 10 digit numbers as quickly and accurately as possible using the respective input methods tried out in balanced order. The experiment was an enactment because detecting of the skin touch was not implemented, thus no sensor error nor delay was considered. The subject performance was recorded by a video camera and measured manually by the experimenter. When the TS was used, the input key layout was displayed on a separate monitor screen in a small scale (as small of a smart watch screen). The subject wore a glove with the input key mapping drawn on it just to aid the experimenter manually measure for the input error while reviewing the recorded video footage. The subjects were instructed to enter the numbers as fast and accurately as possible. When testing for the three TS conditions, they were also instructed to only watch the monitor screen rather than their hands.

## 3.2 Results

The three TS conditions did not differ in the task completion time but TS with the mapping on the back of the hand showed a lower accuracy with a statistical significance. When compared to the smartphone, the TS finger and TS palm were less accurate but actually slightly faster in performance (see Fig. 2). The survey showed that while the smartphone touch screen interface was still superior in most categories, TS still received a very positive response and even preferred over the smartphone. Overall, we can see that given a stable skin event detection method, the TS would exhibit reasonable input performance with satisfactory usability.

# 4 Discussion and Conclusion

In this poster, we propose "Touch Skin (TS)" that enlarges the interaction space of the smart watch using the hand (or skin) surface and proprioceptive sense. While the input interface is displayed on the small smart watch screen, the interaction is carried out by touching on the larger hand surface to which the input interface elements (e.g. graphical buttons and keys) are mapped. The pilot enactment study showed promising results of input performance and usability competent to that of the smart phone. We plan to implement and mount a finger detection sensor on the smart watch and conduct a more formal and full-fledged usability experiment to further validate our approach.

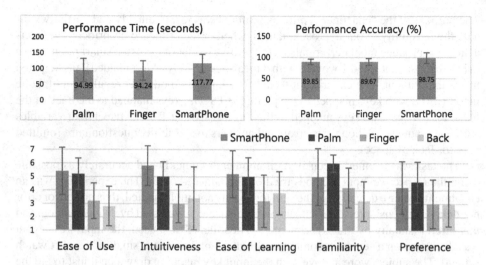

**Fig. 2.** Top: performance results between TS palm, TS finger and smartphone: task completion time (left) and accuracy (right). Bottom: usability survey results.

**Acknowledgements.** This research was funded by the Forensic Research Program of the National Forensic Service (NFS), Ministry of Government Administration and Home Affairs, Korea. (NFS-2015-DIGITAL-04), and the Basic Science Research Program through the National Research Foundation of Korea (NRF) funded by the Ministry of Science, ICT & Future Planning (No. 2011-0030079).

# References

1. Wikipedia: Proprioception (2015). http://en.wikipedia.org/wiki/Proprioception
2. Mine, M., Brooks, F., Sequin, C.: Exploiting proprioception in virtual-environment interaction. In: SIGGRAPH, pp. 19–26 (1997)
3. Gustafson, S., Bierwirth, D., Baudisch, P.: Imaginary interfaces: spatial interaction with empty hands and without visual feedback. In: UIST, pp. 3–12 (2010)
4. Mistry, P., Maes, P.: SixthSense : a wearable gestural interface. In: SIGGRAPH Asia 2009 Sketches, p. 11 (2009)
5. Harrison, C., Tan, D., Morris, D.: Skinput: appropriating the body as an input surface. In: SIGCHI, pp. 453–462 (2010)
6. Laput, G., Xiao, R., Chen, X., Hudson, S., Harrison, C.: Skin buttons: cheap, small, low-powered and clickable fixed-icon laser projectors. In: UIST, pp. 389–394 (2014)

# Towards In-Air Gesture Control of Household Appliances with Limited Displays

Euan Freeman[1]([✉]), Stephen Brewster[1], and Vuokko Lantz[2]

[1] Glasgow Interactive Systems Group, University of Glasgow,
Glasgow, Scotland, UK
{euan.freeman,stephen.brewster}@glasgow.ac.uk
[2] Nokia Technologies, Espoo, Finland
vuokko.lantz@nokia.com

**Abstract.** Recent technologies allow us to interact with our homes in novel ways, such as using in-air gestures for control. However, gestures require good feedback and small appliances, like lighting controls and thermostats, have limited, or no, display capabilities. Our research explores how other output types can be used to give users feedback about their gestures, instead, allowing small devices to give useful feedback. We describe the *Gesture Thermostat*, a gesture-controlled thermostat dial which gives multimodal gesture feedback.

**Keywords:** In-air gestures · Household devices · Multimodal feedback

## 1 Introduction

Our homes are becoming increasingly interactive. Small household appliances, like lighting controls and thermostats, are being enriched with new interaction modalities. Users can now interact with their household environments using their smartphones, speech commands and even in-air gestures. Gesture interaction is especially compelling as users can interact from across the room and without having to first locate their smartphone or a remote control. Unlike speech, gestures do not disturb others and work in noisy household environments, where chatter, music and television may cause speech recognition difficulties.

In-air gesture interaction, like speech, can be uncertain and users require lots of feedback during interaction, so that they can gesture confidently and effectively. Many household appliances have limited ability to give feedback, however. They typically have small displays, or no display at all, meaning visual feedback would be difficult to see from a short distance away. Users would lose the benefits of gesturing from across the room if they had to approach a device first to see feedback about their gestures and the effects they are having.

Changing the form factor of such devices to accommodate a larger screen is undesirable, as doing so increases size, cost and power demands. In our research, we are exploring other ways for household controls to give users feedback during interaction. This paper describes the *Gesture Thermostat*, a gesture-controlled

© IFIP International Federation for Information Processing 2015
J. Abascal et al. (Eds.): INTERACT 2015, Part IV, LNCS 9299, pp. 611–615, 2015.
DOI: 10.1007/978-3-319-22723-8_73

thermostat dial which gives users multimodal feedback about their gestures. Interactive lighting illuminates the surrounding wall to give visual feedback as users gesture (see Fig. 1). We also use sound, from within the device, and vibration, from a smart-watch, to enhance the feedback.

## 2   Related Work

Many have found that users are more willing to interact with small devices from a distance than they are to approach them for input. Valkkynen *et al.* [7] found that users preferred to interact with objects by pointing at them, rather than touching them, when more than a step away. Even when on their feet or walking past objects, users would rather gesture than go out of their way to touch them. Rukzio *et al.* [5] also found that distal interactions were more preferred than approaching objects to interact with them. These distal interactions allow what Koskela *et al.* [2] call *instant control* of household appliances: immediate, convenient access to basic functionality.

Offermans *et al.* [3] looked at interaction with household lighting. They found that access to controls had a strong influence on willingness to interact: users were more likely to interact when controls were easily accessible. They noted that mobile devices – remote controls and smartphones – often required too much effort and had inconsistent availability. We think in-air gestures could be a convenient alternative, allowing direct interaction when desired. Users could gesture from across the room for instant control of basic functionality, like switching lights off or setting the air conditioning to a cooler temperature.

In-air gestures are also available when other interaction modes are inconvenient or unavailable; for example, touch is less appropriate when cooking. *Kinect in the Kitchen* [4] explored this scenario further, allowing users to browse recipes and set cooking timers using in-air gestures. They found that gestures were effective but users required more feedback. Others have used in-air gestures for interacting with lighting controls, [1] and [6]. Both used the lighting itself as functional feedback: users saw immediate feedback from how the lights changed in response to gestures. Functional feedback is often unavailable and gives limited insight into interaction, however. Users receive little feedback during gestures and if movements are unrecognised, they receive none at all.

## 3   Gesture Thermostat

Gestures give users another way to interact with household devices, although they need sufficient feedback to help them interact. Many household appliances have limited display capabilities, which limits their ability to give feedback. Functional feedback is often unavailable and does not give users enough information to help them gesture. We are exploring other ways of giving users feedback during gesture interaction with household devices. We focus on interaction with thermostats as these are common devices with limited displays and no immediately noticeable effects; such devices benefit most from extra feedback.

Our *Gesture Thermostat* prototype (see Fig. 1) has three types of output which can be used for gesture feedback: interactive light, sound and vibration. Lights embedded in the thermostat dial (46 LEDs, approx 7 mm apart) illuminate the surrounding wall, giving visual feedback over a large area which users can easily see from across the room. An internal speaker provides audio feedback. Wearable devices, like smart-watches, could also be used as tactile displays for feedback. We use a simple actuator as a prototype smart-watch. In the rest of this paper and in our poster, we describe the *Gesture Thermostat*, its gestures and feedback designs, and initial findings from a user evaluation.

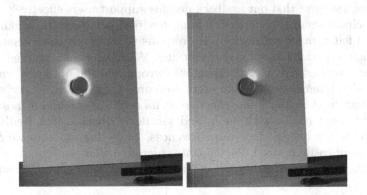

**Fig. 1.** The *Gesture Thermostat* illuminates surrounding areas for visual feedback (Color figure online).

## 3.1 Gesture and Feedback Design

We use gestures for basic functionality – adjusting temperature – as this allows *instant control* [2]. More complex interactions, like programming the thermostat schedule, are less suited for in-air gestures. We give users two ways of adjusting temperature: (1) imprecise "punch" gestures, which increase or decrease temperature by a few degrees; and (2) precise "dial" gestures, which allow finer-grained temperature control.

Users initiate interaction by raising their hand with a closed fist. Upon detecting this gesture, the thermostat plays a short tone, emits a short vibration if a smart-watch is available, and reads the current temperature setting aloud; for example "twenty-two degrees". All lights turn on with a low brightness and pulse slowly to show continued responsiveness. A single area of coloured light shows the temperature setting; blue light for cooler temperatures on the left (Fig. 1, left), red light for warmer temperatures on the right (Fig. 1, right).

From this position, users can quickly move their hand up-then-down or down-then-up to raise or lower the temperature, respectively. Audio and tactile feedback are given to confirm a recognised gesture and lights update to show the new thermostat setting. Alternatively, users can open their hand, as though about to grasp the dial, and turn it left or right to lower or raise the temperature. We use rate-based rather than position-based control due to hand instability and sensing inaccuracy. As users perform the dial gestures, white lights stop pulsing and the coloured area of light pulses instead; this helps users identify between interaction modes. Users are given feedback about their gestures, as before.

## 3.2 Initial Evaluation Results

Our initial evaluation asked eight users to complete tasks using the thermostat. Our findings suggest that our feedback designs support users effectively. Evaluation participants generally understood how feedback related to their hand movements and felt it made the device seem responsive; however, some wanted more information, especially about gesture sensing. When users encountered tracking issues, they were aware that something was wrong, but did not know why. More feedback about sensing could help users overcome these issues.

Although light feedback was effective on its own, users found it most salient and useful when paired with audio and tactile feedback. Light feedback was continuous which helped show responsiveness, while discrete audio and tactile feedback were easily noticed. Participants suggested that non-visual cues made visual changes more noticeable and made the thermostat seem more responsive.

## 4    Summary

In-air gestures allow users to interact with small household devices quickly and from a distance. Users need feedback to gesture effectively, although many household devices have limited feedback capabilities. Our *Gesture Thermostat* exemplifies how embedded lights, sound and vibration from wearables can be used to give gesture feedback. Our initial findings are positive: these outputs help users gesture effectively and make devices fun and responsive.

**Acknowledgements.** This research was part-funded by Nokia Technologies, Finland.

## References

1. Djajadiningrat, T., Geurts, L., Bont, J., Chao, P.: Grace: A gesture-controlled wake-up light. In: Proceedings of the DeSForM 2012, pp. 130–136 (2012)
2. Koskela, T., Väänänen-Vainio-Mattila, K.: Evolution towards smart home environments: empirical evaluation of three user interfaces. Pers. Ubiquit. Comput. **8**, 234–240 (2004)
3. Offermans, S., van Essen, H., Eggen, J.: User interaction with everyday lighting systems. Pers. Ubiquit. Comput. **18**(8), 2034–2055 (2014)
4. Panger, G.: Kinect in the kitchen: testing depth camera interactions in practical home environments. In: CHI 2012 Extended Abstracts, pp. 1985–1990. ACM Press (2012)

5. Rukzio, E., Leichtenstern, K., Schmidt, A.: Mobile interaction with the real world: an evaluation and comparison of physical mobile interaction techniques. In: Proceedings of the Am I 2007, pp. 1–18. Springer (2007)
6. Sørensen, T., Andersen, O., Merritt, T.: "Tangible lights": In-air gestural control of home lighting. In: Proceedings of the TEI 2015, pp. 727–732. ACM Press (2015)
7. Välkkynen, P., Niemelä, M., Tuomisto, T.: Evaluating touching and pointing with a mobile terminal for physical browsing. In: Proceedings of the NordiCHI 2006, pp. 28–37. ACM Press (2006)

# Video-Conferencing in E-commerce Website: Effect on Perceived Service Quality and Trust

Suleman Shahid[1], Abdullah Al Mahmud[2], and Omar Mubin[3(✉)]

[1] Tilburg Center for Cognition and Communication,
Tilburg University, Tilburg, The Netherlands
s.shahid@uvt.nl
[2] Swinburne University of Technology, Melbourne, Australia
[3] University of Western Sydney, South Penrith, Australia
o.mubin@uws.edu.au

**Abstract.** This study investigates the effect of the presence of live video support in an e-commerce environment on online trust, perceived customer friendliness and perceived quality of service. Participants were asked to rent a car at a car rental website. They needed to find specific information, which was offered, in the form of live video, pre-recorded video or text. Results showed that presence of live video increases perceived support in finding information, perceived customer friendliness and perceived quality of service.

**Keywords:** E-commerce · Live video · Service quality

## 1 Introduction

E-commerce has shown rapid growth numbers in the last decade. The market for e-commerce goods has doubled in the period between 2005 and 2010 and is still growing with 15 % [1]. However, there are several aspects of e-commerce, which might withhold consumers from taking part in it. One of the most important disadvantages in e-commerce is based on the lack of personal contact between a customer and a vendor. Salespeople play a key role in the formation of long-term buyer-seller relationships [2]. As the primary link between the buying and selling firms, they have considerable influence on the buyer's perceptions of the seller's reliability and the value of the seller's services and consequently the buyer's interest in continuing the relationship [2]. Personal interaction between customers and vendors does not only affect trust in a company, it also affects perceived service quality by the customer. There are many definitions of the construct 'service quality', but in all definitions personal interaction is a key influencer of service quality [3]. Personal interaction does not only affect online trust. It is also seen as one of the five basic dimensions of service quality [3]. Reference [4] states that customer perceptions of website quality and service quality predict the purchase likelihood for customers. What if there would be more personal contact between the customer and the vendor in e-commerce? Would it

J. Abascal et al. (Eds.): INTERACT 2015, Part IV, LNCS 9299, pp. 616–620, 2015.
DOI: 10.1007/978-3-319-22723-8_74

enhance the trustworthiness of the e-business and the service quality perceived by the customer? This is what we investigate in this study.

The media-richness theory states [6] that a medium can be ranked by its richness, which is based on the possibility to provide direct feedback, the number of cues it can handle, and the opportunity to communicate emotions. Reference [6] also mentioned video conferencing as the richest medium after face-to-face contact. The use of live video streams in e-commerce is an underexposed topic in research. Now that live video is a viable option, there is a need for more research on how it can be implemented in e-commerce environments to make it more personal and how would it affect online trust and service quality.

## 2   Method

The study included a total of 67 participants. Their average age was 27.44 (SD = 6.51) years and all participants were at least 18 years old. The sample was about equally divided between males and females (49 % male). The study used a between subject design. There was one independent variable with three levels. The independent variable was the form in which information was presented (live video, pre- recorded video, text). The dependent variables were perceived trustworthiness and perceived service quality measured by the rating on statements, which could be answered on a 5-point Likert-scale.

A website of a fictitious car rental company was created which was a fully working car rental application which participants can use to book a car, find information about cars, insurance, and information about the company. In the 'live video' condition, participants had a possibility to establish a live video stream between themselves and an employee of the company, played by an assistant of the researcher. The participants had an option to switch on or off their webcam in this condition. In the 'recorded video' condition, videos were made in which the same assistant of the researcher provided information on rental conditions, how to use the website and insurance fees. These videos were embedded on the TempCar website. In the 'text' condition, the same information was given using the text format. A questionnaire with statements on trustworthiness and service quality of TempCar was made. The statements on service quality were taken from the SERVQUAL questionnaire, which were adjusted for websites by [5]. The statements represent different aspects of trust and service quality in e-commerce environments and could be answered on a 5-point Likert-scale with answers varying from 1 being 'Very poor' to 5 'Very good'.

Participants were instructed to find information on renting a car website. The car needed to meet specific requirements. They had to find information on insurance fees, renting costs and whether or not their friend was allowed to drive in the car. In the live video condition, participants could not find the answer to all the questions on the website, but were steered into asking for help in a live video chat. For instance, when they were looking for information about insurance fees, they would find a page with information on insurance which said they could use the live help function on the website for information on insurance fees (see Fig. 1). In the pre-recorded video

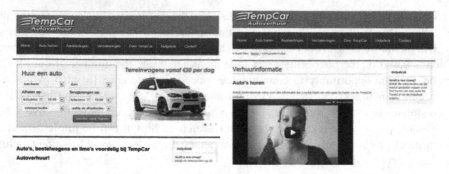

**Fig. 1.** TempCar website and videos

condition, participants could only find the answer in the videos displayed on the helpdesk page. In the 'text condition', the information was presented in a textual form on a FAQ page. For the text page to be as similar as possible, the required information can be found in the middle of a paragraph, instead of the usual 'question-answer' form used in FAQ pages. This mimics the characteristics of video, where you cannot just scan the video to find the information you are looking for. Participants have to watch the video as a whole to find the information.

## 3    Results

A one-way ANOVA was run to find differences in the mean scores on statements on perceived trust and service quality between the three conditions (live video, pre-recorded video, text). All mean scores can be found in Table 1. In all conditions only those participants who used these feature to get actual help were included. When significant differences were found, Gabriel's test was used as a post hoc analysis, because the sample sizes were unequal (4 more participants in the live condition as compared to other two). Gabriel's test can be unreliable when the assumption of homogeneity has been violated. This was tested for by Levene's test and a violation of homogeneity was not the case in the sample used for this study.

**Table 1.** Mean scores of participants in three conditions

|                       | Text        | Video       | Live video  |
|-----------------------|-------------|-------------|-------------|
| Perceived support     | 3.67 (.66)  | 3.33 (.80)  | 4.20 (1.04) |
| Customer friendliness | 3.48 (.68)  | 3.62 (.59)  | 4.56 (.77)  |
| Quality of service    | 2.57 (.60)  | 3.43 (.75)  | 4.04 (.79)  |
| Trustworthiness       | 3.62 (.81)  | 3.48 (.87)  | 3.63 (.84)  |

Significant differences were found between the scores on perceived support in finding the required information in the three conditions. A one-way ANOVA showed a strong effect of the medium used to present the information perceived support, $F(2, 64) = 5.98$, $p = < .01$, $\omega = .35$. A live video increases the perceived support by a company. An even greater effect was found for perceived customer friendliness, $F(2, 64) = 17.16$, $p = < .001$, $\omega = .57$. The perceived customer friendliness was indeed higher in the live video condition. The scores on perceived quality of service were significantly higher among users of the live video help than among the other participants, $F(2, 64) = 4.61$, $p = < .05$, $\omega = .31$. A one-way ANOVA for the trustworthiness dimension showed no significant differences between the three conditions. The post hoc analysis shows that participants in the live video condition rate the perceived support, quality of service and customer friendliness significantly higher than the other two conditions but there was no difference between the text and record video conditions.

## 4 Discussion and Conclusion

This study investigated how the presence of a live video effects perceive support customer friendliness, quality of service and trustworthiness of an e-commerce website. The results clearly show that use of live video has a positive effect on almost all dimensions. Despite being instructed repeatedly to contact the live video helpdesk to find all the required information, 37 % of the participants in the live video condition did not contact the live video help. There seemed to be resistance to contact a company to find information on the Internet, even though participants could not find all the required information needed to complete the task. Although participant were not forced to switch on their webcam and company representative's video stream was enough to get the information, participants stated they were resistant to be seen by somebody, while being in front of a computer. There seemed to be serious privacy issues among the participants when it comes to being seen via a webcam connection. This is a strong indication that all the steps in using live video should be explained very clearly to reduce any uncertainties before users press a button to call for live video help. Interestingly, most participants who did use the live video help rated the experience as very good (M = 4.48, SD = .92). In future research we would like to test live text chat, live audio chat and live video chat to find out which form of live contact scores best on online trust, customer friendliness etc.

## References

1. Internetkassa: Online verkopen trekt weer aan (2011). http://www.internetkassa.nu/nieuws/738-online-verkopen-trekt-weer-aan.html. Accessed 27 March 2015
2. Biong, H., Selnes, F.: The strategic role of the salesperson in established buyer-seller relationships. Working paper report no. 96-118. Marketing Science Institute, Cambridge (1996)
3. Dabholkar, P.A., Thorpe, D.I., Rentz, J.O.: A measure of service quality for retail stores: scale development and validation. J. Acad. Mark. Sci. 24(1), 3–16 (1996)
4. Cao, M., Zhang, Q.Y., Seydel, J.: B2C e-commerce web site quality: an empirical examination. Ind. Manage. Data Syst. 105(5), 645–661 (2005)

5. Cox, J., Dale, B.G.: Service quality and e-commerce: an exploratory analysis. Manag. Serv. Q. **11**(2), 121–131 (2001)
6. Daft, R., Lengel, R.: Organizational information requirements, media richness and structural design. Manage. Sci. **32**, 554–571 (1986)

# Contextual Interaction Design Research:
## *Enabling HCI*

Martin Murer, Alexander Meschtscherjakov, Verena Fuchsberger,
Manuel Giuliani, Katja Neureiter, Christiane Moser, Ilhan Aslan,
and Manfred Tscheligi[✉]

Center for Human-Computer Interaction, Department of Computer Sciences,
University of Salzburg, Sigmund Haffner Gasse 18, 5020 Salzburg, Austria
{Martin.Murer,Alexander.Meschtscherjakov,
Verena.Fuchsberger,Manuel.Giuliani,Katja.Neureiter,
Christiane.Moser,Ilhan.Aslan,
manfred.tscheligi}@sbg.ac.at

**Abstract.** Human-Computer Interaction (HCI) has always been about humans, their needs and desires. Contemporary HCI thinking investigates interactions in everyday life and puts an emphasis on the emotional and experiential qualities of interactions. At the *Center for Human-Computer Interaction* we seek to bridge meandering strands in the field by following a guiding metaphor that shifts focus to what has always been the core quality of our research field: *Enabling HCI*, as a leitmotif, draws our attention to how each research activity may benefit desires, goals and objectives. *Enabling* expresses how human-computer interactions are always situated within someone's life, values, and needs; it emphasizes the power of thoughtful design to enable desired interactions and explore desirable futures and expresses how our research addresses the very essence of contextual qualities. This is facilitated through context-rich lab spaces that foster a maker culture for exploring novel forms of contextual interaction. Being an interdisciplinary research group that is rooted in the rich epistemological tradition of the field allows us to bridge boundaries between contemporary thinking and formerly prevalent domains, between established methodology and current research questions. In this paper we highlight how our organizational structure fosters this viewpoint on human-computer interactions.

## 1 Contextual.Interaction.Design.Research

In our research activities (e.g., a seven-year basic research project on "Contextual Interfaces", focusing on contextual qualities and interaction in factories and cars) we acknowledge that interactions are heavily dependent on the concrete, situated characteristics of the context in which they take place. This understanding results in a methodological viewpoint, which we entitle 'contextual.interaction.design.research'. Contextual research expresses our devotion to rich ethnomethodologically informed studies as well as the development and refinement of according methods. Our interaction designs are on one hand informed by those studies, aiming for user experiences that reflect the situated qualities of the context we address. On the other hand, we

© IFIP International Federation for Information Processing 2015
J. Abascal et al. (Eds.): INTERACT 2015, Part IV, LNCS 9299, pp. 621–623, 2015.
DOI: 10.1007/978-3-319-22723-8_75

consider design methods and processes as legitimate mode of inquiry, as means of critical reflection and exploration. With interaction design research we investigate and discuss the according methodological challenges and opportunities.

## 2 Enabling HCI – the Case of Six Research Groups

The Center is organized in six research groups that address particular aspects of HCI in its relation to specific areas of human life. While the respective epistemologies differ, *Enabling HCI* guides all of them. With **Contextual Persuasion** we seek to *enable* individuals and groups to change their attitude and behavior by means of interactive technologies. Research includes fieldwork in persuasive potentials, design of behavior change systems, and in situ studies of persuasive technologies. With research on **Human-Robot Interaction** we study how multimodal and natural interaction can *enable* social interaction with robots in challenging contexts such as industrial production, tele-operated medicine, and robots in public spaces.

We aim to *enable* new qualities of interaction through enhancing the knowledge about experiential and material use and design practices. This includes theoretical framings of the materiality of interactions, user experience, and constructive design research (**Material and Experiential Foundations**). By **Embodied Interaction Design** we explore sensorimotor skills and couplings to *enable* extended bodily perception and experiences. Through reflective design, engineering, and craft we seek to understand the material qualities of novel technologies.

The group on **Cooperation Experience** aims to *enable* and understand meaningful computer mediated cooperation by investigating needs for successful cooperative processes (e.g., social presence) as well as identifying the nature of resources within social cooperation (social capital). **Enhancing Life Experiences** seeks to *enable* and promote social interaction and health/well-being of selected user groups in the (extended) home by creating valuable technical solutions in a user-centered design approach. The respective focus lies on enhancing peoples' life experiences.

The different research topics are bridged with at the moment two dedicated contextual laboratories (**Car Interaction Lab** and **Fabrication Experience Lab**) that allow our researchers to design, prototype, and study contextual interactions.

## 3 Conclusion

The variety of viewpoints has allowed us to design new experiences through different HCI lenses with a particular focus on the context in which the interaction takes place, emphasizing the essence of interaction through making and reflection processes in our research. It enables us to focus our research on different core topics in HCI and at the same time use dedicated contexts as enabling design and research spaces. By building an environment in which researchers from different HCI domains can collaboratively create meaningful and tangible interaction designs in an atmosphere that is charged with experiential qualities of the contexts we address, we enrich both the design process, as well as the outcome of our research efforts. With *contextual.interaction. design.research* we have been able to identify relevant aspects of the constant, situated interplay between users and artifacts in order to create artifacts that enable humans to experience novel, exceptional, or disruptive interactions, aiming to go beyond current trends and imaginations.

# Organisational Overview: Institute for Design and Assessment of Technology, Vienna University of Technology (TU Wien)

Geraldine Fitzpatrick(✉), H. Tellioglu, W. Zagler, M. Pohl,
F. Güldenpfennig, O. Hödl, R. Ganhör, P. Mayer,
and C. Frauenberger

Argentinierstrasse 8 187-2, 1040 Vienna, Austria
geraldine.fitzpatrick@tuwien.ac.at
http://igw.tuwien.ac.at/

The *Institute for Design & Assessment of Technology* (IGW) is part of the Faculty of Informatics at the Vienna University of Technology and is historically comprised of two groups: *Multidisciplinary Design* and *Human Computer Interaction*, which also includes the *Centre for Applied Assistive Technology*. The institute is highly interdisciplinary, within a traditional computer science faculty. Members come from various backgrounds, enabling us to merge technical engineering and social sciences research with people-centred design. The Institute includes 35 employed faculty/researchers/students and over 10 associated PhD students, engaged in 30 projects funded by the EU and national funding agencies, and supported by administrative staff (Fig. 1).

**Fig. 1.** Members of IGW at an inter-group workshop in 2014.

The *Institute* can look back on more than two decades of research about end-users' participation, acceptance and adoption of new technologies, their motivations and experiences, and about ethics and the social impact of information and communication technologies. Our research is grounded in understanding the challenges of everyday contexts and our contributions are technical, theoretical and practical. We have particular expertise in mobile, tangible and sensor-based technologies and in applying participatory and co-design approaches, with access to cutting-edge technologies, such as eye-trackers, 3D printers, laser cutters and electronics labs. The groups of IGW are

© IFIP International Federation for Information Processing 2015
J. Abascal et al. (Eds.): INTERACT 2015, Part IV, LNCS 9299, pp. 624–625, 2015.
DOI: 10.1007/978-3-319-22723-8_76

united by a commitment to put technology in the service of people, that is, all design activities are initiated with people and contexts in mind.

We complete the second half of this overview by outlining each group's specialties and highlighting exemplary research projects.

The *Multidisciplinary Design Group* studies work practices and organization to design supporting technologies. Besides design thinking, the major intellectual work of the group is to achieve a deeper understanding of (collaborative) work practices and technology in use, e.g., in health care, architecture/urban planning, and other professional contexts. In the project *TOPIC*[1], the group seeks to offer a platform for informal carers' cooperation with formal carers by improving, integrating, making mobile multimodal communication easier and accessible.

The *Human Computer Interaction* group covers a broad agenda including: exploratory design, games design, information visualisation evaluation (in the Laura Bassi project, CVAST[2]), selfcare/healthcare, health/wellbeing, social interaction, older people, sustainability and local communities. Much of our research explores alternative approaches to more technology-driven agendas. An example is the *Give & Take*[2] project, exploring an ICT platform to enable senior citizens to reciprocally exchange services in their local communities. The *Outside the Box*[2] project, similarly steps back from the deficit-oriented view of much assistive technology work to explore possibilities with autistic children to create technologies that are fun and meaningful to the child.

The *Centre for Applied Assistive Technology* (AAT) designs and builds assistive technologies, not exclusively but mainly, for elderly people. The group runs an AAL laboratory for close-to-real-life user-centred research. An example project is *Hobbit*[3], which focuses on assistive robots and is currently running final trials in older people's homes in three EU countries. The robot designed and built as the project's outcome supports older people in living independently and hence aging well at home. AAT also has ethics expertise around these technologies.

---

[1] https://media.tuwien.ac.at/project/; http://www.topic-aal.eu/.

[2] http://igw.tuwien.ac.at/hci/index.php/projects; http://givetake.eu/; http://outsidethebox.at/.

[3] http://www.aat.tuwien.ac.at/de/project.html; http://hobbit-project.eu/.

# Technology Experience Research:
# A Framework for Experience Oriented
# Technology Development

Manfred Tscheligi[(✉)], Sebastian Egger, Peter Fröhlich,
Cristina Olaverri-Monreal, and Georg Regal

Innovation Systems Department, Business Unit Technology Experience,
AIT Austrian Institute of Technology GmbH,
Giefinggasse 2, 1210 Vienna, Austria
{manfred.tscheligi, sebastian.egger, peter.frohlich,
cristina.olaverri-monreal, georg.regal}@ait.ac.at

**Abstract.** The optimization as well as exploitation of various aspects of user experience is crucial for future technological innovation and adoption. As a consequence of individualization, industrialization and lifestyle orientation, user experience is becoming more and more a major paradigm in the industry as well as in research & technology organizations. This applies at the level of products (goods, services), at the level of (public) technical infrastructures as well as on the level of human oriented innovation cultures and approaches. Based on several years of experience in applied HCI research the *Business Unit Technology Experience* within the Innovation Systems Department at the Austrian Institute of Technology (AIT) has been established as a horizontal unit to bridge between innovation in technological infrastructures and the diverse needs of users, costumers or diverse infrastructure contexts. Providing different viewpoints of technology experience and applied HCI thinking is a vehicle to facilitate improved levels of experiential quality.

## 1 Viewpoints Towards a Business Agenda

Specific application areas and application situations comprise specific interaction contexts, which leads to a comprehensive concept of contextual experience. Over the past years, the field of Human-Computer Interaction (HCI) moved beyond the desktop and explored new forms of interaction in different contexts. An in-depth understanding of contextual characteristics and the focused orientation of future experience approaches are the prerequisite for mature applications and technologies. Contexts are built by a variety of technological building blocks. This demands a structured integration of technology experience into development cycles as well as strong movement towards experience oriented thinking rather than pure technological orientation.

An applied research environment has to be supported by a clear definition of dedicated business cases. **Institutional Experience** deals with experience-oriented strategies, methods and tools within organizations. Technology Experience has to be implemented within the organizations in the right way. Current internal mechanisms need improvement under the regime of a user and experience driven mindset.

© IFIP International Federation for Information Processing 2015
J. Abascal et al. (Eds.): INTERACT 2015, Part IV, LNCS 9299, pp. 626–627, 2015.
DOI: 10.1007/978-3-319-22723-8_77

**Experience Innovation Scouting** delivers detailed needs as a prerequisite for successful technologies of the future. Supporting the detailed and contextual understanding of experience needs is a major element in an optimized user-driven development strategy.

**Experience Creation** is transforming requirements, needs and contextual insights into tangible experiences (interfaces) to allow access to the different features of a technological system. There is growing awareness that future market success will highly depend on the quality at the interface level as well as on appropriate ideas for future interaction approaches.

With **Experience Trials** new experience approaches combined with different technological building blocks call for effective and methodological experimentation and evaluation approaches. There is still a gap between a mature setup of such studies and the current practice in technological development.

## 2  Viewpoints Towards a Research Agenda

The Unit is organized in four research streams. **Social and Collaborative Experience** aims to enhance the quality of experience for joint activities using various technologies, with specific technologies as well as induced by technologies. The enhancement and focused consideration of personal values in the existing as well as upcoming information and technology society is forming the second research stream on **Personal Value Enhancing Experience**. Users seek to achieve their values and technological artifacts are used to deliver these values. Technology Experience should support different values at the user side and gain understanding of the importance of different values from the perspective of an individual user.

In addition we are living in a mobile society where technological artifacts are ubiquitous. However, the very essence of needs of users on the move (e.g. intermodal transport information), characteristics of specific user groups (e.g. elderly users on the move) or enhanced experiences of specific mobility situations still offers some challenges. So the research stream of **Mobile User Experience** is dedicated to enhancing the experience of different situations of users on the move. **The Experience Foundations** research stream will complement theses more contextual viewpoints by investigating basic aspects such as key ingredients and understanding of technology experience, future methodological approaches (e.g. including the perspective of Quality of Experience) as well as emerging interaction paradigms.

## 3  Conclusion

The efficient synergy of these two levels of viewpoints allows a methodological driven research and innovation strategy. Technology experience research services are positioned between industrial and research technology providers and different kinds of end users and user groups, which will be more motivated to accept, utilize and invest in technologies with a higher degree of user experience quality.

# Usability Testing Practice
# at MIMOS Usability Lab

Norfarhana Abdollah[1($\boxtimes$)], Ashok Sivaji[1], and Masitah Ghazali[2]

[1] Usability/User Experience Lab, MIMOS Berhad,
Technology Park Malaysia, 57000 Kuala Lumpur, Malaysia
{norfarhana.abdollah,ashok.sivaji}@mimos.my
[2] Faculty of Computing, Universiti Teknologi Malaysia,
81310 Skudai, Malaysia
masitah.ghazali@mimos.my, masitah@utm.my

**Abstract.** This paper presents one of our practices in conducting usability testing. Accredited with ISO/IEC 17025:2005 software testing laboratory, we consider ISO usability sub-characteristics as the metrics for the usability evaluation.

**Keywords:** Usability evaluation · User experience testing · Software testing

## 1 Introduction

Practically, there are many different ways to apply by user experience practitioners to evaluate product's usability; depending on the type of the product; be it a website, a system, a standalone program, hardware devices and many more. We have our own approach to elicit usability of certain product, which depends on several conditions such as number of evaluators/resources available, project schedule, cost, product cycle stage, etc. By referring to [1] which defines usability as a subset of quality in use model consisting of effectiveness, efficiency and satisfaction for consistency with its established meaning, we present one of our usability testing methods we used which incorporates the combination of these three important metrics.

## 2 Usability Testing Practice

### 2.1 Setting up Task to Measure Effectiveness, Efficiency, Satisfaction

In order to evaluate each usability metrics in a more practical manner, setting up a task requires certain technique [2]. For example, to evaluate effectiveness of a product usage, the task will be setup as of how successful the user completed the task, how often the user produces errors and how easy the user can recover. Meanwhile, to evaluate efficiency, the task will be setup with enough repetitions of typical tasks to create realistic work rhythm, or by observing the users at their daily work to look for situations that interrupt or slow them down. For satisfaction, interview or survey will normally be part of the evaluation, or by performing a comparative preference testing.

© IFIP International Federation for Information Processing 2015
J. Abascal et al. (Eds.): INTERACT 2015, Part IV, LNCS 9299, pp. 628–629, 2015.
DOI: 10.1007/978-3-319-22723-8_78

## 2.2    Giving Score

Effectiveness and efficiency are measured by the successful completion of criteria breakdown from a scenario or task. For a task that matches totally to the set criteria, the moderator will mark the score to 'Yes'. A success mark is given the full credit of 100 %. Criteria that does not match at all will be given a 'No' mark, with credit of 0 %. 'No' is normally given for unsuccessful task criteria which may include events such as user giving up, user requires a lot of assistance from moderator, user incompletes the task etc. While partial credit is given based on moderator's discretion, for e.g. moderator decides that the mistake should be given at least 50 % (partial) rather than 0 % (no) mark. Measures of satisfaction are taken using post questionnaires with users. The questions will appear each time the user completed or abandons the pre-setup task.

## 2.3    Calculating Individual Metrics and Usability Score

Following are the calculations for each metric score:

- Effectiveness (%) = (yes + (partial × 0.5))/total × 100 %
- Efficiency (%) = (yes + (partial × 0.5))/total × 100 %
- Satisfaction (%) = answer point/total point × 100 %

The way we calculate the overall usability score is as follows:

- Usability (%) = (effectiveness % + efficiency % + satisfaction %)/3

The total usability score is the sum of the three metrics scores divided by three, i.e. the average.

# 3    Conclusion

We have applied the method discussed in this paper for many different case studies and tested usability for many different types of products. Comfortable with the method, we have developed and configure our own software tool called Mi-UXLab to evaluate usability which incorporates the discussed method.

# References

1. Systems and software engineering – Systems and software Quality Requirements and Evaluation (SQuaRE) – System and software quality models, ref. no.: MS ISO/IEC 25010 (2011)
2. Quesenbery, W.: Balancing the 5Es of usability. Cutter IT J. **17**(2), 4–11 (2004)

# Design, Innovation and Respect in the Global South

Jose Abdelnour-Nocera[1,2]($\boxtimes$), Chris Csikszentmihályi[2],
Torkil Clemmensen[3], and Christian Sturm[4]

[1] Sociotechnical Centre for Innovation and User Experience,
University of West London, London, UK
Jose.abdelnour-nocera@uwl.ac.uk
[2] Madeira Interactive Technologies Institute, Funchal, Portugal
csik@m-iti.org
[3] Copenhagen Business School, Frederiksberg, Denmark
tc.itm@cbs.dk
[4] Hamm-Lippstadt University of Applied Sciences, Hamm, Germany
c.sturm@arolis.com

**Abstract.** The aim of this panel is to facilitate a discussion on the practice of interaction design in the Global South in the context of current global discourses on development, as particularly evidenced in the United Nations' post-2015 development agenda. The panel will generate a thought-provoking debate based on different experiences and cultural and political reflections on designing and innovating in the Global South.

**Keywords:** Interaction design · Innovation · Development · Global south

## 1 Panel Topics and Objective

The aim of this panel is to explore the current global discourse on development and situate these in terms of the real challenges faced by interaction designers 'on the ground'. Through their different perspectives and experiences panelists, will articulate the different ontological, epistemological and methodological dimensions of the concept and practice of interaction design in the Global South. This means questioning (1) 'what' we mean by design; (2) the relationships 'between' designers, what is designed and the intended users of those designs; and (3) 'how' we design.

At different levels the panelists will question the development discourse with a particular focus on the United Nations new universal agenda for post-2015 development goals set in 2013 by a high-level panel of presidents and foreign ministers: To what extent should the field of interaction design and international development (IDID) be underpinned by this agenda? Are development discourses such as the post 2015 agenda limiting innovation and sustainability in the Global South? How can designers in the Global South untangle the cultural and political scripts embedded in imported ID practices and tools? How can the Global South create their own design practices outside of these development discourses?

The panel will provoke different answers and a useful debate around these issues.

© IFIP International Federation for Information Processing 2015
J. Abascal et al. (Eds.): INTERACT 2015, Part IV, LNCS 9299, pp. 630–632, 2015.
DOI: 10.1007/978-3-319-22723-8_79

# 2 Panelists

## 2.1 Chris Csikszentmihályi: Innovating in the Global South

"As a humanist technologist, most of my work has been developed in the US for American users and situations. I have recently taken up the challenge of developing new technologies in the context of Uganda; we hope that what we are creating there might also be useful in much of the rest of the world. But Uganda is awash with the rubric of "development," a fraught set of actors, agendas, and assumptions, and indeed one of the largest and most ubiquitous industries in this and many other countries. So even though my current project, RootIO seeks to create a platform for intra-community dialog in rural areas, when most professionals of any sort working in Uganda are exposed to it, they immediately state that it would be a great platform for development messaging and behavior change. These different goals, while not wholly exclusive, are very different. In this panel I hope to describe why I am less interested in development messaging than in intra-community media, and how we are designing for the latter but constantly forced into the mold of the former. I'll bring in some of the post-colonial theory that informs our work, and how we feel that there is a difference between how users are defined in the Global South versus the North."

Chris Csikszentmihalyi is the current ERA chair at Madeira Interactive Technologies Institute. He has been a professor at colleges, universities, and institutes, including Distinguished Visiting Professor of Art and Design Research at Parsons the New School for Design. He cofounded and directed the MIT Center for Future Civic Media (C4), which was dedicated to developing technologies that strengthen communities. He also founded the MIT Media Lab's Computing Culture group, which worked to create unique media technologies for cultural and political applications. Trained as an artist, he has worked in the intersection of new technologies, media, and the arts for 16 years, lecturing, showing new media work, and presenting installations on five continents and one subcontinent. He was a 2005 Rockefeller New Media Fellow, and a 2007–2008 fellow at Harvard's Radcliffe Institute for Advanced Study, and has taught at the UC San Diego, Rensselaer Polytechnic Institute, and Turku University.

## 2.2 Torkil Clemmensen: Reframing HCI Concepts and Tools

"If we are to support a sustainable development, we need to integrate social, economic and environmental dimensions in our development and use of IT. I want to focus on the importance of reframing HCI from local perspectives by integrating cultural perspectives on HCI research and practice. In particular we need (a) new concepts of usability and UX which are grounded in the practices of local people and local companies, (b) a more diverse toolbox of HCI methods that better covers the diversity of human life, and (c) to develop the UX profession itself (certification, specialization, community building). Paradoxically, to reframe HCI from local perspectives not only requires more empirical studies, but also reconsidering what theories that we use."

Torkil Clemmensen, PhD, Professor mso at Department of IT Management, Copenhagen Business School, Denmark. His interest is in Human-Computer Interaction, in particular psychology as a science of design. The focus of his research is on cultural psychological perspectives on usability and user experience. As Danish representative in IFIP (International Federation of Information Processing) TC 13(Technical committee on Human-Computer Interaction), and chair (2008–2014) of Working Group 13.6 on Human Work Interaction Design (HWID), he co-organizes a series of international working conferences on work analysis and usability/user experiences in organisational, human, social and cultural contexts.

### 2.3   Christian Sturm: Respect-Based Design

"It is not the economy - "It's the respect, stupid!" Contrary to the common perspective that economic development is driving the well-being of people around the world, it is the missing respect that is responsible for the lack of it: lack of respect from employers toward employees, lack of respect from employees toward their employers, lack of respect from politicians toward citizens and vice versa, lack of respect from researchers toward study participants, from developers and designers toward users...the list is almost infinite. I argue that teaching and practicing respect together with raising the level of self-awareness and awareness of others is the closest we can get contributing to the "Post-2015 Development Agenda". Let's think of respect-based design approaches we could develop to get started.

Christian is professor at the Hamm-Lippstadt University of Applied Sciences in Germany. He holds a bachelor in computer science from Furtwangen University and a PhD in cognitive psychology (major), cultural anthropology (minor) and telematics (minor) from the University of Freiburg. His research interests include cross-cultural aspects of HCI, UX and entrepreneurship, based on his experience living for many years in Mexico, Spain and Egypt.

### 2.4   Jose Abdelnour-Nocera: IDID Under a New Development Agenda

"In May 2013 a United Nations High-level panel released a new universal agenda for post-2015 development goals. This agenda sets new goals for poverty eradication and sustainable development. As a sociotechnical designer, I will discuss the relevance, validity and viability of these goals in terms of concrete design experiences with Namibian farmers, South African townships and Venezuelan rural doctors."

José is Associate Professor in Sociotechnical Design and Head of the Sociotechnical Centre for Innovation and User Experience at the University of West London. He is the current Chair for IFIP TC 13.8 working group in Interaction Design for International Development as well as Chair for the British Computer Society Sociotechnical Specialist Group. His interests lie in the sociotechnical and cultural aspects of systems design, development and use. In pursuing these interests, he has been involved as researcher and consultant in several projects in the UK and overseas in the domains of mHealth, e-learning, social development, e-commerce, e-governance and enterprise resource planning systems. Dr. Abdelnour-Nocera gained an MSc in Social Psychology from Simon Bolivar University, Venezuela and a PhD in Computing from The Open University, UK.

# Interaction and Humans in Internet of Things

Markku Turunen[1(✉)], Daniel Sonntag[2], Klaus-Peter Engelbrecht[3],
Thomas Olsson[4], Dirk Schnelle-Walka[5], and Andrés Lucero[6]

[1] University of Tampere, Tampere, Finland
markku.turunen@sis.uta.fi
[2] DFKI, Berlin, Germany
Daniel.Sonntag@dfki.de
[3] Technische Universität Berlin, Berlin, Germany
Klaus-Peter.Engelbrecht@telekom.de
[4] Tampere University of Technology, Tampere, Finland
thomas.olsson@tut.fi
[5] Slnn GmbH & Co. KG, Stuttgart, Germany
Dirk.schnelle@jvoicexml.org
[6] University of Southern Denmark, Odense, Denmark
lucero@mci.sdu.dk

**Abstract.** Internet of Things is mainly about connected devices embedded in our everyday environment. Typically, 'interaction' in the context of IoT means interfaces which allow people to either monitor or configure IoT devices. Some examples include mobile applications and embedded touchscreens for control of various functions (e.g., heating, lights, and energy efficiency) in environments such as homes and offices. In some cases, humans are an explicit part of the scenario, such as in those cases where people are monitored (e.g., children and elderly) by IoT devices. Interaction in such applications is still quite straightforward, mainly consisting of traditional graphical interfaces, which often leads to clumsy co-existence of human and IoT devices. Thus, there is a need to investigate what kinds of interaction techniques could provide IoT to be more human oriented, what is the role of automation and interaction, and how human originated data can be used in IoT.

**Keywords:** IoT · Novel interaction means · Automation

## 1 Introduction

Most successful Internet of Things applications nowadays provide quite straightforward user interfaces in comparison to the vast capabilities a smart device with smart materials, sensors and web access could actually provide. When thinking of the most successful practical IoT applications, human-technology interaction is mostly focused on graphical mobile or web interfaces – and in some cases embedded interaction devices such as touch screen panels. Typical examples include "smart home" devices, such as thermostats, ovens, and light fixtures. Since it is assumed that the IoT devices operate mostly automatically, the control interfaces are mainly targeted for initial setups or other more individual configuration operations. Another frequent task is monitoring of the device

© IFIP International Federation for Information Processing 2015
J. Abascal et al. (Eds.): INTERACT 2015, Part IV, LNCS 9299, pp. 633–636, 2015.
DOI: 10.1007/978-3-319-22723-8_80

state. Situated control of IoT devices is less frequent in current applications, but may gain importance once more of our everyday objects are connected to the IoT. For situated control, it is particularly desirable that we can interact with the device directly, rather than indirectly using graphical user interfaces. Moreover, the smart capabilities of IoT devices should be exploited for a more human-oriented, i.e. natural and tangible, interaction. To make IoT devices more human oriented we need to explore novel ways to interact with them in our daily life, research how user-friendly automation can be achieved, and analyze how human originated data can be utilized. In this panel, the key topics related to interaction in IoT are covered from these perspectives.

## 2    Interaction Techniques for IoT

As stated, most human-technology interfaces in IoT are still rather traditional, and usually based on GUIs. However, more natural multimodal interaction means, such as spoken and gestural interaction, for example, could provide more efficient and pleasant interaction with IoT devices. Still, such interfaces are not studied widely in IoT context, even there are some cases, which are mostly related to "non-serious" applications such as toys and other gadgets. What we need are success stories – or at least some stories – from experiences of different interaction techniques which have been studied in everyday IoT scenarios. The participants of the panel will demonstrate concrete examples and findings from novel IoT interfaces.

## 3    Automation and Interaction

One of the most interesting aspects of many IoT applications is the relation of automation and human control. For example, when IoT devices are used to automate certain functions in home environments, this creates huge challenges for acceptance of the technology, including critical factors such as safety, feeling of control, and privacy, among others. The key question is in which cases automation is more suitable and when human control should be preferred. The major factors for successful design for co-existence of automation and explicit interaction of IoT devices are discussed.

## 4    Human-Related Information in IoT

In addition to the explicit interaction between humans and devices, human originated information is often highly valuable or even crucial in many IoT applications. Most obvious examples include IoT applications monitoring humans. Practical examples include self-monitoring applications, which are typically related to health and well-being. Other examples include applications for monitoring of other people, such as children and elderly. Topics for discussion include novel means to gather, process and distribute human-oriented data, as well as key questions related to the human-factors, such as safety and privacy. Finally, it will be discussed how all of this affects and changes human behavior in the long run.

# 5 Panel Members

**Markku Turunen** is a professor of Interactive Technology at the School of Information Sciences in University of Tampere, Finland. He has been worked in the Tampere Unit for Computer-Human Interaction (TAUCHI) since 1998, leading a group on pervasive interaction. His fields of expertise include novel interaction techniques, software architectures for interactive systems, pervasive applications, interactive solutions for industrial settings, user experience of multimodal interaction, ecological valid evaluation methods (including showrooms, living labs, and long-term pilot studies) with representative user groups, and commercialization or research results. His teaching portfolio includes multiple courses on pervasive and multimodal interaction. He is also a CEO of Multisense Oy, a startup company specializing on advanced human-technology interaction.

**Dr. Daniel Sonntag** is a principal researcher and principal investigator/project leader at DFKI (Intelligent User Interfaces), reader at Saarland University and University of Kaiserslautern, and permanent member of the editorial board of the German Journal on Artificial Intelligence (KI). He has worked in natural language processing, multimodal interface design, dialogue systems, and knowledge representation for over 17 years and leads a team of more than 10 full-time researchers and engineers at DFKI, and 6 (PhD/Msc) students. His research interests include common-sense and machine learning methods for multimodal human computer interfaces and knowledge discovery, mobile interface design, cognitive modelling with ontologies, and usability for the Internet of the Future. He is particularly interested in practical methods for Augmented Cognition and Mixed Reality, Compensating Cognitive Impairments, (Medical) Cyber-Physical Systems, and Human-Machine Collaboration in Production.

**Klaus-Peter Engelbrecht** is working as a Postdoc at the Quality and Usability Lab, Telekom Innovation Laboratories, Technische Universität Berlin. He studied Communication Research and Musicology and received his Magister degree in 2006 from Technische Universität Berlin. In July 2011 he successfully defended his Dissertation thesis "Estimating Spoken Dialog System Quality with User Models". His more recent work deals with modeling how users experience interactions with automated dialog partners, and how this impacts their quality judgments. From 2013 through 2014, he managed the Forschungscampus project "Interaktion & Sensoren" funded by the Federal Ministry of Education and Research of Germany. In this project, novel ways of interacting with technology in the smart home were designed and evaluated.

**Thomas Olsson** is an adjunct professor of User Experience of Socio-Technical Systems at the Department of Pervasive Computing in Tampere University of Technology (TUT), Finland. He received the Dr. Tech. degree in 2012 with a thesis addressing user experience and user expectations of future mobile augmented reality systems. Currently he leads a research team focusing on social technologies that aim to enhance social interaction and collaboration between co-located people, utilizing technologies like proximity sensing, wearables and smart networked objects. His other research interests include user experience in various ubiquitous computing systems, covering, e.g., context awareness, internet of things and smart environments, as well as user-centered design and user expectations of new interactive technology.

**Dr. Dirk Schnelle-Walka** lead the "Talk&Touch" group at the Telecooperation Lab at TU Darmstadt until end of 2014. Since then, he works as a function owner speech&dialog for S1nn in the automotive industry to take his research portfolio to an industrial level. His research focus is on voice-centric multimodal interaction in smart spaces. He authored more than 50 book chapters, journal article and conference papers and is chairing the IUI workshop on Interacting Smart Objects and the EICS Workshop on Engineering interactive Systems with SCXML. He is also the head behind several open source projects around speech technology, e.g. the open source voice browser JVoiceXML.

**Andrés Lucero** is an Associate Professor of interaction design at the University of Southern Denmark in Kolding. His recent work at Nokia focused on the design and evaluation of novel interaction techniques for mobile phones and other interactive surfaces. He got his Masters degree in Visual Communication Design from Universidad Tecnológica Metropolitana (UTEM), Santiago, Chile. In 2004 he received a Professional Doctorate in Engineering (PDEng) degree in User-System Interaction from the Eindhoven University of Technology (TU/e) in the Netherlands, which included a one-year project in Philips Research. In 2009 he completed his PhD at the TU/e on co-designing mixed reality support tools for industrial designers. As part of his PhD work, he was a visiting researcher at the University of Art and Design Helsinki (TAIK) in Finland. His interests lie in the areas of mobile human-computer interaction, co-design, and design research.

# Role of Conferences in Shaping
# the Field of HCI

Jan Gulliksen[1], Simone Diniz Junqueira Barbosa[2], Anirudha Joshi[3],
Shaun Lawson[4], and Philippe Palanque[5(✉)]

[1] KTH Royal Institute of Technology, Stockholm, Sweden
gulliksen@kth.se
[2] PUC Rio, Rio de Janeiro, Brazil
simone@inf.puc-rio.br
[3] IIT Bombay, Mumbai, India
anirudha@iitb.ac.in
[4] LiSC, University of Lincoln, Lincoln, UK
slawson@lincoln.ac.uk
[5] ICS-IRIT, University of Toulouse, Toulouse, France
palanque@irit.fr

**Abstract.** The panel will discuss the role various conferences have played in developing the field of HCI in academic research and industrial practice. It is composed of people who have experience in organising HCI conferences in different parts of the world. It provides a platform to the participants to think and reflect about what they are doing when attending a conference, what their expectations are and how it impacts positively their knowledge, work and career.

**Keywords:** Human-computer interaction · Conferences

## 1 Introduction

Why go to an international conference? Is it because you see it as a good way to justify that your university pays you to travel the world? Is it because you like to hang out and drink beers with a lot of fun people? Is it because you love to be on the stage and talk about yourself and how good you are? Is it because you think you will get new contacts and sneak you way into a research position that you otherwise would not be able to get? Or do you think it is a way to get famous?

This panel aims at scrutinizing whether it is sustainable to continue polluting the planet by making big crowds travel all across the world for conferences. It aims at discussing whether the acceptance of papers in the field is based on excellence, or whether the system is simply corrupt. It aims at discussing whether it is a business for conference organizers to make money on the side or for big international organizations to colonize the world with their views and perspectives.

In the last two decades, HCI conferences have generally done well. Many conferences have grown in numbers. Some have increased their frequency. Some are broad, others are focussed. Some have explored new geographies, new cultures. New, smaller conferences have emerged, either specialising in a domain or catering to the interests of

© IFIP International Federation for Information Processing 2015
J. Abascal et al. (Eds.): INTERACT 2015, Part IV, LNCS 9299, pp. 637–639, 2015.
DOI: 10.1007/978-3-319-22723-8_81

a local community. Meanwhile, the world has gotten more connected by digital technologies, and more people are now online than ever were. Among other changes, virtual meetings have become more of a norm than an exception.

This is an interesting juncture to seek out what lies ahead and also to ponder about what we might be missing out. Many new questions are being raised that are interesting and relevant. Must all conferences have papers? What is an optimal size of a conference – 50, 500, 5,000, or 50,000? Are we focussing too much on the social programme? On the other hand, would it still be a "conference" if everyone were to participate remotely? Do we need to worry about the relatively infrequent participants – industry professionals, students, those with disabilities, new parents (especially mothers), and those from developing countries?

Worldwide, researchers, research units, and Universities are increasingly being subject to research evaluation exercises which often lead to far-reaching implications around funding, promotion and recruitment. Where do conferences fit within such evaluation programs? How are even the best conference publications viewed in such processes? How is the field of HCI influenced by other disciplines with different publication practices?

This panel consists of people with experience in organising small and large conferences in different parts of the world. They will introspect about the historical role of conferences in shaping the field of HCI and ponder about how they see conferences evolving over the next few years.

## 2 Panel Members

**Jan Gulliksen** is professor in Human Computer Interaction and the Dean of the School of Computer Science and Communication at KTH Royal Institute of Technology, in Stockholm, Sweden. He is in charge of a school comprising 350 employed staff, educating about 1200 students each year. Jan teaches various courses in Human Computer Interaction, Usability and User-Centred Design at undergraduate and postgraduate level and does research on Usability, accessibility and user-centred design in practice. He has been associated with various conferences including CHI, INTERACT, NordiCHI, HCSE and others. He is the current chair of IFIP TC13 on HCI which is the organization in charge of the INTERACT conference series. He is also, as the founder of NordiCHI chairing the organization behind the NordiCHI conference.

**Simone Diniz Junqueira Barbosa** is associate professor at the Department of Informatics, PUC-Rio, Brazil. Level 2 researcher in CNPq (National Council for Scientific and Technological Development in Brazil) and chair of the Special Interest Group on Human-Computer Interaction of the Brazilian Computer Society, she has served as chair in several national and international conferences, e.g., Latin-American Conference on Human-Computer Interaction, CHI, INTERACT, EICS, and IHC.

**Anirudha Joshi** is professor in the interaction design stream in the Industrial Design Centre, IIT Bombay, India. His research is in the area of interaction design for people in developing countries. Much of his recent work is in designing text input mechanisms for

Indian languages. He also works in the cusp between human-computer interaction and software engineering. He has been IFIP TC13 representative from India. He has been active in organising several conferences including India HCI, APCHI, INTERACT, and CHI.

**Shaun Lawson** is Professor of Social Computing at the University of Lincoln in the UK where he directs the Lincoln Social Computing (LiSC) Research Centre. His research interests are mainly centred upon the design, use and implications of interactive social applications and social media. In particular he is interested in how these platforms can be used for political, activist and persuasive aims. He has extensive experience of conference management and organisation in HCI and social computing settings; most recently he was General Chair of British HCI 2015 and served on the organising committees for CHI in both 2014 and 2015.

**Philippe Palanque** is professor in Computer Science at the University Toulouse 3 France. He works in the area of interactive systems engineering with a focus on the dependability, safety and usability of critical systems. He is secretary of the IFIP Working group 13.5 on Human Error Safety and System Development and chaired with Chris Johnson the track on that topic within the IFIP WCC 2004. He was the general co-chair of CHI 2014 and full paper co-chair of INTERACT 2015 and has been on the SIGCHI executive committee in charge of specialized conferences since 2007.

# Design and Rapid Evaluation of Interactive Systems in Theory and Practice

Jochen Denzinger[1] and Tom Gross[2(✉)]

[1] ma ma Interactive System Design, Frankfurt, Germany
`jdenzinger@ma-ma.net`
[2] Human-Computer Interaction Group, University of Bamberg,
Bamberg, Germany
`tom.gross@uni-bamberg.de`

**Abstract.** In this half-day tutorial Jochen Denzinger, partner at the design studio ma ma Interactive System Design, and Tom Gross, full professor and chair of the Human-Computer Interaction at the University of Bamberg, present methodologies for understanding users, tasks, and contexts, for designing interactive systems beyond the desktop, and for evaluating them in novel domains.

**Keywords:** User centred design · Design thinking · Usability and user experience · Evaluation · Development processes · Cyber-Physical systems

## 1 Objectives and Contents

Recent trends such as the increasing convergence of the digital and the physical realm expand the scope of Human-Computer Interaction (HCI) to exciting new fields of application. However, they also entail new challenges for understanding users, tasks, and contexts, for designing interactive systems beyond the desktop, and for evaluating them in novel domains and sometimes with limited resources.

This tutorial aims to address those developments and to present paradigms and basic concepts of HCI as well as its design principles supporting development processes. The primary focus is on concepts, methods, and tools for the design, the implementation, and the evaluation of interactive systems for changing tasks and contexts in emerging technological landscapes—with a special focus on rapid and agile approaches.

In particular, this tutorial includes an introduction of the theoretical foundations of interaction design, interface design, and user experience design. It presents practical methods for the analysis of contexts, stakeholders, and goals; for generating ideas and design thinking; for managing and selecting ideas; for generating fast and graspable results by low-fidelity prototyping; as well as for the fast and effective evaluation of interactive systems in the lab and in the field.

The tutorial lasts half and is planned to proceed as follows: a short introduction of presenters and participants; a theoretical block with foundations; an open discussion on participants' personal questions and current challenges; a tour of practical methods (incl. practical exercise of the participants); and a wrap up and outlook [1–10].

© IFIP International Federation for Information Processing 2015
J. Abascal et al. (Eds.): INTERACT 2015, Part IV, LNCS 9299, pp. 640–641, 2015.
DOI: 10.1007/978-3-319-22723-8_82

## 2   Intended Audience

The intended audience are people from academia and industry, and beginners and experts with diverse and cross-disciplinary backgrounds.

## 3   Instructors

Jochen Denzinger is managing partner of the design studio ma ma Interactive System Design, in Frankfurt, Germany. For further information refer to http://www.ma-ma.net.

Dr. Tom Gross is full professor and chair of Human-Computer Interaction at the University of Bamberg, Germany. Further information can be found at: http://www.tomgross.net.

## References

1. Bannon, L.: Reimagining HCI: towards a more human-centred perspective. ACM Interact. **18**(4), 50–57 (2011)
2. Bürdek, B.E.: Design: the History, Theory and Practice of Product Design. Birkhäuser Architecture, Basel (2004)
3. Gross, T.: Towards a new human-centred computing methodology for cooperative ambient intelligence. J. Ambient Intell. Humanised Comput. (JAIHC) **1**(1), 31–42 (2010)
4. Hammond, J., Gross, T., Wesson, J. (eds.): Usability: Gaining a Competitive Edge. Kluwer Academic Publishers, Dordrecht (2002)
5. Hassenzahl, M.: Experience Design: Technology for All the Right Reasons. Morgan and Claypool Publishers, San Rafael (2010)
6. Holtzblatt, K., Wendel, J.B., Wood, S.: Rapid Contextual Design: A How-to Guide to Key Techniques for User-Centred Design. Elsevier, Amsterdam (2005)
7. Jordan, P.W.: Designing Pleasurable Products. Taylor & Francis Group, Boca Raton (2000)
8. Moggridge, B.: Designing Interactions. MIT Press, Cambridge (2007)
9. Norman, D.A.: Living with Complexity. MIT Press, Cambridge (2011)
10. Saffer, D.: Microinteractions: Designing with Details. O'Reilly, Sebastopol (2014)

# How to Design and Build New Musical Interfaces

Sidney Fels[1]([⊠]) and Michael Lyons[2]

[1] University of British Columbia, Vancouver, BC, Canada
ssfels@ece.ubc.ca
[2] Ritsumeikan University, Kyoto, Japan
michael.lyons@gmail.com

**Fig. 1.** Example Case Studies from the New Interfaces for Musical Expression (NIME) conference.

**Abstract.** This **half day** course introduces the field of musical interface design and implementation. Participants will learn and practice key aspects of the theory and practice of designing original interactive music technology with case studies including augmented and sensor based instruments, audio-visual instruments, mobile, and networked music making. Digital technologies offer powerful opportunities for the creation and manipulation of sound, however the flexibility of these technologies implies a confusing array of choices for musical composers and performers. Some artists have faced this challenge by using computers directly to create new musical forms. However, most would agree the computer is not a musical instrument, in the same sense as traditional instruments, and it is natural to ask 'how to play the computer' in a way appropriate to human brains and bodies. To attempt to answer this question in the course, we draw from the International Conference on New Interfaces for Musical Expression (NIME) [1,2], which began as a workshop of CHI 2001 [3] and explore connections with the established field of human-computer interaction.

**Keywords:** New interfaces for musical expression · Digital musical instruments

## 1 Learning Objectives and Structure

The course learning objectives are: 1. Provide a framework for understanding the current research on new musical interface technology; 2. Introduce the theory &

© IFIP International Federation for Information Processing 2015
J. Abascal et al. (Eds.): INTERACT 2015, Part IV, LNCS 9299, pp. 642–643, 2015.
DOI: 10.1007/978-3-319-22723-8_83

practice of NIME; 3. Point to further knowledge resources; 4. Get to know some of the people & work of NIME; 5. Suggest how to begin creating new musical interfaces for a lifetime of challenge & enjoyment. Participants will participate in a NIME design exercise.

The structure of the course is in two modules:

1. **Module A: Introduction, Tools, Design:** 1. Introduction; 2 Practical Guide to Building Musical Interfaces; 3. Video-based Interfaces; 4. Design and Aesthetics
2. **Module B: Case studies, Theory, and Education:** 1. Case studies; 2. Theory; 3. Education
3. **Design Exercise**

## 2  Intended Audience

Our primary objective in presenting this tutorial is to bring participants up-to-speed on the application of interactive techniques to music technology. No specific technical background is required, though some familarity with interactive systems may be helpful. In particular, we do not assume any prior knowledge of sensors, microcontrollers, audio synthesis methods, but rather aim to provide participants with an introduction to these areas, as well as pointers to resources for further study. As such, the tutorial should be well suited to beginning graduate students or advanced undergraduates who are interested in this area of research; composers and performers who wish to expand their repertoire of methods and tools; member of the general public curious about recent developments and ongoing research in music technology.

## 3  Reading List

The course notes will be available for attendees to read prior to the course. Currently, a version of the notes can be found at: http://www.ece.ubc.ca/~ssfels/InteractNIME2015.pdf.

## References

1. Bevilacqua, F., Fels, S., Jensenius, A.R., Lyons, M.J., Schnell, N., Tanaka, A.: Sig nime: music, technology, and human-computer interaction. In: Extended Abstracts CHI 2013, pp. 2529–2532. ACM (2013)
2. Fels, S., Lyons, M.: Interaction and music technology. In: Campos, P., Graham, N., Jorge, J., Nunes, N., Palanque, P., Winckler, M. (eds.) INTERACT 2011, Part IV. LNCS, vol. 6949, pp. 691–692. Springer, Heidelberg (2011)
3. Poupyrev, I., Lyons, M., Fels, S., Blaine, T.: New interfaces for musical expression. In: Extended Abstracts CHI 2001, pp. 491–492. ACM Press (2001)

# Sketching User Experiences Tutorial

Nicolai Marquardt[✉]

UCL Interaction Centre, University College London, Gower Street, London, UK
nicolai.marquardt@acm.org

**Abstract.** When designing novel user interfaces, paper-pencil sketches can support the design thinking process and are valuable for communicating design ideas to others. In this hands-on tutorial we will demonstrate how to integrate sketching into researchers' and interaction designers' everyday practice – with a particular focus on the design of novel user experiences. Participants will learn essential sketching strategies, apply these in practice during many hands-on exercises, and learn the various ways of using sketches as a tool during all stages of the HCI research and design process. Our emphasis is on quick, easy to learn, and easy to apply methods for generating and refining ideas.

## 1 Tutorial Structure

Creating hand drawn paper-pencil sketches [1] can be a valuable tool for finding the right design; before later refining the work and getting the design right [2]. This hands-on tutorial will demonstrate how to integrate sketching into researchers' and interaction designers' everyday practice.

In this half-day tutorial we will guide participants through selected sketching techniques and strategies. These techniques are partially based on the Sketching User Experiences Workbook [3], but also include other techniques and examples not covered in the book. Live sketching demonstrations and step-by-step instructions will illustrate a basic toolset for getting started sketching when working on HCI research projects. In particular, the demonstrated techniques include, for example (also see techniques in [2, 3]):

- **Sketching vocabulary:** learning to quickly draw objects, people, and activities
- **Rapid sketching of people, emotions, gestures, and objects:** learning sketching shortcuts and strategies to rapidly sketch common elements of sketches in HCI
- **10 plus 10 design funnel:** developing 10 different ideas and refinements of selected ideas
- **Photo tracing:** create collections of sketch outlines that form the basis of composed sketches
- **Hybrid sketches:** combining sketches with photos
- **Storyboards for interaction sequences**: creating visual illustrations of an interaction sequence and telling a story about use and context over time
- **Sketch boards:** sharing and discussing sketches with others; running critiques

With a series of hands-on exercises during the tutorial and different provided templates, the participants of the tutorial can directly apply the learned techniques in

© IFIP International Federation for Information Processing 2015
J. Abascal et al. (Eds.): INTERACT 2015, Part IV, LNCS 9299, pp. 644–646, 2015.
DOI: 10.1007/978-3-319-22723-8_84

**Fig. 1.** Activities from previous sketching tutorials and workshops (from top-left to bottom-right): live sketching demonstrations, learning photo tracing, participant's sketch of interactive system, sharing and discussing participants sketches, an rapidly sketching wireframes.

practice (see activities in Fig. 1). We will demonstrate many best practices and sketching shortcuts, and involve all participants in joint sharing and discussion sessions of the sketches created during the different hands-on activities (see examples in Fig. 2). We will demonstrate how we used sketching techniques in our recent research projects when designing interactive systems, and highlight how to apply the learned sketching techniques during all stages of the design and research process. We end the tutorial with an overview of additional resources and books about sketching techniques, and also possible software and hardware for digital sketching.

This tutorial is open for everyone and does not require any previous drawing expertise. We will provide sketching materials, but please feel free to bring your own sketches to share, sketchbooks, pens or paper.

The tutorial instructor Nicolai Marquardt is Lecturer in Physical Computing in the Department of Computer Science at the University College London. At the UCL Interaction Centre he is working in the research areas of ubiquitous computing, physical user interfaces, proxemic interactions, and interactive surfaces. He is co-author (with Saul Greenberg, Sheelagh Carpendale and Bill Buxton) of 'Sketching User Experiences: The Workbook' (Morgan Kaufmann 2011).

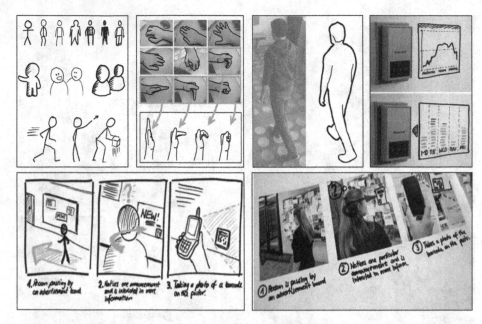

**Fig. 2.** Sketching techniques covered in the course (from top left to bottom right): sketching vocabulary, photo tracing, templates sketches, hybrid sketches, sketching storyboards, and creating photo-based storyboards [3].

# References

1. Baskinger, M.: Pencils before pixels: a primer in hand-generated sketching. Interactions **15**(2), 28–36 (2008)
2. Buxton, B.: Sketching User Experiences: Getting the Design Right and the Right Design. Morgan Kaufmann, Los Altos (2007)
3. Greenberg, S., Carpendale, S., Marquardt, N., Buxton, B.: Sketching User Experiences: The Workbook. Morgan Kaufmann, Los Altos (2011)

# Tutorial on Human Computer Interaction
# for Third Places - THCI-3P

Junia Anacleto[1]($\boxtimes$), Sidney Fels[2], and Roberto Calderon[2]

[1] Advanced Interaction Laboratory, Department of Computer Science, Federal
University of São Carlos, São Carlos, SP, Brazil
junia@dc.ufscar.br
[2] Human Communication Technologies Laboratory,
Electrical and Computer Engineering Department,
University of British Columbia, Vancouver, BC, Canada
ssfels@ece.ubc.ca, roberto@robertocalderon.ca

**Abstract.** Third places are places that are neither home nor work, where people voluntarily come together to socialize. Third places are essential to social life because they provide a common ground where different communities can meet, and they promote a sense of place. Emerging information and communication technologies (ICT) are changing the way we use such third places, altering how we interact with other people and how communities are formed. The goal of the first Tutorial on Human Computer Interaction in Third Places is to provide a forum where researchers can discuss the intersection between computing and third places. We aim to introduce the theoretical basis of third place concepts as well as methods, techniques and tools to support developing a research agenda and to initiate collaboration between researchers to better understand the roles of ICT in such places.

**Keywords:** Third place · Thirdplaceness · Pervasiveness · Ubiquitousness · Socialization

## 1 Introduction

In his seminal book Ray Oldenburg [2] defined "third places" as places where people come together as individuals to socialize and where communities are formed and shaped. These places are low profile, inclusive, accessible, accommodating, filled with regulars and a neutral ground for stimulating playful conversation. These properties can be found in urban third places such as coffee houses, bars, barber shops or community gardens. There is a growing interest in understanding the roles that pervasive technologies play on places where people interact with each other. Some of these places are "third places", or places that are neither home nor work – but are instead places like coffee shops and bars – where people deliberately come together to socialize. Third places are essential to social life because they provide a common ground where people with different interests and backgrounds can interact with each other and create the interpersonal ties that keep communities together. New location based technologies and ever increasing pervasive technologies such as situated displays, mobile devices,

© IFIP International Federation for Information Processing 2015
J. Abascal et al. (Eds.): INTERACT 2015, Part IV, LNCS 9299, pp. 647–650, 2015.
DOI: 10.1007/978-3-319-22723-8_85

passive sensing, or geo-location, enhance such places and affect how we interact with other people. The need to understand how such technologies affect third places has been previously recognized by the HCI community. Yet, we believe that we are at a critical stage wherein it would be beneficial to the research community to discuss a common research agenda tackling common questions regarding human computer interaction in third places. The first Tutorial on Human Computer Interaction in Third Places (THCI-3P) will explore the intersection between different types of third places and human computer interaction. The tutorial will present to participants the theoretical basis of third place concepts as well as methods, techniques and tools to support developing current research and, through a field activity taking place within some of Bamberg third places, provide a common ground to build a research discussion agenda that can lead to collaborative research efforts.

## 2   Motivation and Expected Audience

Over the past decade, computing in public places that are dedicated for sociability has gained a growing interest from the research community [1, 2, 7]. The challenges of collaborative and public interaction within such places, and the benefits of leveraging social technologies within third places, have been outlined by several researchers [4, 8]. Yet, with the increasing number of mobile devices with access to geo-location services, pervasive sensing and place-dependent services, new societal and technical challenges have begun to arise. This has sparked a growing interest from both industry and academia to better understand how humans interact with technologies in third places [3, 5, 6]. We believe that INTERACT2015 is scheduled at an ideal time and possesses an ideal venue to hold a Tutorial on Human Computer Interaction in Third Places. Not only is there a growing interest from the HCI community to understand the role of computing in third places, but there is also a recognition of the challenges that arise when designing third place interactions in novel settings; for example, online communities, non-technical communities, or communities in developing countries. We believe that a forum to introduce theoretical basis to discuss the questions arising from said challenges would not only be beneficial to the community, but would also be indispensible in consolidating a research agenda that reaches into the future of human computer interaction in places promoting the shaping of communities. In particular, the proposed tutorial will focus on the following questions:

   (i)   What are the roles of pervasive computing and sensing in third places?
  (ii)   What are the paradigms to provide crowd interaction within third places?
 (iii)   How can we design technologies that are natural and unobtrusive to existent third places?
  (iv)   How does ICT affect the functioning of existing third places in the long term?
   (v)   What defines a successful technological intervention of third places?
  (vi)   How should ICT adapt to different types of third place communities?
 (vii)   What defines the third place of the future and how should ICT support it?

(viii)  In what ways have ICT already altered existing third places or created new third places?

(ix)  How can ICT create the sense of thirdplaceness independent of architectural and temporal constrains?

## 3  Topics of Interest

HCI-3P will focus on the following topics, but similar topics and discussions will be welcomed for discussion during the tutorial.

- Novel interfaces to support human interaction in third places
- Natural and unobtrusive interfaces to support conversation in third places
- Aesthetic approaches to public interfaces within third places
- Crowd-computing in third places
- Comparison of third places with different cultural rooting
- Supporting third places in special communities (e.g. nomad, non-technical)
- Computing for third places in the developing world
- Properties of Third Places to create the sense of thirdplaceness independent of temporal and architectural constrains.

## 4  Proposed Program

The structure of the tutorial is in four modules:

Module 1: Introduction, Concepts, Methods, Tools, Design for Third places (2 h).

Module 2: Field Study, Exploratory research on thirdplaceness (2 h).

Module 3: Compilation of observations, Discussions on third places' properties evolution into thirdplaceness, methods of evaluation (3 h).

Module 4: Conclusions on how to apply the principles of thirdplaceness to define our next steps to keep the participants connected and engaged as a community that would meet from time to time at INTERACT or other venues, to continue evolving the concept of thirdplaceness, independent of architectural and temporal constrains (1 h).

## 5  Presenters

Dr. Junia Anacleto, Professor, Ph.D. degree in Computational Physics, from the University of São Paulo USP, Brazil. She was a Visiting Researcher at the MediaLab MIT, Massachusetts Institute of Technology in 2006–2007. She is currently an International Visiting Research Scholar from Peter Wall Institute for Advanced Studies at University of British Columbia. She is a Professor at the Federal University of São Carlos, Department of Computing, Brazil. She is also the Coordinator of LIA - Advanced Interaction Laboratory. She has experience in the area of Computer Science, with emphasis on Human Computer Interaction focused on: Natural interactions, Culture, Education, Healthcare, Urban Computing, wearable technologies.

Dr. Sidney Fels, Professor, Electrical and Computer Engineering. Ph.D., Toronto. Sid has worked in HCI, neural networks, intelligent agents and interactive arts for over ten years. He was visiting researcher at ATR Media Integration and Communications Research Laboratories (1996/7). His multimedia interactive artwork, the Iamascope, was exhibited world-wide. Sid created Glove-Talk II that maps hand gestures to speech. He was co-chair of Graphics Interface 2000. He leads the Human Communications Technology Laboratory and is Director of the Media and Graphics Interdisciplinary Centre.

Roberto Calderon is a Ph.D. student at The University of British Columbia. His research focuses on the use of situated computing to support the forming of communities in urban third places. His approach brings together Architectural Design and Human Computer Interaction to the problem of third places. He has previously served on the organizing committee of the Interdisciplinary Workshop on Communication for Sustainable Communities collocated with SIGDOC'2010.

All the presenters have previously served on the organizing committee of The First Workshop on Human Computer Interaction for Third Places HCI3P collocated with CHI'2013 and The Second Workshop on Human Computer Interaction for Third Places (HCI3P) collocated with DIS'2014.

# References

1. Brignull, H., Rogers, Y.: Enticing people to interact with large public displays in public spaces. In: Proceedings of the INTERACT 2003 (2003)
2. Churchill, E.F., Nelson, L., Hsieh, G.: Cafe life in the digital age: augmenting information flow in a cafe-work-entertainment space. In CHI 2006 extended abstracts on Human factors in computing systems, CHI EA 2006. ACM, New York, NY, USA, pp. 123–128 (2006)
3. Holopainen, J., Lucero, A., Saarenpaa, H., Nummenmaa, T., El Ali, A., Jokela, T.: Social and privacy aspects of a system for collaborative public expression. In: Proceedings of the 8th International Conference on Advances in Computer Entertainment Technology, ACE 2011. ACM, New York, NY, USA, pp. 23:1–23:8 (2011)
4. Hosio, S., Kukka, H., Riekki, J.: Leveraging social networking services to encourage interaction in public spaces. In: Proceedings of the 7th International Conference on Mobile and Ubiquitous Multimedia, MUM 2008. ACM, New York, NY, USA, pp. 2–7 (2008)
5. Karnik, M.: Social aspects of music and interactive technologies in facilitating face-to-face interactions in third places. In: Proceedings of the Second Conference on Creativity and Innovation in Design, DESIRE 2011. ACM, New York, NY, USA, pp. 431–432 (2011)
6. McCarthy, J.F., Farnham, S.D., Patel, Y., Ahuja, S., Norman, D., Hazlewood, W.R., Lind, J.: Supporting community in third places with situated social software. In: Proceedings of the Fourth International Conference on Communities and Technologies, C&T 2009. ACM, New York, NY, USA, pp. 225–234 (2009)
7. O'Hara, K., Glancy, M., Robertshaw, S.: Understanding collective play in an urban screen game. In: Proceedings of the 2008 ACM conference on Computer Supported Cooperative Work, CSCW 2008. ACM, New York, NY, USA, pp. 67–76 (2008)
8. Scheible, J., Tuulos, V.H., Ojala, T.: Story mashup: design and evaluation of novel interactive storytelling game for mobile and web users. In: Proceedings of the 6th International Conference on Mobile and Ubiquitous Multimedia, MUM 2007. ACM, New York, NY, USA, pp. 139–148 (2007)

# Tutorial: Modern Regression Techniques for HCI Researchers

Martin Schmettow[✉]

University of Twente, Enschede, The Netherlands
m.schmettow@utwente.nl

## 1 Objectives

Despite a century of progress in statistics since the introduction of ANOVA and Pearson correlation, many researchers are still squeezing their precious data into the tight corset of those dated statistical models. This is particularly limiting in applied disciplines such as HCI, where impact factors can be numerous, heterogeneous and difficult to control experimentally. The proposed tutorial aims at liberating applied researchers from constraints and concerns associated with legacy statistics. After the tutorial, attendees will be able to:

1. build *general linear models*, with multiple categorical and metric predictors
2. model and interpret *interaction effects*
3. identify the optimal set of predictors through *model selection*
4. analyze data from complex research designs using *mixed-effects models*
5. use all above-mentioned techniques to conceive *advanced research models*
6. use all above-mentioned techniques to create more *efficient research designs*

## 2 Content

The tutorial spans one day, divided into four sessions of 90 min. All start with a motivating example, then explain the technique and demonstrate its use in R (or SPSS, if desired). In all sessions, attendees have opportunity to work on exercises.

### 2.1 Session 1: From Classic to General Linear Models (GLM)

Attendees are picked up where they most likely stand: outcome variables are continuous and predictors are either metric or categorical. After briefly rehearsing ANOVA and regression, the *general linear models (GLM)* framework is introduced, which allows to free combinations of any number of categorical and metric predictors.

### 2.2 Session 2: Interaction and Selection

With multiple predictors, the outcome variable sometimes shows non-linear trends, which often can conveniently be modeled as *interaction effects*. First, interactions

© IFIP International Federation for Information Processing 2015
J. Abascal et al. (Eds.): INTERACT 2015, Part IV, LNCS 9299, pp. 651–654, 2015.
DOI: 10.1007/978-3-319-22723-8_86

between factors and metric predictors are introduced. Then, common interaction patterns, such as ceiling effects and amplifiers are explained by examples. Finally, we advance to hypothesis forming with interaction effects. In view of the gain in flexibility, the Akaike Information Criterion (AIC) is introduced as alternative to F-tests.

### 2.3  Session 3: Basic Mixed-Effects Models

In experimental or observational research, repeated measures often are preferable with regard to efficiency and data richness. But, neither classic, nor general linear models can deal with repeated measures. (Tweaks exist, but these are limited in statistical power and flexibility.) *Linear mixed-effects models* as the modern way to deal with repeated measures, efficiently and gracefully (Gueorguieva and Krystal 2004).

### 2.4  Session 4: Advanced Mixed-Effects Models

The final session unleashes the power of mixed-effects models by introducing *hierarchical and cross-classified random effects*. By example of Molich et al. (2010), it is shown how to deal with complex sampling schemes. Finally, a paradigm for *quantitative design research* is introduced, that uses *samples of designs* (Monk 2004).

## 3  Intended Audience

The tutorial is primarily targeted at HCI researchers who are conducting or planning observational and experimental studies. Knowledge of legacy parametric statistical methods is required, such as linear regression and ANOVA. The first part of the tutorial is a rehearsal, bringing all attendees on the same level before proceeding to more advanced techniques. Familiarity with SPSS and/or R is assumed.

## 4  Suggested Readings

For preparation, attendees may best pick their favorite textbook on statistics and review the respective chapters on ANOVA and linear regression. An introduction to everything covered in the tutorial (and beyond) is Gelman and Hill (2007). It is recommended to also take a few hours to get acquainted with the basics of R and Rstudio (www.rstudio.com).

## 5  Background of the Tutor

The instructor, Dr. Martin Schmettow, is assistant professor in psychology at the University of Twente (The Netherlands). He has more than a ten year experience in HCI research and education. At his home university, he gives a number of well received courses in Psychology bachelor and master education. Besides his background in Psychology and HCI, he is an expert in modern statistics, including modern regression techniques, exploratory techniques, maximum likelihood estimation, psychometric methods and Bayesian analysis. He has used advanced regression techniques in several publications (Hund et al. 2012; Schmettow et al. 2013; Schmettow et al. 2014; Schmettow and Havinga 2013), but is also known for his mathematical contributions to the problem of sample size estimation in usability testing studies (Schmettow 2012).

For further background information, visit the instructors page on ResearchGate (https://www.researchgate.net/profile/Martin_Schmettow), as well as the tutorial handout (http://rpubs.com/schmettow/regression_in_r).

# 6  Pedagogical Concept

Generally, the tutorial presents modern statistical techniques in a non-intimidating way. Focus is on understanding practical implications of the techniques and train applications in R (or SPSS). Mathematical formalism is avoided as much as possible. The tutorial consists of four sessions that are structured as follows:

1. Every session starts with a mini lecture that first describes a research problem where a particular limitation of classic statistical techniques exists, for example: *How can one simultaneously compare the impact of age and level of education (factor) on web browsing performance?*
2. Then, the problem is analyzed, and a new technique is introduced, for example: Factors and metric predictors can be mixed, by capitalizing on sum of squares and the by introducing dummy variables.
3. Third, it is demonstrated by an example, how the technique is used in R, for example: General linear models can be estimated using **lm** command with a formula expressions. User don't have to deal with dummy variables themselves.
4. Fourth, attendees will work in pairs, applying the newly learned technique to a given research problem, for example: *Examine the combined effects of sleep deprivation and noise on performance (data set: Sleep).*

The proposed tutorial is based on a lecture unit of the Psychology master course *Research methods in Human Factors and Engineering Psychology*. In January 2013, a compact version has been given to PhD students at the University of Twente. In December 2013, a one-day workshop has been given to PhD students and post docs at the University of Würzburg, Germany (host: Prof. Dr. Jörn Hurtienne).

# 7  Material and Required Resources

Attendees receive the following material:

1. Handout containing more than 100 crafted presentation slides.
2. Online tutorial for regression analysis in R.

3. Written tutorial, explaining linear mixed-effects models by the example of four case studies (23 pages), SPSS instructions included.
4. Collection of ten real and synthetic data sets.
5. Annotated list of recommended books.
6. List of over 50 references for use in publications.

It is assumed that attendees bring a notebook with R and Rstudio installed. Those, who want a SPSS demonstration alongside, need SPSS installed (version 19 upwards). The tutorial uses a very small subset of the R programming language. Basic programming skills are beneficial.

# References

Gelman, A., Hill, J.: Data Analysis Using Regression and Multilevel/Hierarchical Models. Cambridge University Press, New York (2007). http://www.imamu.edu.sa/Scientific_selections/abstracts/Math/Data Analysis Using Regression and MultilevelHierarchical Models.pdf

Gueorguieva, R., Krystal, J.H.: Move over ANOVA. Arch. Gen. Psychiatry **61**, 310–317 (2004)

Hund, A.M., Schmettow, M., Noordzij, M.L.: The impact of culture and recipient perspective on direction giving in the service of wayfinding. J. Environ. Psychol. **32**(4), 327–336 (2012). doi:10.1016/j.jenvp.2012.05.007

Molich, R., Chattratichart, J., Hinkle, V., Jensen, J.J., Kirakowski, J., Sauro, J., Traynor, B.: Rent a car in just 0, 60, 240 or 1,217 seconds? – comparative usability measurement, CUE-8. J. Usability Stud. **6**(1), 8–24 (2010). http://eprints.kingston.ac.uk/16473/

Monk, A.: The product as a fixed-effect fallacy. Hum. Comput. Interact. **19**(4), 371–375 (2004). doi:10.1207/s15327051hci1904_6

Schmettow, M.: Sample size in usability studies. Commun. ACM **55**(4), 64 (2012). doi:10.1145/2133806.2133824

Schmettow, M., Bach, C., Scapin, D.: Optimizing Usability Studies by Complementary Evaluation Methods. In: Proceedings of the 28th British HCI conference. BCS Learning and Development Ltd., Southport, UK (2014)

Schmettow, M., Havinga, J.: Are users more diverse than designs? testing and extending a 25 years old claim. In: Love, S., Hone, K., Tom McEwan (eds.) Proceedings of BCS HCI 2013-The Internet of Things XXVII. BCS Learning and Development Ltd., Uxbridge, UK (2013)

Schmettow, M., Noordzij, M. L., Mundt, M.: An implicit test of UX: individuals differ in what they associate with computers. In: CHI 2013 Extended Abstracts on Human Factors in Computing Systems on - CHI EA 2013, pp. 2039–2048. ACM Press, New York, USA (2013) doi:10.1145/2468356.2468722

# Working with Child Participants in Interaction Design

Janet C. Read[✉]

University of Central Lancashire, Preston, UK
jcread@uclan.ac.uk

**Abstract.** This tutorial will introduce attendees to the challenges and benefits of working with child participants in interaction design and evaluation within the context of HCI. It will outline the most used methods and provide resources to participants so they will be able to carry out effective work with children from 4 to 16 in schools, homes and the outdoors. Delivered by an experienced member of the IFIP WP13.1 SIG in IDC, this tutorial will appeal to researchers and developers working with children and in the design of products for children.

**Keywords:** Participatory design · Teenagers · Child computer interaction · Evaluation · Tutorial

## 1 Introduction

The Child Computer Interaction (CCI) community has long advocated the active participation of children in its research and development practices [1]. When children are introduced into design and evaluation studies, there are ethical, practical and methodological concerns that need to be considered, indeed it was at Interact, in 2005, where these concerns were first discussed [2]. For many in HCI the thought of engaging with children, especially young children and teenagers, can be daunting. The IDC community, over the last 13 or so years, has developed methods and techniques, and has amassed a wealth of knowledge that can mitigate this concern. This tutorial delivers this knowledge to attendees in a lively interactive format from experts who have been at the forefront of training and instruction in CCI [3].

## 2 Learning Objectives, Content and Duration

Individuals attending this tutorial can be expected to be able to:

- Plan, carry out and report design and evaluation studies with children
- Understand the importance of ethical practices when children participate.
- Use appropriate methods including verbalisation, survey methods, participatory design techniques and diary methods for technology report.
- Appreciate where additional material can be found

© IFIP International Federation for Information Processing 2015
J. Abascal et al. (Eds.): INTERACT 2015, Part IV, LNCS 9299, pp. 655–656, 2015.
DOI: 10.1007/978-3-319-22723-8_87

This tutorial will be for half a day. The expectation is that it will proceed as follows:

- 9–9.15 Intro to the instructors, brief introductions around the room
- 9.15–9.45 Talking to children in evaluation studies – a lecture style presentation with video and audio and a short group activity will introduce retrospective think aloud, peer tutoring and participant observation [4].
- 9.45 – 10.30 Surveying children – a group activity where participants will complete surveys including The Fun Toolkit [5], the ABCTT [6], the Group Sorter [7] and the This or That method [8]
- 10.30–11 Coffee
- 11-11.15 Diary methods – diaries will be given out and explanations of how they can be used will be given [9]. The diaries will then be used as self report during the next activity and will be discussed again at the end.
- 11.15 – 12.00 Participatory design using diaries to record activity. Participants will do a design activity as though they are children [10].
- 12.-00–12.30 Ethics, and consent and wrap up [11].

## 3    Audience and Reading List

This tutorial is intended for researchers and developers working with, or expecting to be working with children aged between 4 and 16.

## References

1. Read, J.C., Bekker, M.M.: The Nature of Child Computer Interaction. In: HCI 2011. BCS, Newcastle (2011)
2. Markopoulos, P. et al.: Child Computer Interaction: Methodological Research. In: Interact 2005. Rome, Italy (2005)
3. Markopoulos, P., et al.: Evaluating Interactive Products for and with Children. Morgan Kaufmann, San Francisco (2008)
4. Donker, A., Markopoulos, P.: A comparison of think-aloud, questionnairres and interviews for testing usability with children. In: BHCI 2002. Springer, London (2002)
5. Read, J.C.: Validating the fun toolkit: an instrument for measuring children's opinions of technology. Cogn. Technol. Work 10, 119–128 (2007)
6. Yarosh, S., Markopoulos, P., Abowd, G.D.: Towards a questionnaire for measuring affective benefits and costs of communication technologies. In: CSCW 2014, pp. 84–96 (2014)
7. Soute, I., Markopoulos, P., Magielse, R.: Head up games: combining the best of both worlds by merging traditional and digital play. Pers. Ubiquit. Comput. 14(5), 435–444 (2010)
8. Zaman, B.: Introducing a pairwise comparison scale for UX evaluations with preschoolers. In: Gross, T., Gulliksen, J., Kotzé, P., Oestreicher, L., Palanque, P., Prates, R.O., Winckler, M. (eds.) INTERACT 2009. LNCS, vol. 5727, pp. 634–637. Springer, Heidelberg (2009)
9. Markopoulos, P. et al.: The parent evaluator method. In: Workshop on Child Computer Interaction:Methodological Issues. Rome (2005)
10. Druin, A. (ed.): The Design of Children's technology. Morgan Kaufmann Publishers Inc., San Francisco (1999)
11. Read, J.C., Fitton, D., Horton, M.: Giving ideas an equal chance: inclusion and representation in participatory design with children. In: IDC 2014, pp. 105–114 (2014)

# Fostering Smart Energy Applications

Masood Masoodian[1]([⊠]), Elisabeth André[2], and Thomas Rist[3]

[1] Department of Computer Science, The University of Waikato,
Hamilton, New Zealand
masood@waikato.ac.nz
[2] Human Centered Multimedia, Augsburg University, Augsburg, Germany
andre@hcm-lab.de
[3] Faculty of Computer Science, University of Applied Sciences Augsburg,
Augsburg, Germany
thomas.rist@hs-augsburg.de

**Abstract.** There is an increasing need for smart applications with interactive visual interfaces that allow users to better manage and monitor their energy generation and consumption. This workshop will bring together researchers and practitioners from interaction design, human-computer interaction, visualization, computer games, and media technology to foster research, design, development, and deployment of energy-related applications, tools, services, games, and persuasive technologies.

**Keywords:** Energy usage management · Energy usage monitoring · Visualizations · Visual interfaces · Persuasive technologies · User evaluation

## 1 Introduction

As our reliance on energy is increasing rapidly, and worldwide non-renewable energy resources are depleting, it has become necessary to develop more advanced technologies to better manage and reduce our energy consumption. Many such technologies now exist for both domestic and commercial use. These include tools and services for public displays, dashboards, mobile apps, web-portals, simulation tools, computer games, etc. There is, however, a lack of coordinated effort in terms of research, design, development, and deployment of smart energy-related applications. It is therefore becoming important to foster and coordinate these activities through more targeted gatherings and publications focusing on smart applications for energy systems. This workshop aims to fill this existing gap by bringing together researchers and practitioners from energy-related do- mains, as a follow up to a very successful workshop held last year (FSEA 2014, http://it4se.informatik.fh-augsburg.de/FSEA14/).

## 2 Theme and Topics of Interest

The theme of this workshop is interaction techniques, interfaces, and visualizations for energy-related applications, tools, games, and services. The topics of interest include design and evaluation of visual interfaces for: monitoring and managing energy generation and consumption, analysis of energy generation and consumption data,

© IFIP International Federation for Information Processing 2015
J. Abascal et al. (Eds.): INTERACT 2015, Part IV, LNCS 9299, pp. 657–658, 2015.
DOI: 10.1007/978-3-319-22723-8_88

identifying consumption patterns and behavior, relating energy consumption to other information, sharing and comparing energy-use data with others, influencing choices and stimulating sustainable behavior changes.

## 3 Target Audience

The target audience of this workshop are researchers and practitioners from a range of backgrounds, including interaction design, human-computer interaction, visualization, computer games, media technology, and domain experts from energy-related application areas.

## 4 Workshop Plan

This one-day workshop will include short presentations of accepted position papers, discussion sessions, and a hands-on design exercise session, during which the workshop participants will be divided into small groups and invited to design an interactive application for energy usage management and visualization.

## 5 Expected Outcome and Dissemination

The accepted workshop position papers will be included in the official adjunct conference proceedings published by the University of Bamberg Press. The position papers will also be made available through the workshop website (FSEA 2015, http://it4se. informatik.fh-augsburg.de/FSEA15/). The workshop participants will be invited to submit an extended version of their position papers for a special issue of a journal (currently being organized).

## 6 Key Organizers

*Masood Masoodian* is an associate professor in Computer Science at the University of Waikato. His research interests include visualization of temporal data and interaction design. He has participated in numerous projects on design, development, and evaluation of energy-related interactive visualizations.

*Elisabeth André* is a professor in Computer Science, and the Chair of Human- Centered Multimedia at Augsburg University. She has been involved in organization of numerous conferences. She is an Associate Editor of IEEE Transactions on Affective Computing, and ACM Transactions on Intelligent Interactive Systems. She is also on the editorial board of several international journals.

*Thomas Rist* is a professor in Computer Science at the University of Applied Sciences Augsburg. He has a long track-record in the field of intelligent user interfaces, and interactive media systems. His current research activities comprise work at the intersection of HCI and energy-related applications. He has served as a PC or OC member of various workshops, symposia, and conferences. He has also coordinated a number of EU and German funded projects, including the IT4SE network for energy-related ICT research (http://www.it4se.net).

# Human Work Interaction Design (HWID):
# Design for Challenging Work Environments

Verena Fuchsberger[1(✉)], Martin Murer[1], Manfred Tscheligi[1],
José Abdelnour-Nocera[2], Pedro Campos[3], Frederica Gonçalves[3],
and Barbara Rita Barricelli[4]

[1] Center for Human-Computer Interaction,
University of Salzburg, Salzburg, Austria
{verena.fuchsberger,martin.murer,
manfred.tscheligi}@sbg.ac.at
[2] School of Computing and Technology,
University of West London, London, UK
jose.abdelnour-nocera@uwl.ac.uk
[3] Madeira Interactive Technologies Institute,
Universidade da Madeira, Funchal, Portugal
pedro.campos.pt@gmail.com,
frederica.goncalves@m-iti.org
[4] Department of Computer Science,
Università degli Studi di Milano, Milan, Italy
barricelli@di.unimi.it

**Abstract.** This one-day workshop aims to contribute to the goals of the IFIP 13.6 Human Work Interaction Design (HWID) working group, i.e., to establish relationships between empirical work-domain studies and recent developments in interaction design. This goal translates to the workshop by focusing on work environments that are challenging for research and design; from physically or spatially unusual workplaces (e.g., oil platforms), mentally demanding or specifically boring work (e.g., control rooms, academics) to challenging social situations at work (e.g., in hospitals). The workshop aims to discuss resulting constraints for research and design, e.g., restricted access for research, or difficulties in articulating the specifics of the workplaces to a wider audience that is not familiar with them. Some work environments may even impede forms of design research, e.g., critical or provocative design will be hard to carry out in safety- or efficiency-critical workplaces. Thus, ways to generate knowledge addressing the design of interactive artifacts for challenging workplaces will be discussed.

## 1 Background

HWID is concerned with combining work analysis and interaction design to inform the design of interactive systems. On one hand, work analysis focuses on user goals and requirements, tasks and procedures, human factors, cognitive and physical processes, and contexts (organizational, social, cultural). There are several techniques such as Hierarchical Task Analysis [1] and Work Domain Analysis [3] to study goal-directed tasks and to map work environment constraints and opportunities for behavior. On the other hand, human-computer interaction (HCI) has adapted work analysis methods, but

© IFIP International Federation for Information Processing 2015
J. Abascal et al. (Eds.): INTERACT 2015, Part IV, LNCS 9299, pp. 659–660, 2015.
DOI: 10.1007/978-3-319-22723-8_89

also developed its own approaches, such as Contextual Inquiries [5], Research through Design [8] or Constructive Design Research [6], which apply methods of design practice as modes of inquiry. The situated nature of interactions and practices, i.e., the context that interactions are interwoven with (e.g. [4, 7]) creates challenges for research, as some contexts are highly complex, or difficult to access (e.g. [2]). These challenges we seek to address in the proposed workshop.

## 2 Workshop Aims

We invite participants from industry, academia and design practice, who have experienced challenging work environments, to discuss how they dealt with them, either in research or design. We seek participants with an interest in empirical work analysis, HCI, interaction design, or user experience in workplaces. Topics that participants may want to contribute include: Empirical studies of/in challenging work environments (e.g., based on the HWID framework); Interaction design for and in challenging work environments; Benefits and hindrances for research and design; Theories for and reflections upon interaction design for challenging work settings. In order to participate in the workshop, 4–6 page position papers (University of Bamberg Press Format) should be submitted. During the workshop, challenges will be collected, consolidated and suggestions for how to address them will be established. In order to bring the topic to a broader audience, an interactions magazine paper is planned to create awareness for research and design (practice) in workplace interactions. Extended versions of selected papers will be invited for a special issue in a journal. The organizers of the workshop are part of the HWID working group and have extensive experience in work-related research (e.g., researching contextual interfaces for industrial environments). More information is available on the workshop website: http://projects.hci.sbg.ac.at/hwid2015.

## References

1. Annett, J., Duncan, K.D.: Task analysis and training design. J. Occup. Psychol. **41**, 211–221 (1967)
2. Björndal, P., Ralph, M.: On the handling of impedance factors for establishing apprenticeship relations during field studies in industry domains. In: Proceedings of NordiCHI 2014, pp. 1107–1112 (2014)
3. Clemmensen,T., Campos, P., Katre, D., Abdelnour-Nocera, J., Lopes, A., Orngreen, R., Minocha, S.: CHI 2013 human work interaction design (HWID) SIG: past history and future challenges. In: CHI EA 2013, pp. 2537–2540. ACM, New York, NY, USA (2013)
4. Dourish, P.: What we talk about when we talk about context. Pers. Ubiquit. Comput. **8**(1), 19–30 (2004)
5. Holtzblatt, K., Jones, S.: Contextual inquiry: a participatory technique for system design. In: Participatory Design: Principles and Practices, pp. 177–210. CRC Press, Boca Raton (1993)
6. Koskinen, I., Zimmerman, J., Binder, T., Redström, J., Wensveen, S.: Design Research Through Practice: From the Lab, Field, and Showroom. Elsevier, Amsterdam (2011)
7. Kuutti, K., Bannon, L.J.: The turn to practice in HCI: towards a research agenda. In: Proceedings of CHI 2014, pp. 3543–3552. ACM (2014)
8. Zimmerman, J., Forlizzi, J., Evenson, S.: Research through design as a method for interaction design research in HCI. In: Proceedings of CHI 2007, pp. 493–502, ACM (2007)

# IFIP WG 13.2 Workshop on User Experience and User-Centered Development Processes

Marco Winckler[1]([⊠]), Regina Bernhaupt[1], Peter Forbrig[2], and Stefan Sauer[3]

[1] ICS-IRIT, Université Toulouse 3, 118 Route de Narbonne, 31062 Toulouse, France
{winckler,bernhaupt}@irit.fr
[2] Universität Rostock, Albert-Einstein-Straße 22, Raum 266, Rostock, Germany
peter.forbrig@uni-rostock.de
[3] Universität Paderborn, S-Lab, Zukunftsmeile 1, 33102 Paderborn, Germany
sauer@s-lab.uni-paderborn.de

**Abstract.** This workshop focusses on the interplay of user experience (UX) and user-centered development processes of interactive systems. It is organized by the IFIP Working Group 13.2 on Human-Centered Software Methodologies. It is proposed as a follow-up activity started at an interactive session organized at HCSE 2014. Our ultimate goal is bringing together researchers and practitioners to discuss real-life case studies featuring success and/or failure stories of development processes that take into account UX as an important dimension for the interactive system at concern. Based on these discussions, we expect to deepen the understanding of problems and challenges when dealing with UX in the software development process.

## 1 Overview and Goals

This workshop is motivated by discussions held during an interactive session featuring an open panel organized during the 5th International Conference on Human-Centered Software Engineering (HCSE 2014) which took place in Paderborn, Germany from September 16–18, 2014 [1], where conference participants were invited to formulate questions/comments about problems they are actually experiencing with the development of interactive systems. Questions and comments provided by participants have revealed a two-fold concern involving UX in development processes for the development of interactive systems and, in particular, agile methods. On one hand, it is widely agreed that UX dimensions are subjective, dynamic and context-dependent [2, 3]. For that, existing methods for investigating the impact of UX on the system acceptance often require direct participation of end-users who can report about the use of the system (or at least an advanced prototype) at investigation. On the other hand, agile methods [4] have become popular among software engineers and start to influence the development process of interactive software in industry, in particular by accelerating the cadence of iterations along the development lifecycle and promoting communication mechanisms among members of the development team to reinforce transparence in the decision chain. Nonetheless, UX and agile practices are not always straightforward and pose tricky questions such as:

© IFIP International Federation for Information Processing 2015
J. Abascal et al. (Eds.): INTERACT 2015, Part IV, LNCS 9299, pp. 661–662, 2015.
DOI: 10.1007/978-3-319-22723-8_90

- How do we have to change software engineering processes, including agile, to support effectively UX?
- How can UX activities, which are dependent on user studies, be synchronized with software development activities based on fast sprints?
- Should a role UX expert be added in agile processes? Which roles are needed?
- Which process should one follow when UX is in conflict with other user interface properties (such as usability, dependability, privacy…)?
- How can we convince organizations to adopt user-centered design (UCD) activities and incorporate them in organizational processes?

The ultimate goal of this workshop is to deepen the understanding of the current practice of development of interactive software and identify opportunities for improving development processes.

## 2    Target Audience and Expected Outcomes

This workshop is open to everyone (researchers and practitioners) who are interested in UCD processes, and in particular those who have interests in UX and agile methods. As for practitioners, we invite all possible participants in the development process who may include developers, designers, human factor analysts, stakeholders, etc. As for researchers, we expect a high participation of the members of IFIP WG 13.2 and attendees of HCSE 2014 who contribute to the topics of this workshop. We invite participants to present position papers describing real-life case studies featuring success and/or failure stories, and their experiences using methods and tools for dealing with UX along the development. Experiences with any kind of interactive systems are welcome. Contributions on agile methods are welcome, but we also expect to discuss experiences with any type of development process in use. Position papers will be published in official adjunct conference proceedings at the University of Bamberg Press. In the long run, we also expect to compile individual contributions to feature a book such as it has been done in the past [5] for consolidating the knowledge about UX methods and software development.

## References

1. Sauer, S., Bogdan, C., Forbrig, P., Bernhaupt, R., Winckler, M.: HCSE 2014. LNCS, vol. 8742. Springer, Heidelberg (2014)
2. Law, E., Van Schaik, P.: Modelling user experience – an agenda for research and practice. Interact. Comput. **22**(5), 313–322 (2010)
3. Karapanos, E., Zimmerman, J., Forlizzi, J., Martens, J.-B.: Measuring the dynamics of remembered experience over time. Interact. Comput. **22**(5), 328–335 (2010)
4. Cohn, M.: User Stories Applied: For Agile Software Development, 1st edn, p. 304. Addison-Wesley Professional, Boston (2004)
5. Seffah, A., Gulliksen, J., Desmarais, M.C. (eds.): Human-Centered Software Engineering – Integrating Usability in the Software Development Lifecycle, pp. 17–36. Springer, Netherlands (2005)

# IFIP WG 13.5 Workshop on Resilience, Reliability, Safety and Human Error in System Development

Chris Johnson[1], Mike Feary[2], Célia Martinie[3], Phil Palanque[3(✉)], and Regina Peldszus[4]

[1] University of Glasgow, G12 8QJ Glasgow, Scotland
johnson@dcs.gla.ac.uk
[2] NASA Ames Research Center, Moffett Field, Mountain View, CA 94035-1000, USA
michael.s.feary@nasa.gov
[3] ICS-IRIT, Université Toulouse 3, 118 Route de Narbonne, 31062 Toulouse, France
{martinie,palanque}@irit.fr
[4] MECS, Leuphana University, 21335 Lüneburg, Germany
regina@spaceflightdesign.org

**Abstract.** This workshop focusses on the issues of bringing together several properties to interactive systems. While research in the field of HCI is mainly targeting at Usability and user experience (UX) this workshop focusses on Resilience, Reliability and Safety. It is organized by the IFIP Working Group 13.5 on Resilience, Reliability, Safety and Human Error in System Development. The goal of the workshop is to bring together researchers and practitioners from these various disciplines or their related application domains (such as nuclear, space, aeronautics, healthcare...) to discuss real-life case studies featuring success and/ or failure stories of development processes that target resilient interactive systems and take into reliability, safety and human errors for interactive systems. The objective of the workshop is to produce a structured roadmap and a research agenda for the design, construction and assessment of resilient interactive systems.

## 1 Overview and Goals

In the area of Human-Computer Interaction (HCI) there is large involvement in the design, development and evaluation of interactive systems targeting application domains like entertainment and leisure or standard office work environments. In such contexts, the focus is mainly on usability and user experience properties, leaving other aspects of software such as reliability to other disciplines such as dependable computing or computer science. For this reason, interactive systems that are safety-critical and belong to domains such as Healthcare, Aeronautics, Air Traffic Management or Satellite Control are left with designed interaction techniques that are so poorly engineered that they remain inapplicable. While entertainment and "standard" work interactive systems have a strong focus on usability and user experience, in the area of safety-critical systems factors like safety, reliability, fault-tolerance or dependability are as important as usability and user experience, while usability problems are usually compensated by training.

© IFIP International Federation for Information Processing 2015
J. Abascal et al. (Eds.): INTERACT 2015, Part IV, LNCS 9299, pp. 663–664, 2015.
DOI: 10.1007/978-3-319-22723-8_91

These two distinct views about interactive systems lead to two different communities using different approaches, development processes and methods. Contrary to the current perception that this distinction is important and should remain intact, we argue that methods, approaches, processes and solutions in one area can be fruitfully deployed in the other area. One precise example of such possible cross-fertilization is the design and development of user interfaces including autonomous behavior in safety-critical systems [1]. Solutions from video games can be used to solve some of the major problems when interacting with this type of autonomous behavior in a user interface of safety critical systems.

The main goal of this workshop is to identify areas of meaningful integration between mass market products (consumer focus) and safety-critical systems, to investigate new solutions and to strengthen a community interested in this area.

## 2    Target Audience and Expected Outcomes

We expect participants from:

- Mass market products design and development, user interface design and engineering but also interested in safety-critical systems design, specification and validation.
- Safety-critical system design and development but also interested in new interaction techniques, designing for user experience and usability.
- Academics and practitioners carrying out research around the notion of resilience and human error. Their area of expertise can be related to human-computer interaction, human factors or interactive systems development. Their topic of interest should involve usability, reliability, safety, resilience and/or user experience.
- Students interested in mass market products (including video games) and/or safety-critical systems and willing to learn more about the intersection of these domains.

The upper limit in number of participants is 30, to allow for active participation and a fruitful discussion of topics.

## 3    Participant Solicitation and Selection

Workshop participation will be based on an (up to) six page position paper (LNCS Format) describing interests and previous work in the topics of the workshop. *Selection* will be based on the *quality* of the abstract, answers to the list of issues, the extent (and *diversity*) of participants' backgrounds. We envision two main types of contributions: problems contributions bringing case studies or theoretical problems, and solutions contributions bringing solutions already proven efficient in one of the domains considered.

## Reference

1. Palanque, P., Bernhaupt, R., Montesano, F., Martinie C.: Exploiting gaming research and practice in the design of user interfaces of (partly)-autonomous safety-critical systems. In: Proceedings of ATACCS 2011. ACM Press (2011)

# Learning Beyond the Classroom: For and About Older and Disabled People

Gerhard Weber[1(✉)], Christopher Power[2], Helen Petrie[2], and Jenny Darzentas[3]

[1] Department of Computer Science, Technische Universität Dresden,
Dresden, Germany
gerhard.weber@tu-dresden.de
[2] Department of Computer Science, University of York, York YO10 5GH UK
{christopher.power,helen.petrie}@cs.york.ac.uk
[3] Department of Product and Systems Design Engineering,
University of the Aegean, Syros, Greece
jennyd@aegean.gr

**Abstract.** The workshop will provide a forum for discussion for researchers, practitioners and designers interested in both the accessibility of technology-mediated learning for disabled and older learners or in the use of technology-mediated learning to teach professionals about the needs of disabled and older people. Expected outcome is a better understanding of the processes needed to raise the level of inclusion in higher education.

**Keywords:** Accessibility · MOOC · Elearning · Older learners · Disabled learners

## 1 Overall Concept of the Workshop

A number of studies [1, 2] have shown that eLearning platforms can be made accessible, although barriers require specific attention. While typical tasks such as navigation in learning materials, or participation in a forum or a wiki can be made accessible to learners even if they use assistive technologies or augmentations (e.g. subtitling to videos), more advanced tasks such as assessments (e.g. multiple choice quizzes) and the use of specialist notations (e.g. mathematics, chemistry, music) common in education require more advanced accessibility knowledge.

The right to equal access to the educational system has been strengthened by the UN Convention on the Rights of Persons with Disabilities [3] but only at a high level. Developing an action plan suitable for educational institutions at various levels includes both the need to review institutional approaches to identify and strengthen all stake-holders in order to develop more inclusive approaches in classroom teaching and distance education, as well as the provision of education about accessibility in the education system as well as particularly in technology industries. In addition, in an ageing society, life-long access to education is becoming an important issue.

© IFIP International Federation for Information Processing 2015
J. Abascal et al. (Eds.): INTERACT 2015, Part IV, LNCS 9299, pp. 665–666, 2015.
DOI: 10.1007/978-3-319-22723-8_92

## 2    Goals and Topics for the Workshop

The workshop will identify possibilities for making technology-mediated learning (TML) (learning, blended learning, MOOCs) more accessible and acceptable to disabled and older people. In addition, the workshop will analyse how TML can be used to educate professionals about the needs and wishes of disabled and older people in relation to technology. The accessibility of TML relates both learning design and the learning environment. This includes inclusive approaches to asynchronous/synchronous communication, and the accessibility of microteaching (e.g. in MOOCs). Even if the competence of both teachers and learners can be met, there is still a need to change existing practices related to TML. The workshop will discuss processes to activate all stakeholders related to TML. In particular MOOCs may be a new approach to attract teachers or trainers who encounter a deficit in their practices and who want to become more capable of addressing a wider spectrum of learners.

## 3    Organisers

This Workshop is organized on behalf of IFIP WG 13.3 HCI and Disability by:
Professor Gerhard Weber, Chair in HCI at Technische Universität Dresden. His research focuses on personalization of multimodal systems for the benefit of people with a disability.

Professor Helen Petrie, Chair in HCI at the University of York, current chair of IFIP WG 13.3. Her research focuses on the design and evaluation of technology for disabled and older people.

Dr Christopher Power is a Lecturer at the University of York. His research aims at creating interactive web systems for all, focusing on disabled and older people.

Dr Jenny Darzentas works at the University of the Aegean. Her research focuses on the design of accessible and usable content.

## 4    Expected Outcomes

This workshop will develop a better understanding of the processes needed to raise the accessibility of technology mediated learning for disabled and older learners and the methods and content to introduce accessibility topics into education at all levels.

## References

1. Power, C., Petrie, H., Sakharov, V., Swallow, D.: Virtual learning environments: another barrier to blended and e-learning. In: Miesenberger, K., Klaus, J., Zagler, W., Karshmer, A. (eds.) ICCHP 2010, Part 1. LNCS, vol. 6179, pp. 519–526. Springer, Heidelberg (2010)
2. Bohnsack, M., Puhl, S.: Accessibility of MOOCs. In: Miesenberger, K., Fels, D., Archambault, D., Peňáz, P., Zagler, W. (eds.) ICCHP 2014, Part I. LNCS, vol. 8547, pp. 141–144. Springer, Heidelberg (2014)
3. http://www.un.org/disabilities/default.asp?id=150

# Mediation and Meaning in HCI

Susanne Bødker[1]([✉]), Olav W. Bertelsen[1], Liam Bannon[2],
Clarisse de Souza[3], Simone Barbosa[3], and Raquel Prates[4]

[1] Aarhus University, Aarhus, Denmark
{bodker,olavb}@cs.au.dk
[2] University of Limerick, Limerick, Ireland
liambannon@gmail.com
[3] Pontifical Catholic University, Rio de Janeiro, Brazil
{clarisse,simone}@inf.puc-rio.br
[4] Federal University of Minas Gerais, Belo Horizonte, Brazil
rprates@dcc.ufmg.br

This workshop is about computer mediation in human communication and action. The proponents all look at mediation from different angles, but share the view that meaning is what mediation is about. We aim to dig beneath the surface and touch on the *conception, construction, negotiation and evolution of meaning in and of technology*, for producers and consumers, before and after technology is deployed. Mediation and meaning will thus allow us to discuss how different segments and perspectives in HCI research can be brought together to give us new insights about how people interact with technology.

The workshop will start with three *discussion scenarios* that the proponents will provide. Meaning conception, for example, will be initially discussed against the backdrop of participatory design [4, 5], which accounts for what producers (including owners) and consumers *mean* when they talk about some specific technology that is being created. Meaning construction, in turn, is the focus of semiotic engineering [3], which accounts for how meaning and intent are communicated through technologies and their interfaces. It involves, once again, producers (namely, designers and developers) and consumers (namely end-users and/or application developers and tailors). Finally, meaning evolution gives rise to discussions of technology appropriation and mediation in social activities [1, 2] as well as user-driven technology adaptation and extension [6]. The interest of the proposed approach to the workshop is that not only do the three scenarios highlight the dependency between meaning conception, creation and evolution, but they will also highlight the shapes that meaning negotiation can take. In meaning negotiation, specifically, mediation artifacts and processes play a fundamental role, both between different groups of people and between people and technology.

We invite and expect contributions coming from theories, approaches, methods and empirical studies that focus on computing technology as *mediators of human action and activity,* that is, that can view HCI as *interaction between human beings through computers.* Some other related areas, in addition to the ones already mentioned, include, but are not limited to, computer semiotics, activity theory, meta-design, (micro and macro) cultural adaptation, IT adoption and appropriation.

We propose a one-day workshop based on accepted contributions. We will call for position paper submissions that address mediated meaning in use and design of

© IFIP International Federation for Information Processing 2015
J. Abascal et al. (Eds.): INTERACT 2015, Part IV, LNCS 9299, pp. 667–668, 2015.
DOI: 10.1007/978-3-319-22723-8_93

computer technology, focusing on HCI theory (or theoretical approaches), methods or practical aspects (like empirical cases and examples in design or evaluation). They are reviewed by the organizers and serve as foundation of the workshop. Workshop position papers are published in the official adjunct proceedings. Workshop position papers should have a length of 4 to 6 pages. The workshop website can be found at http://pit.au.dk/news-events/events/upcoming-events/interact-2015-ws-mediation-and-meaning-in-hci/.

## About the Organizers

Susanne Bødker is Professor of Human-Computer Interaction at the Department of Computer Science, Aarhus University. She works with activity theoretical HCI, Participatory Design and Computer Supported Cooperative Work.

Olav W. Bertelsen is Associate Professor of Human-Computer Interaction at the Department of Computer Science, Aarhus University. He works with materialist and pragmatist approaches to technologies in human life.

Liam Bannon is affiliated with the Dept. of Computer Science & Information Systems, University of Limerick and the Department of Computer Science, Aarhus University. He does research in interaction design and CSCW.

Clarisse de Souza is Full Professor at the Informatics Department, PUC-Rio. She created Semiotic Engineering, a semiotic theory of HCI. Her research interests center on meaning negotiation and evolution in human-computer interaction.

Simone Barbosa works at PUC-Rio in the area of Human-Computer Interaction, as seen from a Semiotic Engineering perspective. Her research interests involve: model-based interactive systems design; bridging HCI and software engineering.

Raquel Prates is an Associate professor at the Computer Science Department at the Federal University of Minas Gerais (UFMG) in Brazil. She works with HCI and Collaborative Systems and interests include Semiotic Engineering and sociability.

## References

1. Bødker, S., Andersen, P.B.: Complex mediation. J. Hum. Comput. Interact. **20**(4), 353–402 (2005)
2. Bryant, S.L., Forte, A., Bruckman, A.: Becoming Wikipedian: transformation of participation in a collaborative online encyclopedia. In: GROUP 2005, pp. 1–10 (2005)
3. de Souza, C.S.: The Semiotic Engineering of Human-Computer Interaction. The MIT Press, Cambridge (2005)
4. Dindler, D., Iversen, O.S.: Relational expertise in participatory design. In: PDC 2014, vol. 1, pp. 41–50 (2014)
5. Greenbaum, J., Kyng, M. (eds.): Design at Work: Cooperative Design of Computer Systems. Lawrence Erlbaum Associates, Hillsdale (1991)
6. Lieberman, H., Paternò, F., Wulf, V.: End User Development. Springer, Heidelberg (2006)

# Methods for Undertaking Research on Technology with Older and Disabled People

Helen Petrie[1][(✉)], Blaithin Gallagher[2], and Jenny Darzentas[3]

[1] Human-Computer Interaction Research Group, University of York, York, UK
Helen.Petrie@york.ac.uk
[2] National Council for the Blind, Dublin, Ireland
blaithing@gmail.com
[3] Department of Product and Systems Design Engineering,
University of the Aegean, Syros, Greece
jennyd@aegean.gr

**Abstract.** Developing interactive systems for disabled and older people is an increasingly important topic in HCI, yet there is little discussion of methods used to conduct research with these user groups. The workshop will provide an opportunity for researchers and practitioners to discuss research methods used in HCI when applied to working with older and disabled people for the elicitation of user needs, evaluation of technologies and understanding of the uses of technologies by these important user groups.

## 1 Introduction

Developing interactive systems for people with disabilities and older people is becoming an important topic within HCI research and practice. As the population is aging [1], the pressure to use technology to support people to live independently is increasing. But as yet, little attention has been paid to the methods used to conduct research on mainstream or assistive technologies for disabled or older people. A small number of published papers directly address these issues [e.g. 2, 3] and some papers mention challenges of working with these user groups in passing.

## 2 Objectives and Topics to be Addressed in the Workshop

The workshop will provide an opportunity for researchers and practitioners to discuss the advantages and disadvantages of existing research methods used in HCI when applied to working with older and disabled people for the elicitation of user needs, evaluation of technologies and understanding of the uses of technologies by these important user groups. It will also provide an opportunity to discuss innovations to methods and completely new methods that might have been developed in working with older and disabled people.

Topics to be addressed will include: advantages and disadvantages of methods of undertaking research on technology with older and disabled people, for mainstream or

J. Abascal et al. (Eds.): INTERACT 2015, Part IV, LNCS 9299, pp. 669–670, 2015.
DOI: 10.1007/978-3-319-22723-8_94

assistive technologies; practical problems of using existing methods; adaptations that need to be made for particular user groups; limitations in the application of particular methods; innovations in research methods to meet the requirements of particular user groups and innovative research methods; theories and application of inclusive design, design for all and universal design philosophies. Finally, the workshop is open to discussion of all methods, whether qualitative or quantitative, from participatory design to experimentation, and will include inclusive design approaches.

## 3  Organizers

This Workshop is organized on behalf of IFIP WG 13.3 HCI and Disabilities by:

Helen Petrie, Professor of HCI at the University of York and current chair of IFIP WG 13.3. Her research focuses on the design and evaluation of technology for disabled and older people. Dr. Blaithin Gallagher, Head of Research and Projects at NCBI. She is Vice President of the European Network for Vision Impairment Training Education and Research (ENVITER) and on the Executive Committee of the European Society for Low vision Research and Rehabilitation (ESLRR). Dr. Jenny Darzentas from the University of the Aegean. Her research focuses on the design of accessible and usable content.

## 4  Target Audience

Researchers and practitioners interested in working with disabled or older people in the design and development of mainstream or assistive technologies.

## 5  Expected Outcomes

The workshop will contribute to the development of a better understanding of research methods for working with older and disabled people. In addition, the workshop will plan for further events, including a tutorial for new researchers in the field and a handbook on methods for working with older and disabled people.

## References

1. Giannakouris, K.: Ageing characterizes the demographic perspectives of the European societies. Eurostat Stat. Focus **72** (2008) (Luxembourg: Eurostat)
2. Hendriks, N., Huybrechts, L., Wilkinson, A., Slegers, K.: Challenges in doing participatory design with people with dementia. In: Proceedings of the 13th Participatory Design Conference, vol. 2, pp. 33–36. ACM, Windhoek, Namibia (2014)
3. Inglis, E.A., Szymkowiak, A., Gregor, P., Newell, A.F., Hine, N., Shah, P., Wilson, B.A., Evans, J.: Issues surrounding the user-centred development of a new interactive memory aid. Univ. Access Inf. Soc. **2**(3), 226–234 (2003)

# Social Image Research in the Age of Selfies

Casey Dugan[1(✉)] and Sven Laumer[2]

[1] IBM Research, Cambridge, MA, USA
cadugan@us.ibm.com
[2] University of Bamberg, Bamberg, Germany
sven.laumer@uni-bamberg.de

**Abstract.** Capturing and sharing images of ourselves and others has given rise to many applications and much human-computer interaction research. Social media has made it faster and easier than ever to share such photos, with "selfies", or photographs taken of oneself, invading popular culture. In this workshop, we will bring together researchers studying images of people in the context of HCI, whether thru mining such data, analyzing its use, or creating novel UIs for such.

**Keywords:** Selfies · Faces · Social media · Face detection · Self-representation

## 1 Introduction

The desire to capture photographs of ourselves and others is not new, and many applications have arisen to support this desire; with HCI researchers studying these from photobooths [6] to mobile photoware [1]. Social media has made it faster and easier than ever to share such images. In particular, "selfies" or photographs taken of oneself, have invaded popular culture. Instagram accounts are filled with them [4], U.S. courts have ruled on the ownership of a monkey selfie[1], and the word "selfie" was added to the Oxford English dictionary in 2013, becoming their word of the year.

The abundance of these photos, shared on social media platforms, has facilitated HCI research across a number of disciplines. For example, social scientists have studied cultural differences [8] as well as personality and interaction style recognition [3] through social media profile pictures. They have also shown that photos containing human faces are particularly engaging on these sites, being 38 % more likely to receive likes and 32 % more likely to receive comments on Instagram [2]. Others working in face detection and recognition have taken to mining social media sites for this rich source of data. Facebook itself, with their DeepFace system, has used this data shared on their site to achieve face recognition accuracy beating the current state of the art by more than 27 %.[2] Still other researchers have focused on tools to help users pose for better selfies [7] and interactions to trigger the photos [5].

---

[1] http://www.cnn.com/2014/08/08/opinion/cevallos-monkey-selfie-copyright/.
[2] https://research.facebook.com/publications/480567225376225/deepface-closing-the-gap-to-human-level-performance-in-face-verification.

© IFIP International Federation for Information Processing 2015
J. Abascal et al. (Eds.): INTERACT 2015, Part IV, LNCS 9299, pp. 671–672, 2015.
DOI: 10.1007/978-3-319-22723-8_95

## 2    Goals, Themes, and Target Audience

The current popularity of the "selfie" phenomenon, vast amounts of photos of people shared on social media sites, complex issues around presentation of self, ethics and privacy, along with the breadth of applicability in HCI research warrants further discussion. The goal of this workshop is to create a forum for exchange and learning by bringing together researchers from a variety of disciplines, across industry and academia, who study images of people in the context of HCI and social media. As such, we encourage submissions from a variety of areas, including **data science and image processing** (such as mining or creating datasets of faces from social media sites or quantitative analysis of these), **social science** (such as studying benefits, challenges, and perception of such photos on social media sites), **information systems** (such as studying the business impact and use of selfies in an organizational context), and **novel applications and interfaces** (such as novel interfaces, interactions or hardware for taking pictures of people and using faces in interface design or applications).

## 3    Organizers

The workshop organizers represent both academia (**Sven Laumer, Assistant Professor, University of Bamberg**) and industry (**Casey Dugan, IBM Rese**arch). They have a history of studying the use of social media (Facebook, Twitter) and enterprise social networks. In 2014, they deployed kiosks for taking selfies at IBM locations around the world. Their research, as well as the increasing attention being paid to "selfies" in popular culture, has inspired them to bring together researchers from across disciplines to exchange ideas. They have organized workshops at ICWSM'13, RecSys'09 & '10, served on numerous HCI/IS program committees, and co-edited journals.

## References

1. Ames, M., Eckles, D., Naaman, M., Spasojevic, M., House, N.: Requirements for mobile photoware. In: Personal and Ubiquitous Computing, vol. 14, no. 2, pp. 95–109. Springer, Heidelberg (2010)
2. Bakhshi, S., Shamma, D.A, Gilbert, E.: Faces engage us: photos with faces attract more likes and comments on Instagram. In: Proceedings of CHI 2014, pp. 965–974. ACM (2014)
3. Celli, F, Bruni, E., Lepri, B.: Automatic personality and interaction style recognition from Facebook profile pictures. In: Proceedings of MM 2014, pp. 1101–1104. ACM (2014)
4. Hu, Y., Manikonda, L., Kambhampati, S.: What we Instagram: a first analysis of Instagram photo content and user types. In: Proceedings of ICWSM 2014 (2014)
5. Jain, A., Maguluri, S., Shukla, P., Vijay, P., Sorathia, K.: Exploring tangile interactions for capturing self photographs. In: Proceedings of the India HCI 2014, p. 116. ACM (2014)
6. Salomon, G.B.: Designing casual-user hypertext: the CHI 1989 InfoBooth. In: Proceedings of the SIGCHI Conference on Human Factors in Computing Systems, pp. 451–458 (1990)
7. Yeh, M., Lin, H.: Virtual portraitist: aesthetic evaluation of selfies based on angle. In: Proceedings of MM 2014, pp. 221–224. ACM (2014)
8. Zhao, C., Jiang, G.: Cultural differences on visual self-presentation through social networking site profile images. In: Proceedings of CHI 2011, pp. 1129–1132. ACM (2011)

# The Landscape of UX Requirements Practices

Gregorio Convertino[1], Nancy Frishberg[2], Jettie Hoonhout[3],
Rosa Lanzilotti[4(✉)], Marta Kristín Lárusdóttir[5],
and Effie Lai-Chong Law[6]

[1] Informatica Corporation, 2100 Seaport Blvd, Redwood City, CA 94063, USA
gconvertino@informatica.com
[2] Financial Engines, Inc, 1050 Enterprise Way, 3rd Fl.,
Sunnyvale, CA 95089, USA
nancyf@acm.org
[3] Philips Research, High Tech Campus 34, 5656 AE Eindhoven, Netherlands
Jettie.hoonhout@philips.com
[4] Dipartimento di Informatica, Università di Bari Aldo Moro,
Via Orabona 4, 70125 Bari, Italy
rosa.lanzilotti@uniba.it
[5] School of Computer Science,
Reykjavik University, Reykjavík, Iceland
Marta@ru.is
[6] Department of Computer Science,
University of Leicester, Leicester LE1 7RH, UK
elaw@mcs.le.ac.uk

**Abstract.** Studies of development practices reveal that usability and user experience (UX) are often not addressed consistently or explicitly in current development projects. A key reason is that UX requirements are either omitted or not formalized enough for their implementation to be objectively verifiable. This workshop brings together researchers and practitioners who have faced this problem and have experimented with methods to resolve it. The expected result is a descriptive framework that will summarize the current best practices, differentiate them along key dimensions and in relation to known obstacles. Then, a set of recommendations to formalize and verify UX requirements will be provided.

**Keywords:** Requirements specification · Usability · UX practices

## 1 Workshop Topic and Rationale

The primary motivation for this workshop is the need for systematic methods, based on empirical research, to define and confirm statements of usability and UX requirements for software systems. The problem of omission or poor formalization of UX requirements is limiting the success of projects in the public and private sectors. For example, too many companies have not yet integrated usability and UX methods and approaches as part of the software development process.

For the public sector, studies of ICT companies that work with public authorities in Europe suggest that a critical problem is the lack of formal UX requirements in the Call for Tenders or CfT (cf. Request for Proposals or RFP). In fact, during the implementation, the

© IFIP International Federation for Information Processing 2015
J. Abascal et al. (Eds.): INTERACT 2015, Part IV, LNCS 9299, pp. 673–674, 2015.
DOI: 10.1007/978-3-319-22723-8_96

company that obtained the contract from the public authority is likely to focus only on the requirements agreed upon as part of the CfT. Thus, the contracting company has no incentives to consider additional requirements.

For the private sector, perhaps the hallmark of a successful UX professional is flexibility, due to the recurrent need for negotiation, tighter time constraints and multiple stakeholders. The post hoc narratives of UX contributions to products often sound like the idealized exploratory phase followed by a narrowing of the scope with a steady progress toward a product that meets the requirements expressed by users. In practice, however, the real story often is of projects with processes and methods that differ widely across development projects but follow common principles and lead to similar artifacts, such as personas, story mapping, and prototypes. Some projects may never create a formal requirements document, but will reveal the increasingly formalized UX requirements through a sequence of prototypes and product versions. This is a challenge for requirement formalization methods – i.e., a workshop topic.

For both public and private endeavors, the problem of formalizing requirements is a balancing act among various factors, such as identifying the user classes and competing requirements for such user classes, satisfying the buyer, driving innovation, and keeping consistency among products from the same organization.

As the agile and lean software development processes become pervasive, renewed attention is necessary on defining more suitable methods to build and preserve high-quality UX designs along the development process.

## 2    Target Audience and Expected Outcomes

The workshop aims at bringing together researchers and practitioners who face the problem of formalizing usability or UX requirements and have tried effective methods to resolve it. The expected outcome of the workshop is a descriptive framework that helps to organize the current best practices and a set of recommendations for formalizing and verifying usability/UX requirements in specific contexts.

## 3    Workshop Organizers

*Gregorio Convertino*, PhD, is a Senior User Researcher at Informatica. His research focuses on UX, information visualization, collaborative and social computing.

*Nancy Frishberg*, PhD, heads the User Research Program at Financial Engines, Inc. Her research interests include harnessing the creativity of groups, accessibility (for aging or Deaf populations), and successful UX in agile projects.

*Jettie Hoonhout* is a Senior Scientist at Philips Research. Her research interest is in methodologies, methods and tools that address the UX of products, and that support the development process of products and product-service concepts.

*Rosa Lanzilotti* is a researcher at the University of Bari (IT). Her research interests include usability and UX, accessibility, UX practices in industry and public institutions.

*Marta Kristín Lárusdóttir* is an assistant professor at Reykjavik University (IS). Her main research area is the interplay between usability and UX activities and software development processes.

*Effie Lai-Chong Law* is Reader at the University of Leicester (UK). Her research focuses are usability and UX methodologies and their applications in various contexts including education, health, law, and cultural heritage.

# Workshop on Designing Interaction and Visualization for Mobile Applications (DIViM 2015)

Shah Rukh Humayoun[1](✉), Achim Ebert[1], Steffen Hess[2],
and Gerrit van der Veer[3]

[1] Computer Graphics and HCI Group, University of Kaiserslautern, Kaiserslautern, Germany
{humayoun,ebert}@cs.uni-kl.de
[2] Fraunhofer IESE, Kaiserslautern, Germany
steffen.hess@iese.fraunhofer.de
[3] Sino-European Usability Centre, Dalian Maritime University, Dalian, China
gerrit@acm.org

**Abstract.** The DIViM 2015 workshop focuses on different issues and limitations regarding designing intuitive interaction and visualization for mobile applications and devices, as well as how to overcome these limits through novel approaches and techniques.

**Keywords:** Interaction design · Visualization · Mobile app development

## 1 Motivation and Objectives

Current mobile applications (commonly abbreviated as *mobile apps* or just *apps*) are in many ways different from the conventional desktop applications due to factors like the usage of multi-touch gesture interaction, the availability of different sizes of devices, new operating systems, mobile access, the change of usage context in different circumstances, and so on.

The recent advances in mobile paradigm bring new challenges and open issues in developing intuitive and interactive mobile apps [1]. In this context, designing intuitive interaction and visualization plays an important role for many purposes, e.g., improved user experience and aesthetics. In addition, better interaction modes and suitable visual representations in mobile apps are critical for a successful execution of the users' required tasks [2]. However, this requires not only an intensive collaboration between the responsible parties – especially the interaction/UX designers, visualization and HCI experts – but also needs focusing on novel interaction and visualization approaches and techniques targeting this new mobile paradigm.

Inspired by the critical role of interaction design and visualization in the current mobile app development and the organizers' previous experience with the related fields (i.e., interaction designing, visualization, human experience, perception and multimodal input actions, and mobile apps), the workshop aims at creating awareness in the related communities to start focusing on novel methods, approaches, and techniques for utilizing the full power of interaction design and visualization in the current mobile app

© IFIP International Federation for Information Processing 2015
J. Abascal et al. (Eds.): INTERACT 2015, Part IV, LNCS 9299, pp. 675–676, 2015.
DOI: 10.1007/978-3-319-22723-8_97

development at different levels, from showing the relevant information to enhancing user experience.

## 2 Workshop Details

*Topics and Themes.* DIViM 2015 is dedicated to observations, concepts, approaches, techniques, and practices that allow understanding, facilitating, and increasing the awareness of the role of designing and implementing intuitive interactions and visualizations for mobile apps. In this context, topics of interest for paper submissions include, but are not limited to: novel interaction and visualization techniques and methods targeting current mobile apps and devices; frameworks and approaches for designing new interaction techniques and intuitive visualization; novel visual interactive techniques targeting mobile devices; scalability issues; context and usage issues; accessibility and usability issues; interaction and visualization for mobile smart watches; user-centric interaction/visualization; testing/evaluation; tools and environments to support the designing and building of interactive visualization; case studies and best practices.

*Target Audience.* The workshop targets at researchers and practitioners with a background in interaction design, UX design, visualization, HCI, or mobile app development. The workshop provides a platform for discussing issues and limitations regarding design and implementation of intuitive interaction modes and visualizations for mobile devices as well as how to overcome current limitations and user disaffection through novel approaches and techniques.

*Expected Outcomes.* The workshop aims at achieving the following outcomes:

- Consolidating research and practices related to interaction design and visualization design in the context of current mobile apps and devices;
- Establishing a platform for bringing the interested communities (such as interaction/ UX designers, HCI/visualization experts, etc.) closer together to discuss how to make changes in the existing approaches and frameworks, as well as to examine novel methods for designing useful and intuitive interaction and visualization;
- Growing the body of knowledge related to interaction and visualization design for the current mobile environment and identifying challenges and future avenues for research relevant to both academia and industry;
- Providing a dedicated forum to the relevant communities for exchanging ideas and best practices; thus, foster collaboration between industry and academia.

## References

1. Abolfazli, S., Sanaei, Z., Gani, A., Xia, F., Yang, L.T.: Review: rich mobile applications: genesis, taxonomy, and open issues. Netw. Comput. Appl. **40**, 345–362 (2014)
2. Burigat, S., Chittaro, L.: On the effectiveness of overview+detail visualization on mobile devices. Pers. Ubiquit. Comput. **17**(2), 371–385 (2013)

# Workshop on Interactivity in Healthcare Systems (IHS)

Vicki Hanson[1], Gemma Webster[2(✉)], and Matt Dennis[2]

[1] Rochester Institute of Technology, Rochester, NY, USA
vlhics@rit.edu
[2] University of Aberdeen, Aberdeen, UK
{gwebster,m.dennis}@abdn.ac.uk

**Abstract.** We are all living longer with average life expectancy increasing across the globe [1]. However, chronic conditions such as heart disease, strokes and cancer, coupled with an increasing global obesity problem still cause a growing number of premature deaths [1]. These conditions combined with an aging population cause a huge strain on healthcare provision.

**Keywords:** Healthcare · Interactivity · eHealth · Healthy living

## 1 Workshop Theme

We are all living longer with average life expectancy increasing across the globe [1]. However, chronic conditions such as heart disease, strokes and cancer, coupled with an increasing global obesity problem still cause a growing number of premature deaths [1]. These conditions combined with an aging population cause a huge strain on healthcare provision.

There are two approaches to reduce the burden on healthcare services – encouraging healthy lifestyles through increased knowledge, and improving people's ability to affect the quality of care for those living with long-term conditions and age related illnesses. Although these issues appear to be separate, they have an effect on each other. For example, if someone has a healthier lifestyle they are less likely to develop certain chronic conditions. Furthermore, if someone is used to maintaining a healthy lifestyle then they are more likely to actively engage with their healthcare providers. We have now reached a critical point in healthcare - both healthcare professionals and patients alike recognize the potential for technology to provide them with personalized healthcare and support [2]. The WHO has recognized the importance of using such technology by encouraging investment and forming an internal eHealth division which focuses on promoting and strengthening the use of technology in health [3].

eHealth can be used in a diverse range of areas to promote access, improve efficiency and enhance quality within healthcare [4]. Key goals in this field are to facilitate personalized health information to promote self-management, to identify and act upon support needs, to improve communication between patients and healthcare workers, to assist with the use of medicine and assistive technology and inform decision-making between healthcare workers [5]. Additionally, any health technology has to be designed to be usable, efficient, effective and accepted by the healthcare community. This workshop

© IFIP International Federation for Information Processing 2015
J. Abascal et al. (Eds.): INTERACT 2015, Part IV, LNCS 9299, pp. 677–678, 2015.
DOI: 10.1007/978-3-319-22723-8_98

aims to promote discussion between multidisciplinary researchers on novel, innovative and connective approaches within eHealth, improving engagement and patient outcomes.

## 2    Topics

This workshop is aimed at multidisciplinary researchers and healthcare professionals from all areas interested in novel approaches to interactivity in technology for healthy living, healthcare and eHealth. The areas of interest are, but not limited to:

- Usability of eHealth technologies
- Technologies to support health education, promotion and advice, and healthy independent living
- Personal health technologies or personalized assistance
- Social care
- Novel approaches to health technologies
- Tailored decision support (for patients and practitioners)
- Mobile and wearable healthcare systems for eHealth
- Personalization in online support for health and wellbeing

## 3    Outcomes

This workshop aims to promote discussions within the community around the future of healthy living and healthcare. We are aiming to produce a special issue of a journal, with accepted authors potentially being invited to write extended versions of their papers.

## References

1. World Health Organization: World Health Statistics 2014: A Wealth of Information on Global Public Health. WHO Document Production Services, Geneva, Switzerland (2014)
2. Schraefel, M.C., Mamykina, L., Marsden, G., Shneiderman, B., Szolovits, P., Weitzner, D., André, P., White, R., Tan, D., Berners-Lee, T., Consolvo, S., Jacobs, R., Kohane, I., La Dantec, C.A.: Interacting with eHealth. In: Proceedings of the 27th International Conference Extended Abstracts on Human Factors in Computing Systems - CHI EA 2009 (2009)
3. World Health Organization: eHealth at WHO. http://www.who.int/ehealth/about/en/. Accessed 6 February 2015
4. Churchill, E.F., Schraefel, M.C.: mHealth + proactive well-being = wealth creation. Interactions 22(1), 60–63 (2015)
5. Scottish Government: eHealth Strategy 2011–2017 (Revised July 2012 to include a Sixth Strategic Aim). Scottish Government, St. Andrew's House, Regent Road, Edinburgh (2012)

# Author Index

Printed in the United States
By Bookmasters